PASSTRAK®

Life and Health Insurance

License Exam Manual

5th Edition

Dearborn™
Financial Services
A **Kaplan Professional** Company

This publication is designed to provide accurate and authoritative information in regard to the subject matter covered. It is sold with the understanding that the publisher is not engaged in rendering legal, accounting or other professional service. If legal advice or other expert assistance is required, the services of a competent professional person should be sought.

This text is updated periodically to reflect changes in laws and regulations. To verify that you have the most recent update, you may call Dearborn at 1-800-423-4723.

Library of Congress Cataloging-in-Publication Data

PassTrak life and health insurance. License exam manual.-- 5th ed.
    p. cm.
    Rev. ed. of: Life and health insurance. 4th ed. c1997.
    ISBN 0-7931-4475-2 (pbk.)
    1. Insurance, Life--United States--Examinations, questions, etc. 2.
Insurance, Health--United States--Examinations, questions, etc. 3.
Insurance, Life--Law and legislation--United States--Examinations,
questions, etc. 4. Insurance, Health--Law and legislation--United
States--Examinations, questions, etc.   I. Title: Life and health
insurance. II. Dearborn Financial Institute.
  HG8951 .L98 2001
  368.3'0076--dc21
                                        2001042248

Contents

Acknowledgments

The publisher would like to acknowledge the following individuals for their contributions to the development of this text:

Jeffrey Galper, Dearborn midwest regional director
Barb Gavitt, Dearborn insurance instructor
Ann Heinz, J.D., content reviewer
Wes Schaller, Dearborn branch manager (Minnesota)
Anne Shropshire, CLU, Associate Publisher

Their efforts have resulted in a text that we believe will be an excellent source of knowledge and information about life and accident and health insurance in these early years of the new millennium.

Arthur G. Carvajal, Esq.
Senior Legal Editor

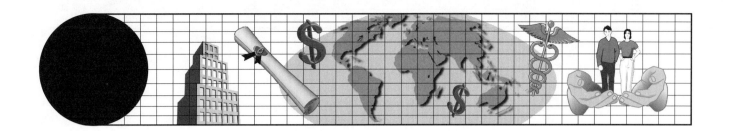

Introduction

Thank you for purchasing PASSTRAK® *Life and Health Insurance License Exam Manual*. This brief introduction will help you get the most out of this book when preparing for your state licensing examination.

Most states require individuals to obtain some education in insurance before taking a state licensing exam. All states require individuals to take an exam to become licensed as an insurance agent or producer. There are some individuals who may be exempt from this licensing exam, usually on the basis of prior insurance education or experience. You can contact the department of insurance for your state to determine its precise licensing requirements.

This new edition includes information that we have added and expanded in the following topics: enhanced whole life insurance, viatical settlements, accelerated death benefits, equity-indexed annuities, Medicare+Choice programs, Medicare supplement policies, the Financial Services Modernization Act of 2000, and the Economic Growth and Tax Relief Reconciliation Act of 2001. Also, the changes necessitated by the repeal of the Social Security earnings limitations on employed persons drawing Social Security payments have been incorporated. Additional examples and highlighted sections called Take Note and Test Topic Alert have been added to highlight key points in an easy-to-use format. Almost every lesson contains at least one Quick Quiz that asks questions about the material just covered in the previous section. Finally, questions have been added at the end of each lesson, the glossary has been updated, and we have included an index for the first time. We hope that these changes will make this book easier to use and your study time more productive.

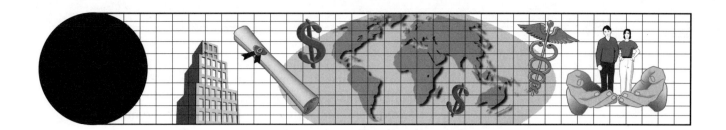

How to Use the License Exam Manual

PASSTRAK® *Life and Health Insurance License Exam Manual* consists of lessons, lesson exams, and practice final exams.

Here is an effective way to use this text for the greatest comprehension:

1. Read the entire text, or at least the lessons that deal with the line of insurance you are studying. For instance, if you are studying for a life insurance licensing examination, study those lessons that cover life insurance and general insurance topics. If you are studying to take a combined life and accident and health insurance exam, study the entire book.
2. Throughout the text, you will see special notes to help your comprehension. These two types of notes have a specific purpose and are denoted with different text markers:

✓ **Take Note:** This note highlights an important point of fact, law, policy or practice that you should know. By reading the Take Note sections by themselves after you have read the book, you can get a quick review of these important points just before you take the licensing exam.

 **Test Topic Alert**   This note alerts you to important information that frequently appears in the licensing exam. This information comes directly from our classroom instructors, and highlights an important point that you should remember for the exam.

✓ **For Example:** This note illustrates the operation of important concepts and principles. It applies a principle or concept to a realistic situation.

3. Each Lesson contains periodic Quick Quizzes. Take these quizzes to ensure that you understand and retain the material covered in the preceding section.

4. At the end of each Lesson, you will find a Lesson Exam. This review test covers all of the topics presented in the preceding Lesson. If you have mastered the Quick Quizzes, you should have no trouble successfully completing the Lesson Exam.

5. Finally, when you have finished reading the book and have mastered the Quick Quizzes and Lesson Exams, you are ready to take the Final Exam at the end of the book. If you are studying for a life insurance license, take the life insurance Final Exam. If you are studying for an accident and health insurance license, take the accident and health insurance Final Exam. If you are studying for both lines, take both final exams. You should strive to get at least 80 percent of the questions correct after careful study of this book.

The state insurance licensing exam is not easy. You must display considerable knowledge of the topics presented in this textbook and the law supplement, which covers state insurance laws and regulations. (If you do not have this law supplement for your state, contact Dearborn's customer service department at 1-800-423-4723.) If you thoroughly understand the information in this book and in the law supplement, you will be well-prepared to take the licensing exam.

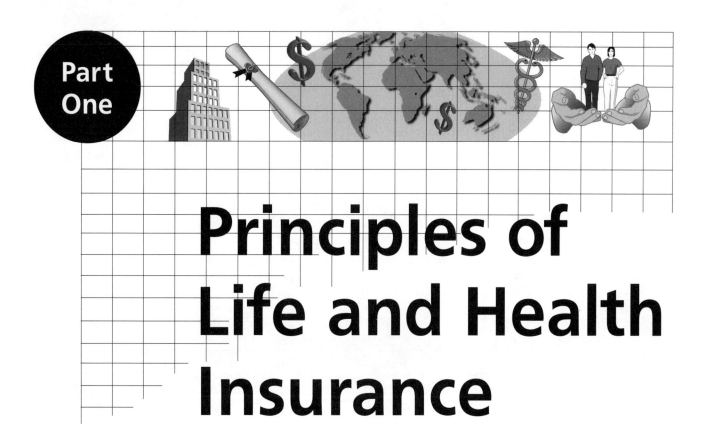

Principles of Life and Health Insurance

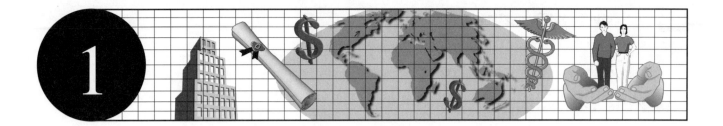

Purpose of Life and Health Insurance

INTRODUCTION

Life and health insurance play an important role in helping attain financial and emotional security throughout people's lives. For instance, life insurance protects against the risk that a person will die too soon and be unable to fulfill his or her obligations to others. It guarantees that a specific sum of money will be available exactly when it is needed: at death, when a family or business may be exposed to certain financial risks, such as burial expenses, loss of personal or business income and debts. In contrast, health insurance protects individuals by assuming the risk that they will incur medical expenses. In this lesson, we will examine the purpose of both types of insurance: providing economic protection against losses resulting from chance happenings like illness, accident or death. We also will take a look at various types of risks and how insurance is designed specifically to replace the uncertainties of risk with guarantees.

LESSON OBJECTIVES

When you complete this lesson, you should be able to:

- explain the importance of life and health insurance to people and to society as a whole;
- explain the concepts of risk pooling and the law of large numbers;
- define speculative risk, pure risk, peril and hazard and give an example of each;
- identify the four methods used to handle risk; and
- list and explain the elements of an insurable risk.

The Role of Insurance

Through the centuries, people have pursued financial security for themselves and their dependents. We all have a compelling need for security; security is peace of mind and freedom from worry. Insecurity is doubt, fear and apprehension. Most economic actions we take are for the purpose of satisfying some need and, thus, attaining some degree of security.

Unfortunately, achieving complete financial security historically has been elusive, in part because of universal problems such as death, sickness, accidents and disability. These problems can strike at any time and without warning. The emotional stress they bring is increased by the financial hardships that almost certainly follow.

Death may strike anyone prematurely. When death takes the life of a family provider, surviving family members often suffer if they are left without adequate income or the means to provide basic necessities. On the other hand, some people face the unpleasant prospect of outliving their incomes—retirement may be forced on them before they have prepared adequately for a non-income-earning existence. Sickness and disability also can leave economic scars, often more intense than death. An accident or illness easily can result in catastrophic medical bills or the inability to work for months or even years.

Insurance evolved to provide a practical solution to the problem of such economic uncertainties and losses. Life insurance, based on actuarial or mathematical principles, guarantees a specified sum of money on the death of the insured person. Health insurance also evolved from scientific principles to provide funds for medical expenses due to sickness or injury and to cover loss of income during a period of disability. Annuities provide a stream of income by making a series of payments to the annuitant for a specific period of time or for his or her lifetime. The true significance of insurance is its promise to substitute future economic certainty for uncertainty and to replace the unknown with a sense of security.

An Industry Overview

The insurance industry plays an important role in our society. In 1998, about 85 percent of U.S. households owned life insurance. The average amount each household owned was $178,600. In 1998, purchases of life insurance, both individual and group, exceeded $2.2 trillion, and benefits paid by the

FIGURE 1.1   Life Insurance per Insured Household, 1970–1998

Year	Life Insurance per Insured Household	Year	Life Insurance per Insured Household
1970	$25,500	1985	$82,200
1971	$27,000	1986	$89,100
1972	$28,300	1987	$98,400
1973	$30,100	1988	$105,600
1974	$32,500	1989	$112,400
1975	$34,900	1990	$124,500
1976	$37,100	1991	$130,000
1977	$40,000	1992	$136,600
1978	$43,200	1993	$143,100
1979	$48,000	1994	$146,500
1980	$51,100	1995	$149,500
1981	$56,300	1996	$158,400
1982	$63,100	1997	$167,600
1983	$69,500	1998	$178,600
1984	$75,700		

Source: *1999 Life Insurance Fact Book*

industry, excluding health insurance, reached $302 billion. Most new life insurance policies are purchased by individuals from life insurance agents. According to the American Council of Life Insurance's *1999 Life Insurance Fact Book*, life insurance in force in the United States at the end of 1998 totaled $14.47 trillion, an increase of 8.3 percent over 1997.

The insurance industry plays an important role in our nation's economy. It is second only to the commercial banking industry as a source of investment funds, because insurance companies invest the billions of premium dollars they receive annually in a wide range of investments.*

As for health insurance, in 1997, 226 million Americans were covered under public and private health insurance, and 43 million were without health insurance. More than 186 million of the insured individuals were covered by private health insurers, including commercial insurance companies, Blue Cross and Blue Shield plans, self-funded employer plans and prepayment plans, such as health maintenance organizations (HMOs). In 1996, private health insurers paid out $292 billion for medical care and disability claims.

The rising cost of health care continues to be one of the most difficult problems currently facing our health care system. For example, according to the Health Insurance Association of America's *1999-2000 Source Book of Health*

---

* As we will see, one of the basic factors in life and health premiums is the interest earned by the insurance company on the premiums it receives and subsequently invests.

Insurance Data, in 1996, Americans spent $1.042 trillion for medical and health care services, research and construction—$561 billion in private funds and $481 billion in public funds. In 1996, spending per person averaged $3,781. In 1997, health care spending in the United States reached $1.092 trillion, with an estimated average of $3,925 per person.

Truly, the insurance industry is a vital one, serving the interests of individuals, businesses and society at large.

The Nature of Insurance

We are exposed to many perils. The purpose of any insurance is to provide economic protection against losses that may be incurred due to a chance happening or event, such as death, illness or accident. This protection is provided through an insurance policy, which simply is a device for accumulating funds to meet these uncertain losses. The policy is a legally binding contract that sets forth the company's promise and obligations as follows:

> Whereby, for a set amount of money (the premium), one party (the insurer) agrees to pay the other party (the insured or his or her beneficiary) a set sum (the benefit) upon the occurrence of some event.

In the case of life insurance, for example, the benefit is paid when the insured dies. In the case of health or disability insurance, the benefit is paid if and when the insured incurs certain medical expenses or becomes disabled, as defined by the contract.

Basic Insurance Principles

Insurance is based on two fundamental principles: the spreading or pooling of risks (also known as *loss sharing*) and the law of large numbers. To understand these principles, consider the following examples.

Risk Pooling   ✓ *For Example:* Assume that 1,000 individuals in the same social club agree that if any member of their group dies, all of the members will pitch in to provide the deceased's family with $10,000. This $10,000, it was determined, would provide the family with enough funds to cover the immediate costs associated with death and to provide a cushion for at least a few months. Because it is not known when any one individual within the group will die, the decision is made to pre-fund the benefit by assessing each member $10, thus creating the $10,000 fund. Without the agreement to help provide for each other's potential loss, each group member (and his or her family) would have to face the economic cost of death alone. But by sharing the burden and spreading the risk of death over all 1,000 group members, the most any one member pays is $10.

This is, of course, a simplified example, but it explains the basic concept of loss sharing. By spreading a risk, or by sharing the possibility of a loss, a large group of people can substitute a small certain cost ($10 in our example) for a large unknown risk (the economic risk of dying). In other words, the risk is transferred from an individual to a group, each member of which shares the losses and has the promise of a future benefit. Insurance companies pool risks among thousands and thousands of insureds and apply certain mathematical principles to guarantee policyowners that the money will be there to pay a claim when it arises.

Law of Large Numbers

In addition to spreading risks, insurance relies on the principle that the larger the number of individual risks (or exposures) in a group, the more certainty there is as to the amount of loss incurred in any given period. In other words, given a large enough pool of risks, an insurer can predict with reasonable accuracy the number of claims it will face during any given time. No one can predict when any one person will die or if any one person will become disabled. However, it is possible to predict the approximate number of deaths or the likelihood that disability will occur among a certain group during a certain period. This principle, known as the law of large numbers, is based on the science of probability and the experience of mortality (death) and morbidity (sickness) statistics. The larger and more homogeneous the group, the more certain the mortality or morbidity predictions.

✓ **For Example:** Statistics may show that among a group of 100,000 40-year-old males, 300 will die within one year. While it is not possible to predict who the 300 will be, the number will prove quite accurate. Conversely, with a small group, an accurate prediction is not possible. Among a group of 100 40-year-old males, it is not statistically feasible to predict if any in the group will die within one year. Because insurers cover thousands and thousands of lives, it is possible to predict when and to what extent deaths and disabilities will occur and, consequently, when claims will arise.

All forms of insurance—life, health, accident, property and casualty—rely on risk pooling and the law of large numbers. These principles form the foundation on which insurance is based and allow for its successful operation.

The Concept of Risk

As we have learned so far, insurance replaces the uncertainty of risk with guarantees. But what exactly does the word risk mean? And how does insurance remove the uncertainty and minimize the adverse effects of risk?

Risk Defined

Risk is defined as the uncertainty regarding loss. Property loss, such as the destruction of a home due to fire, is an example of risk. Negligence or carelessness can give rise to a liability risk if there is potential injury to an individual or damage to property. The inability to work and earn a living due to a disability is another example of risk, as is loss of a family's income due to the death of the breadwinner. The loss inherent in all of these risks is characterized by a lessening (or disappearance) of value.

Risks can be divided into two classes: speculative and pure.

- *Speculative risks.* Speculative risks involve the chance of both loss and gain. Betting at the race track and investing in the stock market are examples of speculative risks.
- *Pure risks.* Pure risks involve only the chance of loss; there is never a possibility of gain or profit. The risk associated with the chance of injury from an accident is an example of pure risk. There is no opportunity for gain if the event does not occur—only the opportunity for loss if it does occur. Only pure risks are insurable.

✓ **Take Note:** The distinction between speculative and pure risks is an important one. Insurance does not protect individuals against losses arising out of speculative risks because these risks are undertaken voluntarily. Keep in mind, however, that not all pure risks are insurable.

With life insurance, the risk involved is when, not if, death will occur. It can be tomorrow, next week, next year or well into the future, but loss can result if death is premature or comes too late. With health insurance, in contrast the risk is not when, but if illness or disability will strike. Losses associated with health risks include medical costs and loss of income. With annuities, the risk is living too long and outlasting one's income. Annuities cover this risk by paying a guaranteed income to the annuitant for life.

 **Test Topic Alert!**   Insurance is designed to protect only against pure risk.

Perils and Hazards

Perils and hazards are factors that cause or give rise to risk.

A peril is the immediate specific event causing loss and giving rise to risk. It is the cause of a risk.

✓ **For Example:** When a building burns, fire is the peril. When a person dies, death is the peril. When an individual is injured in an accident, the accident is the peril. When a person becomes ill from a disease, the disease is the peril.

A hazard is any factor that gives rise to a peril. For purposes of life and health insurance, there are three basic types of hazards: physical, moral and morale.

- *Physical hazards.* Physical hazards are individual characteristics that increase the chance of peril. They may exist because of a person's physical condition, past medical history or condition at birth. Blindness and deafness are physical hazards.
- *Moral hazards.* Moral hazards are tendencies that people may have that increase risk and the chance of loss. Alcoholism and drug addiction are considered moral hazards.
- *Morale hazards.* Morale hazards are also individual tendencies, but they arise from an attitude or state of mind that causes indifference to loss. For instance, driving recklessly without fear of death or injury is a morale hazard.

Treatment of Risk

How risks are treated varies greatly, depending on the situation, the degree of potential loss and the individual. Generally, there are four options: *avoid, reduce, retain* or *transfer* the risk.

Risk Avoidance One method of dealing with risk is avoidance—simply avoiding as many risks as possible. By choosing not to drive or own an automobile, one could avoid the risks associated with driving. By never flying, one could eliminate the risk of being in an airplane crash. By never investing in stocks, one could avoid the risk of a market crash.

✓ **Take Note:** Although risk avoidance may be an effective method of dealing with risk, it is not always practical. If risk avoidance were used extensively, society would ultimately suffer because some risk taking is necessary to achieve personal advancement and economic progress. For this reason, avoidance may be an unsatisfactory way of handling many risks.

Risk Reduction Risk reduction is another means of dealing with risk. Because we cannot avoid risk entirely, we often attempt to lessen the possibility of loss by taking action to reduce the risk. Installing a smoke alarm in a home will not lessen the possibility of fire, but it may reduce the risk of loss from fire.

Risk Retention

Risk retention is another method of coping with risk. This means accepting the risk and confronting it if and when it occurs. One way to handle a retained risk is self-insurance, for instance, setting up a fund to offset the costs of a potential loss.

✓ **Take Note:** Risk retention may be voluntary or involuntary. For instance, when a person recognizes that a risk exists, he or she may agree voluntarily to assume the losses involved. A person may agree to retain a risk voluntarily because the risk might lead to relatively small certain losses that can be borne easily. On the other hand, a person may not even recognize that a risk exists. In this case, the person involuntarily retains the possible financial loss without realizing it.

Risk Transference

The most effective way to handle risk is to transfer it so that the loss is borne by another party. Insurance is the most common method of transferring risk—from an individual or group to an insurance company. Though purchasing insurance will not eliminate the risk of death or illness, it relieves the insured individual or group of the losses these risks bring. Insurance satisfies both economic and emotional needs—it replaces the uncertainty surrounding risk with the assurance of guarantees, and it transfers the financial consequences of death, illness or disability to the insurer.

Test Topic Alert!

A typical question on the license exam may ask you to identify the ways that individuals treat risk.

Quick Quiz 1.1

Match the following terms with the appropriate example below.

A. Speculative risk
B. Risk transference
C. Risk reduction
D. Risk avoidance

_____1. Joan installs a sprinkler system in her new house.

_____2. Because Mary is afraid of drowning, she never swims.

_____3. Bob invests all of his investment money in technology stocks.

_____4. Tom, a stuntman, purchases disability insurance.

Answers   1. **C**   2. **D**   3. **A**   4. **B**

Elements of Insurable Risk

Though insurance may be one of the most effective ways to handle risk, not all risks are insurable. As noted earlier, insurers will insure only pure risks or those that involve only the chance of loss. However, not all pure risks are insurable. Certain characteristics or elements must be evident before a pure risk can be insured:

- *The loss must be due to chance.* To be insurable, a risk must involve a chance of loss that is fortuitous and outside the insured's control.
- *The loss must be definite and measurable.* An insurable risk must involve a loss that is definite as to cause, time, place and amount. An insurer must be able to determine how much the benefit will be and when it will become payable.
- *The loss must be predictable.* An insurable risk must have occurrence that can be predicted statistically. This enables insurers to estimate the average frequency and severity of future losses and set appropriate premiums. Death, illness and disability all are events whose rates of occurrence can be projected, based on statistics.
- *The loss cannot be catastrophic.* Insurers typically will not insure risks that will expose them to catastrophic losses. There must be limits that insurers can be reasonably certain their losses will not exceed. For instance, an insurer would not issue a policy for $1 trillion on a single life, because that one death would create a catastrophic loss to the company.
- *The loss exposures to be insured must be large.* An insurer must be able to predict losses based on the law of large numbers. Consequently, there must be a sufficiently large pool to be insured and those in the pool (the exposures) must be grouped into classes with similar risks. Individuals, for example, are grouped according to age, health, sex, occupation and other classifications.
- *The loss exposures to be insured must be selected randomly.* In addition, the group to be insured must be selected randomly. Insurers must have a fair proportion of good risks and poor risks. A large proportion of poor risks would financially threaten the insurance company because there would be many claims without sufficient premiums to offset them. Keep in mind that there is a tendency, called *adverse selection*, for less favorable insurance risks (for example, people in poor health) to seek or continue insurance to a greater extent than other risks.

Economic Basis of Life and Health Insurance

To fully appreciate the purpose and function of insurance, it is important to understand that its roots lie in economics and the concept of human life value.

It has long been recognized that individuals have an economic value that can be measured in part by their future earning potential. This earning potential is the sum of one's net future earnings or, more precisely, the dollar value of an individual's future earning capability. The true significance of this earning potential extends beyond the individual to those who depend on him or her for their financial security. Thus, by definition, *human life value* is the value today of an individual's future earnings that are devoted to his or her dependents.

In the abstract, human life value is the means by which homes are purchased, college educations are provided, monthly bills are paid—in short, it is the essence of an individual's or family's economic existence. Yet this value is subject to loss through death, retirement, disability or poor health—any one of these perils affects earning capacity in some degree and, consequently, diminishes human life value. It is for this purpose—to conserve and protect human life value—that life and health insurance exist.

Summary

Life and health insurance evolved to provide a practical solution to the economic losses associated with death, sickness and accidents. It does so through an insurance policy, which is a device that accumulates funds to meet these losses. Insurance is based on risk pooling and the law of large numbers, principles that allow insurers to spread risks among thousands of individuals and to predict losses with reasonable accuracy.

Insurance transfers risk, which is one of the most effective ways to deal with risk and its losses. Not all risks are insurable, however. There are certain elements every risk must contain before it can be insured: it must be a pure risk; the loss it entails must be due to chance, definite, measurable, predictable and noncatastrophic; and the loss exposure must be part of a large randomly selected group.

The true worth of insurance lies in its ability to protect human life value—the value associated with an individual's earning potential—and to provide financial security.

Key Concepts

In preparing for their licensing examinations, students should be familiar with the following concepts:

pure risk	peril
speculative risk	risk pooling
law of large numbers	methods of handling risk
elements of insurable risk	adverse selection
hazard	

Lesson Exam One

1. Which of the following insurance concepts is founded on the ability to predict the approximate number of deaths or frequency of disabilities within a certain group during a specific time?

   A. Principle of large loss
   B. Quantum insurance principle
   C. Indemnity law
   D. Law of large numbers

2. The owner of a camera store is worried that new employees may help themselves to items from inventory without paying for them. What kind of hazard is this?

   A. Physical
   B. Ethical
   C. Morale
   D. Moral

3. All of the following actions are examples of risk avoidance EXCEPT

   A. refusing to fly
   B. refusing to invest in stocks
   C. paying an insurance premium
   D. refusing to drive

4. Which of the following statements is CORRECT?

   A. Only speculative risks are insurable.
   B. Only pure risks are insurable.
   C. Both pure risks and speculative risks are insurable.
   D. Neither pure risks nor speculative risks are insurable.

5. Which of the following statements does NOT describe an element of an insurable risk?

   A. The loss must not be due to chance.
   B. The loss must be definite and measurable.
   C. The loss cannot be catastrophic.
   D. The loss exposures to be insured must be large.

6. In the insurance business, risk can best be defined as

   A. sharing the possibility of a loss
   B. uncertainty regarding the future
   C. uncertainty regarding loss
   D. uncertainty regarding when death will occur

7. Buying insurance is one of the most effective ways of

   A. avoiding risk
   B. transferring risk
   C. reducing risk
   D. retaining risk

8. Which of the following best describes the function of insurance?

   A. It is a form of legalized gambling.
   B. It spreads financial risk over a large group to minimize the loss to any one individual.
   C. It protects against living too long.
   D. It creates and protects risks.

9. A tornado is an example of a

    A. physical hazard
    B. speculative risk
    C. peril
    D. moral hazard

10. An insured keeps a $50,000 diamond ring in a safe deposit box at a local bank. This is an example of

    A. avoidance
    B. reduction
    C. retention
    D. transference

Answers & Rationale

1. **D.** The law of large numbers relies on the principle that, given a large enough pool of risks, an insurer can predict with reasonable accuracy the number of claims it will face during a specific time period. This principle is based on the science of probability and the experience of mortality (death) and morbidity (sickness) statistics.

2. **D.** The store owner is concerned about moral hazards; that is, the tendency of her employees to be dishonest and steal inventory. The tendency to be dishonest is a moral hazard that increases risk and the chance of loss.

3. **C.** Risk avoidance occurs when a person simply avoids as many risks as possible. However, when Pat purchases insurance, he is not attempting to avoid risk; rather, he is transferring the loss from a potential risk to another party—the insurance company. Purchasing insurance, therefore, is considered risk transference, not risk avoidance.

4. **B.** Unlike speculative risk, pure risk involves only the chance of loss and never a possibility of gain or profit. Only this type of risk is insurable.

5. **A.** To be an insurable risk, the loss must be due to chance. A risk must involve the chance of loss that is fortuitous and outside the insured's control.

6. **C.** Risk is the uncertainty regarding loss.

7. **B.** Buying insurance enables a person to handle risk by transferring the risk of loss to another party—the insurance company. Although purchasing insurance does not eliminate the risk of death or illness, it relieves the insured of the losses that these risks bring by transferring them to a third party.

8. **B.** Insurance is based in part on risk pooling, which involves spreading risks among thousands of individuals to minimize the loss to any one individual.

9. **C.** A peril is the immediate specific event causing loss and giving rise to risk. In other words, a peril is the cause of a risk. Thus, when a town is destroyed by high winds, a tornado is the peril.

10. **B.** Placing a diamond ring in a safe deposit box is an example of risk reduction. Although the insured cannot avoid the risk of losing the ring altogether when not wearing it, the insured can reduce the risk of loss by putting it in a safe deposit box.

2

The Insurance Industry

INTRODUCTION

The insurance industry in the United States is a large industry, with more than 1,500 life insurance companies operating today. These firms employ over 2.3 million people and administer assets of more than $2.826 trillion. In this lesson, we will examine the insurance industry in general and look at the different types of private insurers and government insurance programs. We also will examine how insurance is sold and the ways in which the industry is regulated at both the federal and state levels. Keep in mind, however, that each state has its own insurance laws and regulations that should be consulted.

LESSON OBJECTIVES

When you complete this lesson you should be able to:

- list and describe the different types of private insurers and government insurance programs;
- describe the different types of systems through which insurance is sold and the agent's role in these systems;
- describe the primary ways that insurance is regulated at the federal and state levels;
- define twisting, misrepresentation, misuse of premiums, replacement and rebating and give an example of each of these prohibited practices; and
- describe the roles of the National Association of Insurance Commissioners (NAIC), state guaranty associations, the National Association of Insurance and Financial Advisors (NAIFA) and the National Association of Health Underwriters (NAHU).

Types of Insurers

Although there are many ways to classify organizations that provide insurance, in the broadest of terms, there are two classifications: private and government. Within these two classes are many categories of insurance providers as well as insurance plans and insurance producers.

Private Insurers

Private insurers offer many lines of insurance. Some sell primarily life insurance and annuities, some sell accident and health insurance and some sell property and casualty insurance. Companies that write more than one line of insurance are known as *multiline insurers.*

Within this broad category of private insurers are specific types of insurance companies. A discussion of each type follows.

Stock Insurers A stock insurance company is a private organization, organized and incorporated under state laws for the purpose of making a profit for its stockholders. It is structured the same as any corporation. Stockholders may or may not be policyholders. When declared, stock dividends are paid to stockholders. In a stock company, the directors and officers are responsible to the stockholders.

Mutual Insurers Mutual insurance companies also are organized and incorporated under state laws, but they have no stockholders. Instead, the owners are the policyholders. Anyone purchasing insurance from a mutual insurer is both a customer and an owner. He or she has the right to vote for the board of director members. By issuing participating policies that pay policy dividends, mutual insurers allow their policyowners to share in any company earnings. Essentially, policy dividends represent a refund of the portion of premiums that remains after the company has set aside the necessary reserves and has made deductions for claims and expenses. Policy dividends also can include a share in the company's investment, mortality and operating profits.

Test Topic Alert!   Policy dividends are paid from participating policies usually sold by mutual insurers.

Occasionally, a stock company may be converted into a mutual company through a process called *mutualization.* Likewise, some mutuals are *demutualizing* by converting to stock companies. Stock and mutual companies often are referred to as *commercial insurers.* They both can write life, health and property and casualty insurance.

Assessment Mutual Insurers

Assessment mutual companies are typified by the way in which they charge premiums. A pure assessment mutual company operates on the basis of loss sharing by group members. No premium is payable in advance; instead, each member is assessed an individual portion of losses that actually occur. An advance premium assessment mutual charges a premium in advance, at the beginning of the policy period. If the original premiums exceed the operating expenses and losses, the surplus is returned to the policyholders as dividends. On the other hand, if total premiums are not enough to meet losses, additional assessments are levied against the members. Normally, the amount of assessment that may be levied is limited, either by state law or simply as a provision in the insurer's bylaws.

Reciprocal Insurers

Similar to mutual insurers, reciprocal insurers are organized on the basis of ownership by their policyholders. However, with reciprocals it is the policyholders themselves who insure the risks of the other policyholders. Each policyholder assumes a share of the risk brought to the company by others. Reciprocals are managed by an attorney-in-fact.

 Take Note: As a member of the group of reciprocal insurers, each policyowner is both an insured and an insurer. Each policyowner's premium is paid into a separate account and his or her share of any losses is paid from this account.

Lloyd's of London

Contrary to popular opinion, Lloyd's of London is not an insurer, but rather an association of individuals and companies that individually underwrite insurance. Lloyd's can be compared to the New York Stock Exchange, which provides the arena and facilities for buying and selling public stock. Lloyd's function is to gather and disseminate underwriting information, help its associates settle claims and disputes and, through its member underwriters, provide coverages that might otherwise be unavailable in certain areas.

Reinsurers

Reinsurers are a specialized branch of the insurance industry because they insure insurers. Reinsurance is an arrangement by which an insurance company transfers a portion of a risk it has assumed to another insurer. Usually, reinsurance takes place to limit the loss any one insurer would face should a very large claim become payable. Another reason for reinsurance is to enable a company to meet certain objectives, such as favorable underwriting or mortality results. The company transferring the risk is called the *ceding* company; the company assuming the risk is the reinsurer.

Risk Retention Group

A risk retention group (RRG) is a mutual insurance company formed to insure people in the same business, occupation or profession, such as pharmacists, dentists or engineers.

Fraternal Benefit Societies

Insurance also is issued by fraternal benefit societies, which have existed in the United States for more than a century. Fraternal societies, noted primarily for their social, charitable and benevolent activities, have memberships based on religious, national or ethnic affiliations. Fraternals first began offering insurance to meet the needs of their poorer members, funding the benefits on a pure assessment basis. Today few fraternals rely on an assessment system, most having adopted the same advanced funding approach other insurers use.

To be characterized as a fraternal benefit society, the organization must be nonprofit, have a lodge system that includes ritualistic work and maintain a representative form of government with elected officers. Fraternal society insurance may be sold only to members of the society. Most fraternals today issue insurance certificates and annuities with many of the same provisions found in policies issued by commercial insurers.

 Take Note: Fraternal societies primarily issue life insurance, although they sometimes sell sickness and accident insurance as well.

Service Insurers   Service insurers, or service providers, offer health insurance and health care services. The best known service providers are Blue Cross and Blue Shield. These two organizations are nonprofit and differ from other insurers in that they sell medical and hospital care services, not insurance. These services are packaged into various plans, and those who purchase these plans are known as subscribers. Blue Cross offers prepayment plans to cover hospital expenses such as room and board and miscellaneous expenses. Blue Shield covers surgical expenses and other medical services performed by physicians.

Another type of service provider is the health maintenance organization (HMO). HMOs offer a wide range of health care services to member subscribers. For a fixed periodic premium paid in advance of any treatment, these subscribers are entitled to the services of certain physicians and hospitals contracted to work with the HMO.

 Take Note: Unlike commercial insurers or Blue Cross and Blue Shield, HMOs are distinct because they provide financing for health care plus the health care itself. HMOs are known for stressing preventive health care and early treatment programs.

A third type of service provider is the preferred provider organization (PPO). Under the usual PPO arrangement, a group desiring health care services—an employer or a union, for example—will obtain price discounts or special services from certain select health care providers in exchange for referring its employees or members to them. PPOs can be organized by employers or by the health care providers themselves. The contract between the employer and the health care professional, be it a physician or a hospital, spells out the kind of services to be provided. Insurance companies also can contract with PPOs to offer services to insureds. (Service providers are discussed in detail in Lesson 15.)

Home Service Insurers Insurance also is sold through a special branch of the industry known as home service (or debit) insurers. These companies specialize in a particular type of insurance called industrial insurance, which is characterized by relatively small face amounts (usually $1,000 to $2,000) with premiums paid weekly. (Industrial insurance will be discussed in Lesson 4.)

Government as Insurer

As noted at the beginning of this lesson, federal and state governments also are insurers, providing what commonly are called social insurance programs. Ranging from crop insurance to bank and savings and loan deposit insurance, these programs have far-reaching effects because they cover millions of people. The major difference between these government programs and private insurance programs is that the government programs are funded with taxes and serve national and state social purposes. Social insurance programs include:

- Old Age, Survivors and Disability Insurance (OASDI), commonly known as Social Security;
- Social Security Hospital Insurance (HI) and Supplemental Medical Insurance (SMI), commonly known as Medicare;
- Medicaid; and
- workers' compensation.

Each of these programs is discussed in Lessons 11 and 19. The federal government also has established life insurance programs to benefit active members and veterans of the armed services. Three of the most notable programs are Servicemembers' Group Life, Veterans' Group Life and National Service Life.

The government plays a vital role in providing social insurance programs. These programs pay billions of dollars in benefits every year and affect millions of people.

Self-Insurers

Though self-insurance is not a method of transferring risk, a discussion is appropriate here. Rather than transfer risk to an insurance company, a self-insurer establishes its own reserves to cover potential losses. Self-insurance often is used by large companies for workers' compensation purposes and for funding pension plans. Many times a self-insurer will look to an insurance company to provide insurance above a certain maximum level of loss, but will bear the amount of loss below that maximum amount.

✓ *Take Note:* The use of self-insurance by businesses to deal with risks has grown significantly over the past three decades. In some areas (such as employer-sponsored health plans), it has become a significant alternative to commercial insurance.

How Insurance Is Sold

Insurance is sold by a variety of companies through a variety of methods. Most consumers purchase insurance through licensed producers who present insurers' products and services to the public via active sales and marketing methods. Insurance producers may be either agents who represent a particular company or brokers who are not tied to any particular company and can represent many companies' products.

✓ **Take Note:** In a sales transaction, agents represent the insurer and brokers represent the buyer. An agent has an agent's contract and a broker must have a broker's contract.

Agents also are classified as *captive* (or *career*) *agents* and *independent agents*. A captive agent works for one insurance company and sells only that company's insurance policies. An independent agent works for himself or herself or for other agents and sells the insurance products of many companies.

There also are solicitors, consultants and special agents. Solicitors act for agents by seeking prospects, receiving applications or collecting premiums, but they usually do not have the authority to bind coverage. A consultant is an independent advisor specializing in the design, implementation and administration of insurance sharing plans. Consultants usually are licensed agents. Special agents, who do not actually solicit insurance business, work as field representatives, helping a company's central office and the agency force in their territory.

✓ **Take Note:** As the financial planning industry has grown rapidly in recent years, financial planners also have become an important source of information on personal risk management and insurance. Although these individuals do not actually sell insurance, their goal is to build their clients' wealth, minimize taxes and protect their clients' estates, among other things.

The agent who solicits an insurance application represents the insurer and not the insured or beneficiary in any dispute between the insured or beneficiary and the insurer. In most states, however, the agent may represent as many insurers as will appoint him or her.

There are three systems that support the sale of insurance through agents and brokers. These are the *career agency system*, the *personal producing general agency system* and the *independent agency system*.

Career Agency System

Career agencies are branches of major stock and mutual insurance companies that are contracted to represent the particular insurer in a specific area. In career agencies, insurance agents are recruited, trained and supervised either by a manager-employee of the company or a general agent (GA) who has a vested right in any business written by his or her agents. GAs may operate strictly as managers or they may devote a portion of their time to sales. The career agency system focuses on building sales staffs.

Personal Producing General Agency System

The personal producing general agency (PPGA) system is similar to the career agency system. However, PPGAs do not recruit, train or supervise career agents. They primarily sell insurance, although they may build a small sales force to assist them. PPGAs generally are responsible for maintaining their own offices and administrative staff. Agents hired by a PPGA are considered employees of the PPGA, not the insurance company, and are supervised by regional directors.

Independent Agency System

The independent agency system, a creation of the property and casualty insurance industry, does not tie a sales staff or agency to any one particular insurance company; rather, independent brokers represent any number of insurance companies through contractual agreements. They are compensated on a commission or a fee basis for the business they produce. This system also is known as the American agency system.

Other Methods of Selling Insurance

While most insurance is sold through agents or brokers under the systems described above, a large volume also is marketed through direct selling and mass marketing methods.

With the *direct selling* method, the insurer deals directly with consumers—no agent or broker is involved—selling its policies through vending machines, advertisements or salaried sales representatives. Insurers that operate using this method are known as *direct writers* or *direct response insurers*.

A large volume of insurance also is sold through *mass marketing* techniques, such as direct mail or newspaper, magazine, radio and television ads. Mass marketing methods provide exposure to large groups of consumers, often using direct selling methods with occasional follow-up by agents.

✏ **Quick Quiz 2.1** True or False?

_____ 1. Mutual insurance companies are owned by their policyowners.

_____ 2. A self-insurer transfers risk to an insurance company to cover all of its potential losses.

_____ 3. Career agencies are branches of major stock and mutual insurance companies that represent the insurer contractually in a particular area.

_____ 4. Blue Cross and Blue Shield are examples of home service insurers.

_____ 5. A fraternal benefit society sells insurance to individuals outside of the society as well as to society members.

_____ 6. Most insurance today is sold through direct selling and mass marketing.

_____ 7. With a reciprocal insurer, the policyholders insure the risks of the other policyholders.

Answers

1. **True**

2. **False**. *A self-insurer establishes its own reserves to cover potential losses although it may use an insurance company to provide insurance above a certain maximum level of loss.*

3. **True**.

4. **False**. *Blue Cross and Blue Shield are examples of service insurers. Service insurers offer health insurance and health care services while home service insurers specialize in a particular type of insurance called industrial insurance.*

5. **False**. *Fraternal society insurance can be sold to members only.*

6. **False**. *Although a large amount of insurance is marketed through direct selling and mass marketing, most insurance today is sold through agents and brokers*

7. **True**.

Regulation of the Insurance Industry

The insurance industry is regulated by a number of authorities, including some inside the industry itself. The primary purpose of this regulation is to promote the public welfare by maintaining the solvency of insurance companies. Other purposes are to provide consumer protection and ensure fair trade practices as well as fair contracts at fair prices. It is very important that insurance agents understand and obey insurance laws and regulations.

History of Regulation

A brief overview of the history of insurance regulation will show a seesaw between the authority of the states and the federal government. Though a balance between these two bodies has been reached and maintained for many years, arguments favoring control by one governing authority over another still are being waged.

- *1868—Paul v. Virginia.* This case, which was decided by the U.S. Supreme Court, involved one state's attempt to regulate an insurance company domiciled in another state. The Supreme Court sided against the insurance company, ruling that the sale and issuance of insurance is not interstate commerce, thus upholding the right of states to regulate insurance.
- *1905—The Armstrong Investigation.* Public outcry over abuses by insurers caused the New York state legislature to investigate life insurers in that state by creating the Armstrong Investigation. The result was the New York Insurance Code, which set a precedent and pattern for insurance regulation by other states throughout the country.
- *1944—United States v. Southeastern Underwriters Association (SEUA).* The decision of *Paul v. Virginia* held for 75 years before the Supreme Court again addressed the issue of state vs. federal regulation of the insurance industry. In the SEUA case, the Court ruled that the business of insurance is subject to a series of federal laws—many of which were in conflict with existing state laws—and that insurance is a form of interstate commerce to be regulated by the federal government. This decision did not affect the power of states to regulate insurance, but it did nullify state laws that were in conflict with federal legislation. The result of the *SEUA* case was to shift the balance of regulatory control to the federal government.
- *1945—The McCarran-Ferguson Act.* The turmoil created by the SEUA case prompted Congress to enact Public Law 15, the McCarran-Ferguson Act. This law made it clear that continued regulation of insurance by the states was in the public's best interest. However, it also made possible the application of federal anti-trust laws to the extent that the insurance business is not regulated by state law. This act led each state

to revise its insurance laws to conform to the federal law. Today, the insurance industry is state regulated.

- *1958—Intervention by the Federal Trade Commission.* In the mid-1950s, the Federal Trade Commission (FTC) sought to control the advertising and sales literature used by the health insurance industry. In 1958, the Supreme Court held that the McCarran-Ferguson Act disallowed such supervision by the FTC, a federal agency. The FTC has made additional attempts to force further federal control, but none have been successful.

- *1959—Intervention by the Securities and Exchange Commission.* In this instance, the issue was whether variable annuities are insurance products to be regulated by the states or securities to be regulated federally by the Securities and Exchange Commission (SEC). The Supreme Court ruled that federal securities laws applied to insurers that issued variable annuities (and variable insurance contracts) and thus required these insurers to conform to both SEC and state insurance regulation. Producers who sell variable contracts must have a National Association of Securities Dealers (NASD) license as well as a life insurance license and must abide by NASD rules for sales and marketing practices.

- *1970—Fair Credit Reporting Act.* In an attempt to protect an individual's right to privacy, the federal government passed the Fair Credit Reporting Act, which requires fair and accurate reporting of information about consumers, including applications for insurance. Insurers must inform applicants about any investigations that are being made, and if any consumer report is used to deny coverage or charge higher rates, the insurer must furnish to the applicant the name of the reporting agency conducting the investigation. Any insurance company that fails to comply with this act is liable to the consumer for actual and punitive damages. (For specific provisions of this act, refer to the section entitled The Fair Credit Reporting Act of 1970 in Lesson 8.)

- *1999—The Financial Services Modernization Act.* The Glass-Steagall Act of 1933, which barred common ownership of banks, insurance companies and securities firms and erected a wall of separation between banks and nonfinancial companies, came under repeated attack in the 1980s. In 1999, Congress enacted the Financial Services Modernization Act, which repealed the Glass-Steagall Act. Under the new legislation, commercial banks, investment banks, retail brokerages and insurance companies now may enter each other's lines of business.

The chronology cited above reflects the roles the courts and the federal government have played in regulating the insurance industry. Some of the ways individual states regulate this business and the industry practices self-regulation follow.

State Regulation of the Insurance Industry

In addition to federal laws, the insurance industry is regulated at the state level by state insurance departments, divisions or boards. These in turn are headed by a commissioner, director or superintendent, depending on the state. Though specific duties vary from state to state, the head of a state insurance department generally is responsible for:

- issuing rules and regulations to enforce the state's insurance laws;
- licensing and supervising insurance companies formed within the state;
- licensing and supervising insurance agents and brokers;
- controlling the kinds of insurance contracts and policies that may be sold in the state;
- determining the amount of reserves an insurer must maintain;
- regulating the investment activity of insurers; and
- overseeing insurance companies' marketing practices and investigating consumer complaints.

Insurance Companies

All insurance companies doing business within a given state must be licensed or certified by that state. Thus, insurance companies are referred to as licensed or nonlicensed.

✓ **Take Note:** In some states, the terms used to designate whether or not a company is licensed are authorized and nonauthorized or admitted and non-admitted.

In addition, the following terms frequently are used to describe insurance companies and their site of incorporation:

- *Domestic insurers.* A company is a domestic insurer in the state in which it is incorporated.
- *Foreign insurers.* A foreign insurer is licensed to conduct business in states other than the one in which it is incorporated.
- *Alien insurers.* Alien insurers are companies incorporated in a country other than the United States, the District of Columbia or any U.S. territorial possession.

✓ **Take Note:** Whether companies are considered domestic, foreign or alien, they must be licensed in each state where they conduct business. State laws restrict insurance companies that are not licensed, or authorized, from doing business within their borders.

Insurance Producers

Every state requires that people who sell insurance have a license from the state. However, before an insurance department will issue such a license—whether it's to a prospective agent or broker—the candidate must pass a producer licensing exam administered by the department. In some states, the agent's or broker's license is perpetual unless revoked; in other states, it must be renewed at stipulated intervals.

Individuals who sell variable contracts—variable annuities, variable life and variable universal health—also must be licensed by the NASD. This requires passing the Series 6 (Investment Company/Variable Contracts Limited Representative) or the Series 7 (General Securities Representative) exam. Variable products are considered both securities and life insurance.

Agent Marketing and Sales Practices

Marketing and selling financial products such as life insurance and annuities require a high level of professionalism and ethics. Every state requires its licensed producers to adhere to certain standards designed to protect consumers and promote suitable sales and application of insurance products. Among these standards are:

- *Selling to needs.* The ethical agent determines what needs the client has and then determines the product best suited to address those needs. Two principles of needs-based selling are:
  – fact-find (learn the client's situation and understand his or her goals, needs and concerns; and
  – educate (teach the client about insurance as a financial tool).
- *Suitability of recommended products.* The ethical agent assesses the correlation between a recommended product and the client's needs and capabilities by asking and answering the following questions:
  – What are the client's needs?
  – What product can help meet those needs?
  – Does the client understand the product and its provisions?
  – Does the client have the capability—financially and otherwise—to manage the product?
  – Is this product in the client's best interest?
- *Full and accurate disclosure.* The ethical agent makes it a practice to inform clients fully about all aspects of the products he or she recommends—their limitations as well as their benefits. There never is any attempt to hide or disguise the nature or purpose of the product nor the company that is being represented. Insurance products are highly effective financial planning tools; they should be presented clearly, completely and accurately.
- *Documentation.* The ethical agent documents each client meeting and transaction. He or she uses fact-finding forms and obtains the client's

written agreement as to the needs determined, the products recommended and the decisions made. Some documentation is required by state law. Ethical agents know these laws and follow them precisely.

- *Client service.* The ethical agent knows that a sale does not mark the end of a relationship with a client, but the beginning. Routine follow-up calls are recommended to ensure that the client's needs always are covered and the products in place still are suitable. When clients contact their agents for service or information, these requests are given top priority. Complaints are handled promptly and fully.

Prohibited Practices

Just as there are standards governing appropriate and ethical sales and marketing practices, certain practices long have been viewed as inappropriate to the business of insurance and are prohibited in virtually all jurisdictions. Practically every state bans twisting, misrepresentation, misuse of premiums and rebating. These are known as prohibited practices.

- *Twisting.* Twisting is the act of persuading a policyowner to drop and replace an existing policy by misrepresenting the terms or conditions of another. Typically, the motivation for twisting simply is to induce the sale of a policy without any regard to the potential disadvantages to the policyowner. Not only is twisting illegal, it is highly unethical.
- *Misrepresentation.* Misrepresentation is a false or misleading statement or representation made by a producer regarding his or her own policies or those of a competitor. Agents are not allowed to misrepresent a policy's terms, benefits or the nature of the coverage it provides. If policy dividends are payable, they cannot be represented as guaranteed.
- *Misuse of premiums.* Misuse of premiums includes diverting premium funds for personal use. Some states require that an agent establish a separate premium account if he or she holds the money for any time before turning it over to the insurer. Commingling premium funds with personal funds is prohibited.
- *Rebating.* Rebating occurs if the buyer of an insurance policy receives any part of the agent's commission or if the agent gives the buyer anything of significant value in exchange for purchasing a policy. For instance, a $25 gift certificate given in exchange for the purchase of a policy would be rebating in some jurisdictions. Most states prohibit the practice of rebating, terming it an *illegal inducement*. Where rebating is allowed, strict guidelines have been imposed to control and monitor its practice.

Replacement

The practice of replacement, which involves convincing a policyowner to lapse or terminate an existing policy and replace it with another, requires special attention. While replacement is not illegal, it rarely is in the best interests of the policyowner. As we will discuss in Lessons 4 and 10, permanent life insurance and annuities build cash value over time. To interrupt one cash value plan and begin another could pose serious financial consequences for the policyowner. On the other hand, if a replacement would result in a

FIGURE 2.1   Insurance Company Rating Systems

A.M. Best Company

A++, A+	Superior; very strong ability to meet obligations
A, A–	Excellent; strong ability to meet obligations
B++, B+	Very good; strong ability to meet obligations
B, B–	Good; adequate ability to meet obligations
C++, C+	Fair; reasonable ability to meet obligations
C, C–	Marginal; currently has ability to meet obligations
D	Below minimum standards
E	Under state supervision
F	In liquidation
S	Suspended

S&P

AAA	Superior; highest safety
AA	Excellent financial security
A	Good financial security
BBB	Adequate financial security
BB	Adequate financial security; ability to meet obligations, may not be adequate for long-term policies
B	Currently able to meet obligations but highly vulnerable to adverse conditions
CCC	Questionable ability to meet obligations
CC, C	May not be meeting obligations; vulnerable to liquidation
R	Under a court order of liquidation; in receivership

Moody's

Aaa	Exceptional security
Aa	Excellent security
A	Good security
Baa	Adequate security
Ba	Questionable security; moderate ability to meet obligations
B	Poor security
Caa	Very poor security; elements of danger regarding payment of obligations
Ca	Extremely poor security; may be in default
C	Lowest security

Fitch

AAA	Highest claims-paying ability; negligible risk
AA+, AA, AA–	Very high claims-paying ability; moderate risk
A+, A, A–	High claims-paying ability; variable risk over time
BBB+, BBB, BBB–	Below average claims-paying ability; considerable variability in risk over time
BB+, BB, BB–	Uncertain claims-paying ability
CCC	Substantial claims-paying ability risk; likely to be placed under state supervision

significant economic benefit for the policyowner, it might be appropriate. If and when a replacement is appropriate, the agent must provide:

- full and fair disclosure to the policyowner of all facts regarding both the new coverage and the existing policy;
- a document signed by the policyowner indicating that he or she has full understanding of the replacement transaction and its implications; and
- notice to the existing insurer and the replacing insurer of the intended replacement.

Generally, most state insurance laws now require all life insurance and annuity sales transactions to include questions about replacement. Product application forms routinely ask if a replacement is involved; if so, additional information is necessary. For example, the agent must provide reason for the replacement and an explanation of why the existing policy cannot meet the client's needs. The additional information gives underwriters and regulators a means of assessing a replacement's suitability and requires consumers to consider the pros and cons of such transactions.

The following questions will guide agents when determining the suitability of policy replacement:

- How does the new insurance need compare with the past need?
- Is the client drawn to contract features in the replacement policy that the existing policy lacks?
- What effect will the replacement policy have on future premiums, cash value accumulations and insurance charges?
- What guarantees are being lost or gained?
- Will the policyowner incur surrender charges if the existing policy is cashed in?
- Is the policyowner's instability or underwriting status different?

While no state has moved to make replacement illegal, most have initiated tracking systems that attempt to identify licensed producers who generate high levels of replacement activity. The burden of proof lies with the agent to demonstrate that a replacement is a suitable recommendation.

Buyer's Guides and Policy Summaries

To help insure that prospective insurance buyers select the most appropriate plan or plans for their needs and to improve their understanding of basic product features, most states require agents to deliver a buyer's guide to the consumer whenever they solicit insurance sales. These guides explain the various types of life insurance products in a way that the average consumer can understand. In addition, a policy summary, containing information about the specific policy being recommended, must be given to a potential buyer. Most states require this be done before the applicant's initial premium is accepted.

The policy summary also contains cost indexes that help the consumer evaluate the suitability of the recommended product. The *net payment cost comparison index* gives the buyer an idea of the cost of the policy at some future point in time, compared to the death benefit. The *surrender cost comparison index* compares the cost of surrendering the policy and withdrawing the cash values at some future time.

 Take Note: Because all states are interested in protecting the interests of the buying public, the actions of individuals soliciting insurance sales are strictly regulated. However, the laws regarding insurance marketing and trade practices vary from state to state. As a result, it is very important that you examine and understand your state's laws.

National Association of Insurance Commissioners

All state insurance commissioners or directors are members of the National Association of Insurance Commissioners (NAIC). This organization has standing committees that work regularly to examine various aspects of the insurance industry and to recommend appropriate insurance laws and regulations.

Basically, the NAIC has four broad objectives:

- to encourage uniformity in state insurance laws and regulations;
- to assist in the administration of those laws and regulations by promoting efficiency;
- to protect the interests of policyowners and consumers; and
- to preserve state regulation of the insurance business.

The NAIC has been instrumental in developing guidelines and model legislation that help ensure that the insurance industry maintains a high level of public trust by conducting its business competently and fairly. This group also develops standards for policy provisions, helping ensure that policies are more uniform than disparate across the country. Notable among the NAIC's accomplishments was the creation of the Advertising Code and the Unfair Trade Practices Act, which have been adopted by virtually every state.

Advertising Code   A principal problem of states in the past was regulating misleading insurance advertising and direct mail solicitations. Many states now subscribe to the Advertising Code developed by the NAIC. The code specifies certain words and phrases that are considered misleading and are not to be used in advertising of any kind and also requires full disclosure of policy renewal, cancellation and termination provisions. Other rules pertain to the use of testimonials, statistics, special offers and the like.

Unfair Trade Practices Act   Most jurisdictions also have adopted the NAIC's Unfair Trade Practices Act. This act, as amended in 1972, gives insurance commissioners the power to investigate insurance companies and producers, to issue cease and desist orders and to impose penalties on violators. The act also gives commissioners the authority to seek a court injunction to restrain insurers from using any methods believed to be unfair or deceptive. Included as of unfair trade practices are misrepresentation and false advertising, coercion and intimidation, unfair discrimination, and inequitable administration or claims settlements.

State Guaranty Associations

All states have established guaranty funds or guaranty associations to support insurers and to protect consumers if an insurer becomes insolvent. Should an insurer be financially unable to pay its claims, the state guaranty association will step in and cover the consumers' unpaid claims. These state associations are funded by insurance companies through assessments.

The NAIFA and NAHU

The National Association of Insurance and Financial Advisors (NAIFA) and the National Association of Health Underwriters (NAHU) are organizations of life and health insurance agents that are dedicated to supporting the life and health insurance industries and advancing the quality of service provided by insurance professionals. Each organization issues a code of ethics that stresses the high professional duty expected of underwriters toward their clients, as well as to their companies, and emphasizes that only by observing the highest ethical balance can conflict between these two obligations be avoided. (See the Appendix for both the NAIFA and NAHU code of ethics.)

Rating Services

The financial strength and stability of an insurance company are two vitally important factors to potential insurance buyers and to insurance companies themselves. Guides to insurance companies' financial integrity and claims-paying ability are published regularly by various *rating services*, such as A.M. Best, Inc., Standard & Poor's, Moody's and Fitch. For example, in *Best's Insurance Reports*, companies are rated A++ to A+ (superior), A to A– (excellent), B++ to B+ (very good), B to B– (good), C++ to C+ (fair), C to C– (marginal), D (below minimum standards), E (under state supervision) and F (in liquidation). Experts generally recommend that insurance buyers purchase policies from companies that have a rating of A++ to A–, because these ratings indicate a strong ability to meet obligations to policyowners.

Summary

There are many types of insurance providers. State and local governments provide insurance, as do private insurers. Private insurers include stock companies, mutual companies, reciprocals, assessment mutuals, fraternal societies, home service insurers and service providers. Special categories of insurers include reinsurers and Lloyd's of London.

Insurance is sold through a variety of methods—most commonly through licensed producers. The systems that support the sale of insurance through agents and brokers are the career agency system, the personal producing agency system and the independent agency system.

To promote public welfare, the insurance industry is regulated by a number of authorities. These authorities include the:

- states and their departments of insurance;
- NAIC and its model legislation; and
- federal government through the application of antitrust laws and the Fair Credit Reporting Act.

All states have enacted laws and regulations that affect the business of insurance, always with consumer interest in mind. Insurance companies as well as agents and brokers are bound by these laws.

Key Concepts

In preparing for their licensing examination, students should be familiar with the following concepts:

types of insurers	state regulation
NAIC	prohibited practices
NAIFA	insurance company rating systems
NAHU	organization and ownership of
McCarran-Ferguson Act	insurers
Fair Credit Reporting Act	types of marketing/distribution
federal regulation	systems
Financial Services Modernization Act	*United States v. Southeastern Underwriters Association*

Lesson Exam Two

1. In some states, an insurance salesperson who offers a $100 gourmet dinner in exchange for the purchase of a life insurance policy would be considered to have committed which of the following prohibited sales practices?

    A. Twisting
    B. Replacement
    C. Rebating
    D. Churning

2. An insurance company organized and headquartered in Indiana can be described as what type of company when practicing in Indiana?

    A. Alien
    B. Home-based
    C. Foreign
    D. Domestic

3. Which of the following statements regarding types of insurers is NOT correct?

    A. Reinsurers work directly with individual policyowners.
    B. Stock insurance companies seek a profit for their shareholders.
    C. Mutual insurance companies are owned by their policyowners.
    D. Service providers generally specialize in health insurance and health care services.

4. Regarding landmark cases and laws involving the regulation of insurance, which of the following statements is NOT correct?

    A. Insurers are required to disclose when an applicant's consumer or credit history is being investigated.
    B. The Securities and Exchange Commission (SEC) may regulate insurers that sell variable annuities and variable life insurance.
    C. The Federal Trade Commission (FTC) directly supervises all insurance marketing activities.
    D. The New York Insurance Code long has been a model for state insurance regulation.

5. Which of the following statements regarding the National Association of Insurance Commissioners (NAIC) is NOT correct?

    A. It is empowered to prosecute and punish criminal violators in the insurance industry.
    B. It seeks to preserve state rather than federal regulation of the insurance industry.
    C. It promotes uniformity in state insurance laws and regulations.
    D. It seeks to promote efficient administration of insurance laws and regulations.

6. In an insurance transaction, licensed agents legally represent which of the following?

    A. The insurer
    B. The applicant and insured
    C. The state insurance department
    D. Themselves

7. In an insurance transaction, licensed brokers legally represent which of the following people?

    A. The insurer
    B. The applicant and insured
    C. The state insurance department
    D. Themselves

8. A life insurance company organized in Illinois, with its home office in Philadelphia, is licensed to conduct business in Wisconsin. In Wisconsin, this company would be considered which of the following types of insurers?

   A. Domestic
   B. Alien
   C. Foreign
   D. Regional

9. Which of the following is not a service insurer?

   A. HMO
   B. Blue Cross
   C. Lloyd's of London
   D. PPO

10. A reinsurer is a company that

    A. accepts all the risk from another insurer
    B. assumes a portion of the risk from another insurer
    C. cedes the risk from another insurer
    D. does not take any risk

11. The head of a state insurance department generally is responsible for all of the following EXCEPT

    A. licensing and supervising agents and brokers
    B. overseeing insurance companies' marketing practices
    C. issuing rules and regulations
    D. making insurance laws

12. In addition to the state, the organization that regulates variable life and variable annuities is the

    A. Federal Trade Commission (FTC)
    B. National Association of Insurance Commissioners (NAIC)
    C. Securities and Exchange (SEC)
    D. Federal Communications Commission (FCC)

13. Which of the following prohibited practices involves the diversion of insurance funds for personal use?

    A. Replacement
    B. Rebating
    C. Misrepresentation
    D. Misuse of premiums

14. What does the state guaranty association guarantee?

    A. That your policy will be issued
    B. That your claim will be paid if your insurer becomes insolvent
    C. That dividends will be paid
    D. Rates of return on your policy

15. Which of the following prohibited practices involves the sale of variable universal life insurance policies as mutual funds?

    A. Twisting
    B. Replacement
    C. Rebating
    D. Misrepresentation

Answers & Rationale

1. **C.** Rebating occurs if an agent gives the buyer anything of significant value in exchange for purchasing a policy. A $100 gourmet dinner offered in exchange for purchasing an insurance policy, therefore, would be considered rebating.

2. **D.** An insurance company is considered a domestic insurer in the state in which it is incorporated. Thus, a company organized and headquartered in Indiana is considered a domestic company in Indiana.

3. **A.** Reinsurers insure other insurance companies. The purpose of reinsurance is to limit the loss an insurer would face if a very large claim becomes payable. Thus, reinsurers work directly with other insurance companies rather than with individual policyowners.

4. **C.** The FTC has attempted to control the advertising and sales literature used by the health insurance industry. However, in 1958 the Supreme Court held that the McCarran-Ferguson Act disallowed such supervision by the FTC.

5. **A.** Although the NAIC assists in administering state insurance laws and seeks to protect policyowners' interests, it does not have any legal authority to prosecute and punish criminal violators in the insurance industry.

6. **A.** A licensed insurance agent legally represents the insurer in a sales transaction and in any disputes between the insured or beneficiary and the insurer.

7. **B.** An insurance broker is not affiliated with any particular company and may represent different companies' products. In an insurance transaction, the broker represents the buyer and not the insurer.

8. **C.** To be considered a domestic company in Wisconsin, the insurance company must be incorporated there. However, because it was incorporated in Illinois and merely is authorized to transact business in Wisconsin, it is considered a foreign company in Wisconsin.

9. **C.** Service insurers such as Blue Cross, HMOs and PPOs offer health insurance and health care services. Lloyd's of London, on the other hand, is not a service insurer but instead is an association of individuals and companies that individually underwrite insurance.

10. **B.** A reinsurer assumes part, but not all, of the risk from another insurer to help limit the loss the insurer would face if a large claim became payable.

11. **D.** The head of a state insurance department generally is responsible for licensing and supervising agents and brokers, overseeing insurance companies' marketing practices and issuing rules and regulations. However, it is the state legislature rather than the head of the state insurance department that is responsible for making insurance laws.

12. **C.** Because federal securities laws apply to insurers that issue variable annuities, they must conform to both SEC and state regulations. The SEC also regulates variable life insurance.

13. **D.** The prohibited practice of misusing premiums involves diverting premium funds for personal use.

14. **B.** If an insurer is insolvent or financially unable to pay its claims, the state guaranty association protects consumers by guaranteeing that its claims will be paid.

15. **D.** Agents are prohibited from misrepresenting a policy's terms or the nature of the coverage it provides. As a result, an agent would be guilty of misrepresentation if he or she sold variable universal life insurance policies but instead represented that they were mutual funds.

3

Law and the Insurance Contract

INTRODUCTION   Life and health insurance policies are legal contracts enforceable by law. As such, they are governed by many of the same legal principles that are applicable to the formation of any contract. However, in addition to these general principles that apply to all contracts, there are other characteristics that apply to insurance contracts specifically. We will begin this lesson by reviewing the general requirements of an enforceable contract and then will look at some of the other elements of an insurance contract in particular. We also will examine the agent's role in the creation of a contract and how the concepts of waiver, estoppel and the parol evidence rule apply to the interpretation of contracts.

LESSON OBJECTIVES   When you complete this lesson you should be able to:

- identify and describe the essential elements of a legally binding contract;
- list and describe the special features of insurance contracts;
- explain the general concepts of agency law, including the difference between express, implied and apparent authority, and give an example of each; and
- explain how waiver, estoppel and the parol evidence rule apply to insurance transactions.

General Law of Contracts

A contract is an agreement enforceable by law. It is the means by which one or more parties bind themselves to certain promises. With a life insurance contract, the insurer binds itself to pay a certain sum on the death of the insured. In exchange, the policyowner pays premiums.

For a contract to be legally valid and binding, it must contain certain elements—*an offer and acceptance, consideration, legal purpose* and *competent parties.* Let's consider each.

Offer and Acceptance

To be legally enforceable, a contract must be made with a definite, unqualified offer by one party and the acceptance of its exact terms by the other party. In many cases, the offer of an insurance contract is made by the applicant when he or she submits the application with the initial premium. The insurance company accepts the offer when it issues the policy as applied for. In other cases, the insurance company will not issue the policy as applied for; instead, it may counteroffer with the issuance of another policy at different premium rates or with different terms. In these situations, the applicant has the right to accept or reject the counteroffer.

If an applicant does not submit an initial premium with the application, he or she simply is inviting the insurance company to make the contract offer. The insurer can respond by issuing a policy (the offer) that the applicant can accept by paying the premium when the policy is delivered.

Until an offer has been accepted, the person making the offer has the right to rescind it. Thus, if an applicant wishes to withdraw his or her application before the insurer accepts it, the offer is terminated, even if the initial premium has been submitted. The insurer must return the premium.

Consideration

For a contract to be enforceable, the promise or promises it contains must be supported by consideration. Consideration is something of value given in exchange for the promises sought. In an insurance contract, consideration is given by the applicant in exchange for the insurer's promise to pay benefits; this consideration consists of the application and the initial premium. This is why the offer and acceptance of an insurance contract are not completed until the insurer receives the application and the first premium.

Legal Purpose

To be legally enforceable, a contract must have a legal purpose. This means that the goal of the contract and the reason the parties enter into the agreement must be legal. A contract in which one party agrees to commit murder for money would be unenforceable in court because the goal or purpose of the contract is not legal.

✓ *Take Note:* In all jurisdictions, insurance is considered to possess a legal purpose.

Competent Parties

To be enforceable, a contract must be entered into by competent parties. With a contract of insurance, the parties to the contract are the applicant and the insurer. The insurer is considered competent if it has been licensed or authorized by the state (or states) in which it conducts business. The applicant, unless proven otherwise, is presumed to be competent, with three possible exceptions:

- minors;
- the mentally infirm; and
- those under the influence of alcohol or narcotics.

Each state has its own laws governing the legality of minors and the mentally infirm entering into contracts of insurance. These laws are based on the principle that some parties are not capable of understanding the contract they agree to.

✓ *Take Note:* In many states, a minor is considered to be any person under age 21. However, in recent years, a majority of states have lowered this age to 18. With respect to insurance contracts, several states have enacted statutes that give minors of a certain age (varying from 14 to 18) the capacity to enter into valid and enforceable life insurance contracts. In the absence of such a statute, however, insurance contracts with minors are voidable at the minor's option.

It should be noted that beneficiaries and insureds (if different from the applicant) are not parties to an insurance contract. As such, they need not have contractual capability.

Other competent parties that may enter into contracts of insurance with an insurance company include business entities, trusts and estates.

 **Test Topic Alert!**

Use this mnemonic device to recall the four elements of a legal contract: CLOC (competent parties, legal purpose, offer and acceptance and consideration).

Special Features of Insurance Contracts

The elements just discussed must be contained in every contract for it to be enforceable by law. In addition to these, insurance contracts have their own distinguishing characteristics that set them apart from other legally binding contracts. Let's review these characteristics.

Aleatory

An aleatory contract is conditioned on the occurrence of an uncertain event beyond the control of the parties involved. Insurance contracts are aleatory in that (1) there is an element of chance for both of the contracting parties and (2) the dollar values exchanged need not be equal. Consequently, the benefits provided by an insurance policy may or may not exceed the premiums paid. For example, an individual who has a disability insurance policy will collect benefits if he or she becomes disabled; if no disability strikes, no benefits are paid.

✓ **Take Note:** The opposite of an aleatory contract is a commutative contract, where there is no element of chance and the parties exchange goods of equal value. A real estate transaction is a commutative contract—the seller agrees to sell property for a certain sum and the buyer agrees to buy the property for the same sum.

Adhesion

Insurance contracts are contracts of adhesion. This means that the contract has been prepared by one party (the insurer), and the terms did not result from negotiation between the parties. In effect, the applicant adheres to the terms of the contract when he or she accepts it.

In contract law, and notably with respect to contracts of adhesion, the contract is to be viewed or interpreted most favorably for the party that did not draft it. The purpose is to overcome or balance any advantage that may result for the party that prepared the contract. Consequently, if there are any ambiguities in the contract, they will be interpreted in favor of the party that did not create the contract. For insurance contracts, this means that any ambiguous provisions will be given the interpretation most favorable to the insured or beneficiary, not the insurer.

Unilateral

Insurance contracts are unilateral in that only one party—the insurer—makes any kind of enforceable promise. Insurers promise to pay benefits when or if a certain event, such as death or disability, should happen. The applicant makes no such promise—he or she does not even promise to pay premiums, and the insurer cannot require that they be paid. Of course, the insurer has the right to, and will, cancel the contract if premiums are not paid.

⋅ᬭᬭ̣- **Test Topic Alert!**   As a unilateral contract, an insurance policy is legally binding on the insurance company only. The terms may be enforced only against the insurance company, which is bound to perform its duties under the contract.

A unilateral contract can be contrasted to a bilateral contract, in which each contracting party makes enforceable promises.

Not a Personal Contract

Life insurance is not a personal contract or personal agreement between the insurer and the insured. For this reason, people who buy life insurance policies are called policyowners rather than policyholders. These people actually own their policies and can give them away if they wish. Such a transfer of ownership is known as *assignment*. To assign a policy, a policyowner simply must notify the company in writing. The company then will accept the validity of the transfer without question. The new owner then is granted all of the rights of policy ownership.

Most other insurance contracts are personal contracts. They constitute a personal agreement between the insured and the insurer, and they cannot be transferred to another person without the insurer's approval. Because of the personal nature of most insurance contracts, they cannot be freely assigned by the policyholder to other parties. To permit a fire insurance contract to be assignable without the insurer's approval, for example, would be unfair to the insurer. Only by knowing and investigating each applicant for insurance can an insurance company accurately appraise the risk it is accepting.

Conditional

An insurance contract is conditional in that the insurer's promise to pay benefits is dependent on the occurrence of the risk insured against. If the risk does not materialize, no benefits are paid. Furthermore, the insurer's obligations under the contract are conditioned on the performance of certain acts by the insured or the beneficiary.

For Example: The timely payment of premiums is a condition of the continuance of the contract. If premiums are not paid, the company is relieved of its obligation to pay a death benefit, though it would be bound by other promises contained in the contract's surrender and reinstatement provisions. Providing proof of death (or proof of disability or medical expenses) is another condition. Until the insurer receives such proof, it is not liable for payment.

The significance of a condition is that, if the policyowner or beneficiary satisfies the condition, it legally binds the insurer to its obligations under the contract. If the condition is not met, the insurer is released from its obligations. However, conditions on a policyowner or beneficiary are not legally binding or enforceable. An insured who does not meet a contractual condition simply gives up the right to make a claim under the contract. If a policyowner stops paying premiums, for example, the insurance company cannot compel further payment. It can only cancel the policy. By contrast, an insurance company that does not meet its contractual obligations once the policyowner or beneficiary satisfies the conditions for making a claim may be liable to the insured for damages.

Valued or Indemnity

An insurance contract is either a valued contract or an indemnity contract. A valued contract pays a stated sum, regardless of the actual loss incurred, when the contingency insured against occurs. Life insurance contracts are valued contracts. If an individual acquires a life insurance policy insuring his life for $1 million, that is the amount payable at his death. There is no attempt to value actual financial loss.

An indemnity contract, on the other hand, pays an amount equal to the loss—it attempts to return the insured to his or her original financial position.

 For Example: Fire and health insurance policies are examples of indemnity contracts. An insured who owns a $100,000 fire insurance policy and suffers a $5,000 loss from fire will be able to collect up to $5,000, not $100,000.

The doctrine of *subrogation* is inherent to indemnity contracts. This means that in the event a claim is paid, the insurer acquires the insured's right to take legal action against any negligent third party that may have caused or contributed to the loss. The right of subrogation does not exist with life insurance contracts. An auto insurer has the right to take legal action against an individual who caused damage to one of the company's insured vehicles (up to the amount of the loss payment); a life insurer has no such recourse if the death of one of its insureds was caused by a negligent third party.

Utmost Good Faith

Insurance is a contract of utmost good faith. Both the policyowner and the insurer must know all material facts and relevant information. There can be no attempt by either party to conceal, disguise or deceive. A consumer purchases a policy based largely on what the insurer and its agent claim are its features, benefits and advantages; an insurer issues a policy based primarily on what the applicant reveals in the application.

The concepts of *warranties, representations* and *concealment* are associated with this idea of utmost good faith. These represent grounds through which an insurer might seek to avoid payment under a contract.

Warranty

A warranty in insurance is a statement made by the applicant that is guaranteed to be true. It becomes part of the contract and, if found to be untrue, can be grounds for revoking the contract. Warranties are presumed to be material because they affect the insurer's decision to accept or reject an applicant.

Representation

A representation is a statement made by the applicant that he or she believes to be true. It is used by the insurer to evaluate whether or not to issue a policy. Unlike warranties, representations are not part of the contract and need be true only to the extent that they are material and related to the risk. Most states require that life insurance policies contain a provision that all statements made in the application be deemed representations, not warranties. If an insurance company rejects a claim on the basis of a representation, the company bears the burden of proving that the representation was material and related to risk.

🔆 Test Topic Alert!

Statements made by a person on an application for life or health insurance generally are representations, not warranties.

The practical distinction between a warranty and a representation is this—if a warranty is untrue, the insurer has the right to cancel the contract; if a representation is untrue, the insurer has the right to cancel the contract only if the representation was material to the creation of the contract.

✔ **For Example:** If an insured falsely stated in a life insurance application that his or her cancer was in remission when the insured was, in fact, terminally ill, this statement would be a misrepresentation. If the insurance company had known this information, it would either have rejected the application or issued the policy on substantially different terms. As a result, this misrepresentation may provide grounds for the insurer to cancel the contract. However, if an insured misstated the age at which a grandparent died, the insurer probably would not be able to rescind the contract because such misrepresentation would have had no influence on the terms of the contract.

Concealment

The issue of concealment also is important to insurance contracts. Concealment is defined as the applicant's failure to disclose a known material fact when applying for insurance. If the purpose for concealing information is to defraud the insurer (that is, to obtain a policy that might not be issued otherwise if the information were revealed), the insurer may have grounds for voiding the policy. Again, the insurer must prove concealment and materiality.

In most instances, life insurers have only a limited period of time to uncover false warranties, misrepresentations or concealment. After that time period passes, usually two years from policy issue, the contract cannot be voided or revoked for these reasons. (See *Incontestable Clause*, Lesson 5.) Health insurance contracts follow slightly different rules. (See *Time Limit on Certain Defenses*, Lesson 21.)

 For Example: An applicant for homeowner's insurance does not disclose that he or she manufactures firecrackers in the basement as a hobby. Although the insurance company did not specifically ask about this hobby, the applicant has an obligation to disclose extraordinary facts such as these that are within his or her scope of knowledge. Not disclosing this fact would be considered concealment.

Insurable Interest

Another element of a valid insurance contract is insurable interest. This means that the person acquiring the contract (the applicant) must be subject to loss on the death, illness or disability of the person being insured. A policy obtained by a person not having an insurable interest in the insured is not valid and cannot be enforced.

 Take Note: Many relationships provide the basis for an insurable interest. Husbands and wives have an insurable interest in each other as do partners in a partnership. Corporations have an insurable interest in their key executives, as well.

Thus, insurable interest must exist between the applicant and the individual being insured. When the applicant is the same as the person to be insured, there is no question that insurable interest exists—individuals are presumed to have insurable interest in themselves. Questions tend to arise when the applicant is not the person to be insured. As a general rule, the consent of the person to be insured is required before a policy is issued, even if the applicant has an insurable interest. Insurers have a legal responsibility to verify insurable interest and obtain the insured's consent. (See also *Does Insurable Interest Exist?* in Lesson 8.)

 **Test Topic Alert!** Insurable interest may have to exist between the policyowner, the insured and the beneficiary for the insurance company to consider the risk a pure risk.

FIGURE 3.1 Elements of an Insurance Contract

Elements Associated with All Legal Contracts

- Offer and Acceptance
- Consideration
- Legal Purpose
- Competent Parties

+

Characteristics of Insurance Contracts

- Aleatory
- Adhesion
- Unilateral
- Not Personal
- Conditional
- Valued or Indemnity
- Utmost Good Faith
- Insurable Interest

One important point to note about insurable interest with life and health contracts is that the interest must exist at the inception of the policy. It need not continue throughout the duration of the policy, nor must it exist at the inception of the policy and at the time of claim. This is in contrast to property and casualty insurance policies, for which insurable interest must exist at the time of claim.

 **Quick Quiz 3.1**

1. To be legally binding, a contract must contain all of the following elements EXCEPT

   A. consideration
   B. offer and acceptance
   C. competent parties
   D. unilateral promises

2. An insured does not disclose a terminal illness when applying for life insurance. This is known as a

   A. guaranteed warranty
   B. concealment
   C. conditional disclosure
   D. revocation of warranty

3. A life insurance contract that pays a set $500,000 death benefit at the insured's death is what kind of contract?

   A. Indemnity
   B. Warranty
   C. Valued
   D. Personal

4. Which of the following parties makes an enforceable promise in an insurance contract?

   A. Insured
   B. Insurer
   C. Insured and the insurer
   D. Agent, the insured and the insurer

5. If an insured makes a material warranty in an insurance application that is later found to be untrue, the insurance company can

   A. cancel the contract
   B. file a lawsuit
   C. increase premiums
   D. assign the contract

Answers

1. **D.** To be legally binding, a contract must contain an offer and acceptance, consideration, a legal purpose and competent parties. Some contracts, such as insurance contracts, are unilateral; that is, only one party makes any type of enforceable promise. However, this is not a required element for a contract to be legally binding.

2. **B.** Concealment occurs when an applicant fails to disclose a known material fact when applying for insurance.

3. **C.** A life insurance contract that pays a set death benefit at the insured's death is called a valued contract. A valued contract pays a stated sum, regardless of the actual loss incurred, when the contingency insured against occurs. In contrast, an indemnity contract pays an amount equal to the loss and attempts to return the insured to his or her original financial position.

4. **B.** In an insurance contract, only one party—the insurer—makes any kind of enforceable promise. The applicant, on the other hand, makes no such promise and does not even promise to pay premiums.

5. **A.** Because the insured's warranties will affect the insurer's decision to accept or reject the application, the insurer could cancel the contract if it discovers an untrue warranty in the application.

Agents and Brokers

Because insurance contracts are binding and enforceable, certain legal concepts extend to those who bring together the contract parties—the applicant and the insurer. In most cases, bringing the parties together is done by an agent or a broker. In Lesson 2, we discussed some of the more important regulations that states impose on those who solicit and sell insurance; here we will focus on legal aspects of negotiating and placing insurance contracts.

The Concept of Agency

As noted earlier, an agent is an individual who has been authorized by an insurer to be its representative to the public and to offer its goods and services for sale. Specifically, this role entails:

- describing the company's insurance policies to prospective buyers and explaining the conditions under which the policies may be obtained;
- soliciting applications for insurance;
- in some cases, collecting premiums from policyowners; and
- rendering service to prospects and to those who have purchased policies from the company.

An agent's authority to undertake these functions is defined clearly in a contract of agency (or agency agreement) between the agent and the company. Within the authority granted, the agent is considered identical with the company. The relationship between an agent and the company he or she represents is governed by agency law.

Principles of Agency Law

By legal definition, an agent is a person who acts for another person or entity (known as the *principal*) with regard to contractual arrangements with third parties. The concept of power is implicit in this definition—an authorized agent has the power to bind the principal to contracts (and to the rights and responsibilities of those contracts). With this in mind, we can review the following main principles of agency law:

- The acts of the agent (within the scope of his or her authority) are the acts of the principal.
- A contract completed by an agent on behalf of the principal is a contract of the principal.
- Payments made to an agent on behalf of the principal are payments made to the principal.

- The agent's knowledge regarding the principal's business is presumed to be the principal's knowledge.

Agent Authority   Note the above parenthetical explanation "within the scope of his or her authority." Authority—that which an agent is authorized to do on behalf of his or her company—is another important concept in agency law. Technically, only those actions for which an agent is authorized can bind a principal. In reality, however, an agent's authority can be quite broad. There are three types of agent authority: *express, implied* and *apparent*. Let's take a look at each.

- *Express authority.* Express authority is the authority a principal intends to—and actually does—give to its agent. Express authority is granted by means of the agent's contract, which is the principal's appointment of the agent to act on its behalf.

✓ **For Example:** The agency contract generally contains clauses dealing with the specific and general powers of the agent, the scale of commissions and the ownership of contracts sold.

- *Implied authority.* Implied authority is authority that is not expressly granted but which the agent is assumed to have to transact the principal's business. Implied authority is incidental to express authority because not every single detail of an agent's authority can be spelled out.

✓ **For Example:** An agent's contract may not specifically state that he or she can print business cards that contain the company's name, but the authority to do so is implied.

- *Apparent authority.* Apparent authority is the appearance or assumption of authority based on the actions, words or deeds of the principal or because of circumstances the principal created.

✓ **For Example:** By providing an individual with a rate book, application forms and sales literature, an insurance company creates the impression that an agency relationship exists between itself and the individual. The company will not later be allowed to deny that such a relationship existed.

✓ **Take Note:** It is important to understand that apparent authority arises only when the buyer has no way of knowing that the agent has exceeded his or her authority. Also, even if the agent did not have the express or implied authority to take a particular action, his or her authority may be extended by ratification. *Ratification* occurs when the insurer accepts the agent's actions that were beyond the scope of his or her authority and acts as if the agent actually had authority to take such actions (e.g., it accepts the premium on coverage the agent wrote while exceeding express authority).

The significance of authority—whether express, implied or apparent—is that it ties the company to the acts and deeds of its agent. The law will view the agent and the company as the same entity when the agent acts within the scope of his or her authority.

Agent as Fiduciary

Another legal concept that governs the activity of an agent is that of fiduciary. A fiduciary is a person who holds a position of special trust and confidence. Agents act in a fiduciary capacity when they accept premiums on behalf of the insurer or offer advice that affects people's financial security. Agents have fiduciary responsibilities to both their clients and the insurance companies they represent. Acting as a fiduciary requires that an agent:

- be fit and proper;
- be honest and trustworthy;
- have a good business reputation;
- be qualified to perform insurance functions;
- have knowledge of, and abide by, state laws and regulations; and
- act in good faith.

Brokers vs. Agents

As noted earlier, unlike agents, brokers legally represent the insureds and do not have the legal authority to bind the insurer. Brokers solicit and accept applications for insurance and then place the coverage with an insurer. The business is not in force and the insurance company is not bound until it accepts the application. Technically, brokers represent themselves in the solicitation of insurance policies; once prospects or clients request coverage, brokers represent their buyers.

In practice, the legal distinction between brokers and agents is insignificant. Both brokers and agents are licensed as insurance producers and both are subject to insurance laws and regulations. In fact, in some states any individual who solicits insurance and places a policy will be considered an agent of the insurer with regard to that policy.

Professional Liability

Just as doctors and lawyers should have malpractice insurance to protect against legal liability arising from their professional services, insurance agents need errors and omissions (E&O) professional liability insurance. Under this insurance, the insurer agrees to pay sums that the agent legally is obligated to pay for injuries resulting from professional services that he or she rendered or failed to render. Under E&O policies, the insurer will defend any suits covered by the policy, even if the suits are groundless, false or fraudulent. Any claim arising from injuries, real or alleged, comes within the scope of this coverage.

Other Legal Concepts

In addition to the principles of contract and agency law, other legal concepts apply to insurance and the power of agents. These are *waiver, estoppel, the parol evidence rule, void vs. voidable contracts* and *fraud.*

Waiver

Waiver is the voluntary giving up of a legal, given right. If an insurer voluntarily waives a legal right it has under a contract, it cannot later deny a claim based on a violation of that right.

✓ **For Example:** Assume a life insurance contract specifies that premium payments are to be made by the policyowner directly to the company at the home office address. John, one of the company's insureds, has instead made his payments over the years to his agent and the company has accepted these payments. In so doing, the company has effectively waived the direct payment provision and cannot later deny payment of claim on John's policy on the grounds that premiums were not remitted directly to the company.

Estoppel

The concepts of waiver and estoppel are closely related. Estoppel prohibits one party from denying the consequences of its own actions or deeds if such actions or deeds result in another party acting in a specific manner or drawing certain conclusions. In other words, estoppel is the loss of defense.

✓ **For Example:** In the preceding example, if the insurer has waived its right to have premiums remitted to it directly, it will be *estopped* from denying John's claim because he gave his premium payments to his agent.

Another example of estoppel is if a company severs its agency relationship with an agent but later accepts an application from this individual, thereby reasserting the agency relationship. The company will be estopped from claiming an agency relationship did not exist at the time it entered into the contract with the insured.

Parol Evidence Rule

Parol evidence is oral or verbal evidence, or that which is given verbally in a court of law. The parol evidence rule states that when parties put their agreement in writing, all previous verbal statements come together in that writing, and a written contract cannot be changed or modified by parol (oral) evidence. This preserves the integrity of the written contract as the final embodiment of the parties' agreement.

✓ **Take Note:** There are a few exceptions to the parol evidence rule. Parol evidence may be admissible in court when the written contract terms are incomplete or ambiguous, or when there has been a mistake or fraud in preparing the written contract. Then parol evidence is used not to change the terms, but to explain or interpret them.

Void vs. Voidable Contracts

The terms void and voidable often are incorrectly used interchangeably. A void contract simply is an agreement without legal effect. In essence, it is not a contract at all, for it lacks one of the elements specified by law for a valid contract. A void contract cannot be enforced by either party.

A contract having an illegal object is void, and neither party to the contract can enforce it.

✓ **For Example:** Tom agrees to steal a car and sell it to Fred. The car is damaged during the theft; Fred refuses to pay the price they agreed upon. Tom cannot sue Fred to get the payment, and Fred cannot sue Tom to get another undamaged car.

In contrast, a voidable contract is an agreement which, for a reason satisfactory to the court, may be set aside by one of the parties to the contract. It is binding unless the party with the right to reject it wishes to do so. Say that a situation develops under which the insured has failed to comply with a condition of the contract: he or she ceased paying the premium. The contract then is voidable, and the insurance company has the right to void the contract and revoke the coverage.

Fraud

In the event of fraud, insurance contracts are unique in that they run counter to a basic rule of contract law. Under most contracts, fraud is a reason to void a contract. With life insurance contracts, an insurer has only a limited period of time (usually two years from date of issue) to challenge the validity of a contract. After that period, the insurer cannot contest the policy or deny benefits based on material misrepresentations, concealment or fraud. (This is explained in more detail in *Incontestable Clause*, Lesson 5 and *Time Limit on Certain Defenses*, Lesson 21.)

Summary

An insurance policy is a legally binding contract between the applicant/owner and the insurance company. As such, it must contain an offer and acceptance, consideration, legal purpose and competent parties—elements required of all enforceable contracts. In addition, insurance contracts are distinguished by other features unique to the purpose and scope of insurance. Among these special features is the element of insurable interest.

Agents and brokers—and the companies they conduct business with—operate under the concept of agency and the principles of agency law. One of the most important aspects of agency law is that it gives the agent the power to act on behalf of the principal (the insurer) and to bind it to contracts. Agents are empowered by three types of authority: express, implied and apparent.

Finally, there are additional legal concepts that have direct application to insurance and insurance contracts. These include waiver, estoppel, the parol evidence rule, void vs. voidable contracts and fraud.

Key Concepts

In preparing for their licensing examination, students should be familiar with the following concepts:

offer and acceptance	consideration
legal purpose	competent parties
aleatory	adhesion
unilateral	conditional
valued vs. reimbursement	insurable interest
warranties	representations
concealment	waiver
estoppel	parol evidence rule
fraud	void vs. voidable contract
express authority	implied authority
apparent authority	personal contract

Lesson Exam Three

1. Which of the following is the authority that an insurer gives to its agents by means of the agent's contract?

    A. Implied
    B. Express
    C. Fiduciary
    D. General

2. "An insurance contract is prepared by one party, the insurer, rather than by negotiation between the contracting parties." This feature means that the insurance contract

    A. is an aleatory contract
    B. is a contract of acceptance
    C. is a contract of adhesion
    D. names only the insurer as the competent party

3. Which of the following statements regarding insurable interest is NOT correct?

    A. Insurable interest exists when the applicant is the insured.
    B. A policy obtained by a person without an insurable interest in the insured can be enforced.
    C. The applicant must be subject to loss on the death, illness or disability of the insured.
    D. Generally, the person to be insured must give his or her consent before a policy is issued, even if the applicant has an insurable interest.

4. Which of the following statements is NOT correct?

    A. Express authority is granted by means of the agent's contract.
    B. Express authority is expressed orally.
    C. Implied authority is not overtly extended in the agent's contract, but does permit many of the agent's operations.
    D. Apparent authority is the appearance of authority based on the principal's actions, words or deeds.

5. Which of the following statements regarding utmost good faith in insurance contracts is CORRECT?

    A. The concept of utmost good faith—that there is no attempt to conceal, disguise or deceive—applies only to the insurer.
    B. Although a warranty is a statement, it technically is not part of the contract.
    C. A representation is a statement that the applicant guarantees to be true.
    D. Most state insurance laws consider statements made in an application for an insurance policy to be representations, not warranties.

6. Which of the following statements describes an insurable interest?

    A. The policyowner must expect to benefit from the insured's death.
    B. The policyowner must expect to suffer a loss when the insured dies or becomes disabled.
    C. The beneficiary, by definition, has an insurable interest in the insured.
    D. The insured must have a personal or business relationship with the beneficiary.

7. Which of the following statements describes the parol evidence rule?

   A. A written contract cannot be changed once it is signed.
   B. An oral contract cannot be modified by written evidence.
   C. A written contract cannot be changed by oral evidence.
   D. An oral contract takes preference over any earlier written contracts.

8. Which of the following is a special element of an insurance contract?

   A. Offer and acceptance
   B. Conditional
   C. Consideration
   D. Competent parties

9. An insurer is considered competent if it

   A. is registered with the NAIC
   B. is licensed or authorized by the state
   C. follows the state department of insurance's code of ethics
   D. is registered with the Securities and Exchange Commission

10. All of the following generally are considered to be competent parties who can enter into insurance contracts EXCEPT

   A. applicants
   B. trusts and estates
   C. business entities
   D. individuals under age 18

11. Which of the following is an example of consideration?

   A. Politeness
   B. Initial premium
   C. Legal purpose
   D. Offer and acceptance

12. With life and health contracts, when must an insurable interest exist?

   A. After the policy is issued
   B. Before the beneficiary is named
   C. While the policy is in force
   D. At the inception of the policy

13. An insurance company only has how many years to challenge the validity of a life insurance contract?

   A. 1
   B. 2
   C. 3
   D. 4

14. Which of the following describes the voluntary giving up of known right?

   A. Estoppel
   B. Adhesion
   C. Waiver
   D. Unilateral

15. Bob and Tom enter into a contract in which Bob agrees to fraudulently induce sick people to sell their insurance contracts to Tom's company. Bob and Tom's contract can best be described as

   A. void
   B. competitive
   C. voidable
   D. conditional

Answers and Rationale

1. **B.** Express authority is granted through the agent's contract in which the principal appoints the agent to act on its behalf.

2. **C.** Insurance contracts are contracts of adhesion. This means that the contract has been prepared by one party (the insurer) rather than as the result of negotiation between the parties.

3. **B.** If a person obtains a policy but does not have an insurable interest in the insured, the contract will not be valid and cannot be enforced.

4. **B.** Express authority is the authority the principal intends for and gives to its agent under a contract. It is not expressed orally.

5. **D.** According to most states, life insurance policies must contain a provision that all statements made in the application are deemed representations, not warranties. If a warranty or representation is untrue, the insurer may cancel the contract; however, the insurer may cancel the contract only if the representation was material to the creation of the contract.

6. **B.** In every insurance contract there must be an insurable interest. This means that the person acquiring the contract (the applicant) must be subject to loss on the death, illness or disability of the person being insured.

7. **C.** According to the parol evidence rule, once an agreement is reduced to writing, it cannot later be modified by any parol (verbal) evidence.

8. **B.** An insurance contract is conditional in that the insurer's promise to pay benefits depends on the occurrence of the risk insured against. The insurer's obligations under the contract also are conditioned on whether the insured performs certain acts, such as paying premiums.

9. **B.** To have an enforceable contract, both the insurer and the applicant must be competent parties. The insurer will be considered competent if it has been licensed or authorized by the state (or states) in which it conducts business.

10. **D.** Applicants are presumed to be competent. However, there are three exceptions: minors, the mentally infirm and those under the influence of alcohol or drugs.

11. **B.** To be enforceable, a contract's promises must be supported by consideration. Consideration means that value has been given in exchange for the promises sought. In the life insurance context, consideration is the initial premium that an applicant gives in exchange for the insurer's promise to pay benefits.

12. **D.** Although an insurable interest does not have to exist when a claim is made or throughout the duration of a policy, it must exist at the inception of the policy.

13. **B.** An insurer generally has only two years from the date of issue to challenge the validity of a contract.

14. **C.** A person who voluntarily gives up a legal, given right is deemed to have waived that right.

15. **A.** Bob and Tom's contract would be considered a void contract because it lacks one of the elements specified by law for a valid contract. In this case, the contract has an illegal purpose (fraudulently inducing sick individuals to sell their insurance policies) and neither part to the contract can enforce it.

Principles of
Life Insurance

4

Life Insurance Policies

INTRODUCTION

Insurers offer several different types of life insurance policies designed to serve different needs. In this lesson, we will examine the traditional forms of life insurance—term, whole life and endowment contracts—that have existed for many years. In addition to these standard policies, a number of specialized insurance products have evolved to serve a variety of needs ranging from family protection to debt repayment guarantees. Finally, we will examine some of the newer, nontraditional policies, such as universal life and variable life, that offer increased flexibility and current market returns.

LESSON OBJECTIVES

When you complete this lesson you should be able to:

- distinguish among the three basic categories of life insurance—ordinary insurance, industrial insurance and group insurance;
- list and identify the basic forms and features of term life insurance;
- describe the features of whole life insurance that distinguish it from term life insurance and identify the basic types of whole life insurance;
- define endowment policies and explain how modified endowment contracts are taxed;
- compare and contrast family income policies, family maintenance policies, family plan policies, multiple protection policies, joint life policies, juvenile insurance and credit life insurance; and
- list and explain the different features of nontraditional life policies, including interest-sensitive whole life, adjustable life, universal life, variable life and variable universal life insurance.

Categories of Life Insurance

Life insurers issue three basic kinds of coverage: *ordinary insurance, industrial insurance* and *group insurance.* Many companies offer all; some companies specialize in one or another. These coverages are distinguished by types of customers, amounts of insurance written, underwriting standards and marketing practices.

Ordinary Insurance

Ordinary life insurance includes many types of temporary (term) and permanent (whole life, endowment, universal life, variable universal life and other interest-sensitive cash value plans) insurance protection plans with premiums paid monthly, quarterly, semiannually or annually. Ordinary life insurance is the principal type of life insurance purchased in the United States. In 1998, ordinary life accounted for 58.8 percent of all life insurance in force in the United States.

Industrial Insurance

Industrial life insurance is characterized by comparatively small issue amounts, such as $1,000, with premiums collected on a weekly basis by the agent at the policyowner's home. Industrial insurance, or debit insurance, offers a way for individuals who cannot afford larger policies to obtain some measure of insurance coverage. Quite often it is marketed and purchased as burial insurance. As mentioned in Lesson 2, industrial insurance is sold by home service companies.

 Take Note: Four decades ago, industrial life insurance comprised more than 10 percent of all life insurance in force. Today, however, this number has fallen to less than 1 percent. This decline is due in part to the rising incomes of workers, the increased awareness of the need for more adequate life insurance and the expansion of group life insurance.

Group Insurance

Group life insurance is written for employer-employee groups, associations, unions and creditors to provide coverage for a number of individuals under one contract. Underwriting is based on the group, not the individuals who are insured. Group insurance, which has grown tremendously over the past few decades, will be discussed in detail in Lesson 9.

Keep in mind that the coverages described above are general categories of insurance. We now turn to the various life insurance plans: *term, whole life* (or *permanent*) and *endowment*.

Term Life Insurance

Term life insurance is the simplest type of life insurance plan. It provides insurance protection for a specified period (or term) and pays a benefit only if the insured dies during that period.

✓ **For Example:** An insured has a 5-year $50,000 level term life insurance policy that names a sibling as beneficiary. If the insured dies at any time within the policy's five-year period, the sibling will receive the $50,000 death benefit. If the insured lives beyond that period, nothing is payable because the policy's term has expired. If the insured cancels or lapses the policy during the 5-year term, nothing is payable because there are no cash values in term policies.

Term life also is called temporary life insurance since it provides protection for a temporary period of time.

The period for which these policies are issued can be defined in terms of years (1-year term, 5-year term or 20-year term, for example) or in terms of age (term to age 45, term to age 55, term to age 70, for example). Term policies issued for a specified number of years provide coverage from their issue date until the end of the years so specified. Term policies issued until a certain age provide coverage from their date of issue until the insured reaches the specified age.

Basic Forms of Term Life

Insurers offer a number of forms of term life insurance. These forms, distinguished primarily by the amount of benefit payable, are known generally as *level term, decreasing term* and *increasing term.*

Level Term Insurance

Level term insurance provides a level amount of protection for a specified period, after which the policy expires.

✓ **For Example:** A $100,000 10-year level term policy provides a straight, level $100,000 of coverage for a period of 10 years. A $250,000 term to age 65 policy provides a straight $250,000 of coverage until the insured reaches age 65. If the insured under the $100,000 policy dies at any time within those 10 years, or if the insured under the $250,000 policy dies before age 65, their

FIGURE 4.1   Level Term Insurance

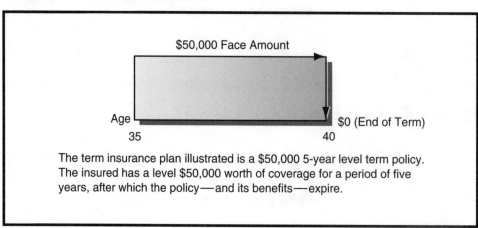

The term insurance plan illustrated is a $50,000 5-year level term policy. The insured has a level $50,000 worth of coverage for a period of five years, after which the policy—and its benefits—expire.

beneficiaries will receive the policies' face amount benefits. If the insureds live beyond the 10-year period or past age 65, the policies expire and no benefits are payable.

Decreasing Term Insurance

Decreasing term policies are characterized by benefit amounts that decrease gradually over the term of protection. A 20-year $50,000 decreasing term policy, for example, will pay a death benefit of $50,000 at the beginning of the policy term; that amount gradually declines over the 20-year term and reaches $0 at the end of the term.

 **Test Topic Alert!**

Decreasing term insurance often is used as credit life insurance and generally has the lowest premiums.

Decreasing term insurance is best used when the need for protection declines from year to year.

✓ **For Example:** A family breadwinner who has a $100,000 30-year mortgage could purchase decreasing term mortgage insurance that would retire the mortgage balance should he or she die during the 30-year mortgage paying period. Credit life insurance, sold to cover the outstanding balance on a loan, also is based on decreasing term.

Increasing Term Insurance

Increasing term insurance is term insurance that provides a death benefit that increases at periodic intervals over the policy's term. The amount of increase usually is stated as specific amounts or as a percentage of the original amount, or it may be tied to a cost of living index, such as the Consumer Price Index. Increasing term insurance may be sold as a separate policy; however, it usually is purchased as a cost of living rider to a policy. (See Cost of Living Rider, Lesson 5.)

FIGURE 4.2 Level Term vs. Decreasing Term

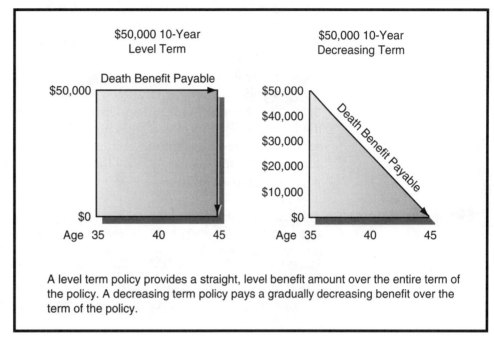

A level term policy provides a straight, level benefit amount over the entire term of the policy. A decreasing term policy pays a gradually decreasing benefit over the term of the policy.

Features of Term Life

Though term policies are issued for a specified period, defined in terms of years or age, most contain two options that can extend the coverage period, if the policyowner desires. These are the *option to renew* and the *option to convert* the policy.

Option to Renew The option to renew allows the policyowner to renew the term policy before its termination date without having to provide evidence of insurability (that is, without having to prove good health).

✓ **For Example:** A 5-year renewable term policy permits the policyowner to renew the same coverage for another five years at the end of the first five-year term.

The premiums for the renewal period will be higher than the initial period, reflecting the insurer's increased risk (see *Term Life Premiums* later in this lesson). Renewal options with most term policies typically provide for several renewal periods or for renewals until a specified age. The advantage of the renewal option is that it allows the insured to continue insurance protection, even if he or she has become uninsurable.

A common type of renewable term insurance is *annually renewable term* (ART)—also called *yearly renewable term* (YRT). Essentially, this type of policy represents the most basic form of life insurance. It provides coverage for one year and allows the policyowner to renew his or her coverage each year, without evidence of insurability. Again, most insurers limit the number of times such a policy can be renewed or specify an age limit. However, it is common for ART policies to be renewable to age 65 or beyond.

Some renewable term plans offer a *re-entry option*. With re-entry term policies, the policyowner is guaranteed to be able to renew his or her coverage at the end of the term without evidence of insurability at a premium rate specified in the policy. However, this policy also provides that, at periodic intervals, the insured may submit evidence of insurability and, if found acceptable by the insurer, qualify for renewed protection at a rate lower than what the contract states.

Option to Convert

The second option common to most term plans is the option to convert. The option to convert gives the insured the right to convert or exchange the term policy for a whole life (or permanent) plan without evidence of insurability. This exchange involves the issuance of a whole life policy at a premium rate reflecting the insured's age at either the time of the exchange (the attained age method) or the time when the original term policy was taken out (the original age method).

✔ **For Example:** If a 30-year-old insured converts a term policy to whole life insurance and pays the whole life premium for age 35, the conversion is based on attained age. But if the same insured converts a term policy that was issued 5 years ago to whole life insurance at the age-30 premium rate, the conversion is based on an original age.

If a conversion is made on the original age basis, the premium for the new policy naturally will be lower. However, the policyowner may have to pay an additional amount to make up the difference between the term and permanent insurance from the date of the term policy's original issue to the time of conversion. By paying the difference, the policyowner enjoys a lower premium and builds cash values more rapidly in the new policy than if conversion had been at the attained age.

✔ **Take Note:** The option to convert generally specifies a time limit for converting, such as three or five years before the policy expires.

☀ Test Topic Alert!

Renewable and convertible options usually are only added to level term insurance.

The option to convert and the option to renew can be (and typically are) combined into a single term policy. For instance, a 10-year convertible renewable policy could provide for renewals until age 65 and be convertible any before age 55.

Term Life Premiums

Though a detailed discussion of premiums appears in Lesson 7, a simplified introduction is appropriate here. To begin, understand that the amount of premium any insurance plan entails reflects, in part, the degree of risk the insurer accepts when it issues a policy. With life insurance, age is a significant risk factor: the higher the age, the more likely is death.

✔ ***For Example:*** Consider two males, one age 25, the other age 55. Both make an application to purchase a 10-year $50,000 term policy. Statistically, it's more likely that the 55-year-old man will die within the 10-year period than the 25-year-old; consequently, it's more likely that the insurance company will pay benefits on the older man's policy than the younger man's. Due to this increased risk (and assuming all other factors are equal), the 55-year-old will pay a higher premium for his protection than will the 25-year-old.

Because the probability of death increases with age, premiums also increase gradually with age. At older ages, this increase becomes quite sharp, reflecting the corresponding higher death rates. Few people could afford the premium rates that would be charged at higher ages; therefore, insurance companies offer term insurance plans on a *level-premium basis*—premiums are calculated and charged so that they remain level throughout the policy's term period. If the policy is renewed, the premium is adjusted upward, reflecting a higher rate for the increased age, and will remain level at that amount for the duration of the renewed term.

✔ ***Take Note:*** The phrase used to describe this method of premium payments is step-rate. If you picture a staircase, the first step represents the premium amount payable for the initial term; at the end of the term, the premium steps up to a higher amount for the second term and remains at that level until the second term expires, and so on.1 An illustration of the step-rate method is found in Figure 4.3.

 **Test Topic Alert!**

Term policies that include the option to renew, the option to convert or both will carry a higher premium than policies that do not have these features.

1An exception to the level-premium approach is *deposit term insurance*. This type of term policy requires a premium payment in the first year that is much higher than the level premiums required in the second and subsequent years. At the end of the policy's term, the policyowner receives some of the premium back; the amount returned typically is a multiple of the difference between the higher first-year premium and the lower second-year premium. Deposit term insurance accounts for a very small percentage of the term insurance sold today.

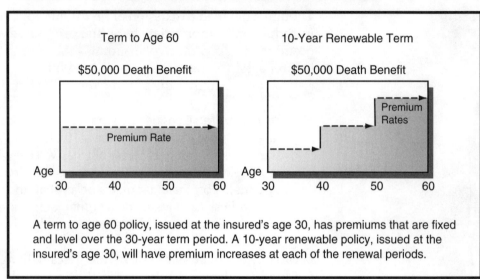

FIGURE 4.3   Level Term Premium vs. Renewable Term Premium

A term to age 60 policy, issued at the insured's age 30, has premiums that are fixed and level over the 30-year term period. A 10-year renewable policy, issued at the insured's age 30, will have premium increases at each of the renewal periods.

Whole Life Insurance

A second type of life insurance plan is whole life insurance (also known as *permanent* or *cash value* insurance). Whole life insurance is so called because it provides permanent protection for the whole of life—from the date of issue to the date of the insured's death—provided premiums are paid. The benefit payable is the face amount of the policy, which remains constant throughout the policy's life. Premiums are set at the time of policy issue and also remain level for the policy's life.

Features of Whole Life

In addition to its permanence, there are certain other features of whole life insurance that distinguish it from term insurance: cash values and maturity at age 100. These two features combine to produce living benefits to the policyowner.

Cash Value   Unlike term insurance, which provides only death protection, whole life insurance combines insurance protection with a savings or accumulation element. This accumulation, commonly referred to as the policy's cash value, builds over the life of the policy. This is because whole life insurance plans are credited with a certain guaranteed rate of interest; this interest is credited to the policy regularly and grows over time.

Though it is an important part of funding the policy, the cash value often is regarded as a savings element because it represents the amount of money the policyowner will receive if the policy ever is canceled. It often is called the cash surrender value. This value is a result of the way premiums are calculated and interest is paid, as well as of the policy reserves that build under this system.

The amount of a policy's cash value depends on a variety of factors, including:

- the face amount of the policy;
- the duration and amount of the premium payments; and
- how long the policy has been in force.

Generally, the larger the face amount of the policy, the larger the cash values; the shorter the premium-payment period, the quicker the cash values grow; and the longer the policy has been in force, the greater the build-up in cash values. The reason for these things can be clarified with an understanding of a whole life policy's maturity.

 **Test Topic Alert!**   A policy matures or endows when the face amount equals the cash value.

Maturity at Age 100   Whole life insurance is designed to mature at age 100. The significance of age 100 is that, as an actuarial assumption, every insured is presumed to be dead by then. (While some people live beyond age 100, the number who do is not statistically significant.) Consequently, the premium rate for whole life insurance is based on the assumption that the insured will be paying premiums for the whole of life, to age 100. At age 100, the cash value of the policy has accumulated to the point that it equals the face amount of the policy, as it was actuarially designed to do. At that point, the policy has completely matured or endowed. No more premiums are owed; the policy is completely paid up.

For those lucky insureds who live to age 100, the insurance company will issue checks for the full value of their policies. At that point, the policy expires; the contract has been completed. Thus, when whole life is defined as a policy that provides a death benefit whenever death occurs, some qualification is required. Whole life insurance provides a death benefit if death occurs before age 100; if the insured has not died by age 100, the full maturity value of the policy is paid out to the insured as a living benefit and the policy terminates. In either event, age 100 defines the point at which the cash value of the policy equals the face amount (or death benefit amount) of the policy. (See Figure 4.4.)

 Take Note: Very few people live to age 100. It's far more likely that a whole life policy will be cashed in for its surrender value or that its face amount will be paid out as a death benefit before maturity.

FIGURE 4.4   Whole Life Insurance

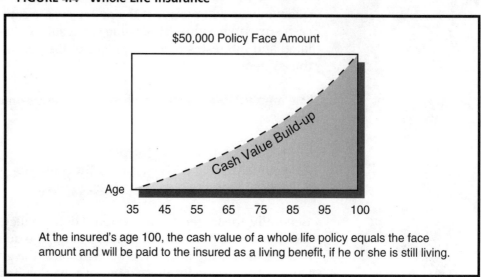

$50,000 Policy Face Amount

Cash Value Build-up

Age

35   45   55   65   75   85   95   100

At the insured's age 100, the cash value of a whole life policy equals the face amount and will be paid to the insured as a living benefit, if he or she is still living.

Living Benefits
Another unique feature of whole life insurance is the living benefits it can provide. Through the cash value accumulation build-up in the policy, a policyowner has a ready source of funds that may be borrowed at reasonable rates of interest. These funds may be used for a personal or business emergency, to help pay for a child's education or to pay off a mortgage. It is not a requirement of the policy that the loan be repaid. However, if a loan is outstanding at the time the insured dies, the amount of the loan plus any interest due will be subtracted from the death benefit before it is paid. Indeed, policy loans are more benefit advances than loans.

In addition, because life insurance is considered property with a quantifiable cash value, it may be used as collateral or security for loans. Also, the policyowner may draw on the cash value to supplement retirement income.

Cash values belong to the policyowner. The insurance company cannot lay claim to these values. This concept is discussed in more detail in Lesson 5, under *Nonforfeiture Values*.

Whole Life Premiums

As noted, whole life is actuarially designed as if the insured will live to age 100. Accordingly, the premium amount for a whole life policy is calculated, in part, on the basis of the number of years between the insured's age at issue and age 100. This time span represents the full premium-paying period, with the amount of the premium spread equally over that period. This is known as a *level premium basis*. As is the case with level premium term insurance, this approach allows whole life insurance premiums to remain level rather than increase each year with the insured's age. To put it simply, the premium amount is calculated so that in the early years it is more than necessary to meet anticipated claims and expenses and is less than adequate in the later years when the claims likely will be paid. The balanced result is a level amount payable over the entire period.

Basic Forms of Whole Life

Just because whole life premiums are calculated as if they were payable to age 100, they do not necessarily have to be paid this way. Whole life is flexible and a number of policy types have been developed to accommodate different premium-paying periods. Three notable forms of whole life plans are *straight whole life, limited pay whole life* and *single-premium whole life.*

Straight Whole Life   Straight whole life is whole life insurance that provides permanent level protection with level premiums from the time the policy is issued until the insured's death (or age 100).

✓ **Take Note:** The main advantage of straight whole life is that it provides permanent protection for permanent needs (such as insurance to provide liquidity for estate tax purposes). It also provides coverage over the insured's entire lifetime and, because it includes a cash value, it offers both protection and savings.

Limited Pay Whole Life   Limited pay whole life policies have level premiums that are limited to a certain period (less than life). This period can be of any duration. For example, a 20-pay life policy is one in which premiums are payable for 20 years from the policy's inception, after which no more premiums are owed. A life paid-up at 65 policy is one in which the premiums are payable to the insured's age 65, after which no more premiums are owed.

The names of the policies denote how long the premiums are payable.

✓ **For Example:** A 30-year-old applicant who purchases a life paid-up at 65 policy will pay premiums for 35 years and then have a paid-up policy. If the same applicant buys a 20-pay life policy, he or she will pay premiums for 20 years and have a paid-up policy at age 50.

Keep in mind that even though the premium payments are limited to a certain period, the insurance protection extends until the insured's death, whenever that may be, or to age 100.

Single-Premium Whole Life   The most extreme form of limited pay policies is a single-premium policy. A single-premium whole life policy involves a large one-time-only premium payment at the beginning of the policy period. From that point, the policy is completely paid for.

FIGURE 4.5 Premium Rates per $1,000 of Insurance

Issue Age	1-Year Term	Straight Whole Life	Life Paid-up at 65	20-Pay Life
35	$1.35	$16.29	$21.07	$26.00
45	$3.10	$23.17	$32.16	$32.16
55	$12.68	$36.44	$70.01	$50.12

 **Test Topic Alert!**   The payment of the single premium for a policy gives it an immediate cash value.

Premium Periods   The shorter the premium-paying period, the higher the premium. The same principle applies when a person purchases an item on a credit installment plan—the shorter the payment period, the higher each payment will be. As Figure 4.5 shows, the premium rates at age 35 for a 20-pay life policy are over one and a half times those for a straight life policy, per $1,000 of insurance coverage. This is because the 20-pay life policy has a premium-paying period of 20 years, while the straight life policy assumes a premium-paying period of 65 years, or until age 100.

The length of the premium-paying period also affects the growth of the policy's cash values. The shorter the premium-paying period (and consequently, the higher the premium), the quicker the cash values grow. This is because a greater percentage of each payment is credited to the policy's cash values. By the same token, the longer the premium-paying period, the slower the cash values grow. Figure 4.6 shows how the cash values grow in a 20-pay, a 30-pay and a straight whole life policy. As this figure also shows, the cash values build up in the limited pay policies faster during the premium-paying years than during the non-premium-paying years. After the premium-paying period, the cash values continue to grow, but more slowly, until the policy matures and the cash value equals the face amount, again, at age 100.

Note that life insurance policies now must meet certain statutory definitions and tests, which are primarily aimed at limited pay policies and single-premium policies.

These rules are explained in a later section of this Lesson, titled *Modified Endowment Contracts*.

 **Test Topic Alert!**   Be careful to note which policy will cost least over the life of the policy, all other considerations being equal. In general, the shorter the premium payment period, the lower the cost of the policy.

FIGURE 4.6 How Cash Values Grow

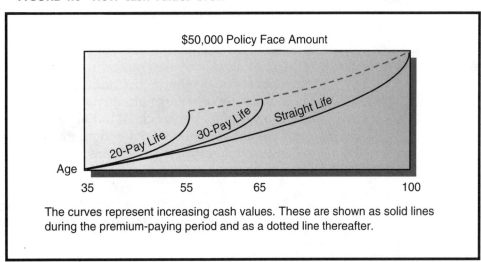

$50,000 Policy Face Amount

20-Pay Life   30-Pay Life   Straight Life

Age

35   55   65   100

The curves represent increasing cash values. These are shown as solid lines during the premium-paying period and as a dotted line thereafter.

Other Forms of Whole Life

There are many other forms of whole life insurance, most of which are characterized by some variation in the way the premium is paid. Let's review these policies next.

Modified Whole Life   Modified whole life policies are distinguished by premiums that are lower than typical whole life premiums during the first few years (usually five) and then higher than typical thereafter. During the initial period, the premium rate is only slightly higher than that of term insurance. Afterward, the premium is higher than the typical whole life rate at age of issue.

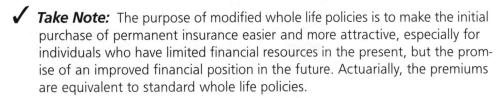 **✓ Take Note:** The purpose of modified whole life policies is to make the initial purchase of permanent insurance easier and more attractive, especially for individuals who have limited financial resources in the present, but the promise of an improved financial position in the future. Actuarially, the premiums are equivalent to standard whole life policies.

Graded Premium Whole Life   Similar to modified whole life, graded premium policies also redistribute premiums. Premiums are lower than typical whole life rates during the preliminary period following issue (usually 5 to 10 years) and increase each year until leveling off after the preliminary period. Again, the premium rates are actuarially equivalent to standard whole life.

 **Test Topic Alert!**   While modified whole life and graded premium whole life insurance are similar, be sure to know their differences.

Minimum Deposit Whole Life   Minimum deposit insurance begins building cash values immediately on payment of the first premium. From that point, the policyowner systematically borrows from the cash value to pay some or all of the premium.

Indeterminate Premium Whole Life   Indeterminate premium whole life policies are those in which the premium rate can be adjusted based on the insurance company's anticipated future experience. The maximum premium that the insurer can charge is stated in the contract, though the premium payable at issue is much lower and is fixed at the lower rate for a specified initial period (typically two to three years). After the initial period, and based on the company's expected mortality, expense and investment projections, the premium may be raised, kept the same or lowered.

> ✓ **Take Note:** The benefit structure for indeterminate premium whole life policies is the same as that for other policies. Only the premium structure differs.

Enhanced (Economatic) Whole Life   Enhanced whole life policies are offered by some mutual insurers. Though the precise composition of these plans differs from company to company, the process is similar in all cases: A mutual company issues a policy with a low premium and face amount that diminishes after a few years. Dividends are used to buy paid-up additions to keep insurance equal to the amount of the reduction. In this manner, the face amount remains constant. (Paid-up additions are explained in Lesson 5.)

Indexed Whole Life   The face amount of indexed whole life insurance increases automatically as the Consumer Price Index (CPI) increases. Two basic pricing methods are used with this type of policy:

- The policyowner assumes the risk of future increases and thus must pay additional premium with each face amount increase; or
- The insurer assumes the risk and thus the policyowner does not pay a higher premium with face amount increases.

Regardless of the method used, the policyowner is not required to furnish evidence of insurability to obtain the face amount increase.

🖉 **Quick Quiz 4.1**   Match the following types of insurance with the appropriate description below.

A. Indexed whole life insurance
B. Limited pay whole life insurance
C. Decreasing term insurance
D. Industrial insurance
E. Minimum deposit whole life insurance

_____ 1. Cash values begin building immediately when the first premium is paid. Thereafter, the policyowner borrows from the cash value to pay premiums.

_____ 2. The face amount increases automatically as the Consumer Price Index (CPI) increases.

_____ 3. Premiums are level and payable over a certain time period (less than life), after which no more premiums are owed.

_____ 4. Benefit amounts decrease gradually over the term of protection.

_____ 5. Small policy amounts are issued and the agent collects premiums on a weekly basis at the policyowner's home.

Answers   *1. E*   *2. A*   *3. B*   *4. C*   *5. D*

Endowment Policies

Besides term and whole life insurance, life insurers also issue endowment policies. An endowment policy is characterized by cash values that grow at a rapid pace so that the policy matures or endows at a specified date (that is, before age 100). An endowment policy provides benefits in one of two ways:

- as a death benefit to a beneficiary if the insured dies within the specified policy period (known as the *endowment period*); or
- as a living benefit to the policyowner if the insured is alive at the end of the endowment period, at which time the policy has fully matured.

Because an endowment policy pays a death benefit if the insured dies during a certain period, it can be compared to level term insurance. The new concept presented here is that of *pure endowment*. Pure endowment insurance is a contract that guarantees a specified sum payable only if the insured is living at the end of a stated time period—nothing is payable in the case of prior death.

✓ **Take Note:** These two elements—level term insurance and endowment—together provide the guarantees endowment contracts offer.

One can compare endowment policies to whole life policies with accelerated maturity dates; age 65 is a common maturity age. At the maturity age, the cash value has grown to match the face amount, just as it does at age 100 with a whole life policy.

FIGURE 4.7 Types of Endowment Policies

Description	Type of Policy
These policies will endow for the face amount at the end of the premium-paying period. That is, premiums are paid to the time of endowment.	• 10-Year Endowment • 20-Year Endowment • 25-Year Endowment • 30-Year Endowment • Endowment at Age 55 • Endowment at Age 60 • Endowment at Age 65
In these policies, the premium payments are completed before the time of endowment. After premiums stop, the cash value increases from interest earnings and equals the face amount at the time of endowment. Insurance protection extends to the time of endowment.	• 20-Pay Endowment at Age 60 • 20-Pay Endowment at Age 65 • Single Premium Endowment

Figure 4.7 shows some of the more common endowment policies that insurers offer. The name of each policy establishes how long premiums are payable, how long the insurance lasts and when the policy endows.

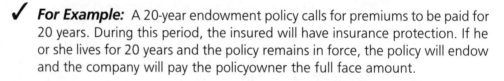 **For Example:** A 20-year endowment policy calls for premiums to be paid for 20 years. During this period, the insured will have insurance protection. If he or she lives for 20 years and the policy remains in force, the policy will endow and the company will pay the policyowner the full face amount.

 **Test Topic Alert!**   Because they are designed to build cash values quickly, endowment policies typically are purchased to provide a living benefit for a specified future time—for retirement, for instance, or to fund a child's college education.

Endowment Premiums

Because of their rapid cash value build-ups to provide early policy maturity, endowment policies have comparatively high premiums. Remember that the shorter the policy term, the higher the premiums. Figure 4.8 shows some typical premium costs for a 20-year endowment and an endowment at age 65, issued at various ages. Compare these premium costs to those shown for term and whole life policies in Figure 4.5.

Note that the purchase of endowment policies has been on the decline for several years. This is because they no longer meet the income tax definition of life insurance and, consequently, no longer qualify for the favorable tax treatment life insurance is given. Essentially, the Internal Revenue Code

FIGURE 4.8   Premium Rates per $1,000 of Endowment Insurance

Issue Age	Endowment at Age 65	20-Year Endowment
20	$15.30	$43.59
30	$22.35	$44.03
40	$36.14	$45.74

specifies that life insurance products cannot endow before age 95. Because one objective of endowment policies is to provide a living benefit by building an endowment fund for a definite future objective (presumably before the insured reaches age 95), they generally do not qualify as life insurance. Though a number of endowment policies still are in force today, very few new policies are sold.

Modified Endowment Contracts

In 1988, Congress enacted the Technical and Miscellaneous Revenue Act (TAMRA). Among other things, this act revised the tax law definition of a life insurance contract, primarily to discourage the sale and purchase of life insurance for investment purposes or as a tax shelter. By redefining life insurance, Congress effectively created a new class of insurance, known as modified endowment contracts (MECs).

For the producer who sells life insurance and for the consumer who purchases life insurance, the significance of this class of insurance is the way a life policy, if it is deemed an MEC, will be taxed. Historically, life insurance has been granted very favorable tax treatment. Specifically:

- Cash value accumulations are not taxed to the policyowner as they build inside a policy.
- Policy withdrawals are not taxed to the policyowner until the amount withdrawn exceeds the total amount the policyowner paid into the contract.
- Policy loans are not considered distributions and are not taxed to the policyowner unless or until a full policy surrender takes place and then only to the extent that the distribution exceeds what was paid into the policy.

However, for those policies that do not meet the specific test (described below) and consequently are considered MECs, the tax treatment is different—and it is the policyowners who pay.

If a policy is deemed an MEC and the policyowner receives any amount from it in the form of a loan or withdrawal, that amount will be taxed first as ordinary income and second as return of premium, if there is any gain in the contract over premiums paid. A 10 percent penalty tax also is imposed on these amounts if they are received before the policyowner's age 59½ and none of the exceptions to the penalty tax apply.

In order to avoid being classified as an MEC, a policy must meet what is known as the *7-pay test*. This test states that if the total amount a policyowner pays into a life contract during its first years exceeds the sum of the net level premiums that would have been payable to provide paid-up future benefits in seven years, the policy is an MEC. And once a policy is classified as an MEC—which it can be at any time during the first seven years—it will remain so throughout its duration.

✓ **For Example:** Suppose a policyowner purchased a $100,000 7-year limited pay whole life policy. The scheduled premiums are $7,500 a year, payable for seven years. At the end of that period, the policy will be completely paid up. The first year, the policyowner pays $7,500. The second year, the policyowner pays $8,000. At that point, the policy would become an MEC because the policyowner paid more into the policy than the net level premiums required to provide paid-up benefits in seven years. From that point on, any withdrawals or loans the policyowner takes from that policy will be taxed as income, to the extent there is gain in the policy. Now let's assume that this policyowner paid $7,500 in the first year and $7,000 in the second year. In the third year, he or she can make an $8,000 payment and not run afoul of the 7-pay test—he or she still is within the guidelines of the sum of the net level premiums payable. However, if that sum total limit ever is exceeded in those first seven years, the policy will become an MEC.

Making sure that policies meet the definition of life insurance and comply with the 7-pay test is the responsibility of insurers and their actuaries. Agents do not have the time or resources; consumers do not have the knowledge or understanding. However, because the potential for misuse—or even abuse—exists with single-pay, limited pay and universal life policies, and because consumers may be lured into purchasing insurance for its tax benefits instead of its protection guarantees, producers must be alert to this law and its implications.

 **Test Topic Alert!**   An insurance company may refund the excess premiums to avoid having a policy become a MEC.

Special Use Policies

In addition to the basic types of life insurance policies—term, whole life and endowment—there are a number of special use policies insurers offer. Many of these are a combination, or packaging, of different policy types, designed to serve a variety of needs.

Family Income Policy

A family income policy is a combination of whole life and decreasing term covering a select period of years. If the insured dies within a specified period, this policy provides a certain monthly income from the date of death until the end of the specified period. This period is known as the *income period* and the monthly payments are accomplished by the term insurance, plus interest from the proceeds of the whole life policy. At the end of the specified income period, the face amount of the whole life policy is payable to the beneficiary. If the insured lives beyond the specified income period, only the face amount of the whole life policy is payable.

Family income insurance usually is sold in monthly *income units*, each valued at $10 or more (per $1,000 of the base whole life policy's face amount). In other words, one unit will include enough insurance to provide $10 or more per month to the family during the income period. Five, 10, 15 and 20 years are commonly used term periods.

The specified income term period starts when the policy is issued. If the insured dies during the term period, monthly income to the family begins at the time of death and continues to the end of the term period, at which time the face amount of the whole life policy is payable. If the insured dies after the end of the term period, no income payments are made; only the whole life base policy is payable.

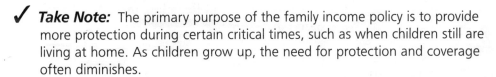 **✓ Take Note:** The primary purpose of the family income policy is to provide more protection during certain critical times, such as when children still are living at home. As children grow up, the need for protection and coverage often diminishes.

Family Maintenance Policy

A family maintenance policy is similar to a family income, but uses level term insurance rather than decreasing term insurance to provide the monthly income payments. At the insured's death, the family maintenance plan provides for payment of monthly income for a selected period of years,

FIGURE 4.9 Family Income vs. Family Maintenance Plans

Family income and family maintenance plans both are designed to provide a period of monthly income following the death of the insured, if death occurs during the specified period. The distinction between the two plans is when the income period begins.

The diagrams above show a family income plan and a family maintenance plan that provide for monthly benefits should the insureds die at any time during the first 20 years. Under the family income plan, the income period begins when the policy is *issued* and ends 20 years later, at the insured's age 50. Thus, if the insured died at age 40, the family income plan would pay monthly benefits for ten years, at which time the base policy's face amount is paid. Under the family maintenance plan, the income period begins when the insured *dies* and continues for the full specified period. Thus, if the insured under the maintenance plan died at age 40, monthly income benefits would be paid for 20 years.

beginning from the date of death. (The face amount of the whole life insurance usually is paid at the beginning of the fixed period, though some plans pay it at the end of the period.) Note that this differs from the family income plan under which the fixed income period begins from the date of issue.

☀ **Test Topic Alert!**   Monthly income is paid from the date of death and lasts for the length of the term, i.e. 10, 15 or 20 years.

A family income policy plan and a family maintenance policy plan are compared in Figure 4.9.

Family Plan Policy

The family plan policy is designed to insure all family members under one policy. Coverage is sold in units. A typical plan would insure the family breadwinner for, say, $10,000 or $15,000, the spouse for $3,000 and each child for $1,000. Usually the insurance covering the family head is permanent insurance; that covering the spouse and children is level or decreasing term. These plans generally cover all children currently in the family within certain age limits—for example, older than 14 days and younger than age 21. Children who are born later are covered automatically at no extra premium. The children's coverage usually is convertible without evidence of insurability.

Multiple Protection Policy

A multiple protection policy pays a benefit of double or triple the face amount if death occurs during a specified period. If death occurs after the period has expired, only the policy face amount is paid. The period may be for a specified number of years—10, 15 or 20, for example—or to a specified age, such as 65. These policies are combinations of permanent insurance and, for the multiple protection period, level term insurance.

Joint Life Policy

A joint life policy is one policy that covers two people. Using some type of permanent insurance (as opposed to term), it pays the death benefit when the first insured dies. The survivor then has the option of purchasing a single individual policy without evidence of insurability. The premium for a joint life policy is less than the premium for two separate policies. The ages of the two insureds are averaged and a single premium is charged for both lives.

A variation of the joint life policy is the *last survivor policy,* also known as a *second-to-die policy.* This plan also covers two lives, but the benefit is paid on the death of the second insured.

 Test Topic Alert!   In a last survivor policy, the beneficiary typically is the estate.

Juvenile Insurance

Insurance written on the lives of children (ordinarily age one day to age 14 or 15 years) is called juvenile insurance. Application for insurance and ownership of the policy rest with an adult such as a parent or guardian. The adult applicant usually is the premium payor as well, until the child comes of age and is able to take over the payments. A payor provision typically is attached to juvenile policies. It provides that, in the event of death or disability of the adult premium payor, the premiums will be waived until the insured child reaches a specified age (such as 25) or until the maturity date of the contract, whichever comes first. (See *Payor Rider,* Lesson 5.)

A special form of juvenile insurance is the *jumping juvenile* or *junior estate builder* policy. These policies typically are written on children ages 1 to 15 years in units of $1,000, which automatically increase to $5,000—or five times the face amount—at age 21. Although the face amount increases automatically, the premium remains the same and no evidence of insurability is required.

✓ **Take Note:** The main advantage of juvenile insurance is that it protects a child's insurability. If a child later becomes uninsurable, a jumping juvenile policy would ensure that the child has at least some minimum amount of lifetime protection.

Note that some states limit the amount of life insurance that can be written on a child at an early age. They do so by specifying a maximum that can be in force on a child's life during his or her early years, such as up to age 5, 10 or 15.

Credit Life Insurance

Credit life insurance is designed to cover the life of a debtor and pay the amount due on a loan if the debtor dies before the loan is repaid. The type of insurance used is decreasing term, with the term matched to the length of the loan period, though usually limited to 10 years or less, and the decreasing insurance amount matched to the declining loan balance.

Credit life sometimes is issued to individuals as single policies, but most often it is sold to a bank or other lending institution as group insurance that covers all of the institution's borrowers. (See *Group Life Insurance*, Lesson 9.)

 Quick Quiz 4.2 True or False?

_____ 1. A multiple protection policy pays a benefit equal to double or triple the policy's face amount if death occurs during a specified period.

_____ 2. A family income policy uses both whole life and level term insurance.

_____ 3. Credit life insurance covers the life of a creditor.

_____ 4. A joint life policy covers two people and uses some type of permanent insurance.

_____ 5. To avoid being classified as a modified endowment contract, a life insurance policy must meet the 7-pay test.

Answers   1. **True**.

2. **False**. *A family income plan uses whole life and decreasing term insurance.*

3. **False**. *Credit life insurance covers the life of a debtor.*

4. **True**.

5. **True**.

Nontraditional Life Policies

In the 1980s, insurance companies introduced a number of new policy forms, most of which are more flexible in design and provisions than their traditional counterparts. The most notable of these are *interest-sensitive whole life, adjustable life, universal life, variable life* and *variable universal life.*

Interest-Sensitive Whole Life

Also known as *current assumption whole life*, this policy is characterized by premiums that vary to reflect the insurer's changing assumptions with regard to its death, investment and expense factors. In this respect, it is similar to indeterminate premium whole life. However, interest-sensitive products also provide that the cash values may be greater than the guaranteed levels, if the company's underlying death, investment and expense assumptions are more favorable than expected. In this way, policyowners have two options: lower premiums or higher cash values.

If underlying assumptions turn out to be less favorable than anticipated, which otherwise would call for a higher premium than that at policy issue, the policyowner either may pay the higher premium or choose to reduce the policy's face amount and continue to pay the same premium.

Adjustable Life

Adjustable life policies are distinguished by their flexibility, which comes from combining term and permanent insurance into a single plan. The policyowner determines how much face amount protection he or she needs and how much premium he or she wants to pay. The insurer then selects the appropriate plan to meet those needs. Or the policyowner may specify a desired plan and face amount, and the insurer will calculate the appropriate premium. As financial needs and objectives change, the policyowner can make adjustments to his or her coverage, such as increasing or decreasing the:

- premium and (or) the premium-paying period; or
- face amount and (or) the period of protection.

Consequently, depending on the desired changes, the policy can be converted from term to whole life or from whole life to term—from a high premium contract to a lower premium or limited pay contract.

✔ ***Take Note:*** Most adjustable life policies contain limits that restrict the changes in face amounts or premium payments to specified minimums and maximums. Typically, increases in the face amounts on these policies require evidence of insurability. Moreover, due to its design and flexibility, adjustable life usually is more expensive than conventional term or whole life policies.

Universal Life

Universal life is a variation of whole life insurance, characterized by considerable flexibility. Unlike whole life, with its fixed premiums, fixed face amounts and fixed cash value accumulations, universal life allows its policyowners to determine the amount and frequency of premium payments and to adjust the policy face amount up or down to reflect changes in needs. Consequently, no new policy need be issued when changes are desired.

Universal life provides this flexibility by unbundling, or separating, the basic components of a life insurance policy—the insurance (protection) element, the savings (accumulation) element and the expense (loading) element. As with any other life policy, the policyowner pays a premium. Each month, a mortality charge is deducted from the policy's cash value account for the cost of the insurance protection. This mortality charge also may include an expense, or loading, charge.

Like term insurance premiums, the universal life mortality charge increases steadily with age. Actually, universal life technically is defined as term insurance with a policy value fund. Even though the policyowner may pay a level premium, an increasing share of that premium goes to pay the mortality charge as the insured ages.

⚬̣̇ **Test Topic Alert!**   The mortality portion of a universal life policy may make it appear similar to an annual renewable term policy.

As premiums are paid and cash values accumulate, interest is credited to the policy's cash value. This interest may be either the current interest rate, declared by the company (and dependent on current market conditions) or the guaranteed minimum rate, specified in the contract. As long as the cash value account is sufficient to pay the monthly mortality and expense costs, the policy will continue in force, whether or not the policyowner pays the premium.

✔ ***Take Note:*** Premium payments must be large enough and frequent enough to generate sufficient cash values. If the cash value account is not large enough to support the monthly deductions, the policy terminates.

At stated intervals (and usually on providing evidence of insurability), the policyowner can increase or decrease the face amount of the policy. A corresponding increase (or decrease) in premium payment is not required, as long as the cash values can cover the mortality and expense costs. By the same token, the policyowner can elect to pay more into the policy, thus adding to the cash value account, subject to certain guidelines that control the relationship between the cash values and the policy's face amount.

Another factor that distinguishes universal life from whole life is the fact that partial withdrawals can be made from the policy's cash value account. (Whole life insurance allows a policyowner to tap cash values only through a policy loan or a complete cash surrender of the policy's cash values, in which case the policy terminates.) Also, the policyowner may surrender the universal life policy for its entire cash value at any time. However, the company probably will assess a surrender charge unless the policy has been in force for a certain number of years.

UL Death Benefit Options

Universal life insurance offers two death benefit options. Under option one, the policyowner may designate a specified amount of insurance. The death benefit equals the cash values plus the remaining pure insurance (decreasing term plus increasing cash values). If the cash values approach the face amount before the policy matures, an additional amount of insurance, called the *corridor*, is maintained in addition to the cash values. (Figure 4.10 illustrates option one.)

Under option two, the death benefit equals the face amount (pure insurance) plus the cash values (level term plus increasing cash values). To comply with the tax code's definition of life insurance, the cash values cannot be disproportionately larger than the term insurance portion. (Figure 4.10 illustrates option two.)

Variable Insurance Products

Introduced in the 1970s, variable insurance products added a new dimension to life insurance: the opportunity for policyowners to achieve higher-than-usual investment returns on their policy cash values by accepting the risk of the policy's performance. This concept is best explained by a comparison to traditional whole life plans.

Under traditional whole life insurance policies, the insurer guarantees a certain minimum rate of return will be credited to the policies' cash values. This is accomplished because the insurer invests the policyowner's premiums in its general account—an investment account composed of investments carefully selected to match the liabilities and guarantees of the contracts they back. (These investments usually are quite conservative: U.S. government securities and investment-grade bonds are common.) Actually, the premiums paid for life insurance are not, in and of themselves, sufficient to cover the benefits promised in the contract. Rather, they will be sufficient only if the insurer can earn a certain interest rate on the invested values. This makes earnings of crucial importance; the insurer is bound to provide the

FIGURE 4.10   Universal Life Death Benefit Options

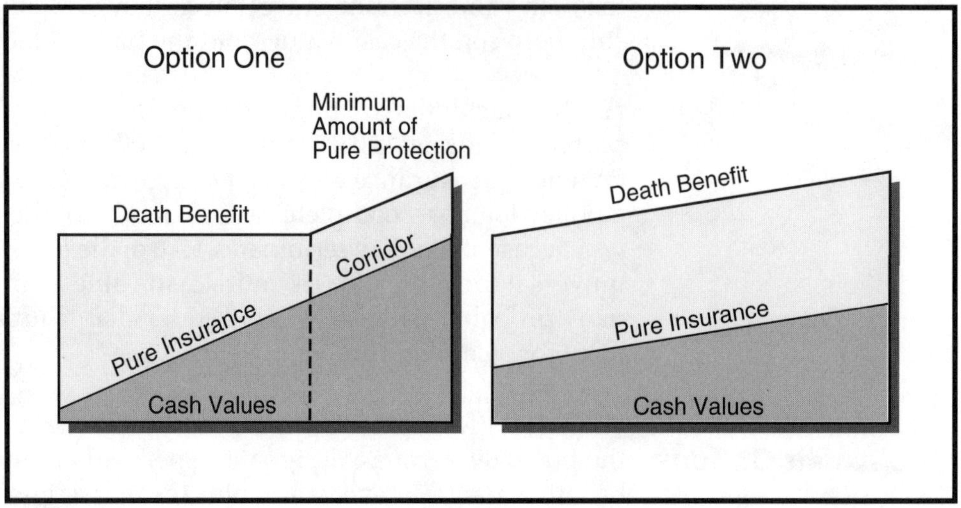

contractually guaranteed values and benefits whether or not it earns its assumed rate of return. Consequently, with traditional whole life policies, it is the insurer that bears the investment risk. That is why the guaranteed rate of return for traditional whole life policies is quite conservative—typically 3 to 5 percent.

In contrast, variable insurance products do not guarantee contract values and it is the policyowner who assumes the investment risk. Variable life insurance contracts do not make any promises as to interest rates or minimum cash values. What these products do offer is the potential to realize investment gains that exceed those available with traditional life insurance policies. This is done by allowing policyowners to direct the investment of the funds that back their variable contracts through *separate account options*. By placing their policy values into separate accounts, policyowners can participate directly in the account's investment performance, which will earn a variable (as opposed to a fixed) return. Functioning on much the same principle as mutual funds, the return enjoyed—or loss suffered—by policyowners through their investment in a separate account is directly related to the performance of the assets underlying the separate account.

✓ **Take Note:** Separate accounts are not insured by the insurer and the returns on their investments are not guaranteed. For the insurer, this presents a means of transferring the investment risk from itself to the policyowner. The insurer can offer policyowners the possibility (though not the guarantee) of competitively high returns without facing the investment risk posed by its guaranteed fixed policies.

FIGURE 4.11   General Accounts vs. Separate Accounts

Understanding the distinctions between an insurer's general account and its separate account is key to understanding the differences between traditional guaranteed contracts and variable contracts.

General account assets are used to support the contractual obligations of an insurer's fixed, traditional policies; they represent the general assets of the company. Though they are the foundation of the insurer's policy reserves, they also are subject to the claims of creditors. If an insurer's general account assets ever fail to support its reserve liability, the company is said to be insolvent and the assets become subject to the claims of the company's creditors—including policyowners. To reduce the likelihood of this occurring, insurers typically invest their general account assets in conservative investment instruments.

Separate accounts are just as their name implies: accounts separate from the insurer's general accounts. Separate accounts are maintained solely for the purpose of allowing policyowners to participate directly in the account's investment performance and contract values earn a variable, rather than a fixed, return. Also, because they are separate from the insurer's general account, separate accounts are not subject to the claims of the insurer's general creditors. This means that policyowners cannot lose the physical assets underlying their variable contracts in the event of the company's insolvency (though the assets' value can be lost by changes in market conditions). Many consumers today purchase variable contracts for this reason. In addition to being able to participate in the investment performance of the assets underlying their contracts, variable contractholders are assured that their share of those assets never will be compromised, even in the event of company insolvency.

Because of the transfer of investment risk from the insurer to the policyowner, variable insurance products are considered securities contracts as well as insurance contracts. Therefore, they fall under the regulation of both state insurance departments and the Securities and Exchange Commission (SEC). To sell variable insurance products, an individual must hold a life insurance license and a National Association of Securities Dealers (NASD) registered representative's license. Some states also may require a special variable insurance license or special addendum to the regular life insurance license.

Because variable insurance policies are securities, full and fair disclosure must be provided to the prospective policyowner. Therefore, by law, a variable insurance sales presentation cannot be conducted unless it is preceded or accompanied by a prospectus, prepared and furnished by the insurance company and approved by the SEC. Also, all other materials used in selling and promoting variable insurance products—direct mail letters, brochures, advertising pieces and the like—must also have prior approval of the SEC. These requirements provide consumer protection and promote meaningful communication between agents and consumers.

Take Note: A prospectus contains information about the nature and purpose of the insurance plan, the separate account and the risk involved. It is a significant source of information for the prospect.

With this introduction in mind, let's look at two types of variable insurance products: *variable life insurance* and *variable universal life insurance*. Keep in mind that while these policies involve investment management and offer the potential for investment gains, they primarily are life insurance policies, not investment contracts. The primary purpose of these plans, like any life insurance plan, is to provide financial protection in the event of the insured's death.

Variable Life Insurance

Variable life insurance is permanent life insurance with many of the same characteristics of traditional whole life insurance. The main difference, as explained previously, is the manner in which the policy's values are invested. With traditional whole life, these values are kept in the insurer's general accounts and invested in conservative investments selected by the insurer to match its contractual guarantees and liabilities. With variable life insurance policies, the policy values are invested in the insurer's separate accounts, which house common stock, bond, money-market and other securities investment options. Values held in these separate accounts are invested in riskier, but potentially higher-yielding, assets than those held in the general account.

As with any permanent insurance product, the growth of the policy's cash values support the death benefit. In traditional whole life products, that benefit is fixed and guaranteed; with variable life insurance, the benefit rises (and falls) in relation to the performance of the policy's values. There is a minimum guaranteed death benefit; this is equal to the face amount at policy issue and is based on an assumed rate of return, usually 3 to 4 percent. However, if the separate account growth (and by extension, the cash value growth) exceeds this assumed rate, the result is an elevated death benefit.

Figure 4.12 shows the effect over time of increases—and decreases—in a variable life insurance policy's separate account rate of return. Each year that the actual return exceeds the assumed rate of return (shown in this example as 4 percent), there is a positive net investment return and the death benefit is increased. In years where the actual return or growth is less than assumed, the death benefit is decreased from any previously attained levels. Note, however, that the death benefit never will drop below the face amount guaranteed at policy issue.

 **Test Topic Alert!**

Like traditional whole life insurance, variable life insurance requires the payment of set premiums on a scheduled basis. Failure to make these premium payments results in policy lapse.

FIGURE 4.12 Variable Life Death Benefit

The following graph shows how the investment performance of a variable life insurance policy's values affect the death benefit. Here, the assumed rate of return is 4 percent. If the net investment results were equal to 4 percent throughout the life of the policy, the death benefit would remain the same—that is, the face amount of the policy at issue. However, as is more likely, the actual investment results will vary. A return greater than 4 percent produces a rise in the death benefit; a return less than 4 percent produces a drop in the death benefit from the previous year.

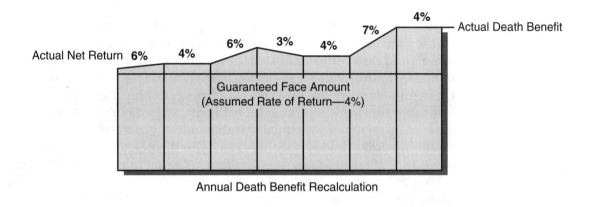

Variable life insurance policyowners can access their policy values through policy loans. However, the amount of the loan is limited—usually 75 to 80 percent of the cash value. (Compare this to conventional whole life policies, which typically permit loans up to 100 percent of the cash value.) The reason for this restriction is to reduce the possibility that falling returns will cause an outstanding policy loan to become greater than the policy's cash value.

Variable Universal Life

Variable universal life (VUL) blends many features of whole life, universal life and variable life. Premium flexibility, cash value investment control and death benefit flexibility are key among these features. These features give VUL its unique characteristics and make it responsive to policyowners' needs.

Every variable universal life insurance policy is issued with a minimum scheduled premium based on an initial specified death benefit. This initial premium establishes the plan, meets first-year expenses and provides funding to cover the cost of insurance protection. Once they pay this initial premium, policyowners can pay whatever premium amount they wish, with certain limitations. Provided adequate cash value is available to cover periodic charges and the cost of insurance, they can suspend or reduce premium payments. Policyowners may even be able to vanish their premiums indefinitely if their cash values realize consistently strong investment returns.

Conversely, policyowners wishing to increase death benefits or take advantage of tax-favored accumulation of cash values can pay additional premiums into their plans. However, most policies contain maximum limits, and if the increase is above a certain amount, proof of insurability may be required.

✓ **Take Note:** These maximum limits are imposed to maintain the corridor between the cash value and the death benefit. This corridor must exist for the policy to qualify as life insurance and retain its tax-sheltered cash value accumulation status.

Cash value in a VUL plan is maintained separately from the rest of the plan. At the time of application, the policyowner elects to have his or her net premiums and cash values allocated to one or more separate account investment options. These accounts usually are mutual funds created and maintained by the insurance company or provided through arrangements between the insurance company and other investment companies. These funds are kept in separate accounts and function independently of the insurance company's assets. Earnings or losses accrue directly to the policyowner's cash value, subject to stated charges and management fees. Policyowners can redirect future premiums and switch accounts periodically, generally once a year, without charge. The result is a life insurance policy that provides policyowners with self-directed investment options.

VUL policies generally offer both a level death benefit, which provides for a fixed death benefit (until the policy values reach the corridor level) and potential higher cash value accumulation, or a variable death benefit, which provides a death benefit that fluctuates in response to the performance of investments.

Under the level death benefit, the policyowner specifies the total death benefit in the policy. This amount remains constant and does not fluctuate as cash values increase or decrease. Instead, cash values build up within the policy until they reach the corridor, at which time the death benefit will increase to corresponding increases in the cash value. Until that point is reached, however, the cash value simply accumulates, with each increase replacing a corresponding amount of pure insurance needed to keep the death benefit at the specified amount.

Under the variable death benefit, the policyowner selects a specified amount of pure insurance coverage. This specified amount remains constant. The death benefit payable at any time is a combination of the specified (or face) amount and the cash value within the policy. Essentially, the cash value is added to the specified amount to create the total death benefit. Under this option, the emphasis is on the potential for both cash value and death benefit growth. This option often is recommended for policyowners who want favorable investment results and additional premiums reflected directly in increased death benefits.

FIGURE 4.13   Loan or Withdrawal?

Partial cash value distributions may be classified as loans or withdrawals; which of the two is chosen depends on several factors.

A *loan* is just that—a loan against one's own money. It is withdrawn with either the presumption that it will be repaid (with accrued interest) or the understanding that by not repaying it the amount of future benefits—including the death benefit—will be reduced by the loaned amount (plus accrued interest).

A *withdrawal* generally has the same impact on policy benefits, but there is no presumption that it will be repaid. The withdrawn amount is treated as a permanent withdrawal, thus immediately reducing the death benefit and, of course, the cash value. The withdrawn amount does not accrue interest against future policy values, as it does with a loan. However, from an actuarial perspective, the impact on future policy values is identical with either approach.

Generally, only universal life and variable universal life policies, with their inherent policy flexibility, permit withdrawals. Traditional whole life and variable life do not lend themselves to this type of flexibility and, though there may be a few exceptions, they typically provide only for loans.

Because cash value withdrawals (as opposed to loans) are recognized as taxable income to the extent they exceed the policyowner's cost basis in the contract, most sizeable withdrawals are technically regarded as withdrawals up to the owner's basis; withdrawn amounts above basis are regarded as loans, which are not taxable. By recognizing withdrawn amounts that exceed basis merely as loans and not permanent withdrawals, this technique defers and possibly avoids income taxation of the full withdrawn amount.

Like universal life, VUL policies permit partial withdrawals, allowing the owner to tap the cash value without incurring any indebtedness. Policyowners need not repay those funds and no interest is incurred on the amount withdrawn. Withdrawals, of course, affect the policy's future earnings, and their effect on the death benefit depends on the death benefit option in force. Partial withdrawals taken in a policy's early years may be subject to surrender charges (when the insurer is trying to recover the costs of issuing the policy).

 **Test Topic Alert!**   Variable universal life insurance may be referred to as *flexible premium variable life insurance.*

Summary

Today's life insurers offer a vast array of life insurance plans, which are designed to serve various functions and meet different needs. Term insurance, the simplest type of plan, provides pure protection only, for a specified temporary period or term. At the end of the term, the protection expires. If a policyowner desires, he or she can extend the coverage through two options: the option to renew the term policy for another term and (or) the option to convert the term policy to a whole life, or permanent, plan.

Whole life insurance provides protection for the whole of life and pays a death benefit if the insured dies at any time before age 100. Whole life insurance is characterized by cash values that accumulate over time, eventually reaching a level equal to the policy's face amount at the insured's age 100. At that point, the policy has matured or endowed. Premiums for whole life insurance are level throughout the policy's period and are calculated as though the insured were to pay them until age 100. A large percentage of whole life policies, known as straight life policies, are purchased on this basis. However, if a policyowner desires, the premium-paying period can be limited to a certain age or for a specified number of years; these policies are known as limited pay life policies. The most extreme example of limited pay life is single-premium whole life. Other types of whole life plans—such as modified whole life, graded premium whole life, minimum deposit whole life and indeterminate premium whole life—also provide permanent protection but vary the way in which premiums are paid.

Endowment insurance combines the principles of term insurance and pure endowment. If the insured dies at any time within the endowment period, the policy pays a death benefit. If the insured lives to the end of the endowment period, the policy matures and is paid off as a completely endowed policy.

Various special use plans, which combine features of term and whole life into single policies, are available to fit different needs. These include family policies, multiple protection policies, joint life policies, juvenile insurance and credit life insurance.

Finally, a number of newer, nontraditional life policies have been introduced over the past decade or so. These policies are characterized in part by increased flexibility and current market returns. Most notable of these newer policy forms are interest-sensitive whole life, adjustable life, universal life, variable life and variable universal life.

Key Concepts

In preparing for their licensing examination, students should be familiar with the following concepts:

ordinary insurance
group insurance
decreasing term
whole life
modified whole life
enhanced whole life
limited pay whole life
modified endowment contract
family maintenance policy
minimum deposit
juvenile insurance
adjustable life
universal life
variable universal life

industrial insurance
level term
increasing term
graded premium whole life
single-premium whole life
indexed whole life
endowment policies
family income policy
joint and last survivor policy
credit life
multiple protection plan
interest-sensitive whole life
variable life

Lesson Exam Four

1. Which of the following life insurance is characterized by low issue amounts and weekly at-home premium collection?

   A. Mini-life
   B. Direct life
   C. Ordinary life
   D. Industrial life

2. All of the following terms correctly apply to a life insurance policy that provides a straight $100,000 of coverage for a period of five years EXCEPT

   A. temporary
   B. term
   C. variable
   D. level

3. Which of the following statements regarding term life insurance is NOT correct?

   A. A three-year renewable policy allows a term policyowner to renew the same coverage for another three years.
   B. A three-year renewable policy allows a term policyowner to increase coverage for the next three years.
   C. An option to convert provides that a term life insurance policy can be exchanged for a permanent one.
   D. Both the option to renew and the option to convert relieve the insured from furnishing evidence of insurability.

4. "When level premium insurance is renewed, the premium amount rises to reflect the increased mortality risk of the insured's older age." What phrase best describes this approach to increasing premiums?

   A. Variable rate
   B. Targeted rate
   C. Step rate
   D. Seniority rate

5. Which of the following statements describing whole life insurance is NOT correct?

   A. The face amount of the policy stays the same as long as the policy remains in force.
   B. The shorter a premium period is, the faster the cash value will grow.
   C. The policy's cash value decreases each year the policy is in force.
   D. Whole life insurance is designed to mature at age 100.

6. The cash values of life insurance policies belong to which of the following entities?

   A. Policyowner
   B. Insured
   C. Insurer
   D. Beneficiary

7. Which of the following statements regarding basic forms of whole life insurance is NOT correct?

   A. Generally, straight life premiums are payable, at least annually, for the duration of the insured's life.
   B. The owner of a 30-pay life policy will owe no more premiums after the 30th year the policy is in force.
   C. Limited payment life provides protection only for the years during which premiums are paid.
   D. A single-premium life policy is purchased with a large one-time-only premium.

8. Which of the following statements regarding modified endowment contracts (MECs) is CORRECT?

   A. A 1988 revenue act, commonly known as TAMRA, greatly increased the popularity of MECs.
   B. Congress has granted the MEC the most favorable tax status among all life insurance policies.
   C. To avoid being classified as an MEC, a life insurance policy must satisfy the 7-pay test.
   D. According to the 7-pay test, if the total amount a policyowner pays into a life contract during its first seven years is less than the sum of the net level premiums that would have been payable to provide paid-up future benefits in seven years, the policy is an MEC.

9. All of the following whole life insurance policies attempt to make insurance premiums more manageable by offering lower premiums during the first few years following issue EXCEPT

   A. graded premium whole life
   B. modified whole life
   C. indexed whole life
   D. indeterminate premium whole life

10. Which of the following statements regarding special use policies is NOT correct?

    A. A family income policy combines whole life and decreasing term insurance into one policy package.
    B. A family maintenance policy combines whole life and level term insurance into one policy package.
    C. A joint life policy is available using term insurance only.
    D. A multiple protection policy pays double or triple death proceeds if the insured dies during a specified period.

11. What type of policy would be the best choice to insure the declining balance on a home mortgage?

    A. Level term
    B. Decreasing term
    C. Whole life
    D. Universal life

12. Which of the following statements about term insurance is NOT correct?

    A. It pays a benefit only if the insured dies during a specified period.
    B. Level, decreasing and increasing are basic forms of term insurance.
    C. Cash values build during the specified period.
    D. It provides protection for a temporary period of time.

13. An insured purchases a $50,000 5-year level term policy. Which of the following statements about this coverage is NOT correct?

    A. The policy provides a straight, level $50,000 of coverage for five years.
    B. If the insured dies at any time during the five years, the beneficiary will receive the policy's face value.
    C. If the insured dies after the specified five years, only the policy's cash value will be paid.
    D. If the insured lives beyond the five years, the policy expires and no benefits are payable.

14. An insured purchases a 5-year $50,000 decreasing term policy with an option to renew. Which of the following statements about the policy's renewability is CORRECT?

    A. The premium for the renewal period will be the same as the initial period.
    B. The premium for the renewal period will be higher than the initial period.
    C. The premium for the renewal period will be the same as the initial period, but a one-time service charge will be assessed on renewal.
    D. The premium for the renewal period will be lower than the initial period.

15. Which of the following statements about variable insurance policies is NOT correct?

    A. Sales presentations must be preceded or accompanied by a prospectus.
    B. SEC laws protect consumers and promote meaningful communication
    C. Materials used in selling variable policies need approval from the state department of insurance.
    D. Full and fair disclosure must be provided to prospective policyowners.

16. In contrast to traditional whole life insurance policies, with variable life insurance products

    A. premiums are invested in an insurer's general account
    B. investments match the insurer's contractual guarantees and liabilities
    C. contract values are not guaranteed
    D. the insurer assumes the investment risk

17. Which of the following statements about variable insurance policies is NOT correct?

    A. They are considered insurance contracts.
    B. Those who sell it must hold a state insurance license.
    C. They are not considered securities contracts.
    D. Those who sell it must hold a National Association of Securities Dealers registered representative license.

18. At age 30, an insured buys a 20-year family maintenance policy that pays $1,000 a month. The insured dies at age 48. How much will the family receive?

    A. $12,000
    B. $24,000
    C. $120,000
    D. $240,000

19. Which of the following is a policy covering two lives that only pays a death benefit when the second insured person dies?

    A. Joint life
    B. Family
    C. Family maintenance
    D. Joint and last survivor

20. Which of the following is a policy that pays double or triple the face amount if death occurs during a specified period?

    A. Multiple protection
    B. Credit life
    C. Family
    D. Joint

Answers and Rationale

1. **D.** Industrial life insurance is characterized by comparatively small issue amounts (e.g., $1,000) with premiums collected by the agent on a weekly basis at the policyowner's home. This type of insurance offers protection to individuals who cannot afford larger policies.

2. **C.** Because this policy provides a set amount of protection ($100,000) for a specified period only (five years), it will be considered a level term policy. Term life also is called temporary life insurance because it provides protection for a temporary period of time only.

3. **B.** An option to renew allows the policyowner to renew the same coverage before the policy's termination date, without having to show evidence of insurability. A three-year renewable policy, therefore, would allow a term policyowner to renew the same coverage for another three years.

4. **C.** When level premium insurance is renewed, the premium will be increased, reflecting a higher rate because of the insured's increased age. The phrase used to describe this method of premium payments is step-rate.

5. **C.** The shorter the premium-paying period (and consequently, the higher the premium), the faster the cash values grow in a whole life insurance policy. This is because a greater percentage of each payment is credited to the policy's cash values.

6. **A.** Ownership of a policy's cash value rests solely with the policyowner. A policy's cash value is nonforfeitable; that is, policyowners are assured that they are fully entitled to the accrued cash values of their policies.

7. **C.** Even though premium payments are limited to a certain period, the insurance protection under a limited pay whole life policy extends until the insured's death, or to age 100.

8. **C.** To avoid being classified as a modified endowment contract, a life insurance policy must meet the 7-pay test. According to this test, if the total amount a policyowner pays into a life contract during its first year exceeds the sum of the net level premiums that would have been payable to provide paid-up future benefits in seven years, the policy is an MEC.

9. **C.** With indexed whole life insurance, the policyowner assumes the risk of future increases and thus must pay additional premium with each face amount increase. Alternatively, the insurer assumes the risk and the policyowner does not pay a higher premium with face amount increases. This type of insurance does not offer lower premiums during the first few years following issue.

10. **C.** Joint life policies cover two people and use some type of permanent insurance, as opposed to term.

11. **B.** Decreasing term insurance is best suited for an individual whose need for protection declines from year to year. It therefore would be a good choice to insure the declining balance on a home mortgage.

12. **C.** Term life insurance offers protection for a specified period and pays a benefit only if the insured dies during that time. No cash values are generated in term life insurance.

13. **C.** If the insured dies after the end of the five-year period, the beneficiary will receive nothing. A term life policy has no cash value.

14. **B.** When a term policy is renewed, the premiums for the renewal period will be higher than the initial period. This is because the insured now is older and the insurer's risk, therefore, is greater.

15. **C.** Because variable insurance policies are securities, state insurance departments and the Securities and Exchange Commission (SEC) regulate them. All materials used in selling and promoting variable insurance products must have prior approval of the SEC.

16. **C.** Variable insurance products do not guarantee contract values. This is because policy-owners can direct the investment of the funds backing their variable contracts through separate account options. Instead of a fixed return, the investment account will earn a variable return depending on the account's investment performance.

17. **C.** Variable insurance contracts are considered securities contracts as well as insurance contracts. Therefore, both state insurance departments and the SEC regulate them.

18. **D.** If an insured buys a family maintenance policy at age 30 and dies at age 48, the income period will begin upon death and will continue thereafter for the specified period. Thus, the monthly benefit ($1,000) will be paid for 20 years beginning at the date of the insured's death. The total amount of payments will be $240,000 ($12,000/year × 20 years).

19. **D.** Under a joint and last survivor policy, two lives are covered but the benefit is paid only on the death of the second insured.

20. **A.** A multiple protection policy pays a benefit of double or triple the face amount if death occurs during a specified period. If death occurs after the period has expired, only the policy's face amount is paid.

5

Life Insurance Policy Provisions, Options and Riders

INTRODUCTION

Life insurance is property, and policyowners have important rights, as well as responsibilities, inherent in the ownership of this special type of property. Although no standard policy form must be used in life insurance, states have enacted strict guidelines as to what must and must not be included in a policy. As a result, all life insurance policies contain certain standardized policy provisions that identify the rights and obligations of the policyowner and the insurer. Of course, life insurance can be customized to meet the specific needs of the owner through policy riders and options. In this lesson, we will examine the standard provisions found in most life insurance contracts as well as some of the common riders and options that can be added to give a life insurance contract its form and flexibility.

LESSON OBJECTIVES

When you complete this lesson you should be able to:

- list and describe the standard provisions in a life insurance policy;
- describe the most common types of policy exclusions;
- compare and contrast the three nonforfeiture options—cash surrender, reduced paid-up insurance and extended term insurance;
- explain the different options policyowners have for receiving dividends; and
- list and describe the different types of policy riders.

Rights of Policy Ownership

Before we discuss specific policy provisions, it is important to mention the rights of ownership that policyowners have. Although there are no provisions in a life insurance policy specifically titled Rights of Ownership, the fact is, owning a life insurance policy does entail important rights. These rights are woven throughout the policy in various clauses and provisions. The most significant rights of ownership include the right to:

- designate and change the beneficiary of the policy proceeds;
- select how the death proceeds will be paid to the beneficiary;
- cancel the policy and select a nonforfeiture option;
- take out a policy loan, assuming the policy is a whole life or other permanent plan and a cash value exists;
- receive policy dividends and select a dividend payment option, if it is a participating policy; and
- assign ownership of the policy to someone else.

The clauses and provisions that set forth these rights will be examined in this and later lessons.

Standard Policy Provisions

Despite insurance companies' efforts to offer products distinctive from their competitors', insurance policies are more notable for their many similarities than differences. This high degree of uniformity is rooted in the state-level regulation of the industry and the adoption of National Association of Insurance Commissioners (NAIC) guidelines.

As discussed in Lesson 2, regulators in each state protect consumers by establishing strict guidelines as to what must, and must not, be included in an insurance policy. Furthermore, in an effort to promote state-by-state uniformity of insurance industry regulation, most states have adopted, to one degree or another, the standard wording of NAIC model regulations. Accordingly, policy language is strikingly similar among the many different life insurance contracts available to consumers.

We will begin this section with a discussion of the standard provisions that appear in most life insurance contracts, then take a look at some of the common exclusions. Note that while the provision names used here are commonly accepted terms, individual contracts may use different wording. For example, the Entire Contract clause falls under the heading The Contract in one company's policy, Entire Contract in another's and General in a third. (It may be helpful to review the sample policy in the Appendix as you read this section.)

Entire Contract Provision

The entire contract provision, found at the beginning of the policy, states that the policy document, the application (which is attached to the policy) and any attached riders constitute the entire contract. Nothing may be incorporated by reference, meaning that the policy cannot refer to any outside documents as being part of the contract.

✓ **For Example:** An insurance company could not claim that a special rider, not attached to the policy but on file in the home office, is part of the policy.

The entire contract clause has another important function—it prohibits the insurer from making any changes to the policy, either through policy revisions or changes in the company's bylaws, after the policy has been issued.

✓ **Take Note:** A typical entire contract provision reads:

This policy and the application, a copy of which is attached when issued, constitute the entire contract. All statements in the application, in the absence of fraud, shall be deemed representations and not warranties. No statement shall void this policy or be used in defense of a claim under it unless contained in the application.

This clause does not prevent a mutually agreeable change from being made to the policy if the policy specifically provides a means for modifying the contract after it has been issued (for example, changing the face amount of an adjustable life policy).

 **Test Topic Alert!**

A change made by the policyowner after the policy is issued is called an *amendment*. Amendments become part of the contract by virtue of the entire contract clause.

Insuring Clause

The insuring clause, or provision, sets forth the company's basic promise to pay benefits on the insured's death. Generally, this clause is not actually titled as such, but appears on the cover of the policy.

✓ **For Example:** A typical insuring clause reads:

The Insurance Company agrees, in accordance with the provisions of this policy, to pay to the beneficiary the death proceeds upon receipt at the Principal Office of due proof of the insured's death prior to the maturity date.

Further, the Company agrees to pay the surrender value to the owner if the insured is alive on the maturity date.

The insuring clause typically is undersigned by the president and secretary of the insurance company.

 Test Topic Alert!   The insuring clause usually is found on the first page of the policy and identifies the parties to the contract.

Free Look Provision

The free look provision, required by most states, gives policyowners the right to return the policy for a full premium refund within a specified period of time, if they decide not to purchase the insurance. Most policies provide for a 10-day free look period.

 Take Note: It is important to note that the free look period begins when the policy document actually is received by the policyowner, not when the application is signed or when the policy is issued by the insurance company.

 **Test Topic Alert!**   A policyowner may cancel a policy at any time, of course. However, doing so during the free look period entitles the policyowner to a refund of the premium.

Consideration Clause

As we learned in Lesson 3, consideration is the value given in exchange for a contractual promise. The consideration clause, or provision, in a life insurance policy specifies the amount and frequency of premium payments that the policyowners must make to keep the insurance in force. Often, the amount and frequency of required premiums are listed on the Schedule or Specifications page. A separate page will provide details on the manner in which premiums must be paid (as well as the consequences of not making a premium payment).

Grace Period Provision

The grace period provision undoubtedly has saved many life insurance policies from lapsing. If policyowners forget or neglect to pay their premiums by the date they are due, the grace period allows an extra 30 days or one month (possibly less for some industrial policies) during which premiums may be paid to keep policies in force.

 Take Note: If an insured dies during the grace period and the premium has not been paid, the policy benefit is payable. However, the premium amount due is deducted from the benefits paid to the beneficiary.

Reinstatement Provision

It always is possible that, due to nonpayment of premiums, a policy may lapse, either deliberately or unintentionally. In cases where a policyowner wishes to reinstate a lapsed policy, the reinstatement provision allows him or her to do so, with some limitations. With reinstatement, a policy is restored to its original status and its values are brought up to date.

✓ **Take Note:** Most insurers require the following to reinstate a lapsed policy:

- all back premiums must be paid;
- interest on past-due premiums may be assessed;
- any outstanding loans on the lapsed policy may be required to be paid; and
- the policyowner may be asked to prove insurability.

In addition, there is a limited period of time in which policies may be reinstated after lapse. This period usually is three years but may be as long as seven years, in some cases. A new contestable period usually goes into effect with a reinstated policy, but there is no new suicide exclusion period. (See Incontestable Clause and Suicide Provision in this lesson.)

Policy Loan Provision

State insurance laws require that cash value life insurance policies include a policy loan provision. This means that, within prescribed limits, policyowners may borrow money from the cash values of their policies if they wish to do so.

Actually, a policy loan is more an advance on proceeds than a true loan. As such, these loans may not be called by the company and can be repaid at any time by the policyowners. If not repaid by the time the insured dies, the loan balance and any interest accrued are deducted from the policy proceeds at the time of claim. If the policy is surrendered for cash, the cash value available to the policyowner is reduced by the amount of any outstanding loan plus interest.

Interest rates on policy loans vary, but most states stipulate a maximum allowable rate. Some newer policies are issued with a variable interest rate tied to current market rates; older policies still in force stipulate a flat rate of interest, such as 5 to 8 percent.

Loan values and cash surrender values are shown as identical amounts in a policy and often are listed under the single column heading of Cash or Loan Value. (See Figure 5.1.)

FIGURE 5.1   Table of Guaranteed Values

Face Amount: $100,000   Annual Premium: $2,000

End of Policy Year	Cash or Loan Value	Reduced Paid-up	Extended Term Years	Extended Term Days
1	$0	$0	0	0
2	$50	$210	0	66
3	$960	$3,600	2	290
4	$2,150	$7,250	6	9
5	$4,000	$12,000	8	111
6	$5,975	$16,110	10	147
7	$7,210	$19,880	12	22
8	$9,340	$23,800	14	18
9	$11,415	$27,620	15	312
10	$13,005	$30,990	16	362
11	$14,770	$34,010	17	202
12	$16,785	$37,880	18	116
13	$19,430	$40,940	18	1
14	$23,000	$43,985	17	144
15	$26,990	$47,010	16	302
16	$30,215	$50,600	15	347
17	$34,600	$53,815	15	88
18	$38,910	$56,910	14	117
19	$43,020	$60,010	13	361
20	$47,910	$63,715	13	47
Age 65	$56,770	$78,700	11	36

This table shows how the guaranteed (nonforfeitable) values are presented in a life insurance policy. These figures reflect the values available to the policyowner at different points in the policy's life for purposes of surrendering the policy for cash, taking out a loan against the policy, purchasing a reduced paid-up policy or purchasing an extended term policy. (See also the sample policy in the Appendix.)

Incontestable Clause

The incontestable clause, or provision, provides that after a specified period of time (usually two years from the issue date and while the insured is living), the insurer no longer has the right to contest the validity of the life insurance policy so long as the contract continues in force. This means that after the policy has been in force for the specified term, the company cannot contest a death claim or refuse payment of the proceeds even on the basis of a material misstatement, concealment or fraud. Even if the insurer learns that an error was deliberately made on the application, it must pay the death benefit at the insured's death if the policy has passed the contestable period.

✓ **Take Note:** Although the incontestable clause applies to death benefits, it generally does not apply to accidental death benefits or disability provisions if they are part of the policy. Because conditions relating to accidents vary and often are uncertain, the right to investigate them usually is reserved by the company.

The incontestable clause applies to the policy face amount, plus any additional death benefit added by rider that is payable in the case of normal death.

It should be noted that there are three situations to which the incontestable clause does not apply. A policy issued under any of these circumstances is not a valid contract, which gives the insurer the right to contest and possibly void the policy at any time:

- *Impersonation.* When application for insurance is made by one person but another person signs the application or takes the medical exam, the insurer can contest the policy and its claim.
- *No insurable interest.* If no insurable interest existed between the applicant and the insured at the inception of the policy, the contract is not valid to begin with; as such, the insurer can contest the policy at any time.
- *Intent to murder.* If it is subsequently proven that the applicant applied for the policy with the intent of murdering the insured for the proceeds, the insurance company can contest the policy and its claim.

Assignment Provision

People who purchase life insurance policies commonly are referred to as policyowners rather than policyholders because they actually own their policies and may do with them as they wish. They can even give them away, just as they can give away any other kind of property they own. This transfer of ownership is known as assignment.

The assignment provision in a life insurance contract sets forth the procedure necessary for ownership transfer. This procedure usually requires that the policyowner notify the company in writing of the assignment. The company then will accept the validity of the transfer without question. A policyowner need not have the insurer's permission to assign a policy. The new owner is known as the *assignee*.

 For Example: If an individual gave a policy to his church as a donation, the church would be the assignee. An insurable interest need not exist between the insured and the assignee.

As the owner of the policy, the assignee is granted all the rights of policy ownership, including the right to name a beneficiary. If the assignee does not change the beneficiary designation, the proceeds will be paid to the beneficiary named by the original owner.

Take Note: The assignee has the right to change the beneficiary as long as the original beneficiary designation was revocable.* If a policyowner names an irrevocable beneficiary (meaning the beneficiary cannot be changed), he or she must get the beneficiary's agreement to any assignment. (See Lesson 6.)

Within the guidelines set forth for assignments in any given policy, a policyowner generally has two options. Under the first, *absolute assignment*, the transfer is complete and irrevocable, and the assignee receives full control over the policy and full rights to its benefits. Under the second, *collateral assignment*, the policy is assigned to a creditor as security, or collateral, for a debt. If the insured dies, the creditor is entitled to be reimbursed out of the benefit proceeds for the amount owed. The insured's beneficiary then is entitled to any excess of policy proceeds over the amount due the creditor. Once the debt is repaid, the policyowner is entitled to the return of the rights assigned.

 **Test Topic Alert!**   An absolute assignment is common in key employee policies, policies that parents own on their children and accelerated death benefits.

Accelerated Benefits Provision

Until recently, traditional whole life insurance policies provided cash benefit payments in the event of the insured's death (or in the rare case of an insured living to a contract's maturity date). The only way an insured could access the policy's cash value while living was through a policy loan or policy surrender. If an insured was faced with a life-threatening medical condition, the life insurance policy, by design, could provide no immediate financial relief.

Today, accelerated benefits provisions are standard in life insurance policies. They provide for the early payment of some portion of the policy face amount should the insured suffer from a terminal illness or injury. The death benefit, less the accelerated payment, still is payable.

 For Example: A $250,000 policy that provides for a 75 percent accelerated benefit would pay up to $187,500 to the terminally ill insured, with the remaining $62,500 payable as a death benefit to the beneficiary when the insured dies. An accelerated payment can be made in a lump sum or in monthly installments over a special period, such as one year.

This provision is provided at no increase in premium. Some companies deduct an interest charge from the proceeds paid out to make up for what the

---

*Though there may be exceptions, most jurisdictions will not allow an assignee to change the beneficiary designation if it was originally designated irrevocable. (See Changing a Beneficiary, Lesson 6.)

company would have earned had the money not been withdrawn from the contract.

 **Test Topic Alert!**   The money an insured receives from accelerated death benefits need not be spent on final expenses or medical expenses. The insured can spend this money as he or she wishes.

Suicide Provision

The suicide provision, found in most life policies, protects the company and its policyowners against the possibility that a person might buy an insurance policy and deliberately commit suicide to provide a sum of money for the beneficiary. With this provision, a life insurance policy discourages suicide by stipulating a period of time (usually one or two years from the date of policy issue) during which the death benefit will not be paid if the insured commits suicide. If that happens, however, the premiums paid for the policy will be refunded.

Of course, if an insured takes his or her own life after the policy has been in force for the period specified in the suicide clause, the company will pay the entire proceeds, just as if death were from a natural cause.

 Take Note: Because of the instinct for self-preservation, most courts will assume a death was unintentional unless there is strong evidence to the contrary. So even if death occurs during the suicide exclusion period and suicide is suspected, the company must prove that suicide was more likely than not the cause of death; otherwise, the policy proceeds generally must be paid to the beneficiary.

Misstatement of Age or Sex Provision

The misstatement of age or sex provision is important because the age and sex of the applicant are critical factors in establishing the premium rate for a life insurance policy. To guard against a misunderstanding about the applicant's age, the company reserves the right to make an adjustment at any time. Likewise, an adjustment is made if an applicant's sex is incorrectly indicated in a policy because, age for age, premium rates for females generally are lower than for males. Normally, such adjustments are made either in the premium charged or in the amount of insurance.

Assume an error in age is discovered after the death of an insured. If the insured was younger than the policy showed, the amount of proceeds would be increased to a sum the premium paid would have bought at the correct age. On the other hand, if the insured was older than the policy indicated, the amount of proceeds would be decreased to whatever the premium paid would have purchased at the correct age.

If an error is discovered while the insured is living, the premium will be adjusted downward if the insured is younger than the policy shows and a refund of the premium overpayments will be made. By the same token, if the insured is older than the policy indicates, the company will either adjust the premium upward and require the difference in premium or it will reduce the amount of insurance to what it should be for the amount of premium being paid.

 **Test Topic Alert!**   The misstatement of age provision allows the insurer to adjust the death benefit whenever it discovers a misstatement. This provision extends beyond the incontestability period.

Automatic Premium Loan Provision

A provision that is now commonly added to most cash value policies is the automatic premium loan. This provision authorizes the insurer to withdraw from the policy's cash value the amount of premium due if the premium has not been paid by the end of the grace period. The amount withdrawn becomes a loan against the cash value, bearing the rate of interest specified in the contract.

Depending on the insurer, this provision may be standard to the contract or added as a rider, with no additional charge to the policyowner.

Note that this provision may be very beneficial for a policyowner who forgets to pay the premium within the grace period or who cannot pay the current premium because of financial difficulties. Most importantly, the policy does not lapse and coverage continues.

-Ω- **Test Topic Alert!**   If the policyowner allows the automatic premium loan to continually pay the premiums, of course, the policy eventually will lapse when the cash value is reduced to nothing. The owner then would have to reinstate the policy and pay back the loans.

Other Policy Provisions

There are two additional provisions that appear in all policies: the *beneficiary designation*, whereby the policyowner indicates who is to receive the proceeds, and *settlement options*, whereby the ways in which the proceeds can be paid out, or settled, are explained. Beneficiaries are discussed in Lesson 6; settlement options are discussed in Lesson 7.

🖊 **Quick Quiz 5.1** Match the following terms with the appropriate description.

A. Automatic premium loan provision
B. Assignment provision
C. Incontestable clause
D. Policy loan provision
E. Grace period provision
F. Free look provision

_____ 1. A policyowner may return the policy for a full premium refund within a specified period of time if he or she does not want to buy the insurance.

_____ 2. This policy provision gives a policyowner the right to borrow money from his or her policy's cash values.

_____ 3. A policyowner can give away or transfer ownership of the policy.

_____ 4. The insurer can withdraw the amount of premium due from the policy's cash value if the premium has not been paid during the grace period.

_____ 5. The insurer cannot contest the validity of a life insurance policy after a specified period of time.

_____ 6. This policy provision gives a policyowner extra time to pay premiums that are due to prevent the policy from lapsing.

Answers   *1. F*   *2. D*   *3. B*   *4. A*   *5. C*   *6. E*

Policy Exclusions

Most life insurance policies contain restrictions that exclude from coverage certain types of risks from coverage. If no exclusions existed, premium rates would be much higher. Exclusions can be stated in the policy itself or attached as riders. The most common types of exclusions include:

- *War.* This exclusion provides that the death benefit will not be paid if the insured dies as a result of war.
- *Aviation.* This exclusion commonly is found in older policies; very few policies issued today exclude death as a result of commercial aviation. However, some insurers will exclude aviation deaths for other than fare-paying passengers.
- *Hazardous occupations or hobbies.* Individuals who have hazardous occupations, such as stunt people, or who engage in hazardous hobbies, such as auto racing, may find that their life insurance policies

exclude death as a result of their occupation or hobby. Or, these risks may be covered, but an increased, or rated, premium will be charged.

- *Commission of a felony.* Some contracts will exclude death when it results from the insured committing a felony.
- *Suicide.* As previously noted, almost all policies exclude payment of the benefit if the insured commits suicide during the specified time period. After that period passes, death by suicide is covered.

Because these exclusions are allowed by state regulators to be included in policies at the discretion of the insurance company, they also are called *optional provisions.* Note, however, the term exclusions more precisely defines their purpose.

Nonforfeiture Values and Options

In Lesson 4 we learned that an important feature of whole life insurance is its cash value, which is created in part by the level premium funding method. As a policy matures, cash values grow until, when the policy endows, the cash value equals the face amount of the policy. Ownership of a policy's cash value rests solely with the policyowner. Even though the cash value is an important part of the underlying funding of the policy, the policyowner is entitled to receive the accrued cash value at any time. When a policy is active, the owner can borrow from the cash value. If a policy is lapsed or surrendered, the owner is entitled to the cash surrender value.

Until the beginning of the 20th century, it was common for insurers to keep part or all of the cash value in a surrendered policy. The idea that it was the policyowner, not the insurer, who was entitled to a policy's cash value did not gain universal acceptance until the 1905 Armstrong Investigation looked at a number of insurer abuses, including the practice of keeping policy cash values on policy surrender.

 Take Note: Today every state has legislated laws, modeled after the NAIC Standard Nonforfeiture Law, assuring policyowners that they are fully entitled to the accrued cash values of their policies.

The term nonforfeiture value refers to the fact that a policy's cash value is not forfeitable. Nonforfeiture options are the ways in which cash values can be paid out to or used by policyowners, if they choose to lapse or surrender their policies.

FIGURE 5.2 Reduced Paid-up Option

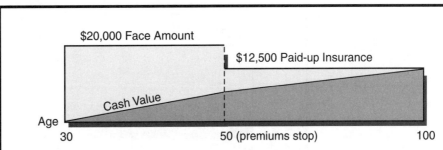

$20,000 Face Amount

$12,500 Paid-up Insurance

Cash Value

Age

30   50 (premiums stop)   100

Using the above diagram as an example, assume Lyman purchased a $20,000 whole life policy at age 30 and now, at age 50, decides to discontinue premium payments and use the accumulated cash value to make a single payment to purchase a reduced amount ($12,500) of permanent paid-up insurance. Lyman has exercised the "reduced paid-up" nonforfeiture option. (Amounts shown are illustrative only.)

Nonforfeiture Options

There are three nonforfeiture options from which policyowners can select: *cash surrender, reduced paid-up insurance* and *extended term insurance*.

Cash Surrender Option

If they desire, policyowners may request an immediate cash payment of their cash values when their policies are surrendered. A table of cash surrender values is included in every permanent life insurance policy, as illustrated in Figure 5.1, under the heading Cash or Loan Value. The amount of cash value the policyowner receives is reduced by any outstanding policy indebtedness.

Insurers are required to make cash surrender values available for ordinary whole life insurance after the first three policy years and, for industrial insurance, after five years. In practice, however, most policies begin to generate cash values in as little as one year.

 Take Note: Most states permit insurers to postpone payment of cash surrender values for up to six months after policyowners request payment. This *delayed payment provision* is a protective measure for companies should an economic crisis arise, but such delays rarely are invoked.

Reduced Paid-up Option

A second nonforfeiture option is to take a paid-up policy for a reduced face amount of insurance. By doing this, the policyowner does not pay any more premiums but still retains some amount of life insurance. In essence, the cash value is used as the premium for a single-premium whole life policy, at a lesser face amount than the original policy.

FIGURE 5.3 Extended Term Option

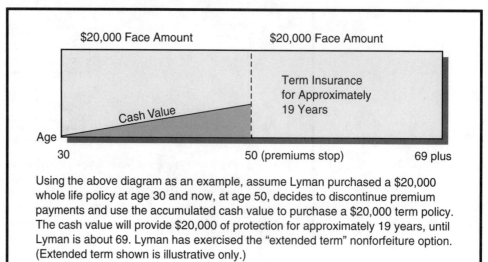

$20,000 Face Amount $20,000 Face Amount

Cash Value

Term Insurance for Approximately 19 Years

Age

30 50 (premiums stop) 69 plus

Using the above diagram as an example, assume Lyman purchased a $20,000 whole life policy at age 30 and now, at age 50, decides to discontinue premium payments and use the accumulated cash value to purchase a $20,000 term policy. The cash value will provide $20,000 of protection for approximately 19 years, until Lyman is about 69. Lyman has exercised the "extended term" nonforfeiture option. (Extended term shown is illustrative only.)

When this option is exercised, the paid-up policy is the same kind as the original, but for a lesser amount of coverage.

 For Example: If the original policy was a participating whole life policy, the paid-up policy also will be a participating whole life policy. The paid-up policy is computed as a single-premium policy at the attained-age rate. Any term insurance rider and disability or accidental death benefits from the original policy are excluded when the amount of paid-up life insurance is calculated.

Once the paid-up policy has been issued, the new face value remains the same for the life of the policy, which also builds cash values. (See Figure 5.2.)

Extended Term Option

The third nonforfeiture option is to use the policy's cash value to purchase a term insurance policy in an amount equal to the original policy's face value, for as long a period as the cash value will purchase. When the term insurance expires, no more protection exists. Moreover, all supplemental benefits included with the original policy, such as a term rider or accidental death or disability benefits, are dropped. (See Figure 5.3.)

 **Test Topic Alert!**   The extended term option is not renewable or convertible.

In the case of endowment insurance, the extended term insurance will not be provided beyond the maturity date of the original endowment policy. The cash value of an endowment policy eventually will exceed the amount needed to buy extended term insurance so, in that case, the excess cash value is used to purchase a pure endowment policy with the same maturity date as the original policy.

Policy Dividends

As noted previously, life insurance policies may be either participating or nonparticipating, and it is important to distinguish between the two to understand the source of policy dividends. At any given age, people who buy participating (par) policies normally pay premiums that are slightly higher than premiums paid by those who purchase nonparticipating (non-par) policies. This is because an extra charge to cover unexpected contingencies is built into premiums for par policies.

At the end of each year, the insurance company analyzes its operations. If fewer insureds have died than was estimated, a *divisible surplus* results and the company can return to the policyowners a part of the premiums paid for participating policies. A company also can issue returns stemming from positive operating or investment income. These payments are called dividends but should not be confused with the dividends paid on stocks.

✓ **Take Note:** Insurance policy dividends really are a return of part of the premiums paid. As such, policy dividends are not taxable income, unlike corporate dividends, which are reportable for income tax purposes.

Because the payment of policy dividends hinges on several unexpected contingencies that will affect the amount of the dividend, policy dividends normally will vary from year to year and cannot be guaranteed.

Thus, when an insurance company gives a policy illustration that includes dividends, it is purely an estimate or approximation of what future dividends might be. To protect life insurance buyers against the misuse of dividend illustrations, most states require life insurance proposals containing a dividend illustration to state clearly that future dividends are not guaranteed.

Dividends usually become payable at the end of the first or second policy year. A provision in each participating policy states when the policyowner can expect to begin receiving any dividends.

 **Test Topic Alert!**   Policy dividends usually are paid by mutual insurers on an annual basis.

FIGURE 5.4   Paid-up Additions: A Popular Option

The *paid-up additions* dividend option is popular with many policyowners. A close look at the benefits of this option will explain why.

When a dividend is declared, it is used in effect as the premium for a single-payment whole life policy of the same type as the base policy under which the dividend is declared. The face amount of this paid-up addition generally is small, but over time the sum of these additions can be substantial.

The paid-up addition enjoys all the advantages of any whole life policy. It will accrue a cash value. It possesses all the tax advantages of whole life insurance. Most significantly, it is issued to the policyowner without any additional premium requirement beyond the premium being paid for the base policy.

Consider the example of a policyowner with a $100,000 par policy who is paying a level premium of $1,300 annually. As each year passes, a paid-up addition is added. In time, the total face amount of the policy will grow as more paid-up additions are added; perhaps after 10 years the total face amount may be $115,000. The cash value of this policy will increase at an ever-faster rate as the paid-up additions' cash values are added to the base policy's cash value. And all of this will occur with the same $1,300 annual outlay as was required when the policy was first purchased.

Dividend Options

Policyowners generally are permitted by insurers to utilize their dividends through one of five options:

- *Take dividends in cash.* When dividends become payable, they usually are paid on policy anniversary dates. Policyowners who elect to take their dividends in cash automatically receive their dividend check after the company approves a dividend.
- *Apply dividends against premium payments.* Dividends also can be applied directly to the policyowner's premium payments, lowering the owner's out-of-pocket expense.
- *Allow dividends to accumulate at interest.* A third option is to leave the dividends with the company to accumulate with interest, for withdrawal at any time. Note that while policy dividends are not taxable, any interest paid on them is taxable income in the year the interest is credited to the policy, whether or not it actually is received by the policyowner.
- *Use dividends to buy paid-up additions.* Dividends also can be used to purchase paid-up additions of life insurance, of the same kind as the original or base policy. The premium rate is based on the attained age of the insured at the time the paid-up additions are purchased.

• *Use dividends to purchase one-year term insurance.* A fifth option, though not utilized as frequently as the others, is to use dividends to purchase as much one-year term insurance as possible or to purchase one-year term insurance equal to the base policy's cash value. This is done through specific application for and issue of a separate rider. Sometimes called the *fifth dividend option,* this provision allows for any excess dividend portions to be applied under any of the other regular options.

 Test Topic Alert!

The only dividend option with a potential tax consequence is the option to allow dividends to accumulate at interest. While the dividend is not taxable, the interest will be taxed.

Quick Quiz 5.2   True or False?

1. _____ Policy riders excluding death as a result of commercial aviation typically are found in older policies.

2. _____ Under most state insurance laws, policyowners are fully entitled to the accrued cash values of their policies.

3. _____ Like corporate dividends, insurance policy dividends constitute taxable income.

4. _____ Policyowners cannot apply dividends against premium payments.

5. _____ When a policy is surrendered, the policyowner may use the policy's cash value to buy a term insurance policy in an amount equal to the original policy's face value.

Answers

1. **True**.

2. **False**. Every state, not simply most states, has laws modeled after the NAIC Standard Nonforfeiture Law. These laws assure policyowners that they are fully entitled to their policies' accrued cash values.

3. **False**. Insurance policy dividends really are a return of part of the premiums paid and therefore do not constitute taxable income.

4. **False**. Dividends can be applied directly to the policyowner's premium payments, which lowers the owner's out-of-pocket expense.

5. **True**.

Policy Riders

The flexibility of life insurance policies is well demonstrated by the ability policyowners have to customize a policy to meet their specific needs. Imagine buying a new car without being able to purchase optional features, such as air conditioning or a CD player. Chances are good you might not even buy that car. Insurers offer their applicants the privilege of adding options—in the form of policy riders—to their policies to meet their unique needs. Like new car options, policy riders are available at an extra cost (through increased premiums) but are justified because of the increased value the riders give to the base policy.

Most of the optional riders described below must be selected at the time the policy is applied for. The automatic premium loan rider (if it is an option and not a standard policy feature) is the only optional rider available at no cost to the policyowner. It sometimes can be added after the policy is in force.

Guaranteed Insurability Rider

For an extra premium, the guaranteed insurability rider may be attached to a permanent life insurance policy at the time of purchase. It permits the insured, at specified intervals in the future, to buy specified amounts of additional insurance without evidence of insurability.

Typically, this option allows the insured to purchase additional life insurance at stated policy intervals or ages. The amount of insurance that can be purchased at each option date is subject to minimums and maximums specified in the rider, but the insurance is available at standard premium rates, whether or not the insured still is insurable.

These riders generally allow the insured to buy additional life insurance at three-year intervals, beginning with the policy anniversary date nearest his or her age 25 and terminating at the anniversary date nearest age 40. (Guaranteed insurability options usually do not extend past age 40.) Thus, the option dates listed in the rider are for the insured's ages 25, 28, 31, 34, 37 and 40. The insured normally has 90 days in which to exercise an option to purchase. If no purchase is made within that time, the option for that particular age expires automatically. The expiration of one option will not affect the exercise of future options.

✔ **For Example:** Assume that an insured purchases a $10,000 ordinary life policy at age 21 with a guaranteed insurability rider. At ages 25, 28, 31, 34, 37 and 40, this insured can exercise the option to add $10,000 of insurance at each of these six dates, even if he or she has become uninsurable in the meantime and thereby add up to $60,000 of coverage to the original $10,000 policy.

Company practice varies, but if a waiver of premium or accidental death benefit (both are explained below) is included with the original policy, most companies allow these benefits to be added to the additional life insurance purchased under the guaranteed insurability option, if the policyowner wants to pay the additional premium.

Waiver of Premium Rider

The waiver of premium rider provides valuable added security for policyowners. It can prevent a policy from lapsing for nonpayment of premiums while the insured is disabled and unable to work.

Under the waiver of premium, if the company determines that the insured is totally disabled, the policyowner is relieved of paying premiums as long as the disability continues. Some companies include the waiver of premium as part of the contract, with the cost built into the overall premium. In other companies, the waiver may be added to a policy by rider or endorsement for a small, additional premium.

Some policies specify that an insured must be totally and permanently disabled for the waiver to take effect. It does not apply to short-term illnesses or injuries. In fact, an insured generally must be seriously disabled for a certain length of time, called the *waiting period* (usually 90 days or six months). The policyowner continues paying premiums during the waiting period. If the insured still is disabled at the end of this period, the company will refund all of the premiums paid by the policyowner from the start of the disability.

 **Test Topic Alert!**

The waiting period under a waiver of premium rider is retroactive. Therefore, if the disability continues beyond the waiting period, the premiums paid from the date of disability forward will be refunded to the policyowner.

The company then continues to pay all premiums that become due while the insured's disability continues. If the insured recovers and can return to work, premium payments then must be resumed by the policyowner. No premiums paid by the company, however, have to be repaid by the policyowner.

✓ *Take Note:* For the waiver to become operative, the insured must meet the policy's definition of totally disabled, which may be defined as the insured's inability to engage in any work for which he or she is reasonably fitted by education, training or experience. Or, as with some policies, the definition is worded in terms of the insured's inability to work at his or her own occupation for a stated period (such as 24 months) and at any occupation thereafter.

FIGURE 5.5   Which Rider to Purchase?

Riders can work in tandem. Consider the insured policyowner who has both a *guaranteed insurability* and *waiver of premium* rider on her policy. At age 29, she becomes totally and permanently disabled. Because she meets the definition of total disability in her policy, her premiums will be waived and in two years, when she is 31, she can increase the face amount of her policy to the maximum permitted under the guaranteed insurability rider—all without paying any premiums.

A waiver of premium rider generally remains in effect until the insured reaches a specified age, such as 60 or 65. When the provision expires, the policy premium is reduced accordingly. If an insured becomes disabled before the specified age, all premiums usually are waived while the disability continues—even those premiums falling due after the insured passes the stipulated age.

Although premiums are waived for a disabled insured, the death benefit remains the same, cash values increase at their normal rate and dividends for a participating policy are paid as usual. In fact, cash values continue to be available to the policyowner at all times while the insured's disability continues.

Automatic Premium Loan Rider

The automatic premium loan rider, discussed earlier in this lesson, is a standard feature in some life insurance policies; in others, its provisions are added to the policy by rider. In either case, it is available to the policyowner at no additional charge. As noted previously, it allows the insurer to pay premiums from the policy's cash value if premiums have not been paid by the end of the grace period. These deductions from cash values are treated as loans and are charged interest; in time, if the loan is not repaid, the interest also will be deducted from the cash value. Should the insured die, the loan plus interest will be deducted from the benefits payable.

Automatic premium loans provide that, as long as premiums are not paid, the loan procedure will be repeated until the cash value of the policy is exhausted. When the cash value is depleted, the policy lapses.

An automatic premium loan option can be elected at the time of application or, with some insurers, added after the policy is issued.

Payor Provision or Rider

As noted earlier in the discussion of juvenile insurance, a payor provision usually is available with such policies, providing for waiver of premiums if the adult premium-payor should die or, with some policies, become totally disabled.

Typically, this payor provision, also known as a *death and disability payor benefit*, extends until the insured child reaches a specified age, such as 21 or 25. It is available for a small extra premium, but before it is issued the adult who is to pay the premium usually must show evidence of insurability.

 **Test Topic Alert!**
Under the payor provision, the premium will be waived if the premium payor dies or becomes disabled. The death or disability of the juvenile insured does not invoke the waiver.

Accidental Death Benefit Rider

The accidental death benefit rider (sometimes called a double indemnity provision) provides an additional amount of insurance, usually equal to the face amount of the base policy, if death occurs under stated conditions. Consequently, if the insured died as a result of the stated circumstances, and he or she had a double indemnity rider, the total benefit paid would be double the policy's face—the benefit payable under the policy plus the same amount payable under the rider. A triple indemnity provision would provide a total death benefit of three times the face amount. Any policy loans are subtracted from the policy's face amount and not from the accidental death riders.

Accidental death is strictly defined and it does not include accidents resulting, directly or indirectly, from an ailment or physical disability of the insured. The additional proceeds are paid only if the insured dies as a result of bodily injury from some external, violent and purely accidental cause. Also, death must occur within a specified time (usually 90 days) following the accident. Deaths that might be considered accidental, such as those resulting from self-inflicted injury, war or private aviation activities, are excluded.

Many companies do not offer the accidental death benefit to anyone older than age 55 or 60, and the extra protection generally expires after the insured reaches age 60 or 65. While in effect, the additional insurance does not build any cash value.

The extra premium for this benefit is not payable beyond the date when the additional benefit expires, nor does the benefit apply to any paid-up additions that may be purchased with policy dividends. The benefit also drops off in the event the policyowner surrenders the policy and selects one of the non-forfeiture options.

 **Test Topic Alert!**   If the insured dies from natural causes or some cause not related to an accident, the accidental death benefit rider will not double or triple the benefits, though the policy still will pay the claim.

Return of Premium Rider

A return of premium rider provides that in the event of the insured's death within a specified period of time, the policy will pay, in addition to the face amount, an amount equal to the sum of all premiums paid to date. In actuality, this rider does not return premiums but pays an additional benefit equal to premiums paid on the date of death. The policyowner simply is purchasing term insurance that increases as the total amount of premiums paid increases.

Cost of Living Rider

Some companies offer their applicants the ability to guard against the eroding effects of inflation. A cost of living (COL) or cost of living adjustment (COLA) rider can provide increases in the amount of insurance protection without requiring the insured to provide evidence of insurability. The amount of increase is tied to an increase in an inflation index, most commonly the Consumer Price Index (CPI). Depending on the type of base policy, these riders can take several different forms.

For standard whole life policies, a COL rider usually is offered as an increasing term insurance rider that is attached to the base policy. The COL rider provides for automatic increases in the policy death benefit in proportion to increases in the CPI. Generally there is a maximum percentage increase, such as 5 percent, allowed in any one year. When the increase becomes effective, the policyowner is billed for the additional coverage.

 Take Note: Declines in the CPI are not matched by a decline in the amount of coverage; instead, future increases are held off until the CPI again exceeds its prior high point.

Adjustable life insurance, which is characterized in part by giving the policyowner limited freedom to increase and decrease the policy's face amount, frequently includes a COL agreement. The COL agreement waives the need for evidence of insurability for limited face amount increases that are intended to match increases in the CPI. The face amount increase is accompanied by an increase in premium, although the agreement itself usually is offered at no charge to the policyowner.

The COL agreement also can be used, with certain restrictions, with term and whole life policies. They are not practical with universal life policies, however, because of the high degree of flexibility already present in UL policies.

 **Test Topic Alert!** Increasing term insurance almost always is sold as a cost of living rider.

Other Insureds Rider

A rider that is useful in providing insurance for more than one family member is the other insureds rider. Usually this rider is offered as a term rider, covering a family member other than the insured, and is attached to the base policy covering the insured. Sometimes this is called a *children's rider* if it covers only the children; otherwise, it often is referred to as a *family rider*. This type of rider is used in family plan policies, discussed in Lesson 4.

Summary

All life insurance policies are characterized by standardized policy provisions that identify the rights and obligations of the policyowner and the insurance company. Many standard provisions are required by state insurance regulators to be included in policies. Other provisions, dealing with exclusions and restrictions of coverage, are optional and can be included at the discretion of the insurer.

Whole life policies generate cash values to which policyowners are entitled. Policyowners may borrow from a policy's cash value or, on lapse or surrender of the policy, select one of three possible nonforfeiture options.

Participating policies share in the divisible surplus of company operations by returning part of the premium to the owner as a policy dividend. There are five dividend options available to policyowners in deciding how to use their policy dividends.

Policyowners can customize their policy to meet their specific insurance needs by including, generally at a cost, one or more policy riders.

Key Concepts

In preparing for their licensing examination, students should be familiar with the following concepts:

owner's rights
insuring clause
consideration clause
reinstatement
incontestable clause
suicide provision
policy exclusions (optional
    provisions)
policy dividends and options
waiver of premium
payor benefit
cost of living adjustments

accelerated benefits rider
entire contract provision
free look
grace period
policy loans
assignment provision
misstatement of age or sex clause
nonforfeiture options
guaranteed insurability rider
automatic premium loan
accidental death benefit
other insureds rider

Lesson Exam Five

1. In which of the following situations does the incontestable clause apply?

   A. Impersonation of the applicant by another
   B. No insurable interest
   C. Intent to murder
   D. Concealment of smoking

2. If after the death of an insured, but before any death benefits are distributed, the insurance company discovers that the insured was older than stated in the policy, how would it handle the situation?

   A. No adjustment would be made because the contestable period had passed.
   B. The amount of death proceeds would be reduced to reflect the statistically diminished mortality risk.
   C. The amount of death proceeds would be reduced to reflect whatever benefit the premium paid would have purchased at the correct age.
   D. The beneficiary would be required to pay all underpaid back premiums before the death benefit is received.

3. Which of the following allows an extra 30 days or one month (possibly less for some industrial policies) during which premiums may be paid to keep policies in force?

   A. Grace period
   B. Reinstatement clause
   C. Incontestable clause
   D. Waiting period

4. Which of the following statements regarding the assignment of a life insurance policy is NOT correct?

   A. Absolute assignment involves a complete transfer, which gives the assignee full control over the policy.
   B. Under a collateral assignment, a creditor is entitled to be reimbursed out of the policy's proceeds only for the amount of the outstanding credit balance.
   C. Under a collateral assignment, policy proceeds exceeding the collateral amount pass to the insured's beneficiary.
   D. All beneficiaries must expressly approve any assignments of life insurance policies.

5. All of the following are common life insurance policy exclusions today EXCEPT

   A. war
   B. death during commission of a felony
   C. death as a result of commercial aviation
   D. death as a result of a hazardous occupation

6. All of the following are standard life insurance policy nonforfeiture options EXCEPT

   A. cash surrender
   B. one-year term insurance
   C. extended term insurance
   D. reduced paid-up (permanent) insurance

7. Which of the following statements best describes life insurance policy dividends?

   A. They represent earnings to shareowners who hold stock in insurance companies.
   B. They affect the costs of virtually all insurance policies issued today.
   C. They are an intentional return of a portion of the premiums paid.
   D. They provide policyowners with a level, known annual cash inflow.

8. The most common guaranteed insurability riders allow additional life insurance to be purchased on the insured within a range of ages. The common age range in which guaranteed insurability is available is from age

   A. 16 to 65
   B. 21 to 59½
   C. 25 to 40
   D. 30 to 70½

9. Which life insurance provision allows the policyholder to inspect and, if dissatisfied, to return the policy for a full refund?

   A. Waiver of premium
   B. Facility of payments
   C. Probationary period
   D. Free look

10. Which of the following statements regarding a cost of living (COL) rider on a life insurance policy is NOT correct?

    A. A COL rider provides for automatic increases of the policy's face amount.
    B. To acquire additional amounts of life insurance under a COL rider, evidence of insurability will be required.
    C. An inflation index, usually the Consumer Price Index (CPI), determines the amount of inflation adjustment that is made to the policy up to a maximum percentage increase.
    D. Declines in the CPI do not cause corresponding declines in the amount of insurance coverage.

11. "If an insurance company determines that the insured is totally disabled, the policyowner is relieved of paying the policy premiums as long as the disability continues." This above statement describes the

    A. premium suspension clause
    B. waiting period exemption
    C. disability income rider
    D. waiver of premium rider

12. A ten-day free look provision would apply to the first ten days after the

    A. application has been signed by the applicant
    B. application has been received by the insurer
    C. policy has been issued by the insurer
    D. issued policy has been received by the insured

13. Which of the following statements regarding assignment of a life insurance policy is NOT correct?

    A. To secure a loan, the policy can be transferred temporarily to the lender as security for the loan.
    B. The policyowner must obtain approval from the insurance company before a policy can be assigned.
    C. The life insurance company assumes no responsibility for the validity of an assignment.
    D. The life insurance company must be notified in writing by the policyowner of any assignment.

14. Which provision of a life insurance policy states that the application is part of the contract?

    A. Consideration clause
    B. Insuring clause
    C. Entire contract clause
    D. Incontestable clause

15. Ron, the insured under a $100,000 life insurance policy, dies during the grace period. What happens, considering that he has not paid the premium on the policy?

    A. The premium is canceled because the insured died during the grace period.
    B. The amount of the premium is deducted from the policy proceeds paid to the beneficiary.
    C. The premium due, plus a 10 percent penalty, is charged against the policy.
    D. The beneficiary must pay the premium after the death claim is paid.

16. Which of the following is stated in the consideration clause of a life insurance policy?

    A. Insured's risk classification
    B. Insured's general health condition
    C. Amount and frequency of premium payments
    D. Benefits payable on the insured's death

17. John stopped paying premiums on his permanent life insurance policy eight years ago, though he never surrendered it. He still is insurable and has no outstanding loan against the policy. The company probably will decline to reinstate the policy because the time limit for reinstatement has expired. The limit usually is

    A. six months
    B. one year
    C. two years
    D. three years or as long as seven years

18. Which of the following statements about reinstatement of a life insurance policy is NOT correct?

    A. A suicide exclusion period is renewed with a reinstated policy.
    B. When reinstating a policy, the insurer will charge the policyowner for past-due premiums.
    C. When reinstating a policy, the insurer will charge the policyowner for interest on past-due premiums.
    D. A new contestable period becomes effective in a reinstated policy.

19. Leland elects to surrender his whole life policy for a reduced paid-up policy. The cash value of his new policy will

    A. continue to increase
    B. decrease gradually
    C. remain the same as in the old policy
    D. be forfeited

20. If, after an insured dies, it is discovered that he or she was younger than the policy state, what will the insurance company do?

    A. Reduce the death benefits
    B. Reduce premiums
    C. Waive the difference
    D. Increase the death benefits

21. Which of the following statements about the incontestable clause in a life insurance policy is NOT correct?

    A. The clause gives people assurance that when their policies become claims they will be paid without delays or protests.
    B. The incontestable clause means that after a certain period an insurer cannot refuse to pay the proceeds of a policy or void the contract.
    C. Incontestable clauses usually become effective two years from the issue date of the policy.
    D. Insurers can void a contract even after the specified period, provided they can prove the policy was purchased fraudulently.

22. If it is discovered that an insured is older than a policy states, what can the insurance company do?

    A. Increase premiums
    B. Reduce premiums
    C. Waive the difference
    D. Increase the benefits

23. Which of the following is the rider that provides for a waiver of premiums if the adult
premium payor dies or becomes disabled?

    A. Guaranteed insurability rider
    B. Payor rider
    C. Waiver of premium rider
    D. Automatic premium loan rider

24. Which of the following statements about
a life insurance policy's cash values is
CORRECT?

    A. In many but not all states, policyowners
       are fully entitled to the accrued cash val-
       ues of their whole life policies.
    B. When a whole life insurance policy is
       active, the owner can borrow from the
       cash value.
    C. Owners of term and whole life insur-
       ance are entitled to the cash surrender
       value when a policy is lapsed or surren-
       dered.
    D. If a policyowner lets his or her whole
       life policy lapse, the insurer will be enti-
       tled to part of the policy's cash value.

Answers & Rationale

1. **D.** If an applicant did not reveal that he or she smoked and the specified time period passed, the insurer cannot contest the validity of the life insurance policy, even though the applicant concealed this material information.

2. **C.** A misstatement of age provision gives the insurer the right to make an adjustment at any time if the applicant's age was stated incorrectly in a policy. Thus, if an insurer discovers that the insured was older than previously thought, it could reduce the amount of death proceeds to reflect whatever benefit the premium paid would have purchased at the correct age.

3. **A.** An insurance policy's grace period allows an extra 30 days or one month during which premiums may be paid to keep a policy in force. The grace period may be less for some industrial policies.

4. **D.** If irrevocable beneficiaries are named under an insurance contract, the policyowner must obtain their consent before assigning the policy. However, consent need not be obtained before a policy is assigned if there are only revocable beneficiaries.

5. **C.** Exclusions for death resulting from commercial aviation commonly are found in older policies. Very few policies issued today contain such exclusions.

6. **B.** Standard nonforfeiture options include cash surrender options, reduced paid-up options and an extended term option. A one-year term insurance option does not exist. The extended term option permits the policyowner to use the policy's cash value to purchase a term insurance policy in an amount equal to the original policy's face value, for as long a period as the cash value will purchase.

7. **C.** Insurance policy dividends constitute a return of part of the premiums paid and normally will vary from year to year. They differ from dividends paid on stocks because they do not represent corporate earnings.

8. **C.** Guaranteed insurability options allow the insured to buy additional life insurance at three-year intervals beginning at age 25 and continuing every three years until age 40.

9. **D.** The free look provision gives policyowners the right to return a policy for a full premium refund within a specified period of time, if they decide not to purchase the insurance. This period usually is ten days.

10. **B.** A cost of living rider can provide increases in the amount of insurance protection without requiring the insured to provide evidence of insurability.

11. **D.** A waiver of premium rider prevents a policy from lapsing because the insured cannot pay premiums while he or she is disabled and unable to work. This waiver continues as long as the insured is disabled.

12. **D.** Most policies provide for a 10-day free look provision beginning when the policyowner actually receives the policy document, not when the application is signed or when the insurance company issues the policy.

13. **B.** While a policyowner must notify the insurance company in writing of an assignment, he or she need not obtain the insurer's approval before assigning a policy.

14. **C.** The entire contract clause states that the insurance policy documents, the application and any attached riders constitute the entire contract.

15. **B.** If Ron has not paid the premium and dies during the grace period, the policy benefit still is payable. However, the premium amount that was due will be deducted from the benefits paid to his beneficiary.

16. **C.** The consideration clause specifies the amount and frequency of premium payments that the policyowner must make to keep the insurance in force.

17. **D.** If an insurance policy lapses due to non-payment of premiums, the policy may be reinstated. However, there usually is a three-year time period in which the policy may be reinstated, although some policies provide for as long as seven years.

18. **A.** If a policy is reinstated, a new contestable period usually goes into effect, but there is no new suicide exclusion period.

19. **A.** If Leland surrenders his whole life policy for a reduced paid-up policy, the face value of the new policy remains the same for the life of the policy, and cash values will continue building.

20. **D.** If an insured died but was younger than the policy stated, the amount of death proceeds would be increased to an amount that the premium would have bought at the correct age.

21. **D.** There are three situations in which the incontestable clause does not apply and an insurer can void a policy: impersonation when applying for the insurance, no insurable interest between the applicant and insured at the policy's inception and the applicant purchased the policy intending to murder the insured. Because a contract that was purchased fraudulently does not fall within any of these exceptions, the insurer only has two years after the policy issue date to contest the policy's validity. Thereafter, the policy becomes incontestable.

22. **A.** If an insured is older than the policy states and this error is discovered while the insured is living, the company either can increase the premium or reduce the amount of insurance to what it should be for the amount of premium being paid.

23. **B.** In juvenile insurance, a payor rider provides for waiver of premiums if the adult premium payor dies or becomes disabled. The premiums will be waived until the insured child reaches a specified age (such as 25) or until the maturity date of the contract, whichever comes first.

24. **B.** When a whole life policy is active, the policyowner can borrow from the cash value. If the policy is lapsed or surrendered, the owner is entitled to the entire cash surrender value. However, the insurer is not entitled to any part of a policy's cash value.

6

Life Insurance Beneficiaries

INTRODUCTION

One of a policyowner's most important rights is the ability to name the beneficiary of his or her life insurance policy. When a specific beneficiary is named, the proceeds will not be subject to estate administration with all probate's delays. Instead, the proceeds will be paid to the designated person immediately after the insured's death. Perhaps most importantly, the payment of the proceeds will not be delayed until the insured's entire estate has been settled. In this lesson, we will look at the kinds of entities that commonly are named beneficiaries as well as the ways in which beneficiaries are classified. We also will examine a few special situations that occasionally arise when paying proceeds; namely, what happens if the insured and beneficiary die simultaneously, how to prevent the proceeds from being attached by creditors and situations in which proceeds can be paid to nondesignated beneficiaries.

LESSON OBJECTIVES

When you complete this lesson you should be able to:

- list the different kinds of entities that commonly are designated beneficiaries of life insurance policies;
- describe the differences between primary, secondary and tertiary beneficiaries;
- define *per stirpes* and *per capita* and give an example of each method of distribution;
- explain the differences between revocable and irrevocable beneficiaries; and
- describe the purpose of spendthrift clauses and facility of payment provisions and explain how proceeds are paid in the event of simultaneous death.

Who Can Be a Beneficiary?

Life insurance companies place very few restrictions on who may be named the beneficiary of a life insurance policy. The decision rests solely with the owner of the policy. However, in some cases, the insurer must consider the issue of insurable interest.

As we have learned, insurable interest is not a concern when the applicant for a policy also is the insured. In those cases, a person can apply for as much life insurance as the company will issue and can name anyone as beneficiary, whether or not insurable interest exists between the applicant-insured and the beneficiary. This is because, by law, individuals are presumed to have an unlimited insurable interest in their own lives.

The situation is different when the policy applicant is not the insured (that is, with a third-party applicant). When a third-party applicant names himself or herself as beneficiary, insurable interest must exist between the applicant and insured. When a third-party applicant names yet another as beneficiary, most states require that insurable interest must exist between that beneficiary and the insured.

✓ **For Example:** If Bill were to apply for life insurance coverage on Sue and name himself as beneficiary, insurable interest would have to exist between Bill and Sue. If Bill were to apply for life insurance coverage on Sue but name Jason as beneficiary, insurable interest would probably have to exist between Jason and Sue.

With this in mind, let's take a look at what kinds of entities commonly are designated beneficiaries.

Individuals as Beneficiaries

In most cases, an individual is selected to be the sole or proportional beneficiary of a life insurance policy. There may be one named individual or more than one.

✓ **For Example:** A policyowner could designate his wife as the sole beneficiary or designate that she receive half the proceeds of his policy, with the remainder to be split equally between his two children.

Businesses as Beneficiaries

There is no question that insurable interest exists in business relationships. Professional sports clubs have an insurable interest in the lives of their best players. Partnerships have an insurable interest in the lives of their partners. Small corporations have an insurable interest in the lives of their key employees. Creditors have an insurable interest in the lives of people who owe them money. Life insurance policies may designate businesses as beneficiaries.

Trusts as Beneficiaries

A trust is a legal arrangement for the ownership of property by one party for the benefit of another. Designating a trust as the beneficiary of a life insurance policy means that the proceeds will be paid to the trust for the ultimate benefit of and use by another. Trusts are managed by trustees, who have the fiduciary responsibility to oversee and handle the trust and its funds for its beneficiaries.

Estates as Beneficiaries

Policyowners may designate their estates as beneficiaries, so that upon death the proceeds can be used to meet federal estate taxes, debts and other administrative costs, leaving other assets intact to pass on to heirs.

✔ **Take Note:** The primary drawback to leaving proceeds to an estate is that the value of the policy will be included in the value of the insured's gross estate for estate tax purposes.

Charities as Beneficiaries

Naming a charity as the beneficiary of a life insurance policy is another commonly accepted practice. Life insurance is one of the most attractive and flexible ways to make a contribution to a church, educational institution, hospital, public welfare agency or similar nonprofit organization. One of the benefits of making a contribution of life insurance proceeds—in contrast to leaving a bequest in a will—is that the gift cannot be contested by disgruntled heirs. This is because life insurance proceeds are not part of the insured-donor's probate estate.

Minors as Beneficiaries

Naming minors as life insurance beneficiaries can present some legal and logistical complications. For instance, the minor may not have the legal capacity to give the insurance company a signed release for receipt of the policy proceeds. (Some states have adopted special laws that allow only minors of specified ages, such as age 15, to sign a valid receipt.) If an insurer were to pay out the proceeds and not receive a receipt, the minor legally could demand payment a second time, once he or she has reached the age of majority. Furthermore, the minor simply may lack the judgment or expertise to manage the proceeds properly.

Nonetheless, insurers recognize that policyowners may want minors to benefit from an insurance policy. In those cases, and in accordance with the laws of the particular state, insurers may:

- make limited payments to an adult guardian for the benefit of the minor beneficiary;
- retain the policy proceeds at interest and pay them out when the child reaches majority or when an adult guardian is appointed; or
- place the proceeds in a trust for the present or future benefit of the minor, as determined by the trustee.

Classes as Beneficiaries

There also is a beneficiary designation known as a *class designation*. This means that rather than specifying one or more beneficiaries by name, the policyowner designates a class or group of beneficiaries.

✔ **For Example:** *Children of the insured* and *my children* are class designations.

Types of Beneficiary Designations

A number of ways to classify beneficiary designations exist: by the order of succession (or preference); by the number named; by line of descent; or by whether or not the designation(s) can be changed. A discussion of these various types of designations follows. In any event, it is important to select and arrange beneficiary designations carefully, because once they are in effect, the insurance company must follow them to the letter.

Order of Succession

It always is possible that a beneficiary to a life insurance policy may predecease the insured. To meet this contingency, policyowners are encouraged to designate *primary, secondary* and, occasionally, *tertiary* beneficiaries.

Primary Beneficiaries

A primary beneficiary is the party designated to receive the proceeds of a life insurance policy when they become payable. There may be more than one primary beneficiary, and how the proceeds are to be split is up to the policyowner.

Secondary (Contingent) Beneficiaries

A secondary beneficiary also may be named and stands second in line to receive the proceeds of a life insurance policy if the primary beneficiary dies before the insured. Secondary beneficiaries are entitled to policy proceeds only if no primary beneficiaries are living. Secondary beneficiaries also are known as *contingent* or *successor* beneficiaries.

Tertiary (Contingent) Beneficiaries

A tertiary beneficiary stands third in line to receive the proceeds of a life insurance policy, in cases where all primary and secondary beneficiaries predecease the insured.

✓ **For Example:** Deborah takes out a $150,000 life policy on herself and designates the following beneficiaries: her husband, Rob, is to receive the full benefit; if he predeceases her, their two children are to share equally in the benefit; if her husband and both her children predecease her, the benefit is payable to Homestate College, her alma mater. In this situation, Rob is the primary beneficiary; the children are contingent secondary beneficiaries; Homestate College is the contingent tertiary beneficiary.

🔆 **Test Topic Alert!**

If no beneficiary is named, or if all primary and contingent beneficiaries are deceased at the time of the insured's death, the proceeds are paid to the policyowner or to his or her estate, if the policyowner is deceased.

More than One Beneficiary per Category

Policyowners may name more than one beneficiary in any category, whether the category is primary, secondary or tertiary. When they do so, however, they should specify the percentage or dollar amount of the proceeds that each is to receive. Most companies recommend that each beneficiary's share be indicated as a fraction.

✓ **For Example:** Harry specifies that the proceeds of his $50,000 life insurance policy are to be paid out as follows: $25,000 to his wife, Louise, and the remaining $25,000 to his son, Jack. When Harry dies, there is a $20,000 loan against the policy. Consequently, in accordance with the way Harry designated his beneficiaries, Louise will receive $25,000 and Jack will receive $5,000. Had Harry specified that his wife and his son were to share equally

(50 percent) in the proceeds, the remaining death benefit would have been distributed more equitably—$15,000 to each—which probably was Harry's intent.

Now let's take a look at a beneficiary designation that properly takes the proportioning of the proceeds into account.

✓ **For Example:** One-half to my wife, Shirley Dawn Brown; one-fourth to my son, Curtis Rodney Brown; one-fourth to my daughter, Mary Lee Brown. In the event of the death of any beneficiary, his or her share shall be divided equally between the survivors or all shall go to the sole survivor.

Distribution by Descent

When life insurance policy proceeds are to be distributed to a person's descendents, a *per stirpes* or a *per capita* approach generally is used.

Per Stirpes   The term *per stirpes* means *by* or *by way of branches*. A *per stirpes* distribution means that a beneficiary's share of a policy's proceeds will be passed down to his or her living child or children in equal shares should he or she (the named beneficiary) predecease the insured.

Per Capita   The term *per capita* means *per person* or *by head*. A *per capita* distribution means that a policy's proceeds are paid only to the beneficiaries who are living and have been named in the policy.

✓ **For Example:** Assume that Arthur makes the following designation with respect to the proceeds of his life insurance policy: To his four children—Amy, Brian, Charlie and Denise—as co-beneficiaries to share equally in the proceeds, and to the surviving children of any deceased children of Arthur, *per stirpes*. Brian predeceases Arthur, leaving two children, Xavier and Yolanda. The *per stirpes* distribution means that the surviving co-beneficiaries—Amy, Charlie and Denise—will each receive a quarter share of the proceeds. Brian's quarter will be shared between Xavier and Yolanda, who will take their share by right of their father's representation. On the other hand, Arthur could have made the following designation: To Amy, Brian, Charlie and Denise in equal shares. If they survive him, and to the surviving children of his children who predecease him, or *per capita*. If Brian predeceases Arthur, Brian's children—Xavier and Yolanda—would be counted among the surviving beneficiaries to take an equal share. Consequently, the proceeds would be divided among Amy, Denise, Xavier and Yolanda, with each beneficiary taking a one-fifth share.

In short, the *per capita* beneficiary claims proceeds in his or her own right, while the *per stirpes* beneficiary receives the proceeds through the rights of another. Today, the *per stirpes* method of distribution is by far the more common approach.

FIGURE 6.1 Comparison of *Per Stirpes* and *Per Capita* Distribution

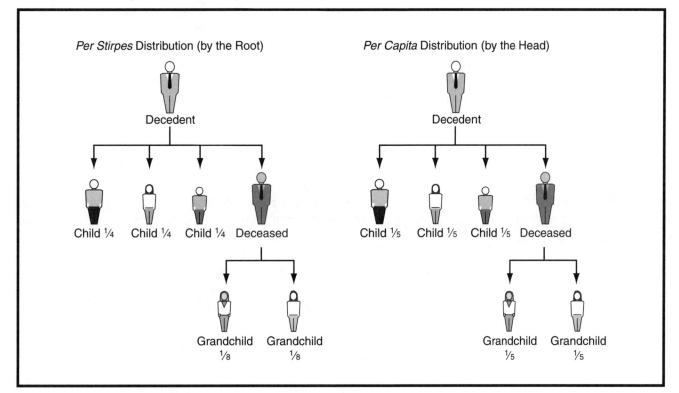

Changing a Beneficiary

Beneficiary designations are classified according to whether they can be changed after a policy is issued. Recall that the right to change beneficiary designations is a right of ownership. It is a right the policyowner may retain or relinquish. The terms used to indicate this right are *revocable* and *irrevocable beneficiary.*

Revocable Beneficiary

When beneficiaries are designated revocable, the policyowner may change the designation at any time. It also means that the policyowner remains the complete owner of the policy. The policyowner can make policy changes whenever needed or desired. A revocable beneficiary has no vested claim on the policy or its proceeds as long as the insured (or policyowner, if different) is living.

✔ **Take Note:** The revocable beneficiary designation is used in the vast majority of life insurance contracts today. Note that the insured may change a revocable beneficiary at any time and any number of times during the term of the policy.

Irrevocable Beneficiary

When a beneficiary is designated irrevocable, the policyowner gives up the right to change the beneficiary. For all practical purposes, the policy is owned by both the policyowner and the beneficiary. An irrevocable beneficiary has a vested right in the policy and the policyowner cannot exercise any right that would affect the vested rights of the beneficiary without the beneficiary's consent. For instance, a policyowner cannot borrow from the policy, assign the policy or surrender it without the written consent of the beneficiary.

Irrevocable clauses can be *absolute* or *reversionary.* When absolute, the beneficiary has an absolute vested interest in the life insurance contract even if the beneficiary predeceases the insured. When reversionary, the right to modify the beneficiary clause as well as all other rights of ownership revert to the insured if and when the beneficiary predeceases the insured.

Procedure for Changing Beneficiaries

Each life insurance policy describes the procedure for changing a beneficiary. Here, for example, is the beneficiary change clause that appears in the sample life insurance policy in Appendix A:

> A change of beneficiary may be made by written request while the insured is living. The change will take place as of the date the request is signed even if the insured is not living on the day the request is received. Any rights created by the change will be subject to any payments made or actions taken by Superior Mutual before the written request is received.

This is the common method in use today for changing beneficiaries. It's called the *recording method.* Following this method, the policyowner notifies the insurance company in writing of the beneficiary change. When the insurer records the change, it becomes effective as of the date the insured signed the notice.

✎ Quick Quiz 6.1 True or false?

_____ 1. When life insurance proceeds are left to the insured's estate, the value of the proceeds will be included in the insured's gross estate for estate tax purposes.

_____ 2. Partnerships generally cannot be designated as beneficiaries of a policy on a partner's life.

_____ 3. A policyowner can name more than one primary or secondary beneficiary but only one tertiary beneficiary.

_____ 4. The *per stirpes* method of distribution by far is the more common approach used today.

_____ 5. Revocable beneficiaries have no vested claim on a policy or its proceeds while the insured is living.

Answers   1. ***True***.

2. ***False***. *An insurable interest exists between a partnership and a partner. As a result, a partnership could own a policy on the life of a partner as long as it is the named beneficiary.*

3. ***False***. *A policyowner can name more than one beneficiary in any category, whether primary, secondary or tertiary. If more than one beneficiary is named, the policyowner should specify the percentage or dollar amount of the proceeds that each is to receive.*

4. ***True***.

5. ***True***.

Special Situations

There are a few special situations that insurers must occasionally address with regard to the payment of policy proceeds. These include the simultaneous deaths of the insured and the beneficiary, how to prevent the proceeds paid to a beneficiary from being attached by creditors and situations in which insurers can pay proceeds to nondesignated beneficiaries.

Simultaneous Death

When an insured dies and the death benefit is payable to a named beneficiary, usually there is nothing to complicate the transaction. But the situation is complicated if the insured and the primary beneficiary die in the same accident and there is no evidence to show which one died first. In such cases, the insurer must determine how and to whom to pay the proceeds.

To address this problem, the Uniform Simultaneous Death Act has been enacted in most states. This law stipulates that if the insured and the primary beneficiary are killed in the same accident and there is not sufficient evidence to show who died first, the policy proceeds are to be distributed *a*s if the insured died last. This law allows the insurance company to pay the proceeds to a secondary or other contingent beneficiary. If no contingent beneficiary has been named, the insured's estate will receive the proceeds.

The Uniform Simultaneous Death Act is only a partial solution to the problem, however. There are situations in which the primary beneficiary clearly outlives the insured, but only for the briefest time—minutes, hours or a few days. In these cases where the beneficiary obviously outlived the insured, if the provisions of the insurance contract were followed strictly, the insurer would pay the proceeds to the estate of the recently deceased primary beneficiary. Chances are, this would be contrary to the policyowner's wishes. The policyowner likely would have preferred that the proceeds be paid to a secondary beneficiary or to his or her own estate.

The problems resulting from the proximate but not (proven) simultaneous death of both the insured and the primary beneficiary prompted insurance companies to develop and offer a *common disaster provision* that gives policyowners greater control over payment of the policy proceeds. This provision, which may be part of the policy itself or incorporated into the beneficiary designation, activates only when the insured and the primary beneficiary die as a result of the same accident. It provides that:

- If the insured and primary beneficiary die in the same accident, it is presumed that the insured died last. (This coincides with the Uniform Simultaneous Death Act.)
- In addition, the primary beneficiary must outlive the insured by a definite period of time, as stipulated by the policyowner—14 days or 30 days are typical choices—or it still is assumed that the insured died last.

Thus, with a common disaster provision operating, a policyowner can be sure that if both the insured and the primary beneficiary die within a short period of time, the death benefits will be paid to the secondary beneficiary (if there is one) or to the insured's estate.

✓ **For Example:** Burt and Carol, his wife by a second marriage and the primary beneficiary of his $100,000 life insurance policy, both are killed in the same auto accident. Carol survives Burt by only 24 hours. Without a common disaster clause, the proceeds of Burt's policy would be paid to Carol's estate and possibly go to her children by her first marriage. Burt's children by his first marriage could be left out entirely. But because a common disaster provision was in effect in Burt's policy, the proceeds instead were paid to his estate, and distribution of the estate's assets were made according to his wishes by virtue of his will.

 **Test Topic Alert!**   Both the Uniform Simultaneous Death Act and the common disaster clause are designed to pay the death benefit to the policyowner's intended beneficiary.

Spendthrift Trust Clause

The spendthrift trust clause is another commonly used clause in life insurance policies. Its purpose is to help protect beneficiaries from the claims of their creditors. More precisely, it shelters life insurance proceeds that have not yet been paid to a named beneficiary from the claims of either the beneficiary's or policyowner's creditors.

The spendthrift clause does not apply to proceeds paid in one lump sum. As we will learn in the next lesson, proceeds may be held in trust by the insurer and paid to the beneficiary in installments over a period of time. The spend-thrift clause pertains to these installment payment arrangements. Generally, the clause states that policy distributions payable to the beneficiary after the insured dies are not assignable or transferable and may not be attached in any way.

 ✓ **For Example:** Al is receiving monthly installment income payments from the proceeds of his late wife's life insurance policy. He buys an expensive sports car and later finds out that he cannot meet the payments on the car. If the finance company is awarded a judgment when it sues Al, his unpaid life insurance proceeds are protected against the judgement. Of course, the finance company still can go after Al's other assets.

The spendthrift trust clause does not operate to protect proceeds that belong to the policyowner and are payable as income to the policyowner. It applies only to money held in trust by the insurance company that is earmarked to be paid to the named beneficiary at some future time. Spendthrift trust clauses are valid in the majority of states and are found in many life insurance policies.

 **Test Topic Alert!**   The spendthrift trust clause protects life insurance proceeds that have not yet been paid to a beneficiary from the claims of the beneficiary's creditors, and only when the proceeds are payable in installments.

Facility of Payment Provision

There are a few limited situations in which an insurer must pay proceeds to someone not designated as a beneficiary. A facility of payment provision, most typically found in industrial policies, permits an insurer to pay all or a portion of the proceeds to someone who, though not named in the policy, has a valid right. These situations include cases in which:

- the named beneficiary is a minor;
- the named beneficiary is deceased;
- no claim is submitted within a specified period of time; or
- costs were incurred by another party for the deceased insured's final medical expenses or funeral expenses.

Summary

Designating an individual or entity as the beneficiary of a life insurance policy is one of the policyowner's most important rights. Insurance companies place very few conditions on this right, but care must be taken because the insurer is bound to follow the designation once it is established.

There are many ways to classify beneficiary designations: by order of succession—primary, secondary or tertiary; by the number named within each order; and by descent—*per stirpes* or *per capita*. Whether or not a beneficiary designation can be changed is also a consideration.

Insurers must address a few special situations regarding the payment of life insurance proceeds. Should the insured and the primary beneficiary die simultaneously or within a short time of each other, the appropriate and fair disbursement of proceeds could be compromised. The Uniform Simultaneous Death Act and the common disaster provision help assure that the proceeds will be paid in line with the insured's wishes, as far as possible. The spendthrift trust clause protects unpaid insurance proceeds from claims by the beneficiary's creditors. Finally, the facility of payment provision allows an insurer to pay proceeds to someone not named in the policy but who, due to special circumstances, has a right to them.

Key Concepts

In preparing for their licensing examination, students should be familiar with the following concepts:

beneficiary designation options	classifications of beneficiaries
per stirpes	*per capita*
revocable beneficiary	irrevocable beneficiary
Uniform Simultaneous Death Act	common disaster provision
spendthrift trust clause	facility of payment provision

Lesson Exam Six

1. Sandra has a life insurance policy that states that her husband, Gerald, is to receive the full death benefit. If he predeceases her, their three children are to share the benefit equally. If her husband and all three children predecease her, the benefit is payable to the First Community Church. Which of the following statements is NOT correct?

   A. Gerald is the primary beneficiary.
   B. The three children all are secondary beneficiaries.
   C. The First Community Church is the tertiary beneficiary.
   D. The designation of the First Community Church can be contested by any of Sandra's relatives who survive the children.

2. The beneficiary designation on Walter's life insurance policy reads, *children of the insured*. Which of the following phrases best describes this type of beneficiary designation?

   A. Juvenile beneficiaries
   B. Class beneficiaries
   C. Generational beneficiaries
   D. Attractive nuisance beneficiaries

3. Which of the following statements is NOT correct?

   A. A *per capita* distribution specifies that a policy's proceeds are paid only to those beneficiaries who are living and have been named in the policy.
   B. A *per stirpes* distribution means that a beneficiary's share of a policy's proceeds will be passed down to his or her living child or children if the named beneficiary predeceases the insured.
   C. The *per capita* method of distribution is the more common approach used today.
   D. A *per stirpes* or *per capita* approach generally is used when life insurance proceeds are to be distributed to a person's descendents.

4. If an irrevocable beneficiary dies before the insured, which of the following gains control of the life insurance policy with a revisionary clause?

   A. Insurer
   B. Insured
   C. Policyowner
   D. Irrevocable beneficiary's children

5. Christine's policy has a clause that reads as follows: "Should the primary beneficiary and the insured die in the same accident and the primary beneficiary fails to survive the insured by 14 days, it will be assumed that the beneficiary predeceased the insured." Which of the following phrases best describes this clause?

   A. Secondary beneficiary provision
   B. Facility of payment provision
   C. Uniform Simultaneous Death Act
   D. Common disaster provision

6. Kevin, the insured under a $200,000 life insurance policy, and his sole beneficiary, Lynda, are killed instantly in a car accident. Under the Uniform Simultaneous Death Act, to whose estate will the policy proceeds be paid?

   A. Lynda's estate
   B. Kevin's estate
   C. Both Kevin's and Lynda's estate, equally
   D. The proceeds will escheat to the state.

7. When a policyowner cannot exercise his or her rights of ownership without the policy beneficiary's consent, the beneficiary is designated

   A. vested
   B. contractual
   C. irrevocable
   D. primary

8. Mr. Williams names his son, John, a beneficiary of his life insurance policy. What designation should he use if he wants to make sure that John's children would receive John's share of the life insurance policy proceeds should John predecease his father?

   A. *Per capita*
   B. All my children
   C. *Per stirpes*
   D. Grandchildren

9. What is the beneficiary designation that can only be changed with the beneficiary's written agreement?

   A. Revocable beneficiary
   B. Wife of the insured
   C. *Per stirpes*
   D. Irrevocable beneficiary

10. Which of the following statements concerning a common disaster provision is NOT correct?

    A. It activates when the insured and primary beneficiary die as a result of the same accident.
    B. It stipulates that if the insured and primary beneficiary die in the same accident, it is presumed that the insured died last.
    C. It gives a policyowner assurance that proceeds will be distributed according to his or her wishes.
    D. It stipulates that if the primary beneficiary outlives the insured by more than 48 hours, then the proceeds will be paid to his or her estate.

11. Which of the following is a clause that states that policy distributions payable to a beneficiary after the insured dies are not assignable or transferable and may not be attached in any way?

    A. Facility of payment
    B. Debtors protection
    C. Spendthrift trust
    D. Assignment

12. Which of the following statements about facility of payment provisions is NOT correct?

    A. They often are found in group life insurance policies.
    B. They permit an insurer to pay all or part of the proceeds to a party who is not named in the policy.
    C. They typically are found in industrial policies.
    D. They permit insurance proceeds to be paid to someone who is not named in the policy when the named beneficiary is a minor.

13. Mary names her husband, Rick, as primary beneficiary of her insurance policy and their two children, Pam and Matt, as contingent beneficiaries. Rick dies in March. Pam and Matt are killed simultaneously in a car accident later that month. Hearing the news, Mary has a fatal heart attack. In this case, Mary's life insurance proceeds will be paid

    A. to Rick's estate
    B. to Mary's estate
    C. in equal shares to Rick's, Pam's and Matt's estates
    D. one-half to Rick's estate and one-quarter each to Pam's and Matt's estates

14. Which of the following statements about beneficiary designations is NOT correct?

    A. A business can be designated as beneficiary.
    B. Minors cannot be named life insurance beneficiaries.
    C. When a charity is named beneficiary, the policyowner's heirs cannot contest the gift.
    D. When a trust is named beneficiary, a trustee will manage the insurance proceeds.

15. Which of the following is the method used today to change beneficiaries?

    A. Recording method
    B. Assignment method
    C. Beneficiary alteration method
    D. *Change* of designation method

Answers & Rationale

1. **D.** In this case, Gerald is the primary beneficiary, the three children are secondary beneficiaries and the First Community Church is the tertiary beneficiary. Sandra's surviving relatives would not have the right to contest the gift to the church because the life insurance proceeds would not pass by will. Instead, the proceeds would pass outside of the probate process and could not be contested by disgruntled heirs.

2. **B.** Rather than specifying one or more beneficiaries by name, a policyowner may designate a class or group of beneficiaries. Thus, if Walter names children of the insured as his beneficiaries, this type of beneficiary designation would be called class beneficiaries.

3. **C.** The *per stirpes* method of distribution, rather than the *per capita* method, is the more common approach used today.

4. **B.** If the beneficiary predeceases the insured and the irrevocable clause is reversionary, the right to modify the beneficiary clause as well as all other rights of ownership revert to the insured.

5. **D.** A clause in which the beneficiary is assumed to have predeceased the insured if both the insured and the beneficiary die in the same accident but the beneficiary does not survive the insured by 14 days is called a common disaster provision. This provision assures the policyowner that if both the insured and primary beneficiary die within a short period of time, the death benefits will be paid to the secondary beneficiary or to the insured's estate.

6. **B.** According to the Uniform Simultaneous Death Act, if Kevin and Lynda are killed in the same accident and there is insufficient evidence to show who died first, the policy proceeds are to be distributed as if the insured—Kevin—died last. This means that the proceeds will be paid to a secondary beneficiary if one was named; otherwise, Kevin's estate will receive the proceeds.

7. **C.** When an irrevocable beneficiary is named, the policyowner cannot exercise any rights of ownership that would affect the beneficiary's rights without the beneficiary's consent.

8. **C.** Mr. Williams should use the *per stirpes* distribution method. Under this method, if John predeceased his father, John's share of the insurance proceeds would be passed down to his children in equal shares. If John's father designated the proceeds to be distributed *per capita*, John's children would not receive any of the proceeds. Instead, the other primary beneficiaries would receive John's share.

9. **D.** When a beneficiary is designated irrevocable, the policyowner can change the beneficiary designation only with the beneficiary's consent. This is because an irrevocable beneficiary has a vested right in the policy and the policyowner cannot exercise any right that would affect the beneficiary without the beneficiary's consent.

10. **D.** A common disaster provision usually stipulates that the primary beneficiary must outlive the insured by a definite time period. Although 14 or 30 days are common time periods in these provisions, a policy generally will not contain a period as short as 48 hours.

11. **C.** A spendthrift clause protects life insurance proceeds from the claims of either the beneficiary's or policyowner's creditors.

12. **A.** Facility of payment provisions typically are found in industrial policies rather than group life insurance policies.

13. **B.** If Mary's primary and contingent beneficiaries all predecease her, the insurance proceeds will be paid to Mary's estate.

14. **B.**   Although naming minors as life insurance beneficiaries may present some legal and logistical complications, they still can be named beneficiaries. To protect itself and the minor, the insurer may make payments to an adult guardian, retain the proceeds until the minor reaches majority or place the proceeds in trust for the minor's benefit.

15. **A.**   The most commonly used method today for changing beneficiaries is called the recording method. The policyowner simply notifies the insurer in writing of the beneficiary change. When the change is recorded, it becomes effective as of the date the insured signed the notice.

7

Life Insurance Premiums and Proceeds

INTRODUCTION

When people buy life insurance, they must, of course, pay premiums. In this lesson, we will examine the three primary factors that affect an insured's premium rates: the mortality charge, interest earnings and an expense charge. We also will look at some of the other premium factors that come into play when evaluating individual applications for life insurance. After a policy is in force, the owner may surrender it at any time or keep it active by paying premiums. When an insured dies, the policy proceeds can be paid to the beneficiary in a variety of ways, depending on the beneficiary's needs and personal situation. After reviewing the different settlement options a beneficiary may select, we will examine the important topic of life insurance taxation. Specifically, we will look at how premiums, cash values and life insurance proceeds are taxed.

LESSON OBJECTIVES

When you finish this lesson you should be able to:

- explain how mortality, interest and expenses affect premium rates and list the other factors affecting premiums;
- describe the different approaches used to rate substandard cases;
- explain how level premium funding works;
- describe how life insurance premiums, cash values and proceeds are taxed;
- list and explain the various options for paying death proceeds to beneficiaries; and
- describe the tax treatment of accelerated death benefits, viatical settlements, 1035 exchanges and policy surrenders.

Life Insurance Premiums

The task of determining an insurance company's premium rates rests with the company's actuaries. Actuaries are mathematicians by education who are responsible for bringing together the financial and statistical data that have an influence on life (and health) insurance premium rates. Establishing realistic premium rates is a critical function in any life insurance company. Rates must be high enough to cover the costs of paying claims and doing business, yet low enough so that they are competitive with other insurers' rates.

FIGURE 7.1   How the Life Insurance Premium Dollar Is Used

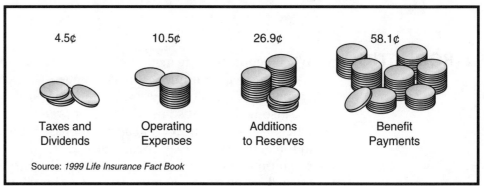

4.5¢	10.5¢	26.9¢	58.1¢
Taxes and Dividends	Operating Expenses	Additions to Reserves	Benefit Payments

Source: *1999 Life Insurance Fact Book*

Life insurance premium rates generally are expressed as an annual cost per $1,000 of face amount.

✓ **For Example:** One company's rate for a male, age 35, is $13.73. What exactly does this mean? It means that for the particular policy in question (say, a $50,000 participating straight whole life policy), the policyowner, a male who was 35 when he purchased the policy, pays an annual premium of $13.73 for every $1,000 of face amount he purchased, or $686.50 ($13.73 × 50). Because it is a straight whole life policy, this policyowner will pay $686.50 per year for his life (or to age 100, if he lives that long).

Primary Factors in Premium Calculations

Three primary factors are considered when computing the basic premium for life insurance: *mortality, interest* and *expense*. Of these, the mortality factor has the greatest effect on premium calculations (commonly termed *rate-making*). That is, while an insurer's interest and expense factors generally are the same for all of its policyholders, the mortality factor can vary greatly, depending on personal characteristics of individual insureds.

Mortality Factor

A basic principle of life insurance is that it must be based on an accurate prediction of mortality, that is, the average number of deaths that will occur each year in each age group. Throughout the years, statistics have been compiled, showing how many and at what ages people generally can be expected to die. Compiled, these statistics become mortality tables, which reflect death rates at each age.

✓ **Take Note:** For a mortality table to be accurate, it must be based on two things—a large cross section of people and a large cross section of time.

Figure 7.2 is a sample mortality predictions table, taken from the 1980 Commissioner's Standard Ordinary, or CSO, Mortality Table. For easier reading, the starting group has been reduced to 100,000. (The complete CSO table reflects 10,000,000 lives.) Also, only 10-year age intervals are shown and the ages in between (except age 99) are not included.

Two primary purposes of a mortality table are to indicate: (1) the expectation of life at given ages—the average number of years remaining for a group of persons of the same age and (2) the probability of death—the average number of deaths for a group of persons in given years. Obviously, the significance of mortality predictions to an insurance company is that they provide a basis to estimate how long its insureds will live, how long they will be paying premiums and at what future dates the company will have to pay out benefits. Consequently, the portion of the premium associated with mortality reflects the pure cost of providing death protection. Large insurance companies typically base their rates on their own statistics and experience or construct their own mortality tables from a data pool based on the experience of many insurers. Actuaries use the experience of several years to determine the mortality data that will be incorporated into premium rates.

💡 **Test Topic Alert!**

The mortality table arbitrarily sets the upper age limit at 100, because statistics show that very few people live to that age. Therefore, for purposes of determining mortality, age 100 is deemed to be the age at which the last person in an original population of 100,000 dies. Whole life insurance will mature or endow at age 100 because insurance is not designed to provide coverage beyond that age.

Interest Factor

When policyowners pay premiums to a life insurance company, the funds do not sit idle in the insurer's vaults. They are combined with other funds and

FIGURE 7.2   1980 CSO Mortality Table

Age	Number Living at Start of Year	Deaths Within Year
0	100,000	418
10	98,783	72
20	97,542	185
30	95,800	166
40	93,772	283
50	89,666	602
60	80,842	1,300
70	62,742	2,479
80	32,745	3,237
90	6,458	1,432
99	108	108
100	0	0

The figures above are a sampling from the 1980 CSO Mortality Table, showing how many individuals are expected to die within certain years out of a starting group of 100,000. For example, out of 100,000 people, 93,772 are expected to be living at the age of 40; during that 40th year, 283 are expected to die.

Notice the mortality patterns this table reveals. The first year of life is one of relatively high mortality. The mortality rate of 418 deaths during the year out of the original group of 100,000 is not matched again until age 45 (not shown here).

At age 1 (not shown), the number dying is 107, and the rate continues to decline until age 10 (with 72 deaths, it is the lowest in the table). Then begins the climb up. Older teens and young adults face an increased risk of death. But from a rate of 185 deaths at age 20, the mortality actually decreases as this population matures through its 20s. The rate at age 29 is 164, the lowest it will be for the remainder of this population's average life expectancy.

From a high of 3,300 at age 78 (the highest rate in the table), the rate once again begins to decline—a sign that if one can make it this long, the odds of making it to 100 actually improve.

Actuaries know that many people live longer than the average life expectancy. Nonetheless, it is an indisputable fact that everyone dies eventually, so actuaries have set age 100 as the somewhat arbitrary age at which the last person in the original population of 100,000 dies. It is at age 100, therefore, that whole life policies mature or endow.

invested to earn interest. Among other things, this interest earned helps hold down the cost of life insurance premiums.

An insurer makes two assumptions with regard to interest. First, it assumes that a specific net rate of interest will be earned on all its investments. Actually, some investments will earn more than the assumed rate and some will earn less, so the company selects an average rate for its assumption. The assumed interest rate may seem low (generally, 3½ to 4½ percent), but it directly affects the premium levels that are guaranteed to policyowners for years into the future. Thus, the assumed rates must be reasonably conservative.

The second assumption made by the company is that one full year's interest will be earned by each premium policyowners pay. Therefore, it must be assumed that all premiums are paid at the beginning of the year.

 Take Note: There is no reliable basis for predicting future interest rates or trends, therefore a company must remain conservative in its interest assumptions, because it is committed to the interest rate guaranteed in its life insurance policies for as long as those policies remain in force. Interest earnings on invested premiums is the second consideration in premium rate calculations; the higher the assumed rate of interest, the lower the premium rate charged to policyowners.

Expense Factor

The third factor affecting premium rates is expenses. As does any business, an insurance company has various operating expenses. Personnel must be hired and paid; sales forces must be recruited, trained and compensated; supplies must be purchased; rent must be paid; and buildings must be maintained. Local, state and federal taxes also must be paid. Each premium must carry its small proportionate share of these normal operating costs.

 **Test Topic Alert!**   An expense factor is computed and included in the premium rates for life insurance. Sometimes the expense factor is called the *loading charge*.

Net vs. Gross Premiums

The factors basic to premium calculations—mortality, interest and expense—are only a portion of the equation. Actuaries use the assumptions underlying these factors and translate them into *net single premium, net level premiums* and *gross premiums*.

The net single premium can be defined as the single amount needed today to fund the future benefit. Basically, it is the amount of premium, when combined with interest, that will be sufficient to pay the future death benefit. However, only rarely do people purchase life insurance with a single premium because of the large cash outlay required. Most pay premiums over a number of years. Thus, the net single premium is converted into net annual level premiums, with some adjustments due to a lesser amount of interest these smaller premiums will earn. Finally, the gross premium is determined, which reflects the addition of the expense factor. The gross premium is what the policyowners are required to pay.

In very general terms, actuaries deduct the assumed interest earnings from the mortality cost. The mortality cost less the assumed interest earnings equals the net premium. The expense factor then is added to the net premium to arrive at the gross premium.

✔ **Take Note:** The two key formulas to keep in mind are:

- Net single premium = Mortality cost – Interest
- Gross premium = Net single premium + Expense (or Premium = Mortality cost – Interest + Expense)

Other Premium Factors

The preceding discussion focused on the three primary factors underlying all life insurance premiums. When evaluating individual applications for life insurance, other premium factors come into play, all of which influence mortality to one degree or another:

- *Age.* As we have seen, the age of an individual has a direct bearing on mortality, and mortality is figured directly into premium calculations. The older the insured, the greater the mortality risk.
- *Sex.* The sex of the applicant also has a bearing on mortality. Experience has shown that, on the average, women live five or six years longer than men. Statistically, then, they are considered better life insurance risks than men and their premium rates usually been lower than those for men.*
- *Health.* Another factor influencing mortality is the health of the applicant. Obviously, those in poorer health represent a higher risk than those in good health.
- *Occupation or avocation.* An applicant's occupation or avocation also can affect mortality. Those employed in hazardous occupations pose a greater risk to an insurer, as do those who engage in dangerous hobbies.
- *Habits.* An individual's personal habits also may influence the premium rate he or she will be assessed. Habits such as smoking or overeating adversely affect health and may increase the risk of death.

Factors such as these are considered carefully by insurance company underwriters, whose job it is to evaluate and select risks. In those cases where an individual applicant represents a higher-than-normal risk to the insurer due to one or more of these personal characteristics, he or she is known as a substandard risk. Of course, insurers can reject a substandard risk, and some applicants are denied. However, another way to treat a substandard case is

---

* Note that many insurance companies have adopted unisex rating tables, which effectively disregard the difference in mortality rates between men and women of the same age.

to adjust the premium to reflect the increased risk. This approach is known as *rating*.

Methods of Rating Substandard Risks

There are a number of approaches insurance companies use to set or adjust premiums for substandard cases. These methods include *extra percentage tables, permanent flat extra premiums, temporary flat extra premiums, rate-up in age* and *liens*. Let's briefly review each.

Extra Percentage Tables

Although the extra percentage tables rating system varies somewhat from company to company, it is the one used most extensively today. This method involves a numerical system for rating substandard cases, so the premium charged, for example, may be from 125 percent to 500 percent of standard. A number of premium rates usually are established for each age and type of policy. The system assumes there are a certain number of extra deaths per thousand that will increase with age for all kinds of cases.

Permanent Flat Extra Premiums

The permanent flat extra premiums rating system adds a fixed charge of so many dollars per $1,000 of insurance for substandard cases. This additional charge is assessed for the extra risk, which is measured in extra deaths per thousand. The flat extra premiums do not increase the policy's cash or non-forfeiture values. Any extra premium may be removed when the insured's condition is believed to have changed to a point where the risk is reduced.

Temporary Flat Extra Premiums

The temporary flat extra premiums rating system is identical to the permanent flat extra premium system, except that the fixed additional premium is charged for a specified number of years. With either permanent or temporary flat extra premiums, the amount of the additional charge generally will vary with the type of policy. A temporary extra premium may be charged when most of the extra risk is anticipated during the early years the policy is in force (e.g., perhaps the first few years following surgery).

Rate-up in Age

Though the rate-up in age system of rating substandard cases no longer is used widely, it warrants mention. Under this method, the proposed insured is assumed to be a number of years older than he or she really is and the policy is issued with a correspondingly higher premium.

Lien System

Under the lien system, a policy is issued at standard rates on a substandard applicant, but with a lien against the policy. This lien automatically reduces the amount of insurance in the event the insured dies from a cause cited in the policy (and which resulted in the rating). Generally, this system is used now only with some money-purchase pension plans where premiums are uniform.

✓ **Take Note:** This system has had major drawbacks, primarily because insureds have not understood that they are getting less protection than is shown as the face amount of their policies.

✎ **Quick Quiz 7.1**   Match the following methods of rating substandard risks with the appropriate description below.

A. Rate-up in age
B. Extra percentage tables
C. Temporary flat extra premiums
D. Permanent flat extra premiums
E. Lien system

_____ 1. This system of setting premiums for substandard cases generally is used now only with money-purchase pension plans where premiums are uniform.

_____ 2. Under this system of rating substandard cases, the applicant is assumed to be older than he or she actually is and the policy is issued with a correspondingly higher premium.

_____ 3. A fixed charge of a certain dollar amount per $1,000 of insurance is added for substandard cases for a specified number of years.

_____4. This rating system is used most extensively today for rating substandard cases.

_____ 5. This premium rating system adds a fixed charge of so many dollars per $1,000 of insurance for substandard cases.

Answers   *1. E   2. A   3. C   4. B   5. D*

Level Premium Funding

As mentioned earlier, the age of an insured has direct influence on the mortality charge—the higher the age, the higher the mortality charge. Because the mortality charge has a direct impact on the amount of premium, it stands to reason that as a person ages, the premium rate for that person should increase.

In Lesson 4, it was pointed out that term insurance is characterized, in part, by steadily increasing premiums. The most dramatic example of this is annually renewable term insurance (ART). With ART policies, policyowners are paying for one year of pure insurance protection only, meaning that they will pay, in any given year, the cost of insurance for that year. The older an insured becomes, the higher the mortality charge becomes and, thus, the higher the premium becomes.

In Lesson 4, the concept of level premiums also was introduced. As we discussed, life insurance is issued with premiums calculated and payable on a level basis for the policy's life. If the policy is a term policy, the premiums are level for the duration of the term; if the policy is a whole life policy, the premiums are level for life or, in the case of a limited pay policy, for the duration of the premium-paying period.

How is this possible? If the mortality rate (and consequently the mortality charge) for an insured increases each year, how can any type of life insurance permit its premiums to remain level for the life of the policy? The answer lies in the funding method underlying the policy.

All forms of permanent insurance (and those types of term whose periods extend beyond one year) are based on the level premium funding method. A full explanation of this complex actuarial concept is beyond the scope of this book; however, it is possible to simplify the explanation. Under the level premium funding method, the insured pays more than the insurance protection requires in the policy's early years; in the policy's later years, when the increasing mortality charge normally would increase the premium to a very high level, the excess paid in the early years is used to help fund the additional cost now required.

✓ **Take Note:** Interest plays an important role in this process. The excess funds paid in the early years will earn interest, thus making it possible to keep the actual premium level lower than if interest were not considered. In essence, the level premiums collected under a permanent policy are actuarially (that is, mathematically) equivalent to the sum of the increasing annual renewable term rates for the same insured risk and for the same period of time.

Because of the time value of money, (that is, the influence of interest) the actual sum of out-of-pocket premiums paid under a permanent policy (or a term policy that extends for a number of years) will be significantly less than those paid under an ART policy, all other factors (age and policy face amount, for instance) being equal.

Reserves vs. Cash Values

What happens to those excess funds that are paid in the early years of a permanent policy? Because they are not actually required to cover the insurance risk at that time, they are set aside for the future time when they will be required. As one might guess, the unused funds belong to the policyowner;

they constitute the policy's cash value. It is easy to see how important these funds are to the overall funding of the policy, especially in the policy's later years. This also explains why any loan against the cash value must be offset by a reduction in the proceeds paid out of the policy, unless the policyowner returns the borrowed funds, with interest.

People sometimes confuse the term policy cash value with policy reserve. While the two are similar in concept, there are some important differences. Basically, the cash value is a tangible amount that represents the additional funds paid in the early years of a whole life policy. It is, quite literally, the savings element of a whole life policy. The policy reserve is more intangible; it is a fund required by each state's insurance laws to be set aside to ensure that money will be available to pay future claims.

Literally, the policy reserve is the amount which, when added to the present value of future net premiums, will equal the present value of future claims. A very simple example will better illustrate this. Note that the term present value simply means the value today of a sum which will be larger in the future, after it accrues interest.

✓ **For Example:** A policyowner is 38 years old, owns a $50,000 permanent policy and is actuarially expected to live to age 78. The annual net premium is $450, and the company is using an assumed interest rate of 4 percent.

Present value of the future claim	$10,400
Present value of the future premiums	−$8,900
Reserve liability	$ 1,500

This example shows that, with a 4 percent interest rate assumption, the present value of the $50,000 death benefit is $10,400. In other words, if $10,400 were invested at 4 percent interest for the next 40 years, it would grow to $50,000. The present value of future premiums is $8,900. If this amount were set aside to earn 4 percent interest, it would accumulate to an amount actuarially equivalent to the $450 premium the owner is paying each year. The difference—$1,500—is the required policy reserve.

Reserves are treated as a liability, meaning that companies must keep the reserve amount as a liability, not an asset, on their books. It is money that must be set aside to assure policyowners (and state regulators) that sufficient funds will be available when a claim arises.

Modes of Premium Payment

Policyowners ordinarily may pay their premiums under one of four modes: annually, semiannually, quarterly or monthly. On any policy anniversary date (or at other times, if company rules permit) a policyowner may change from one payment mode to another, provided the payment is not less than a minimum specified by the company.

✓ *Take Note:* There is a slight extra charge when premiums are not paid annually, as all gross premiums are calculated on an annual basis. The extra charge is to cover the additional paperwork and to make up for interest lost by the company because it does not have the full annual premium to invest in advance.

All premiums are payable in advance. The first premium is due on the day the policy is issued. Subsequent premiums become payable at the end of the period for which the preceding premium was paid. The first premium usually is paid to the agent at the time of application. If not paid then, it must be paid at the time of policy delivery. Premiums have to be paid to keep a policy in force, although policyowners have the right to stop paying premiums at any time.

 Test Topic Alert!   The more often a premium becomes due, the more expensive the mode of the premium will be for the insurance company to administer. The insurer passes these costs on to the policyowner.

Tax Treatment of Premiums

As a general rule, premiums paid for personal life insurance policies by individual policyowners are considered to be personal expenses and, therefore, are not deductible from gross income. Also, premiums paid for business life insurance usually are not deductible.

✓ *For Example:* ABC Corporation purchased a key-person life insurance policy on the life of its president. The premiums are not deductible by the corporation.

There are a few exceptions to this general rule:

- Premiums paid for life insurance owned by a qualified charitable organization are deductible.
- Premiums paid for life insurance by an ex-spouse as part of an alimony decree are deductible (as alimony).
- Premiums paid by a business creditor for life insurance purchased as collateral security for a debt are deductible.
- Premiums paid by an employer for employee group life insurance are deductible as an employee benefit business expense, as long as certain conditions are met.

FIGURE 7.3 The Claims Process

It is the duty of the insurance company's claims department to make sure that a death claim is handled promptly and properly. At the very least, the claims examiner will require a certified death certificate, which states in part the cause of the insured's death. The examiner will review the policy to determine if there is a reason to contest the claim. If the cause of death was suicide, the claims examiner will want to know if the policy still is within the suicide exclusion period. If the insured was murdered, the laws of most states prevent life insurance proceeds from being paid to the beneficiary if the beneficiary was an accomplice to the murder.

Even if death resulted from natural causes, the examiner will review the policy carefully, especially if it is within the contestable period, to determine if the insured's application contained any misrepresentations that could void the contract. At the very least, the claims examiner will make sure that the actual age and sex of the insured agree with company records. Assuming that there is no reason to contest the claim (which is true in the majority of cases), the examiner will authorize payment of the death benefit to the policy beneficiary.

The next question the examiner will seek to answer is: Did the policyowner wish the proceeds to be paid in any particular manner, or can the beneficiary select the manner of proceeds distribution, more properly called the *settlement option*? If the policyowner did not specify a particular option, and if the beneficiary does not wish to select any settlement option, the claim will be paid as a lump sum. Often, though, either the policyowner or the beneficiary will select a settlement option.

Tax Treatment of Cash Values

The yearly increase in the cash value of a whole life insurance policy is not taxed during the period it accumulates inside the policy. If the cash value is taken out while the insured still is living—for example, as retirement income—a portion of each retirement income payment is received tax free, because it represents a return of principal. Let's look at this in more detail.

With regard to the taxation of surrendered cash values, a policyowner is allowed to receive tax free an amount equal to what he or she paid into the policy over the years in the form of premiums. The sum of the premiums paid is known as the policyowner's *cost basis*. However, when the accumulated cash value exceeds the premiums paid—when the cash value is greater than the policyowner's cost basis—the difference is taxable.

 For Example: At the age of 65, Mel decides to surrender his whole life policy and take the $28,000 accumulated cash value in a lump sum. He paid a total of $19,000 in premiums over the years. The difference between his cost basis and the accumulated value ($28,000 − $19,000 = $9,000) will be treated as taxable income in the year Mel actually receives it.

As long as a policy is not surrendered, the cash value continues to accumulate tax free. There never is a tax imposed on the policyowner, even if the cash value exceeds the cost basis, as long as the cash value remains in the policy.

Life Insurance Policy Proceeds

One thing that distinguishes life insurance from other forms of insurance is that a life insurance policy kept in force long enough is inevitably going to pay a benefit. When this benefit is payable due to the death of the insured, it is known as the policy's death proceeds. Certainly, the payment of death proceeds is how many policies deliver their benefit; however, today life insurance policy proceeds also are available to the living through such means as accelerated benefits and viatical settlements as well as through traditional policy surrenders.

Death Benefits

The death proceeds of a life insurance policy can be paid out in a variety of ways. The choice is up to the policyowner, as a right of ownership, or he or she may leave the decision to the beneficiary.

 Take Note: Payment options are known as settlement options. The selection of the appropriate settlement option should be based on the wishes of the insured and the needs of the beneficiary.

The variety of options insurers offer makes the selection fairly easy, because the decision usually rests on whether the beneficiary will need the entire amount at once or as income, payable over time. There are five settlement options available: *lump-sum, interest only, fixed period, fixed amount* and *life income.*

Lump-Sum Cash Option   Many years ago, all life insurance policy proceeds were paid out in single lump-sum cash settlements. Today, this option still is available, though not used to the extent of some of the others.

Interest-Only Option   Under the interest-only option, the insurance company holds the death proceeds for a specified period of time and, at regular intervals, pays the beneficiary a guaranteed rate of interest on the proceeds. The proceeds themselves then are paid out at the end of the specified period, either in cash or under one of the other settlement options.

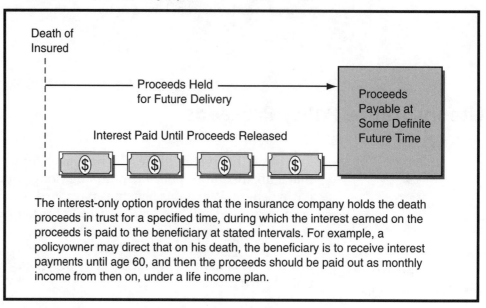

FIGURE 7.4 Interest-Only Option

Death of Insured

Proceeds Held for Future Delivery

Interest Paid Until Proceeds Released

Proceeds Payable at Some Definite Future Time

The interest-only option provides that the insurance company holds the death proceeds in trust for a specified time, during which the interest earned on the proceeds is paid to the beneficiary at stated intervals. For example, a policyowner may direct that on his death, the beneficiary is to receive interest payments until age 60, and then the proceeds should be paid out as monthly income from then on, under a life income plan.

Test Topic Alert!

If the interest-only option is selected, the policyowner must select another option to specify how the death benefit proceeds should be paid.

Because the interest is paid out rather than accumulated, the proceeds of the policy remain the same and intact. Interest payments to the beneficiary may be made monthly, quarterly, semiannually or annually. The interest rate never will be lower than the guaranteed rate specified in the policy, but it can be higher. If the company has sufficiently high earnings, it might pay additional interest over and above the guaranteed minimum. (See Figure 7.4.)

Fixed-Period Option

Under the fixed-period (or fixed-time) option, the company pays the beneficiary equal amounts of money at regular intervals over a specified period of years. This option pays out both principal (proceeds) and the interest earned. The amount of each installment payment is determined by the length of the desired period of income. Thus, the longer the period of income, the smaller each payment will be. Conversely, the shorter the period, the larger each payment amount.

If company earnings are large enough to permit paying excess interest, the excess interest will be used to make each payment larger. It will not be used to extend the payment period. If company earnings are lower than expected, the guaranteed payments to the beneficiary cannot be reduced. Guaranteed life insurance payments may always be more but may never be less. (See Figure 7.5.)

FIGURE 7.5   Fixed-Period Option

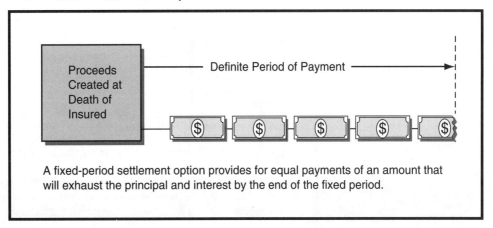

A fixed-period settlement option provides for equal payments of an amount that will exhaust the principal and interest by the end of the fixed period.

Fixed-Amount Option

Under a fixed-amount option, the policy proceeds plus interest are used to pay out a specified amount of income at regular intervals for as long as the proceeds last. The policyowner or beneficiary requests the size of payment desired. The amount of each income payment is fixed, and the duration of the payment period varies according to the payment amount. If excess interest is credited, it will be used to extend the payment period; the amount of each payment remains the same. (See Figure 7.6.)

Life Income Options

Under a life income option, of which there are many, the beneficiary receives a guaranteed income for life—no matter how long he or she lives. This unique concept is successful because the principal and interest of life insurance proceeds are paid out together, with the amount of payment actuarially calculated and guaranteed to last a lifetime. Even if the principal is depleted, income payments will continue, so long as the primary beneficiary lives. Essentially, the insurance company uses the death benefit to purchase a single payment immediate annuity for the beneficiary. As you will learn in Lesson 10, the purpose of annuities is to provide an income stream for the duration of an individual's life.

Because the life income settlement options are the same as annuity income options, a detailed discussion is reserved for Lesson 10. For now, note that these options are:

- straight life income option;
- cash refund option;
- installment refund option;
- life with period certain option;
- joint and survivor option; and
- period certain option.

FIGURE 7.6   Fixed-Amount Option

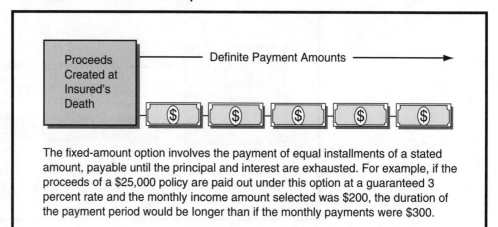

The fixed-amount option involves the payment of equal installments of a stated amount, payable until the principal and interest are exhausted. For example, if the proceeds of a $25,000 policy are paid out under this option at a guaranteed 3 percent rate and the monthly income amount selected was $200, the duration of the payment period would be longer than if the monthly payments were $300.

Living Benefits

In addition to the cash surrender option discussed earlier in Lesson 5 under Nonforfeiture Values and Options, policy benefits are available to living insureds through accelerated benefits and viatical settlements.

Accelerated Benefits

Accelerated benefit provisions are standard in most individual and group life insurance policies. Through these provisions, people who are terminally or chronically ill have access to policy death benefits. People suffering from AIDS, cancer, heart disease, Alzheimer's disease or other terminal or severe chronic illnesses often experience devastating financial hardship. During such times, funds from accelerated benefits help them maintain their independence and dignity. These funds usually are used for such necessities as rent, food and medical services.

To be considered terminally ill, a physician must certify that the person has an illness or condition that can reasonably be expected to result in death in two years. To be considered chronically ill, a licensed health care practitioner must have certified within the previous 12 months that the person (1) is unable to perform, without substantial assistance, as least two activities of daily living for at least 90 days, due to a loss of functional capacity; (2) has a similar level of disability as defined by regulations; or (3) requires substantial supervision to protect the person from threats to health and safety because of severe cognitive impairment.

Viatical Settlements

Through viatical settlements, individuals with a terminal illness or severe chronic illness sell their life insurance policies to viatical companies. The policies, of course, must have been in force beyond the contestable period. The price viatical companies pay for policies depends on the insured's life expectancy and the cost of future premiums. The NAIC has adopted model guidelines for fair payment. Under these guidelines, insureds receive anywhere from 50 percent to 80 percent of the policy face value. When a viatical company purchases a policy, it becomes the policyowner and is responsible for paying premiums. The company receives the death benefit when the insured dies.

Before the enactment of the Health Insurance Portability and Accountability Act of 1996 (HIPAA), the amount a chronically or terminally ill individual received after selling or assigning his or her life insurance contract was treated as a sale of property. This meant that the gain—the amount received that was more than the person's basis in the contract—was subject to federal income tax. However, beginning in 1997, under HIPAA, the proceeds from the sale of life insurance by a chronically or terminally ill individual to a qualified viatical settlement provider are exempt from federal income tax, as are accelerated death benefits.

This exclusion from gross income applies only if the policy is sold to a qualified viatical settlement provider. A provider will be considered qualified if it regularly engages in the business of buying or taking assignment of life insurance contracts on the lives of insured individuals who are terminally or chronically ill.

Quick Quiz 7.2 True or False?

_____ 1. A policy's cash value represents the savings element of a whole life policy.

_____ 2. Policy reserves must be set aside to assure policyowners that sufficient funds will be available when a claim arises.

_____ 3. No extra charges generally will be assessed if a policyowner pays premiums semiannually, quarterly or monthly.

_____ 4. Premiums paid for business life insurance never are deductible by the employer.

_____ 5. Under the fixed-period settlement option, a beneficiary's guaranteed payments cannot be reduced if the insurer earns less than expected.

_____ 6. If Susan chooses a life income settlement option, she will receive a guaranteed income for life, up to age 100.

Answers
1. **True**.

2. **True**.

3. **False**. *Policyowners ordinarily may pay their premiums annually, semiannually, quarterly or monthly. If premiums are not paid annually, however, the insurer charges a small extra fee for two reasons: to cover the additional paperwork and to make up for interest it loses because it does not have the full annual premium in advance to invest.*

4. **False**. *Although premiums paid for business life insurance usually are not deductible, there is an exception. An employer may deduct premiums it pays for employee group life insurance, as long as certain conditions are met.*

5. **True**.

6. **False**. *Under any one of the many life income settlement options, the beneficiary receives a guaranteed income for life, no matter how long he or she lives. As a result, even if Susan lives past 100, she still will receive a guaranteed income.*

Tax Treatment of Proceeds

To understand the taxation of life insurance proceeds, remember one basic principle: death benefits paid under a life insurance policy to a named beneficiary are free of federal income taxation. However, interest paid by an insurance company on death benefit proceeds left with the company is taxable income, just as interest payments any financial institution makes are taxable. The same principle applies in the case of life insurance policy dividends; the dividends themselves are free of income taxation, but interest under a dividend option is taxable in the year the interest is paid.

Proceeds Paid at the Insured's Death

When an insured dies, life insurance policy proceeds paid as a lump-sum death benefit to a beneficiary are exempt from federal income tax. The amount paid under a double indemnity provision and the benefits from any paid-up additions to a life insurance policy also are tax exempt.

When proceeds are paid out to an individual on an installment basis—as is the case with the fixed-amount, fixed-period or life income options—a portion of each payment consists of principal and a portion consists of interest. The portion of the proceeds attributed to interest is taxable; the remaining portion is received tax free.

✓ **Take Note:** This method of taxing life insurance proceeds is consistent with the annuity rule.

Under the annuity rule, a fixed, unchanging fraction of each payment is considered a return of principal and is excluded from gross income for tax purposes. Thus, that portion of the proceeds representing principal is received tax free. The balance of each payment representing interest income is taxable as ordinary income. The percentage of each payment to be exempted is determined by dividing the insured's investment in the contract by the expected return. The expected return is based on the insured's life expectancy.

On the other hand, when the insurance company holds the death proceeds of a policy under the interest-only option (the company holds the proceeds for a specified period of time and pays the beneficiary a guaranteed rate of interest on the proceeds at regular intervals), the interest payments are taxable to the beneficiary as ordinary income. When the principal amount is finally paid out, it still represents tax-free income.

✓ **Take Note:** Accumulated dividends, which are not properly classed as life insurance proceeds, also are exempt from federal income tax. The interest element in installment payments, as explained previously, is taxable income.

Transfer for Value Rule
In certain cases another tax provision, called the transfer for value rule, applies. If a policy is transferred by assignment or otherwise for valuable consideration (i.e., the policy is sold to another party) and the insured dies, the person who then owns the policy will be taxed on the excess of the proceeds over the consideration paid, including any premiums paid by the transferee. However, the rule does not apply to certain transfers, including transfers for value to the insured, to a partner (or partnership) of the insured or to a corporation in which the insured is a shareholder or an officer.

Proceeds Paid During the Insured's Lifetime

There are three reasons why an insured policyowner might receive proceeds from (or by reason of) a life insurance policy while he or she still is living: as a result of a policy surrender, as accelerated benefits or as payment received in a viatical settlement. Let's review the tax treatment of such proceeds paid during the insured's lifetime.

Policy Surrender
As noted earlier in this lesson under Tax Treatment of Cash Values, the taxation of accumulated values received when a policyowner surrenders a policy is determined by his or her cost basis. Only the excess of such proceeds over the cost of the policy is taxable.

✓ **Take Note:** Remember that the policyowner's cost basis is figured as total premiums paid, less policy dividends received, less any policy loan and less extra premiums paid for supplementary benefits, such as waiver of premium or accidental death benefits.

Endowment policy proceeds, even though left with the company at maturity under an interest-only option, will be taxable partially under the rule of constructive receipt. The taxable amount will be the excess of the proceeds over the premiums paid, the rationale being that the insured has the right to withdraw the endowed proceeds and so has them in constructive receipt.

The policyowner has 60 days after the policy maturity date to exercise an annuity option before the rule of constructive receipt takes effect.

Accelerated Death Benefits and Viatical Arrangements

As noted, with the passage of the Health Insurance Portability and Accountability Act of 1996 (HIPAA), which became effective on January 1, 1997, accelerated death benefits that terminally or chronically ill individuals receive from life insurance policies may be tax free.

✔ **Take Note:** For chronically ill individuals there is a limit on the maximum amount of accelerated benefits that can be excluded from income. In 2001, this limit is $200 per day ($73,000 annually) and is adjusted annually for inflation. Any amounts received that exceed this dollar limit must be included in gross income. This limit does not apply, however, to accelerated death benefits paid to terminally ill individuals.

Although accelerated death benefits generally are not included in a terminally or chronically ill person's income, there is one exception. The exclusion does not apply to any amount paid to a person other than the insured if that other person has an insurable interest in the life of the insured because the insured:

- is a director, officer or employee of the other person; or
- has a financial interest in the business of the other person.

✔ **Take Note:** If a terminally or chronically ill person receives an accelerated death benefit, the death benefit still will be paid to the beneficiary, less the amount of the accelerated payment.

A terminally or chronically ill person also can assign or sell a life policy to a viatical settlement provider and not pay federal taxes on amounts received. These provisions remove tax barriers for policyowners who need access to policy values because of terminal or chronic illness.

Income tax treatment of viaticals varies by state. California and New York, for example, treat viatical settlements as tax-free transactions for viators. With the passage of the Health Insurance Portability and Accountability Act, other states are expected to adopt similar legislation.

1035 Policy Exchanges

Another provision of the Internal Revenue Code pertains to life insurance policies that are exchanged or transferred for another like-kind policy. Typically, when an individual realizes a gain on a financial transaction, that gain is taxed. As we just learned, if a policyowner surrenders a life insurance policy and receives the cash value, he or she will realize a gain to the extent that the cash value exceeds the amount of premiums paid. That gain is considered ordinary income and is fully taxable. However, if a policy is exchanged for another, Section 1035 of the Tax Code stipulates that no gain (or loss) will be recognized. Consequently, the transaction is not subject to any tax. The following kinds of exchanges are allowed under this provision:

- a life insurance policy for another life insurance policy, endowment policy or annuity contract;
- an endowment policy for an annuity contract or an endowment contract under which payments will begin not later than payments would have begun under the contract exchange; and
- an annuity contract for another annuity contract.

✓ *Take Note:* If a life insurance policy is exchanged for another life insurance policy, the policies must be on the life of the same insured. Thus, if Tim exchanged a policy insuring only his life for a policy that insured the lives of both himself and his wife, this exchange would not qualify as a tax-free exchange under Section 1035. To constitute a nontaxable exchange, Tim would have to exchange his current policy for one insuring his life only.

Life Insurance and the Insured's Estate

When an insured dies, the value of any life insurance policy he or she owned is included in his or her gross estate for federal estate tax purposes. State death taxes also may be payable. The proceeds payable at death to a beneficiary, as explained previously, are not subject to federal income tax.

Any accumulated policy dividends, although exempt from income tax, also are included in the insured's gross estate for federal estate tax purposes.

Summary

There are three primary factors in a life insurance premium. The mortality charge has the greatest influence in making one insured's premium different from another insured's, assuming the two people represent different risks to the insurance company. The mortality charge is reduced by expected interest earnings, which is the second premium factor; these two factors constitute the net premium. The insurer's cost of doing business is recouped partly through an expense charge, the third premium factor, which, when added to the net premium, equals the gross premium.

Life insurance premiums generally are not tax deductible unless the premiums qualify as some other form of expense that is tax deductible (alimony payments or charitable contributions, for instance).

Life insurance proceeds can be paid out in a variety of ways. The standard means of paying a death benefit is in a lump sum. However, either the policyowner or the beneficiary can select another settlement option as an alternate method of paying a policy's proceeds.

Life insurance death benefits are paid without income tax consequence, with one exception. If the transfer for value rule applies, the recipient of the proceeds will be taxed on a portion of the proceeds that exceeds the amount paid for the policy.

Federal income taxes are payable on interest earnings credited to a policy on either death benefit proceeds or policy dividends that have been left with the company.

Key Concepts

In preparing for their licensing examination, students should be familiar with the following concepts:

level premium funding	cash value
premium factors	1035 exchange
policy reserves	settlement options
accelerated benefits	tax treatment of premiums, cash values
viatical settlements	and proceeds

Lesson Exam Seven

1. A mortality table would reveal which of the following pieces of information?

   A. That there is no death rate for persons age 99
   B. Who will die in any given year
   C. The average number of deaths that will occur each year in any age group
   D. That the death rate normally is higher in the lower age groups

2. All of the following are primary premium factors EXCEPT

   A. expense
   B. interest
   C. dividends
   D. mortality

3. Which of the following statements pertaining to life insurance premiums is CORRECT?

   A. Premium rates usually are lower for men than women.
   B. The most significant factor in premium rate calculation is interest.
   C. Harold and Billy, both age 25, each buy a whole life policy from the same company. However, Harold has a participating policy, while Billy's policy is nonparticipating. Harold will pay a higher premium.
   D. Lucy, who is substantially overweight, has applied for a life insurance policy. Her weight may affect her insurability but not the amount of premium on her policy.

4. Which of the following statements pertaining to life insurance premiums is CORRECT?

   A. The premiums for a policy that insures a spouse are tax deductible.
   B. A company may purchase key-person life insurance and deduct the premiums as a business expense.
   C. Premiums for group term insurance covering employees are tax deductible, assuming certain requirements are met.
   D. Premiums for policies in which the insured is someone other than the policyowner are tax deductible.

5. Art, the owner and insured under a $75,000 life policy, is killed in an accident. He had paid total premiums of $26,000. How much of the death benefit will be included in his gross estate for estate tax purposes?

   A. $0
   B. $26,000
   C. $49,000
   D. $75,000

6. With regard to the situation described in Question 5, how much of the $75,000 death benefit that was paid to Art's wife in a lump sum is taxable income to her?

   A. $0
   B. $26,000
   C. $49,000
   D. $75,000

7. Which of the following statements pertaining to life insurance policy settlement options is NOT correct?

    A. By using the interest-only option, two or more settlement options can be combined for added flexibility.

    B. Payments under the interest-only option may be made at a rate higher than the guaranteed minimum.

    C. Diane and Rhonda each are receiving monthly income from their deceased husbands' identical life insurance policies under the fixed-period option. Diane's payments are to be made for 15 years and Rhonda's for 20 years. Diane receives the larger monthly payments.

    D. Under the fixed-period option, the payment of excess interest will lengthen the payment period.

8. Assume the following persons buy identical life insurance policies from the same company. Who will pay the lowest premium, if all have standard ratings?

    A. Linda, age 28
    B. Thomas, age 28
    C. Louise, age 40
    D. Joe, age 45

9. Sarah, age 65, the owner of a $150,000 whole life policy, decides to surrender the policy and take the $90,000 cash value in a lump sum. Over the years, she has paid a total of $54,000 in premiums. How much, if any, of the payment will be taxed?

    A. $0
    B. $36,000
    C. $54,000
    D. $90,000

10. Beth, age 50, the beneficiary of her late husband's life insurance policy, has elected to receive the proceeds in monthly installments over the next five years. Due to the insurer's interest earnings, Beth notices that the amount of the payments often is more than what she was guaranteed. What kind of settlement option did Beth select?

    A. Life income
    B. Fixed-amount
    C. Cash value
    D. Fixed-period

11. Under which option does the insurer hold the death proceeds for a specified period of time and pay the beneficiary a guaranteed rate of interest on the proceeds at regular intervals?

    A. Fixed-period
    B. Interest-only
    C. Fixed-amount
    D. Life income

12. Bill names his church as the beneficiary of his $300,000 life insurance policy. When Bill dies, who is responsible for the income taxes payable on the lump-sum proceeds received by the church?

    A. His estate
    B. His church
    C. No income tax is payable on the death proceeds
    D. His estate and the beneficiary share the tax liability equally

13. Which of the following factors is most important when computing basic premiums for life insurance?

    A. Expense
    B. Interest
    C. Mortality
    D. Reserves

14. Which of the following statements about accelerated death benefits and viatical settlements is NOT correct?

   A. A terminally ill person receives accelerated death benefits tax-free.
   B. An insured who sells an insurance policy to a viatical company usually receives 100 percent of the policy's face value.
   C. A chronically ill person receives funds from a viatical settlement tax-free.
   D. Accelerated benefit provisions are standard in most individual and group life insurance policies.

15. Which of the following statements about the taxation of insurance proceeds is NOT correct?

   A. Accumulated dividends are exempt from income tax.
   B. A beneficiary will not be taxed on insurance proceeds paid as a lump sum death benefit.
   C. A policyowner who receives the cash value for a surrendered policy must pay capital gains tax on any gain.
   D. Generally, no gain or loss is realized when one insurance policy is exchanged for another.

Answers & Rationale

1. **C.** A mortality table is used to compute life insurance premiums. Mortality tables show the average number of deaths that will occur each year in each age group.

2. **C.** The three primary factors used to compute basic premiums for life insurance include mortality, interest and expense. The amount of dividends does not affect an insurance policy's premium rates.

3. **C.** Because participating life insurance policies pay dividends, they are more expensive than nonparticipating policies which do not pay dividends.

4. **C.** Although premiums paid for business life insurance usually are not deductible, there are a few key exceptions. For example, an employer may generally may take a deduction for premiums that are paid for employee group life insurance.

5. **D.** When Art dies, the entire value of the life insurance policy he owned ($75,000) is included in his gross estate for federal estate tax purposes. However, the proceeds will not be subject to income tax.

6. **A.** At Art's death, the $75,000 of insurance proceeds paid as a lump-sum death benefit to Art's wife will not be subject to federal income tax. If she had chosen another settlement option instead (such as fixed-amount, fixed-period or life income options), a portion of each payment would consist of principal and interest. The portion attributed to interest would be taxable while the remaining part would be tax free.

7. **D.** Under the fixed-period option, any excess interest will be used to make each payment larger, not to extend the payment period.

8. **A.** Linda will pay the lowest premium. Of all these individuals, Linda and Thomas are the youngest. The younger the insured, the less the mortality risk; conversely, the older the insured, the greater the mortality risk. However, Linda's premium will be lower than Thomas' because she is a woman. Generally, the average woman lives longer than the average man. As a result, women are considered better insurance risks than men and usually have lower premium rates.

9. **B.** If Sarah surrenders her policy, she can receive the amount she paid into the policy (i.e., her premiums) tax free. However, because the accumulated cash value exceeds the amount of premiums she paid, the difference between these two amounts is taxable. In Sarah's case, the taxable portion would be calculating by taking the difference between her cost basis and the policy's accumulated value ($90,000 – $54,000 = $36,000).

10. **D.** Under a fixed-period option, a beneficiary's payments may be larger than guaranteed if company earnings are big enough to permit paying excess interest. In Beth's case, her payments were more than what she was guaranteed because she selected a fixed-period option.

11. **B.** Under an interest-only option, the insurance company holds the death proceeds for a specified period of time and, at regular intervals, pays the beneficiary a guaranteed rate of interest on the proceeds.

12. **C.** When Bill dies, the proceeds paid to the church as a lump-sum death benefit are exempt from federal income tax. This is true whether the beneficiary is a person or a charitable organization.

13. **C.** Of the three primary factors that are considered when computing the basic premium for life insurance—mortality, interest and expense—the mortality factor has the greatest effect on premium calculations. This is because while an insurer's interest and expense factors

generally are the same for all of its policyholders, the mortality factor can vary greatly depending on the personal characteristics of individual insureds.

14. **B.** When an insured sells a life insurance policy to a viatical company, he or she will receive from 50 to 80 percent of the policy face value.

15. **C.** If a policyowner surrenders a life insurance policy and receives the cash value, he or she will realize a gain to the extent that the cash value exceeds the amount of premiums paid. However, that gain is considered ordinary income, not capital gain, and is fully taxable.

8

Life Insurance Underwriting and Policy Issue

INTRODUCTION

To determine who is qualified to purchase life insurance and who is not, insurance company underwriters must engage in a process called risk selection. This involves reviewing each applicant to determine whether or not and on what basis it will accept an application for insurance. In many cases the underwriter places much weight on the agent's or broker's recommendations. In this lesson, we will examine how the underwriting process works and look at the agent's role in this process. We also will discuss what happens after underwriting is finished; namely, how policies are issued and delivered.

LESSON OBJECTIVES

When you complete this lesson you should be able to:

- define underwriting and explain its purpose;
- list and describe the most common sources of underwriting information;
- explain the agent's role in the underwriting process; and
- describe the agent's role after a policy has been issued.

The Purpose of Underwriting

Insurance companies would like nothing more than to be able to sell their policies to anyone wishing to buy them. However, they must exercise caution in deciding who is qualified to purchase insurance. Issuing a policy to someone who is uninsurable is an unwise business decision that can easily mean a financial loss for the company.

Each insurer sets its own standards as to what constitutes an insurable risk versus an uninsurable risk, just as each insurer determines the premium rates it will charge its policyowners. Every insurance applicant is reviewed individually by a company underwriter to determine if he or she meets the standards established by the company to qualify for its life insurance coverage.

Underwriting, another term for risk selection, is the process of reviewing the many characteristics that make up an applicant's risk profile to determine if he or she is insurable and, if so, at standard or substandard rates.

✔ ***Take Note:*** There are two basic questions underwriters seek to answer about an applicant:

- Is the applicant insurable?
- If the applicant and insured are two different people, does an insurable interest exist between the two of them?

Insurable Interest

As discussed in Lessons 3 and 6, insurable interest is extremely important in life insurance. Without this requirement, people could purchase life insurance and the policy would be nothing more than a wagering contract. As we have established, an insurable interest exists when the death of the insured would have a clear financial impact on the policyowner. (See Figure 8.1.) Individuals are presumed to have an insurable interest in themselves. Therefore, when the applicant and proposed insured are the same person, there is no question that insurable interest exists. Questions are raised, however, with third-party contracts—those in which the applicant is not the insured.

✔ ***Take Note:*** Some relationships automatically are presumed to qualify as having an insurable interest—spouses, parents, children and people in certain business relationships. In most other cases, the burden is on the applicant to show that an insurable interest exists.

It bears repeating that with life insurance, an insurable interest must exist only at the policy inception; it need not exist when the policy proceeds actually are paid. Thus, a policyowner could assign a life policy to someone who has no insurable interest in the insured, and the assignment nonetheless would be valid.

Insurability

Once the underwriter determines that insurable interest exists, he or she must next determine the applicant's insurability. The underwriting process is the way an underwiter determines insurability.

FIGURE 8.1 **What Constitutes Insurable Interest?**

Though laws differ slightly from state to state, in general the following types of relationships automatically carry insurable interest:

- An individual has an insurable interest in his or her life.

- A husband or wife has an insurable interest in his or her spouse.

- A parent has an insurable interest in his or her child.

- A child has an insurable interest in a parent or grandparent.

- A business has an insurable interest in the lives of its officers, directors and key employees.

- Business partners have an insurable interest in each other.

- A creditor has an insurable interest in the life of a debtor, but only to the extent of the debt.

The Underwriting Process

The underwriting process is accomplished by reviewing and evaluating information about an applicant and applying what is known about the individual against the insurer's standards and guidelines for insurability and premium rates.

Underwriters have several sources of underwriting information available to help them develop a risk profile of an applicant. The number of sources checked usually depends on several factors, most notably the size of the requested policy and the risk profile developed after an initial review of the application. The larger the policy, the more comprehensive and diligent the underwriting research. Regardless of the policy size, if the application raises questions in the underwriter's mind about the applicant, that also can trigger a review of other sources of information.

✔ **Take Note:** The most common sources of underwriting information include the application, the medical report, an attending physician's statement, the Medical Information Bureau, special questionnaires, inspection reports and credit reports.

🔆 **Test Topic Alert!**   Underwriting is the process of selecting, classifying and rating risks.

The Application

The application for insurance is the basic source of insurability information. Regardless of what other sources of information the underwriter may draw from, the application—the first source of information to be reviewed—will be evaluated thoroughly. Thus, it is the agent's responsibility to see that an applicant's answers to application questions are recorded fully and accurately. (A sample application appears in the Appendix.) There are three basic parts to a typical life insurance application: *Part I—General, Part II—Medical* and *Part III—Agent's Report.*

Part I—General

Part I of the application asks general questions about the proposed insured, including name, age, address, birth date, sex, income, marital status and occupation. Also to be indicated here are details about the requested insurance coverage:

- type of policy;
- amount of insurance;
- name and relationship of the beneficiary;
- other insurance the proposed insured owns; and
- additional insurance applications he or she has pending.

Other information sought may indicate possible exposure to a hazardous hobby, foreign travel, aviation activity or military service. Whether the proposed insured smokes also is indicated in Part I.

Part II—Medical

Part II focuses on the proposed insured's health and asks a number of questions about the health history of not only the proposed insured, but also his or her family. This medical section must be completed in its entirety for every application. Depending on the proposed policy face amount, this section may or may not be all that is required in the way of medical information. The individual to be insured may be required to take a medical exam.

Part III—Agent's Report

Part III of the application often is called the agent's report. This is where the agent reports his or her personal observations about the proposed insured. Because the agent represents the interests of the insurance company, he or she is expected to complete this part of the application fully and truthfully.

In this important section, the agent provides firsthand knowledge about the applicant's financial condition and character, the background and purpose of the sale and how long the agent has known the applicant.

The agent's report also usually asks if the proposed insurance will replace an existing policy. If it will, most states demand that certain procedures be followed to protect the rights of consumers when policy replacement is involved.

 **Test Topic Alert!**   In a typical life insurance application, the applicant signs Parts I and II. He or she does not see Part III, the agent's report.

The Medical Report

A policy often is issued on the basis of the information provided in the application alone. Most companies have set nonmedical limits, meaning that applications for policies below a certain face amount (perhaps $50,000 or even $100,000) will not require any additional medical information other than what is provided by the application. However, for larger policies (or smaller policies when the applicant is older than a certain age) a medical report may be required to provide further underwriting information.

✔ *Take Note:* If the application's medical section raises questions specific to a particular medical condition, the underwriter also may request an *attending physician's statement* (APS) from the physician who has treated the applicant. The statement will provide details about the medical condition in question.

Medical reports must be completed by a qualified person, but that person does not necessarily have to be a physician. Many companies accept reports completed by a paramedic or a registered nurse. Usually the applicant can select the physician or paramedic facility to perform the exam; insurers also are prepared to recommend paramedic facilities where the exam can be given. In almost all cases, the expense for the exam is borne by the insurance company.

When completed, the medical report is forwarded to the insurance company, where it is reviewed by the company's medical director or a designated associate.

The Medical Information Bureau

Another source of underwriting information that focuses specifically on an applicant's medical history is the Medical Information Bureau (MIB). The MIB is a nonprofit central information agency established by a number of insurance companies to aid in the underwriting process and is supported by more than 600 member insurance companies.

The MIB's purpose is to serve as a reliable source of medical information concerning applicants and to help disclose cases where an applicant either forgets or conceals pertinent underwriting information, or submits erroneous or misleading medical information with fraudulent intent. The MIB operations help to hold down the cost of life insurance for all policyowners through the prevention of misrepresentation and fraud.

This is how the system works: If a company finds that one of its applicants has a physical ailment or impairment listed by the MIB, the company is pledged to report the information to the MIB in the form of a code number. By having this information, home office underwriters will know that a past problem existed should the same applicant later apply for life insurance with another member company. The information is available to member companies only and may be used only for underwriting and claims purposes.

 **Test Topic Alert!**   Information sent to the MIB may concern adverse medical histories, hazardous hobbies and occupations and even the insured's driving habits.

Each member company and its medical director sign a pledge to follow the rules and principles of the MIB. The basic requirements are:

- Applicants for life insurance must be notified in writing that the insurance company may make a brief report on their health to the MIB.
- Applicants must be advised that, should they apply to another MIB company for coverage or if a claim is submitted to such a company, the MIB will supply any requested information in its files to the company.
- Applicants must sign authorization forms for information from the MIB files to be given to a member company.
- The MIB will arrange the disclosure of any information it has concerning an applicant on request by the applicant. Medical information, however, will be disclosed only to the individual's physician, who then can interpret best the facts for the applicant (patient).

 **Test Topic Alert!**   The rules regarding disclosure of information from the MIB are enforced by the federal Fair Credit Reporting Act.

Special Questionnaires

When necessary, special questionnaires may be required for underwriting purposes to provide more detailed information related to aviation or avocation, foreign residence, finances, military service or occupation.

 For Example: If an applicant's hobby is skydiving, the insurance company needs detailed information about the extent of his or her participation to determine whether or not the insurance risk is acceptable.

The most common of these special questionnaires is the aviation questionnaire required of any applicant who spends a significant amount of time flying, such as an airline pilot.

Inspection Reports

Inspection reports usually are obtained by insurance companies on applicants who apply for large amounts of life insurance. These reports contain information about prospective insureds, which is reviewed to determine their insurability. Insurance companies normally obtain inspection reports from national investigative agencies or firms.

The purpose of these reports is to provide a picture of an applicant's general character and reputation, mode of living, finances and exposure to abnormal hazards. Investigators or inspectors may interview employees, neighbors and associates of the applicant as well as the applicant.

Inspection reports ordinarily are not requested on applicants who apply for smaller policies, although company rules vary as to the sizes of policies that require a report by an outside agency.

Credit Reports

Some applicants may prove to be poor credit risks, based on information obtained before a policy is issued. Thus, credit reports obtained from retail merchants' associations or other sources are a valuable underwriting tool in many cases.

Applicants who have questionable credit ratings can cause an insurance company to lose money. Applicants with poor credit standings are likely to allow their policies to lapse within a short time, perhaps even before a second premium is paid. An insurance company can lose money on a policy that is lapsed quickly, because the insurer's expenses to acquire the policy cannot be recovered in a short period of time. It is possible, then, that home office underwriters will refuse to insure persons who have failed to pay their bills or who appear to be applying for more life insurance than they reasonably can afford.

The Fair Credit Reporting Act of 1970

To protect the rights of consumers for whom an inspection report or credit (or consumer) report has been requested, Congress enacted the Fair Credit Reporting Act (FCRA) in 1970. As previously mentioned, this federal law applies to financial institutions that request these types of consumer reports, including insurance companies.

The FCRA established procedures for the collection and disclosure of information obtained on consumers through investigation and credit reports; it seeks to ensure fairness with regard to confidentiality, accuracy and disclosure. The FCRA is quite extensive. Included in it are the following important requirements pertaining to insurers:

- Applicants must be notified (usually within three days) that the report has been requested. The insurer also must notify the applicant that he or she can request disclosure of the nature and scope of the investigation. If the applicant requests such disclosure, the insurer must provide a summary within five days of the request.
- The consumer must be provided with the names of all people contacted during the preceding six months for purposes of the report. People contacted who are associated with the consumer's place of employment must be identified as far back as two years.
- If, based on an inspection or consumer report, the insurer rejects an application, the company must provide the applicant with the name and address of the consumer reporting agency that supplied the report.
- If requested by the applicant (more formally, the consumer), the consumer reporting agency—not the insurance company—must disclose the nature and substance of all information (except medical) contained in the consumer's file. Note that the file may be more extensive than the actual report that was provided to the insurer. The FCRA does not give consumers the right to see the actual report, although most reporting agencies do provide copies of the report routinely, if requested.
- If the applicant/consumer disagrees with information in his or her file, he or she can file a statement giving his or her opinion on the issue.

Classification of Applicants

Once all the information about a given applicant has been reviewed and evaluated, the underwriter seeks to classify the risk that the applicant poses to the insurer. In a few cases, an applicant represents a risk so great that he or she is considered uninsurable and his or her application will be rejected. However, the vast majority of insurance applicants fall within an insurer's underwriting guidelines and accordingly will be classified as a *standard risk*, *substandard risk* or *preferred risk*.

Standard Risk   Standard risk is the term used for individuals who fit the insurer's guidelines for policy issue without special restrictions or additional rating. These individuals meet the same conditions as the tabular risks on which the insurer's premium rates are based.

Substandard Risk   A substandard risk is one below the insurer's standard or average risk guidelines. An individual can be rated as substandard for number of reasons: poor health, a dangerous occupation or attributes or habits that could be hazardous.

✓ *Take Note:* Some substandard applicants are rejected outright; others will be accepted for coverage but with an increase in their policy premium.

Preferred Risk   Many insurers today reward exceptionally good risks by assigning them to a preferred risk classification. Preferred risk premium rates generally are lower than standard risk rates. Personal characteristics that contribute to a preferred risk rating include not smoking, weight within an ideal range and favorable cholesterol levels.

🖉 **Quick Quiz 8.1**   Fill in the blanks with the appropriate terms.

1. An individual who is rated below the insurer's standard or average risk guidelines is called a _____ risk.

2. If an applicant applies for a large amount of life insurance, the insurance company may request a(n) _____, which provides a picture of the applicant's general character, reputation, mode of living, finances and exposure to abnormal hazards.

3. The part of the application that describes the agent's personal observations about the proposed insured is called the _____.

4. If an applicant is a military fighter pilot, an insurance company may need additional detailed information about the applicant's job and may require a _____, to determine whether or not the insurance risk is acceptable.

5. If an applicant has a questionable credit rating, an insurance company may request a _____, which shows whether the applicant has paid his or her bills on time or if he or she is applying for more life insurance than can be reasonably afforded.

Answers   1. *substandard*

2. *inspection report*

3. *agent's report*

4. *special questionnaire*

5. *credit report*

Field Underwriting Procedures

As noted earlier, an agent plays an important role in underwriting. As a field underwriter, he or she initiates the process and is responsible for many important tasks: proper solicitation, completing the application thoroughly and accurately, obtaining appropriate signatures, collecting the initial premium and issuing a receipt. Each of these tasks is vitally important to the underwriting process and policy issue.

Proper Solicitation

As a representative of the insurer, an agent has the duty and responsibility to solicit good business. This means that an agent's solicitation and prospecting efforts should focus on cases that fall within the insurer's underwriting guidelines and represent profitable business to the insurer. At the same time, the agent has a responsibility to the insurance-buying public to observe the highest professional standards when conducting insurance business. All sales solicitations should be open and aboveboard, with the agent identifying the insurer he or she represents and the reason for the call clearly. In addition, good sales practices avoid high pressure tactics and are aimed at helping applicants select the most appropriate policies to meet their needs.

False advertising is prohibited as an unfair trade practice in all states. In this context, *advertising* encompasses almost any kind of communication used to promote the sale of an insurance policy.

✓ **For Example:** Descriptive literature, sales aids, slide shows, prepared group talks, brochures, sales illustrations and policy illustrations all are considered advertising.

All advertising must be truthful. Insurance products should be described properly and accurately, without exaggerating benefits or minimizing drawbacks.

Sales presentations must not be deceptive. What is a deceptive sale? Any presentation that gives a prospect or client the wrong impression about any aspect of an insurance policy or plan is deceptive. Any presentation that does not provide complete disclosure to a prospect or client is deceptive. Any presentation that includes misleading or inconclusive product comparisons is deceptive.

✓ **Take Note:** Even if a sales presentation is unintentionally deceptive, the agent has done the consumer a disservice. In addition, it's likely the agent has violated some aspect of the state insurance code.

In many states, an agent is required to deliver to the applicant a buyer's guide and a policy summary. These documents usually are delivered before the agent accepts the applicant's initial premium. Typically, the buyer's guide is a generic publication that explains life insurance in a way that average consumers can understand. It speaks of the concept in general and does not address the specific product or policy being considered.

The policy summary addresses the specific product being presented for sale. It identifies the agent, the insurer, the policy and each rider. It includes information about premiums, dividends, benefit amounts, cash surrender values, policy loan interest rates and life insurance cost indexes for the specific policy being considered.

Completing the Application

As mentioned earlier, the application is one of the most important sources of underwriting information, and it is the agent's responsibility to see that it is completed fully and accurately. Statements made in the application are used by insurers to evaluate risks and decide whether or not to insure the life of the applicant. Such statements are considered representations: statements an applicant represents as being substantially true to the best of his or her knowledge and belief, but which are not warranted to be exact in every detail. Representations must be true only to the extent that they are material to the risk.

✔ **Take Note:** In most states, statements made in insurance applications are considered representations, not warranties. Warranties are statements that are considered literally true. A warranty that is not literally true in every detail, even if made in error, is sufficient to render a policy void.

If an insurer rejects a claim based on a representation, it bears the burden of proving materiality. Representations are considered fraudulent only when they relate to a matter material to the risk and when they were made with fraudulent intent.

Several signatures are required to complete an application, and to overlook a needed signature will cause delay in issuing a policy. Note that in some jurisdictions a child must be a minimum age (for example, 15 or 18) to sign a life insurance application; otherwise, an adult, such as a parent, must sign.

✔ **Take Note:** Each application requires the signatures of the proposed insured, the policyowner (if different from the insured) and the agent who solicits the application. If the policyowner is to be a firm or corporation, one or more partners or officers, other than the proposed insured, generally must sign the application.

If additional questionnaires regarding an applicant's aviation or avocation activities are required for underwriting purposes, the signatures of the applicant and the agent also are required.

Where required by state law, the agent also must sign a form attesting that a disclosure statement has been given to the applicant. Moreover, a form authorizing the insurance company to obtain investigative consumer reports or medical information from investigative agencies, physicians, hospitals or other sources generally must be signed by the proposed insured and the agent as witness.

When premiums are to be paid according to an automatic check plan, forms for that purpose also must be signed by the applicant.

Changes in the Application The application for insurance must be completed accurately, honestly and thoroughly, and it must be signed by the insured and witnessed. The completed application is important because the information in it is used, sometimes exclusively, to evaluate risks and determine whether or not to issue a policy. When attached to the insurance policy, the application becomes part of the legal contract between the insurer and the insured. Consequently, the general rule is that no alterations of any written application can be made by any person other than the applicant without the applicant's written permission.

When an applicant makes a mistake in the information he or she has given to an agent in completing the application, the applicant can have the agent correct the information, but the applicant must initial the correction. If the company discovers a mistake, it usually returns the application to the agent, who then corrects the mistake with the applicant and has the applicant initial the change. If the company accepts an application and then, before the policy's incontestable clause takes effect, discovers incorrect or incomplete information in it, the company may rescind or cancel the contract.

✓ **Take Note:** Some states permit insurers to make insertions in applications for administrative purposes, provided the insurer clearly indicates that those insertions are not to be ascribed to the applicant.

Initial Premium and Receipts

It is generally in the best interests of both the proposed insured and the agent to have the initial premium (or a portion of it) paid with the application. For the agent, this usually will help solidify the sale and may accelerate the payment of commissions on the sale. The proposed insured benefits by having the insurance protection become effective immediately, with some important restrictions.

FIGURE 8.2 Conditional Receipts

When a conditional receipt is given, the applicant and the company form what might be called a *conditional contract*—contingent upon conditions that exist at the time the application is signed (or when the medical exam is completed, if required). In providing early coverage, the insurer conditionally assumes the risk and will provide coverage from the specified date, on the condition that the applicant is approved for policy issue.

For example, assume an agent sells a $50,000 nonmedical life insurance policy to Matthew, who hands the agent his signed application with a check for the first premium. In turn, Matthew receives from the agent a conditional receipt for the premium. Two days later, Matthew becomes seriously ill and enters the hospital. So long as the company finds that Matthew qualifies for the policy as applied for, the company will issue the policy, regardless of his condition in the hospital. In fact, if Matthew died before the policy was issued, but was qualified at the time of application, his beneficiary still would receive the $50,000 death benefit.

However, in this example, if the company's underwriter determined that Matthew was uninsurable, and thus rejected the application, then there is no coverage, even during the period when the receipt was effective.

On the other hand, if a premium deposit is not paid with the application, the policy will not become valid until the initial premium is collected. Recall from the discussion in Lesson 3 that one of the requirements for a valid contract is consideration. In the case of an insurance contract, the consideration is the first premium payment plus the application. An insurer will not allow an applicant to possess a policy without receipt of the initial premium.

✓ **Take Note:** There is one exception to this rule. The applicant may be allowed to sign an inspection receipt and obtain the policy for inspection purposes. However, the 10-day free look policy provision generally makes this unnecessary.

Applicants who pay a premium deposit with the application are entitled to a premium receipt. It is the type of receipt given that determines exactly when and under what conditions an applicant's coverage begins. The two major types of receipts are *conditional receipts* and *binding receipts* (sometimes called *temporary insurance agreements*).

Conditional Receipts

The most common type of premium receipt is the conditional receipt. A conditional receipt indicates that certain conditions must be met for the insurance coverage to go into effect. There are two types of conditional receipts: *insurability* and *approval*. Both specify the conditions required for coverage. The primary distinction between the two is when the coverage goes into effect.

Insurability Receipt

The insurability receipt provides that coverage is effective when the applicant pays the initial premium—on the condition that the applicant proves to be insurable—either on the date the application was signed or the date of the medical exam, if one is required.

✓ **For Example:** If the applicant dies between the date of application or of the medical exam and the date the insurer approves the application, the coverage is retroactively effective, as long as the applicant proved to be insurable on the specified date. On the other hand, with the insurability type of receipt, if the applicant proves to be uninsurable as of the date of application or of the medical exam, no coverage takes effect and the premium is refunded.

Approval Receipt

An approval receipt is more restrictive than the insurability. In general, with an approval receipt, coverage is effective only after the application has been approved by the insurer and before the policy is delivered to the policyowner. Because they offer only a short period of special protection and usually are frowned upon by the courts, approval receipts are used rarely.

With either kind of conditional receipt, if the applicant is found to be insurable, but only on a substandard or rated basis, no retroactive protection is provided. This is because the applicant did not qualify for the policy he or she applied for (and to which the receipt pertains). Instead, the insurer will counter with an offer of another policy at a different rate. Consequently, if an applicant who has a conditional receipt is found to be substandard, and dies before accepting the rated policy counteroffered by the insurer, there would be no coverage.

Companies usually impose a limit on the amount of coverage provided under a conditional receipt (generally $100,000 or less). Therefore, even if the applicant is applying for a policy with a much higher face amount, the insurer usually will restrict the conditional coverage to a specified limit.

Binding Receipts   Under the binding receipt (or temporary insurance agreement), coverage is guaranteed, even if the proposed insured is found to be uninsurable, until the insurer rejects the application formally. Because the underwriting process often can take several weeks or longer, this can place the company at considerable risk. Accordingly, binding receipts often are reserved only for a company's most experienced agents.

Like the conditional receipt, a binding receipt typically stipulates a maximum amount that would be payable during the special protection period.

FIGURE 8.3 Life Insurance Policy Cost Comparison Methods

Insurance producers sometimes encounter a competitive situation in which a prospect is considering two or more policies. In a situation like this, producers who can accurately compare the true costs of each policy may have an advantage.

Two policies rarely are so closely alike that a true "apples to apples" comparison can be made (one company may provide a free waiver of premium provision, for example). Fortunately, however, established methods of comparing policy costs exists. While it is beyond the scope of this book to provide a thorough review of each, producers should be familiar with the two primary methods: *traditional net cost* and *interest adjusted net cost*.

Traditional Net Cost Method

Under the *traditional net cost method*, projected premiums for a certain time period (say, 20 years) are totalled. Projected policy dividends (if any) and the cash value at the end of that period are subtracted from the total. The resulting number, divided by the number of years in the comparison, yields the net cost per thousand per year.

This method no longer is permitted in many states because of one significant flaw—it ignores the time value of money. Money placed in an investment vehicle (like insurance) earns interest. Different companies apply different interest rates to their policies. By ignoring this fact, traditional net cost comparison falls short in projecting the real cost of a policy.

Interest Adjusted Net Cost Method

The *interest adjusted net cost method* is used widely today to compare policy costs. It is calculated in much the same way as the traditional net cost method, except that it adds the extra component of *interest* to the formula. The interest factor used is based on each company's projected interest rate. In this way, the cost estimates reflect the actual cost of a policy more accurately.

The provisions a binding receipt contains can vary slightly from company to company. Generally, however, upon payment of the initial premium at time of application, the receipt provides the following:

- The applicant is covered at the time of application (or on the date a later medical examination is completed, if required) for the amount of insurance applied for—usually not to exceed a maximum of $100,000 under all outstanding receipts. The temporary coverage continues until the policy is issued as requested, until the company offers a different policy or until the company rejects the application—but in no event for more than 60 days from the date the agreement was signed.

- If a medical examination is required, the temporary insurance coverage does not begin until the examination has been completed. But if death accidentally occurs within 30 days from the date of the agreement, the death benefit is paid even though the medical examination was not taken.
- The applicant must pay in advance at least one month's premium for the policy being applied for. Furthermore, there must be no material misrepresentations in the application, and the death must not result from suicide.

Policy Effective Date

The policy effective date—the date the policy goes into effect—is another important factor that must be addressed in any life insurance sale. The effective date is important for two reasons: it identifies when the coverage is effective and establishes the date by which future annual premiums must be paid.

If a receipt (either conditional or binding) was issued in exchange for the payment of an initial premium deposit, the date of the receipt generally will be noted as the policy effective date in the contract.

If a premium deposit is not given with the application, the policy effective date usually is left to the discretion of the insurer. Often, it will be the date the policy is issued by the insurance company. However, the policy will not be truly effective until it is delivered to the applicant, the first premium is paid and a statement of continued good health is obtained.

Back Dating   As we have learned, the premiums required to support a life insurance policy are determined, in part, by the insured's age. If an applicant can be treated by the insurance company as being a year younger, the result can be a lifetime of slightly lower premiums. Thus, it is understandable that applicants might want to back date a policy, making it effective at an earlier date than the present, in order to save age.

As surprising as it may seem, many insurers are willing to let an applicant back date a policy. As one might guess, though, there are some important conditions the applicant must meet before this step can be taken.

First of all, the insurer must allow back dating. Second, the company usually will impose a time limit on how far back a policy can be back dated (typically six months, the limit imposed by most states' laws). More importantly, the policyowner is required to pay all back-due premiums and the next premium is due at the back-dated anniversary date (which can be as close as six months in the future).

Preliminary Term for Interim Coverage

Some applicants for life insurance desire immediate protection but, for one reason or another, want to defer the issue dates of their policies for several months or to some specific date in the future. This usually can be accomplished by using preliminary (or interim) term insurance.

Companies ordinarily allow preliminary term to be used to defer the effective date of the original policy from 1 to 11 months. Premiums for preliminary term are based on the age of the insured at the time of application. The premium for the principal policy involved is based on the insured's age at the end of the interim period.

 Take Note: By using preliminary term, the applicant can be insured without delay and still postpone payment of premium on the principal policy for one or more months.

Policy Issue and Delivery

After the underwriting is complete and the company has decided to issue the policy, other departments in the company assume the responsibility for issuing the policy. Once issued, the policy document is sent to the sales agent for delivery to the new policyowner. The policy usually is not sent directly to the policyowner, because as an important legal document it should be explained by the sales agent to the policyowner.

Constructive Delivery

From a legal standpoint, policy delivery may be accomplished without physically delivering the policy into the policyowner's possession. Constructive delivery, which satisfies the legal interpretation of delivery, is accomplished if the insurance company intentionally relinquishes all control over the policy and turns it over to someone acting for the policyowner, including the company's own agent. Mailing the policy to the agent for unconditional delivery to the policyowner also constitutes constructive delivery—even if the agent never personally delivers the policy. However, if the company instructs the agent not to deliver the policy unless the applicant is in good health, there is no constructive delivery.

FIGURE 8.4   **From Application to Policy Delivery**

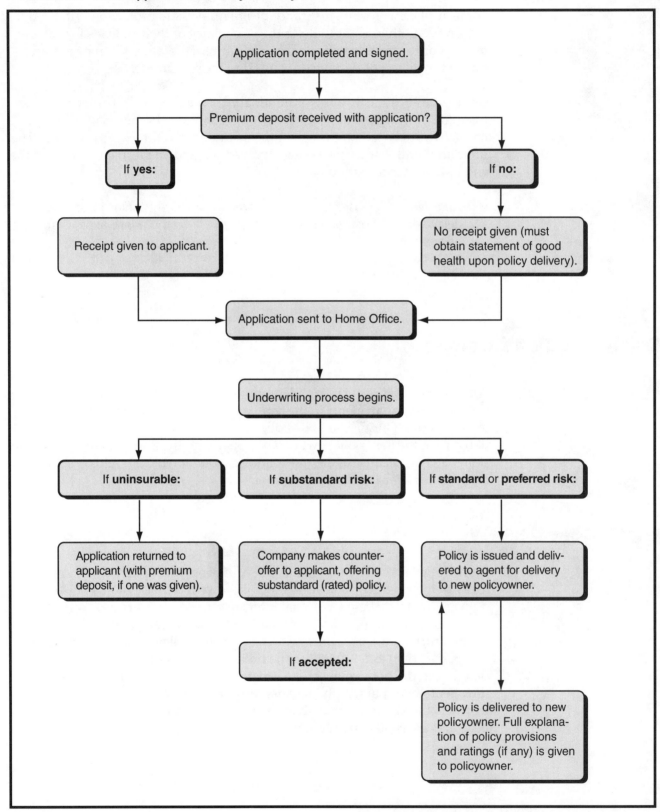

Test Topic Alert!   Constructive delivery is made when the insurer physically sends the policy on its way to the policyowner, without placing any condition or restriction on the delivery. Whether the policyowner actually receives the policy is irrelevant; the insurer's actions are controlling.

Mere possession of a policy by the client does not actually establish delivery if all conditions have not been met.

✓ **For Example:** A policy may be left with an applicant for inspection and an inspection receipt obtained to indicate that the policy is neither in force during the inspection period nor will it be in force until the initial premium has been paid.

Explaining the Policy and Ratings to Clients

Most applicants will not remember everything they should about their policies after they have signed the application. This is another reason agents should deliver policies in person. Only by personally delivering a policy does the agent have a timely opportunity to review the contract and its provisions, exclusions and riders. In fact, some states (and most insurers) insist that policies be delivered in person for this very reason.

✓ **Take Note:** The agent's review is especially important, for it helps reinforce the sale. It also can lead to future sales by building the client's trust and confidence in the agent's abilities and desire to be of genuine service.

Explaining the policy and how it meets the policyowner's specific objectives helps avert misunderstandings, policy returns and potential lapses. Agents sometimes may have a chance to prepare applicants in advance when it appears that policies may be rated as substandard. And sometimes both agent and policyowner may be surprised when the policy is issued as a rated contract. In either case, the agent usually can stress reasons why the insured has an even greater need for insurance protection because of the physical impairment or condition. Indeed, it may be the policyowner's last chance to purchase such coverage, because a worsening of the condition responsible for the rating could render the person completely uninsurable.

Obtaining a Statement of Insured's Good Health

In some instances, the initial premium will not be paid until the agent delivers the policy. In such cases, common company practice requires that, before leaving the policy, the agent must collect the premium and obtain from the insured a signed statement attesting to his or her continued good health.

The agent then is to submit the premium with the signed statement to the insurance company. Because there can be no contract until the premium is paid, the company has a right to know that the policyowner has remained in reasonably good health from the time he or she signed the application until receiving the policy. In other words, the company has the right to know if the policyowner represents the same risk to the company as when the application was first signed.

Summary

An insurance company decides if it is going to issue a policy to an applicant during the underwriting process. The underwriter seeks to determine if the proposed insured is insurable and, if so, at standard, substandard or preferred rates. Underwriters assign rates to proposed insureds, based on the risks the applicants represent to the insurers.

The effective date of the policy depends on whether or not an initial premium deposit was paid with the application (thus requiring the agent to issue either a conditional or binding receipt) as well as the date requested by the applicant (policies can be back dated in some situations).

Policy delivery is an important responsibility of the sales agent.

Key Concepts

In preparing for their licensing examination, students should be familiar with the following concepts:

underwriting process	standard vs. substandard (rated)
insurable interest	policies
consumer and investigative	Medical Information Bureau
reports	Fair Credit Reporting Act
application	standard risk
substandard risk	preferred risk
required signatures	initial premium deposits
conditional receipts	binding receipts
policy delivery	effective date of coverage
statement of good health	explanation of the policy to the client
proper solicitation	traditional net cost method
interest adjusted net cost method	

Lesson Exam Eight

1. Underwriting is a process of

   A. selection and issue of policies
   B. evaluation and classification of risks
   C. selection, reporting and rejection of risks
   D. selection, classification and rating of risks

2. Which of the following statements about a life insurance policy application is CORRECT?

   A. The names of both the insured and the beneficiary are indicated on the application.
   B. If an applicant's age is shown erroneously on a life insurance application as 28 instead of 29, the result may be a premium quote that is higher than it should be.
   C. The size of the policy being applied for does not affect the underwriting process.
   D. The agent's report in the application must be signed by the agent and the applicant.

3. If a medical report is required on an applicant, it is completed by

   A. a home office underwriter
   B. a paramedic or examining physician
   C. the agent
   D. the home office medical director

4. Which of the following statements about the Medical Information Bureau (MIB) is CORRECT?

   A. The MIB is operated by a national network of hospitals.
   B. Information obtained by the MIB is available to all physicians.
   C. The MIB provides assistance in the underwriting of life insurance.
   D. Applicants may request that MIB reports be attached to their policies.

5. Which of the following statements regarding the Fair Credit Reporting Act (FCRA) is CORRECT?

   A. Applicants must be notified within a short period of time that their credit report has been requested.
   B. If an applicant for insurance is rejected based on a consumer report, the name of the reporting agency must be kept confidential.
   C. If requested to do so, the insurance company must provide the actual consumer report to the applicant.
   D. Consumer reports are final in nature and cannot be disputed by an applicant.

6. Which of the following statements about the classification of applicants is NOT correct?

   A. A substandard applicant never can be rejected outright by the insurer.
   B. Applicants who are preferred risks have premium rates that generally are lower than standard rate risks.
   C. An individual can be rated as a substandard risk because of a dangerous occupation.
   D. A standard applicant fits the insurer's guidelines for policy issue without special restrictions.

7. Which of the following statements about the Fair Credit Reporting Act is CORRECT?

   A. It prohibits insurance companies from obtaining reports on applicants from outside investigative agencies.
   B. It provides that consumers have the right to question reports made about them by investigative agencies.
   C. It applies to reports about applicants that are made by insurance agents to their companies.
   D. It prohibits insurance companies from rejecting an application based on a credit report.

8. Elaine signs an application for a $50,000 nonmedical life policy, pays the first premium and receives a conditional insurability receipt. If Elaine were killed in an auto accident two days later,

   A. the company could reject the application on the basis that death was accidental
   B. her beneficiary would receive $50,000, if Elaine qualified for the policy as applied for
   C. the premium would be returned to Elaine's family because the policy had not been issued
   D. the company could reject the death claim because the underwriting process never was completed

9. Generally, the party who delivers an insurance policy to the new policyowner is the

   A. insurance company's home office
   B. sales agent
   C. state insurance commissioner's office
   D. underwriter

10. The primary distinction between insurability and approval conditional receipts is when the

   A. applicant pays the initial premium
   B. coverage goes into effect
   C. medical exam is given
   D. applicant proves insurable

Answers & Rationale

1. **D.** Underwriting is the process of reviewing the many characteristics that make up an applicant's risk profile to determine if the applicant is insurable at standard or substandard rates. It therefore can be considered a process of selection, classification and rating of risks.

2. **A.** In the application, the proposed insured must provide details about the requested insurance, including the type of policy, amount of insurance, name and relationship of the beneficiary, other insurance owned and any additional insurance applications that are pending.

3. **B.** A physician, paramedic or registered nurse typically can complete a medical report on an applicant.

4. **C.** The Medical Information Bureau is a nonprofit central information agency that aids in the underwriting process. Its purpose is to provide reliable medical information concerning applicants and to help disclose cases where an applicant either forgets or conceals pertinent underwriting information, or fraudulently submits erroneous or misleading medical information.

5. **A.** If an insurance company requests an inspection or credit report, the applicant must be notified (usually within three days) that the report has been requested.

6. **A.** Some substandard applicants can be rejected outright while others will be accepted for coverage but with an increase in their policy premium.

7. **B.** If an applicant disagrees with information in his or her MIB file, he or she can file a statement giving his or her opinion on the issue.

8. **B.** Because a conditional insurability receipt was issued in exchange for Elaine's payment of an initial premium deposit, her policy will become effective as of the date the application was signed, provided she later proves to be insurable. As a result, when she is killed two days later, her coverage would become effective retroactively and her beneficiary would be entitled to receive the $50,000 death proceeds.

9. **B.** Once a policy has been issued, the insurer sends the policy to the sales agent for delivery to the new policyowner. It usually is not sent directly to the policyowner.

10. **B.** The primary difference between the two types of conditional receipts is when the coverage goes into effect. With insurability receipts, the coverage is effective either on the date the application was signed or the date of the medical exam. In contrast, with approval receipt, coverage is effective only after the insurer has approved the application and before the policy is delivered to the policyowner.

9

Group Life Insurance

INTRODUCTION

Up to this point, we have focused our discussion on individual life insurance plans, policies and underwriting. However, there is another important category of insurance: group insurance. Group insurance provides life and health insurance coverage for a number of people under one contract. Because business owners generally recognize that employee benefits—or the lack of them—vitally affect their businesses in numerous ways, they usually are quick to realize the importance of group insurance. Like individual life insurance coverage, a group plan can be tailored to meet the employer's needs. By its very nature, group insurance has several features that set it apart from individual plans, including the nature of the contract, the cost of the plan, the form of premium payments and eligibility requirements. In this lesson, we will look at the principles of group insurance in general, focusing specifically on group life insurance plans. Employers also may adopt group health and disability plans, which are discussed in detail in Lesson 23.

LESSON OBJECTIVES

When you complete this lesson you should be able to:

- explain how group insurance differs from individual insurance plans;
- describe the types of groups eligible for group insurance coverage and the various plans insurers may offer them;
- explain how group life insurance premiums and proceeds are taxed;
- explain how group life insurance benefits are determined under the earnings, employment position and flat benefit schedules; and
- identify and describe the main characteristics of franchise life insurance, credit life insurance, blanket life, multiple employer trusts and multiple employer welfare arrangements.

Principles of Group Insurance

The basic principle of group insurance is that it provides insurance coverage for a number of people under a single master contract or master policy. Because a group policy insures a group of people, it is the group—not each individual—that must meet the underwriting requirements of the insuring company.

Group insurance most typically is provided by an employer for its employees as a benefit. In these cases, the employer is the applicant and contract policyholder. The employees, as group members, are not parties to the contract—in fact, they are not even named in the contract. Instead, each employee who is eligible to participate in the plan fills out an enrollment card and is given a certificate of insurance, which summarizes the coverage terms and explains the employee's rights under the group contract. A list of individual employees covered under the contract is maintained by the insurer.

 **Test Topic Alert!**

In the case of an employer's group insurance policy, the employer receives the master policy. Each employee receives a certificate of insurance.

In most cases, it is the policyholder—the employer—that selects the type of insurance coverage the group will have and determines the amount of coverage the contract will provide for covered group members. In addition, the employer typically pays all or a portion of the premium.

✔ *Take Note:* When an employer pays all of the premium, the plan is a *noncontributory* plan because the employees are not required to contribute to premium payments. If a group plan requires its members to pay a portion of the premium, it is a *contributory plan.*

Features of Group Insurance

To individual members covered by a group life or health insurance plan, the function the insurance serves is identical to an individual plan. In the case of group life, should the covered member die, his or her beneficiary will receive a stated amount in death proceeds. In the case of group health, should the covered member become ill or disabled, the plan will provide a stated benefit amount to help cover the corresponding medical costs or replace income lost due to the disability. Thus, the purpose of group life and health plans is the same as individual life and health plans. However, group plans have a number of features that set them apart from individual plans.

Master Policy

As noted, the foremost distinction of a group plan is that it insures a number of people under one contract. Because of this, individual underwriting and individual evidence of insurability are generally are not required. When it comes to underwriting, the insurer looks at the group as a whole, not at the health, habits or characteristics of individual members.

 Take Note: Group insurance involves experience rating, which is a method of establishing a premium for the group based on the group's previous claims experience. The larger and more homogeneous the group, the closer it comes to reflecting standard mortality and morbidity rates.

Low Cost

Another characteristic of group insurance is that, per unit of benefits, it is available at lower rates than individual insurance, due primarily to the lower administrative, operational and selling expenses associated with group contracts. And because most employers pay all or part of the group premium, individual insureds are able to have insurance coverage for far less than what they normally would pay for an individual or personal plan.

Flow of Insureds

Finally, group insurance is distinguished by a flow of insureds, entering and exiting under the policy as they join and leave the group. In fact, for it to operate effectively, group insurance requires a constant influx of new members into the group, to replace those who leave and to keep the age and health of the group stable.

Eligible Groups

What kinds of groups are eligible for group insurance coverage? Generally, almost any kind of natural group—those formed for a purpose other than to obtain insurance—will be considered by an insurer.

Insurable groups most typically fall into one of the following categories:

- single-employer groups;
- labor unions;
- trade associations;

- creditor and debtor groups; and
- fraternal organizations.

In years past, only groups of a certain size, such as 50 or more, were eligible for group insurance. Today, in accordance with NAIC guidelines that do not set a minimum size limit, insurers often issue coverage to groups with as few as 10 (or even fewer) members.

✔ *Take Note:* Remember that most states impose regulations on group insurance and often stipulate a minimum number of participants, usually 10, that constitute an eligible group.

It is important to note, however, that once a group policy is issued, insurers usually require that a certain number or percentage of eligible members must participate to keep the coverage in force.

 **Test Topic Alert!**   Each state sets the minimum number of members that a group must have to be eligible for group insurance.

Eligibility of Group Members

By its very nature, group insurance provides for participation by virtually all members of a given insured group. Whether or not an individual member chooses to participate usually depends on the amount of premium he or she must pay, if the plan is contributory. If the plan is noncontributory and the employer pays the entire premium, full participation is the general rule.

On the other hand, employers and insurers are allowed some latitude in setting minimum eligibility requirements for employee participants. For instance, employees must be full-time workers and actively at work to be eligible to participate in a group plan. If the plan is contributory, the employee must authorize payroll deductions for his or her share of premium payments. In addition, a probationary period may be required for new employees, which means they must wait a certain period of time (usually from one to six months) before they can enroll in the plan.

The probationary period is designed to minimize the administrative expense involved with those who remain with the employer only a short time. The probationary period is followed by the enrollment period, the time during which new employees can sign up for the group coverage. If an employee does not enroll in the plan during the enrollment period (typically 31 days), he or she may be required to provide evidence of insurability if he or she wants to enroll later. This is to protect the insurer against adverse selection.

With these basics in mind, let's turn our attention to group life insurance plans. As noted, group health plans are discussed in Lesson 23.

Group Life Insurance

Today, approximately 40 percent of life insurance in force in the United States is group life insurance and billions of dollars more are purchased every year. In fact, as far as coverage amounts go, group life insurance is the fastest growing life insurance line. According to the American Council of Life Insurance *1999 Life Insurance Fact Book*, at the end of 1998, group life insurance in force in the United States totaled more than $5.73 trillion. This represents an 8.6 percent increase in one year and is nearly twice the amount in force at the end of 1988. More and more, employees look to their group coverage to provide the foundation for their life insurance programs.

Types of Group Life Plans

There are many types of group life plans that insurers offer employers. The appropriate choice depends on the employer's objectives, needs and resources. Group life can be either term or permanent.

Group Term Life   Most group life plans are term plans, which use annual renewable term (ART) insurance as the underlying policy. This gives the insurer the right to increase the premium each year (based on the group's experience rating), and it gives the policyholder the right to renew coverage each year. As is characteristic of ART policies, coverage can be renewed without evidence of insurability.

 **Test Topic Alert!**   Most group life insurance is written as term life insurance.

 ✔ *Take Note:* The prevalent use of ART insurance is another reason for the low cost of group insurance.

Group Permanent Life   Some group life plans are permanent plans, using some form of permanent or whole life insurance as the underlying policy. The most common types of permanent group plans are *group ordinary, group paid-up* and *group universal life*.

Group ordinary insurance is any type of group life plan—and there are many variations—that uses cash value life insurance. In some cases, the employees are allowed to own the cash value portion of the policy if they contribute to the plan. In other instances, an employee's termination results in the forfeiture of the cash value, which then is used to help fund the plan for the remaining employees.

With group paid-up plans, a combination of term and whole life insurance is used. Usually the employer pays for the term portion of the plan and

FIGURE 9.1   Taxation of Group Life Premiums and Proceeds

To encourage employers to provide employee benefits—such as a group life insurance plan—the federal government has granted these plans favorable tax treatment. To begin with, an employer may deduct the group plan premiums as a business expense. Secondly, the employee does not have to report the employer-paid premiums as income, as long as the insurance coverage is $50,000 or less. (Employees who are provided with more than $50,000 of coverage must declare the premiums paid by the employer for the excess coverage as taxable income.)

Proceeds paid under a group life plan to a deceased employee's beneficiary are exempt from income taxation if they are paid in a lump sum. If the proceeds are paid in installments, consisting of principal and interest, the interest portion is taxed.

For a group life insurance plan to receive favorable tax treatment, the government imposes some requirements to ensure that rank-and-file employees are not discriminated against in favor of select key employees. Basically, these requirements apply to eligibility and the type and amount of benefits provided.

Regarding eligibility, the requirements are that:

- the plan must benefit at least 70 percent of all employees; or

- at least 85 percent of all participating employees must not be key employees.

Regarding benefits, the requirements state that, again, the plan cannot discriminate in favor of key employees. For example, the amount of life insurance provided to all employees must bear a uniform relationship to their level of compensation or position.

If a group life insurance plan fails to meet these nondiscrimination requirements, the cost of the first $50,000 of coverage—normally excluded from gross income—will be included in a key employee's gross income for tax purposes. Rank-and-file employees are not so penalized.

employee contributions are used to purchase units of single-premium whole life. The sum of the employees' paid-up insurance and the employer-paid term insurance (usually decreasing term, to offset the annually increasing amount of paid-up insurance) equals the amount of life insurance the employees are entitled to under the plan. At retirement or termination, employees possess their paid-up policies.

A growing number of group life plans use universal life insurance policies, due to the flexibility these policies provide. The underlying policy contains the same features as individual universal life, but the policy is administered in much the same way as any group ordinary policy. Characteristically, the employees pay most of the premium in group universal life plans; however, they are given certain rights to policy ownership that are not found in ordinary group life plans.

How Benefits Are Determined

The type and amount of benefits provided to each insured member under a group life plan typically are predetermined by the employer as policyholder. Most employers will establish benefit schedules according to *earnings*, according to *employment position* or as a *flat benefit*. A set schedule, such as one of these, helps protect the insurer against adverse selection, because the employees do not have the option to insure themselves for any more or any less than the schedule allows.

Earnings   Under an earnings schedule, the amount of life insurance provided to individual employees is based on their salary or earnings. It can be a flat amount per earnings level or a percentage of earnings.

✔ *For Example:* An earnings schedule could provide each employee with life insurance coverage equal to 1½ times his or her salary.

Employment Position   An employment position schedule sets the amount of life insurance according to an employee's position with the company.

✔ *For Example:* General staff employees may be provided with $30,000 of life insurance, managers with $50,000, account supervisors with $75,000 and vice presidents with $100,000.

Flat Benefit   A flat benefit schedule provides the same amount of life insurance to all employees, regardless of their earnings or position. Flat benefit schedules most frequently are used when the employer wants to provide only a small amount of insurance to its employees.

Conversion to Individual Plan

Once coverage becomes effective for an individual under a group life plan, it remains effective until he or she leaves the employer group or the plan is terminated. Most group life policies contain a conversion provision that allows individual insured members to convert to an individual plan without evidence of insurability, if their employment is terminated. Usually, the employee has a limited period of time following termination (typically 31 days) in which to exercise the conversion privilege. This means that the group coverage will continue in force for the terminated employee for the duration of the conversion period, even if no conversion takes place.

✔ *For Example:* If a group-insured ex-employee were to die within 31 days after termination of employment, the group insurance death benefit would be payable to his or her beneficiary.

Most group conversion provisions require the individual to convert to a whole life policy, as opposed to term. The premium for the new policy is based on the individual's attained age at the time of conversion.

✓ **Take Note:** There is a growing trend among employers to offer more than just a conversion privilege. Many employers now are offering portable group term life insurance. This means that employees can take (or *port*) their insurance with them. The insurance coverage remains a term life benefit with no cash value.

With portable group term life insurance, all of the ported policies are pooled together rather than remaining in the employer's plan. The rates, therefore, are more like group rates and are much lower than individually sold coverage. In contrast, most group conversion provisions require the individual to convert to a whole life policy, as opposed to term. As a result, the policy's rates will mirror individual rates and generally will be much higher.

Quick Quiz 9.1   True or False?

_____ 1. Bob and three of his friends, who all are self-employed, could form a group to be eligible for group life insurance coverage.

_____ 2. Group life plans can use either term or permanent insurance, although permanent insurance generally is used.

_____ 3. An employee generally can exclude the amount of employer-paid premiums from income, provided the group life insurance coverage is $50,000 or less.

_____ 4. If Jane's employment is terminated on May 15, she has 31 days after this date to covert her group life coverage to an individual plan without evidence of insurability.

_____ 5. XYZ Company provides $30,000 of life insurance coverage to all of its administrative assistants, $50,000 to its managers and $100,000 to its top executives. The company's benefits are based on an earnings schedule.

Answers
1. **False**. *Almost any type of natural group can be eligible for group insurance coverage. However, a group cannot be formed simply for the purpose of obtaining insurance coverage. Also, most states stipulate that there must be a minimum number of participants, usually 10, that constitute an eligible*

group. As a result, if Bob and his friends formed a group to obtain insurance coverage, they probably would not be considered an eligible group.

2. ***False****. Group life insurance plans can offer either term or permanent insurance. However, most group life plans are term plans and use annual renewable term insurance as the underlying policy.*

3. ***True****.*

4. ***True****.*

5. ***False****. XYZ Company's group life insurance benefits are based on an employment position schedule rather than an earnings schedule. An employment position schedule bases the amount of life insurance on an employee's position with the company. All similarly situated employees receive the same amount of insurance coverage (e.g., all administrative assistants would receive the same amount as would all managers, etc.).*

Other Forms of Group Life Coverage

Several other kinds of group life insurance plans exist, three of which should be noted—*franchise life insurance plans, credit life insurance plans* and *blanket life insurance plans*. In addition, as alternatives to traditional insured plans, *multiple employer trusts* and *multiple employer welfare arrangements* are becoming popular options.

Franchise Life Insurance

Franchise life insurance, sometimes called wholesale insurance, is a form of group insurance in that those covered are employees of a common employer or members of a common association or society. However, franchise insurance deviates from the typical group insurance arrangement in that the employer or association is not the master policyholder. Rather, it simply serves as the sponsor of the plan, collects premiums from its employees or members and remits them to the insurance company. (A franchise plan may provide for employer contributions.) Each individual insured under a franchise arrangement is given an individual policy. As long as he or she maintains a valid relationship with the employer or association and continues to pay the premiums, the insurance policy remains in force. Under a franchise plan, the type and amount of insurance available to individual members is determined by the sponsoring association.

Take Note: Franchise life plans commonly are used for small groups whose numbers are less than the minimum required by state law for group insurance coverage.

Group Credit Life Insurance

Group credit life insurance is another form of group insurance. A type of decreasing term insurance, it is issued by insurance companies to creditors to cover the lives of debtors in the amounts of their respective loans. Typically, it is provided through commercial banks, savings and loan associations, finance companies, credit unions and retailers.

If an insured dies before his or her loan is repaid, the policy proceeds are paid to the creditor to settle the remaining loan balance. Unlike regular group life insurance, premiums for group credit life may be paid wholly by the individual insureds. State laws, which vary, generally set a maximum amount of group credit life insurance per individual creditor (generally the creditor must have a minimum of 100 debtors per year) and limit the amount of insurance per borrower, which may not exceed the amount of indebtedness. Debtors cannot be forced to take the coverage from any particular insurance company, but have the right to choose their insurers.

Blanket Life Insurance

Blanket life insurance covers a group of people exposed to a common hazard. Individuals need not apply for blanket coverage and insurers need not provide each person with a certificate of coverage. Insureds are not named specifically in the policy because coverage is temporary. In fact, individuals may be covered for only a few hours at a time. Members of the group are covered automatically, but only while participating in the specific hazards named in the policy.

 For Example: A blanket policy can be issued to the owner of an airline to cover its passengers. A person is covered by the blanket policy only while he or she is a passenger on that airline.

State insurance laws generally allow a number of groups to hold blanket life insurance policies. Some common policyholders include the following:

- college, school or its principal, covering students, teachers or employees;
- religious, recreational or civic organization, covering its members while participating in specific hazards as part of an activity sponsored by the organization;
- employer, covering any group of employees who participate in specified hazards of employment;

- sports team, covering members while they are participating on the team;
- volunteer fire department, covering its firefighters while participating in specific hazards related to membership (such as fighting fires); and
- newspaper, covering its carriers.

✔ ***Take Note:*** Note the fundamental difference between franchise life insurance and blanket life insurance. In both types of insurance, coverage extends to a group of persons. Persons covered by franchise life insurance, however, apply for and are given individual policies. They pay premiums to the sponsor of the plan, usually an employer or association, which remits them to the insurer. In contrast, persons covered by blanket life insurance do not apply for or receive individual policies. They are covered automatically when they join the group. They remain covered only for as long as they belong to the group or participate in the specific hazards named in the policy. Coverage can be so temporary that protection lasts for only a few minutes.

Multiple Employer Trusts and Multiple Employer Welfare Arrangements

A method of marketing group benefits to employers who have a small number of employees is the multiple employer trust (MET). METs may provide either a single type of insurance (such as health insurance) or a wide range of coverages (such as, life, medical expense and disability income insurance). In some cases, alternative forms of the same coverage are available (such as comprehensive health insurance or basic health insurance).

An employer who wants to get coverage for employees from an MET first must become a member of the trust by subscribing to it. The employer is issued a joinder agreement, which spells out the relationship between the trust and the employer and specifies the coverages to which the employer has subscribed. An employer need not subscribe to all the coverages offered by an MET.

An MET may either provide benefits on a self-funded basis or fund benefits with a contract purchased from an insurance company. In the latter case, the trust, rather than the subscribing employers, is the master insurance contractholder. In either case, the employees of subscribing employers are provided with benefit description (certificates of insurance) in a manner similar to the usual group insurance agreement.

In addition to alternative methods of funding benefits, METs can be categorized according to how they are administered, that is, whether by an insurance company or a third-party administrator.

✔ ***Take Note:*** There also is another type of MET called a multiple employer welfare arrangement (MEWA). It covers union employees, is self-funded and has tax-exempt status. Employees covered under an MEWA are required by law to have an "employment related common bond."

Summary

Group insurance is a way to provide insurance coverage for a number of individuals under one master policy. It generally is purchased by an employer as a benefit for employees. Usually the employer pays all or a portion of the premium on behalf of its employees. Employer-pay-all plans are known as noncontributory plans; plans that require partial premium contributions from employees are contributory plans.

When a group plan initially is installed, all employees who meet the eligibility requirements are eligible for coverage. Individual underwriting usually is not done; instead, the insurer looks at the characteristics of the group as a whole. New employees who are hired after the plan is in effect usually are subject to a probationary period before they are allowed to enroll.

Most group life insurance plans are term plans that use annually renewable term insurance as the underlying policy. Permanent group life plans include group ordinary, group paid-up and group universal life. The amount of life insurance coverage individual employees receive is determined by the employer based on earnings, employment position or flat benefit schedule.

Other types of group plans are franchise life, group credit life, blanket life, multiple employer trusts and multiple employer welfare arrangements.

Key Concepts

In preparing for their licensing examination, students should be familiar with the following concepts:

master policy	certificate of insurance
experience rating	probationary period
enrollment period	annually renewable term
group ordinary	group paid-up
group universal life	franchise life insurance
group credit life insurance	blanket life insurance
multiple employer trusts	multiple employer welfare arrangements

Lesson Exam Nine

1. With regard to group insurance plans, which of the following statements is CORRECT?

   A. Employees generally pay for all of the premium.
   B. The sponsoring employer of a group insurance plan is given a master certificate of insurance that lists the names of all employees covered by the plan.
   C. Per unit of benefits, group insurance generally is available at rates lower than those for individual plans.
   D. Group insurance plans are a means for employers to provide a benefit for their key employees, without having to include all employees.

2. Group insurance plans that require employees to pay a portion of the premium are called

   A. underwritten
   B. contributory
   C. participatory
   D. shared

3. Which of the following statements pertaining to the conversion privilege of group term life insurance is NOT correct?

   A. An insured employee typically has 31 days following termination of employment in which to convert the group insurance.
   B. An insured employee must convert to the same type of coverage as was provided under the group plan (that is, term).
   C. Insureds who convert their coverage to individual plans pay a premium rate according to their attained age.
   D. An insured employee may exercise the conversion privilege regardless of his or her insurability.

4. Jackie has just signed up to participate in her employer's franchise life insurance program. Which of the following will she receive?

   A. Certificate of insurance
   B. Individual policy
   C. Joinder agreement
   D. Individual policy and a certificate of insurance

5. The type of insurance used in group life plans is most frequently

   A. annually renewable term
   B. ten-year renewable term
   C. limited pay whole life
   D. single-premium whole life

6. ABC Company offers a group life insurance plan to its employees. Bob and Mary, two key executives, receive $500,000 of coverage while five other employees each receive $50,000 of coverage. Fifty employees receive no coverage whatsoever. Which of the following statements is CORRECT?

   A. Bob and Mary can exclude the cost of the first $50,000 in life insurance coverage from income.
   B. If Bob dies, his beneficiary will have to include any lump sum benefits in income.
   C. ABC Company's group insurance plan will not be considered discriminatory because Bob and Mary are key executives.
   D. Bob and Mary must include the entire cost of the insurance coverage in their taxable income.

7. Which of the following statements about blanket life insurance is NOT correct?

   A. It covers a group of people exposed to a common hazard.
   B. Insureds are not specifically named in the policy because coverage is temporary.
   C. Each person covered by a blanket insurance policy receives a certificate of coverage.
   D. Schools may own blanket life insurance policies covering students, teachers and employees.

8. Which of the following statements about multiple employer trusts (METs) is NOT correct?

   A. Only an insurance company can administer an MET.
   B. METs can provide several different types of coverage, including life, medical expense and disability income insurance.
   C. Employers with a small group of employees typically use METs.
   D. Employees covered by an MET receive a certificate of insurance.

9. A group life insurance plan that uses a combination of term and whole life insurance is called a group

   A. ordinary plan
   B. universal life plan
   C. variable life plan
   D. paid-up plan

10. The type and amount of benefits provided to each employee under a group life plan may be determined by all of the following benefit schedules EXCEPT

   A. earnings
   B. employment position
   C. years of service
   D. flat benefit

Answers & Rationale

1. **C.** Group insurance is available at lower rates than individual insurance, per unit of benefits, because of the lower administrative, operational and selling expenses associated with group contracts. The cost also is lower because annually renewable term insurance typically is used as the underlying policy, rather than permanent life insurance.

2. **B.** Plans where employees pay part of the premium are called contributory. In contrast, if the employer pays all of the premium, the plan is a noncontributory plan.

3. **B.** Most group conversion provisions require the individual to convert to a whole life policy, as opposed to term.

4. **B.** Franchise life insurance differs from the typical group insurance plan in that the employer is not the master policyholder; rather, it serves as the sponsor of the plan. Each individual insured under a franchise plan is given an individual policy.

5. **A.** Most group life plans are term plans that use annually renewable term insurance as the underlying policy.

6. **D.** This is an example of a discriminatory plan. It does not benefit at least 70 percent of ABC Company's employees and only 28 percent of participating employees are key employees. The benefits also are discriminatory because there is no uniform relationship between the amount of life insurance provided and the employees' level of compensation or position. As a result, Bob and Mary must include the cost of the entire amount insurance coverage as taxable income.

7. **C.** Individuals need not apply for blanket life insurance coverage and insurers need not provide each person with a certificate of coverage. Because coverage is only temporary, insureds are not named specifically in the policy.

8. **A.** An insurance company or a third-party administrator can administer an MET.

9. **D.** A group paid-up plan uses a combination of term and whole life insurance. Typically, the employer pays for the term part of the plan while employee contributions are used to purchase single-premium whole life.

10. **C.** Employers typically establish group life insurance benefit schedules according to an employee's earnings, employment position or as a flat benefit. Benefits are not based on how long an employee has been employed by the sponsoring company.

10

Annuities

INTRODUCTION

As noted in Lesson 7, a beneficiary can choose among several different options for receiving the proceeds from a life insurance policy. One option is the life income option, which actually consists of about half a dozen choices. Beneficiaries who select this option receive an important guarantee: they can never outlive the income provided under the contract.

When a beneficiary selects a life income option, he or she actually is using the proceeds to purchase an annuity and selecting an annuity payout option. Annuities provide a way to receive a stream of income for a guaranteed period of time, a period that most typically is defined in terms of the recipient's life. In this lesson, we examine how annuities can be structured to meet a person's financial needs and also look at the different payout options available. Finally, we will examine the different ways in which annuities typically are used and how payments are taxed.

LESSON OBJECTIVES

When you complete this lesson you should be able to:

- explain how annuities can be funded and the differences between immediate and deferred annuities;
- list and explain the various annuity payout options;
- compare and contrast fixed and variable annuities;
- explain how annuity payments are taxed using the exclusion ratio; and
- identify how annuities are used by individuals, in qualified plans and in structured settlements.

Purpose and Function of Annuities

An annuity is a mathematical concept that is quite simple in its most basic definition. Start with a lump sum of money, pay it out in equal installments over a period of time until the original fund is exhausted and you have an annuity. An annuity simply is a vehicle for liquidating a sum of money. Of course, in practice the concept is more complex. An important factor not mentioned above is interest. The sum of money that has not yet been paid out is earning interest, and that interest also is passed on to the income recipient, or the *annuitant*.

Anyone can provide an annuity. By knowing the original sum of money (the principal), the length of the payout period and an assumed rate of interest, it is a fairly simple process to calculate the payment amount. Actuaries have constructed tables of annuity factors that make this process even easier.

✔ **For Example:** The present value interest factor for a $1 annuity (a formal name for one of the aforementioned tables; see Figure 10.1) shows that the factor for a 20-year annual payment of $1, based on a 7 percent interest factor, is 10.59. This means that if a person set aside $10.59, and could earn 7 percent interest while the fund was being depleted, an annual income of $1 could be paid for 20 years. The income recipient would receive a total of $20 for the original $10.59 invested in the annuity.

Other tables solve for related problems (for example, how long income can be paid for any given amount of principal). The basic underlying principle, however, is the same in every case—the amount of an annuity payment depends on three factors: starting principal, interest and income period.

One important element is absent from this simple definition of an annuity, and it is the one distinguishing factor that separates life insurance companies from all other financial institutions. While anyone can set up an annuity and pay income for a stated period of time, only life insurance companies can do so and guarantee income for the life of the annuitant.

Because of their experience with mortality tables, life insurance companies are uniquely qualified to combine an extra factor into the standard annuity calculation. Called a *survivorship factor*, it is, in concept, very similar to the mortality factor in a life insurance premium calculation. Thus, it provides insurers with the means to guarantee annuity payments for life, regardless of how long that life lasts.

FIGURE 10.1   Present Value of $1 Payable

The following is a present value annuity table that shows the amount which, if deposited today at 7 percent interest, would produce an annual income of $1 for the specified number of years. In other words, this table reflects the value today of a series of payments tomorrow. For example, the present value of $1 payable for 25 years, at 7 percent interest, is $11.65. This means that $11.65 deposited today at 7 percent interest would generate a payment of $1 for 25 years.

Years	Present Value (at 7 percent)	Years	Present Value (at 7 percent)
5	$4.10	30	$12.40
10	$7.02	35	$12.94
15	$9.10	40	$13.33
20	$10.59	45	$13.60
25	$11.65	50	$13.80

In more practical terms, suppose you wanted to know how much money you should have on hand at age 65 to generate $5,000 a year in income for 10 years, assuming you could earn 7 percent interest while the fund was being paid out. The present value of $1 payable for 10 years is $7.02; therefore, the present value of $10,000 payable for 10 years is $70,200 ($10,000 × $7.02).

Annuities vs. Life Insurance

It is important to realize that annuities are not life insurance contracts. In fact, it can be said that an annuity is a mirror image of a life insurance contract—they look alike but actually are exact opposites.

 **Test Topic Alert!**

Whereas the principal function of a life insurance contract is to create an estate (an estate being a sum of money) by the periodic payment of money into the contract, an annuity's principal function is to liquidate an estate by the periodic payment of money out of the contract.

Life insurance is concerned with how soon one will die; life annuities are concerned with how long one will live.

It is easy to see the value of annuities in fulfilling some important financial protection needs. Their role in retirement planning should be obvious; guaranteeing that an annuitant cannot outlive the payments from a life annuity has brought peace of mind to countless people over the years. Annuities can play a vital role in any situation where a stream of income is needed for only a few years or for a lifetime.

Annuity Basics

An annuity is a cash contract with an insurance company. Unlike life insurance products, where policy issue and pricing are based largely on mortality risk, annuities primarily are investment products. Individuals purchase or fund annuities with a single sum amount or through a series of periodic payments. The insurer credits the annuity fund with a certain rate of interest, which currently is not taxable to the annuitant. In this way, the annuity grows. The ultimate amount that will be available for payout is, in part, a reflection of these factors. Most annuities guarantee a death benefit payable in the event the annuitant dies before payout begins; however, it usually is limited to the amount paid into the contract plus interest credited.

With any annuity, there are two distinct time periods involved: the accumulation period and the payout or annuity period. The accumulation period is that time during which funds are being paid into the annuity in the form of payments by the contractholder and interest earnings credited by the insurer. The payout or annuity period refers to the point at which the annuity ceases to be an accumulation vehicle and begins to generate benefit payments on a regular basis.

✓ **Take Note:** Typically, benefits are paid out monthly, though a quarterly, semiannual or annual payment arrangement can be structured.

Structure and Design of Annuities

Annuities are flexible in that the purchaser has a number of options that enable him or her to structure and design the product to best suit his or her needs:

- *Funding method*—Single lump-sum payment or periodic payments over time.
- *Date annuity benefit payments begin*—Immediately or deferred until a future date.
- *Investment configuration*—A fixed (guaranteed) rate of return or a variable (nonguaranteed) rate of return.
- *Payout period*—A specified term of years or for life, or a combination of both.

Let's take a closer look at each of these options. (They are illustrated in graphic form in Figure 10.2.)

FIGURE 10.2 Annuities Classification Chart

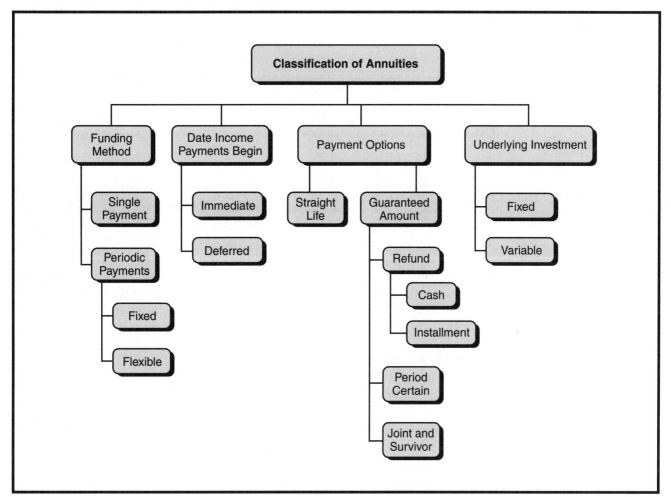

Funding Method An annuity begins with a sum of money, called the principal. Annuity principal is created (or funded) in one of two ways: immediately with a single premium or over time with a series of periodic premiums.

Single Premium Annuities can be funded with a single, lump-sum premium, in which case the principal is created immediately.

> ✓ **For Example:** An individual nearing retirement whose financial priority is retirement income could surrender his or her whole life policy and use the cash value as a lump-sum premium to fund an annuity.

Periodic Payments Annuities also can be funded through a series of periodic premiums that, over time, will create the annuity principal fund. At one time, it was common for insurers to require that periodic annuity premiums be fixed and level, much like insurance premiums.

FIGURE 10.3   Types of Annuities

FPDA	Flexible-premium deferred annuity
SPIA	Single-premium immediate annuity
SPDA	Single-premium deferred annuity
TSA	Tax-sheltered annuity

The purpose of this type of funding is to create a certain amount of periodic annuity income. In other words, the contract defines the premium required to generate a specified amount for a specified period of time upon contract maturity.

Today, it is more common to allow annuity owners to make flexible premium payments. An annuity might require a certain minimum initial premium but then will allow the contractholder to add deposits as often as he or she wishes.

 For Example: An annuity contract may require an initial deposit of $1,000 or $2,500 but then will allow the owner to make additional premium payments of as little as $25, whenever and as often as desired.

With flexible premium annuities, the ultimate accumulation amount cannot be defined. Therefore, these contracts specify the benefit per $1,000 of accumulated value. For instance, a contract might specify that it will provide for guaranteed lifetime monthly payments of $5.06 per $1,000 at the annuitant's age 65. This means that a contract that has grown to $100,000 on the annuitant's age 65 would generate $506 per month for his or her life.

 Test Topic Alert!   Flexible premium annuities can only be deferred.

Date Annuity Income Payments Begin

Annuities can be classified by the date the income payments to the annuitant begin. Depending on the contract, annuity payments can begin immediately or they can be deferred to a future date.

Immediate Annuities   An immediate annuity is designed to make its first benefit payment to the annuitant at one payment interval from the date of purchase. Because most annuities make monthly payments, an immediate annuity typically would pay its first payment one month from the purchase date. Thus, an immediate annuity has a relatively short accumulation period.

As you might guess, immediate annuities can only be funded with a single payment and often are called single-premium immediate annuities, or SPIAs. An annuity cannot accept periodic funding payments and pay out income to the annuitant simultaneously.

✓ **Take Note:** The income flow from immediate annuities can be either fixed or variable. Under a fixed immediate annuity, the annuitant is guaranteed an income flow without risk of market fluctuations affecting the amount of the income. The insurance company absorbs the market risk associated with the investment of the annuity funds. In contrast, a variable immediate annuity transfers the investment risk to the annuitant. This means that once an income stream is created the payments can increase or decrease depending on the performance of the underlying investments.

Deferred Annuities

Deferred annuities provide income payments at some specified future date. Unlike immediate annuities, deferred annuities can be funded with periodic payments over time. Periodic payment annuities commonly are called flexible premium deferred annuities, or FPDAs. Deferred annuities also can be funded with single premiums, in which case they are called single-premium deferred annuities, or tax-sheltered annuities (TSAs).

Most insurers charge contractholders for liquidating deferred annuities in the early years of the contract. These surrender charges cover the costs associated with selling and issuing contracts as well as costs associated with the insurer's need to liquidate underlying investments at a possibly inappropriate time.

✓ **Take Note:** Surrender charges for most annuities are of limited duration, applying only during the first five to eight years of the contract. However, for those years in which surrender charges are applicable, most annuities provide for an annual free withdrawal, which allows the annuity owner to withdraw up to a certain percentage, usually 10 percent, of his or her annuity account with no surrender charge applied.

Insurance companies impose restrictions on how far into the future income benefit payments may be deferred. Typically, deferred annuities must be annuitized (that is, converted from the accumulation mode to an income-paying mode) before the annuity owner reaches a maximum age, such as 75 years.

Annuity Payout Options

Just as life insurance beneficiaries have various settlement options for the disposition of policy proceeds, so too do annuitants have various income payout options to specify how an annuity fund is to be paid out. In fact, as noted in Lesson 7, selecting any of the life income options as a life insurance settlement (see the section titled *Life Income Options* in Lesson 7) is the same

FIGURE 10.4 Life Income Option

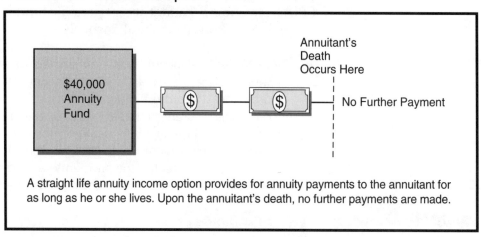

A straight life annuity income option provides for annuity payments to the annuitant for as long as he or she lives. Upon the annuitant's death, no further payments are made.

as using the policy proceeds to purchase a single-premium immediate annuity and selecting an annuity income option.

A number of annuity income options are available: *straight life income, cash refund, installment refund, life with period certain, joint and survivor* and *period certain.*

Straight Life Income Option

A straight life income annuity option (often called a life annuity or a straight life annuity) pays the annuitant a guaranteed income for his or her lifetime. When the annuitant dies, no further payments are made to anyone. If the annuitant dies before the annuity fund (the principal) is depleted, the balance, in effect, is forfeited to the insurer. It is used to provide payments to other annuitants who live beyond the point where the income they receive equals their annuity principal. (See Figure 10.4.)

 **Test Topic Alert!**

The straight life income annuity pays the most income per month, in comparison with the other annuity payout options.

Cash Refund Option

A cash refund option provides a guaranteed income to the annuitant for life and, if the annuitant dies before the annuity fund (the principal) is depleted, a lump-sum cash payment of the remainder is made to the annuitant's beneficiary. Thus, the beneficiary receives an amount equal to the beginning annuity fund less the amount of income already paid to the deceased annuitant. (See Figure 10.5.)

Installment Refund Option

Like the cash refund, the installment refund option guarantees that the total annuity fund will be paid to the annuitant or to his or her beneficiary. The difference is that under the installment option, the fund remaining at the annuitant's death is paid to the beneficiary in the form of continued annuity payments, not as a single lump sum. (See Figure 10.6.)

FIGURE 10.5 Cash Refund Option

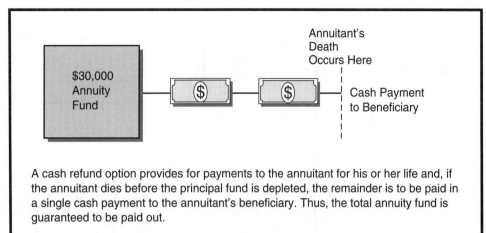

A cash refund option provides for payments to the annuitant for his or her life and, if the annuitant dies before the principal fund is depleted, the remainder is to be paid in a single cash payment to the annuitant's beneficiary. Thus, the total annuity fund is guaranteed to be paid out.

✓ **Take Note:** Under either the cash refund or installment refund option, if the annuitant lives to receive payments equal to the principal amount, no future payments will be made to a beneficiary.

Life with Period Certain Option

Also known as the life income with term certain option, this payout approach is designed to pay the annuitant an income for life but guarantees a definite minimum period of payments. (See Figure 10.7.)

✓ **For Example:** If an individual has a life and 10-year certain annuity, he or she is guaranteed payments for life or 10 years, whichever is longer. If the individual receives monthly payments for six years and then dies, his or her beneficiary will receive the same payments for four more years. Of course, if the annuitant died after receiving monthly annuity payments for 10 or more years, his or her beneficiary would receive nothing from the annuity.

FIGURE 10.6 Installment Refund Option

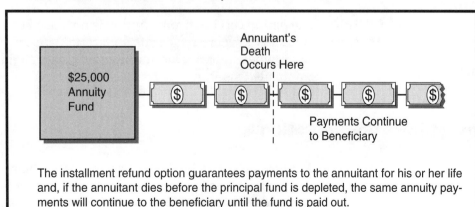

The installment refund option guarantees payments to the annuitant for his or her life and, if the annuitant dies before the principal fund is depleted, the same annuity payments will continue to the beneficiary until the fund is paid out.

FIGURE 10.7   Life with Period Certain Option

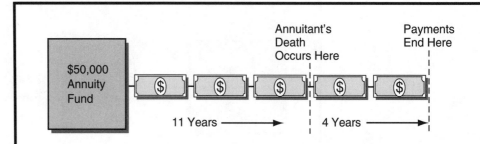

The life with period certain annuity option provides income to the annuitant for life but guarantees a minimum period of payments. Thus, if the annuitant dies during the specified period, benefit payments continue to the beneficiary for the remainder of the period. For example, if an individual has a 15-year life with period certain annuity, receives monthly benefit payments for 11 years and then dies, his or her beneficiary will receive the same payments for the remainder of the period certain, or four years.

Joint and Full Survivor Option

The joint and full survivor option provides for payment of the annuity to two people. If either person dies, the same income payments continue to the survivor for life. When the surviving annuitant dies, no further payments are made to anyone. (See Figure 10.8.)

There are other joint arrangements offered by many companies.

Joint and Two-Thirds Survivor

This is the same as the above arrangement, except that the survivor's income is reduced to two-thirds of the original joint income.

Joint and One-Half Survivor

This is the same as the above arrangement, except that the survivor's income is reduced to one-half of the original joint income.

Period Certain Option

The period certain income option is not based on life contingency. Instead, it guarantees benefit payments for a certain period of time, such as 10, 15 or 20 years, whether or not the annuitant is living. At the end of the specified term, payments cease.

Investment Configuration

Annuities also can be defined according to their investment configuration, which affects the income benefits they pay. The two classifications are fixed annuities, which provide a fixed, guaranteed accumulation or payout, and variable annuities, which attempt to offset inflation by providing a benefit

FIGURE 10.8   Joint and Survivor Option

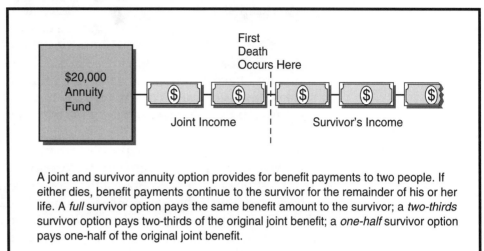

A joint and survivor annuity option provides for benefit payments to two people. If either dies, benefit payments continue to the survivor for the remainder of his or her life. A *full* survivor option pays the same benefit amount to the survivor; a *two-thirds* survivor option pays two-thirds of the original joint benefit; a *one-half* survivor option pays one-half of the original joint benefit.

linked to a variable underlying investment account. Equity indexed annuities, a type of fixed annuity, are fairly new but have become quite popular.

Fixed Annuities   Fixed annuities provide a guaranteed rate of return. During the period in which the annuitant is making payments to fund the annuity (the accumulation period), the insurer invests these payments in conservative, long-term securities (typically bonds). This, in turn, allows the insurer to credit a steady interest rate to the annuity contract. The interest rate payable for any given year is declared in advance by the insurer and is guaranteed to be no less than a minimum specified in the contract.

✔ **Take Note:** A fixed annuity typically has two interest rates: a minimum guaranteed rate and a current rate. The current rate is what the insurer credits to the annuity on a regular schedule (typically each year); the current rate never will be lower than the minimum rate, which the insurer guarantees. In this way, the accumulation of funds in a fixed annuity is certain and the contract-owner's principal is secure.

When converted to a payout mode, fixed annuities provide a guaranteed fixed benefit amount to the annuitant, typically stated in terms of dollars per $1,000 of accumulated values (such as $7 for each $1,000 of accumulated value). This is possible because the interest rate payable on the annuity funds is fixed and guaranteed at the point of annuitization. The amount and duration of benefit payments are guaranteed. Because they provide a specified benefit, payable for life (or any other period the annuitant desires), fixed annuities can offer security and financial peace of mind. On the other hand, because the benefit amount is fixed, annuitants may see the purchasing power of their payments decline over the years, due to inflation. Many annuitants prefer a variable annuity.

Equity Indexed Annuities

The equity indexed annuity is another type of annuity product that bears mention. These annuities have most of the features of fixed annuity contracts, except that the interest credited to the annuity owner's account is tied to a stock market related (equity) index, such as the Standard & Poor's 500 Index. However, unlike variable annuities, an equity indexed annuity cannot decrease in value. Besides having a fixed minimum guarantee (somewhat similar to a fixed annuity), the value of an annuity owner's account can only increase because of stock market appreciation. If the market is flat or declining, the account value will not decrease in value.

Variable Annuities

In the early 1950s, a group of people representing a teacher's association reviewed the annuity principle that was the foundation of their pension plan. The question of protection against inflation arose; it was noted that someone who retired with a given amount of income (say, $200 per month) would find that after a decade or so of inflation, the real purchasing power of that income would diminish. Attention then turned to solving the problem, and the birth of the variable annuity was the solution.

In Lesson 4, we discussed variable life insurance. The same underlying principles of variable life insurance apply to variable annuities. As is true with variable life, variable annuities shift the investment risk from the insurer to the contract owner. If the investments supporting the contract perform well (as in a bull market), the owner probably will realize investment growth that exceeds what is possible in a fixed annuity. However, the lack of investment guarantees means that the variable annuity owner can see the value of his or her annuity decrease in a depressed market or in an economic recession.

Variable annuities invest deferred annuity payments in an insurer's separate accounts, as opposed to an insurer's general accounts, which allow the insurer to guarantee interest in a fixed annuity. Because variable annuities are based on non-guaranteed equity investments, such as common stock, a sales representative who wants to sell such contracts must be registered with the National Association of Securities Dealers (NASD) and also hold a state insurance license.

Not only can the value of a variable annuity fluctuate in response to movements in the market, so too will the amount of annuity income fluctuate, even after the contract has annuitized. It was for that reason the product was developed in the first place. In spite of inevitable dips in the amount of benefit income, the theory is that the general trend will be an increasing amount of income over time as inflation pushes up the price of stocks—a theory that generally has held true.

To accommodate the variable concept, a new means of accounting for both annuity payments and annuity income was required. The result is the accumulation unit (which pertains to the accumulation period) and the annuity unit (which pertains to the income payout period).

Accumulation Units In a variable annuity, during the accumulation period, contributions made by the annuitant, less a deduction for expenses, are converted to accumulation units and credited to the individual's account. The value of each accumulation unit varies, depending on the value of the underlying stock investment.

> ✓ **For Example:** Assume that the accumulation unit initially is valued at $10, and the holder of a variable annuity makes a payment of $200. This means she has purchased 20 accumulation units. Six months later, she makes another payment of $200, but during that time, the underlying stocks have declined and the value of the accumulation unit is $8. This means that the $200 payment now will purchase 25 accumulation units.

The value of one accumulation unit is found by dividing the total value of the company's separate account by the total number of accumulation units outstanding.

> ✓ **For Example:** If a company had $20 million in its separate account and a total of 4 million accumulation units outstanding, the value of one accumulation unit would be $5.

As the value of the account rises and falls, the value of each accumulation unit rises and falls.

Annuity Units At the time the variable annuity benefits are to be paid out to the annuitant, the accumulation units in the participant's individual account are converted into annuity units. At the time of initial payout, the annuity unit calculation is made and, from then on, the number of annuity units remains the same for that annuitant. The value of one annuity unit, however, can and does vary from month to month, depending on investment results.

> ✓ **For Example:** An annuitant has 1,000 accumulation units in her account by the time she is ready to retire and these units have been converted into 10 annuity units. She always will be credited with 10 annuity units—that number does not change. What does change is the value of the annuity units, in accordance with the underlying stock. Assume when she retired, each annuity unit was valued at $40. That means her initial benefit payment is $400 (10 × $40). As long as the value of the annuity unit is $40, her monthly payments will be $400. But what if the value of the stock goes up and her annuity unit value becomes $45? Her next monthly payment will be $450 (10 × $45).

The theory has been that the payout from a variable annuity over a period of years will keep pace with the cost of living and thus maintain the annuitant's purchasing power at or above a constant level. As with fixed annuities, the variable annuity owner has various payout options from which to choose. These options usually include the life annuity, life annuity with period certain, unit refund annuity (similar to a cash refund annuity) and a joint and survivor annuity.

Retirement Income Annuities

While all annuities are well suited to provide retirement income, one annuity is designed especially for retirement planning uses. Called the retirement income annuity, this plan basically is a deferred annuity policy to which a decreasing term life insurance rider is added.

If the policyowner reaches retirement age (usually age 65), the term insurance expires and the deferred annuity is used to provide retirement income under standard annuity principles. The unique feature of this plan is the death protection it provides. If the insured dies before retirement, the combination of the deferred annuity values and the term insurance benefits are paid to the beneficiary. The beneficiary may use the combined benefits to select any settlement option.

Quick Quiz 10.1 Match the following annuity payout options with the appropriate example below.

A. Installment refund option
B. Straight life income option
C. Cash refund option
D. Period certain option
E. Life with period certain option

_____ 1. At Bob's death, the remaining annuity funds will be paid to his wife in the form of continued annuity payments, but not as a lump sum.

_____ 2 Jane receives a guaranteed income from her annuity for life. At her death, no further payments are made.

_____ 3. John's annuity is designed to pay him an income for life, but guarantees payments for 10 years.

_____ 4. Fran's annuity guarantees benefits for 20 years whether or not she is living.

_____ 5. Ted's annuity provides a guaranteed income for life. If he dies before the annuity fund is depleted, a lump-sum cash payment of the remainder will be made to his beneficiary.

Answers   1. *A*   2. *B*   3. *E*   4. *D*   5. *C*

Income Taxation of Annuity Benefits

Annuity benefit payments are a combination of principal and interest. Accordingly, they are taxed in a manner consistent with other types of income: the portion of the benefit payments that represents a return of principal (i.e., the contributions made by the annuitant) are not taxed. However, the portion representing interest earned on the declining principal is taxed. The result, over the benefit payment period, is a tax-free return of the annuitant's investment and the taxing of the balance.

Though a detailed discussion of how to compute the taxable portion of an annuity payment is beyond the scope of this text, the basics are not difficult to understand. An exclusion ratio is applied to each benefit payment the annuitant receives:

$$\frac{\text{Investment in the contract}}{\text{Expected return}} = \text{Exclusion ratio}$$

The investment in the contract is the amount of money paid into the annuity; the expected return is the annual guaranteed benefit the annuitant receives, multiplied by the number of years of his or her life expectancy. The resulting ratio is applied to the benefit payments, allowing the annuitant to exclude a like percentage from income.

✓ **For Example:** Joan purchased an annuity for $10,800. Under its terms, the annuity will pay her $100 a month for life. If Joan is age 65, her life expectancy, as taken from the applicable tables, is 20 years. Her expected return is $24,000 ([20 × 12] × $100). Her cost ($10,800) divided by her expected return of $24,000 equals 45 percent. This is the percentage of each annuity payment that she will not have to include in income. Each year until Joan's net cost is recovered, she will receive $540 (45 percent of $1,200) tax-free. She must include $660 ($1,200 − $540) in her income.

Deferred annuities accumulate interest earnings on a tax-deferred basis. While no taxes are imposed on the annuity during the accumulation phase, taxes are imposed when the contract begins to pay its benefits (in accordance with the exclusion ratio just described). To discourage the use of deferred annuities as short-term investments, the Internal Revenue Code imposes a penalty (as well as taxes) on early withdrawals (and loans) from annuities. Partial withdrawals are treated first as earnings income (and are thus taxable as ordinary income); only after all earnings have been taxed are withdrawals considered a return of principal.

✓ **Take Note:** A 10 percent penalty tax is imposed on withdrawals from a deferred annuity before age 59½. Withdrawals after age 59½ are not subject to the 10 percent penalty tax, but still are taxable as ordinary income.

1035 Contract Exchanges

As discussed in Lesson 7, Section 1035 of the Internal Revenue Code provides for tax-free exchanges of certain kinds of financial products, including annuity contracts. Recall that no gain will be recognized (meaning no gain will be taxed) if an annuity contract is exchanged for another annuity contract or if a life insurance or endowment policy is exchanged for an annuity contract.

✓ **Take Note:** An annuity contract cannot be exchanged tax-free for a life insurance contract. This is not an acceptable exchange under Section 1035.

Uses of Annuities

Annuities have a variety of uses. They are suited to a variety of circumstances that require a large sum of money to be converted into a series of payments over a set time, particularly a lifetime. Now let's look at some of the common uses of annuities.

Individual Uses

The principal use of an annuity is to provide income for retirement. The advantage of the structured, guaranteed life income provided by annuities for retirement purposes is obvious and is one of the primary reasons the annuity is so popular. Many individuals, especially those in retirement, may be reluctant to use the principal of their savings, fearing it may become depleted. However, if they choose to conserve the principal, they run the risk of never deriving any benefit from it at all—and ultimately are obliged to pass it on to others at their deaths. An annuity is designed to liquidate principal—but in a structured, systematic way that guarantees it will last a lifetime.

Besides being able to guarantee a lifetime income, annuities make excellent retirement products because they are conservative in nature, reliable and flexible enough to meet nearly all needs. As accumulation vehicles, they offer safety of principal, tax deferral, diversification, competitive yields (enhanced by tax deferral) and liquidity. As distribution vehicles, they offer a variety of payout options, which can be structured to conform to certain payment amounts or certain payment periods. They can cover one life or two. They can be arranged so that a beneficiary will receive a benefit if the annuitant dies before receiving the full annuity principal.

✓ **Take Note:** While annuities are designed to create and accumulate income for retirement, they can be used for other purposes as well. For instance, they can be used to create and accumulate funds for a college education. Annuities serve a variety of purposes for which a stream of income is needed for a few years or a lifetime.

Qualified Annuity Plans

A qualified plan is a tax-deferred arrangement established by an employer to provide retirement benefits for employees. The plan is qualified by reason of having met government requirements. A qualified annuity is an annuity purchased as part of a tax-qualified individual or employer-sponsored retirement plan, such as an individual retirement account (IRA), which will be discussed in Lesson 12, a tax-sheltered annuity (TSA) or other IRS-recognized plans.

A TSA is a special type of annuity plan reserved for nonprofit organizations and their employees. It also is known as a 403(b) plan or a 501(c)(3) plan, because it was made possible by those sections of the Internal Revenue Code. For many years, the federal government, through its tax laws, has encouraged specified nonprofit charitable, educational and religious organizations to set aside funds for their employees' retirement. Regardless of whether the money actually is set aside by the employers for the employees of such organizations or the funds are contributed by the employees through a reduction in salary, such funds may be placed in TSAs and are excludable from the employees' current taxable income.

Upon retirement, payments received by employees from the accumulated savings in tax-sheltered annuities are treated as reportable income. However, as the total annual income of the employees likely is less after retirement, the tax to be paid by such retirees likely is less than while they were working. Furthermore, the benefits can be spread out over a specified period of time or over the remaining lifetime of the employee so that the amount of tax owed on the benefits in any one year generally will be small.

✓ **Take Note:** In addition to TSAs and IRAs, annuities are an acceptable funding mechanism for other qualified plans, including pensions and 401(k) plans.

Structured Settlements

Annuities also are used to distribute funds from the settlement of lawsuits or the winnings of lotteries and other contests. Such arrangements are called structured settlements.

Court settlements of lawsuits often require the payment of large sums of money throughout the rest of the injured party's life. Annuities are perfect vehicles for these settlements because they can be tailored to meet the needs of the claimant. Annuities also are suited for distributing the large awards people win in state lotteries. These awards usually are paid out over a period of 10 or 20 years. Because of the extended payout period, the state can advertise large awards and then provide for the distribution of the award by purchasing a structured settlement from an insurance company at a discount. The state can get the discounted price because a $1 million award distributed over a 20-year period is not worth $1 million today. Trends indicate that significant growth can be expected from both these markets for annuities.

Summary

Annuities are suited ideally for providing peace of mind to anyone who is concerned about receiving income for life. The exact opposite of the life insurance concept, annuities start with a large fund and reduce it through a series of payments. Life insurance companies are the only financial institutions that can guarantee annuity payments will be made to the annuitant for life. Like beneficiaries of life insurance policies, annuitants have a variety of payout options as to how they can receive their annuity benefit payments.

While many annuitants find comfort in the guarantees of a traditional fixed annuity, many others prefer the potential investment gains possible with equity indexed annuities or variable annuities. Because variable annuities are recognized by the Securities and Exchange Commission as an investment, people who want to sell them must be licensed by and registered with the NASD. All states also require salespeople to hold a valid life insurance license to sell any type of annuity.

Key Concepts

In preparing for their licensing examination, students should be familiar with the following concepts:

single-premium annuities	periodic payment annuities
immediate and deferred annuities	fixed and variable annuities
annuity payout options	taxation of annuities
tax-sheltered annuities	exclusion ratio
equity indexed annuities	

Lesson Exam Ten

1. Which of the following statements regarding annuities are is NOT correct?

   A. Generally, annuity contracts issued today require fixed, level funding payments.
   B. Annuities are sold by life insurance agents.
   C. An annuity is a periodic payment.
   D. Annuitants can pay the annuity premiums in lump sums.

2. What annuity payout option provides for lifetime payments to the annuitant but guarantees a certain minimum term of payments, whether or not the annuitant is living?

   A. Installment refund option
   B. Life with period certain
   C. Joint and survivor
   D. Straight life income

3. Which of the following statements regarding annuity payout options is NOT correct?

   A. Under a straight life annuity option, all annuity payments stop when the annuitant dies.
   B. In a cash refund annuity, upon the annuitant's death, the beneficiary always receives an amount equal to the beginning annuity fund.
   C. A period certain annuity guarantees a definite number of payments.
   D. Joint and survivor annuities guarantee payments for the duration of two lives.

4. James died after receiving $180 monthly for six years from a $25,000 installment refund annuity. His wife, Lucy, as beneficiary, now will receive the same monthly income until her payments total

   A. $2,160
   B. $12,040
   C. $12,960
   D. $25,000

5. Annuity payments are taxable to the extent that they represent interest earned rather than capital returned. What method is used to determine the taxable portion of each payment?

   A. Exclusion ratio
   B. Marginal tax formula
   C. Surtax ratio
   D. Annuitization ratio

6. Before he died, Gary received a total of $9,200 in monthly income payments from his $15,000 straight life annuity. He also was the insured under a $25,000 life insurance policy that named his wife, Darlene, as primary beneficiary. Considering the two contracts, Darlene would receive death benefits totaling

   A. $15,000
   B. $25,000
   C. $30,800
   D. $40,000

7. When a cash value life insurance policy is converted into an annuity in a nontaxable transaction, that event generally is known as a

   A. rollover
   B. 1035 exchange
   C. modified endowment
   D. pension enhancement

8. Joanna and her husband, Tom, have a $40,000 annuity that pays them $200 a month. Tom dies and Joanna continues receiving the $200 monthly check as long as she lives. When Joanna dies, the company ceases payment. This is an example of what kind of annuity?

   A. Installment refund
   B. Joint and full survivor
   C. Life
   D. Cash refund

9. Which kind of the following statements about variable annuities is NOT correct?

   A. Individuals selling variable annuities must be registered with the NASD.
   B. The contract owner, rather than the insurer, bears the investment risk.
   C. Once a variable annuity contract has been annuitized, the amount of annuity income will not fluctuate.
   D. During the accumulation period, the annuitant's contributions are converted to accumulation units and credited to his or her account.

10. Which of the following statements about annuities is CORRECT?

    A. Most annuities do not guarantee a death benefit if the annuitant dies before payout begins.
    B. Deferred annuities are used primarily to accumulate funds for retirement.
    C. Immediate annuities can be funded with payments made over an extended period of time.
    D. The amount of an individual's annuity payments depends on how much principal was invested, the amount of interest earned and the income period selected.

Answers & Rationale

1. **A.** Years ago, insurers typically required that annuity premiums be fixed and level. Today, annuitants have much more flexibility as to when and how much they pay into their annuity contracts.

2. **B.** The life with period certain payout option pays the annuitant an income for life and guarantees a definite minimum period of payments regardless of whether the annuitant is living.

3. **B.** In a cash refund option, the annuitant receives a guaranteed income for life, and, if he or she dies before the principal is depleted, the annuitant's beneficiary will receive a lump-sum cash payment of the remainder. The beneficiary will receive an amount equal to the beginning annuity fund less the amount of income that already has been paid to the annuitant.

4. **B.** Under an installment refund option, the total annuity fund is paid to the annuitant or to his or her beneficiary. If James received $180 a month for six years before he died, he would have received a total of $12,960 ([$180 × 12] × 6). As beneficiary, his wife will receive the remaining balance of the annuity ($25,000 − $12,960 = $12,040) in monthly annuity payments.

5. **A.** The taxable portion of each annuity payment is determined by using the exclusion ratio. This ratio is determined by dividing the investment in the contract (the amount of money paid into the annuity) by the expected return.

6. **B.** Under Gary's straight life annuity, he will receive a guaranteed income only during his lifetime. At his death, no further payments are made to anyone. Darlene therefore will receive only $25,000, the proceeds paid to her as beneficiary of his life insurance policy.

7. **B.** A life insurance policy can be exchanged for an annuity in a nontaxable transaction known as a 1035 exchange.

8. **B.** Joanna and Tom have a joint and full survivor annuity. The joint and full survivor option provides for payment of an annuity to two people. At either person's death, the same income payments continue to the survivor for life. When the surviving annuitant dies, no further payments are made.

9. **C.** Even after a variable annuity contract has been annuitized, the amount of annuity income will fluctuate. This is because the value of one annuity unit can and will vary from month to month, depending on investment results.

10. **D.** The amount of an individual's annuity payment will depend on how much money was invested, the length of the payout period and the rate of interest earned. The more invested and the shorter the period of distribution, the larger the payout.

11

Social Security

INTRODUCTION   The challenge of accumulating funds for retirement and protecting a person's family from the financial loss that often accompanies death, disability or old age has been made a little easier thanks to the federal Social Security program. In this lesson, we will examine how this program works and see who it covers, how benefits are determined and the different benefits that are available.

LESSON OBJECTIVES   When you complete this lesson you should be able to:

- describe Social Security eligibility and coverage requirements;
- explain how Social Security benefits are funded and calculated;
- list and describe the various types of survivor, retirement and disability benefits; and
- explain how Social Security benefits are taxed.

Purpose of Social Security

Much confusion and misunderstanding surrounds the Social Security program and role in our society. This misunderstanding has led to unrealistic expectations of Social Security benefits and what they mean to an individual's overall financial plan. Life insurance producers have the important duty of making sure their clients understand the true function of Social Security and recognize the purpose for which it was designed.

The Social Security system was enacted in 1935—in the throes of the Great Depression—for one purpose: to provide basic protection for all working

Americans against the financial problems brought on by death, disability and aging. That remains the primary objective of Social Security. Its purpose always has been to augment—not replace—a sound personal insurance plan. Unfortunately, too many Americans have come to expect Social Security to fulfill all their financial needs. The consequence of this misunderstanding has been the disillusionment of many Americans who found, often too late, that they were covered inadequately when they needed life insurance, disability income or retirement income.

The Social Security program, administered at the federal level by the Social Security Administration, more formally is called OASDI. This acronym aptly identifies the types of protection provided under the program: Old Age (retirement), Survivors (death benefits) and Disability Insurance*. Social Security is an entitlement program, not a welfare program; Americans are entitled to participate in the program's benefits, provided they meet basic eligibility requirements. With few exceptions, most gainfully employed people are covered by Social Security and are, or will be, eligible for the program's benefits. It is estimated that over 45 million Americans currently are receiving benefits under the system.

Social Security Coverage

With only a few exceptions, Social Security extends coverage to virtually every American who is employed or self-employed. Those not covered include:

- most federal employees hired before 1984 who are covered by Civil Service Retirement or another similar pension plan;
- approximately 25 percent of state and local government employees who are covered by a state pension program and have elected not to participate in the Social Security program (each state and local government unit decides for itself whether or not to participate); and
- railroad workers who are covered under a separate federal program, the Railroad Retirement System.

It is easy to see that Social Security is quite broad in its reach, excluding only a small fraction of the working population. In addition to covering workers, Social Security provides for spouses, dependent children and, in some cases, dependent parents of covered workers.

---

*Social Security also provides health insurance (HI) through its Medicare program.

✓ *Take Note:* A basic condition for coverage is index FICA tax instead that a person must work. OASDI is funded by a payroll tax (called the FICA tax after the Federal Income Contribution Act that established it) and eligibility for benefits is contingent upon a person contributing to the system during his or her working years.

Coverage vs. Eligibility

There is a significant difference between being covered by Social Security and being eligible for Social Security benefits. Being covered means that a worker is actively participating in the program actively through FICA tax contributions, but he or she may or may not be eligible for benefits. Eligibility for benefits is based on a person's insured status, which can be described either as fully insured or currently insured. Being fully insured entitles a worker and his or her family to full retirement and survivor (that is, death) benefits. A currently insured status qualifies a worker for a limited range of survivor benefits.

Quarters of Coverage

One's insured status—currently or fully—is based on his or her accrued credits. A credit is earned for each $830 of annual earnings on which FICA taxes are paid. (This $830 was the amount in 2001; it is adjusted frequently and almost certainly will increase.) Up to four credits can be earned in any one year.

✓ *For Example:* A worker who earned $2,490 in 2001 received three credits; someone who earned $3,320 or more was credited with the maximum of four credits.

Fully Insured vs. Currently Insured

A worker is fully insured if he or she has accumulated the required number of credits based on his or her age. For most persons, the required number of credit is 40 (representing approximately 10 years of work). Again, fully insured status provides eligibility for full retirement and survivor benefits.

To be considered currently insured and thus eligible for limited survivor (such as death) benefits, a worker must have earned six credits during the 13-quarter period ending with the quarter in which the worker died.

How Social Security Benefits Are Determined

The amount of benefits to which a worker is entitled under Social Security is based on his or her earnings over the years. There is a direct relationship between the amount of FICA taxes paid and the level of benefits earned. Workers who pay the maximum FICA tax over their lifetimes will receive higher benefits than those who pay less than the maximum. However, the FICA tax is not necessarily applied to all of a worker's earnings; the FICA tax is assessed only up to a maximum amount of earnings (known as the maximum taxable wage base, discussed later). Accordingly, Social Security benefits actually bear an inverse relationship to earnings: the more the person makes over his or her lifetime in excess of the maximum taxable wage base, the less Social Security provides in benefits as a proportion of total earnings. Conversely, a person who earned relatively little will receive a higher level of benefits in proportion to his or her total earnings.

Critics of Social Security sometimes complain of the apparent unfairness of a system in which the rich do not have to pay taxes above the maximum taxable wage base. These critics fail to point out, however, that those same wealthy people will receive benefits no greater than a worker who earned only the amount of the maximum taxable wage base.

Social Security Taxes

To understand Social Security, one must understand the basis upon which it is funded. Social Security is a pay-as-you-go system; the taxes paid by workers today are used to provide benefits today. Excess contributions are placed in a fund for future benefits, but are not earmarked for individual contributors. As noted, OASDI is supported by a payroll tax, paid by employees, employers and self-employed individuals.

This payroll, or FICA tax, is applied to employees' incomes up to a certain limit, called the *taxable wage base*. A portion of the FICA tax funds OASDI benefits; the other portion funds Medicare benefits. Employers pay an equal amount on behalf of each employee. Self-employed workers pay a higher rate (roughly equal to the sum of an employee's plus an employer's rate), but on annual income up to the same taxable wage base.

✓ *Take Note:* When a worker's salary exceeds the taxable wage base in a calendar year, no more FICA tax is deducted from his or her salary for the remainder of that year.

The maximum taxable wage base was, until 1971, quite stable. However, since 1972, the wage base has increased every year, meaning that more and more of a worker's earning are subject to FICA taxes. Up until 1991, the same

FIGURE 11.1   Calculating FICA Taxes

Let's look at some examples of how FICA taxes are levied on workers. In 2001, Bill earned $26,000, Janice earned $80,400 and Sam earned $140,000. All are covered by Social Security.

All of Bill's earnings were subject to the full FICA tax, so in 2001 he paid:

$$\$26{,}000 \times .0620 = \$1{,}612 \text{ toward OASDI}$$
$$\$26{,}000 \times .0145 = \$\underline{\ \ 377} \text{ toward Medicare}$$
$$\text{Total} \quad \$1{,}989$$

All of Janice's earnings were subject to the full FICA tax, so in 2001 she paid:

$$\$80{,}400 \times .0620 = \$4{,}984.80 \text{ toward OASDI}$$
$$\$80{,}400 \times .0145 = \$\underline{1{,}165.80} \text{ toward Medicare}$$
$$\text{Total} \quad \$6{,}150.60$$

Now as to Sam, only the first $80,400 of his earnings were subject to the OASDI portion of the FICA tax. There no longer is a limit on the earnings on which one pays the Medicare tax. In 2001, Sam paid:

$$\$80{,}400 \times .0620 = \$4{,}984.80 \text{ toward OASDI}$$
$$\$140{,}000 \times .0145 = \$\underline{2{,}030.00} \text{ toward Medicare}$$
$$\text{Total} \quad \$7{,}014.80$$

wage base was used to calculate FICA taxes for both OASDI and Medicare; now, however, the wage base to which the Medicare portion of the tax applies has been extended greatly. In 2001, the taxable wage base for OASDI was $80,400. This means that, in 2001, the first $80,400 of an employee's earnings was subject to the full FICA tax—OASDI and Medicare. No cap exists on earnings for the Medicare portion of the FICA tax. Currently, all wages and self-employment income are subject to the full Medicare payroll tax.

The FICA tax rate also is subject to increases, though not as often as the wage base. In 2001, the rate for employees and employers alike was 7.65 percent, of which 6.20 percent applied to OASDI and 1.45 percent applied to Medicare. The tax rate for self-employed persons in 2001 was 15.3 percent.

Calculating Benefits

Social Security benefits were computed on a worker's *average monthly wage* (AMW) if the person became eligible for benefits before 1979. For people becoming eligible in 1979 or later, the calculation is based on the worker's *average indexed monthly earnings* (AIME). The AIME, like the AMW, is an average of the worker's lifetime earnings that were subject to the FICA tax. The

AIME adds the additional, and critical, step of weighting a worker's past earnings to take inflation into account and to bring them up to current economic standards; failure to do so would result in exceptionally small benefits.

Consider, for instance, the worker now retiring who never earned any more than the taxable wage base in, say, 1970. At the time, the taxable wage base was $7,800. If the worker's retirement benefit today were directly based on earnings of $7,800 in 1970 it is easy to see how painfully small his or her level of retirement income would be by today's economic standards. Through weighting, the AIME adjusts past earnings to what they would be worth by current economic standards.

The averaged monthly earnings figure derived by the AIME next is applied to a formula to yield the *primary insurance amount* (PIA). The PIA actually is the amount equal to the worker's full retirement benefit at age 65 (benefits are reduced for early retirement) or benefits to a disabled worker. Benefits payable to workers and their spouses and dependents usually are expressed as a percentage of the worker's PIA. For example, a person who elects to retire at age 62 with Social Security retirement benefits will receive benefits equal to 80 percent of his or her PIA.

✓ **Take Note:** There are advantages and disadvantages to retiring early. The disadvantage is that this reduced amount does not increase to 100 percent of the PIA when the worker reaches his or her full retirement age; the reduction stays in effect for the remainder of the worker's life. The advantage is that benefits can be collected for a longer period of time.

🖉 Quick Quiz 11.1 True or False?

_____ 1. Social Security can be described as a pay-as-you-go system in which taxes paid by workers today are used to provide current benefits.

_____ 2. In 2001, Ellen earned $90,000. All of her wages will be subject to the OASDI and Medicare payroll tax.

_____ 3. John earns $100,000 in 2001. All of his compensation will be subject to the Medicare payroll tax.

_____ 4. Social Security benefits currently are based on a worker's average monthly wage.

_____ 5. Individuals who retire before their full retirement age will receive a permanently reduced amount of benefits.

Answers
1. **True**.

2. **False**. *If Ellen earns $90,000 in 2001, only the first $80,400 of her compensation is subject to both the OASDI and Medicare tax. The amount of her compensation exceeding this limit will be subject only to the full Medicare tax.*

3. **True**.

4. **False**. *Social Security benefits used to be based on a worker's average monthly wage. For people becoming eligible in 1979 or later, the calculation is based on the worker's averaged indexed monthly earnings.*

5. **True**.

Types of OASDI Benefits

Now that you have a basic understanding of how Social Security benefits are determined, let's take a closer look at the benefits themselves. Specifically, we will review the *death*, *retirement* and *disability* benefits provided under Social Security. (Medicare benefits will be discussed in Lesson 19.)

Death Benefits

Upon the death of an eligible worker, Social Security provides death benefits to a surviving spouse, dependent children and dependent parents. These death benefits more commonly are called *survivor benefits*.

Lump-Sum Death Benefit Social Security provides a one-time, lump-sum death benefit to a deceased worker's surviving spouse or children. The amount of this benefit is equal to three times the worker's PIA, up to a maximum of $255. This benefit is designed to help defray funeral expenses. Only surviving spouses or eligible children may receive this benefit.

Surviving Spouse's Benefit The eligible surviving spouse of a fully insured deceased worker is entitled, at age 65, to a monthly life income equal to the worker's PIA at death. Or, if he or she wishes to receive these benefits early, the surviving spouse can elect reduced benefits starting as early as age 60.

If the surviving spouse has a child under age 16 (or age 22, if disabled) and the child was a dependent of the deceased worker, an additional benefit of 75 percent of the worker's PIA is payable, regardless of the spouse's age, until the child reaches age 16. Disabled children entitle the surviving spouse to this benefit indefinitely, as long as the child remains disabled and under the care of the surviving spouse.

Child's Benefit   A child who is under age 18 (or disabled before age 22) whose parent is a deceased worker may receive a benefit equal to 75 percent of the worker's PIA until he or she turns age 18 (age 19 if still in high school). If the child marries before age 18, the benefit terminates.

Parents' Benefits   Beginning at age 62, each parent of a deceased fully insured worker is eligible to receive a monthly benefit if the parent was at least one-half supported by the worker at the time of death. When two parents are eligible, each receives 75 percent of the worker's PIA; if only one parent is eligible, he or she receives 82.5 percent of the worker's PIA.

Test Topic Alert!   The *blackout period* is the period of years during which no Social Security benefit is payable to the surviving spouse of a deceased, fully insured worker between the time the youngest child of the worker (in the spouse's case) attains the age of 18 and the spouse's age 60.

Maximum Survivor Benefits   Social Security has placed limits on the total amount of survivor benefits that any one family may receive. This limit is known as the *maximum family benefit*, and it varies according to the PIA. If the sum of the individual benefits paid to members of one family exceeds this maximum limit, they will be reduced proportionately to bring the total within the limit.

Retirement Benefits

Social Security also provides old age, or retirement, benefits to qualified (fully insured) workers and their families. These benefits are paid monthly.

Worker's Retirement Benefit   Fully insured workers are eligible for full retirement income benefits (i.e., 100 percent of the PIA) at their full retirement age (currently age 65). Permanently reduced benefits are available from age 62 for those who elect to retire early and draw benefits; slightly greater benefits are available for those who delay retirement beyond age 65.

✓ **For Example:** Persons turning age 65 in 2000 or 2001 received a delayed retirement credit (DRC) of 6 percent per year for each full year that they did not receive Social Security benefits.

Note that the normal retirement age for receiving Social Security benefits will increase gradually from age 65, eventually reaching age 67 for individuals born after 1959.

✓ **Take Note:** The full retirement age is being increased in gradual steps because of longer life expectancies.

Spouse's Benefit   The spouse of any worker eligible for retirement benefits is entitled to an old age income at his or her age 65, or a reduced benefit at age 62. At age 65, the spouse's benefit is 50 percent of the retired worker's PIA; at age 62, the spousal benefit is 37.5 percent of the PIA.

If there is a dependent child under age 16 (or disabled before age 22), the spouse is eligible to receive the 50 percent spousal benefit, regardless of his or her age.

Child's Benefit   An unmarried child of a worker on retirement income generally is eligible to receive a monthly benefit of 50 percent of the worker's PIA until he or she turns 18 years old. If the child is disabled before age 22, his or her benefit continues indefinitely.

Maximum Retirement Benefits   As is the case with survivor benefits, a maximum family benefit amount also applies to Social Security retirement benefits. If the total benefits due to a spouse and child exceed this limit, their benefits will be reduced proportionately.

Earnings Test

Under prior law, anyone under age 70 who was receiving Social Security retirement benefits but continued to work could earn only so much each year without having his or her benefits reduced. However, this law was repealed in 2001. Under the new rules, starting with the month a person reaches full retirement age, he or she can continue working and receive Social Security benefits, with no limit on earnings. However, if a person is under the full retirement age when he or she begins receiving Social Security benefits and continues to work, his or her benefits still will be reduced.

✔ **Take Note:** In this case, $1 in benefits will be deducted for each $2 earned above the annual limit. For 2001, this limit was $10,680. However, in the year a worker reaches full retirement age, $1 in benefits will be deducted for each $3 earned above a different limit ($25,000 in 2001). Only earnings received before the month the worker reaches the full benefit retirement age will be counted.

✔ **For Example:** Bill, age 62, started getting his Social Security benefits in January 2001 and is entitled to $600 each month ($7,200 for the year). He works and earns $20,000 ($9,320 over the $10,680 limit) during the year. Bill would have to give up $4,660 of his Social Security benefits ($1 for every $2 over the limit). He still would receive $2,240. Now, let's assume Bill was 64 at the beginning of 2001 and reached full retirement age in August 2001. He earns $46,000 during the year, with $30,000 of it in the seven months from January through July. He would have to give up $1,667 in benefits ($1 for every $3 of the $5,000 he earned above the $25,000 limit) through July. With benefits of $600 a month, Bill still would receive $2,533 out of his $4,200 benefits for the first seven months. He would receive his entire Social Security benefits

($3,000) for the remaining months of August through December after he turned 65, because the earnings limitations do not apply once he reached full retirement age.

Disability Benefits

A fully insured worker who becomes disabled is entitled to disability benefits under Social Security, as are his or her spouse and dependent children.

Disabled Worker's Benefit
A disabled worker is entitled to a monthly benefit equal to his or her PIA at the time the disability occurred. There is no reduction in benefits if they begin before age 65. However, if the worker becomes disabled after age 63 and had been receiving a reduced retirement benefit, his or her disability benefits will be reduced to take into account the retirement benefits already received.

Spouse's Benefit
The spouse of a qualified disabled worker also may receive benefits from Social Security, depending on his or her age. If the spouse is age 65, the benefit is equal to 50 percent of the worker's PIA. A spouse who is age 62 can elect reduced benefits equal to 37.5 percent of the worker's PIA.

If there is a dependent child under age 16 (or who is disabled, regardless of age), the spouse can receive the 50 percent spousal benefit, regardless of his or her age.

Child's Benefit
A disabled worker's unmarried dependent child who is under age 18 (or a child who was disabled before age 22) is eligible for monthly benefits equal to 50 percent of the worker's PIA.

Maximum Disability Benefits
Again, a maximum family benefit applies, limiting the amount of disability benefits one family can receive on the worker's earnings record. The earnings test also applies and pertains individually to each family member.

Qualification for Social Security disability benefits is subject to rigid requirements. To begin with, the worker must meet Social Security's definition of disability, which is the inability to engage in any substantial gainful work. The disability must be the result of a medically determinable physical or mental impairment that can be expected to last at least 12 months or to result in an earlier death.

Disability benefits begin after the worker has satisfied a waiting period of five consecutive months, during which he or she must be disabled. The benefits may be paid retroactively for as long as 12 months (excluding the waiting period) preceding the date an application for benefits is filed.

FIGURE 11.2   Calculating the Tax on Social Security Benefits

Assume Fred and Julia are a retired couple, both age 66. In 2001, they received $70,000 in income: $27,000 from investment earnings, $23,000 from Fred's pension plan and $20,000 in Social Security retirement benefits. The amount of their Social Security subject to income tax is calculated this way.

Step 1	Determine *modified adjusted gross income*	$ 27,000
	(total of all earnings, pension benefits, dividends, taxable	23,000
	investment earnings, interest on tax-exempt bonds plus	+ 10,000
	50 percent of Social Security benefits)	$ 60,000
Step 2	Excess of modified AGI over first threshold	$ 60,000
	($25,000 for singles; $32,000 for joint filers)	– 32,000
		$ 28,000
Step 3	Excess of modified AGI over second threshold	$ 60,000
	($34,000 for singles; $44,000 for joint filers)	– 44,000
		$ 16,000
Step 4	Determine the *smallest* of:	
	a. 50 percent of excess over first threshold *plus*	
	35 percent of excess over second threshold	$19,600
	or	
	b. 85 percent of Social Security benefit	$17,000
	or	
	c. 50 percent of total Social Security benefit *plus*	
	85 percent of excess over second threshold	$23,600

The *smallest* of these three figures—$17,000—is the amount of Social Security benefits subject to income tax.

Taxation of Social Security Benefits

Until 1984, all Social Security benefits were exempt from federal income taxes. Today, however, up to 85 percent of Social Security benefits may be treated as taxable income for recipients whose income exceeds certain base amounts. Certain step-rate thresholds determine the amount on which a worker's benefits might be taxed.

✓ **Take Note:** The step-rate thresholds are $25,000 and $34,000 for single individuals and $32,000 and $44,000 for married individuals filing jointly.

Figure 11.2 explains how to figure the amount of Social Security income subject to tax.

Summary

The federally managed Social Security program, more formally called Old Age, Survivors, and Disability Insurance (OASDI), is the government's attempt to provide a basic floor of financial protection to all working Americans. It is a pay-as-you-go system funded by a mandatory FICA payroll tax on almost all workers. While Social Security benefits do provide an important source of income for retirees and the surviving spouses and children of covered workers, these benefits alone are not sufficient to maintain a meaningful standard of living. Social Security benefits augment, but do not replace, a well-founded personal insurance program.

Key Concepts

In preparing for their licensing examination, students should be familiar with the following concepts:

OASDI benefits	FICA tax
fully insured status	currently insured status
taxable wage base	credits
PIA earnings test	AIME
full retirement age	taxation of Social Security benefits

Lesson Exam Eleven

1. Ellen works part time to supplement her family's income. In 2001, she earned $3,000 and worked at least part of every month. With how many quarters of coverage will she be credited for 2001?

   A. One
   B. Two
   C. Three
   D. Four

2. Anne earned $85,000 in 2001. Assuming 2001 Social Security rates, how much did her employer deduct from her salary for FICA taxes that year?

   A. $5,270
   B. $6,050
   C. $6,218
   D. $6,503

3. Which of the following statements regarding Social Security survivor benefits is NOT correct?

   A. A surviving widow, age 66, is entitled to a life income equal to her husband's PIA.
   B. A healthy dependent child of a deceased worker is entitled to an income benefit until age 18, or to age 22 if he or she attends college.
   C. A surviving widower, age 47, has a 13-year-old child who also was a dependent of the deceased worker. The widower is entitled to monthly income until the child reaches age 16, at which time benefits will cease to the widower until the widower reaches at least age 60.
   D. A deceased covered worker was providing one-half of the support for a 62-year-old parent who is confined to a nursing home. The parent is entitled to a survivor's benefit.

4. Which of the following statements about Social Security benefits is CORRECT?

   A. Simon has a Social Security PIA of $700 at the time of his death. His surviving spouse will receive a lump-sum death benefit of $2,250.
   B. Lola, age 30, has a daughter, age 10. Her husband, who is covered under Social Security, died unexpectedly last month following surgery. Both Lola and her daughter are entitled to receive monthly survivor benefits until her daughter reaches age 18.
   C. Mason, who is married with one son, age 16, is a fully insured retired worker receiving Social Security benefits. In addition, his spouse is eligible for benefits at age 62 and his son, normally, is eligible for benefits until he is 18 years old.
   D. Arlene, the 20-year-old daughter of a fully insured retired worker, becomes totally and permanently disabled from injuries she receives in a car accident. Because her disability occurred after age 16, Arlene is not eligible for her father's Social Security benefits.

5. In determining Social Security retirement benefits, which of the following statements is NOT correct?

   A. Average indexed monthly earnings (AIME) are adjusted for inflation.
   B. Average monthly wages (AMW) are adjusted for inflation.
   C. The primary insurance amount (PIA) is a determination of the amount equal to the worker's full retirement benefit at his or her full retirement age.
   D. A worker retiring at age 62 will not receive 100 percent of his or her PIA.

6. Rudy is eligible for full death, retirement and disability benefits under Social Security. His worker status is

    A. completely insured
    B. currently insured
    C. fully insured
    D. partially insured

7. Which of the following statements does NOT describe the purpose of Social Security correctly?

    A. It provides a source of income for a meaningful standard of living during retirement.
    B. It provides basic protection against financial problems accompanying death, disability and retirement.
    C. It augments a sound personal insurance plan.
    D. It provides retirement and survivor benefits to a worker and his or her family.

8. What is the 2001 FICA tax rate for self-employed individuals?

    A. 6.20 percent
    B. 7.65 percent
    C. 15.0 percent
    D. 15.3 percent

9. Jan, a single working mother, dies at age 40. Dave, her only son, would receive a one-time, lump-sum death benefit of

    A. $255
    B. $500
    C. $1,000
    D. $2,000

Answers & Rationale

1. **C.** In 2001, a worker earned one credit for each $830 of annual earnings on which FICA taxes are paid. If Ellen earns $3,000 during the year, she will be credited with three quarters of coverage.

2. **C.** In 2001, the first $80,400 of Anne's taxable wages are subject to the OASDI portion of the FICA tax. All of her earnings are subject to the 1.45 percent Medicare tax. As a result, Anne's FICA taxes for 2001 are $6,218 ([$80,400 × .0620] + [$85,000 × .0145])

3. **B.** A child who is under age 18 (or disabled before age 22) can receive survivor benefits until he or she turns 18 (19 if still in high school).

4. **C.** Mason's spouse, age 62, is eligible for retirement benefits at age 62, although the benefits will be reduced permanently. Mason's son also is eligible to receive a monthly benefit until he turns 18.

5. **B.** Social Security benefits used to be computed based on a worker's average monthly wage (AMW) for people who became eligible for benefits before 1979. Unlike the average indexed monthly earnings that is now used to determine benefits, the AMW did not take inflation into account.

6. **C.** If Rudy is eligible for full death, retirement and disability benefits under Social Security, he will be considered fully insured. If he only qualified for a limited range of survivor benefits, he would be considered currently insured.

7. **A.** The purpose of Social Security is to provide basic protection to all working Americans against the financial problems caused by death, disability and aging. It is not designed to provide a source of income for a meaningful standard of living during retirement.

8. **D.** In 2001, the FICA tax rate was 15.3 percent for self-employed persons.

9. **A.** Social Security provides a one-time, lump-sum death benefit of $255 to a deceased worker's surviving spouse or children. As Jan's only child, Dave would receive this lump sum benefit.

12

Retirement Plans

INTRODUCTION

As noted in the last lesson, Social Security alone does not provide enough benefits to ensure a meaningful standard of living for retired individuals. To meet the financial challenges of retirement, individuals must take the initiative and begin preparing early if they want full security down the road. This preparation involves maintaining adequate life insurance to meet the costs of death, enough health insurance to cover illnesses and a well-planned retirement program to ensure a desired standard of living when employment income ceases. For many individuals, saving through an employer-sponsored plan or a personal plan likely is the most effective way to accumulate retirement assets. In this lesson, we will discuss the many options employers can choose from when establishing retirement plans for their employees. Although this subject is complex and can be covered only briefly here, it is important for financial professionals to recognize the role a well-structured retirement plan plays in an individual's overall insurance and financial plan.

LESSON OBJECTIVES

When you complete this lesson you should be able to:

- compare and contrast qualified and nonqualified plans;
- explain the basic ERISA concepts of participation, coverage, vesting, funding and contributions;
- explain how defined contribution plans differ from defined benefit plans;
- identify the basic features of 401(k) plans, tax-sheltered annuities and Section 457 plans;
- list and describe the different types of qualified plans available to small employers; and
- explain the differences between traditional IRAs, Roth IRAs and education IRAs.

Qualified vs. Nonqualified Plans

The field of retirement planning has grown tremendously in both scope and significance. In various ways, the federal government encourages businesses to set aside retirement funds for their employees and provides incentives for individuals to do likewise. Many kinds of retirement plans exist, each designed to fulfill specific needs. Life insurance companies play a major role in the retirement planning arena, as the products and contracts they offer provide ideal funding or financing vehicles for both individual and employer-sponsored plans.

Retirement plans can be divided into two categories: qualified plans and nonqualified plans. Qualified plans, by design or by definition, meet certain requirements established by the federal government and, consequently, receive favorable tax treatment:

- Employer contributions to a qualified retirement plan are considered a deductible business expense, which lowers the business' income taxes.
- The earnings of a qualified plan are exempt from income taxation as they accumulate in the plan.
- Employer contributions to a qualified plan currently are not taxable to the employee in the years they are contributed, but are taxable when they are paid out as a benefit and, typically, when the employee is retired and in a lower tax bracket.
- Contributions to an individual qualified plan, such as an individual retirement account (IRA) or annuity, are deductible from income under certain conditions.
- Employee contributions to certain types of employer plans, such as 401(k) plans, are not included in the employee's gross income, which lowers his or her income taxes.

If a plan does not meet the specific requirements the federal government sets forth, it is termed a nonqualified plan and, thus, is not eligible for favorable tax treatment.

✓ **For Example:** Bill, age 42, decides he wants to start a retirement fund. He opens a new savings account at his local bank, deposits $150 a month in that account and vows not to touch that money until he reaches age 65. Although his intentions are good, they will not qualify his plan. The income he deposits and the interest he earns still are taxable every year.

In this lesson our discussion will focus on qualified retirement plans, both individual and employer-sponsored.

Qualified Employer Retirement Plans

An employer retirement plan is one that a business makes available to its employees. Typically, the employer makes all or a portion of the contributions on behalf of its employees and is able to deduct these contributions as ordinary and necessary business expenses. The employees are not taxed on the contributions made on their behalf, nor are they taxed on the benefit fund accruing to them until it is actually paid out. By the same token, contributions made by an individual employee to a qualified employer retirement plan are not included in his or her ordinary income and therefore are not taxable.

Basic Concepts

Many of the basic concepts associated with qualified employer plans can be traced to the Employee Retirement Income Security Act of 1974, commonly called ERISA. The purpose of ERISA is to protect the rights of workers covered under an employer-sponsored plan.

✔ **Take Note:** Before the passage of ERISA, workers had few guarantees to assure them that they would receive the pension benefit they thought they had earned. A sad but common plight was the worker who had devoted many years to one employer, only to be terminated within a few years of retirement and not be entitled to a pension benefit.

ERISA imposes a number of requirements that retirement plans must follow to obtain IRS approval as a qualified plan eligible for favorable tax treatment. (See Figure 12.1.) While an in-depth discussion of these requirements is beyond the scope of this text, the basic concepts of *participation, coverage, vesting, funding* and *contributions* should be noted.

Participation Standards

All qualified employer plans must comply with minimum participation standards designed to determine employee eligibility. In general, employees who have reached age 21 and have completed one year of service must be allowed to enroll in a qualified plan. Or, if the plan provides for 100 percent vesting upon participation, they may be required to complete two years of service before enrolling.

Coverage Requirements

The purpose of coverage requirements is to prevent a plan from discriminating against rank-and-file employees in favor of the elite—shareholders, officers and highly compensated employees—whose positions often enable them to make basic policy decisions regarding the plan. The IRS will subject qualified employer plans to coverage tests to determine if they are discriminatory. A qualified plan cannot discriminate in favor of highly paid employees in its coverage provisions or in its provisions for contributions and benefits.

FIGURE 12.1   General Qualification Requirements for Employer-Sponsored Retirement Plans

1. A plan must be written.

2. A plan must be in effect.

3. A plan must be communicated to employees.

4. A plan must be established by the employer.

5. Contributions must be made by the employer, the employees or both.

6. A plan must be for the exclusive benefit of the employees.

7. A plan must be permanent.

8. Any life insurance benefits must be incidental to retirement benefits.

9. Minimum participation standards must be met.

10. A plan must not discriminate in coverage.

11. A plan must not discriminate in contributions or benefits on the basis of income or sex.

12. Annuity payments under a plan must be available in the form of a joint and survivor annuity.

13. Comprehensive vesting standards concerning the vesting of an employee's benefits must be followed.

14. Minimum funding standards must be met.

15. A plan must comply with limitations on contributions and benefits.

16. There must be no assignment or alienation of benefits.

17. A plan must meet Social Security integration rules.

18. A plan must meet rules for mergers and consolidations.

19. A plan must meet rules for multi-employer plans.

20. A plan must meet rules pertaining to the reduction of benefits because of Social Security.

21. A plan must fulfill plan termination requirements.

22. A plan must fulfill special requirements for particular plans.

23. A top-heavy plan must contain contingency provisions.

FIGURE 12.2   Vesting Schedules for Qualified Plans

To meet qualification standards, an employer retirement plan must provide for a *vesting schedule,* which sets forth the time period by which an employee-participant becomes entitled to nonforfeitable benefits under the plan. In general, two schedules are available:

1. Cliff Vesting	Years of Service	Vested Percentage		2. Graded Vesting	Years of Service	Vested Percentage
	1	0			1	0
	2	0			2	0
	3	0			3	20
	4	0			4	40
	5	100			5	60
					6	80
					7	100

As an alternative, a plan can provide for a different vesting schedule, as long as it is no less favorable to the participants than those above.

Note: For plans that include matching employer contributions, two new schedules are required: 3-year cliff vesting and 2- to 6-year graduated vesting. Under the former, a participant is 100 percent vested in employer matching contributions after three years. Under the latter, the participant is gradually vested in 20 percent increments, and is 100 percent vested in six years.

The new vesting schedules apply only to employer matching contributions in defined contribution plans. For all other types of plans and employer contributions, the 5-year and 7-year schedules continue to apply.

Vesting Schedules

All qualified plans must meet standards that set forth the employee vesting schedule and nonforfeitable rights at any specified time. Vesting means the right each employee has to his or her fund; benefits that have vested belong to the employee even if he or she terminates employment before retirement.

✓ **Take Note:** For all plans, an employee always has a 100 percent vested interest in benefits that accrue from his or her own contributions. Benefits that accrue from employer contributions must vest according to vesting schedules established by law. These schedules have been modified. (See Figure 12.2.)

Funding Standards

For a plan to be qualified, it must be funded. In other words, there must be real contributions on the part of the employer, the employee or both, and these funds must be held by a third party and invested. The funding vehicle is the method for investing the funds as they accumulate. Federal minimum funding requirements are set to ensure that an employer's annual contributions to a pension plan are sufficient to cover the costs of benefits payable during the year, plus administrative expenses.

Contributions   Qualification standards regarding the amount and type of contributions that can be made to a plan vary, but all plans must restrict the amount of contributions that can be made for or accrue to any one plan participant.

With these basics in mind, let's turn to the two major categories of qualified employer retirement plans, used primarily by corporate employers. They are the *defined contribution plan,* which obligates the plan sponsor to make periodic contributions for each participant per a defined formula, and the *defined benefit plan*, which defines the amount of retirement income each participant will receive.

Defined Contribution Plans

The provisions of a defined contribution plan address the amounts currently going into the plan and identify the participant's vested (nonforfeitable) account. These predetermined amounts contributed to the participant's account accumulate to a future point (such as retirement) and the final fund available to any one participant depends on total amounts contributed, plus interest and dividends earned.

Three types of defined contribution plans exist: *profit-sharing plans, stock bonus plans* and *money-purchase plans*.

Profit-Sharing Plans   Profit-sharing plans are established and maintained by an employer that allows employees to participate in the profits of the company. They provide for a definite predetermined formula for allocating plan contributions among the participants and for distributing the funds upon retirement, death, disability or termination. Because contributions are tied to the company's profits, it is not necessary that the employer contribute every year or that the amount of contribution be the same. However, the IRS states that to qualify for favorable tax treatment, the plan must be maintained with "recurring and substantial" contributions.

Stock Bonus Plans   A stock bonus plan is similar to a profit-sharing plan, except that contributions by the employer do not depend on profits, and benefits are distributed in the form of company stock.

Money-Purchase Plans   Money-purchase plans provide for fixed contributions with future benefits to be determined and thus most truly represent a defined contribution plan. A money-purchase plan must meet three requirements:

- Contributions and earnings must be allocated to participants in accordance with a definite formula.
- Distributions can be made only in accordance with amounts credited to participants.
- Plan assets must be valued at least once a year, with participants' accounts being adjusted accordingly.

Defined Benefit Plans

In contrast to a defined contribution plan that sets up predetermined contributions, a defined benefit plan establishes a definite future benefit, predetermined by a specific formula. When the term *pension* is used, the reference typically is to a defined benefit plan. Usually the benefits are tied to the employee's years of service, amount of compensation or both.

✓ **For Example:** A defined benefit plan may provide for a retirement benefit equal to 2 percent of the employee's highest consecutive five-year earnings, multiplied by the number of years of service. Or the benefit may be defined simply as $100 a month for life.

To qualify for federal tax purposes, a defined benefit plan must meet the following basic requirements:

- The plan must provide for *definitely determinable benefits*, either by a formula specified in the plan or by actuarial computation.
- The plan must provide for *systematic payment of benefits* to employees over a period of years (usually for life) after retirement. Thus, the plan has to detail the conditions under which benefits are payable and the options under which benefits are paid.
- The plan must primarily provide *retirement benefits*. The IRS will allow provisions for death or disability benefits, but these benefits must be incidental to retirement.
- The *maximum annual benefit* an employee may receive in any one year is limited to an amount set by the tax law. This amount is indexed for inflation. In 2001, the indexed amount was $140,000. This amount will increase to $160,000 in 2002.

The appropriate choice of qualified corporate retirement plan—defined contribution or defined benefit—requires an understanding of the operation and characteristics of each plan as they relate to the employer's objectives.

Cash or Deferred Arrangements (401(k) Plans)

Another popular form of qualified employer retirement plan is commonly known as the 401(k) plan, whereby employees can elect to take a reduction in their current salaries by deferring amounts into a retirement plan. These plans are called cash or deferred arrangements because employees cannot be forced to participate; they may take their income currently as cash, or defer a portion of it until retirement, with favorable tax advantages.

The amounts deferred are not included in the employees' gross incomes and earnings credited to the deferrals grow tax free until distribution. Typically, 401(k) plans include matching employer contributions: for every dollar the employee defers, for example, the employer will contribute 50 cents.

✓ ***Take Note:*** The maximum annual amount an employee could defer in 2001 was $10,500. This amount is indexed for inflation and will vary from year to year as follows:

Year	Contribution Limit
2001	$10,500
2002	$11,000
2003	$12,000
2004	$13,000
2005	$14,000
2006	$15,000*

* The $15,000 limit is indexed for inflation in $500 increments after 2006.

A cash or deferred arrangement must be part of a profit-sharing or stock bonus plan. In addition to meeting the qualification rules that apply to defined contribution plans, 401(k) plans also must qualify under a special set of rules:

- Amounts deferred can be distributed penalty free only because of retirement, death, disability, separation from service or attainment of age 59½.
- Employee-deferred contributions are nonforfeitable.
- Special nondiscrimination requirements must be met to prevent highly compensated employees from deferring disproportionately higher amounts of their salaries.

Employer contributions to a qualified cash or deferred profit-sharing plan currently are not taxed to the employee.

Tax-Sheltered Annuities (403(b) Plans)

Another type of employer retirement plan is the tax-sheltered annuity, or 403(b) plan. This was explained in Lesson 10, but it is appropriate to review it here.

A tax-sheltered annuity is a special tax-favored retirement plan available only to certain groups of employees. Tax-sheltered annuities may be established for the employees of specified nonprofit charitable, educational, religious and other 501(c)(3) organizations, including teachers in public school systems. Such plans generally are not available to other kinds of employees.

Funds are contributed by the employer or by the employees (usually through payroll deductions) to tax-sheltered annuities and, thus, are excluded from the employees' current taxable income.

✓ **Take Note:** The maximum annual salary reduction for an employee under a 403(b) plan is the same as that for a 401(k) plan: currently $10,500 in 2001. (Similarly, this amount is indexed for inflation and will vary from year to year in the same manner as for a 401(k) plan.)

IRC Section 457 Deferred Compensation Plans

Deferred compensation plans for employees of state and local governments and nonprofit organizations became popular in the 1970s. Congress enacted Internal Revenue Code Section 457 to allow participants in such plans to defer compensation without current taxation as long as certain conditions are met.

If a plan is eligible under Section 457, amounts deferred will not be included in gross income until they actually are received or made available. Life insurance and annuities are authorized investments for these plans.

The annual amounts an employee may defer under a Section 457 plan are similar to those available for 401(k) plans. In 2001, this amount was $8,500. It is scheduled to increase to $11,000 in 2002 and rises an additional $1,000 each year until it reaches $15,000 in 2006. After 2006, this amount (like that for 401(k) plans) is indexed for inflation in $500 increments. For the three years preceding retirement, the deferral limit in each year will be twice the applicable limit.

 Quick Quiz 12.1 True or False?

_____ 1. Both qualified and nonqualified plans receive favorable tax treatment.

_____ 2. ERISA's coverage requirements are designed to prevent retirement plans from discriminating against lower-paid employees in favor of key employees.

_____ 3. In a profit-sharing plan, the employer need not contribute the same amount every year.

_____ 4. Under a money-purchase plan, the employer makes varying contributions each year that depend in part on the company's profits.

_____ 5. A 403(b) plan may be established only for employees of certain nonprofit charitable, educational and religious organizations.

Answers
1. **False**. *Only qualified plans receive favorable tax treatment. Earnings of a qualified plan are exempt from income taxation and employer contributions are not currently taxable to the employee in the year contributed.*

2. **True**.

3. **True**.

4. **False**. *A money purchase plan provides for fixed, not varying, contributions by the employer. Contributions do not depend on the company's profits.*

5. **True**.

Qualified Plans for the Small Employer

Before 1962, many small business owners found that their employees could participate in, and benefit from, a qualified retirement plan, but the owners themselves could not. Self-employed individuals were in the same predicament. The reason was that qualified plans had to benefit employees. Because business owners were considered employers, they were excluded from participating in a qualified plan.

The Self-Employed Individuals Retirement Act, signed into law in 1962, rectified this situation by treating small business owners and self-employed individuals as employees, thus enabling them to participate in a qualified plan, if they chose to do so, just as their employees. The result was the Keogh or HR-10 retirement plan.

Keogh Plan (HR-10)

A Keogh plan is a qualified retirement plan designed for unincorporated businesses that allows the business owner (or partner in a business) to participate as an employee. These plans may be set up either as defined contribution or defined benefit plans.

In the first years following enactment of the Keogh bill, a great deal of disparity existed between the rules for Keogh plans and those for corporate plans. However, the law eliminated most of the rules unique to Keogh plans, thereby establishing parity between qualified corporate employer retirement plans and noncorporate plans. This change means that Keogh plans:

- are subject to the same maximum contribution limits and benefit limits as qualified corporate plans;

- must comply with the same participation and coverage requirements as qualified corporate plans; and
- are subject to the same nondiscrimination rules as qualified corporate plans.

Simplified Employee Pension (SEP)

Another type of qualified plan suited for the small employer is the simplified employee pension (SEP) plan. Due to the many administrative burdens and the costs involved with establishing a qualified defined contribution or defined benefit plan as well as maintaining compliance with ERISA, many small businesses have been reluctant to set up retirement plans for their employees. SEPs were introduced in 1978 specifically for small businesses to overcome these cost, compliance and administrative hurdles.

Basically, an SEP is an arrangement whereby an employee (including a self-employed individual) establishes and maintains a traditional IRA to which the employer contributes. Employer contributions are not included in the employee's gross income. A primary difference between a SEP and an IRA is the much larger amount that an employer can contribute each year to a SEP—currently, up to 100 percent of the employee's compensation or $40,000, whichever is less.

In accordance with the rules that govern other qualified plans, SEPs must not discriminate in favor of highly compensated employees with regard to contributions or participation.

Salary Reduction SEP Plan

A variation of the SEP plan is the salary reduction SEP, or SARSEP. SARSEPs incorporate a deferral/salary reduction approach in that the employee can elect to have employer contributions directed into the SEP or paid out as taxable cash compensation. The limit on the elective deferral to a SARSEP is the same as a 401(k) ($10,500 in 2001, and is indexed for inflation in the same manner as for a 401(k) plan.)

 Take Note: SARSEPs are reserved for small employers—those with 25 or fewer employees—and had to be established before 1997. As a result of tax legislation, no new SARSEPs can be established; however, plans that already were in place as of the end of 1996 may continue to operate and accept new employee participants.

SIMPLE Plan

The same legislation that did away with SARSEPs also created a new form of qualified employer retirement plan. Known as a Savings Incentive Match Plan for Employees, or SIMPLE plan, these arrangements allow eligible employers to set up tax-favored retirement savings plans for their employees without addressing many of the usual (and burdensome) qualification requirements.

SIMPLE plans are available to small businesses (including tax exempt and government entities) that employ no more than 100 employees who received at least $5,000 in compensation from the employer during the previous year. In addition, to establish a SIMPLE plan, the employer must not have a qualified plan in place.

A SIMPLE plan may be structured as an IRA or as a 401(k) cash or deferred arrangement. Under these plans, employees who elect to participate may defer up to a specified amount each year ($6,000 in 2001 increasing in $1,000 increments each year up to $10,000 by 2005) and the employer then makes a matching contribution, dollar-for-dollar, up to an amount equal to 3 percent of the employee's annual compensation. All contributions to a SIMPLE IRA or SIMPLE 401(k) plan are nonforfeitable; the employee is vested immediately and fully. Taxation of contributions and their earnings is deferred until funds are withdrawn or distributed.

✓ **Take Note:** In place of the dollar-for-dollar matching contributions, an employer can choose to make nonelective contributions of 2 percent of compensation on behalf of each eligible employee. Only the first $170,000 of the employee's compensation can be taken into account when determining the contribution limit. (This amount will gradually increase to $200,000 with adjustments for inflation in $5,000 increments. The base period is July 1, 2001.)

Individual Retirement Plans

In much the same way that it encourages businesses to establish retirement plans for their employees, the federal government provides incentives for individuals to save for their retirement by allowing certain kinds of plans to receive favorable tax treatment. Individual retirement accounts (IRAs) are the most notable of these plans. Available IRAs include the traditional tax-deductible IRA and the traditional non-tax-deductible IRA, as well as the Roth IRA (named after IRA advocate William Roth, Jr., Chairman of the Senate Finance Committee) and the education IRA. The Roth and education IRAs were created by the Taxpayer Relief Act of 1997. Both of these IRAs require nondeductible contributions but offer tax-free earnings and withdrawals.

Traditional IRA

An IRA is a means by which individuals can save money for retirement and receive a current tax break. Basically, the amount contributed to an IRA accumulates and grows tax deferred. IRA funds are not taxed until they are taken out at retirement. In addition, depending on the individual's earnings and whether or not he or she is covered by an employer-sponsored retirement plan, the amount he or she contributes to a traditional IRA may be fully or partially deducted from current income, resulting in lower current income taxes.

IRA Participation

Anyone under age 70½ who has earned income may open a traditional IRA and contribute each year an amount up to the contribution limit or 100 percent of compensation, whichever is less. (The limit was $2,000 in 2001.) A non-wage-earning spouse is allowed to open an IRA and contribute up to the contribution limit each year.

Under the Economic Growth and Tax Relief Reconciliation Act of 2001 (TRRA), the annual limit on contributions that an individual can make to a traditional (or Roth) IRA is scheduled to increase from its 2001 level ($2,000). The increases will be phased in, beginning in 2002:

Year	IRA Contribution Limit
2001	$2,000
2002	$3,000
2003	$3,000
2004	$3,000
2005	$4,000
2006	$4,000
2007	$4,000
2008 and thereafter	$5,000

After 2008, the contribution limit will be adjusted annually for inflation. These limits will also apply to any combined contributions that might be made to a traditional IRA and a Roth IRA.

 Take Note: Contributions exceeding these limits are subject to a 6 percent excise tax.

Also beginning in 2002, persons who are age 50 and older will be allowed to make "catch-up" contributions to their IRAs, above the scheduled $3,000, $4,000 or $5,000 limit, enabling them to save even more for retirement. These catch-up payments can be either deductible or made to a Roth IRA. The additional catch-up amount allowed in 2002 through 2005 is $500. In 2006 and after, the amount increases to $1,000.

Deduction of IRA Contributions

In many cases, the amount an individual contributes to a traditional IRA can be deducted from his or her income in the year it is contributed. The ability of an IRA participant to take a deduction for his or her contribution rests on two factors:

- whether or not he or she is covered by an employer-sponsored retirement plan; and
- the amount of income he or she makes.

Individuals who are not covered by an employer-sponsored plan may contribute up to the annual limit to a traditional IRA and deduct the full amount of the contribution from their current income, no matter what their income level. Married couples who both work and have no employer-sponsored plan can contribute and deduct up to a combined total of $4,000 in 2001 to any and all of his or her IRAs. These contribution limits will increase each year through 2008, by which time the limit for individuals will be $5,000. Consequently, the most that married couples can contribute to any and all of their IRAs will be $10,000. After 2008, the limits will be adjusted annually for inflation.

Individuals who are covered by an employer-sponsored plan are subject to different rules regarding deductibility of traditional IRA contributions. For them, the amount of income they make is the determining factor: the more they make, the less IRA deduction they can take.

✓ **For Example:** A single taxpayer covered by an employer plan whose adjusted gross income is $33,000 or less may take up to the $2,000 maximum deduction in 2001. As income exceeds $33,000, the amount of allowable IRA deduction gradually is phased down. Single taxpayers covered by an employer plan lose IRA deductibility completely when adjusted gross income reaches $43,000 (in 2001). This range ($33,000 to $43,000) gradually will increase to $50,000 to $60,000 by 2005. In other words, in 2005 and thereafter, single taxpayers covered by an employer plan, whose adjusted gross income is $50,000 or less, may take the maximum deduction ($4,000 in 2005), and single taxpayers covered by an employer plan will lose IRA deductibility completely when adjusted gross income reaches $60,000.

✓ **For Example:** For married individuals filing jointly, when either or both are covered by an employer plan, the full deduction is available if their adjusted gross income is less than $53,000 in 2001. Again, the deduction is phased down gradually as income rises. Once joint income reaches $63,000, there no deduction is allowed for IRA contributions. The Tax Reform Act of 1997 provides for the gradual increase of this range from $53,000/$63,000 to $80,000/$100,000 by the year 2007.

 **Test Topic Alert!**

Do not confuse contribution deductibility with the ability to make contributions. Again, anyone under age 70½ who has earned income (as well as his or her non-wage-earning spouse) can contribute to a traditional IRA. However, level of income and participation in an employer plan may affect the traditional IRA owner's ability to deduct the contributions.

✓ **Take Note:** A traditional IRA owner must file Form 8606 with his or her tax return to report any nondeductible contributions that have been made. If an individual does not report nondeductible contributions, all contributions made to the traditional IRA will be treated as deductible. This means that when withdrawals are made from the IRA, all of the amounts withdrawn will be subject to tax.

Traditional IRA Withdrawals

Because the purpose of an IRA is to provide a way to accumulate retirement funds, a number of rules discourage IRA owners from withdrawing these funds before retirement. By the same token, traditional IRA owners are discouraged from sheltering their accounts from taxes perpetually by rules that mandate when the funds must be withdrawn.

Traditional IRA owners must begin to receive payment from their accounts no later than April 1 following the year in which they reach age 70½. The law specifies a minimum amount that must be withdrawn every year. Failure to withdraw the minimum amount can result in a stiff penalty tax on the difference between the amount that should have been withdrawn and the amount that was actually withdrawn.

With a few exceptions, any distribution from a traditional IRA before age 59½ will have adverse tax consequences. In addition to income tax, the taxable amount of the withdrawal will be subject to a 10 percent penalty (similar to that imposed on early withdrawals from deferred annuities). Early distributions taken for any of the following reasons or circumstances will not be assessed the 10 percent penalty:

- if the owner dies or becomes disabled;
- if the owner is faced with a certain amount of qualifying medical expenses;
- to pay for higher education expenses;
- to cover first-time home purchase expenses (up to $10,000);
- to pay for health insurance premiums while unemployed;
- if the distribution is taken in equal payments over the owner's lifetime; or
- to correct or reduce an excess contribution.

At retirement, or any time after age 59½, a traditional IRA owner can elect to receive either a lump-sum payment or periodic installment payments from his or her fund. IRA distributions are taxed in much the same way as annuity benefit payments are taxed. That is, the portion of an IRA distribution that is attributed to nondeductible contributions is received tax free; the portion that is attributed to interest earnings or deductible contributions is taxed. The result is a tax-free return of the IRA owner's cost basis and a taxing of the balance.

If an IRA owner dies before receiving full payment, the remaining funds in the deceased's IRA will be paid to the named beneficiary.

IRA Funding

A flexible premium fixed deferred annuity is an ideal funding vehicle for IRAs. Other acceptable IRA funding vehicles include bank time deposit open accounts, bank certificates of deposit, insured credit union accounts, mutual fund shares, face amount certificates, real estate investment trust units and certain U.S. gold and silver coins.

Roth IRA

In 1997, a new kind of IRA was introduced: the Roth IRA. Roth IRAs are unique in that they provide for back-end benefits. No deduction can be taken for contributions made to Roth IRAs, but the earnings on those contributions are entirely tax free when they are withdrawn.

An amount up to the contribution limit for the year ($2,000 in 2001) can be contributed to a Roth IRA for any one eligible individual. Active participant status is irrelevant—an individual can contribute to a Roth regardless of whether he or she is covered by an employer plan or maintains and contributes to other IRA accounts. (Note, however, that the annual limit on contributions applies collectively to both traditional and Roth IRAs. No more than this amount can be contributed in any year for any account or combination of accounts.)

Unlike traditional IRAs, which are limited to those people under age 70½, Roth IRAs impose no age limits. At any age, an individual with earned income can establish a Roth and make contributions. On the other hand, Roth IRAs subject participants to earnings limitations which traditional IRAs do not. High income earners may not be able to contribute to a Roth IRA because the maximum annual contribution which can be made begins to phase out for individuals whose modified adjusted gross incomes reach certain levels. Above these limits, no Roth contributions are allowed. Figure 12.3 explains how these phaseout limits are applied, using the contribution limit for 2001 of $2,000.

Qualified Roth Withdrawals

Withdrawals from Roth IRAs are either qualified or nonqualified. A qualified withdrawal provides for the full tax advantage that Roths offer: tax-free distribution of earnings. To be a qualified withdrawal, two requirements must be met:

- The funds must have been held in the account for a minimum of five years; and
- The withdrawal must occur for one of the following reasons:
  - the owner has reached age 59½;
  - the owner dies;
  - the owner becomes disabled; or
  - the distribution is used to purchase a first home.

If these requirements are met, no portion of the withdrawal is subject to tax.

Nonqualified Roth Withdrawals

A nonqualified withdrawal does not meet the previously discussed criteria. The result is that distributed Roth earnings are subject to tax. This would occur when the withdrawal is taken without meeting the above requirements and the amount of the withdrawal exceeds the total amount that was contributed. Because Roth contributions are made with after-tax dollars, only the *earnings* on those contributions are subject to taxation. Furthermore, they are taxed only when those earnings are removed from the account

FIGURE 12.3 AGI Phaseout Limits for Roth IRAs

Eligibility to contribute to a Roth IRA is based on one's adjusted gross income and filing status. Individuals with AGIs above certain limits will find that the maximum they can contribute is phased down from the annual limit and then eliminated entirely once AGI reaches a certain point. These phaseout ranges follow, using contribution limits effective in 2001:

	Full Contribution Available for AGIs:	Partial Contribution Available for AGIs:	No Contribution Allowed for AGIs:
Single Taxpayers	$0–$95,000	$95,000–$110,000	Above $110,000
Married Taxpayers, Filing Jointly	$0–$150,000	$150,000–$160,000	Above $160,000

For AGIs that fall into the "partial contribution available" category, the maximum amount that can be contributed to a Roth IRA is determined as follows:

Single Filers

$$\$2,000 - \left[\frac{AGI - \$95,000}{\$15,000} (2,000) \right]$$

Joint Filers

$$\$2,000 - \left[\frac{AGI - \$150,000}{\$10,000} (2,000) \right]$$

For example, a single individual with an AGI of $98,000 could contribute up to $1,600 to a Roth IRA; a couple with an AGI of $156,000 could contribute up to $800. (Unless an individual's or a couple's contribution limit is reduced to zero, the Code allows a minimum contribution of $200.) Roth contributions that are phased down due to income levels can be "made up" with corresponding contributions to traditional IRAs. For example, if the individual in the above example contributed the maximum he could of $1,600 to a Roth IRA, he could also contribute $400 to a traditional IRA; combined, the contributions would equal the $2,000 limit. (If the individual in this case is an active participant, the traditional IRA contribution would be nondeductible because his AGI exceeds the threshold for deductible contributions to traditional IRAs.)

without having met the above requirements. If the owner of the Roth IRA is younger than 59½ when the withdrawal is taken, it will be considered premature and (if it does not qualify as an exception to the premature distribution rule) the earnings will be assessed a 10 percent penalty.

No Required Distribution   Unlike traditional IRAs, Roth IRAs do not require mandatory distributions. No minimum distribution requirement exists for the account owner—the funds can remain in the account as long as the owner desires. In fact, the account can be left intact and passed on to heirs or beneficiaries.

FIGURE 12.4   Taxation of Distributions from Roth IRAs

Type of Distribution	Roth IRA Held Less Than 5 Years		Roth IRA Held 5 Years or More	
	Earnings Taxed	10% Penalty	Earnings Taxed	10% Penalty
Pre 59½	Yes	Yes	Yes	Yes
Pre 59½, but distribution due to death, disability, or for a first home purchase	Yes	No	No	No
Post 59½	Yes	No	No	No

Spousal IRA

Persons eligible to set up IRAs for themselves may create a separate spousal IRA for a nonworking spouse and contribute up to $2,000 (in 2001) to the spousal account, even if the partner is in an employer-sponsored plan. This means that a couple can contribute up to $4,000 (in 2001) to their IRAs in a single year—$2,000 for the working spouse's IRA and $2,000 for·the non-working spouse's IRA. (Before 1997, the maximum amount that could have been contributed annually to a spousal IRA was $250.) However, there are a number of limitations. If the spousal account is a traditional IRA, the amount of the deduction that can be taken for contributions may be reduced or eliminated if the partner is an active participant and the couple's adjusted gross income exceeds certain amounts. If the spousal account is a Roth IRA, the maximum contribution may be reduced or eliminated if the couple's adjusted gross income exceeds certain thresholds. The spousal IRA contribution must be reported on the couple's joint tax return, as would be the IRA contribution for the working spouse.

The contribution limit is scheduled to increase (from $2,000 in 2001) each year through 2008, by which time the annual limit for any IRA will be $5,000. After 2008, the limit will be adjusted annually for inflation.

Education IRA (Coverdell Education Savings Account)

Education IRAs, or education savings accounts, are special investment accounts that allow individuals and families to fund formal education expenses on a tax-favored basis.

Beginning in 2002, education IRAs are exempt from tax as long as they are used for qualified education expenses of the account's beneficiary, such as tuition, tutoring, books, room and board, computer equipment, uniforms, extended day program costs and any other supplies required for attendance at any public or private elementary or secondary school, as well as at any college, university, vocational school or other postsecondary educational institution.

Education IRAs were originally designed to fund higher education expenses of a designated beneficiary by allowing after-tax (nondeductible) contributions to accumulate on a tax-deferred basis. When distributions are taken from an education IRA, the earnings portion of the distribution is excluded from income to the extent it is used to pay qualified education expenses. Earnings are taxed when they are not used to pay qualified education expenses, and then they are also subject to a 10-percent penalty.

Contributions to education IRAs are not deductible, currently are limited to $500 each year per child and must be made before the beneficiary turns 18. In 2002 and thereafter, the annual contribution limit increases to $2,000 per beneficiary. Single taxpayers whose adjusted gross incomes are $95,000 or less and joint filers with adjusted gross incomes of $150,000 or less can take full advantage of the maximum contribution. The AGI limit for joint filers rises to $190,000 in 2002. As income exceeds these levels, the amount of allowable education IRA contribution is phased down until it is eliminated at $110,000 for single taxpayers and at $160,000 for joint filers. Beginning in 2002, joint filers will not be allowed to contribute once their AGI reaches $220,000. (See Figure 12.5).

FIGURE 12.5   Contributions to Education IRAs

Year	Contribution Limit	AGI Phaseout Range for Single Filers	AGI Phaseout Range for Joint Filers
2001	$ 500	$95,000 – $110,000	$150,000 – $160,000
2002 and later	$2,000	$95,000 – $110,000	$190,000 – $220,000

If the child for whom an account has been established does not use the funds for education, or if there are any amounts remaining in an account when the beneficiary reaches age 30, remaining funds can be rolled over to another education IRA benefiting another family member with no penalty. Any IRA distributions that are not used to pay for a beneficiary's education expenses will be included in the recipient's income and will be subject to a 10 percent penalty.

✓ **For Example:** Christine, the beneficiary of an education IRA, uses the funds to pay for her university expenses. She applies the funds toward tuition, room and board, and computer equipment. She graduates with some funds remaining in the account. When she turns 30 years old, her parents roll these funds over to another education IRA that they established for her younger sister, Lucy. Lucy uses the funds to pay for truck-driving school, computer-simulation fees, and even a uniform. She also finishes school with some funds remaining in the account. Her parents divide the balance and give it to Christine and Lucy for them to use in buying their first homes. This balance is taxed as ordinary income to both Christine and Lucy because it is not used for qualified education expenses. Furthermore, a 10-penalty is also assessed against the balance.

Nothing prevents more than one individual from contributing to an education IRA. The annual limit applies to each beneficiary only. Consequently, parents and grandparents can contribute to a single account, so long as the annual limit is not exceeded in any year. Excess contributions will still be subject to a 6 percent excise penalty.

Rollover IRA

Normally, benefits withdrawn from any qualified retirement plan are taxable the year in which they are received. However, certain tax-free rollover provisions of the tax law provide some degree of portability when an individual wishes to transfer funds from one plan to another, specifically to a rollover IRA.

Essentially, rollover IRAs provide a way for individuals who have received a distribution from a qualified plan to reinvest the funds in a new tax-deferred account and continue to shelter those funds and their earnings from current taxes. Rollover IRAs are used by individuals who, for example, have left one employer for another and have received a complete distribution from their previous employer's plan or by those who had invested funds in an individual IRA of one kind and want to roll over to another IRA for a higher rate of return.

A distribution received from an employer-sponsored retirement plan or from an IRA is eligible for a tax-free rollover if it is reinvested in an IRA within 60 days following receipt of the distribution and if the plan participant does not actually take physical receipt of the distribution. The entire amount need not be rolled over; a partial distribution may be rolled over from one IRA or eligible plan to another IRA. However, if a partial rollover is executed, the part retained will be taxed as ordinary income and subject to a 10 percent tax.

✓ **Take Note:** Only the person who established an IRA is eligible to benefit from the rollover treatment—with one exception. A surviving spouse who inherits IRA benefits or benefits from the deceased spouse's plan is eligible to establish a rollover IRA in his or her own name.

Summary

Individuals prepare for the financial challenges of retirement in a variety of ways. They may be covered under any one (or more) of a variety of employer-sponsored qualified retirement plans, including defined benefit and defined contribution pension plans, 403(b) plans, 457 deferred compensation plans, simplified employee pension (SEP) plans, SIMPLE plans, Keogh plans and 401(k) plans. Even if they are not covered under an employer-sponsored plan, individuals can save for retirement with a traditional or Roth individual retirement account (IRA) or annuity.

Key Concepts

In preparing for their licensing examination, students should be familiar with the following concepts:

qualified vs. nonqualified retirement plans	tax-sheltered annuity plans—403(b) plans
defined benefit plans	defined contribution plans
minimum participation standards	401(k) plans
457 plans	Keogh plans
SEP plans	vesting
traditional IRAs	spousal IRAs
rollover IRAs	SIMPLE plans
Roth IRAs	education IRAs

Lesson Exam Twelve

1. All of the following employed persons who have no employer-sponsored retirement plan would be eligible to set up and contribute to a traditional IRA EXCEPT

   A. Miriam, age 26, secretary
   B. Brent, age 40, medical technician
   C. Jack, age 60, plumber
   D. Edna, age 72, nurse

2. David is age 40 and single. He earns $45,000 annually as an engineer with a company that has a group life plan but no employer-sponsored retirement plan. If David sets up a traditional IRA, what is the maximum contribution he can make and deduct from taxes in 2001?

   A. $0
   B. $1,000
   C. $2,000
   D. $4,000

3. Herbert and Olga have been married 10 years. They have no children and each has a well-paying job. However, neither is covered by an employer retirement plan. What is the maximum amount they may set aside together in tax-deductible traditional IRA funds in 2001?

   A. $2,200
   B. $2,250
   C. $3,000
   D. $4,000

4. Which of the following scenarios pertaining to IRAs is NOT correct?

   A. June has accumulated $30,000 in her traditional IRA. At age 55 she withdraws $2,500 to take a vacation. She will have to include the $2,500 in her taxable income for the year and pay a $250 penalty.
   B. Bradley, age 72, is covered by an employer-sponsored retirement plan. He cannot establish a traditional IRA.
   C. Peter inherits $15,000 in IRA benefits from his father, who died in 1997. Peter can set up a tax-favored rollover IRA with the money and defer current income tax on the benefits received.
   D. Walter is age 60. He may take a distribution from his traditional IRA without having to worry about an early withdrawal penalty.

5. Which of the following statements regarding Roth IRAs is NOT correct?

   A. They provide for tax-free accumulation of funds.
   B. They limit contributions each year.
   C. They mandate distributions no later than age 70½.
   D. They are not available to those in the upper-income tax brackets.

6. Which of the following statements regarding Keogh plans is NOT correct?

   A. They must comply with the same participation and coverage requirements as qualified corporate plans.
   B. They apply to self-employed persons.
   C. They may be funded by an individual retirement annuity.
   D. Distributions before age 59½ are tax deductible.

7. Which of the following statements does NOT describe correctly the tax advantages of a qualified retirement plan?

   A. The earnings of a qualified plan are exempt from the employee's current income taxation.
   B. Employer contributions to a qualified plan are considered a deductible business expense.
   C. An employee's contribution to his or her retirement plan is included in ordinary income
   D. Earnings from a qualified retirement plan are taxable when paid out as a benefit.

8. Vesting can be best described as which of the following?

   A. The time at which a worker meets the eligibility requirements for plan participation
   B. The age at which an employee must begin to make withdrawals from retirement plans
   C. The right of an employee's spouse to be accounted for in the employee's qualified plan benefits
   D. The employee's right to funds or benefits contributed by the employer

9. Marvin is single and earned $24,000 in 2001. The company where he is employed has a pension plan in which he participates. For that year, he is eligible to set up a traditional IRA and deduct annual contributions of up to

   A. $0
   B. $1,000
   C. $2,000
   D. $4,000

10. All of the following should be eligible to establish a Keogh retirement plan EXCEPT

    A. a dentist in private practice
    B. partners in a furniture store
    C. a sole proprietor of a jewelry store
    D. a major stockholder-employee in a family corporation

11. All of the following types of plans are reserved for small employers EXCEPT

    A. 401(k)
    B. SARSEP
    C. SIMPLE IRA
    D. SIMPLE 401(k)

12. The maximum amount that can be contributed to a child's education IRA each year is

    A. $500 in 2001; $2,000 thereafter
    B. $1,000 in 2001; $2,000 thereafter
    C. $2,000 in 2001; $4,000 thereafter
    D. $5,000 in 2001; $10,000 thereafter

13. All of the following statements about SIMPLE plans are correct EXCEPT

    A. an employer may establish a SIMPLE plan if another qualified plan is not already in place.
    B. they can be structured as an IRA or as a 401(k) cash or deferred arrangement.
    C. employers must make a matching contribution, dollar-for-dollar, up to 2 percent of each employee's annual compensation.
    D. only employers with no more than 100 employees can establish SIMPLE plans.

14. Which of the following statements about 401(k) plans is CORRECT?

    A. All of a company's employees must participate in the plan.
    B. An employee's deferred contributions become nonforfeitable according to the plan's vesting schedule.
    C. Employer contributions are included in an employee's income for the year.
    D. As of 2001, the limit on employee deferrals to a 401(k) plan was $10,500 per year.

15. Bob owns a traditional IRA and a Roth IRA. What is the maximum combined amount that he can contribute to both accounts in 2001 without being penalized?

    A. $1,000
    B. $2,000
    C. $3,000
    D. $4,000

Answers & Rationale

1. **D.** Anyone under age 70½ may open a traditional IRA. Because Edna is 72 years old, she is not eligible to set up and contribute to a traditional IRA.

2. **C.** David can contribute the maximum amount ($2,000 in 2001) and take a full deduction for his entire contribution to his traditional IRA. When an individual is not covered by any employer-sponsored retirement plan, he or she may contribute the maximum amount to a traditional IRA and take a deduction for this amount, regardless of income level.

3. **D.** Because neither Herbert nor Olga is covered by an employer retirement plan, they can contribute $2,000 each in 2001 to a traditional IRA and take a full deduction for this amount. This means that they can contribute and take a $4,000 deduction. These limits will gradually increase through 2008.

4. **C.** Peter cannot establish a rollover IRA with the IRA funds he inherited from his father. Only a surviving spouse who inherits IRA benefits or benefits from a deceased spouse's qualified plan can establish a rollover IRA.

5. **C.** Unlike traditional IRAs, Roth IRAs do not require mandatory distribution. There is no minimum distribution requirement, and the account owner may leave funds in the account as long as desired. In fact, the account can be left intact and passed on to heirs or beneficiaries.

6. **D.** As with other qualified retirement plans, distributions from a Keogh plan before age 59½ are subject to a 10 percent penalty tax and are not tax deductible.

7. **C.** An employee's contributions to an individual qualified plan are deductible from income under certain conditions.

8. **D.** Vesting means the right each employee has to his or her retirement fund. Benefits that have vested belong to the employee even if he or she terminates employment prior to retirement. Although an employee always has a 100 percent vested interest in benefits that he or she has contributed, an employer's contributions will vest according to a vesting schedule established by law.

9. **C.** Single taxpayers like Marvin, who are covered by an employer sponsored retirement plan, can take the $2,000 maximum deduction of 2001, provided adjusted gross income is $32,000 or less.

10. **D.** Keogh plans are designed for unincorporated businesses that allow the business owner (or partner in a business) to participate as an employee. A major stockholder-employee in a family corporation, therefore, would not be eligible to establish a Keogh plan.

11. **A.** SARSEPs and SIMPLE plans both were designed to be used for small businesses employing no more than 25 and 100 employees, respectively. No similar restrictions exist on the number of employees that may be employed by a company with a 401(k) plan.

12. **A.** In 2001, an individual can contribute up to $500 per child to an education IRA until the child reaches age 18. This contribution limit increases to $2,000 per year in 2002.

13. **C.** With a SIMPLE plan, an employer has two options for making contributions. First, it can make a matching contribution of up to 3 percent, dollar-for-dollar, of an employee's annual compensation. Alternatively, it can make nonelective contributions of 2 percent of compensation on behalf of each eligible employee.

14. **D.** In 2001, an employee could defer up to $10,500 to his or her 401(k) plan account. The limit of this deferral will increase each year beginning in 2002 ($11,000), until it reaches $15,000 in 2006.

15. **B.** Although Bob can own a traditional and Roth IRA and make contributions to both, he can contribute no more than $2,000 total in 2001. This limit is scheduled to slowly increase beginning in 2002 ($3,000) until it reaches $5,000 in 2008, after which it will be adjusted annually for inflation.

13

Uses of Life Insurance

INTRODUCTION

For most people, the best solution to the adverse financial consequences that result when a breadwinner dies is to have an adequate amount of life insurance. Without question it remains the most efficient way to guarantee a family's or business' continued financial integrity. What often is overlooked or not understood are the many living benefits of life insurance—especially whole life insurance. For example, the cash value feature of permanent insurance and the owner's right to borrow from the cash value make these policies an important source of funds to meet living needs. In this lesson, we will review some of the more common ways that life insurance is used to meet individual needs as well as business needs, not only at the death of the policyowner but also during the owner's life.

LESSON OBJECTIVES

When you complete this lesson you should be able to:

- explain how the human life approach and the needs approach are used to determine the amount of life insurance needed;
- list and describe the different ways life insurance can be used to meet an individual's financial needs; and
- explain how businesses use life insurance as a funding vehicle for buy-sell agreements, to provide protection when a key employee dies and as an employee benefit.

Determining Proper Insurance Amounts

Life insurance has many uses, some obvious, others not so apparent. A family's desire to provide protection against the loss of its breadwinner (or breadwinners) is perhaps the most obvious function of life insurance, as is a small business' need to protect itself against the death of a key employee. Few people, however, realize that life insurance can be used as a vehicle to facilitate saving for retirement or funding a child's education. As we will see in this lesson, the uses of life insurance extend far beyond the realm of death benefits.

When deciding how much insurance is enough for a given client, professional insurance producers know that affordability, while important, is not the only consideration. Accurately determining the proper amount of life insurance requires the consideration of a number of factors, including the planned uses for the insurance, the client's long-range goals, and the ways insurance may or may not be able to help meet those goals.

Two basic approaches are used today to help insurance buyers and producers determine the proper amount of life insurance. The older method, known as the *human life value approach*, has been replaced largely by the more practical *needs approach*—but both methods can be effective in answering the primary question, How much life insurance is needed?

Human Life Value Approach

The concept of human life value was first mentioned in Lesson 1, where we discussed the purpose and function of insurance. This concept was formulated by the late Dr. Solomon S. Heubner in 1924 as a philosophical framework for understanding the services that can be performed by life and health insurance, for people both in and out of the insurance business. The result of Dr. Heubner's work is that everyone can have a better idea of how an insurance plan can be tailor-made to meet specific objectives.

Dr. Heubner pointed out that the value of a human life can and should be expressed as a dollar valuation; that is, determining the economic value of a person by discounting estimated future net earnings used for family purposes at a reasonable rate of interest.

A relatively simple method of accomplishing this is to:

- estimate an individual's average annual future earnings after deducting taxes and personal living costs;
- estimate the number of years the individual expects to work until retirement;
- select a reasonable interest rate (comparable to current rates paid on insurance proceeds held by insurers) at which future earnings should be discounted; and
- multiply the present value of one dollar payable annually for the number of years until expected retirement, using the selected interest rate, by the estimated average future annual earnings. The result is a

reasonably accurate estimate of the individual's economic value to his or her family. (Tables that show the present value of one dollar at various interest rates are available.)

✔ **For Example:** George, who is 35 years old, estimates that he will earn an average of $40,000 a year until retirement at age 65. Of that $40,000, $25,000 is devoted to the care and maintenance of his family; the remaining $15,000 goes for taxes and his personal living costs.

Based on these assumptions, we can see that George's family will need and use $750,000 over George's working lifetime ($25,000 per year × 30 years). Essentially, this is George's economic value to his family over the next 30 years. However, what if today George were to die or become so severely disabled that he could not work? What source could his family rely on to continue to provide them with $25,000 a year for the next 30 years? What George needs today is a fund that, when compounded at a certain rate of interest, will produce a constant $25,000 a year for the next 30 years.

Figure 13.1 shows the amount of money that must be on hand today to produce annual incomes of $10,000, $15,000, $20,000 and $25,000 for various terms, assuming a 4 percent interest factor. For George, who needs a fund that will generate $25,000 a year for 30 years, the amount needed today is $432,300. Thus, George's human life value to his family is $432,300—the amount required today that, at 4 percent interest, would produce the same annual income his family consumes over the same length of time that George plans to work. This $432,300 is a measurement of how much financial protection—insurance—George's family needs to replace the income that will be lost if he dies or becomes disabled.

✔ **Take Note:** This human life value approach has come under criticism by some industry experts who point out that it does not take into account inflation or the likelihood of increases in wages or standards of living. In other cases, it may actually overstate the amount of insurance needed if it does not take into consideration other sources of income or family situations changing. Consequently, the method most typically used today is the needs approach.

Needs Approach

Fundamentally, the needs approach for determining how much insurance protection a person should have requires first analyzing the family's (or business') financial needs and objectives should the breadwinner (or businessperson) die or become disabled. Then, those needs are weighed against the ability of the family (or business) to meet them out of current or anticipated assets. For example, the death of a family's breadwinner will necessitate a new source of funds to replace the earnings that are now lost. The obvious answer is life insurance. However, the amount of life insurance required must take into account the amount of monthly benefits the family

FIGURE 13.1   Amounts Necessary to Produce Future Income Streams

This table illustrates the amount of capital that must be on hand today to produce various annual incomes for specified time periods. The assumed interest rate is 4 percent.

| Number of Years | Annual Income Streams (4 Percent Interest) | | | |
of Income	$10,000	$15,000	$20,000	$25,000
20	$135,903	$203,855	$271,306	$339,758
25	$156,221	$234,332	$312,442	$390,553
30	$172,920	$259,380	$345,840	$432,300
35	$186,646	$279,969	$373,292	$466,615
40	$197,928	$296,892	$395,856	$494,820

For example, to generate $25,000 a year for 30 years, one needs $432,300 on hand today, earning 4 percent interest.

will be receiving from Social Security, from the deceased's pension plan, from personal savings and any other source. The difference between what is owned now (or will ultimately be available) and what is needed in terms of funds then is used to help the insurance producer recommend an insurance program that may involve the use of term insurance, permanent insurance, annuities or a combination of all three.

 Take Note: The needs approach is not limited to fulfilling objectives in the event of death only. It also considers a family's (or business') living needs, such as providing for a child's education and planning for retirement. Again, the amount of life insurance required to meet these needs is coordinated with other assets that may be available.

In the remainder of this lesson, we will look at the many uses for life insurance. Insurance producers should consider all these concerns when helping a person or a business determine the proper insurance program to meet anticipated needs. In some cases, such as planning for education or retirement, the producer must consider the need for funds not only if the insured dies, but also if he or she lives. A whole life policy, for instance, can provide funds either in the form of a death benefit or cash value when those funds are needed. If the insured should die prematurely, the beneficiary can take comfort in knowing that funds will be available to meet the planned objectives. If the insured lives, the policy's cash value can be used to meet the same objectives.

A family's or business' ability to pay for the insurance deemed necessary to meet its objectives is, of course, an important consideration. It may be decided that only part of the insurance plan can be purchased immediately and the rest will be put into effect at a later date. For this reason, and because a family's or business' needs change over time, a needs approach insurance program usually includes plans for periodic reviews (usually annually) to update the program as needed.

Individual Uses for Life Insurance

The number of uses for life insurance in meeting personal and family financial needs really is quite impressive. The following list of common uses can be met with term insurance if the need is temporary (such as providing an additional protection fund while the children are growing up and living at home), with whole life insurance if the need is permanent (such as meeting estate planning objectives and for any living financial need) or with annuities if the need is for future income (such as retirement income).

In some cases, different products can be mixed to strengthen the protection. For example, a person may use a deferred annuity to plan for retirement, but also use a whole life policy to provide protection before retirement and additional retirement funds, through the policy's cash value, at retirement. Health insurance, covered later in this text, also plays an important role in a balanced insurance program.

When working with a client, the insurance producer should consider the following individual needs.

Final Expense Fund

A final expense fund is the amount of cash that is required (and should be on hand) at death to pay for a deceased breadwinner's last illness and funeral costs, outstanding debts, federal and state death taxes and any other unpaid taxes, legal fees, court costs and executor's fees, etc. These last expenses usually will total at least several thousand dollars.

 Take Note: Social Security provides only a very small amount as a death benefit—a maximum lump sum of $255—and only to an eligible surviving spouse or child.

Housing Fund

In the case of a breadwinner's death, there may be the need for a home mortgage or rental allowance fund. With this cash fund, a surviving family can, for instance, pay off the mortgage or continue mortgage payments. If the family rents its home, the need may be for a monthly amount that will continue rental payments for a certain number of years.

Education Fund

How much, where and how expensive a child's education will be—together with how it is to be paid for—are goals that vary widely from family to family. However, most people want their children to obtain a good education and studies prove that a college education is vitally important for today's young people.

The cost of a college education has continued to spiral in recent years, currently ranging from about $28,000 or more for four years in state universities to approximately $78,000 or more in private institutions. An adequate education fund is a typical family need.

Monthly Income

The income a breadwinner provides for his or her family obviously will cease upon his or her death. However, the income needs of the surviving family continue. Monthly income will be needed during the years that the children are growing and living at home and then for the surviving spouse after the children are self-supporting. Thus, there are two distinct income needs periods: the dependency period and the blackout period. Ensuring a source of monthly income during these two critical periods is another use for life insurance.

Dependency Period The dependency period refers to that period following the death of a breadwinner during which the children are living at home. The need for family income is greatest while the children are growing up. When a breadwinner dies, a surviving spouse with small children usually will be eligible for Social Security benefits. However, as we have seen, Social Security benefits, while helpful, generally will not meet the total family need.

Moreover, an eligible spouse with an eligible child receives Social Security income only while the child is under age 16 (or disabled). Once the child turns 16, his or her Social Security benefits will continue another two years, but income to the spouse ceases and will not resume until, at the earliest, the spouse reaches age 60.

Blackout Period The period in which there are no Social Security benefits for the surviving spouse is known as the blackout period. Again, the blackout period begins when the youngest child turns 16. If there are no eligible children with the surviving spouse when the breadwinner dies, the blackout period starts immediately and continues until, at the earliest, the spouse reaches age 60.

Emergency Fund

Every family faces emergencies from time to time, so a fund is needed to provide money for various miscellaneous costs and expenses that may arise, but cannot be foreseen.

Income Needs If Disabled or Ill

Basically, the same cash (except a final expense fund) and monthly income needs that arise at the death of a breadwinner exist when disability strikes a breadwinner. In both cases, the family loses the breadwinner's earnings. However, the need for income often is greater with disability because most of the disabled person's expenses continue and the family generally is faced with additional medical expenses. Medical expense insurance and disability income insurance (discussed in Lessons 16 and 17), also should be considered in a personal insurance program.

Life-threatening or severe chronic diseases, such as Alzheimer's disease, cancer, heart disease and AIDS, can wipe out a person's life savings in a short time and have other devastating effects on a person's life. People suffering such illnesses often face the loss of their job and their home as well as their independence and dignity. Funds from a life insurance policy under an accelerated death benefits provision can relieve the immediate financial hardships and help people preserve their possessions and lifestyle. Care must be taken, however, to ensure that the financial well-being of dependents is not compromised.

Retirement Income

The happy eventuality is that both spouses will live to a ripe old age. If so, they also will need income to supplement their Social Security or other retirement benefits. The same holds true for single individuals as well.

🖉 **Quick Quiz 13.1**   Fill in the blanks below with the appropriate terms.

1. The older method used to determine the amount of life insurance a person should have is known as the _____.

2. The _____ period refers to the time after a breadwinner's death when minor children still are living at home.

3. The _____ is the amount of cash that is needed to pay for a deceased breadwinner's last illness and funeral costs, debts, federal and state death taxes and any other outstanding debts.

4. Most insurance buyers use the _____ approach today to determine the amount of life insurance protection needed.

5. The period during which the surviving spouse receives no Social Security benefits is called the _____ period.

Answers

1. *human life value approach*

2. *dependency*

3. *final expense fund*

4. *needs*

5. *blackout*

Business Uses for Life Insurance

Continued financial well-being for families depends not only on income from breadwinners, but also on the continued good health of the businesses in which they are engaged. So life insurance also plays an important role in the business world. The reasons for buying life insurance for business uses are the same as those for buying personal insurance—in one word, protection. Business owners wish to protect the condition of their businesses to provide security for their families. When people buy insurance for personal reasons, their families are concerned; when they buy it for business reasons, their employees, their associates and their families are involved.

Life insurance is used in businesses in a variety of ways:

- *As a funding medium.* For example, life insurance can be used to fund a business continuation (buy-sell) agreement to transfer ownership between partners or stockholders or to fund a deferred compensation plan.
- *As a form of business interruption insurance.* Life insurance cannot prevent the interruption of business activity caused by death or disability; however, it can indemnify the business for losses created by these interruptions.

- *As an employee benefit.* Life insurance can protect employees and their families from the financial problems of death, disability, illness and retirement.

Health insurance also plays a vital role in the business arena, primarily as an employee benefit. In this lesson, we will focus on business uses of life insurance; Lesson 24 covers business (and personal) uses of health insurance.

A Funding Medium

When a business owner dies, the business itself may terminate, or at least its ownership and management personnel will change. The death of a business owner often creates havoc—not only with the business, but also with the deceased owner's estate.

Insured buy-sell agreements can ensure the orderly continuation of a business, while family survivors receive a fair cash settlement for a deceased owner's interest in the business. Such an agreement guarantees that cash will be available at the owner's death to purchase the deceased owner's interest, so the business can continue without financial disruption.

 Take Note: Buy-sell plans may be used in any form of business—sole proprietorship, partnership or close corporation—so long as there are potential buyers.

Sole Proprietor Buy-Sell Plans

When a sole proprietor dies, his or her business generally comes to a sudden halt unless some arrangement has been made beforehand to continue the business. There are three alternatives. First, a member of the proprietor's family may be willing and able to operate the business at the proprietor's death. If so, the proprietor may wish to leave the business to one or more family survivors as a gift. Second, there may be no interested taker, so the only thing to do is close down the business at the proprietor's death. The third, and often most desirable alternative, is for the business to be sold to a competent and faithful employee.

Employees who have been active in the operation or the management of the business are the most likely buyers. Many times, the employee's talent is recognized by customers, creditors and suppliers, and it is obvious that the employee has helped build the good reputation enjoyed by the business. As a result, there is every indication that the business can continue successfully under the employee's direction.

A *two-step buy-sell plan* then can be arranged to sell the business to the employee at the proprietor's death:

- A buy-sell agreement is drafted by an attorney, setting forth the employee's obligation to buy and the responsibility of the proprietor's estate to sell the business interest at an agreed-upon price.
- An insurance policy is purchased by the employee on the life of the proprietor. The employee is the owner, premium-payor and beneficiary of the policy, the proceeds from which will be used to buy the business at the proprietor's death.

In addition, when cash value life insurance is used to fund the agreement, the plan may call for a transfer of ownership should the proprietor prefer to retire at some future time. The employee then could use the policy's cash value to make a substantial down payment toward the purchase of the business. The balance of the purchase price might be paid in installments over a period of years.

Partnership Buy-Sell Plans

By law, partnerships are dissolved automatically upon the death of a partner. Thus, it is vital that a binding buy-sell agreement be established by the partners while they are living. Under such an agreement, the interest of any partner who dies will be sold to and purchased by the surviving partners. The price (or a formula to determine one) is agreed upon in advance and stipulated in the buy-sell plan.

When properly executed—and funded with life insurance—a partnership buy-sell plan benefits all parties involved and no uncertainty as to the outcome exists. The deceased has agreed beforehand to the sale of his or her interest. The surviving partners know they will have a legal right to buy, and the deceased's family and heirs are certain that the partnership interest will be disposed of at a fair price. Furthermore, with life insurance as the funding vehicle, the money needed to purchase the deceased partner's interest will be available at precisely the moment it is needed. So, at the death of any partner, the surviving partners are able to maintain the business while the deceased partner's estate receives full value for the deceased's interest.

Two kinds of partnership insured buy-sell agreements exist: the *cross-purchase plan* and the *entity plan*.

Partnership Cross-Purchase Plan

Under the cross-purchase buy-sell plan, which is the more common approach to a buyout, the partners agree individually to purchase the interest of a deceased partner, and the executor of the deceased partner's estate is directed to sell the interest to the surviving partners. The partnership itself is not a party to the agreement.

FIGURE 13.2 Partnership Cross-Purchase Buy-Sell Plan

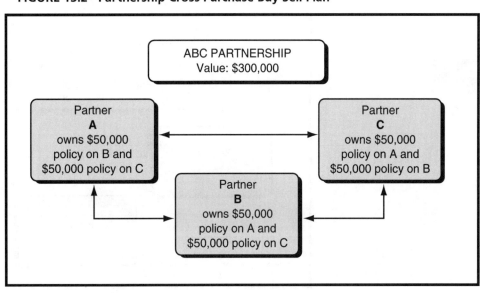

With these plans, each partner owns, is the beneficiary of and pays the premiums for life insurance on the other partner or partners in an amount equal to his or her share of the purchase price.

 For Example: A partnership worth $300,000 is owned equally by Partners A, B and C. Under an insured cross-purchase plan, each partner insures the life of each of the other partners for $50,000. As a result, the total insurance on each partner's life equals his or her share—$100,000—which would approximate the total purchase price the surviving partners would pay to the deceased's estate. (See Figure 13.2.)

 **Test Topic Alert!**

To calculate the total number of policies needed to fund a partnership cross-purchase plan, use the following formula: No. of Partners × (No. of Partners – 1)

Partnership Entity Plan

Under the entity buy-sell plan, the business itself—the partnership—owns, pays for and is the beneficiary of the policies that insure the lives of the individual partners. The partnership is a party to the buy-sell agreement.

With an entity plan, when a partner dies, his or her interest is purchased from his or her estate by the partnership. This interest then is divided among the surviving partners in proportion to their own interest.

 For Example: The XYZ Partnership is worth $600,000 and each partner has an equal interest. The partnership purchases a $200,000 insurance policy on the life of each partner. If Partner X dies first, the partnership buys X's interest

FIGURE 13.3 Partnership Entity Buy-Sell Plan

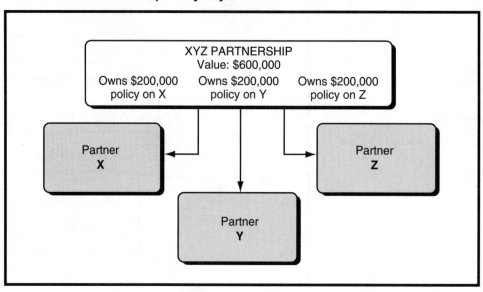

from his estate with the $200,000 insurance proceeds and divides this interest equally between Partners Y and Z. The proportionate share of Y and Z then would be increased from 33.33 percent to 50 percent. (See Figure 13.3.)

Close Corporation Buy-Sell Plans

In a close corporation (generally an incorporated family business), an insured buy-sell agreement can provide multiple advantages for all concerned. Unlike a partnership, a corporation does not cease to exist after the death of one of its owners. It is, by law, a separate entity apart from its owners, the stockholders. Nevertheless, problems are certain to develop if an agreement is not made in advance as to the disposition of a deceased stockholder's interest.

So buy-sell agreements are every bit as important to a close corporation as to a partnership. Just as in partnerships, the corporate insured buy-sell plan can take one of two forms, cross-purchase or entity. In a corporate plan, however, the entity type of agreement is known as a stock redemption plan.

✓ **Take Note:** It does not matter which plan—cross-purchase or stock redemption—is used, for the corporate insured buy-sell plan, although a close corporation with a relatively large number of stockholders usually will find the stock redemption plan more suitable. The decision about the type of plan should be left to the stockholders themselves, their attorney and their accountant.

Close Corporation Cross-Purchase Plan

The close corporation cross-purchase agreement is similar to that used in a partnership. The agreement calls for the surviving stockholders to purchase the interest of the deceased stockholder as individuals and for the estate of the deceased stockholder to sell the interest to the surviving stockholders directly. The corporation itself is not a party to the agreement. To fund a cross-purchase plan, each stockholder owns, pays for and is the beneficiary of insurance on the life of each of the other stockholders in amounts equivalent to his or her share of the purchase price.

Close Corporation Stock Redemption Plan

The corporation stock redemption plan operates in much the same manner as an entity plan in a partnership. The corporation, rather than the individual stockholders, is owner, premium-payor and beneficiary of policies on the lives of the stockholders. The corporation is a party to the agreement.

The amount of insurance carried by the corporation on the lives of the stockholders is equal to each stockholder's proportionate share of the purchase price. When a stockholder dies, the proceeds of the policy insuring that person are paid to the corporation. The corporation then uses the proceeds to buy the deceased's business interest represented by the stock in the deceased's estate. As with other life insurance, the premiums paid by the corporation are not tax deductible. The proceeds, however, generally are received income tax free, as is the case in a partnership plan.

Key-Person Insurance

Another important use of life insurance is to protect a business against interruptions caused by the loss of one of its valuable assets—a key employee or key executive.

When an individual dies, the primary function of life insurance is to offset the economic loss. We have noted how important life insurance is to the family. Key-employee or key-executive life insurance provides similar benefits—not to the family, but to the business. When an insured key person dies, the insurance beneficiary is the business itself.

✓ **Take Note:** A key person is any person in an organization whose contribution to the operation and success of the business is essential. Therefore, an owner-executive or highly skilled employee generally may be considered a key person.

With key-person insurance, the owner, premium-payor and beneficiary of the policy is the business organization. Complete control of the policy rests with the business, which means key-person insurance can be considered a company-owned asset not earmarked for any specific purpose. The death proceeds, or even the policy's cash value, may be used for a variety of business purposes. In fact flexibility is one of the outstanding features of this type of insurance. However, it usually is employed for some major purposes that, rather than being distinct from one another, actually work together to make the life insurance a practical company investment.

In general, the following are the primary purposes that key-person insurance serves:

- *Business indemnification.* Key-person insurance indemnifies a business; that is, it compensates a business for any financial loss caused by the death of a valuable key person. The death of a key person—whether an owner or employee—may result in less liberal credit terms from suppliers; banks may be less willing to lend the business money; valuable accounts once served by the key person may be lost. The proceeds from a key-person policy can be utilized to avoid some or all of these problems before they occur or to ease the financial burden they bring about.
- *A reserve fund.* Key-person life insurance also provides a business with a living benefit. When a business purchases key-person insurance, it automatically acquires an asset that can perform valuable services for the business while the key person still is alive. For example, when whole life insurance is purchased, the cash values increase steadily to provide a cash reserve fund for the business, which appears each year as an asset on the company's balance sheet.
- *Business credit.* Disruption of a business by the death of a key person can affect a business' credit seriously. Key-person life insurance, however, can offset this danger in two ways: as tangible evidence of business character and as a guarantee of loan repayment at the death of the key person.
- *Favorable tax treatment.* Finally, key-person life insurance receives favorable tax treatment. The death proceeds received by the business are not taxable. Premiums, of course, are not deductible for income purposes.

 **Test Topic Alert!**

If a key person leaves an employer, the employer can surrender the policy for cash, assign the policy or keep it in force, as there is no need to maintain an insurable interest.

Employee Benefit Plans

Life insurance also serves an important role in the area of employee benefits. Basically, employee benefits are plans established by employers who pay all or a portion of the cost of the plans to benefit their employees and, in some cases, to obtain favorable tax treatment. Let's review a few of these plans.

Split-Dollar Plans   Many business organizations have found split-dollar life insurance plans to be an effective and economical way to encourage young employees to join the organization and to discourage the established executive from taking his or her talents and knowledge elsewhere.

Split-dollar insurance plans enable an employer and any employee of the employer's choosing to share premium payments toward the purchase of insurance on the employee's life. Therefore, the split-dollar policy is a method of buying life insurance rather than a reason for buying it. The employee already has determined the need for the insurance, but cannot afford the entire premium. The employer has the funds to help finance the purchase of the insurance and has a specific reason for doing so—the desire to attract and hold key employees.

The split-dollar plan is informal in nature; it requires no qualification or approval by the Internal Revenue Service. A split-dollar plan has a low premium outlay. It is a single contract that uses cash value whole life and term insurance protection (dividends generally are used to purchase one-year term; any dividend excess is applied to the year's premium) to guarantee the return of the premium money to one party while ensuring a death benefit to the policy beneficiary.

In a typical split-dollar plan, the employer and the employee share the premium cost. Though there are variations, the employer generally contributes to the premium each year the amount equal to the increase in the policy's cash value. The employee pays only the balance of the premium. Upon the insured employee's death, the amount of death proceeds equal to the cash value generally goes to the employer, and the balance of the proceeds goes to the insured's beneficiary. On the other hand, if the plan is terminated while the insured is living, the cash value generally goes to the employer to compensate for the portion of premiums paid.

 **Test Topic Alert!**

The employer and employee share the premium cost in a typical split-dollar plan. In general, the employer contributes to the premium each year the amount equal to the increase in the policy's cash value. The employee pays the balance of the premium.

This method permits a financially able person or entity to help another person buy insurance, generally in the favorable interest of both parties. Thus, split-dollar may be used as an incentive plan by an employer for an employee, by an employer for a stockholder/employee, for business partners, for business co-owners or by a parent for a child or child-in-law.

Deferred Compensation Plans

Deferred compensation plans are a popular way for businesses to provide an important benefit for their owners or for select employees. Basically, a deferred compensation plan is an arrangement whereby an employee (or owner) agrees to for go some portion of his or her current income (such as annual raises or bonuses) until a specified future date, typically retirement. Life insurance is a popular funding vehicle for deferred compensation plans, in that the amounts deferred are used to pay premiums on cash value life insurance. At retirement, the cash values are available to the employee to supplement income. If the employee dies before retirement, his or her beneficiary receives the policy's proceeds. Deferred compensation plans can be employer-motivated or established at the employee's request.

A deferred compensation plan is an example of a nonqualified plan. Recall that a nonqualified plan does not receive favorable tax treatment by the IRS.

✓ **Take Note:** Because a deferred compensation plan is nonqualified, a company can pick and choose who among its employees and owners may participate in the plan, without regard to years of service, salary levels or any other criteria. A nonqualified plan allows a business to provide proportionate benefits for officers, executives and other highly paid employees; a qualified plan is not nearly as flexible.

Salary Continuation Plans

Deferred compensation and salary continuation plans appear similar in nature, but in fact, are quite different. Deferred compensation gives employees deferred benefits in lieu of a current raise or bonus. Salary continuation, on the other hand, is an additional fringe benefit that augments an employee's salary. In simple terms, the employee funds the deferred compensation plan; the employer funds the salary continuation plan.

A salary continuation plan may be set up between an employer and its employees or between a business and an independent contractor. Typically, the employer agrees to pay the employee (or his or her assignee) continuing payments at retirement, death or disability. This is subject to the condition that the employee continues employment with the employer. Or the plan may require that the employee provide continuing consultant services after his or her retirement. The plan is informally funded through life insurance.

Other Employee Benefit Plans

Many other types of employee benefit plans and programs exist. These programs include retirement plans (pensions, profit-sharing plans, employer-sponsored IRAs, 401(k) and 403(b) plans), group life and health plans, child care plans, educational assistance programs, disability plans, survivor benefit plans and wellness programs, to name just a few. Some might even argue that an employer's FICA contributions to the Social Security system and payments to workers' compensation programs, though they are mandatory, are forms of employee benefits.

Throughout this text, we have discussed many of these benefit plans and in the next lesson, we will focus specifically on health and disability programs. Therefore, we will not go into any additional detail here, other than to emphasize that insurance helps make a lot of these employee benefits possible, either as the funding vehicle or as the benefit itself.

✎ Quick Quiz 13.2 True or False?

_____ 1. Under a cross-purchase buy-sell plan, the partners individually agree to buy a deceased partner's interest, and the executor of the deceased partner's estate is directed to sell the interest to the surviving partners.

_____ 2. Buy-sell plans can be used only in partnerships and close corporations.

_____ 3. In a key-person insurance policy, the business itself is the beneficiary, not the family of the key person.

_____ 4. As with other business life insurance, a business can take an income tax deduction for the amount of premiums paid for key-person insurance and will not be taxed on the death proceeds.

_____ 5. Under a split-dollar insurance plan, the employer and employee share premium costs on the purchase of life insurance for the employee.

_____ 6. Salary continuation plans and deferred compensation plans are very similar employee benefit plans.

Answers

1. *True*.

2. *False*. Buy-sell plans can be used in any form of business—sole proprietorship, partnerships and close corporations—to ensure the orderly continuation of the business.

3. *True*

4. *False*. The premiums paid for key person insurance are not deductible for income tax purposes but the death proceeds are received tax-free.

5. *True*.

6. *False*. Although salary continuation and deferred compensation plans appear similar, they are quite different. For instance, deferred compensation plans give employees deferred benefits instead of a current raise or bonus. In contrast, salary continuation is an additional fringe benefit that augments an employee's salary. The employee funds a deferred compensation plan, and the employer funds the salary continuation plan.

Summary

Beyond the obvious use for life insurance—to provide a source of funds for an insured's beneficiary—there are a number of other uses for this versatile product in meeting individual needs as well as business needs. Some producers find that they are most comfortable working in the individual or family market, while others prefer the business market.

An important duty of the professional insurance producer is to determine the proper amount of insurance needed to meet a client's needs. The two most common methods used to evaluate how much insurance is appropriate in a given situation are the human life value and the needs approaches.

Life insurance can be used in a variety of ways to meet personal and family financial needs. The cash values of a whole life insurance policy make it especially helpful in meeting permanent insurance needs such as estate planning objectives and financial needs that arise at death. On the other hand, term insurance is suited ideally for meeting temporary needs. Annuities are the perfect answer to a future income need, such as retirement.

Businesses also have many needs for life insurance. It can provide the foundation for business continuation agreements or buy-sell plans, for key-person protection or for any number of employee benefit programs.

Key Concepts

In preparing for their licensing examination, students should be familiar with the following concepts:

human life value approach	key-person insurance
needs approach	split-dollar life insurance
individual uses for life insurance	deferred compensation plans
business uses for life insurance	employee benefits
buy-sell plans	salary continuation plans

Lesson Exam Thirteen

1. Which of the following statements regarding ways to determine the proper amount of life insurance is CORRECT?

   A. The most popular method today for determining the proper amount of life insurance is the human life value approach.
   B. When using the needs approach to determine the proper amount of life insurance to purchase, non-insurance-type assets, such as pension benefits or personal savings, are not factors in the calculation.
   C. The human life approach takes into account inflation and likely increases in wages.
   D. The needs approach takes into account family financial goals such as college education for children or retirement income for a surviving spouse.

2. Which of the following statements regarding survivor financial needs is NOT correct?

   A. The term *dependency period* refers to the 20-year period immediately following the insured's death during which the widowed spouse must depend on Social Security.
   B. The period for which there are no Social Security benefits for the surviving spouse is known as the blackout period.
   C. A final expense fund addresses a deceased breadwinner's last illness and funeral costs, death taxes, outstanding debts and more.
   D. A housing fund addresses a family's rental or home mortgage needs.

3. Three business partners individually agree to acquire the interest of a deceased partner and own life insurance on each of the other partners in the amount of his or her share of the business' buyout value. What kind of plan is this an example of?

   A. Entity buy-sell
   B. Stock redemption buy-sell
   C. Cross-purchase buy-sell
   D. 401(k)

4. Which of the following statements regarding key-person insurance is NOT correct?

   A. Key-person life insurance indemnifies a business for financial loss caused by the death of a key employee or key executive.
   B. The business may borrow from the cash value of a permanent key-person life insurance policy.
   C. The policy's death proceeds received by the business are not taxable.
   D. Premiums for a key-person life insurance policy are a tax deductible expense to the business.

5. Which of the following statements regarding deferred compensation plans is CORRECT?

   A. A deferred compensation plan always must be designed as a qualified plan.
   B. Life insurance is not a permissible funding vehicle, but annuities are.
   C. They permit a business to provide extra benefits to officers, executives and other highly paid employees.
   D. A deferred compensation plan must be made available to all employees who are at least 21 years old and have one year of service to the business.

6. With three partners in a business, how many life insurance policies would be required to insure a cross-purchase buy-sell plan?

   A. 3
   B. 6
   C. 9
   D. 12

7. Robert and his employer agree on the purchase of a split-dollar life insurance policy and the usual split-dollar approach to premium payments. Each year, the employer will contribute to the premium an amount equal to

   A. one-half the premium
   B. the annual dividend
   C. the increase in the policy's cash value
   D. two-thirds of the premium

8. Roland is 45 years old and married. He has a son, age 19, a freshman at a local university and a daughter, age 8. Decreasing term insurance could be recommended for Roland in order to accomplish which of the following?

   A. Supplement retirement income
   B. Guarantee a college education for the son
   C. Provide payment protection
   D. Provide a college education fund for the daughter

9. A partnership owns, pays for and is the beneficiary of the life insurance policies on the lives of its individual partners. What kind of plan is this an example of?

   A. Entity buy-sell
   B. Stock redemption buy-sell
   C. Cross-purchase buy-sell
   D. Keogh

10. Which of the following statements about key-person insurance is CORRECT?

    A. The key employee's family is the beneficiary of the policy.
    B. The death proceeds are taxable.
    C. The business can take a tax deduction for premiums paid.
    D. Because the business has complete control over the policy, a key-person policy can be considered a business asset.

Answers & Rationale

1. **D.** The human life value approach is the older method used to determine the proper amount of life insurance. It does not take into account inflation and likely wage increases. In contrast, the needs approach takes into account a family's financial goals if the breadwinner dies. This approach also takes into account the amount of monthly benefits the family will receive from other sources such as pension benefits, Social Security and personal savings.

2. **A.** The dependency period refers to the period after the breadwinner's death during which children are living at home. During this period, the need for family income is greatest while the children are growing up.

3. **C.** In a partnership cross-purchase buy-sell plan, the partners individually agree to buy a deceased partner's interest. The executor of the deceased partner's estate is directed to sell the interest to the surviving partners. The partnership itself is not party to the agreement.

4. **D.** A business cannot take an income tax deduction for premiums paid on key person life insurance. However, it receives the death proceeds tax-free.

5. **C.** Because a deferred compensation plan is a nonqualified plan, a company can pick and choose who will participate in it. As a result, it can be used to provide extra benefits for owners and select employees.

6. **B.** If a partnership has three partners, they will need a total of six life insurance policies to insure a cross-purchase buy-sell plan. This is because each partner owns, is the beneficiary of and pays premiums for life insurance on the other partners. In a three person partnership, each partner would have to buy insurance on the other two partners, for a total of six policies.

7. **C.** In a split-dollar life insurance arrangement, the employer and employee share the cost of life insurance. Generally, the employer contributes an amount equal to the increase in the policy's cash value to the premium each year. The employee pays the balance of the premium.

8. **B.** Because the cost of a college education continues to increase every year, Roland actually would need more insurance protection by the time his daughter goes to college. Decreasing term insurance could be used, however, to guarantee a college education for his son, who already has started school.

9. **A.** Under an entity buy-sell plan, the partnership itself, rather than the individual partners, owns, pays for and is the beneficiary of the policies that insure the lives of the individual partners. When a partner dies, the partnership buys his or her partnership interest from the estate. This interest then is divided among the surviving partners in proportion to their own interest.

10. **D.** With key-person insurance, the business itself is the beneficiary, and death proceeds are not taxable. Because the business is the owner, premium-payor and beneficiary of the policy, it retains complete control of the policy. This means that the key-person insurance can be considered a company-owned asset.

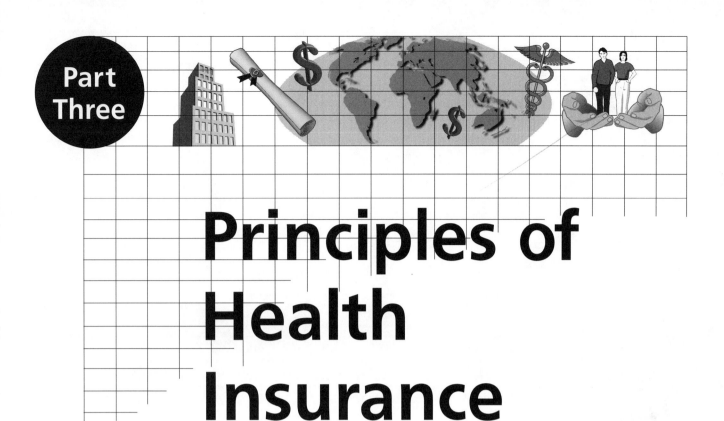

Part Three

Principles of Health Insurance

14

Introduction to Health Insurance

INTRODUCTION

The terms *health and accident insurance, accident and sickness insurance* and *health insurance* are used interchangeably in the health insurance industry, from state to state and company to company. But no matter how this type of insurance is referred to in the industry, it all means the same thing to consumers—a critically important type of insurance that provides financial protection from the high costs of illness and injury.

The remainder of this text is devoted to the principles of health insurance. We will take a look at the types of health insurance plans that exist (including plans for the elderly), the providers of health insurance coverages, policy provisions, underwriting standards, and more. This lesson is designed to provide an overview of the broad field of health insurance, focusing on the basics.

LESSON OBJECTIVES

When you complete this lesson you should be able to:

- explain the main features of medical expense insurance, disability income insurance and accidental death and disability insurance;
- describe the typical ways in which individuals and families purchase health insurance; and
- explain the main ways in which health insurance differs from life insurance.

Basic Forms of Health Insurance Coverage

Health insurance (as it will be called in this text) refers to the broad field of insurance plans that provide protection against the financial consequences of illness, accidents, injury and disability. Statistics reveal that approximately 226 million Americans were protected by one or more forms of health coverage at the end of 1997. Health insurance claims payments made to insureds amount to billions of dollars every year, and approximately half of these claims payments are made by commercial insurance companies.

Within the broad field of health insurance, three distinct categories of health coverage exist: *medical expense insurance, disability income insurance* and *accidental death and dismemberment insurance*. Each of these coverages will be discussed in detail in subsequent lessons, but an introduction is appropriate here.

FIGURE 14.1   Health Coverages and What They Provide

Type of Coverage	Provisions and Benefits
Medical Expense Insurance	Provides benefits for the cost of medical care. Depending on the type of policy (and its specific provisions), coverage can range from limited (coverage for hospital costs only, for example) to very broad (coverage for all aspects of medical services and care).
Disability Income Insurance	Provides a specified periodic income to the insured—usually on a monthly basis—in the event he or she becomes disabled.
Accidental Death and Dismemberment Insurance	Provides a lump-sum payment in the event the insured dies due to an accident or suffers the loss of one or more body members due to an accident.

Medical Expense Insurance

Medical expense insurance provides financial protection against the cost of medical care by reimbursing the insured, fully or in part, for these costs. It includes many kinds of plans that cover hospital care, surgical expenses, physician expenses, medical treatment programs, outpatient care and the like. Medicare supplement insurance and long-term care insurance, two types of health insurance coverage designed for the elderly, also are examples of medical expense insurance plans, and are discussed in detail in Lesson 20.

Disability Income Insurance

Disability income insurance is designed to provide a replacement income when wages are lost due to a disability. As such, it does not cover the medical expenses associated with a disability; rather, it provides the disabled insured with a guaranteed flow of periodic income payments while he or she is disabled.

Accidental Death and Dismemberment (AD&D) Insurance

Accidental death and dismemberment insurance (AD&D) is the purest form of accident insurance, providing the insured with a lump-sum benefit amount in the event of accidental death or dismemberment under accidental circumstances.

✓ **Take Note:** Typically, AD&D coverage is part of a group insurance plan.

Within each of these three categories are many forms and variations of coverage that have evolved to meet unique insurance needs. Even the type of health insurance provider—of which there are many—can make a difference in the basic makeup of any of these kinds of coverages. Each of these basic coverages, as well as the many types of health insurance providers, will be discussed in later lessons. They are introduced here to help acquaint you with the health insurance field in general.

How Health Insurance Is Purchased

As is the case with life insurance, health insurance is available to individuals and families through individual plans and policies or group plans and policies, including blanket policies and franchise policies.

Individual health insurance is issued by commercial insurers and service organizations as contracts between the insured and the company. Though all companies have standard policies for the coverages they offer, most allow an individual to select various options or benefit levels that will meet his or her needs most precisely. Individual health contracts require an application, and the proposed insured usually must provide evidence of insurability.

Group health insurance, also issued by commercial insurers and service organizations, provides coverage under a master contract to members of a specified group. Like group life plans, group health plans are available to employers, trade and professional associations, labor unions, credit unions and other organizations. Insurance is extended to the individuals in the group through the master contract, usually without individual underwriting and usually without requiring group members to provide evidence of insurability. The employer or the association is the policyowner and is responsible for premium payments. The employer may pay the entire premium or may require some contribution from each member to cover the insurance cost.

✓ **Take Note:** In general, the provisions and coverages of group health insurance contracts are more liberal than individual health contracts.

Health insurance also is provided through state and federal government programs. At the state level, Medicaid is available to assist low-income individuals in meeting the costs of medical care. The federal government offers health insurance protection through Medicare and OASDI disability provisions, components of the Social Security system.

Characteristics of Health Insurance

Though closely related to life insurance in purpose, health insurance differs from it in several important ways. A review here of the distinguishing characteristics of health insurance will set the stage for the more in-depth discussion to follow in later lessons.

Renewability Provisions

Life insurance (particularly whole life insurance) and annuities are characterized by their permanence; the policies cannot be canceled by the insurer unless the policyowner fails to make a required premium payment. Even term life policies are guaranteed effective for the duration of the term, as long as premiums are paid. Health insurance is not as permanent in nature. Health insurance policies may contain any one of a wide range of renewability provisions, which define the rights of the insurer to cancel the policy at different points during the life of the policy.

✓ **Take Note:** Five principal renewability classifications exist: cancelable, optionally renewable, conditionally renewable, guaranteed renewable and noncancelable.

The distinguishing characteristics of each type will be covered in Lesson 21, but, in general, the more advantageous the renewability provisions are to the insured, the more expensive the coverage.

Premium Factors

Like life insurance, health insurance is funded by the regular payment of premiums. Unlike life insurance, however, relatively few payment options are available with a health policy. For instance, health policies do not offer any sort of limited payment option, as one would find with, say, a 10-pay or paid-up-at-65 life policy. Health insurance policies are paid for on a year-by-year basis. Health premiums can be paid under one of several different payment modes, including annual, semiannual, quarterly and monthly. Monthly premiums often are paid through some form of preauthorized check method, by which the insurer automatically obtains the premium directly from the policyholder's checking account.

✓ **Take Note:** Except for the noncancelable type of policy cited previously, health insurance premium rates are subject to periodic increases.

Various factors enter into premium calculations for health insurance. These include interest, expense, types of benefits and morbidity. Morbidity is the expected incidence of sickness or disability within a given age group during a given period of time; it is to health insurance what mortality is to life insurance. Other health insurance premium factors are claims experience and the age, sex and occupation of the insured. All of these factors are discussed in detail in Lesson 22.

Participating vs. Nonparticipating Policies

Health insurance policies may be written on either a participating or nonparticipating basis. Most individual health insurance is issued on a nonparticipating basis. Group health insurance, on the other hand, generally is participating and provides for dividends or experience rating.

Group health plans issued by mutual companies usually provide for dividends, while stock companies frequently issue experience-rated plans. A group policy that is experience-rated may make premium reductions retroactive for 12 months. Premium increases for such policies are not retroactive. Experience-rated refunds may be contingent upon renewal of the master policy, but the payment of dividends usually is not contingent upon renewal.

Cost-accounting formulas are complex and vary from insurer to insurer. However, the two major factors that influence whether or not dividends or experience-rated refunds are payable are expenses and claims costs of the insurer. If these cost items are less than anticipated, the group policyowner benefits by receiving a dividend or refund credit. If expenses and claims costs are higher than expected, the group policyowner may not qualify for a dividend or refund credit.

Reserves

Reserves are set aside by an insurance company and designated for the payment of future claims. Part of each premium is designated for the reserves.

Two types of health insurance reserves are *premium reserves* and *loss* (or *claims*) *reserves*. Premium reserves reflect the liability of the insurer for losses that have not occurred but for which premiums have been paid. Reserves earmarked as loss (or claims) reserves represent the insurer's liability for losses that have occurred, but for which settlement is not yet complete. The details of how reserves are handled and recorded by the company are very technical. State laws dictate the minimum requirements for reserves for both life and health insurance. The annual statements required by state insurance departments break down a company's reserves in considerable detail.

Claims

The role of the health insurance claims examiner differs somewhat from that of the life insurance claims examiner. In the case of life insurance, most claims are fairly well defined: the amount of insurance coverage is readily determined by the policy and benefits are payable if the insured has died. With health insurance, though, the claims process is not as clearly defined. Medical expense insurance, for example, typically is based on a *reimbursement contract*, meaning that the benefit an insured receives is not fixed but instead is dependent on the amount of the loss. Its purpose is to reimburse the insured for the amount of loss sustained (within limits). This is in contrast to life insurance, AD&D and disability income insurance, which all are *valued contracts*—they pay the amount stated in the contract if a defined event, such as death or disability, occurs.

The health claims examiner also must decide if, in fact, a loss actually has occurred. This is especially challenging in disability income cases, where a subjective assessment of disability can create misunderstandings.

Summary

This lesson introduced the important field of health insurance. Many hybrid plans offer health protection in three different forms: medical expense, disability income and accidental death and dismemberment. Health insurance is available to individuals and families on an individual basis, through a group plan or through the federal government. It is distinguished by many factors, including its provisions for renewability, premium factors, whether or not the contract is participating, reserves and its claims procedures. In the following lessons, we will review the different types of health insurance and health insurance providers in greater detail.

Key Concepts

In preparing for their licensing examination, students should be familiar with the following concepts:

medical expense insurance	disability income insurance
reserves	valued vs. reimbursement contracts
morbidity	renewability provisions
accidental death and dismemberment insurance	participating vs. nonparticipating policies

Lesson Exam Fourteen

1. Which of the following statements pertaining to health insurance policy premium factors is CORRECT?

   A. A *policy fee* is another term for policy premium.
   B. A policyowner has an individual health plan; therefore, the policy most likely is a participating policy.
   C. Age and sex of the individual insureds would have the most influence on a group health insurance policy's experience rating refund credit.
   D. Pearl files a claim against her major medical policy for a $9,800 hospital bill. The claim likely will be paid out of the insurer's reserves.

2. All of the following are basic forms of health insurance coverage EXCEPT

   A. medical expense
   B. limited pay health
   C. disability income
   D. accidental death and dismemberment

3. Which of the following premium factors is distinctive to health insurance (as opposed to life insurance)?

   A. Age
   B. Sex
   C. Morbidity
   D. Interest

4. Which of the following statements regarding health insurance is CORRECT?

   A. Once issued, health insurance policies cannot be canceled by the insurer.
   B. Numerous premium-payment options are available with health insurance policies.
   C. Most medical expense policies are contracts of reimbursement.
   D. Disability income policies are designed to pay the medical expenses associated with a disability.

5. Assume a health insurance contract states that it will pay $350 a month to the insured, should he or she become totally disabled. Which term most aptly defines this kind of contract?

   A. Participating
   B. Valued
   C. Inclusive
   D. Reimbursement

Answers & Rationale

1. **D.** Each health insurance company must set aside reserves that are designated for paying future claims. If Pearl files a claim for a $9,800 hospital bill, the claim likely will be paid out her insurance company's reserves.

2. **B.** Three distinct categories of basic health insurance coverage exist: medical expense, disability income and accidental death and dismemberment.

3. **C.** One factor that enters into premium calculations for health insurance but not life insurance is morbidity. Morbidity is the expected incidence of sickness or disability within a given age group during a given period of time.

4. **C.** Most medical expense insurance pays for medical care by reimbursing the insured, either fully or in part, for his or her costs.

5. **B.** A valued contract pays an amount stated in the contract if a defined event, such as death or disability, occurs. A contract that pays $350 a month to the insured upon his or her total disability, therefore, would be considered a valued contract.

15

Health Insurance Providers

INTRODUCTION

Most Americans regard medical insurance as the most important form of insurance protection to own, and with good reason. As the cost of medical care increases, an uninsured illness or injury could result in financial disaster for many families.

A number of sources are available for individuals seeking health insurance protection. In general, health insurance providers can be divided into three main categories: commercial insurers, service providers and state and federal government. In all cases, though, the objective is the same: to provide protection against the financial costs associated with illness, injury or disability. In this lesson, we will look at some of the specific types of providers in each of these groups. We also will introduce Medicare and Medicaid, which play an important role in providing health insurance for a large segment of our population.

LESSON OBJECTIVES

When you complete this lesson you should be able to:

- explain the main characteristics of Blue Cross and Blue Shield, HMOs and PPOs, and describe how they differ from each other;
- identify the purpose of Medicare, Social Security Disability Income, Medicare and state workers' compensation programs and explain how each program works; and
- describe how self-insured plans, multiple employer trusts and MEWAs are used to provide health insurance.

Commercial Insurance Providers

Health insurance may be written by a number of commercial insurers, including life insurance companies, casualty insurance companies or mono-line companies that specialize in one or more types of medical expense and disability income insurance. This includes both individual and group insurance policies. Among life insurance companies, health insurance is offered by ordinary companies as well as debit (or home service) companies. (Recall that debit companies sell what are known as industrial policies.)

Commercial insurance companies function on the reimbursement approach; that is, policyowners obtain medical treatment from whatever source they feel is most appropriate and, per the terms of their policy, submit their charges to their insurer for reimbursement. The right of assignment built into most commercial health policies lets policyowners assign benefit payments from the insurer directly to the health care provider, thus relieving the policyowner of first having to pay the medical care provider. The right to assign a policy's benefits, however, does not change the fact that the policy is reimbursing the insured for covered medical expenses.

Service Providers

Service providers are not insurers per se; rather, they operate on the principle that their subscribers (the term used in place of policyholders) receive medical care services as a result of their payment of premiums. Subscribers typically are not billed for services rendered by a medical care provider. Instead, the care provider—who has entered into an agreement with the service organization to provide medical care—is paid by the service organization directly.

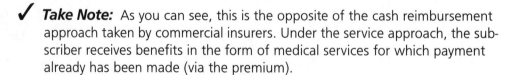 **Take Note:** As you can see, this is the opposite of the cash reimbursement approach taken by commercial insurers. Under the service approach, the subscriber receives benefits in the form of medical services for which payment already has been made (via the premium).

This service approach is used primarily by three types of organizations: *Blue Cross* and *Blue Shield organizations, health maintenance organizations* (HMOs) and *preferred provider organizations* (PPOs).

Blue Cross and Blue Shield

Blue Cross and Blue Shield are voluntary not-for-profit health care service organizations. Blue Cross offers prepayment plans designed to cover hospital services. Blue Shield covers surgical expenses and other medical services performed by physicians.

Generally, Blue Cross and Blue Shield plans work in close cooperation with each other, within a given state or region within a state. In fact, in the past few years, most Blue Cross and Blue Shield plans merged into single plans. Unlike commercial insurance companies, Blue Cross and Blue Shield organizations have contractual arrangements with hospitals and physicians. These contracts provide for payments for services rendered to subscribers with agreed-upon rates or fee schedules.

Consequently, to obtain full value from their service plans, subscribers usually are required to utilize the contracted hospitals and physicians for medical care. Payments for services are made by Blue Cross or Blue Shield directly to the hospitals and physicians; subscribers are responsible only for services not covered by their particular plans. (Blue Cross and Blue Shield plans offer a broad and comprehensive range of services from which the subscriber can choose.)

✓ **Take Note:** Blue Cross and Blue Shield plans are available on an individual, family or group basis.

Health Maintenance Organization (HMO)

A health maintenance organization (HMO), is another type of organization offering comprehensive prepaid health care services to its subscribing members. HMO participants can be members under a group insurance plan or individual or family members.

HMOs are distinguished by the fact that they not only finance health care services for their subscribers on a prepayment basis, but also organize and deliver the health services. Subscribers pay a fixed periodic fee to the HMO (as opposed to paying for services only when needed) and are provided with a broad range of health services, from routine doctor visits to emergency and hospital care. This care is rendered by physicians and hospitals that participate in the HMO.

 **Test Topic Alert!**   HMOs are known for stressing preventive care, with the objective of reducing the number of unnecessary hospital admissions and duplication of services.

Unlike commercial insurers and Blue Cross and Blue Shield organizations, HMOs rarely assess deductibles. When they do, the charges are nominal, such as $2 for prescription drugs or $5 for an office visit.

Two basic types of HMOs exist: an open-panel HMO and a closed-panel HMO.

- *Open-panel HMO.* An open-panel HMO is characterized by a network of physicians who work out of their own private offices and participate in the HMO on a part-time basis.
- *Closed-panel HMO.* A closed-panel HMO is represented by a group of physicians who are salaried employees of the HMO and work out of its facilities.

Health maintenance organizations may be self-contained and self-funded based on dues or fees from their subscribers, or they may contract for excess insurance or administrative services provided by insurance companies. In fact, some HMOs are sponsored by insurance companies.

The Health Maintenance Act of 1973, which provided some federal funding for these organizations, spurred the HMO movement forward. One of its provisions requires employers with 25 or more employees to offer enrollment in an HMO if they provide health care benefits for their workers.

Preferred Provider Organization (PPO)

Another relatively new type of health insurance provider is the preferred provider organization (PPO). A preferred provider organization is a collection of health care providers, such as physicians, hospitals and clinics, who offer their services to certain groups at prearranged prices. In exchange, the group refers its members to the preferred providers for health care services.

Unlike HMOs, preferred provider organizations usually operate on a fee-for-service-rendered basis, not on a prepaid basis. Members of the PPO select from among the preferred providers for needed services. Also in contrast to HMOs, PPO health care providers normally are in private practice. They have agreed to offer their services to the group and its members at fees that typically are less than what they normally charge. In exchange, because the group refers its members to the PPO, the providers broaden their patient and service base.

 **Test Topic Alert!**

One of the features that attracts groups to PPOs is the discounted fees that are negotiated in advance. Although an insured can receive treatment from any doctor of his or her choice, the benefit will be reduced if the doctor is not in the PPO.

Groups that contract with PPOs often are employers, insurance companies or other health insurance benefits providers. While these groups do not mandate that individual members must use the PPO, a reduced benefit is typical if they do not. For instance, individuals may pay a $100 deductible if they use PPO services and a $500 deductible if they go outside the PPO for health care services.

Government Insurance Programs

For many people, health care cost protection is made available through a state or federal government program. At the federal level, Medicare is the primary source of health insurance. It is a part of the Social Security program that also provides disability income to qualified workers under OASDI. At the state level, Medicaid offers protection to financially needy individuals, and state workers' compensation programs provide benefits for workers who suffer from occupational injuries or illnesses. Let's take a brief look at each. Because of their significance to the health care needs of seniors, a detailed discussion of Medicare and Medicaid is included in Lesson 19.

Medicare

The federally administered Medicare program took effect in 1966. Its purpose is to provide hospital and medical expense insurance protection to those aged 65 and older, to those of any age who suffer from chronic kidney disease or to those who are receiving Social Security disability benefits.

Social Security Disability Income

In addition to Medicare, the federal government also provides disability-related benefits through the Social Security OASDI program. Although this subject was covered in Lesson 11, let's review some of the important points here.

Disability income benefits are available to covered workers who qualify under Social Security requirements. One of the requirements is that the individual must be so mentally or physically disabled that he or she cannot perform any substantial gainful work. In addition, the impairment must be expected to last at least 12 months or result in an earlier death. The determination of disability for Social Security purposes usually is made by a government agency. In addition to meeting the definition of disabled, the individual must have earned a certain minimum number of quarters of coverage under Social Security. A five-month waiting period is required before an individual will qualify for benefits, during which time he or she must remain disabled.

✓ **For Example:** Jerry became disabled in January. He must wait five full months—February through June—before he will qualify for disability benefits. His first benefit payment would be for July, and it would be paid in August. No second five-month waiting period is required if the disabled worker recovers and then is disabled again within five years.

Medicaid

Medicaid is Title XIX of the Social Security Act, added to the Social Security program in 1965. Its purpose is to provide matching federal funds to states for their medical public assistance plans to help needy persons, regardless of age. If family income is below a specified level, Medicaid benefits generally are available. Although each state has some leeway in establishing eligibility requirements, Medicaid benefits generally are payable to low-income individuals who are blind, disabled or under age 21. The benefits may be applied to Medicare deductibles and copayment requirements.

State Workers' Compensation Programs

All states have workers' compensation laws, which were enacted to provide mandatory benefits to employees for work-related injuries, illness or death. Employers are responsible for providing workers' compensation benefits to their employees and do so by purchasing coverage through state programs private insurers or by self-insuring.

Although each state's laws differ with regard to procedures, requirements and minimum benefits, there is uniformity to the following extent:

- If a worker is killed in an industrial accident, the law provides for payment of burial expenses, subject to a maximum amount, and compensation for the surviving spouse or other dependents of the worker at the time of death.
- Regardless of any negligence by the employer, he or she is liable for work-related disabilities that employees suffer.
- Under the law, a disabled employee is entitled to benefits as a matter of right, without having to sue the employer for benefits. However, in return for the benefits provided under the law, the employee gives up the right to sue the employer.
- Under most laws, a disabled employee is paid benefits on a weekly or monthly basis, rather than in a lump sum.
- The employer must provide the required benefits; the employee does not contribute to the plan.

The law provides for a schedule of benefits, the size of which is based on such factors as the severity of the disability and the employee's wages.

✏️ **Quick Quiz 15.1** True or False?

_____ 1. Tina, age 30, is unemployed and has been blind since birth. She would probably would qualify for workers' compensation benefits.

_____ 2. If Mary obtains her health insurance through a commercial insurer, she must submit her medical charges to the insurer for reimbursement.

_____ 3. Blue Cross and Blue Shield plans are available to individuals, families and groups.

_____ 4. With a PPO, a reduced benefit will be paid if a member uses a doctor who is not part of the network.

_____ 5. In January, Tom becomes disabled while working and begins receiving Social Security disability income benefits five months later. He recovers and returns to work that fall. If Tom re-injures himself a year later, he can receive Social Security benefits only after another five-month waiting period passes.

Answers

1. **False**. _Workers' compensation benefits are available to employees who suffer work-related injuries, illness or death. Although Tina would not be eligible for these benefits because she is unemployed, she might be eligible for Medicare or Medicaid._

2. **True**.

3. **True**.

4. **True**.

5. **False**. _If a disabled worker recovers but then becomes disabled again within five years, a second five-month waiting period is not required. As a result, Tom could immediately begin receiving Social Security benefits the second time he becomes disabled._

Alternative Methods of Providing Health Insurance

As the cost of health insurance has increased, businesses and individuals have turned to nontraditional methods of providing health insurance, including self-insured plans, Multiple Employer Trusts (METs) and Multiple Employer Welfare Arrangements (MEWAs).

Self-Insurance

For businesses and individuals, an alternative to a commercial or service health insurance plan is self-insurance. Large corporations especially will self-insure their sick-leave plans for their employees. Labor unions, fraternal associations and other groups often self-insure their medical expense plans through dues or contributions from members. Others may self-insure part of a plan and use insurance to protect against large, unpredictable losses.

Many of these self-insured plans are administered by insurance companies or other organizations that are paid a fee for handling the paperwork and processing the claims. When an outside organization provides these functions, it is called an *administrative services only* (ASO) or *third-party administrator* (TPA) plan.

To bolster a self-insured plan, some groups adopt a *minimum premium plan* (MPP). These plans are designed to insure against a certain level of large, unpredictable losses, above and beyond the self-insured level. As the name implies, MPPs are available for a fraction of the insurer's normal premium.

Multiple Employer Trust (MET)

As mentioned in Lesson 9, a method of marketing group benefits to employers who have a small number of employees is the MET. METs can provide a single type of insurance (such as health insurance) or a wide range of coverages (for example, life, medical expense and disability income insurance). In some cases, alternative forms of the same coverage are available (such as comprehensive health insurance or basic health insurance).

An employer who wants to get coverage for employees from an MET first must become a member of the trust by subscribing to it. The employer is issued a joinder agreement, which spells out the relationship between the trust and the employer and specifies the coverages to which the employer has subscribed. An employer need not subscribe to all the coverages offered by an MET.

An MET may either provide benefits on a self-funded basis or fund benefits with a contract purchased from an insurance company. In the latter case, the trust, rather than the subscribing employers, is the master insurance contractholder. In either case, the employees of subscribing employers are provided with benefit descriptions (certificates of insurance) in a manner similar to the usual group insurance agreement.

In addition to alternative methods of funding benefits, METs can be categorized according to how they are administered, that is, whether by an insurance company or a third-party administrator.

Multiple Employer Welfare Arrangements

A MEWA is a type of MET for union employees. MEWAs are self-funded and tax exempt. Employees covered under a MEWA are required by law to have an employment related common bond.

 Test Topic Alert!   METs often are funded fully and claims are guaranteed. In contrast, MEWAs often are self-funded and claims are not guaranteed.

Summary

People seeking health insurance protection has a number of resources. Commercial insurance companies, which include life insurance companies as well as mono-line and casualty insurance companies, are one source. Service providers, including the Blue Cross and Blue Shield organizations and the more recently introduced health maintenance organizations, are others. Preferred provider organizations provide an additional option by contracting their services with employer groups or insurers.

For many people, health insurance protection is obtained through a government-sponsored program. At the federal level, the Social Security program (OASDI) provides both disability income benefits and medical expense protection, the latter through the Medicare program.

At the state level, medical expense insurance is provided through the Medicaid program to financially needy citizens who are blind, disabled or under age 21. Because Medicaid is state-administered (and only partially federally supported), each state has some leeway in setting the qualification standards for its program. All states also have enacted workers' compensation programs, which provide benefits to workers for occupational illnesses and disabilities.

Some large employers prefer to retain the risk of covering their employees' medical care expenses, or at least part of the expenses, and thus self-insure their plan.

Key Concepts

In preparing for their licensing examination, students should be familiar with the following concepts:

commercial health insurers

health maintenance organizations (HMOs)

third-party administrator (TPA) plans

self-insured plans

Social Security disability income

workers' compensation

service providers

preferred provider organizations (PPOs)

administrative services only (ASO) plans

Medicare

Medicaid

multiple employer trusts (METs)

multiple employer welfare arrangements (MEWAs)

Lesson Exam Fifteen

1. HMOs are known for stressing

   A. preventive medicine and early treatment
   B. state-sponsored health care plans
   C. in-hospital care and services
   D. health care services for government employees

2. Which of the following statements regarding Blue Cross and Blue Shield organizations is CORRECT?

   A. Blue Cross provides surgical expense prepayment plans.
   B. Blue Shield provides hospital expense prepayment plans.
   C. Both Blue Cross and Blue Shield plans are available on a group basis.
   D. Reimbursement for hospital and medical expenses is made by Blue Cross and Blue Shield directly to the subscriber.

3. Which of the following organizations would make reimbursement payments directly to the insured individual for covered medical expenditures?

   A. Blue Cross/Blue Shield
   B. Commercial insurer
   C. Preferred provider organization
   D. Health maintenance organization

4. Marty just received his first Social Security disability payment. From this, we can assume

   A. he had applied for Medicaid previously
   B. he is at least age 65
   C. his disability is expected to last at least 12 months
   D. his disability commenced three months ago

5. Which of the following statements about health maintenance organizations is CORRECT?

   A. An insurance company that also markets group health insurance is known as an HMO.
   B. If a person joins an HMO and undergoes a physical examination, he or she will be billed for the exam and each subsequent medical service as it is performed.
   C. An insurance company may sponsor an HMO or assist an HMO by providing contractual services.
   D. Like commercial insurers, HMOs generally assess deductibles.

6. The waiting period before qualifying for Social Security disability benefits is how many months?

   A. 3
   B. 5
   C. 6
   D. 12

7. Which of the following statements regarding workers' compensation plans is CORRECT?

   A. Benefit amounts are mandated by the federal government.
   B. A worker will qualify for benefits only if his or her disability or illness was a result of employer negligence.
   C. Benefits may be financed by private insurers, state funds or self-insurance.
   D. If a worker is killed in an industrial accident, his or her family is entitled only to a specified benefit amount to pay for burial expenses.

8. Which of the following statements about Medicaid is NOT correct?

   A. It provides federal matching funds to states for medical public assistance plans.
   B. Its purpose is to help eligible needy persons with medical assistance.
   C. Medicaid benefits may be used to pay the deductible and coinsurance amounts of Medicare.
   D. It limits financial assistance to persons age 65 or older who are in need of medical services they cannot afford.

9. Jerry is injured while working for his employer. Under state workers' compensation laws, we can assume that

   A. his employer will not be liable for Jerry's work-related disabilities if the employer's negligence did not contribute to the injuries
   B. Jerry probably will receive workers' compensation benefits on a monthly or weekly basis
   C. Jerry must sue his employer to receive workers' compensation benefits
   D. both Jerry and his employer are required to contribute to the cost of workers' compensation coverage

Answers & Rationale

1. **A.** HMOs are known for stressing preventive care, the objective being to reduce the number of unnecessary hospital admissions and duplication of services.

2. **C.** Blue Cross and Blue Shield plans are available on a group basis as well as to individuals. While Blue Cross offers prepayment plans to cover hospital services, Blue Shield covers surgical expenses and other medical services performed by physicians. Payments for services are made directly to the hospitals and physicians.

3. **B.** Commercial insurance companies use the reimbursement approach; that is, policyowners obtain medical treatment from whatever source they want and, per the terms of their policy, submit their charges to their insurer for reimbursement.

4. **C.** To receive Social Security disability payments, Marty's disability must be expected to last at least 12 months.

5. **C.** HMOs may contract for excess insurance or administrative services provided by insurance companies. Some HMOs also are sponsored by insurance companies.

6. **B.** There is a five-month waiting period before an individual will qualify for benefits. During this time, the individual must remain disabled.

7. **C.** Employers are responsible for providing workers' compensation benefits to their employees and do so by purchasing coverage through state programs or private insurers or by self-insuring.

8. **D.** Medicaid benefits generally are payable to low-income individuals who are blind, disabled or under age 21. Medicaid does not only benefit persons age 65 or older.

9. **B.** If Jerry is injured while working for his employer, he probably will receive workers' compensation benefits on a weekly or monthly basis rather than in a lump sum. Jerry need not sue his employer to receive benefits, nor is he required to contribute to the cost of such program. Finally, Jerry's employer will be liable for his work-related disabilities, regardless of whether it was negligent.

16

Medical Expense Insurance

INTRODUCTION

When people speak of their health insurance, they usually are referring to insurance that protects against the costs of medical care. Medical expense insurance, which is available in several different forms, reimburses policy-owners for part or all of the costs of obtaining medical care. It is a vital form of insurance considered by many to be the one type of insurance they cannot do without.

LESSON OBJECTIVES

When you complete this lesson you should be able to:

- describe the different types of coverage available under basic medical expense plans;
- explain the difference between supplementary major medical and comprehensive major medical plans;
- list and describe the three types of major medical deductibles;
- explain the concepts of coinsurance, stop-loss features and preexisting conditions; and
- describe the main features of hospital indemnity policies and limited risk policies.

Purpose of Medical Expense Insurance

Medical expense insurance provides financial protection against the cost of medical care for accidents and sickness. In this broad context, medical care includes hospital care, physician services, surgical expenses, drugs, nursing and convalescent care, diagnostic treatment, laboratory services, rehabilitative services, dental care, physical therapy—in short, all medical treatment and services. The extent to which a given medical expense policy covers medical care—the specific types of services and treatments covered and the benefits provided—depends on the policy. In general, medical expense insurance is available through one of two different policy plans: *basic medical insurance* or *major medical insurance*. Basic medical insurance limits coverage to select types of medical care. Major medical insurance, which can work either as a supplement to a basic plan or as a comprehensive stand-alone plan, provides broader, more complete coverage.

Reimbursement vs. Indemnity Approach

Medical expense plans typically pay benefits as a reimbursement of actual expenses, although some benefits are paid as fixed indemnities, regardless of the actual loss.

✓ *For Example:* Karl owns a reimbursement-type medical expense policy that pays a maximum benefit of $200,000. He is hospitalized for 10 days and incurs covered medical expenses totaling up to $10,000. The policy would provide benefits of $10,000—the expenses incurred.

✓ *For Example:* Doris owns an indemnity-type medical expense policy that provides a $100-per-day benefit for each day of hospitalization. She is hospitalized for ten days, incurring medical expenses of $10,000. Her policy will indemnify her by providing benefits of $1,000: ten days at $100 per day. Indemnity medical expense policies do not pay expenses or bills; they merely provide the insured with a stated benefit amount for each day he or she is confined to a hospital as an inpatient. The money may be used by the insured for any purpose.

With this foundation, we are ready to take a look at the two kinds of medical expense insurance policies: *basic* and *major medical*. Many types of plans fall within these two categories.

Basic Medical Expense Plans

Basic medical expense insurance sometimes is called first dollar insurance because, unlike major medical expense insurance, it provides benefits up front, without requiring the insured to satisfy a deductible first. For many years it was the leading type of medical expense insurance sold, but today it is overshadowed by major medical insurance. This is due largely to the fact that basic medical expense policies limit the type and duration of services covered and dollar amounts that will be paid (or reimbursed) to the insured. Major medical plans are not as limiting.

 **Test Topic Alert!**   Basic medical expense insurance often is referred to as first dollar insurance.

Basic medical expense policies classify their coverages according to general categories of medical care: *hospital expense, surgical expense* and *physicians' (nonsurgical) expense*. Additional plans cover *nursing expenses* and *convalescent care*. While it is common to find all categories contained under the umbrella of one policy, they can be written as separate coverages.

Basic Hospital Expense

Basic hospital expense insurance reimburses policyowners for the cost of hospital confinement. (Many policies today also provide coverage for outpatient care if it is provided in lieu of hospitalized care.) Basic hospital policies cover costs associated with daily room and board and other miscellaneous expenses.

Daily Room and Board Basic hospital expense policies cover the daily cost of room and board. These policies follow no set standards; they vary by daily amount payable and by the length of time the benefits are payable.

✔ **For Example:** Some policies will pay an in-hospital benefit for as long as 365 days, while others pay benefits for 90 days or 30 days only. Some policies reimburse the insured for the daily room and board charge up to a specified dollar amount. Others provide a service type of benefit, paying an amount equal to the hospital's daily charge for a semiprivate room.

Miscellaneous Expenses In addition to room and board, basic hospital expense policies cover hospital extras, or miscellaneous charges, up to a specified limit. Covered miscellaneous expenses include drugs, x-rays, anesthesia, lab fees, dressings, use of the operating room and supplies.

In general, the maximum miscellaneous expense benefit is expressed as a multiple of the daily room and board benefit (10 times room and board or 20 times room and board, for instance) or it may be a stated dollar amount. Some policies may even specify individual maximums for certain expenses within the maximum miscellaneous benefit.

✔ **For Example:** The overall maximum for the miscellaneous expense benefit may be $1,000, with maximums of $150 for use of the operating room, $125 for anesthesia, $75 for drugs and so on, but the total miscellaneous benefit would be limited to $1,000.

It is important to note that physicians' services are not covered under a basic hospital expense policy, even in the case of surgery. The cost for a physician is covered under a basic surgical expense or basic physicians' (nonsurgical) expense policy.

Basic Surgical Expense

Basic surgical expense policies provide coverage for the cost of a surgeon's services, whether the surgery is performed in the hospital or out. The surgeon's fees, anesthesiologist's fees and any postoperative care generally are included in the coverage.

Three different approaches are used by insurers in providing this type of coverage and determining the benefits payable. These are the *surgical schedule* approach, the *reasonable and customary* approach and the *relative value scale* approach.

 **Test Topic Alert!**   The approach used by an insurer in providing basic surgical expense coverage and determining the benefits payable is described in the back of the policy.

Surgical Schedule   Under the surgical schedule method, every surgical procedure is assigned a dollar amount by the insurer. Although the policy itself will contain only a representative sampling of common surgical procedures and their prices, a complete listing of all established surgical procedures is maintained in the insurer's claims department, for use by its claims examiners. When a claim is submitted to the insurer, the claims examiner reviews the policy to determine the amount payable; if the surgeon's bill is more than the allowed charge set by the insurer, it is up to the insured to pay the surgeon the difference. If the surgeon's bill is less than the allowed charge, the insurer will pay only the full amount billed; the claim payment never will exceed the amount charged.

Reasonable and Customary Approach   Whereas the surgical schedule method pays up to a stated dollar amount regardless of the actual charge, the reasonable and customary approach is more open in its determination of benefits payable. Under this approach, the surgical expense is compared to what is deemed reasonable and customary for the geographical part of the country where the surgery was performed. If the charge is within the reasonable and customary parameters, the expense is paid, usually in full.

 **Take Note:**   If the charge for a procedure is more than what is reasonable and customary, the patient must absorb the difference.

Relative Value Scale   The relative value scale is similar to the surgical schedule method, except that instead of a flat dollar amount being assigned to every surgical procedure, a set of points is assigned.

The number of points assigned to any one procedure is relative to the number of points assigned to a maximum procedure.

 **For Example:** An operation like a triple heart bypass typically would be considered a maximum procedure and assigned a high number of points (usually 500 or 1,000). Every other procedure also is assigned a set of points relative to that; an appendectomy, which is a major procedure but not as serious as a triple bypass, might be assigned 200 points. Setting a broken finger might rate five points.

How are benefit amounts determined? The policy will carry a stated dollar-per-point amount, known as the *conversion factor,* to determine the benefit. For example, a plan with a $5-per-point conversion factor would pay $1,000 for a 200-point procedure. Generally the larger the conversion factor, the larger the policy's premium.

Basic Physicians' (Nonsurgical) Expense

Basic physicians' expense insurance provides benefits for nonsurgical physicians' services. Examples of services covered include office visits and the care by a physician while the insured is hospitalized for a nonsurgical reason. Benefits usually are based on the indemnity approach.

 For Example: A plan might pay a flat fee of $50 per visit (not to exceed the actual charge, if less).

These policies typically carry a number of exclusions, such as x-rays, drugs and dental treatment.

Other Basic Plans

Two other basic medical expense plans are worth noting: *nurses' expense benefits* and *convalescent care facility benefits.*

Nurses' expense benefits coverage generally is limited to private duty nursing care arranged in accordance with a doctor's order while the insured is a hospital patient. It may cover both registered professional and licensed practical nurses.

Convalescent care facility benefit coverage provides a maximum daily benefit for confinement in a skilled nursing facility for a specified recovery period following discharge from a hospital. Rest cures and normal custodial care are not covered.

FIGURE 16.1   Basic Medical Expense Coverages

Medical Expense Category	What Is Covered
Hospital expense	• Daily room and board • Miscellaneous expenses
Surgical expense	• Cost of surgeon's services • Anesthesiologist
Physicians' expense	• Office visits • Nonsurgical care by a physician while hospitalized
Nurses' expense	• Private duty nursing care
Convalescent care expense	• Skilled nursing facility expenses

Basic medical expense policies provide coverage according to general categories of medical care. Policies covering all categories are available, as are policies that cover only select categories.

Major Medical Expense Plans

Major medical expense insurance, often called simply major medical, has made it possible for many people to achieve substantial protection against the high cost of medical care. It offers broad coverage under one policy, typically paying benefits for hospital room and board, hospital extras, nursing services in-hospital or at home, blood, oxygen, prosthetic devices, surgery, physicians' fees, ambulance services and more. In addition, it provides for high benefit limits. It generally is available on both an individual basis and a group basis.

The services and supplies covered under a major medical policy must be performed or prescribed by a licensed physician and necessary for the treatment of an insured's illness or injury. The benefit period may be defined on a calendar-year basis or may be specified as a two- to five-year period. In contrast to basic medical expense insurance, major medical policies provide total maximum lifetime benefits to individual insureds from $250,000 to $1 million or more.

Major medical expense insurance usually picks up where basic medical expense insurance leaves off, in one of two ways: as a supplement to a basic plan or as a comprehensive stand-alone plan.

Supplementary Major Medical

A supplementary major medical plan covers expenses not included under a basic plan. It also provides coverage for expenses that exceed the dollar maximums specified in the basic policy as well as those expenses no longer covered by the basic plan because the benefits have been exhausted.

With a supplemental plan, major medical coverage is coordinated with various basic medical expense coverages, picking up where the basic plan leaves off.

✓ **For Example:** A basic plan may provide for hospital room and board benefits for a maximum of 45 days. If that basic plan were supplemented with a major medical plan, the supplementary major medical plan would cover hospital room and board expenses beginning on the 46th day. Or, if a basic plan provides a maximum benefit of $1,500 for a specific surgical procedure and the actual cost of the procedure was $2,000, a major medical supplement would cover the additional $500.

In addition, because of the broad coverage associated with most major medical supplements, a supplement likely will cover expenses that are either beyond the scope of the basic plan or excluded from its coverage.

Comprehensive Major Medical

The second type of major medical plan is the comprehensive major medical plan. Comprehensive plans are distinguished by the fact that they cover virtually all medical expenses—hospital expenses, physician and surgeon expenses, nursing care, drugs, physical therapy, diagnostic x-rays and laboratory services, medical supplies and equipment, transfusions and more—under a single policy.

Major medical plans, whether supplementary or comprehensive, typically include two important features: *deductibles* and *coinsurance*. Both of these features require the insured to absorb some of the cost of his or her medical expenses, thus allowing the insurer to avoid small claims and keep the cost of premiums down.

✓ **Take Note:** A basic medical plan usually does not include either a deductible or coinsurance; instead it imposes limitations in the form of maximum benefit amounts that will be paid.

Deductibles

A deductible is a stated initial dollar amount that the individual insured is required to pay before insurance benefits are paid.

For Example: If a plan has a flat $250 annual deductible, the insured is responsible for the first $250 of medical expenses every year. Covered expenses exceeding $250 then are paid by the major plan (subject to any coinsurance).

Depending on the type of major medical policy, the deductible may be one of three kinds: *flat, corridor* or *integrated*.

Flat Deductible

A flat deductible is a stated amount that the insured must pay before policy benefits become payable.

 For Example: If an insured has a policy with a $500 deductible and incurs $2,000 of covered medical expenses, he or she must pay $500 toward the total. The insurer then will base its payments on the remaining $1,500.

Quite often, policies will include a family deductible, usually equal to three times the individual deductible amount. In a family of four, for example, if three members each satisfied the individual deductible in one year, no deductible would be applied to medical expenses incurred by the fourth member.

Corridor Deductible

A corridor deductible is typical for a supplementary major medical policy that works in conjunction with a basic medical expense policy. The first covered medical expenses the insured incurs are paid by the basic policy. After the basic policy benefits are exhausted, the insured pays the full deductible, and then the major medical benefits are payable.

 For Example: Linda has a supplementary major medical policy that provides for a corridor deductible of $500. The deductible applies after full payment of up to $2,000 by the basic medical expense policy and before additional expenses are shared on a coinsurance basis by the insurer and Linda (see *Coinsurance* in this lesson). Linda incurs a medical bill of $8,500. Responsibility for payment is as follows:

Total expenses:	$8,500
Basic medical expense pays:	−2,000
	$6,500
Corridor deductible paid by Linda:	− 500
Basis for major medical expense payment and coinsurance:	$6,000

As you can see, the basic medical expense policy paid for the first $2,000 of Linda's medical bills. The corridor deductible, which the insured is responsible for, is applied next. To the extent that additional medical expenses remain—in this case, $6,000—they become the basis for the major medical payment. This usually is accomplished on a coinsurance or copayment basis, whereby the insured shares some percentage of the cost. This process is explained on the following page.

FIGURE 16.2 Types of Major Medical Deductibles

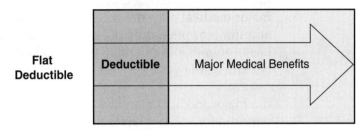

Flat Deductible

Typically used with comprehensive policies, a flat deductible is a stated amount that the insured must pay before any policy benefits are paid.

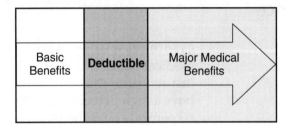

Corridor Deductible

Typically used with supplemental plans, a corridor deductible is the deductible imposed after all basic benefits have been paid but before any major medical benefits will be paid.

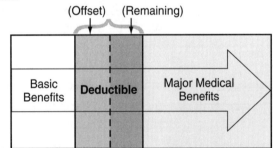

Integrated Deductible

Occasionally used with supplemental plans, this deductible is the amount that must be satisfied before major medical benefits are paid, but it is "offset" dollar-for-dollar by any benefits paid under the basic plan.

 **Test Topic Alert!** It is important to know when a deductible applies to the basic benefits policy and when a deductible applies after that policy's benefits are exhausted and before the supplementary major medical policy pays benefits.

Integrated Deductible An integrated deductible also is used with a supplementary major medical plan, but it is integrated into the amounts covered by the basic plan. For example, if a supplementary plan carries a $500 deductible and the insured incurs $500 or more of covered expenses under the basic plan, the deductible is satisfied. If the basic policy benefits do not cover the entire deductible amount specified in the major medical policy, the insured is compelled to make up the difference.

Each of the preceding deductibles may be figured on one of two bases. If a major medical plan provides for a *calendar year deductible*, the deductible amount is applied only once during each calendar year. Once the deductible has been met in a calendar year, all claims submitted will be treated for the balance of the year without regard to any deductibles.

If a major medical plan has a *per cause deductible*, separate deductibles are required for each separate illness or accident. Per cause deductibles are common in policies that define causes of loss as each sickness or each injury.

Coinsurance

Coinsurance, or percentage participation, is another characteristic of major medical policies. It is, simply, a sharing of expenses by the insured and the insurer. After the insured satisfies the deductible, the insurance company pays a high percentage of the additional (covered) expenses—usually 75 or 80 percent—and the insured pays the remainder.

✓ **For Example:** Joe has an 80 percent/20 percent major medical policy, with a $200 flat annual deductible. This year, he incurs $1,200 in medical expenses, all of which are covered by his policy. The responsibility for payment would be as follows:

Total expenses:	$1,200
Deductible Joe pays:	– 200
Basis for insurer's payment:	$1,000
	× .80
Amount insurer pays:	$ 800
Coinsurance amount Joe pays:	$ 200

Thus, the insurer will pay 80 percent of the charges after the deductible has been satisfied, or $800. Joe must pay the $200 deductible and 20 percent of the remaining expenses, for a total cost share of $400.

Now let's assume that Joe experiences two separate medical problems this year. The first, which required hospitalization and surgery, totaled $7,500. Under his major medical policy, Joe submitted his claim and paid his $200 deductible. The policy would pay 80 percent of the charges above the deductible, or $5,840; Joe is responsible for the remaining $1,460. Three months later, Joe incurs another round of medical expenses amounting to $900. Because his policy stipulates a flat annual deductible, which Joe has paid already, the policy will base its 80 percent payment on the full $900; Joe must pay the remaining 20 percent, or $180.

Coinsurance provisions are effective throughout the duration of a policy.

Stop-Loss Feature

To provide a safeguard for insureds, most major medical policies contain a stop-loss feature that limits the insured's out-of-pocket expenses. Once the insured has paid a specified amount toward his or her covered expenses—usually $1,000 to $2,000—the company pays 100 percent of covered expenses.

How a stop-loss cap is defined depends on the policy. For instance, one policy may stipulate that the contract will cover 100 percent of eligible expenses after the insured incurs $1,000 in out-of-pocket costs. Another policy may specify that the coinsurance provision applies only to the next $5,000 of covered expenses after the deductible is paid, with full coverage for any remaining expenses.

✓ **For Example:** Bill has a major medical policy with a stop-loss feature. It calls for a $500 deductible, followed by an 80 percent/20 percent coinsurance on the next $5,000 in covered expenses. Amounts above that are fully absorbed by the policy. If Bill were to incur hospital and surgical bills of $20,000 this year, this is how payment would be assigned:

Total expenses:	$20,000
Deductible Bill pays:	– 500
	$19,500
Coinsurance Bill pays (20 percent of the next $5,000 in expenses):	– 1,000
Amount insurer pays:	$18,500

Thus, with a $500 deductible and $1,000 in coinsurance for the next $5,000, Bill's plan provides for a maximum out-of-pocket expenditure by the insured of $1,500.

Preexisting Conditions

Another feature characteristic of most major medical policies is the exclusion for preexisting conditions. For individual plans, a preexisting condition is an illness or physical condition that existed before the policy's effective date and one that the applicant did not disclose on the application. (A condition that is noted on the application may be excluded by rider or waiver.) Consequently, medical costs incurred due to a preexisting condition are excluded from coverage under plans that contain this exclusion. However, the exclusion applies for only a limited time. After that time limit passes, any existing conditions no longer are considered preexisting and will be covered in full, subject to any other policy limitations. (See also *Time Limit on Certain Defenses*, Lesson 21.)

✓ **Take Note:** The rules regarding preexisting conditions are different for group health insurance plans. On July 1, 1997, the Health Insurance Portability and Accountability Act limited the ability of employer-sponsored groups and insurers to exclude individuals from health insurance coverage due to preexisting medical conditions. These rules will be discussed in more detail in Lesson 23.

🔅 **Test Topic Alert!**   The exclusion for preexisting conditions is designed to protect insurers against adverse selection by those who know they have a medical ailment and are facing certain medical costs.

✎ Quick Quiz 16.1   True or False?

_____ 1. If Susan has surgery, the cost of services provided by her doctor will not be covered under a basic hospital policy.

_____ 2. Tom has an appendectomy that costs $5,000. Under his insurance policy, $4,000 to $4,500 is considered a reasonable and customary charge for this procedure. Because the cost of Tom's surgery falls outside this parameter, his insurance will not pay for his operation.

_____ 3. If Mark has surgery, the costs of surgical care provided by his doctor will be covered under a physicians' expense policy.

_____ 4. Jane is hospitalized. Her nurses' expense benefits plan will cover the cost of the private duty nursing care she receives.

_____ 5. Bill is in the hospital for 10 days. His daily room and board expenses will be covered by his basic hospital expense insurance.

Answers   1. **True**.

2. **False**. *Even though Tom's surgery costs more than what is considered reasonable and customary, his insurance still will pay for part of the cost of operation. However, Tom must pay for the amount that is not covered by insurance.*

3. ***False***. *If Mark has surgery, the cost of his surgeon's services will not be covered by physicians' expense insurance. Instead, a surgical expense policy will cover the cost of his surgeon's services.*

4. ***True***.

5. ***True***.

Other Types of Medical Expense Coverage

As we've discussed, basic medical expense plans and major medical expense plans are the two primary kinds of health policies that provide coverage for accidents and illness. However, a discussion of medical expense plans would not be complete without mentioning a couple of other plans, most notably *hospital indemnity policies* and *limited risk* (or *dread disease*) *policies.*

Hospital Indemnity Policy

A hospital indemnity policy simply provides a daily, weekly or monthly indemnity of a specified amount based on the number of days the insured is hospitalized.

✓ ***Take Note:*** A hospital indemnity plan may provide the insured $100 a day for every day he or she is confined in a hospital irrespective of the actual expenses incurred. The insured can apply the benefits to any purpose.

This insurance has been available for many years but has been promoted more heavily in recent years largely due to rapidly increasing health care costs. Many companies can offer high benefit indemnity plans at reasonable premiums because underwriting and administration are greatly simplified and claim costs are not affected by increases in medical costs.

Benefits may run as high as $4,500 per month, based on a daily hospital confinement benefit of $150, and some are even higher. Maximum benefit periods range from about six months to several years or for a lifetime. Benefits are payable directly to the insureds and may be used for any purpose. Hospital indemnity policies also usually are exempt from most state laws that apply to specific kinds of insurance contracts.

Limited Risk Policy

Policies that provide medical expense coverage for specific kinds of illnesses are known as limited risk or dread disease policies. They are available primarily due to the high costs associated with certain illnesses, such as cancer or heart disease. Note, however, that some states prohibit the sale of these policies, because they invite questionable sales and marketing practices that take advantage of people's fear of these diseases.

Limited risk policies that cover specified accidents also are available and are discussed in Lesson 18.

Summary

The need for medical expense insurance—health care insurance in current vernacular—is greater today than at any time in the past, because of the high cost of medical care. Basic medical expense insurance, once the predominant form of health insurance, now is overshadowed by major medical insurance in terms of premium dollars and total coverage. Offered as individual and group policies, medical expense insurance is an indispensable part of a total insurance portfolio.

Key Concepts

In preparing for their licensing examination, students should be familiar with the following concepts:

deductibles	stop-loss feature
preexisting condition	hospital indemnity policy
basic medical expense policies	limited risk policy
basic surgical expense	coinsurance
basic physicians' (nonsurgical) expense	supplementary and comprehensive major medical expense policies
basic hospital expense	

Lesson Exam Sixteen

1. The miscellaneous expense benefit in a basic hospital expense policy normally will cover

   A. physicians' bedside visits
   B. private duty nursing care
   C. drugs and medicine administered in the hospital
   D. hospital room and board

2. Clarence is to enter the hospital for a thyroidectomy. His basic medical expense policy includes a relative value schedule for surgical expense. The schedule lists 55 units for a thyroidectomy and a conversion factor of $8. How much will the policy pay?

   A. $400
   B. $440
   C. $540
   D. $550

3. Which of the following statements about deductible provisions in medical insurance policies is NOT correct?

   A. They help to eliminate small claims.
   B. They provide that initial expenses up to a specified amount are to be paid by the insured.
   C. They are most common in basic medical expense policies.
   D. They help to hold down premium rates.

4. An insured has a basic hospital/surgical expense policy, which provides benefits of $50 per day for up to 30 days of hospitalization and $750 for miscellaneous charges. It bases its surgical benefits on a schedule approach. The insured is hospitalized for a severely broken leg that requires surgery. The surgical procedure has been assigned $500 by the policy, although the customary charge in the area is $600. The insured incurs the following covered expenses:

   $80 per day for seven days hospital charge
   $675 for the surgical procedure
   $800 for miscellaneous expenses

   The insured's policy will pay

   A. $1,600
   B. $1,700
   C. $1,810
   D. $2,035

5. When a medical expense policy pays benefits on an indemnity basis, it pays

   A. a certain percentage of whatever the hospital room charges are
   B. for total hospital expenses, less a deductible
   C. a flat amount per day for hospital room and board
   D. only for surgery and miscellaneous hospital expenses

6. Wilbur's basic medical expense policy limits the miscellaneous expense benefit to 20 times the $90 daily room and board benefit. During his recent hospital stay, Wilbur's miscellaneous expenses totaled $2,100. How much, if any, of this amount will Wilbur have to pay?

   A. $0
   B. $210
   C. $300
   D. $2,100

7. Which of the following examples about major medical policy deductibles is CORRECT?

   A. Eric's major medical policy has a $500 flat deductible provision. He incurs covered expenses totaling $350. He will pay nothing and his major medical policy will pay $350.
   B. Sarah has a major medical policy with a $500 flat deductible and an 80/20 coinsurance provision. Her covered expenses total $1,800. Of that amount, she will pay $500 and her insurance will pay $1,300.
   C. Valerie incurs a hospital bill of $8,300. Her basic medical expense insurance pays $2,400. Valerie pays a $200 deductible and her major medical plan takes care of the balance of covered expenses. Her deductible would be classified as a corridor deductible.
   D. An integrated deductible amount is $2,000. With this deductible, after the basic policy benefits are exhausted, the insured pays the full $2,000 deductible and then the major medical benefits are payable.

8. Arthur incurs total hospital expenses of $9,500, all of which are covered by his major medical policy. The policy includes a $500 deductible and a 75/25 coinsurance feature. Of the total expense, how much will Arthur have to pay?

   A. $2,375
   B. $2,750
   C. $2,875
   D. $6,675

9. All of the following are types of deductible provisions associated with major medical policies EXCEPT

   A. corridor
   B. integrated
   C. flat
   D. stop-loss

10. If the coinsurance feature in a major medical insurance policy is 75/25 with a $100 deductible, how much of a $2,100 bill would the insured pay?

   A. $100
   B. $500
   C. $600
   D. $1,500

Answers & Rationale

1. **C.** In addition to room and board, hospital expense policies cover miscellaneous charges such as drugs, x-rays, anesthesia, lab fees and supplies.

2. **B.** To determine the amount that Clarence's policy will pay for his operation, he would take the number of points assigned to the procedure (55) and multiply it by the conversion factor ($8). Using this calculation, the policy will pay $440.

3. **C.** Basic medical expense plans do not require the insured to satisfy a deductible first. Instead, they impose limitations in the form of maximum benefit amounts that will be paid.

4. **A.** Under a basic hospital/surgical expense policy, limits are imposed on the maximum amount of benefits that will be paid. Any expenses incurred above these dollar amounts must be paid by the insured. In this case, the insured's policy will pay $1,600, broken down as follows: $50/day for 7 days = $350; $500 for the surgical procedure; and $750 for miscellaneous expenses.

5. **C.** Under a medical expense policy, when benefits are paid on an indemnity basis, the policy will pay a flat amount per day for hospital room and board.

6. **C.** If Wilbur's basic medical expense policy limits the miscellaneous expense benefit to 20 times the $90 daily room and board benefit, it will pay $1,800 (20 × $90) for such expenses. Wilbur must pay any amount above this limit. In this case, he will have to pay $300 ($2,100 – $1,800).

7. **C.** Valerie's deductible would be considered a corridor deductible. With this type of deductible, the first covered medical expenses ($2,400) that Valerie incurs are paid by her basic medical expense policy. After that, she pays her full deductible ($200) and then her major medical plan takes care of the remaining covered expenses.

8. **B.** Arthur will have to pay $2,750. After he pays his $500 deductible, his insurance company would pay 75 percent of the remaining $9,000 in expenses while Arthur would pay 25 percent of this amount, or $6,750 and $2,250, respectively.

9. **D.** Major medical policies may use one of three types of deductible: flat, corridor or integrated. A stop-loss deductible does not exist.

10. **C.** In an insurance policy with a 75/25 coinsurance feature and a $100 deductible, the insured would pay $600 of a $2,100 bill. This would be calculated as follows: $100 deductible plus $500 (25 percent of $2,000, the remaining amount of the bill).

17

Disability Income Insurance

INTRODUCTION

All too often, what is thought to be a well-planned insurance program—a program consisting of life insurance, annuities and medical expense coverage—is proven completely inadequate when disability, the one risk not covered, materializes. The risk associated with disability is not merely the loss of income; there also is the additional cost of caring for a disabled breadwinner who no longer can earn an income. Because a disability can be permanent, the financial consequences rank in severity with the death of the wage earner. The sudden loss of income resulting from a disabling accident or illness would, in most cases, lead to serious financial consequences. Fortunately, protection is available. The purpose of this lesson is to describe the important role disability income insurance serves and to explain the different features found in these types of policies.

LESSON OBJECTIVES

When you complete this lesson you should be able to:

- explain how the percent-of-earnings and flat amount methods are used to determine the amount of disability income benefits;
- compare and contrast the *any occupation* and *own occupation* definitions of total disability;
- describe how partial disability benefits are determined;
- list and describe the standard provisions typically found in a disability income policy; and
- list and describe the different types of riders that may be purchased with disability income policies.

Purpose of Disability Income Insurance

Disability income insurance is designed to provide an individual with a stated amount of periodic income in the event he or she cannot work due to a disabling illness or accident. Statistics prove that the probability of disability greatly exceeds the probability of death during an individual's working years. The need for protection against the economic consequences of a wage earners death cannot be overemphasized, and it is this need that disability income insurance fills.

Disability income policies provide coverage for disabilities resulting either from accidents alone or from accidents and sickness. Because sickness-related disabilities represent only a small fraction of all disabilities, it is not economically feasible to issue sickness-only disability policies. To obtain sickness income protection, one normally has to purchase accident income coverage as well.

Disability income policies are available as individual plans and group plans. They also serve a very important function for businesses and businessowners. In this lesson, we will focus on the basics of individual disability policies; group disability is discussed in Lesson 23 and business uses of disability income insurance are discussed in Lesson 24.

Disability Income Benefits

The benefits paid under a disability income policy are in the form of monthly income payments. Unlike life insurance, which insurers will issue for almost any amount the applicant applies and qualifies for disability income insurance is characterized by benefit limits. Insurers typically place a ceiling on the amount of disability income protection they will issue on any one applicant, defined in terms of the insured's earnings. And with few exceptions, this benefit ceiling is less than the insured's regular income.

✓ **Take Note:** Without a benefit ceiling, a disabled insured could conceivably receive as much income as he or she did while working, with little incentive to return to work and much incentive to prolong the disability.

 Test Topic Alert!   Disability income benefits are based on the insured's earnings and are designed to replace lost income.

Insurers use two methods to determine the amount of benefits payable under their disability income policies. The first method determines the benefit using a percentage of the insured's predisability earnings, and takes into account other sources of disability income.

> ✓ **For Example:** An individual earning $2,000 a month may be limited by Company A to a monthly benefit of 60 percent of income, or $1,200. If that individual already has an existing disability income policy from Company X that provides for $400 in monthly income, the amount payable by Company A would be limited to $800 each month.

Some policies that use the percent-of-earnings formula provide a benefit that varies with the length of the disability. For instance, the benefit amount may equal 100 percent of the insured's predisability earnings for the first month and then reduce the benefit amount to 70 percent thereafter.

The second method used to establish disability benefits is the flat amount method. Under this approach, the policy specifies a flat income benefit amount that will be paid if the insured becomes totally disabled. Normally, this amount is payable regardless of any other income benefits the insured may receive.

> ✓ **Take Note:** The percent of earnings approach typically is used in group disability income plans. The flat amount method is more common in individual plans.

Disability Defined

With one exception (partial disability), an insured must be totally disabled before benefits under a disability income policy are payable. What constitutes total disability varies from policy to policy. The insured must meet the definition set forth in his or her policy. Basically, there are two definitions: *any occupation* or *own occupation*.

Any Occupation The any occupation definition of total disability requires the insured to be unable to perform any occupation for which he or she is reasonably suited by reason of education, training or experience to qualify for disability income benefits.

Own Occupation The own occupation definition of total disability requires that the insured be unable to work at his or her own occupation as a result of an accident or sickness.

> ✓ **Take Note:** Obviously from a policyowner's point of view, an own occupation disability income policy is more advantageous—it also is more expensive and difficult to qualify for.

FIGURE 17.1   Distribution of Disability Claims by Impairment

Disability Claims, 1996

Impairment	Claims	Percent of total
Back	13,243	18.2
Emotional/psychiatric	9,216	12.7
Neurological	8,201	11.3
Extremities	6,582	9.0
Heart	3,003	4.1
Diabetes	2,605	3.6
Substance Abuse	2,437	3.3
Hearing	2,094	2.9
Vision	1,911	2.6
Blood disorders (including HIV)	1,883	2.6
Cancer	1,706	2.3
Asthma	1,266	1.7
Other	18,560	25.7
Total	72,687	100.0

Source: Equal Employment Opportunity Commission, HIAA *Sourcebook of Health Insurance Data 1999-2000*

Disability income policies often qualify total disability in two stages, using both the own occupation and any occupation definitions. These policies will provide initial benefits based on the own occupation definition for a specified period of time (for example, during the first two years of the disability), then change the qualifying basis to the any occupation definition.

 **Test Topic Alert!**   From the insured's viewpoint, the any occupation definition is more restrictive than the own occupation definition. The insurer is less likely to pay a benefit if the insured's disability must prevent him or her from engaging in *any* reasonably suitable occupation.

Presumptive Disability   Most policies today contain a presumption of disability provision. Basically, this provision specifies certain conditions that automatically qualify the insured for the full benefit, because the severity of the conditions presumes the insured is totally disabled even if he or she is able to work. Presumptive disabilities include blindness, deafness, loss of speech and loss of two or more limbs.

✓ **For Example:** If Janet has a stroke and loses her ability to speak she has suffered a presumptive disability and would be entitled to total disability benefits for the rest of her policy's benefit period.

Partial Disability

The exception to the total disability requirement is a policy that also pays benefits in the event of a partial disability. It is not uncommon for disability income policies to make provision for partial disability, either as part of the basic coverage or as an optional rider for an additional premium. By most definitions, partial disability is the inability of the insured to perform one or more important duties of his or her job or the inability to work at that job on a full-time basis, either of which results in a diminished income.

✓ *Take Note:* Normally, partial disability benefits are payable only if the policy-owner first has been totally disabled. This benefit is intended to encourage disabled insureds to get back to work, even on a part-time basis, without fear that they will lose all their disability income benefits.

The amount of benefit payable when a policy covers partial disabilities depends on whether the policy stipulates a *flat amount* or a *residual amount*.

Flat Amount Benefit A flat amount benefit is a set amount stated in the policy. Usually this amount is 50 percent of the full disability benefit.

✓ *For Example:* Helen, who has a disability income policy with an own occupation definition, is injured severely after falling down a flight of stairs. She is unable to work for four months, during which time her disability income policy pays a full benefit. After four months she is able to return to work, but only on a part-time basis, earning substantially less than she did before her injury. If her policy did not contain a partial disability provision, her benefits would cease entirely because she no longer meets the definition of totally disabled. However, if her policy provides for partial disability benefits to be paid as a flat amount, she will be able to work on a part-time basis and continue to receive half of her disability benefits.

Residual Amount Benefit A residual amount benefit is based on the proportion of income actually lost due to the partial disability, taking into account the fact that the insured is able to work and earn some income. The benefit usually is determined by multiplying the percentage of lost income by the stated monthly benefit for total disability.

✓ *For Example:* If the insured suffered a 40 percent loss of income because of the partial disability, the residual benefit payable would be 40 percent of the benefit that the policy would provide for total disability. This percentage is subject to change as the disabled insured's income varies.

Generally, residual benefits are provided through a rider to the policy, which specifies that no residual benefits are paid if the loss of income is less than 20 or 25 percent. Usually, residual benefits are payable even if the insured was not first totally disabled.

✓ *For Example:* Larry, a printer, suffered a severe back injury following a car accident. Though he was able to continue working, it was on a limited part-time basis, at only 60 percent of his predisability salary. If Larry's disability income policy provided for residual disability benefits, he would receive monthly payments from the insurer equal to 40 percent of the total disability benefit.

Insurers require proof of an insured's total or partial disability before they will pay benefits. To be eligible for benefits, the disabled insured must be under the care of a physician.

Cause of Disability

Another important aspect of disability income policies is the way in which they define the cause of disability. As noted above, disability income insurance policies cover accidents only or accidents and sickness. Thus, how a disability occurs is an important consideration for disability income policies, as well as any other kind of policy covering injury due to accident.

Generally, disability income policies state that benefits are payable when injuries are either caused by external, violent and accidental means or result in accidental bodily injury.

Policies that use the *accidental means provision* require that the cause of the injury must have been unexpected and accidental. Policies that use the accidental bodily injury provision require that the result of the injury—in other words, the injury itself—has to be unexpected and accidental. This also is known as the *results provision*.

✓ *For Example:* Jim, the insured, took an intentional dive off a high, rocky ledge into a lake. He struck his head on some rocks and was partially paralyzed. If his policy had an accidental means provision, the benefits probably would not be payable because the cause of his injury—the dive—was intentional. However, if his policy had an accidental bodily injury (or results) provision, benefits would be payable because the result of the accident—his injury—was unintentional and accidental.

Today, most disability income policies (and other policies providing accident protection) use the accidental bodily injury or results provision, which is far less restrictive than the accidental means provision. In fact, many states now require all accident-based insurance benefits to be based on the accidental bodily injury provision.

Disability Income Policy Provisions

In addition to specifying the amount of benefit payable and the circumstances under which a benefit is payable (plus complying with required provisions standards), disability income policies contain a number of other important provisions. The most notable of these are as follows.

Probationary Period

The probationary period specified in a disability insurance policy is the period of time that must elapse following the effective date of the policy before benefits are payable. It is a one-time-only period that begins on the policy's effective date and ends 15 or 30 days after the policy has been in force. The purpose of the probationary period is to exclude preexisting sicknesses from coverage and provide a guidepost in borderline cases when there is a question as to whether an insured became ill before or after the effective date of the policy. Just as important, it helps protect the insurer against adverse selection, because those who know they are ill are more likely to try to obtain insurance coverage.

 Take Note: A disability income probationary period applies to sickness only; it does not apply to accidents. Whereas a person may be able to anticipate a sickness-related disability (after a visit to the doctor, for example), it is not possible to anticipate an accident.

Elimination Period

Similar in concept to a deductible, the elimination period is the time immediately following the start of a disability when benefits are not payable. Elimination periods eliminate claims for short-term disabilities for which the insured usually can manage without financial hardship and save the insurance company from the expense of processing and settling small claims. This, in turn, helps keep premiums down. The longer the elimination period, the lower the premium for comparable disability benefits. An elimination period can be compared to a deductible because both are cost-sharing devices that can have a direct bearing on the amount of premium required of the policyowner.

Depending on the policy, elimination periods may apply only to disabilities caused by sickness and not to disabilities caused by accident. In either event, elimination periods usually range from one week to one year or longer, but most are at least 30 days.

 **Test Topic Alert!**   An elimination period begins after a disability occurs and is not retroactive. Like a deductible, it is a cost-sharing device that can affect the amount of the premium.

Benefit Period

The benefit period is the maximum length of time that disability income benefits will be paid to the disabled insured. The longer the benefit period, the higher the cost of the policy. For individual policies, there are basically two types of benefit periods and accordingly they serve to classify a disability income policy as either short term or long term. Individual short-term policies provide benefits for six months to two years, after which payments cease. Individual long-term policies are characterized by benefit periods of more than two years, such as 5, 10 or 20 years. In some cases, a long-term policy will provide for benefits until the insured reaches age 65. The classifications of short term and long term are not necessarily the same for individual and group plans. See Lesson 23 for a discussion of group disability plans.

Delayed Disability Provision

In some cases, total disability does not occur immediately after an accident, but develops some days or weeks later. Most policies allow a certain amount of time during which total disability may result from an accident and the insured still will be eligible for benefits. The amount of time allowed for a delayed disability may be 30, 60 or 90 days, for example.

Recurrent Disability Provision

It is not unusual for a person who experienced a total disability to recover and then, weeks or months later, undergo a recurrence of the same disability. Most policies provide for recurrent disabilities by specifying a period of time during which the recurrence of a disability is considered a continuation of the prior disability. If the recurrence takes place after that period, it is considered a new disability and will be subject to a new elimination period before benefits are again payable.

 For Example: Rachel has a short-term disability policy that stipulates a new benefit-paying period begins if the insured is disabled, recovers, returns to work for six months and then becomes disabled again. Rachel is totally disabled and off work from January 15 to April 15, when she returns to work. She is stricken again the same year and is off work from September 1 to November 10. Rachel's policy would resume paying benefits, classifying her recurrence as a continuation of her prior disability, because her return to work did not last six months. She would not be subject to a new elimination period.

Nondisabling Injury

Frequently, a person covered by a disability income policy will suffer an injury that does not qualify for income benefits. Many such policies include a provision for a medical expense benefit that pays the actual cost of medical treatment for nondisabling injuries that result from an accident.

The benefit generally is limited to a percentage of the weekly or monthly income benefit specified in the policy. It is payable to eligible insureds in lieu of other benefits under the policy.

✎ Quick Quiz 17.1 True or False?

_____ 1. If Susan is blind but is able to teach school, she will be considered to have a presumptive disability.

_____ 2. If Matt is injured in a sky-diving accident and as a result is unable to work, he likely will receive benefits under most disability income policies today.

_____ 3. If Paul is injured in a car accident 10 days after obtaining disability income insurance, he will be subject to a 30-day probationary period before disability benefits will be paid.

_____ 4. If Mary is injured in a train accident but does not develop back problems that prevent her from working until two weeks later, she probably will be eligible for disability benefits under most policies.

_____ 5. The percent of earnings approach generally is used in group disability insurance plans while the flat-amount method is more common in individual plans.

Answers

1. **True**.

2. **True**.

3. **False**. _The probationary period in a disability income policy applies to sickness only; it does not apply to accidents. This is because while it is possible to expect a sickness-related disability, it is not possible to anticipate an accident. As a result, Paul will be entitled to disability income benefits immediately after the accident._

4. **True**.

5. **True**.

Disability Income Policy Riders

As is true with life insurance policies, disability income policies may be purchased with riders or options that will enhance their value to the insured. Some of the more common riders are discussed below.

Waiver of Premium Rider

A waiver of premium rider generally is included with guaranteed renewable and noncancelable individual disability income policies. It is a valuable provision because it exempts the policyowner from paying the policy's premiums during periods of total disability. To qualify for the exemption, the insured must experience total disability for more than a specified period, commonly three or six months. In some cases, the waiver applies retroactively to the original date of disability and any premiums paid for that period are refunded. The trend is to have the waiver apply to the entire period of total disability, rather than to just the benefit period.

✓ **Take Note:** The waiver of premium generally does not extend past the insured's age 60 or 65. When the waiver is added, policy premiums are adjusted upward to cover the additional risk. Premiums then are reduced when the waiver is dropped due to the insured reaching the specified age limit.

Social Security Rider

The Social Security rider, sometimes called the social insurance substitute rider, provides for the payment of additional income when the insured is eligible for social insurance benefits but those benefits have not yet begun, have been denied or have begun in an amount less than the benefit amount of the rider. Usually covered under the definition social insurance are disability benefits from Social Security as well as state and local government programs or workers' compensation programs.

When applying for the rider, the applicant states the amount of benefit expected from Social Security and any other programs for which he or she might be eligible. Of course, the level of expected benefits must be realistic in light of the applicant's earnings level. When total disability strikes, the applicant must show that social insurance benefits have been applied for. After the Social Security Administration (or comparable administrative body of a state or local program) determines the benefit payable, the difference between the actual benefit and the expected benefit listed in the rider is payable as an additional disability income benefit.

Cost of Living Adjustment (COLA) Rider

The cost of living adjustment (COLA) rider links the monthly or weekly benefit payable under a disability policy to changes in the Consumer Price Index (CPI). Typically, the benefit amount is adjusted on each disability anniversary date to reflect changes in the CPI (though often a minimum CPI change, such as 4 percent, is required to trigger a disability income benefit increase).

✓ *Take Note:* When the disability ceases, the policyowner can elect to maintain the disability policy at the new (increased) benefit level by paying additional premiums or can choose to let the benefit return to the originally scheduled amount for the same premium as was paid before the disability commenced.

Guaranteed Insurability Rider

A disability income policy is the only type of health insurance policy to which a guaranteed insurability rider may be attached. This option guarantees the insured the right to purchase additional amounts of disability income coverage at predetermined times in the future without evidence of insurability. The guarantee may be contingent upon the insured meeting an earnings test prior to each purchase—a condition stipulated by the insurer to avoid overinsurance.

Most guaranteed insurability riders require the insured to exercise the option for additional coverage before reaching a specific age.

Summary

Often called "the forgotten need," disability income insurance is an important part of a complete insurance program. Monthly or weekly benefits are paid when the insured is totally disabled, as determined by either the *any occupation* or the more liberal *own occupation* definition. If the policy has a partial disability provision, benefits may be payable if the insured is able to work only part time or suffers a less-than-total disability. Another feature of disability income policies is that they define the cause of a disabling accident on an accidental means or accidental results basis.

Disability income contracts are characterized by probationary periods, which exclude preexisting sickness from immediate coverage, and elimination periods, which specify the time after the start of a disability when benefits are not payable, thereby excluding very short-term disabilities from coverage. Like life insurance, disability income policies may be purchased with policy riders that can increase their value to the insured.

Disability income coverage may be purchased as individual or group policies. Its uses for businesses and business owners will be discussed in Lesson 24.

Key Concepts

In preparing for their licensing examination, students should be familiar with the following concepts:

total disability	*any occupation*
own occupation	partial disability
presumptive disability	residual disability
probationary period	elimination period
waiver of premium rider	Social Security rider
cost of living adjustment rider	guaranteed insurability rider

Lesson Exam Seventeen

1. Assume an insurer will issue a maximum monthly disability income benefit of $5,000 of an insured's monthly income, provided the total of such benefits payable by all companies does not exceed 60 percent of the insured's regular monthly income. Ted earns $4,500 per month and has no existing disability income policy. The maximum monthly disability income benefit this insurer would issue to Ted is

   A. $2,500
   B. $2,700
   C. $4,500
   D. $5,000

2. Which of the following is NOT a basis for occupational suitability when determining total disability?

   A. Education
   B. Training
   C. Experience
   D. Job interest

3. Which of the following statements about elimination periods in disability income policies is NOT correct?

   A. Elimination periods apply to disabilities due to sickness and not accidents.
   B. Benefits are not payable during an elimination period, but are paid retroactively to the beginning of the period if the insured remains disabled throughout the period.
   C. An elimination period follows the start of a disability.
   D. Elimination periods help keep premiums down.

4. Which of the following riders provides for changes in the benefit payable based on changes in the consumer price index (CPI)?

   A. Guaranteed insurability
   B. Cost of living adjustment
   C. Social Security
   D. Waiver of premium

5. Benefit periods for individual short-term disability policies typically vary from

   A. 1 to 12 months
   B. 3 months to 3 years
   C. 6 months to 2 years
   D. 1 to 5 years

6. Which of the following statements about waiver of premium in health insurance policies is NOT correct?

   A. It exempts an insured from paying premiums during periods of permanent and total disability.
   B. It may apply retroactively.
   C. It generally drops off after the insured reaches age 60 or 65.
   D. It normally applies to both medical expense and disability income policies.

7. Which of the following terms relates to disability income insurance?

   A. Service basis
   B. First-dollar
   C. Residual basis
   D. Coinsurance

8. Which of the following statements pertaining to recurrent disabilities for disability insurance is NOT correct?

   A. A recurrent disability is one that the insured experiences more than once.
   B. Recurrent disability policy provisions have no effect on the payment of benefits.
   C. A new elimination period may or may not be required for a recurrent disability.
   D. A recurrent disability may begin a new benefit period.

9. Sidney has a monthly benefit of $2,500 for total disability under a residual disability income policy. If Sidney suffers a 40 percent loss of his predisability income, how much will his benefit be?

   A. $0
   B. $1,000
   C. $1,500
   D. $2,500

10. What is the initial period of time specified in a disability income policy that must pass, after a policy is in force, before a loss due to sickness can be covered?

    A. Preexisting term
    B. Probationary period
    C. Temporary interval
    D. Elimination period

Answers & Rationale

1. **B.** The insurer will issue a disability income policy to Ted that determines the benefit using a percentage of his predisability earnings, and takes into account other sources of disability income. If it will pay no more than 60 percent of his regular monthly income ($4,500), the policy will provide a maximum monthly benefit of $2,700 (60 percent of $4,500).

2. **D.** The *any occupation* definition of total disability requires the insured to be unable to perform any occupation for which he or she is reasonably suited by reason of education, training or experience in order to qualify for disability income benefits.

3. **B.** During the elimination period, benefits are not payable. This eliminates claims for short-term disabilities for which the insured can usually manage without financial hardship. If the insured remains disabled throughout the period and thereafter, benefits will not be paid retroactively.

4. **B.** A cost of living adjustment rider provides for indexing monthly or weekly disability benefits to changes in the Consumer Price Index.

5. **C.** Individual short-term disability policies typically have benefit periods ranging from 6 months to 2 years, after which payments stop. In contrast, individual long-term policies provide for benefit periods of more than two years.

6. **D.** A waiver of premium rider generally is included with guaranteed renewable and noncancelable individual disability income policies. It normally does not apply to medical expense policies.

7. **C.** The term *residual basis* applies to disability income insurance. The amount of benefit payable when a policy covers partial disabilities depends on whether the policy stipulates a flat amount or a residual basis. A residual amount benefit is based on the proportion of income actually lost due to the partial disability, taking into account the fact that the insured can work and earn some income.

8. **B.** Recurrent disability policy provisions affect the payment of benefits. Under most policies, a recurrence of a disability is considered a continuation of the prior disability. If the recurrence takes place after that period, it is considered a new disability and will be subject to a new elimination period before benefits become payable again.

9. **B.** Sidney's benefit under his residual disability income policy will be determined by multiplying the percentage of lost income by the stated monthly benefit for total disability. Because he suffered a 40 percent loss of income, the residual benefit payable would be 40 percent of the policy's benefit (40 percent × $2,500), or $1,000.

10. **B.** The probationary period is the period of time that must elapse before benefits due to sickness become payable. It is a one-time-only period that ends 15 or 30 days after the policy has been in force. Its purpose is to exclude preexisting sicknesses from coverage.

18

Accidental Death and Dismemberment Insurance

INTRODUCTION

The third major type of health insurance coverage is accidental death and dismemberment insurance (AD&D). It pays benefits in the event of a fatal accident or if dismemberment results from an accidental injury. Although the circumstances under which benefits are paid are somewhat limited, it is a widely used form of insurance protection and often is attached as a rider on a basic life or health insurance policy. AD&D policies are widely used in group insurance plans as well. In this lesson we will examine the typical features of and benefits provided by AD&D policies and some of the other more specific forms of AD&D policies.

LESSON OBJECTIVES

When you complete this lesson you should be able to:

- explain the purpose of accidental death and dismemberment insurance and the types of benefits that typically are payable;
- explain the difference between policies that base benefits on injuries due to accidental means versus accidental results; and
- compare and contrast limited risk policies and special risk policies and give an example of each type of policy.

Nature of AD&D Policies

Accidental death and dismemberment insurance is the primary form of pure accident coverage. As such, it serves a somewhat limited purpose: it provides a stated lump-sum benefit in the event of accidental death or in the event of loss of body members due to accidental injury. This latter event includes loss of hands or feet or the loss of sight in one or both eyes. (Loss of body member typically is defined as actual severance from the body, though it may include loss of use, depending on the policy.) Separate benefits for hospital, surgical and other medical expenses generally are not included in AD&D policies, although some may pay a medical reimbursement benefit up to a stated amount.

AD&D Benefits

Because an AD&D policy pays a specified benefit to the insured in the event of accidental death or dismemberment due to accidental injury, it is necessary for the policy to make distinctions between these two contingencies and to define the benefits accordingly. Consequently, AD&D policies make benefits payable in the form of a principal sum and a capital sum.

- *Principal Sum.* The principal sum under an AD&D policy is the amount payable as a death benefit. It is the amount of insurance purchased—$10,000, $25,000, $50,000, $100,000 or more. The principal sum represents the maximum amount the policy will pay.
- *Capital Sum.* The capital sum paid under an AD&D policy is the amount payable for the accidental loss of sight or accidental dismemberment. It is a specified amount, usually expressed as a percentage of the principal sum, that varies according to the severity of the injury. The benefit for the loss of one foot or one hand typically is 50 percent of the principal sum. The benefit for the loss of one arm or one leg usually is two-thirds of the principal sum. The most extreme losses, such as the loss of both feet or sight in both eyes, generally qualify for payment of the full benefit, which is 100 percent of the principal sum.

✓ **For Example:** Kevin has an accidental death and dismemberment policy that pays $50,000 for accidental loss of life and the same for accidental loss of two limbs or the sight in both eyes. Thus, $50,000 is the policy's principal sum. The same policy pays $25,000 for accidental loss of sight of one eye or dismemberment of one limb. Therefore, $25,000 is the policy's capital sum.

Some AD&D policies provide for payment of double, triple or even quadruple the principal sum if the insured dies under specified circumstances. A double payment is referred to as double indemnity. If three times the principal sum is payable, it is called triple indemnity. However, do not let these terms confuse you. AD&D policies, because they pay a stated benefit, are valued contracts. They are not contracts of indemnity.

Accidental Means vs. Accidental Results

As we learned in the last lesson, an insurance policy that provides benefits in the event of an injury due to an accident must stipulate what is considered an insurable accident. In all cases, an accident is external and violent, but accidental death and dismemberment policies (like disability income policies) make a distinction between injuries due to accidental means and those due to accidental results (or accidental bodily injury).

By way of a review, policies that base their benefit payments on accidental means require that both the cause and the result of an accident must be unintentional. Policies that use the more liberal accidental results definition stipulate that only the injury resulting from an accident must be unintentional.

✓ **For Example:** If Ted, the insured under an AD&D policy, intentionally jumps from the roof of his house after fixing his antenna (instead of climbing down the ladder) and so severely injures his leg that it must be amputated, he would be paid the appropriate percentage of the capital sum only if his policy used the results definition. If his policy used the means definition, no benefit would be payable because Ted intentionally performed the action (the jump) that resulted in the injury.

As noted in the discussion of disability income policies, most states require that policies that provide any form of accident benefit, as do AD&D policies, base the definition of accident on the results definition, not the means definition.

Other Forms of AD&D

Accidental death and dismemberment coverage is made available in a variety of ways. It can be purchased by individuals as a single policy or it may be a part of an individual disability income policy. Quite typically, however, it is an aspect of a group insurance plan—either group life or group health—or it may in and of itself constitute a group plan. Usually, AD&D benefits are payable whether the injury resulted on or off the job.

By their very nature, AD&D policies are somewhat narrow, providing benefits only in the event of death or dismemberment due to an accident. There is another type of AD&D coverage, even more narrow in scope, that provides protection against accidental death or dismemberment only in the event of certain specified accidents. These are *limited risk policies* and *special risk policies*.

Limited Risk Policies

As noted in Lesson 16, limited risk policies set forth a specific risk and provide benefits to cover death or dismemberment due to that risk. For example, an aviation policy provides benefits for accidental death or dismemberment if death or injury results from an aviation accident during a specified trip. An automobile policy provides benefits for accidental death or injury while riding in a car. Travel accident covers most kinds of travel accidents, but only for a specified period of time, such as one year.

Special Risk Policies

A distinction should be made between limited risk and special risk policies. A special risk policy covers unusual hazards normally not covered under ordinary accident and health insurance. An actress who insures her legs for $1 million or a pilot test-flying an experimental airplane who obtains a policy covering his life while flying that particular plane, both are purchasing special risk policies. But a traveler who purchases an accident policy at the airport to provide coverage while he or she is a passenger on a commercial airlines flight is purchasing a limited risk policy.

Summary

Accidental death and dismemberment insurance (AD&D) represents the purest form of accident coverage. It provides a stated sum benefit in the event of accidental death or accidental loss of one or more body members or accidental loss of sight. The benefit payable in the event of death is known as the principal sum; the benefit payable in the event of dismemberment or loss of sight is the capital sum.

Like all policies that provide accident benefits, AD&D policies must define the term accident on either a means basis (in which both the cause and the result of the accident must be unintentional) or on a results basis (requiring only that the injury itself be accidental). Most states stipulate the use of the results definition.

AD&D coverage may be purchased as an individual policy but usually is part of a larger group life or health plan. In some cases, it is offered as a separate group plan. Specialized forms of AD&D coverage, known as limited risk and special risk insurance, provide accident protection in the event of specified limited risks, such as travel or aviation.

Key Concepts

In preparing for their licensing examination, students should be familiar with the following concepts:

capital sum

special risk policies

accidental death and
  dismemberment coverage

principal sum

limited risk policies

accidental means vs. accidental
  results

Lesson Exam Eighteen

1. The amount payable as a death benefit in an accidental death and dismemberment policy is known as the

   A. primary amount
   B. capital sum
   C. indemnity amount
   D. principal sum

2. Theodore received a $15,000 cash benefit from his $50,000 accidental death and dismemberment policy for the accidental loss of one eye. The amount he received could be identified as the policy's

   A. principal sum
   B. secondary sum
   C. capital sum
   D. contingent amount

3. Which of the following examples about accidental death and dismemberment insurance is CORRECT?

   A. Merrill is the insured under a $50,000 AD&D policy and dies unexpectedly of a heart attack. His beneficiary will receive $50,000 as the death benefit.
   B. Linda has a $40,000 AD&D policy that pays triple indemnity. If she should be killed in a train wreck, her beneficiary would receive $120,000.
   C. Paula has an AD&D policy that pays $15,000 for the loss of one hand or foot or the sight of one eye. That benefit is called the principal sum.
   D. Eric has an AD&D policy. He is killed in an auto accident. The $30,000 his beneficiary receives as a death benefit is the policy's capital sum.

4. Agnes purchases a round-trip travel accident policy at the airport before leaving on a business trip. Her policy would be which type of insurance?

   A. Limited risk
   B. Business overhead expense
   C. Credit accident and health
   D. Industrial health

5. Paul has an accidental death and dismemberment policy that paid him $100,000 after he was injured in a skydiving accident. His policy bases its benefit payments on accidental

   A. means
   B. results
   C. methods
   D. means and methods

Answers & Rationale

1. **D.** The principal sum under an AD&D policy is the amount payable as a death benefit. It is the amount of insurance purchased and represents the maximum amount the policy will pay.

2. **C.** The $15,000 cash benefit Theodore received for the accidental loss of one eye is the policy's capital sum. This is the amount payable for the accidental loss of sight or accidental dismemberment. It is a specified amount that usually is expressed as a percentage of the principal sum and varies according to the severity of the injury.

3. **B.** If Linda's $40,000 AD&D contract pays triple indemnity, her beneficiary will receive three times this amount ($120,000) if she dies in a train accident.

4. **A.** Agnes purchased a limited risk policy that sets forth a specific risk (death or dismemberment from an aviation accident) and provides benefits to cover death or dismemberment due to that risk.

5. **B.** Paul's AD&D policy bases its benefit payments on accidental results. Policies using this definition stipulate that only the injury resulting from an accident must be unintentional. If Paul's policy used the accidental means definition, it would not pay any benefits because Paul intentionally performed the action (skydiving) that resulted in injury.

19

Government Health Insurance Programs

INTRODUCTION

Because of limited resources and the need for more extensive care than younger members of society, senior citizens often face special problems when paying health care bills. To help provide affordable health care for elderly Americans, the federal government enacted Medicare in 1965, which established a health insurance program for aged persons. Since its creation, Medicare has undergone numerous changes affecting its financing, its method of operation, its benefits and its methods of cost control. Despite these changes, the basic mission of Medicare remains the same: to provide a system for the delivery and payment of medical and hospital care for people age 65 and over (and for people with certain disabilities). Today, Medicare covers around 95 percent of our nation's elderly population, as well as many people who are on Social Security because of disability.

We will begin our discussion in this lesson with the Original Medicare Plan, and will then review Medicare+Choice, a program designed to provide Medicare beneficiaries with a variety of health plan options. We also will look at another government program, called Medicaid, which reimburses hospitals and physicians for providing care to needy and low income people who cannot finance their own medical expenses. The lesson ends with a brief discussion of state workers' compensation programs, which provide benefits for work-related injuries, illness or death.

LESSON OBJECTIVES

When you complete this lesson you should be able to:

- explain the types of coverage available under Medicare Part A and Part B;
- identify the different health plan options available under the Medicare+Choice Program;
- explain the purpose of Medicaid and how it differs from Medicare; and
- describe the goal of state workers' compensation laws.

Original Medicare Plan

The Original Medicare Plan consists of two parts: Medicare Part A and Medicare Part B. Medicare Part A is compulsory hospitalization insurance (HI) that provides specified in-hospital and related benefits. It is compulsory in that all workers covered by Social Security finance its operation through a portion of their FICA taxes and automatically are provided with benefits once they qualify for Social Security benefits.

Medicare Part B is a voluntary program designed to provide supplementary medical insurance (SMI) to cover physician services, medical services and supplies not covered under Part A. Those who desire the coverage must enroll and pay a monthly premium. Medicare Part B is financed by monthly premiums from those who participate and by tax revenues.

Medicare Part A Coverages

Medicare Part A provides coverage for inpatient hospitalization and posthospital skilled facility care and home care. For the first 60 days of hospitalization during any one benefit period, Medicare pays for all covered services, except for an initial deductible ($792 in 2001). Covered services include semiprivate room, nursing services and other inpatient hospital services.

For the 61st through the 90th day of hospitalization, Medicare pays a reduced amount of the covered services. The patient is responsible for a daily copayment ($198 per day in 2001).

This 90-day hospitalization coverage is renewed with each benefit period. A benefit period starts when a patient enters the hospital and ends when the patient has been out of the hospital for 60 days. If a patient reenters a hospital before the end of a benefit period, the deductible is not reapplied, but the 90-day hospital coverage period is not renewed. However, if the patient reenters a hospital after a benefit period ends, a new deductible is required and the 90-day hospital coverage period is renewed.

Medicare patients also have a lifetime reserve of 60 days of hospital coverage. If a patient is hospitalized longer than 90 days in a benefit period, he or she can tap into the 60-day reserve. The lifetime reserve is a one-time benefit; it does not renew with a new benefit period. If a patient is hospitalized and taps into the reserve days, he or she is required to pay a higher copayment ($396 per day in 2001). If a patient is hospitalized beyond the 60th lifetime reserve day, thereby exhausting the reserve, he or she is responsible for all hospital charges.

FIGURE 19.1   What Medicare Covers

Part A	Part B
• Inpatient hospital services, including semiprivate room and board and nursing services	• Physicians' and surgeons' services, whether in a hospital, clinic or elsewhere
• Posthospital skilled nursing care, in an accredited care facility	• Medical and health services, such as X-rays, diagnostic lab tests, ambulance services, medical supplies, medical equipment rental and physical and occupational therapy
• Posthospital home health services, including nursing care, therapy and part-time home health aides	
• Hospice benefits for the care of terminally ill patients (to the exclusion of all other Medicare benefits, except for physician services)	
• Inpatient psychiatric care, on a limited basis	

 **Test Topic Alert!**   Medicare Part A is available when an individual turns 65 and automatically is provided when he or she applies for Social Security benefits.

✔ *Take Note:* Most of the people enrolled in Medicare Part A are elderly. In 1999, of the 39 million people who received Medicare Part A benefits, 34 million were over age 65. However, some individuals under age 65 also are eligible for Medicare. For instance, a person under age 65 who receives Social Security or Railroad Retirement disability checks is eligible for Medicare Part A and may enroll in Medicare Part B. Persons with permanent kidney failure who are treated with dialysis or a transplant also are eligible.

In addition, Part A provides benefits for skilled nursing facility care, hospice care, home health services and, to a limited degree, inpatient psychiatric care. In all cases, Part A covers only those services that are medically necessary and only up to amounts deemed reasonable by Medicare.

Part A covers the costs of care in a skilled nursing facility as long as the patient was first hospitalized for three consecutive days. Treatment in a skilled nursing facility is covered in full for the first 20 days. From the 21st to the 100th day, the patient must pay the daily copayment ($99 per day in 2001). No Medicare benefits are provided for treatment in a skilled nursing facility beyond 100 days.

✓ **Test Topic Alert!**   Medicare Part A deductibles and copayments are applied per benefit period, not on an annual basis.

Medicare Part B Coverages

For those who desire, additional coverage is available under Medicare Part B for physician services, diagnostic tests, physical and occupational therapy, medical supplies and the like.

✓ **Take Note:**   Some preventive services, such as mammograms and flu shots, also are covered. However, Medicare Part B does not cover routine physical exams, eyeglasses, dental care, hearing aids, most prescription drugs, orthopedic shoes or routine foot care.

Part B participants are required to pay a monthly premium ($50 in 2001) and are responsible for an annual deductible ($100 in 2001). After the deductible, Part B will pay 80 percent of covered expenses, subject to Medicare's standards for reasonable charges.

 **Test Topic Alert!**   Medicare Part B deductibles and copayments are applied on an annual basis. Part B is an optional coverage.

Primary Payor and Secondary Payor

Anyone aged 65 who is eligible for Medicare and who works for an employer of 20 or more employees is entitled to the same health insurance benefits as the employer offers to younger employees. In these cases, the employer-sponsored plan is the primary payor and Medicare is the secondary payor. This means that Medicare pays only those charges that the employer-sponsored plan does not cover. This also applies to any disabled Medicare enrollee who also is covered by an employer-provided health care plan as a current employee or as a family member of an employee, but only if the employer plan covers 100 or more employees.

Medicare+Choice Program

While Medicare is facing many challenges, the most pressing are the financial pressures resulting from changing demographics. Today, and in the future, the number of people becoming eligible for Medicare will increase rapidly and the number of workers paying taxes to support Medicare will decrease.

In 1997, Congress passed a law to reduce the financial strain on Medicare funds and provide Medicare beneficiaries with a variety of new health plan options. The Original Medicare Plan and Medicare supplement insurance (discussed in the next lesson), which is purchased from private insurance companies, still are available. However, new options are available through what is called the Medicare+Choice Program. These options include a variety of Medicare managed care choices, a private-fee-for-service plan (PFFS) and a Medicare Medical Savings Account Plan (MSA).

Managed Care System

Medicare's managed care system consists of a network of approved hospitals, doctors and other health-care professionals who agree to provide services to Medicare beneficiaries for a set monthly payment from Medicare. The health care providers receive the same fee every month, regardless of the actual services provided. As a result of this arrangement, health care providers try to manage care in such a way that they achieve a balance between budgetary and health care concerns.

✓ **Take Note:** The options available include health maintenance organizations (HMOs), preferred provider organizations (PPOs) and provider sponsored organizations (PSOs). Some HMOs and all PPOs offer a point of service option (POS). With this option, beneficiaries can use providers outside the network for an additional fee.

Private Fee-for-Service Plan

Another Medicare+Choice option is a private-fee-for-service plan (PFFS). This type of plan offers a Medicare-approved private insurance plan. Medicare pays the plan for Medicare-covered services while the PFFS plan determines, up to a limit, how much the care recipient will pay for covered services. The Medicare beneficiary is responsible for paying the difference between the amount Medicare pays and the PFFS charges.

Medical Savings Account

Medicare beneficiaries have the most control over their health care expenditures with Medicare Medical Savings Accounts (MSAs). A Medicare+Choice MSA consists of two parts: a high-deductible insurance policy (the policy) and a savings account (the account). The policy pays for at least all Medicare-covered items and services after an enrollee meets the annual deductible. Medicare pays the premium for the policy and deposits the difference between the premium and the fixed amount Medicare allots for each Medicare+Choice enrollee in the individual's account. Money in the account may earn interest or dividends and can be withdrawn tax free to pay for services covered under the Medicare benefit package, as well as services listed as qualified medical expenses in the Internal Revenue Code. MSA funds can also be used to buy long-term care insurance.

MSAs are available on a first-come, first-served basis to 390,000 Medicare beneficiaries. Note that health care providers can charge whatever they want above what is paid by the Medicare MSA policy. Furthermore, unlike other Medicare+Choice options, individuals who choose an MSA must enroll in the Medicare MSA Plan for at least one year, from January to December. They then can withdraw by December 15 of the following year. Although sales of MSAs have been slow the federal government has extended the program.

✓ **Take Note:** To be eligible for any Medicare+Choice options, a Medicare beneficiary must be enrolled in both Medicare Part A and Part B. Individuals with end-stage renal disease (kidney failure) cannot enroll in most Medicare+Choice plans.

Medicaid

Medicaid is a government-funded, means-tested program designed to provide health care to poor people of all ages. The goal of Medicaid is to offer medical assistance to those whose income and resources are insufficient to meet the costs of necessary medical care. Individuals claiming benefits must prove they do not have the ability or means to pay for their own medical care.

Applicants must complete a lengthy questionnaire, disclosing all assets and income. To qualify for Medicaid, a person must be poor or become poor. Such people frequently include children born to low-income parents, babies born addicted to drugs, AIDS patients and the indigent elderly.

Individual states design and administer the Medicaid programs under broad guidelines established by the federal government. On average, the federal government contributes about 56 cents for every Medicaid dollar spent; however, the amount contributed may be lower or higher. State governments contribute the balance and the extent of coverage and the quality of services vary widely from state to state.

Qualifying for Medicaid Nursing Home Benefits

Unlike Medicare, Medicaid does provide for custodial care or assisted care in a nursing home. However, as explained earlier, individuals claiming a need for Medicaid must prove that they cannot pay for their own nursing home care. In addition, the potential recipient must:

- be at least age 65, blind or disabled (as defined by the recipient's state);
- be a U.S. citizen or permanent resident alien;
- need the type of care that is provided only in a nursing home; and
- meet certain asset and income tests.

✓ **Take Note:** People meeting these basic criteria usually will have their long-term nursing home care paid for by Medicaid. However, each state (and even some counties within certain states) evaluates an individual's ability to pay by looking at the nursing home resident's (and spouse's) income and assets. The specific limits for each of these sources vary by state and change annually.

 **Test Topic Alert!**   Eligibility for Medicaid is based not on an applicant's age, but on his her income.

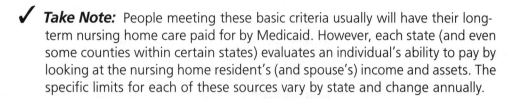

State Workers' Compensation Programs

All states have workers' compensation laws, which were enacted to provide mandatory benefits to employees for work-related injuries, illness or death. Employers are responsible for providing workers' compensation benefits to their employees and do so by purchasing coverage through state programs, private insurers or by self-insuring.

Workers' compensation laws are designed to help injured workers recover and return to work. They are based on the principle that work-related injuries are compensable by the employer without regard to fault. However, the amount of compensation payable is limited and fixed by law. In general, such compensation encompasses medical care costs, disability income, rehabilitation benefits and, for certain specified injuries, specific lump-sum benefits. These benefits relieve injured workers of the burden of medical expenses, replace some of the wages lost due to the disability and provide rehabilitation services to return the person to work. Because of the wide variation among state programs, the laws of each state must be examined to discover available coverages and benefits. See Lesson 15 for a listing of common procedures, requirements and benefits.

Summary

The Original Medicare Plan provides hospital and medical expense insurance protection to those aged 65 and older, to those of any age who suffer from chronic kidney disease or to those who are receiving Social Security disability benefits. Medicaid is a joint federal and state program to pay health care expenses for the poor. To qualify for Medicaid benefits, an individual must meet certain asset and income limitation tests. However, even if a person qualifies for Medicaid, finding an adequate nursing home is difficult because Medicaid does not pay for the full cost of care. Medicaid patients are limited in choice regarding which nursing home they go to.

Key Concepts

In preparing for their licensing examination, students should be familiar with the following concepts:

Medicare	Medicare Part B
Medicaid	lifetime reserve
benefit period	Medicare+Choice program
Medicare Part A	

Lesson Exam Nineteen

1. Which of the following statements pertaining to Medicare is CORRECT?

   A. Bob is covered under Medicare Part B. He submitted a total of $1,100 of approved medical charges to Medicare after paying the required deductible. Of that total, Bob must pay $880.

   B. Each individual covered by Medicare Part A is allowed one 90-day benefit period per year.

   C. For the first 90 days of hospitalization, Medicare Part A pays 100 percent of all covered services, except for an initial deductible.

   D. Medicare Part A is provided automatically when a qualified individual applies for Social Security benefits.

2. Under Medicare Part B, the participant must pay all of the following EXCEPT

   A. an annual deductible
   B. a per benefit deductible
   C. 20 percent of covered charges above the deductible
   D. a monthly premium

3. Which of the following statements about Medicare Part B is NOT correct?

   A. It is a compulsory program.
   B. It covers services and supplies not covered by Part A.
   C. It is financed by monthly premiums.
   D. It is financed by tax revenues.

4. For how many days of skilled nursing facility care will Medicare pay benefits?

   A. 25
   B. 60
   C. 75
   D. 100

5. Which of the following statements concerning workers' compensation is NOT correct?

   A. Workers' compensation laws are designed to return injured persons to work.
   B. Benefits include medical care costs and disability income.
   C. A worker receives benefits only if the work-related injury was not his or her fault.
   D. All states have workers' compensation laws.

Answers & Rationale

1. **D.** When an individual turns age 65, Medicare Part A is available and is provided automatically when he or she applies for Social Security benefits.

2. **B.** Under Medicare Part B, a participant must pay a monthly premium and an annual deductible. Once the deductible has been met, Part B will pay 80 percent of covered expenses and the participant must pay the remaining 20 percent.

3. **A.** Medicare Part B is an optional program that provides additional coverage for physician services, diagnostic tests, physical and occupation therapy, medical supplies and the like.

4. **D.** Medicare Part A covers the cost of care in a skilled nursing facility for 100 days. For the first 20 days, treatment is covered in full. From the 21st to the 100th day, the patient must pay a daily copayment. No Medicare benefits are provided for treatment beyond this period.

5. **C.** All states have workers' compensation laws that are designed to help injured workers recover and return to work. They are based on the principle that the employer should provide compensation for work-related injuries, regardless of who was at fault.

20

Private Insurance Plans for Seniors

INTRODUCTION

As the U.S. population ages, individuals inevitably encounter more medical problems that require additional and costly health care services. As health care costs have increased at a dizzying rate, there has been an ever-growing concern over how to pay for these costs. Because the coverage and benefits provided by Medicare are by no means comprehensive, insurance companies have stepped in to fill these gaps in coverage by offering Medicare supplement policies. As a result, most Medicare recipients supplement their health care through a Medicare supplement policy that picks up coverage where Medicare leaves off.

As we saw in the last lesson, although Medicare was designed to cover physician and hospital costs associated with acute illness and injuries, it never was intended to cover chronic conditions requiring long-term care, whether at home or in a nursing facility. To finance this level of care, many individuals purchase long-term care insurance. In this lesson, we will look at typical features and benefits of long-term care policies and we also will focus on Medicare supplement policies, which are designed to protect elderly people from the high cost of health care.

LESSON OBJECTIVES

When you complete this lesson you should be able to:

- explain the purpose of Medicare supplement policies and describe the types of coverage they provide;
- list and describe the different types of coverage provided under long-term care policies;
- identify the basic provisions and typical limits and exclusions found in most long-term care policies; and
- explain the tax treatment of long-term care benefits.

Medicare Supplement Policies

As is apparent from the discussion of Medicare in the previous lesson, Medicare leaves many gaps in its coverage. With its structure of limited benefit periods, deductibles, copayments and exclusions, the coverage it provides is limited at best. To help fill these gaps, private insurance companies market Medicare supplement insurance policies to consumers. Medicare supplement (or Medigap) policies are designed to pick up coverage where Medicare leaves off.

The term Medicare supplement implies that the policy is supposed to cover what Medicare does not. Unfortunately, until recently some policies did not live up to what was expected of them. To combat this, in 1990 Congress passed a far-reaching Medigap law that required the National Association of Insurance Commissioners (NAIC) to address the subject of Medicare supplement policies. Specifically, the NAIC's task was to develop a standardized model Medicare supplement policy, which would provide certain core benefits, plus as many as nine other supplement policies that would provide increasingly more comprehensive benefits. These 10 model policies then could be adopted by the states as prototype policies for their insurers. (See Figure 20.1)

Each of the 10 plans developed by the NAIC has a letter designation ranging from A (the most basic policy) to J (the most comprehensive policy). Plan A is the core benefits plan; each of the remaining nine plans incorporates these core benefits and adds various other combinations of benefits. Insurers may not alter these combinations of benefits, nor may the letter designations be changed (although insurers may add names or titles to the letter designations).

The purpose of this law was to reduce the variety of Medicare supplement policies being offered for sale and to eliminate some of the questionable marketing practices associated with these policies. It was intended that these model policies would help consumers better understand Medicare supplement policies, thereby allowing them to make more informed buying decisions by:

- standardizing coverages and benefits from one policy to the next;
- simplifying the terms used in these policies;
- facilitating policy comparisons; and
- eliminating policy provisions that may be misleading or confusing.

Qualifying for Medigap Coverage

People age 65 or older who enroll in Medicare Part B are afforded a six-month open enrollment period for purchasing a Medicare supplement

FIGURE 20.1   Standard Medicare Supplement Plans

BASIC BENEFITS: Included in All Plans
Hospitalization: Part A coinsurance plus coverage for 365 additional days after Medicare benefits end
Medical Expenses: Part B coinsurance (20% of Medicare-approved expenses)
Blood: First three pints of blood each year

A	B	C	D	E	F	G	H	I	J
Basic Benefits	Basic Benefits	Basic Benefits	Basic Benefits	Basic Benefits	Basic Benefits	Basic Benefits	Basic Benefits	Basic Benefits	Basic Benefits
		Skilled Nursing Coinsurance	Skilled Nursing Coinsurance	Skilled Nursing Coinsurance	Skilled Nursing Coinsurance	Skilled Nursing Coinsurance	Skilled Nursing Coinsurance	Skilled Nursing Coinsurance	Skilled Nursing Coinsurance
	Part A Deductible	Part A Deductible	Part A Deductible	Part A Deductible	Part A Deductible	Part A Deductible	Part A Deductible	Part A Deductible	Part A Deductible
		Part B Deductible			Part B Deductible				Part B Deductible
					Part B Excess (100%)	Part B Excess (80%)		Part B Excess (100%)	Part B Excess (100%)
		Foreign Travel Emergency	Foreign Travel Emergency	Foreign Travel Emergency	Foreign Travel Emergency	Foreign Travel Emergency	Foreign Travel Emergency	Foreign Travel Emergency	Foreign Travel Emergency
			At-Home Recovery			At-Home Recovery		At-Home Recovery	At-Home Recovery
							Basic Drugs ($1,250 Limit)	Basic Drugs ($1,250 Limit)	Basic Drugs ($3,000 Limit)
				Preventive Care					Preventive Care

Source: National Association of Insurance Commissioners.

policy. They may select any of the Medigap policies available in their state and they cannot be denied coverage because of health problems. In fact, insurers may not discriminate in the pricing of the policy or condition the issuance of the policy on good health.

✓ ***Take Note:*** An insurer may exclude certain preexisting conditions, such as health problems treated within the six months before the policy went into effect.

In general, people under age 65, disabled and enrolled in Medicare Part B are not eligible for open enrollment unless their state mandates otherwise.

Protecting the Consumer

As stated earlier, the standardization of Medigap policies was intended to help consumers understand what these policies cover and, more importantly, what they do not cover. Consumers now are encouraged to do some comparison shopping before they purchase a Medicare supplement policy. Prospective insureds should compare benefits, the coverage limitations, the exclusions and the premiums of several insurers before they buy a policy. In many cases, policies that provide the same coverage will not necessarily have the same premiums.

As further protection for the consumer, purchasers have the option of reviewing their policies and canceling the coverage. Consumers can receive a refund of their premium if they notify the insurer within a specified number of days after the policy is delivered. In most states, this free look period is 30 days, but some states have shorter periods.

 **Test Topic Alert!**   Medicare supplement insurance is not social insurance. It is offered through private insurers to supplement Medicare. An additional premium is charged for this coverage under the various supplement plans.

Long-Term Care Policies

Americans are living longer and many can expect to live a substantial portion of their lives in retirement. That's the good news. The bad news is, although statistics regarding longevity for older Americans may be improving, many individuals over age 65 still have to deal with poor health during their retirement years. As people age, they consume a larger proportion of health care services because of chronic illness, such as Alzheimer's disease, heart disease and stroke. The cost of the extended day-in, day-out care some older people need can be staggering: as much as $40,000 or $50,000 each year or more for nursing home care and upwards of $1,200 a month—or more— for aides who come to one's home.

As beneficial as Medicare and Medicare supplement insurance are to the elderly in protecting them against the costs of medical care, neither of these programs covers long-term custodial or nursing home care. Medicaid covers some of the costs associated with long-term care, but a person is ineligible for

Medicaid until he or she is practically destitute. How can these costs be paid? The solution for many is long-term care insurance.

What Is Long-Term Care?

You often will see nursing home care referred to as long-term care. However, long-term care (LTC) refers to a broad range of medical, personal and environmental services designed to assist individuals who have lost their ability to remain completely independent in the community. Although care may be provided for short periods of time while a patient is recuperating from an accident or illness, LTC refers to care provided for an extended period of time, normally more than 90 days. And, depending on the severity of the impairment, assistance may be given at home, at an adult care center or in a nursing home.

 **Test Topic Alert!**   Long-term care is care rendered for an extended period of time, usually more than 90 days.

A large percentage of the elderly population will spend time in a nursing home. In fact, the Department of Health and Human Services estimated that, in 2000, expenditures on nursing home care exceeded $85.8 billion. The cost of care for elderly or disabled people who remained at home but required some type of home care exceeded $34.7 billion in 2000.

What Is Long-Term Care Insurance?

Long-term care insurance is a relatively new type of insurance product. However, more and more insurance companies are beginning to offer this coverage as the need for it grows. It is similar to most insurance plans, in that the insured, in exchange for a certain premium, receives specified benefits in the event he or she requires LTC, as defined by the policy. Most LTC policies pay the insured a fixed dollar amount for each day he or she receives the kind of care the policy covers, regardless of what the care costs.

✓ **For Example:** If the daily benefit amount is $125 per day and the facility charges $110 per day, the insurance company will pay the full $125 per day. The claimant decides what to do with the funds.

Insurers offer a wide range of benefit amounts, ranging from, for example, $40 each day to $200 each day for nursing home care. The daily benefit for at-home care typically is half the nursing home benefit. Many policies include an inflation rider or option to purchase additional coverage, enabling the policies to keep pace with increases in LTC costs.

Long-Term Care Coverages

As individuals age, they are likely to suffer from acute and (or) chronic illnesses or conditions. An acute illness is a serious condition, such as pneumonia or influenza, from which the body can recover fully with proper medical attention. The patient also may need some assistance with chores for short periods of time until recovery and rehabilitation from the illness are complete.

Some people will suffer from chronic conditions, such as arthritis, heart disease or hypertension, that are treatable but not curable illnesses. When chronic conditions such as diabetes or heart disease initially manifest, many people ignore the inconvenience or pain they cause. Over time, however, a chronic condition frequently goes beyond being a nuisance and begins to inhibit a person's independence.

Typically, the need for LTC arises when physical or mental conditions, whether acute or chronic, impair a person's ability to perform the basic activities of daily living—eating, toileting, transferring, bathing, continence and dressing. This is the risk that long-term care insurance is designed to protect.

✓ **Take Note:** Activities of daily living (ADLs) provide an excellent means to assess an individual's need for nursing home care, home health care or other health-related services. A policy should indicate what number and type of ADLs will be used to trigger benefits. When the insured cannot perform these ADLs independently, benefits will be paid to cover expenses for assistance with those activities.

The kinds of services and support associated with long-term care are provided at three levels: institutional care, home-based care and community care. The appropriate level of care depends, of course, on the individual's medical or health care needs. Within each of these broad levels are many types of care, any or all of which may be covered by a long-term care insurance policy. Typical types of coverages are explained below.

Skilled Nursing Care   Skilled nursing care is continuous around-the-clock care provided by licensed medical professionals under the direct supervision of a physician. Skilled nursing care is usually is administered in nursing homes.

Intermediate Nursing Care   Intermediate nursing care is provided by registered nurses, licensed practical nurses and nurse's aides under the supervision of a physician. Intermediate care is provided in nursing homes for stable medical conditions that require daily, but not 24-hour, supervision.

Custodial Care   Custodial care provides assistance in meeting daily living requirements, such as bathing, dressing, getting out of bed, toileting, etc. Such care does not require specialized medical training, but it must be given under a doctor's order. Custodial care usually is provided by nursing homes but also can be given by adult day care centers, by respite centers or at home.

Home Health Care Home health care is care provided in the insured's home, usually on a part-time basis. It can include skilled care (such as nursing, rehabilitative or physical therapy care ordered by a doctor) or unskilled care (such as help with cooking or cleaning).

Adult Day Care Adult day care is designed for those who require assistance with various activities of daily living, while their primary caregivers (usually family or friends) are absent. These day care centers offer skilled medical care in conjunction with social and personal services, but custodial care usually is their primary focus.

Respite Care Respite care is designed to provide a short rest period for a family caregiver. There are two options: either the insured is moved to a full-time care facility or a substitute care provider moves into the insured's home for a temporary period, giving the family member a rest from his or her caregiving activities.

Continuing Care A fairly new kind of LTC coverage, continuing care coverage, is designed to provide a benefit for elderly individuals who live in a continuing care retirement community. Retirement communities are geared to senior citizens' full-time needs, both medical and social, and often are sponsored by religious or nonprofit organizations. It provides independent and congregate living and personal, intermediate and skilled nursing care and attempts to create an environment that allows each resident to participate in the community's life to whatever degree desired.

Quick Quiz 20.1 True or False?

_____ 1. Long-term care insurance usually only covers the cost of care provided in a nursing home.

_____ 2. Jim has a long-term care policy that pays $80 per day. If his nursing home costs $60 per day, his policy most likely still will pay him $80 per day in benefits.

_____ 3. The daily benefit for at-home care under a long-term care policy usually is equal to one-third the nursing home benefit.

_____ 4. Jane is in a nursing home and receives 24-hour around-the-clock care. This type of care is known as skilled nursing care.

_____ 5. Medicare and Medicare supplement policies provide a significant amount of long-term care coverage.

Answers

1. *False*. Long-term care insurance provides a broad range of coverage for services rendered at home, at adult care centers or in nursing homes.

2. *True*.

3. *False*. The daily benefit for at-home care under most long-term care policies typically is equal to half the nursing home benefit.

4. *True*.

5. *False*. Medicare and Medicare supplement policies are designed to protect the elderly against the costs of medical care. However, neither program covers a significant part of the costs of long-term custodial or nursing home care.

LTC Policy Provisions and Limits

As we have stated, a number of LTC policies are on the market today, each characterized by some distinguishing feature or benefit that sets it apart from the rest. However, there are enough similarities to allow us to discuss the basic provisions of these policies and their typical limits or exclusions.

In addition, as a result of the passage of the Health Insurance Portability and Accountability Act (HIPAA) of 1996, all LTC policies now must contain certain provisions for their benefits to qualify for tax-exempt treatment. These provisions include, for example, a definition of the types of services offered by the plan and when an individual becomes eligible for benefits under the plan. Both provisions, of course, must conform to qualifying standards under HIPAA. In addition, LTC policies also must adopt certain provisions of the NAIC's long-term care insurance model regulation. (See Figure 20.2.)

LTC Services Qualified LTC services are defined as the necessary diagnostic, preventive, therapeutic, curing, treating, mitigating and rehabilitative services, and maintenance or personal care services that are required by a chronically ill individual and are provided under a plan of care set forth by a licensed health care practitioner.

Qualifying for Benefits When LTC policies first were introduced, insurers frequently required at least three days of prior hospitalization or skilled nursing home stays before the LTC policy benefits were triggered. The benefit trigger is an event or condition that must occur before policy benefits become payable. As a result of HIPAA, prior hospitalization no longer can be used as a benefit trigger; instead, the individual must be diagnosed as chronically ill.

FIGURE 20.2 NAIC Model LTC Regulations

The Health Insurance Portability and Accountability Act (HIPAA) of 1996 laid to rest concerns about how the benefits payable under a long-term care policy would be treated for tax purposes. Essentially, the question was whether such benefits were taxable. HIPAA determined that LTC policies are to be treated as other health insurance contracts—that benefits payable under LTC policies are considered reimbursement for expenses incurred for medical care—and therefore, are not taxable to the insured. However, there is an important caveat: to be treated this way, the LTC policy must be qualified. This means that the policy's provisions must conform to certain standards and guidelines as set forth by the Internal Revenue Code and HIPAA. Among the qualifying standards is the requirement to conform to the NAIC's long-term care insurance model regulations. In brief, the NAIC model addresses such things as:

- policy renewability (the policy must be guaranteed renewable)
- prohibitions on limits and exclusions
- policy replacement
- policy conversion
- prohibitions against post-claims underwriting
- the requirement to offer inflation-adjusted benefits
- proper marketing standards
- suitability and appropriateness of the recommended purchase
- a standard format for the outline of coverage

Diagnosis of chronically ill can be made on two levels: physically and (or) cognitively. The physical diagnosis of a chronically ill individual is one who has been certified as being unable to perform at least two activities of daily living. A long-term care policy must take into account at least five of these ADLs. In addition, an individual would be considered chronically ill if he or she requires substantial supervision to protect his or her health or safety owing to severe cognitive impairment and this condition was certified within the previous 12 months.

Test Topic Alert!

A benefit trigger in a long-term care policy is an event or condition that must occur before benefits become payable. An insured who is diagnosed as chronically ill triggers these benefits. Chronic illness can arise from a physical or cognitive illness or condition.

Benefit Limits

Almost all LTC policies set benefit limits, in terms of how long the benefits are paid or how much the dollar benefit will be for any one covered care service or a combination of services. Maximum dollar amounts vary considerably from policy to policy. Maximum coverage periods also vary.

In fact, with LTC policies, it is not unusual for one policy to include separate maximum coverage periods for nursing home care and home health care.

FIGURE 20.3   The Impairment Continuum—Activities of Daily Living

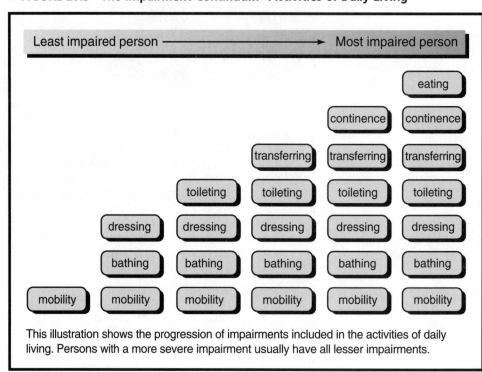

This illustration shows the progression of impairments included in the activities of daily living. Persons with a more severe impairment usually have all lesser impairments.

✓ **Take Note:** Maximum coverage periods extend anywhere from two to six years. Some policies offer unlimited lifetime coverage.

Age Limits   LTC policies typically set age limits for issue, with an average age of about 79. However, some newer policies can be sold to people up through age 89. Many policies also set a minimum purchase age, with an average of age 50.

Renewability   As a result of the 1996 Health Insurance Portability and Accountability Act, all long-term care policies sold today must be guaranteed renewable. This means the insurance company cannot cancel the policy and must renew coverage each year, as long as premiums are paid. A guaranteed renewable policy allows the insurer to raise premiums, but only for entire classes of insureds.

Probationary Periods   LTC probationary periods can range from 0 to 365 days, and many insurers give the insured the option of selecting the period that best serves his or her needs. The longer the deductible or probationary period, the lower the premium.

Specified Exclusions   Most LTC policies exclude coverage for drug and alcohol dependency, acts of war, self-inflicted injuries and nonorganic mental conditions. Organic cognitive disorders, such as Alzheimer's disease, senile dementia and Parkinson's disease, almost always are included.

Premiums   The cost for an LTC policy is based on a number of factors: the insured's age and health, the type and level of benefits provided, the inclusion or absence of a deductible or probationary period and the length of that period, and whether or not options or riders are included with the policy (such as the option to purchase additional coverage in the future or the inflation-adjustment rider, which increases the policy's coverage to match inflation levels automatically).

Taxation of LTC Benefits

As noted earlier, qualified LTC insurance contracts are treated in the same manner as accident and health insurance contracts. Consequently, amounts received under an LTC contract are excluded from income because they are considered amounts received for personal injuries and sickness. However, there is a limit on these amounts. The limit is $200 each day or $73,000 each year. (These amounts apply for 2001 and will be adjusted for inflation in later years.) In other words, benefits payable under LTC policies are not taxable at all to the extent that they cover incurred costs. If an LTC policy pays a benefit that exceeds actual costs, the excess above $200 a day (or $73,000 a year) is taxable to the insured.

Summary

Medicare supplement or Medigap policies are designed to make up for what Medicare doesn't cover and also are becoming increasingly popular. In 1990, the NAIC developed 10 Medicare standard supplement plans, ranging from the basic core policy, Plan A, to those with more comprehensive coverage.

As beneficial as Medicare and Medicare supplement insurance are to the elderly in protecting them against the costs of medical care, long-term care insurance still is needed to offer a broad range of medical and personal services to individuals who need assistance with daily activities for an extended period of time.

Key Concepts

In preparing for their licensing examination, students should be familiar with the following concepts:

Medicare supplement policies	continuing care
long-term care policies	acute illness
chronically ill	activities of daily living (ADLs)
skilled nursing care	intermediate nursing care
custodial care	home health care
adult day care	respite care

Lesson Exam Twenty

1. The core policy (Plan A) developed by the NAIC as a standard Medicare supplement policy includes all of the following EXCEPT

   A. the Medicare Part A deductible
   B. Part A coinsurance amounts
   C. the first three pints of blood each year
   D. the 20 percent Part B coinsurance amounts for Medicare-approved services

2. Which of the following is a serious condition from which a patient can fully recover with proper medical attention?

   A. Chronic illness
   B. Long-term illness
   C. Acute illness
   D. Terminal illness

3. Skilled nursing care differs from intermediate care in which of the following ways?

   A. It must be performed by skilled medical professionals, whereas intermediate care does not require medical training.
   B. It must be available 24 hours a day, while intermediate care is daily, but not 24-hour care.
   C. It typically is given in a nursing home, while intermediate care usually is given at home.
   D. It encompasses rehabilitation, while intermediate care is for meeting daily personal needs, such as bathing and dressing.

4. All of the following conditions typically are covered in a long-term care insurance policy EXCEPT

   A. Alzheimer's disease
   B. senile dementia
   C. alcohol dependency
   D. Parkinson's disease

5. Which of the following statements about long-term care policies is NOT correct?

   A. Maximum coverage periods generally extend from two to six years.
   B. Long-term care policies sold today must be guaranteed renewable.
   C. A long-term care policy with a long probationary period will have a lower premium than one with a shorter probationary period.
   D. Premiums for a long-term care policy are based solely on the insured's age, the insured's health and the type of benefits provided.

Answers & Rationale

1. **A.** Plan A covers the Medicare Part A coinsurance amounts, the first three pints of blood each year and the 20 percent Part B coinsurance amounts. It does not cover the Medicare Part A deductible.

2. **C.** An acute illness is a serious condition from which a person can fully recover with proper medical attention. In contrast, a chronic illness is one that is treatable but not curable.

3. **B.** Skilled nursing care involves continuous around-the-clock care while intermediate care is provided in nursing homes for stable medical conditions that require daily, but not 24-hour, supervision.

4. **C.** Most long-term care policies exclude coverage for drug and alcohol dependency. Organic cognitive disorders, such as Alzheimer's disease, senile dementia and Parkinson's disease, almost always are included.

5. **D.** The cost of a long-term care policy is based on a number of factors, including the insured's age and health, the type and level of benefits provided, the inclusion or absence of a deductible or probationary period and the length of that period, and whether or not riders or options are included with the policy.

21

Health Insurance Policy Provisions

INTRODUCTION

Health insurance is characterized by a number of mandatory provisions that must be included in the contract. These provisions were developed by the National Association of Insurance Commissioners (NAIC) to protect the rights of individual health insurance policyholders. In this lesson, we will review the 12 mandatory provisions and 11 optional provisions that the NAIC developed to add uniformity to health insurance contracts. This lesson also will discuss some of the more common exclusions and restrictions found in health policies as well as typical renewability provisions that allow the insurer to continue or discontinue coverage. (It might be helpful to review the sample health policy in the Appendix as you read this lesson.)

LESSON OBJECTIVES

When you complete this lesson you should be able to:

- list and describe the 12 mandatory policy provisions for individual health insurance contracts;
- list and describe the 11 option policy provisions for individual health insurance contracts;
- explain the purpose of the insuring clause, consideration clause, conversion privilege for dependents and free look provision in a health insurance contract;
- identify the typical exclusions that are not covered by health insurance policies; and
- list and describe the five types of renewability provisions found in health insurance policies.

NAIC Model Health Insurance Policy Provisions

In 1950, the National Association of Insurance Commissioners (NAIC) developed a model Uniform Individual Accident and Sickness Policy Provisions Law. Almost all states have adopted this model law or similar legislation or regulations.

The purpose of the NAIC law was to establish uniform or model terms, provisions and wording standards for inclusion in all individual health insurance contracts or all contracts that provide insurance against loss resulting from sickness or from bodily injury or death by accident or both. The result was 12 mandatory policy provisions and 11 optional policy provisions.

✓ *Take Note:* Because these provisions are to be followed in substance, insurers may employ different wording from that of the law, as long as the protection is provided and is no less favorable to the insured than the law stipulates.

Similar to a life insurance contract, a health insurance contract obligates the insurer to pay the insured (or a beneficiary) a stipulated benefit under circumstances specified in the contract. The specifics of the benefit and the requisite circumstances are set forth in the contract's provisions. Let's take a look at these provisions.

Twelve Mandatory Policy Provisions

In accordance with the NAIC model law, there are 12 mandatory provisions that must be in all health insurance contracts. These are as follows:

Entire Contract Like its counterpart in a life insurance policy, the entire contract provision in a health insurance policy protects the policyowner in two ways. First, it states that nothing outside of the contract—which includes the signed application and any attached policy riders—can be considered part of the contract; that is, nothing can be incorporated by reference. Second, it assures the policyowner that no changes will be made to the contract after it has been issued, even if the insurer makes policy changes that affect all policy sales in the future.

Time Limit on Certain Defenses Under the time limit on certain defenses provision, the policy is incontestable after it has been in force a certain period of time, usually two years. This is similar to the incontestable clause in a life insurance policy. However, unlike life policies, a fraudulent statement on a health insurance application is grounds for contest at any time, unless the policy is guaranteed renewable, in which case it cannot be contested for any reason after the contestable period expires.

Another part of this provision concerns any preexisting conditions (conditions that existed before the policy's effective date) an insured may have. Under the provision, the insurance company cannot deny a claim on the basis of a preexisting condition after expiration of the stated contestable period—unless such preexisting condition has been excluded specifically from the policy by name or description.

Grace Period   Per the grace period provision, the policyowner is given a number of days after the premium due date during which time the premium payment may be delayed without penalty and the policy continues in force.

> ✓ ***Take Note:*** Depending on the state, the minimum grace periods that may be specified typically are seven days for policies with weekly premium payments (i.e., industrial policies), 10 days for policies with premiums payable on a monthly basis and 31 days for other policies. Some states, however, require a standard grace period of 31 days, regardless of the frequency of premium payment or policy term.

Reinstatement   Under certain conditions, a policy that has lapsed may be reinstated. Reinstatement is automatic if the delinquent premium is accepted by the company or its authorized agent and the company does not require an application for reinstatement.

If a company does require such an application, it may or may not approve the application. If it takes no action on the application for 45 days, the policy is reinstated automatically. To protect the company against adverse selection, losses resulting from sickness are covered only if the sickness occurs at least 10 days after the reinstatement date.

 **Test Topic Alert!**   The probationary period may apply when a new application is required. The probationary period excludes claims arising from illness within 10 days of the policy's reinstatement. Losses arising from accidents are covered immediately.

Notice of Claim   The notice of claim provision describes the policyowner's obligation to the insurer to provide notification of loss within a reasonable period of time. Typically, this period is 20 days after the occurrence or a commencement of the loss, or as soon thereafter as is reasonably possible. If the loss involves disability income payments that are payable for two or more years, the disabled claimant must submit proof of loss every six months. Such proof may be submitted to either the company or an authorized agent of the company.

Claim Forms   It is the company's responsibility to supply a claim form to an insured within 15 days after receiving notice of claim. If it fails to do so within the time limit, the claimant may submit proof of loss in any form, explaining the occurrence, the character and the extent of the loss for which the claim is submitted.

Proof of Loss   After a loss occurs, or after the company becomes liable for periodic payments (for example, disability income benefits), the claimant has 90 days in which to submit proof of loss. The claim will not be affected in any way, however, if it is not reasonably possible for the claimant to comply with the 90-day provision.

There is a time limit for submitting proof of loss—whether or not it is reasonably possible to do so—and that is one year after the company becomes liable for the loss. The only exception to the one-year limit is if the claimant does not have the legal capacity to comply.

Test Topic Alert!   The proof of loss, or claim form, must be submitted within 90 days of the date of loss, unless it is not reasonably possible to do so.

Time of Payment of Claims   The time of payment of claims provision provides for immediate payment of the claim after the insurer receives notification and proof of loss. If the claim involves disability income payments, they must be paid at least monthly, if not at more frequent intervals specified in the policy. In some states, the time of payment of claims is 60 days; in other states, it is 30 days.

Payment of Claims   The payment of claims provision in a health insurance contract specifies how and to whom claim payments are to be made. Payments for loss of life are to be made to the designated beneficiary. If no beneficiary has been named, death proceeds are to be paid to the deceased insured's estate. Claims other than death benefits are to be paid to the insured.

 Take Note: In accordance with this required provision are two optional provisions that insurers may add. One gives the insurer the right to expedite payment of urgently needed claim funds and pay up to $1,000 in benefits to a relative or individual who is considered to be equitably entitled to payment. The other optional provision allows the insured to have medical benefits assigned—or paid directly—to the hospital or physician rendering the covered services.

Physical Exam and Autopsy   The physical exam and autopsy provision entitles a company, at its own expense, to make physical examinations of the insured at reasonable intervals during the period of a claim. In the case of death, the insurer has the right to conduct an autopsy on the body of the insured, provided it is not forbidden by state law.

Legal Actions   The insured cannot take legal action against the company in a claim dispute until after 60 days from the time the insured submits proof of loss. The same rule applies to beneficiaries. Also, if legal action is to be taken against the company, it must be done within a certain time after proof of loss is submitted (usually two or three years).

FIGURE 21.1   NAIC Uniform Health Insurance Policy Provisions

Mandatory Provisions	Optional Provisions
1. Entire Contract	1. Change of Occupation
2. Time Limit on Certain Defenses	2. Misstatement of Age
3. Grace Period	3. Other Insurance in This Insurer
4. Reinstatement	4. Insurance with Other Insurer
5. Notice of Claims	5. Insurance with Other Insurers
6. Claims Forms	6. Relation of Earnings to Insurance
7. Proof of Loss	7. Unpaid Premiums
8. Time of Payment of Claims	8. Cancellation
9. Payment of Claims	9. Conformity with State Statutes
10. Physical Exam and Autopsy	10. Illegal Occupation
11. Legal Actions	11. Intoxicants and Narcotics
12. Change of Beneficiary	

Change of Beneficiary

The insured, as policyowner, may change the beneficiary designation at any time, unless a beneficiary has been named irrevocably. So long as the insured reserves the right to change beneficiaries, he or she also may surrender or assign the policy without obtaining the consent of the beneficiary.

Eleven Optional Provisions

There are 11 optional health policy provisions, and companies may ignore them or use only those that are needed in their policy forms. The provisions pertaining to "other insurance in this insurer," "insurance with other insurers," and "relation of earnings to insurance" seldom are used. They were intended to deal with the problem of overinsurance but generally proved to be ineffective.

Change of Occupation

The change of occupation provision sets forth the changes that may be made to premium rates or benefits payable should the insured change occupations. Many insurers include this provision in their disability income policies because an individual's occupation has a direct bearing on his or her risk profile and one's risk profile has a direct bearing on premium charges. Consequently, this provision allows the insurer to reduce the maximum benefit payable under the policy if the insured switches to a more hazardous occupation or to reduce the premium rate charged if the insured changes to a less hazardous occupation.

Take Note: These benefit and premium changes take effect at the time the insured changes occupations. If a change in jobs is discovered after a disability begins, the changes are made retroactively.

Misstatement of Age

The misstatement of age provision allows the insurer to adjust the benefit payable if the age of the insured was misstated when application for the policy was made. Benefit amounts payable in such cases will be what the premiums paid would have purchased at the correct age. The older the applicant is, the higher the premium would be; therefore, if the insured was older at the time of application than is shown in the policy, benefits would be reduced accordingly. The reverse would be true if the insured were younger than listed in the application.

Other Insurance in This Insurer

The purpose of the other insurance in this insurer provision is to limit the company's risk with any individual insured. Under this provision, the total amount of coverage to be underwritten by a company for one person is restricted to a specified maximum amount, regardless of the number of policies issued. Premiums that apply to any such excess of coverage must be returned to the insured or the insured's estate.

Insurance with Other Insurer

In attempting to deal with the potential problem of overinsurance, the insurance with other insurer provision states that benefits payable for "expenses incurred" will be prorated in cases where the company accepted the risk without being notified of other existing coverage for the same risk. When premiums are paid that exceed the amount needed to cover what the company determines it will pay, the excess premiums must be refunded to the policyowner.

Insurance with Other Insurers

Similar to the above, the insurance with other insurers provision calls for the prorating of benefits that are payable on any basis other than "expenses incurred." It also provides for a return of premiums that exceed the amount needed to pay for the company's portion of prorated benefits.

Relation of Earnings to Insurance

If disability income benefits from all disability income policies for the same loss exceed the insured's monthly earnings at the time of disability (or the average monthly earnings for two years preceding disability), the relation of earnings provision states that the insurer is liable only for that proportionate amount of benefits as the insured's earnings bear to the total benefits under all such coverage.

 Take Note: Total indemnities payable to the insured may not be reduced below $200 or the sum total benefits under all applicable coverage, whichever is less. Any premiums paid for the excess coverage are refunded.

Unpaid Premiums

If there is an unpaid premium at the time a claim becomes payable, the amount of the premium is to be deducted from the sum payable to the insured or beneficiary. Or, if the premium is covered by a note when a claim is submitted, the note payment will be subtracted from the amount payable for the claim.

Cancellation   Though prohibited in a number of states, the provision for cancellation gives the company the right to cancel the policy at any time with five days' written notice to the insured. It also provides that the insured may cancel the policy anytime after the policy's original term has expired. Any unearned premium is to be refunded to the insured. If a claim is pending at the time of cancellation, the claim cannot be affected by the cancellation. (See also *Renewability Provisions*, later in this lesson.)

Conformity with State Statutes   Any policy provision that conflicts with state statutes in the state where the insured lives at the time the policy is issued automatically is amended to conform with the minimum statutory requirements.

Illegal Occupation   The illegal occupation provision specifies that the insurer is not liable for losses attributed to the insured's commission of, or being connected with, a felony or participation in any illegal occupation.

Intoxicants and Narcotics   The insurer is not liable for any loss attributed to the insured while intoxicated or under the influence of narcotics, unless such drugs were administered on the advice of a physician.

Other Health Insurance Policy Provisions

The 12 mandatory provisions and 11 optional provisions just described comprise the substantive elements of individual health insurance policies. However, a number of other very important clauses and provisions should be noted.

Insuring Clause   Generally, the insuring clause is a broad statement on the first page of the health policy, stipulating conditions under which benefits are to be paid. While these critical provisions vary considerably in health insurance contracts, they basically represent a company's promise to pay benefits for specific kinds of losses resulting from sickness or accidents. They usually specify that benefits are subject to all provisions and exclusions stated in the policy.

Consideration Clause   The consideration clause states the amount and frequency of premium payments. If the first premium has not been paid—even though the application has been completed and signed by the applicant—the necessary consideration is partially lacking.

✓ *Take Note:* As is the case with life insurance, the legal consideration for a health policy consists of the application and payment of the initial premium. A copy of the application is attached to the policy.

Frequently, the consideration clause also lists the effective date of the contract and defines the initial term of the policy. In addition, it may specify the insured's right to renew the policy.

Conversion Privilege for Dependents

A single health policy may insure one person, or more than one if the applicant is an adult family member and the others to be covered are members of his or her family. Thus, additional persons who may be insured include the husband, wife, dependent children or others dependent on the adult applicant. To be eligible, children must meet certain age requirements.

Generally, children of the insured are eligible for coverage under a family policy until they attain a specified age, usually age 19 or, if they are in school full time, age 23. Adopted children, stepchildren and foster children usually are eligible for coverage. As long as a policy is in force, coverage for a child generally continues until the child marries or reaches the limiting age. However, a number of states have enacted special laws that require insurers to retain as insureds under the parent's individual health policy any child who reaches the limiting age but is dependent on the insured and incapable of self-support because of mental or physical impairment.

Attaining a minimum age, such as 14 days, may be required for coverage. However, legislation in some states mandates that health policies insuring family members also provide coverage for newborn children from the date of birth. Typically, such legislation permits the insurer to require that notice of the child's birth be given and an application and additional premium be submitted within a specified period.

If the insurance on a covered individual is terminated because he or she no longer fits the policy definition of a family member, that person has a right to take out a conversion policy without evidence of insurability.

 For Example: Faye divorces Stanley and thus no longer can be covered under his family policy. She has a right to obtain a conversion policy. When their children reach the limiting age for children's coverage, they also will be eligible for a conversion policy.

Free Look Provision

Most states mandate that their health insurance policies contain a free look provision permitting policyowners either 10 or 20 days in which to examine their new policies at no obligation. If they decide not to keep their policies, they may return them within the prescribed time limit and receive full refunds of premiums paid.

 **Test Topic Alert!**

The state may require that policies sold to seniors have a free look period that is longer than 20 days.

Common Exclusions or Restrictions

Health insurance policies frequently cite a number of exclusions or conditions that are not covered. The common ones are injuries due to war or an act of war, self-inflicted injuries and those incurred while the insured is serving as a pilot or crew member of an aircraft.

Other exclusions are losses resulting from suicide, hernia (as an accidental injury), riots or the use of drugs or narcotics. Losses due to injuries sustained while committing a felony, or attempting to do so, also may be excluded. Foreign travel may not be excluded in every instance, but extended stays overseas or foreign residence may cause a loss of benefits.

Maternity Benefits

Maternity benefits generally are handled differently in individual health policies than in group health policies. When available for individual policies, a maternity provision may provide a fixed amount for childbirth or a benefit based upon a specified multiple of the daily hospital room benefit.

 **Test Topic Alert!**   Individual health policies often offer the maternity benefit only as an added benefit for an additional premium.

Maternity coverage in group health plans is discussed in Lesson 23.

Preexisting Conditions

As we have learned, medical expense and disability income policies usually exclude paying benefits for losses due to preexisting conditions pertaining to illness, disease or other physical impairments. For purposes of issuing individual health policies, insurers consider a preexisting condition to be one that the insured contracted (or one that was manifested) before the policy's effective date. Consequently, in the event the insured did not cite the condition on the application specifically and the insurer did not exclude the condition from coverage expressly, the preexisting condition provision would serve to exclude the condition nonetheless. However, such exclusions are subject to the "time limit on certain defenses" provision.

✓ **Take Note:** Any preexisting condition that the insured has disclosed clearly in the application usually is not excluded or, if it is, the condition is named specifically in an excluding waiver or rider.

The treatment of preexisting conditions under group health plans is a little different and is discussed in Lesson 23.

Waivers for Impairments

The majority of health policies are standard and are issued as applied for. However, a few people have an existing impairment that increases the risk and so are required to pay an extra premium. A few people are uninsurable and must be declined. Others, however, fall in between and would not be able to obtain health insurance if waivers were not in use. Waivers usually are stated in simple language. For example: "This policy does not cover or extend to any disability resulting directly or indirectly from . . ." A waiver is dated and bears the signature of an officer of the company and, in many cases, the applicant. This usually is called an impairment rider.

If the insured's condition improves, the company may be willing to remove the waiver. Meanwhile, the person at least has health protection from other hazards that he or she otherwise could not obtain.

✓ **Test Topic Alert!** The impairment rider allows for coverage despite a preexisting condition, when such coverage might not otherwise be available to the insured, or only at prohibitive cost.

🖉 **Quick Quiz 21.1**   True or False?

_____ 1. The time of payment of claims provision in a health policy provides that if a claim involves disability income payments they must be paid at least monthly.

_____ 2. If an insurer fails to take action on an application for reinstatement within 30 days, the policy will be reinstated automatically.

_____ 3. If Jane names her brother as revocable beneficiary under her health policy, she may surrender the policy at any time without first obtaining her brother's consent.

_____ 4. Adopted children, stepchildren and foster children usually are eligible for health insurance coverage under a family policy.

_____ 5. Once Jan's son Bill reaches age 19 and no longer is eligible for family health coverage, he can take out a conversion policy but first must provide evidence of insurability.

Answers

1. ***True***.

2. ***False***. *If an application is required for reinstatement and an insurer takes no action on the application for 45 days, the policy will be reinstated automatically.*

3. ***True***.

4. ***True***.

5. ***False***. *Once Bill reaches the limiting age for children's coverage under his family's health policy, he may take out a conversion policy without evidence of insurability.*

Renewability Provisions

One of the distinguishing features of health insurance policies is the provisions they contain that allow the insurer to continue or discontinue coverage. Known as renewability provisions, they vary from policy to policy. Generally, the more favorable the renewability provision is to the insured policyholder, the higher the premium.

Cancelable Policies

The renewability provision in a cancelable policy allows the insurer to cancel or terminate the policy at any time, simply by providing written notification to the insured and refunding any advance premium that has been paid. Cancelable policies also allow the insurer to increase premiums.

Optionally Renewable Policies

The renewability provision in an optionally renewable policy gives the insurer the option to terminate the policy on a date specified in the contract. Furthermore, this provision allows the insurer to increase the premium for any class of optionally renewable insureds.* Usually termination or premium increases take place on policy anniversary dates or premium due dates.

---

* A class of insureds includes all insureds of policies of a particular kind or all insureds of a specific group. For example, a class of insureds may be those of a particular age or in a specific geographic region.

Conditionally Renewable Policies

A conditionally renewable policy allows an insurer to terminate the coverage, but only in the event of one or more conditions stated in the contract. These conditions cannot apply to the insured's health; most frequently, they are related to the insured reaching a certain age or losing gainful employment. Usually, the premium for conditionally renewable policies may be increased, if such an increase applies to an entire class of policies.

Guaranteed Renewable Policies

The renewal provision in a guaranteed renewable policy specifies that the policy must be renewed, as long as premiums are paid, until the insured reaches a specified age, such as 60 or 65. Premium increases may be applied, but only for the entire class of insureds; they cannot be assessed to individual insureds.

Noncancelable Policies

A noncancelable, or noncan policy cannot be canceled nor can its premium rates be increased under any circumstances; these rates are specified in the policy. The term of most noncancelable policies is to the insured's age 65. Noncan provisions most commonly are found in disability income policies; they rarely are used in medical expense policies.

 **Test Topic Alert!**   Applicants for guaranteed renewable policies and noncancelable policies are subject to the most stringent underwriting qualifications.

Summary

To protect the rights of individual health insurance policyholders, the NAIC developed a set of 12 mandatory and 11 optional policy provisions. These provisions help assure consumers that the health policies they buy will meet at least a minimum level of standards. Other provisions, though not categorized as required or optional, are equally important. Of special note are the renewability provisions—absent from life insurance policies, but an essential feature of health policies.

Key Concepts

In preparing for their licensing examination, students should be familiar with the following concepts:

entire contract	time limit on certain defenses
grace period	reinstatement
notice of claims	claims forms
proof of loss	time of payment of claims
payment of claims	physical examination and autopsy
legal actions	change of beneficiary
change of occupation	misstatement of age
other insurance in this insurer	relation of earnings to insurance
insurance with other insurer(s)	cancellation
unpaid premiums	illegal occupation
conformity with state statutes	insuring clause
intoxicants and narcotics	conversion privilege
consideration clause	exclusions and waivers
free look	cancelable
preexisting conditions	conditionally renewable
optionally renewable	noncancelable
guaranteed renewable	

Lesson Exam Twenty-one

1. A company may change the wording of a uniform policy provision in its health insurance policies only if the

    A. company's board of directors approves the change
    B. modified provision is not less favorable to the insurer
    C. applicant directs that it be changed
    D. modified provision is not less favorable to the insured

2. Children of the insured are eligible for health insurance coverage until they attain age 19 or, if they remain in school full time, age

    A. 20
    B. 21
    C. 22
    D. 23

3. Which of the following statements about the grace period and reinstatement provisions in health insurance policies is NOT correct?

    A. Craig's health policy has a grace period of 31 days. He had a premium due June 15, while he was on vacation. He returned home July 7, mailed his premium the next day and the insurer received it July 10. His policy would have remained in force.
    B. Warren's medical expense policy was reinstated on September 30 and he became ill and entered the hospital on October 5. His hospital expense will not be paid by the insurer.
    C. Under a health policy's reinstatement terms, insured losses from accidental injuries and sickness are covered immediately after reinstatement.
    D. States may require grace periods of 7, 10 or 31 days, depending on the mode of premium payment or term of insurance; however, many states require a 31-day grace period in any case.

4. Which of the following is the usual grace period for a semiannual premium policy?

    A. 7 days
    B. 20 days
    C. 31 days
    D. 60 days

5. Diana, the beneficiary under her husband's AD&D policy, submits an accidental death claim on May 1, 2001, following his death. However, the company denies the claim on the basis that death was due to natural causes. She decides to talk to her attorney. When is the earliest she could bring legal action against the insurer?

    A. May 2, 2001
    B. June 1, 2001
    C. July 1, 2001
    D. May 1, 2002

6. All of the following are required uniform provisions in individual health insurance policies EXCEPT

   A. change of occupation
   B. grace period
   C. entire contract changes
   D. reinstatement

7. Under the misstatement of age provision in a health insurance policy, what can a company do if it discovers that an insured gave a wrong age at the time of application?

   A. Cancel the policy
   B. Increase the premium
   C. Adjust the benefits
   D. Assess a penalty

8. The conformity with state statutes provision in a health insurance policy stipulates that any policy provision that conflicts with the statutes of the state where the insured resides is

   A. to be submitted to the insurance commissioner for approval
   B. cause for the insured's policy to be voided
   C. automatically amended to conform to the minimum requirements of the state's statutes
   D. to be rewritten if the policy is returned to the company

9. Which section of a health insurance policy specifies the conditions, times and circumstances under which the insured is NOT covered by the policy?

   A. Coinsurance provision
   B. Coverages
   C. Insuring clause
   D. Exclusions

10. Which kind of health insurance policy assures renewability up to a specific age of the insured, although the company reserves the right to change the premium rate on a class basis?

    A. Noncancelable
    B. Guaranteed renewable
    C. Optionally renewable
    D. Cancelable

11. According to the notice of claims provision in a health insurance policy, a claimant normally must notify the insurance company of loss within how many days after the loss occurs?

    A. 10
    B. 20
    C. 40
    D. 60

12. Which of the following types of health insurance policies prevents the company from changing the premium rate or modifying the coverage in any way?

    A. Optionally renewable
    B. Noncancelable
    C. Guaranteed renewable
    D. Cancelable

13. After an insurer receives a notice of claim, it must supply a claim form to the insured within how many days?

    A. 10
    B. 15
    C. 20
    D. 30

14. A cancellation provision gives an insurer the right to cancel a policy at any time after giving how many days' notice to the insured?

   A. 5
   B. 10
   C. 15
   D. 30

15. Which of the following statements about the insuring clause in a health insurance policy is NOT correct?

   A. It is found on the first page of a health policy.
   B. It represents an insurer's promise to pay benefits.
   C. It specifies that benefits will be subject to the exclusions stated in the policy.
   D. It is one of the 11 NAIC optional provisions.

Answers & Rationale

1. **D.** An insurer need not use the exact wording contained in the 12 mandatory provisions. Instead, it may use different wording as long as the same protection is provided and is no less favorable to the insured than the law stipulates.

2. **D.** Generally, an insured's children are eligible for health insurance coverage under a family policy until they attain a certain age, usually age 19 or, if they are in school full time, age 23.

3. **C.** A policy that has lapsed may be reinstated. However, to protect the insurer against adverse selection, losses resulting from sickness are covered only if the sickness occurs at least 10 days after the reinstatement date.

4. **C.** A semiannual premium policy usually has a 31-day grace period in which the policyowner can pay the premium due. For policies with weekly premium payments, the grace period is seven days, and policies with monthly premiums have 10-day grace periods.

5. **C.** Diana cannot take legal action against the insurer until after 60 days from the date she submitted an accidental death claim. She submitted a claim on May 1 and will have to wait 60 days until July 1 to bring a legal action against the insurer.

6. **A.** The grace period, entire contract changes and reinstatement provisions are mandatory uniform provisions. The change of occupation provision sets forth the changes that may be made to premium rates or benefits payable if the insured changes occupations. This provision is optional.

7. **C.** The misstatement of age provision allows the insurer to adjust the benefit payable if the insured's age was misstated when the policy application was made. The benefit amounts payable in such cases will be what the premiums paid would have purchased at the correct age.

8. **C.** Any policy provision that conflicts with the statutes of the state where the insured resides will be amended automatically to conform with the minimum statutory requirements.

9. **D.** The exclusions section of a health insurance policy specifies the conditions, times and circumstances under which the insured is not covered by the policy. Common exclusions include injuries due to war and self-inflicted injuries.

10. **B.** In a guaranteed renewable policy, the renewal provision states that the policy must be renewed, as long as premiums are paid, until the insured reaches a specified age, such as 60 or 65. Premiums may be increased, but only for the entire class of insureds.

11. **B.** A policyowner typically must notify the insurer within 20 days after a loss has occurred.

12. **B.** A noncancelable policy prevents the insurance company from canceling or modifying the coverage or changing the premium rate.

13. **B.** After an insurer receives a notice of claim, it must supply a claim form to the insured within 15 days. If it fails to do so, the claimant may submit proof of loss in any form, explaining the occurrence, character and extent of the loss for which the claim is submitted.

14. **A.** A cancellation provision gives an insurer the right to cancel a policy at any time by giving five days' written notice to the insured. It also allows the insured to cancel the policy any time after the policy's original term has expired.

15. **D.** The insuring clause in a health insurance policy is not one of the 11 optional provisions developed by the NAIC. It is a broad statement found on a policy's first page that stipulates the conditions under which benefits are to be paid. It also usually specifies that benefits are subject to all provisions and exclusions stated in the policy.

22

Health Insurance Underwriting and Premiums

INTRODUCTION

Health insurers often are faced with balancing two conflicting demands: charging adequate premiums to cover the increasingly high cost of health insurance claims while keeping rates as low as possible in response to consumer sentiment and competition within the industry. Health insurers have done this by tightening their underwriting requirements, becoming more selective in the risks they will accept and controlling claims through innovative measures. In this lesson, we will examine how the underwriting process works in the health insurance arena, including the factors that influence the premiums charged. We also will take a look at the important topic of health insurance taxation, that is, how premiums and benefits are taxed under individual and group policies as well as the rules that apply to self-employed individuals. Finally, we will review some of the methods that managed care uses to contain rising health care costs.

LESSON OBJECTIVES

When you complete this lesson you should be able to:

- explain how a person's lifestyle, occupation and physical condition affect the underwriting of a health insurance policy;
- list and describe the four risk categories in which health insurance applicants may be classified;
- explain how morbidity, interest and expenses affect health insurance premiums and identify the other factors influencing premium rates;
- explain the tax treatment of health insurance premiums and benefits; and
- list and describe the common techniques that managed care organizations use to contain health care costs.

Risk Factors in Health Insurance

While most of the underwriting factors that apply to life insurance also apply to health insurance, they take on greater significance in the context of health risks. With life insurance, there is only one death claim per insured. But with health insurance, multiple claims per insured is the rule rather than the exception. Thus, the classification of health insurance risks is critically important. Data accumulated over the years by insurance companies in underwriting health insurance serves as the primary basis for classifying risks.

Classifying risks for health insurance is more complex than simply deciding whether a risk is acceptable or not acceptable. The degree of risk is highly important when considering the probable future health of an individual applicant and the amount of premium to be charged. So home office underwriters are charged with the responsibility of scrutinizing health insurance applications with special care.

Many factors are reviewed in underwriting health insurance policies. Three of the most important factors are *physical condition, moral hazards* and *occupation*.

Physical Condition

An applicant's present physical condition is of primary importance when evaluating health risks. The underwriter must know whether the individual has been treated for any chronic conditions, and any physical impairments of the applicant are checked out carefully. Hernias or ulcers, for example, may require surgical correction or treatment in the future and, thereby, represent an additional risk. Persons with an unusual body build, including obesity or extreme height, also represent higher risks to the insurer.

Moral Hazards

The habits or lifestyles of applicants also can flash warning signals that there may be additional risk for the insurer. Personalities and attitudes may draw attention in the underwriting process. Excessive drinking and the use of drugs represent serious moral hazards. Applicants who are seen as accident-prone or potential malingerers (feigning a continuing disability in order to collect benefits) likewise might be heavy risks, particularly those applying for disability income insurance. Other signals of high moral hazard can be a poor credit rating or dishonest business practices.

Occupation

A third significant factor involved with health insurance risks is the applicant's occupation. This is because occupation has a direct bearing on both the probability of disability and the average severity of disability.

Experience shows that disability benefit costs for insurers can vary considerably from occupation to occupation. Little physical risk is associated with professional persons, office managers or office workers, but occupations involving heavy machinery, strong chemicals or high electrical voltage, for example, represent a high degree of risk for the insurer.

Jobs requiring manual labor also can influence the length of recuperation periods for disabled workers and how soon they can return to work. Further, the sporadic nature of employment in certain occupations can have a bearing on claim costs because the number and size of such claims tend to rise when insureds are unemployed.

Some occupations involve irregular hours, uncertain earnings and, in some cases, not even a definite place of business—all of which contribute to higher risks for insurers. Examples are entertainers and authors, who generally do not have regular business hours. In addition, disability benefit costs to insurers also can be influenced by the social and economic character of persons in some occupational classifications.

✓ **Take Note:** For underwriting purposes, many insurers divide occupations into five classes: AAA, AA, A, B and C. The five classes range from the top classification (AAA), which includes professional and office workers, to more hazardous occupations in the lower (B and C) classes. Persons in a few occupations, such as steeplejacks, airplane test pilots or stunt flyers, usually are uninsurable.

The applicant's occupation and the renewability factor of a policy also are connected from an underwriting standpoint. According to the change of occupation provision, if the insured changes to a less hazardous job, the insurer will return any excess unearned premium; however, if the change is to a more hazardous occupation, the benefits are reduced proportionately and the premium remains the same. The change of occupation clause generally is not included in guaranteed renewable policies, especially long-term disability income policies. Noncancelable policies are sold only to individuals in the higher occupational classes in which change of occupation seldom is a factor. Limited and industrial health policies usually are available at standard rates for all occupations, except those excluded by specific policy provisions.

Other Risk Factors

Additional health insurance risk factors include the applicant's age, sex, medical and family history and avocations.

- *Age.* Generally, the older the applicant, the higher the risk he or she represents. Most individual health insurance policies limit the coverage to a specified age such as 60 or 65 (although some lifetime coverages are available).
- *Sex.* An applicant's sex also is an underwriting consideration. Men show a lower rate of disability than women, except at the upper ages.
- *History.* An applicant's medical history may point to the possibility of a recurrence of a certain health condition. Likewise, an applicant's family history may reflect a tendency he or she has toward certain medical conditions or health impairments.
- *Avocations.* Certain hobbies an applicant may have—such as skydiving or mountain climbing—may increase his or her risk to the insurer. An applicant's avocations are evaluated carefully.

Insurable Interest

Finally, when evaluating health insurance risks, the underwriter must determine whether an insurable interest exists between the applicant and the individual to be insured. In health insurance, an insurable interest exists if the applicant is in a position to suffer a loss should the insured incur medical expenses or be unable to work due to a disability. As with life insurance, insurable interest is a prerequisite for issuing a health insurance policy.

Classification of Applicants

Once an underwriter has reviewed the various risk factors associated with an individual applicant and has measured them against the company's underwriting standards, there are four ways to classify the applicant and his or her request for health coverage: as a *standard risk,* a *preferred risk*, an *uninsurable risk* or a *substandard risk.*

Standard risk applicants usually are issued a policy at standard terms and rates. Preferred risks generally receive lower rates than standard risks, reflecting the fact that people in this class have a better-than-standard risk profile. Uninsurable applicants usually are rejected and denied coverage. Substandard risk applicants—those who pose a higher-than-average risk for one or more reasons—are treated differently. Substandard applicants may represent a very low risk on moral and occupational considerations and still pose a high risk because of their physical condition. Other substandard applicants may be in top physical condition, but work at a hazardous occupation. Besides outright rejection, three techniques commonly are used by insurers in issuing health insurance policies to substandard risks:

- attaching an exclusion (or impairment) rider or waiver to a policy;
- charging an extra premium; or
- limiting the type of policy.

Exclusion or impairment riders rule out coverage for losses resulting from chronic conditions or physical impairments. With the questionable risks excluded, policies then are issued at standard rates. When some occupational hazard exists, applicants may be charged an extra premium to compensate for the additional risk. The same may be true when applicants are over-weight or show signs of high blood pressure, etc. Extra premiums may be charged for only a few years or on a permanent basis.

When applicants represent a substandard risk, the type of policy requested may be modified in some manner. For example, a policy may exclude all sickness or a specific kind of sickness, but cover all losses from accidental injuries. In other cases, a policy may provide protection for a lower amount than requested or provide a shorter benefit period. Or a provision may be inserted calling for a longer waiting period than indicated in the application.

✓ **Take Note:** Only a small percentage of applicants are classified as substandard risks. And, with years of experience to guide them, insurers today reject a smaller percentage of applicants for health insurance than in the past.

Health Insurance Premium Factors

Rate making is more complex for health insurance policies than for life insurance, primarily because it involves more than one type of benefit. The average frequency of covered health insurance losses further complicates premium computations. There are a number of variables—primary and secondary—all insurers take into account when determining the premium rate for a particular health insurance product.

Primary Premium Factors

At the base level, three primary factors affect health insurance premiums: *morbidity, interest* and *expenses*. Note how closely these correspond to basic life insurance premium factors, except that morbidity is substituted for mortality.

Morbidity   Whereas mortality rates show the average number of persons within a larger group of people who can be expected to die within a given year at a given age, morbidity rates indicate the average number at various ages who can be expected to become disabled each year due to accident or sickness. Morbidity statistics also reveal the average duration of disability, so insurers can approximate not only how many in a large group will become disabled, but how long the disabilities can be expected to last.

Morbidity statistics, which are available to companies offering health insurance, have been collected over many years and reflect the disabilities of hundreds of thousands of people. They are compiled into morbidity tables.

Test Topic Alert!   Morbidity statistics serve the same purpose for health insurance that mortality statistics do for life insurance.

Interest   Just as with life insurance, interest is a major element in establishing health insurance premiums. A large portion of every premium received is invested to earn interest. The interest earnings reduce the premium amount that otherwise would be required from policyowners.

Expenses   Every business has expenses that must be paid, and the insurance business is no different. Each health insurance policy an insurer issues must carry its proportionate share of the costs for employees' salaries, agents' commissions, utilities, rent or mortgage payments, maintenance costs, supplies and other administrative expenses.

Secondary Premium Factors

In addition to these three primary factors, the actual rate assigned to a specific health policy by the underwriter depends on several other factors, including the benefits provided under the policy, past claims experience, the age and sex of the insured and the insured's occupation and hobbies.

Benefits   A health insurance policy may offer a specific type of benefit or a variety of benefits. For example, a hospital expense-only policy offers benefits to cover just hospitalization expenses while a comprehensive major medical policy covers a much broader range of medical expenses. The number and kinds of benefits provided by a policy affect the premium rate.

Another aspect is that, while two policies may provide identical types of benefits, the amount of protection or benefits in one policy may be higher than in another. So, the greater the benefits, the higher the premium, or, to state it another way, the greater the risk to the company, the higher the premium.

Claims Experience   Before realistic premium rates can be established for health insurance, the insurer must know what can be expected as to the dollar amount of the future claims. The most practical way to estimate the cost of future claims is to rely on claims tables based on past claims experience. For instance, experience tables have been constructed for hospital expenses based on the amounts paid out in the past for the same types of expenses. Such tables, along with an added factor to account for rising hospital costs, enable companies to estimate the average amounts of future hospital expenses. Similarly, experience tables have been developed for surgical benefits, covering various kinds of surgery based on past experience. The same procedure is followed to estimate average claims expected in the future for other medical expenses. Such tables must be adjusted periodically, of course, to reflect more recent experience.

Age and Sex of the Insured

As discussed earlier, experience has shown that health insurance claims costs tend to increase as the age of the insured increases. For any given coverage, the older the insured, the higher the applicable premium rate.

Also, disabilities among women under age 55, on the average, have a greater frequency and longer duration than among men, so female premium rates for certain coverages are higher than the premium rates for males. At the older ages, however, that generally is not true.

Occupation and Hobbies

Because some types of work are more hazardous than others, the premium rates for a person's health insurance policy may be affected by his or her occupation. If an insured's occupation indicates a higher than normal risk to the company, the policy may carry an extra premium charge. (Insurers establish their own occupational classifications, which represent another element in the premium structure.) The same holds true for any dangerous hobbies in which the insured may participate.

✓ **For Example:** Jim is a certified scuba diver and dives almost every weekend, and his best friend Tom golfs in his free time. All other things being equal, an insurance company may sell health insurance policies to both men, but probably will add a surcharge to Jim's premiums because of his high-risk hobby.

Tax Treatment of Health Insurance Premiums and Benefits

The tax treatment of health insurance premiums and benefits depends, to a large degree, on the type of insurance in question.

Taxation of Disability Income Insurance

Premiums paid for personal disability income insurance are not deductible by the individual insured, but the disability benefits are tax free to the recipient.

When a group disability income insurance plan is paid for entirely by the employer and benefits are paid directly to individual employees who qualify, the premiums are deductible by the employer. The benefits, in turn, are taxable to the recipient. On the other hand, if an employee contributes to any portion of the premium, his or her benefit will be received tax free in proportion to the premium contributed.

✔ **For Example:** An employee pays 40 percent of the premium and the employer pays 60 percent. Forty percent of the benefit is tax free to the employee and 60 percent is taxable.

Also in 2001, a self-employed individual may deduct 60 percent of amounts paid for health insurance covering the individual, spouse and dependents.* The deduction cannot exceed self-employment net earnings and is not available where the individual or spouse is eligible to participate on a subsidized basis in an employer-sponsored health plan.

Persons under age 65 who are retired on permanent and total disability may be eligible for a tax credit on their disability income. The credit is equal to 15 percent of an initial base amount ($5,000 if married with one spouse eligible or unmarried), less:

- amounts received under pensions, annuities or Social Security disability benefits; and
- one-half the excess of the individual's adjusted gross income over specified amounts (for example, $10,000 if married and filing a joint return or $7,500 if single).

 **Test Topic Alert!**

Premiums paid for personal disability income insurance are not deductible by the insured, but the disability benefits are received tax free. Employers who pay the premium for a group disability income insurance plan can deduct the premium payments, but employees are taxed on the benefits. If employees pay part of the premium, they receive benefits tax free in proportion to the amount of the premium they pay.

---

*When this deduction first was introduced, it included an expiration date, after which the deduction would not be allowed. This expiration date consistently has been extended through various pieces of legislation, the latest being the Revenue Reconciliation Act of 1993.

Taxation of Medical Expense Insurance

Incurred medical expenses that are reimbursed by insurance may not be deducted from an individual's federal income tax. Furthermore, incurred medical expenses that are not reimbursed by insurance may only be deducted to the extent they exceed 7.5 percent of the insured's adjusted gross income. For example, an individual who has an adjusted gross income of $35,000 would be able to deduct only the amount of unreimbursed medical expenses over $2,625.

For purposes of figuring any deductible medical expenses, prescription drugs, insulin, hospital expenses, physician and surgeon fees, nursing care, dental care, rehabilitative treatments and medical insurance premiums (including long-term care insurance premiums, within limits) all can be considered.

Benefits received by an insured under a medical expense policy are not included in his or her gross income, because they are paid to offset losses he or she incurred. However, medical expense insurance benefits must be included in gross income to the extent that reimbursement is received for medical expenses deducted in a prior year.

For self-employed individuals and their families, the rules are slightly different. Amounts paid for medical care (including insurance premiums) are deductible, within limits. The deductible percentage of health insurance expenses is as follows:

Beginning Tax Year	Deduction
2000–2001	60%
2002	70%
2003 and after	100%

 Quick Quiz 22.1 1. Jim is self-employed. In 2001, what percentage of his medical care expenses can he deduct?

    A. 40
    B. 60
    C. 70
    D. 80

2. Insurers commonly will use all of the following techniques when issuing health insurance policies to substandard risks EXCEPT

   A. attaching an impairment rider to a policy
   B. charging an extra premium
   C. limiting the type of policy
   D. requiring additional collateral to pay for extraordinary claims

3. Which of the following statements about the taxation of medical expense insurance is CORRECT?

   A. An individual may not take an income tax deduction for medical expenses that are reimbursed by insurance.
   B. An individual cannot take an income tax deduction for the cost of prescription drugs, dental care and rehabilitative treatments.
   C. Reimbursed medical expenses may be deducted only if they exceed 7.5 percent of an insured's adjusted gross income.
   D. Benefits that an insured receives under a medical expense policy must be included in gross income.

4. Which of the following statements about health insurance premiums is NOT correct?

   A. The older the insured, the higher the premium rate.
   B. A person's hobbies may affect his or her health insurance premium rates.
   C. The age and sex of the insured are considered primary factors that affect health insurance premium rates.
   D. Women under age 55 will pay a higher premium for disability income insurance than men of the same age, all other things being equal.

Answers

1. **B**. *In 2001, Jim can deduct 60 percent of his medical expense costs. This percentage will increase to 70 percent in 2002 and will reach 100 percent thereafter.*

2. **D**. *When issuing health insurance policies to substandard risks, insurers commonly will attach an impairment rider to the policy, charge an extra premium or limit the type of policy benefits. They will not require the applicant to pay additional collateral to pay for extraordinary claims.*

3. **A**. *An individual may not take an income tax deduction for medical expenses that are reimbursed by insurance. Only unreimbursed expenses, to the extent they exceed 7.5 percent of a person's adjusted gross income, may be deducted.*

4. **C**. *The age and sex of the insured are considered secondary rather than primary factors that affect health insurance premium rates. The three primary factors are morbidity, interest and expenses.*

Managed Care

With the support and involvement of government, business and the insurance industry, managed care has become the key strategy for containing rising health care costs that were threatening the country's competitive position in global markets. The success of this strategy was revealed in a recent survey conducted by benefit consultants Foster Higgins. The survey found that managed care costs grew at a consistently slower pace than traditional indemnity costs. Indemnity plan costs for active and retired employees of private- and public-sector employers with 10 or more employees rose a cumulative 29 percent from 1993 through 1996, while for the same period the costs of preferred provider organizations (PPO) rose 8 percent and the costs of health maintenance organizations (HMO) rose only 3 percent. PPOs and HMOs exemplify methods or systems of managed care; indemnity plans do not.

Managed care organizations (MCOs) achieve these results because they integrate the financing and delivery of health care services to contain and control costs and to provide health care and services as efficiently as possible.

✓ **Take Note:** Common techniques MCOs use to achieve their objectives include selectively contracting with efficient and effective health care professionals and organizations; establishing financial incentives for members to use providers and procedures sanctioned by the plan; controlling expensive hospital admissions and lengths of stay; using utilization management tools such as utilization review, standardized medical practices guidelines and clinical pathways to achieve better outcomes and case management; and emphasizing disease prevention and health promotion programs.

These characteristics are typical of HMOs, PPOs and exclusive provider organizations (EPOs), which were discussed in Lesson 15.

Other important and related actions insurers are taking to contain health care costs address policy design and medical cost management techniques. The medical cost management techniques discussed below are common practices in managed care organizations.

Policy Design

The design or structure of a policy and its provisions will greatly affect an insurer's cost containment efforts. A higher deductible will help limit claims, for instance, and in fact the average deductible has increased in recent years. Whereas the typical deductible was $100 for an individual and $300 for a family just a few years ago, it is more common now to find deductibles in the $300 to $500 range for an individual and $900 or higher for a family.

Coinsurance is another important means of sharing the cost of medical care between the insured and the insurer. Shortened benefit periods also can prove beneficial from a cost containment standpoint in that they can reduce the tendency some people have to seek medical attention for a condition that has long since been resolved.

Medical Cost Management

Medical cost management is being recognized widely and applauded as the most promising means of controlling claims expenses. Basically, it is the process of controlling how policyowners utilize their policies. Insurers use four general approaches for cost management: *mandatory second opinions, precertification review, ambulatory surgery* and *case management*.

Mandatory Second Opinions

In an effort to reduce unnecessary surgical operations, many health policies today contain a provision requiring the insured to obtain a second opinion before receiving non-life-threatening surgery. Benefits often are reduced if a second opinion is not obtained.

Precertification Review

To control hospital claims, many policies today require policyowners to obtain approval from the insurer before entering a hospital on a nonemergency basis. Even if the admission was on an emergency basis, most policies with this type of provision require the insured to notify the insurer within a short period of time (usually 24 hours) after being admitted. The insurer then will determine how much of the hospital stay it will cover, depending on the reason for the admission. If the insured wants to stay longer, the additional expense will be the responsibility of the insured, not the insurer.

Ambulatory Surgery

The advances in medicine now permit many surgical procedures to be performed on an outpatient basis where once an overnight hospital stay was required. To encourage insureds to utilize less expensive outpatient care, many policies offer some sort of inducement. For instance, a policy may waive the deductible or coinsurance if the policyowner elects to be treated on an outpatient basis rather than as an admitted patient.

Case Management

Case management, as referred to here, involves a specialist within the insurance company, such as a registered nurse, who reviews a potentially large claim as it develops to discuss treatment alternatives with the insured.

 For Example: The insured's policy might state that treatment for a kidney ailment can only be performed in a hospital or registered hemodialysis center. However, if it makes economic sense to the insurer—and practical sense to the insured—to have treatments conducted at the insured's home, the case manager might negotiate with the insured to allow treatment to be performed at home as long as certain conditions are met.

The purpose of case management is to let the insurer take an active role in the management of what potentially could become a very expensive claim.

Summary

The escalating cost of medical care makes it imperative that insurers exercise precaution in their underwriting. A number of important factors come together during the health underwriting process. Preexisting medical conditions as well as circumstances that may affect future medical losses are reviewed carefully by health underwriters. Health insurance premium rates are affected not only by the three primary factors of morbidity, interest and expenses, but also by secondary factors, including the particular benefits provided by the policy and characteristics of the insured. As is true with all aspects of life and health insurance, the tax treatment of health insurance premiums and benefits is an important consideration from a personal financial standpoint. Typically, premiums paid for personal health insurance are not deductible and benefits received are not taxable. The exception is self-employed individuals, whose insurance is regarded partly as employer-sponsored. These individuals may deduct the cost of medical care up to certain limits.

In an effort to control health claims expenses, many insurers exercise some form of cost management, from requiring second surgical opinions to instituting full case management.

Key Concepts

In preparing for their licensing examination, students should be familiar with the following concepts:

health insurance risk factors	substandard risks
health insurance premium factors	tax treatment of premiums and
cost containment measures	benefits

Lesson Exam Twenty-two

1. Susan is covered under her employer-sponsored disability group plan. The premium is $50 a month: Susan pays $10 and the employer pays $40. Assuming Susan were to become disabled and receive monthly disability benefits of $700 from the plan, how much, if any, of the monthly benefit would be taxable income?

   A. $0
   B. $70
   C. $140
   D. $560

2. Assume the following individuals are issued health insurance policies with varying renewability provisions. All other factors being equal, who would pay the highest premium?

   A. Dan—cancelable
   B. Jim—optionally renewable
   C. Henry—conditionally renewable
   D. Jack—noncancelable

3. Which of the following is the purpose of medical cost management?

   A. To influence hospital charges and doctors' fees.
   B. To discourage individuals from utilizing health care services.
   C. To control health claims expenses.
   D. To encourage individuals to seek medical help only as a last resort.

4. All of the following are primary risk factors in underwriting individual health insurance policies EXCEPT

   A. geographical location
   B. moral hazard
   C. occupation
   D. physical condition

5. Which of the following statements most aptly describes health insurance benefits?

   A. Each policy offers a single type of benefit.
   B. Claims, not benefits, affect premium rates.
   C. Policyowners who have policies with identical benefits pay the same premiums.
   D. The greater the benefits, the higher the premium.

6. Which of the following probably would NOT be considered in underwriting a health insurance risk?

   A. Personal habits
   B. Credit rating
   C. Medical history
   D. Marital status

7. All of the following factors would affect a health policy's premium rate EXCEPT

   A. age of the insured
   B. occupation of the insured
   C. type of benefit provided
   D. location of the insured's residence

8. Rick, who has no health insurance, experienced $3,000 in medical expenses this year. Assuming his adjusted gross income was $29,000, how much of those medical expenses can he deduct from his income taxes, if any?

   A. $0
   B. $825
   C. $2,175
   D. $3,000

9. What kind of table reflects the average number of disabilities due to sickness or accidents at various ages?

    A. Mortality
    B. Morbidity
    C. Claims underwriting
    D. Underwriting

10. What is the effect of an impairment rider attached to a health insurance policy?

    A. To increase the premium rate charged
    B. To decrease the amount of benefits provided
    C. To exclude from coverage losses resulting from specified conditions
    D. To increase the policy's waiting period

Answers & Rationale

1. **D.** Susan will receive part of her disability benefit tax free in proportion to the premium she contributed. Because Susan contributed 20 percent of the total premium ($10 of $50), she will receive 20 percent of the benefit tax free (20 percent of $700 = $140). The remaining amount ($560) will constitute taxable income.

2. **D.** In general, the more favorable the renewability provision is to the insured policyholder, the higher the premium. Dan's cancelable policy, therefore, will have the lowest premium while Jack's noncancelable policy will have the highest premium.

3. **C.** The purpose of medical cost management is to control health claims expenses. Four approaches are used: mandatory second opinions, precertification review, ambulatory surgery and case management.

4. **A.** The three primary risk factors affecting individual health insurance underwriting are moral hazards, occupation and physical condition.

5. **D.** The more benefits that a health insurance policy offers, the higher the premiums. Because the insurer is taking on more risk, it will charge a higher premium.

6. **D.** When underwriting a health insurance policy, an insurer will consider a person's personal habits or lifestyle, his or her credit rating and medical history. However, a person's marital status probably will not be considered.

7. **D.** The insured's age and sex will affect the premium rate, as will the amount of protection provided under the policy. For example, the older the insured, the higher the premium. Similarly, premiums will increase as more benefits are provided. Also, premiums will be higher if a person is employed in a hazardous occupation. Where a person lives will not affect the premium he or she is charged.

8. **B.** Rick can take a deduction for medical expenses that exceed 7.5 percent of his adjusted gross income. Because he earned $29,000 this year, he could take a deduction for any expenses exceeding $2,175 (7.5 percent of $29,000). Therefore, he could therefore deduct $825.

9. **B.** Morbidity tables show the average number of disabilities due to sickness or accidents at various ages. Mortality tables, on the other hand, show the average number of persons within a larger group of people who can be expected to die within a given year at a given age.

10. **C.** If an impairment rider is attached to a health insurance policy, coverage will not be provided for losses resulting from chronic conditions or physical impairments. With the questionable risks excluded, policies then can be issued at standard rates.

23

Group Health Insurance

INTRODUCTION

Most of our discussion of health and accident insurance so far has focused on individual coverage. However, because of the high cost of purchasing insurance, many people are unable to purchase individual coverage. As a result, most Americans rely on employer-sponsored plans as their sole source of health insurance.

Group health insurance, like individual health insurance coverage, can be tailored to meet the employer's needs. By its very nature, however, group insurance has several features that set it apart from individual plans, including the nature of the contract, the cost of the plan, the form of premium payments and eligibility requirements. In this lesson, we will examine the characteristics of this type of insurance protection and review the favorable tax treatment given to group plans.

LESSON OBJECTIVES

When you complete this lesson you should be able to:

- list and describe the principal characteristics of group health insurance;
- explain the general underwriting factors that are considered when issuing a group health insurance policy;
- compare and contrast group and individual medical expense, disability income and AD&D insurance;
- explain the rights given to terminated employees under COBRA; and
- explain the tax treatment of group health premiums and benefits.

Nature of Group Health Insurance

In Lesson 9, we introduced the subject of group life insurance and discussed its basic principles. Like group life, group health is a plan of insurance that an employer (or other eligible group sponsor) provides for its employees. The contract for coverage is between the insurance company and the employer, and a *master policy* is issued to the employer. The individual insureds covered by the policy are not given separate policies; instead, they receive *certificates of insurance* and an outline or booklet that describes their benefits. Generally, the benefits provided under a group health plan are more extensive than those provided under an individual health plan. Group health plans typically have higher benefit maximums and lower deductibles.

Characteristics of Group Health Insurance

The characteristics of group health insurance are similar to those of group life. These include eligibility standards for groups and for individuals within the groups, method of premium payments (contributory vs. noncontributory), lower cost, predetermined benefits, underwriting practices, conversion privileges and preexisting conditions provisions. Let's briefly review each.

Eligible Groups   To qualify for group health coverage, the group must be a *natural group.* This means that it must have been formed for some reason other than to obtain insurance. Qualifying groups include employers, labor unions, trade associations, creditor-debtor groups, multiple employer trusts, lodges and the like.

State laws specify the minimum number of persons to be covered under a group policy. One state may stipulate 15 persons as a minimum number, while another state may require a minimum of 10.

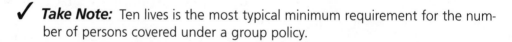 **✓ Take Note:** Ten lives is the most typical minimum requirement for the number of persons covered under a group policy.

Individual Eligibility   Like group life, group health plans commonly impose a set of eligibility requirements that must be met before an individual member is eligible to participate in the group plan. It is common to find the following requirements:

- minimum of one to three months employment service; and
- full-time employment status

Contributory vs. Noncontributory   Group health plans may be contributory or noncontributory. If the employer pays the entire premium, the plan is noncontributory; if the employees share a portion of the premium, it is contributory. Almost universally, noncontributory group health plans require 100 percent participation by eligible members, whereas contributory group health plans require participation by 75 percent of eligible members. The reason for these minimum participation requirements is to protect the insurer against adverse selection and to keep administrative expenses in line with coverage units.

Lower Cost   Benefit for benefit, the cost of insuring an individual under a group health plan is less than the cost of insurance under an individual plan. This is because the administrative and selling expenses involved with group plans are far less.

Predetermined Benefits   Another characteristic of group health plans is that the benefits provided to individual insureds are predetermined by the employer in conjunction with the insurer's benefit schedules and coverage limits. For example, group disability benefits are tied to a position or earnings schedule, as are accidental death and dismemberment benefits.

Underwriting Practices   Generally, the approach in underwriting group health plans is the same as underwriting group life plans: the insurer evaluates the group as a whole, rather than individuals within the group. Based on the group's risk profile, which is measured against the insurer's selection standards, the group is either accepted or rejected.

However, there are some changes taking place with regard to underwriting group medical expenses plans, especially for small groups. Whereas for large group medical plans it is common to accept all currently eligible members and new members coming into the group, this is not necessarily true for smaller groups. In smaller groups the presence of even one bad risk can have a significant impact on the claims experience of the group. Consequently, most insurers today reserve the right to engage in individual underwriting to some degree with groups they insure.

As the term implies, individual underwriting is the process of reviewing a group member's individual risk profile. This is done most commonly on two occasions: when a group first is taken on by an insurer and when a group member (for example, an employee) tries to enter the plan after initially electing not to participate. In the latter case, the underwriter's objective is to reduce the risk of adverse selection. In the former case, individual underwriting is done only on members for whom the initial application indicates a potential risk problem (such as a preexisting condition). If the member is found to represent too great a risk, the insurer often retains the right to reject the member from participating in the plan, or at least charge an increased premium (or exclude coverage for the specified condition). It is important to note that if an insurer does reserve this right of individual underwriting, most states require the insurer to explain, in the policy, how it will exercise this right.

FIGURE 23.1   General Group Underwriting Considerations

In spite of the many differences between types of groups, certain general underwriting considerations apply to all or most types of groups:

• the reason for the group's existence (purchasing group insurance must be incidental to the group's formation, not the reason for it)

• the stability of the group (underwriters want to see a group of stable workers without an excessive amount of turnover)

• the persistency of the group (groups that change insurers every year do not represent a good risk)

• the method of determining benefits (it must be by a schedule or method that prevents individual selection of benefits)

• how eligibility is determined (insurers want to see a sickness-related probationary period, for example, to reduce adverse selection)

• the source of premium payments, whether contributory or noncontributory (noncontributory plans are preferred because they require 100 percent participation, which helps spread the risk and reduces adverse selection)

• the prior claims experience of the group

• the size and composition of the group

• the industry or business with which the group is associated (hazardous industries are typified by higher-than-standard mortality and morbidity rates)

✓ **Take Note:** An entire group rarely is rejected on the basis of one bad risk, unless the group is very small. The underwriter reviews a number of factors to determine whether or not the group should be accepted. (See Figure 23.1.)

Conversion Privilege

Group health plans that provide medical expense coverage universally contain a conversion privilege for individual insureds, which allows them to convert their group certificate to an individual medical expense policy with the same insurer, if and when they leave their employment. Insurers are permitted to evaluate the individual and charge the appropriate premium, be it a standard rate or substandard rate; however, an individual cannot be denied coverage, even if he or she has become uninsurable.

The conversion must be exercised within a given period of time, usually 30 or 31 days, depending on the state. During this time, the individual remains insured under the group plan, whether or not a conversion ultimately takes place. Conversion privileges generally are reserved for those who were active in the group plan during the preceding three months.

Test Topic Alert!   The conversion privilege is exercised when the insured no longer is eligible for coverage under the group plan. The insured converts the group certificate of coverage to an individual medical expense policy with the same insurer.

Preexisting Conditions   In the past, group health insurance plans typically excluded a person from coverage because of preexisting conditions. A preexisting condition generally was defined as any condition for which a participant received treatment at any time during the three months before the effective date of the group coverage. Group plans also specified when a condition would stop being considered preexisting.

However, the Health Insurance Portability and Accountability Act (HIPAA) has changed the rules governing preexisting conditions for group health plans. On July 1, 1997, HIPAA limited the ability of employer-sponsored groups and insurers to exclude individuals on the basis of preexisting medical conditions. The exclusion for preexisting conditions now is limited to conditions for which medical advice or treatment was recommended or received within the six-month period ending on the enrollment date. However, the exclusion can extend for no more than 12 months (18 months for late enrollees).

✓ **Take Note:** This exclusion period must be reduced by one month for each that the employee was covered at a previous job. For example, if an employee had prior group health coverage for eight months, he would be subject to only a four-month exclusion period when he changes jobs. Thereafter, the employee's new plan must cover all of his medical problems. In contrast, if the employee was covered by a group health plan for 12 straight months, the new plan could not invoke the preexisting condition exclusion at all. It must cover the new employee's medical problems as soon as he enrolls in the plan.

Group Health Insurance Coverages

All of the types of health insurance coverages discussed in this text—medical expense, disability income and accidental death and dismemberment—are available for group plans. Rather than repeat the discussion of these policies—their purpose and functions are the same whether it's a group product or an individual product—let's focus on the features of these coverages when they are part of a group plan.

FIGURE 23.2   Dental and Vision Care—Popular Group Benefits

Relatively new to the array of health care benefits offered to groups are coverages for *dental care* and *vision care.*

Dental care coverage is designed to cover the costs associated with normal dental maintenance as well as oral surgery, root canal therapy and orthodontia. The coverage may be on a reasonable and customary charge basis or on a dollar-per-service schedule approach. Deductible and coinsurance features are typical (although some policies will cover routine cleaning and exams at 100 percent), as are maximum yearly benefit amounts, such as $1,000 or $2,000.

Vision care coverage usually pays for reasonable and customary charges incurred during eye exams by opthalmologists and optometrists. Expenses for the fitting or cost of contact lenses or eyeglasses often are excluded.

Group Basic Medical Expense

The three standard forms of basic medical expense insurance—hospital, surgical and physicians' expenses—are available for group insurance. In addition, a number of newer coverages have been developed in recent years, including dental and vision care, prescription drugs, home health care, extended care facilities, diagnostic x-rays and laboratory services. In fact, some of these specified coverages, such as vision and dental care, are available only on a group basis.

A group basic medical expense plan can combine two or more of these coverages or it may consist of only one type of coverage, such as hospital expense only.

Group Major Medical Plans

Like individual major medical plans, group major medical plans may be offered as a single, extensive plan (comprehensive major medical) or superimposed over a group basic plan (supplemental major medical). Participants usually are required to satisfy an initial deductible with comprehensive plans and either a corridor or an integrated deductible with supplemental plans.

Benefits provided by group major medical plans usually are more extensive than those of individual plans. For example, it is not uncommon to find group plans that offer individual benefit maximums of $1 million; still others do not set any maximum benefit limits. Also, deductibles usually are lower for group plans, typically ranging from $100 to $250, whereas deductibles for individual policies can be $500 or more.

Two other characteristics of group medical expense plans distinguish them from individual plans. These are the *coordination of benefits provision* and the treatment of *maternity benefits*.

Coordination of Benefits

The purpose of the coordination of benefits (COB) provision, found only in group health plans, is to avoid duplication of benefit payments and overinsurance when an individual is covered under more than one group health plan. The provision limits the total amount of claims paid from all insurers covering the patient to no more than the total allowable medical expenses.

✓ **For Example:** An individual who incurs $700 in allowable medical expenses would not be able to collect any more than $700, no matter how many group plans he or she is covered by.

The COB provision establishes the primary plan, that is, the plan that is responsible for providing the full benefit amounts as it specifies. Once the primary plan has paid its full promised benefit, the insured may submit the claim to the secondary provider for any additional benefits payable. In no case, however, will the total amount the insured receives exceed the costs incurred, or the total maximum benefits available under all plans. Coordinating benefits is appropriate for married couples, when each is covered by an employer group plan.

✓ **For Example:** John and Cindy, a married couple, each are participants in their own company's health plan and also are covered as dependents under their spouse's plan. John's plan would specify that it is the primary plan for John; Cindy's plan would be his secondary plan. Likewise, Cindy's plan would specify that it is the primary plan for Cindy; John's plan would be her secondary plan.

Maternity Benefits

Whereas it is common for individual health plans to exclude routine maternity care from coverage, group medical expense plans must provide maternity benefits. This is the result of a 1979 amendment to the Civil Rights Act, which requires plans covering 15 or more people to treat pregnancy-related claims no differently than any other allowable medical expense.

 **Test Topic Alert!**

Although individual health plans commonly exclude coverage for routine maternity care, group medical expense plans must provide maternity benefits.

COBRA Continuation of Benefits

Participants in group medical expense plans are protected by a federal law that guarantees a continuation of their group coverage if their employment is terminated for reasons other than gross misconduct. Practically, the law protects employees who are laid-off, but not those who are fired for cause. (The circumstances that qualify for this continued coverage are noted in Figure 23.3.)

This law, known as the Consolidated Omnibus Budget Reconciliation Act of 1985 (or COBRA), requires employers with 20 or more employees to continue

FIGURE 23.3   COBRA Continued Coverage for Former Employees

The following events would qualify for extended medical expense coverage under COBRA for a terminated employee:

- Employment is terminated (for other than gross misconduct):
  18 months of continued coverage (or up to 29 months if disabled).

- Employee's hours are reduced (resulting in termination from the plan):
  18 months of continued coverage (or up to 29 months if disabled).

- Employee dies:
  36 months of continued coverage for dependents.

- Dependent child no longer qualifies as dependent child under the plan:
  36 months of continued coverage.

- Employee becomes eligible for Medicare:
  36 months of continued coverage.

- Employee divorces or legally separates:
  36 months of continued coverage for former spouse.

group medical expense coverage for terminated workers (as well as their spouses, divorced spouses and dependent children) for up to 18 months (or 36 months, in some situations) following termination.

✓ *Take Note:* COBRA is not the same as the policy conversion privilege by which an employee may convert a group certificate to an individual policy. COBRA permits the terminated employee to continue his or her group coverage.

The law does not require the employer to pay the cost of the continued group coverage; the terminated employee can be required to pay the premium, which may be up to 102 percent of the premium that otherwise would be charged. (The additional 2 percent is allowed to cover the insurer's administrative expenses.) The schedule of benefits will be the same during the continuation period as under the group plan.

 **Test Topic Alert!**

COBRA is a continuation of benefits formerly provided under the group plan. The insured may have to pay up to 102 percent of the premium that would otherwise be charged.

Group Disability Income Plans

Group disability income plans differ from individual plans in a number of ways. Individual plans usually specify a flat income amount, based on the person's earnings, determined at the time the policy is purchased. In contrast, group plans usually specify benefits in terms of a percentage of the individual's earnings.

Like individual plans, group disability can include short-term plans or long-term plans. The definitions of short term and long term, however, are different for group and individual.

Group short-term disability plans are characterized by maximum benefit periods of rather short duration, such as 13 or 26 weeks. Benefits typically are paid weekly and range from 50 to 100 percent of the individual's income.

✓ **Take Note:** A group short-term disability policy typically will pay benefits from the first day of a disability resulting from an accident but will impose a waiting period from one to seven days for a disability due to sickness.

Group long-term disability plans provide for maximum benefit periods of more than two years, occasionally extending to the insured's retirement age. Benefit amounts usually are limited to about 60 percent of the participant's income.

If an employer provides both a short-term plan and a long-term plan, the long-term plan typically begins paying benefits only after the short-term benefits cease. Often, long-term plans use an *own occupation* definition of total disability for the first year or two of disability and then switch to an *any occupation* definition.

Most group disability plans require the employee to have a minimum period of service, such as 30 to 90 days, before he or she is eligible for coverage. In addition, most group plans include provisions making their benefits supplemental to workers' compensation benefits, so that total benefits received do not exceed a specified percentage of regular earnings. In some cases, group disability plans actually limit coverage to nonoccupational disabilities, because occupational disabilities normally qualify for workers' compensation benefits.

✓ **Take Note:** Group disability plans also contain specific exclusions under which benefits will not be paid, even if the definition of disability is otherwise met. For example, common exclusions include self-inflicted injuries, disabilities during periods when the employee is not under a physician's care, disabilities resulting from war and those beginning before the employee was eligible for plan coverage.

Group AD&D

Accidental death and dismemberment insurance is a very popular type of group coverage, frequently offered in conjunction with group life insurance plans. It also may be provided as a separate policy, in which case it normally is paid for entirely by the employee. Such employee-pay-all plans are called voluntary group AD&D, because plan participation is voluntary. Benefits may be provided for both occupational and nonoccupational losses, or for nonoccupational losses only. Voluntary group AD&D typically provides benefits for both types of losses.

Like individual AD&D, group AD&D pays a principal sum upon the insured's accidental death (or loss of any two body members). A capital sum is payable upon the accidental loss of one body member. Some group AD&D plans specify a higher death benefit if the insured dies while on company business.

 Take Note: Group AD&D, unlike group life and group medical, normally does not include a conversion privilege.

Other Types of Group Health Plans

In addition to the typical group health insurance plan—as would be utilized by an employer, for instance—are four types of plans are worth noting: *blanket health insurance, franchise* (or *wholesale*) *health insurance, credit accident and health insurance* and *medical savings accounts.*

Blanket Health Plans Blanket health insurance is issued to cover a group who may be exposed to the same risks, but the composition of the group—the individuals within the group—is constantly changing. A blanket health plan may be issued to an airline or a bus company to cover its passengers or to a school to cover its students.

Franchise Health Plans Franchise health plans, sometimes called wholesale plans, provide health insurance coverage to members of an association or professional society. Individual policies are issued to individual members; the association or society simply serves as the sponsor for the plan. Premium rates usually are discounted for franchise plans.

Credit Accident and Health Plans Like credit life plans, credit accident and health plans are designed to help the insured pay off a loan in the event he or she is disabled due to an accident or sickness. If the insured becomes disabled, the policy provides for monthly benefit payments equal to the monthly loan payments due.

Medical Savings Accounts Medical savings accounts (MSAs) were designed to help employees of small businesses and the self-employed to pay for health care expenses. Available since January 1, 1997, a maximum of 750,000 MSAs can be established on a first-come, first-served basis by self-employed individuals or companies that have 50 or fewer employees.

The purpose of the MSA is to enable individuals to set aside funds on a tax-advantaged basis to help defray health care costs. In general, neither contributions to the MSA nor distributions from the MSA are taxable to the MSA owner, as long as distributions are used to cover qualified medical expenses for the individual, a spouse or dependents. Distributions used for other purposes will be taxed and also could incur a 15 percent penalty. MSA funds belong to the insured and, if they are not spent, they accumulate to prefund future health care expenses.

MSAs are designed to cover routine medical expenses; they are not meant to provide catastrophic coverage. Consequently, participation in an MSA is conditioned on being covered by a high-deductible contribution plan. The minimum and maximum deductibles for these plans must be $1,500 and $2,250 for individual coverage and $3,000 and $4,500 for family coverage. These deductibles provide a measuring rod for the amount of contribution that can be made to an account. For instance, with individual coverage, the annual MSA contribution is limited to 65 percent of the deductible; with family coverage, the contribution is limited to 75 percent of the deductible.

✓ **For Example:** Bob is single and self-employed. The deductible for his health insurance plan is $2,000. He can contribute $1,300 to his MSA this year (65 percent of $2,000).

✎ Quick Quiz 23.1   True or False?

_____ 1. XRT Company wants to help its 55 employees pay for health care expenses. To do this, it could create medical savings accounts for the employees.

_____ 2. John, an attorney, obtains health insurance coverage through the local bar association. The type of health plan sponsored by the bar association is called a franchise health plan.

_____ 3. Most group disability plans contain provisions making their benefits supplemental to workers' compensation benefits.

_____ 4. Maria is covered by a group medical plan with a $250 deductible. If she purchases individual medical coverage instead, the deductible probably will be lower.

_____ 5. Vision and dental care insurance generally are available only on a group basis.

Answers   1. *False*. *Only self-employed individuals or companies with 50 or fewer employees can establish medical savings accounts. Because XRT Company has 55 employees, it is not eligible for the MSA program.*

2. *True*.

3. *True*.

4. *False*. *Deductibles usually are lower for group plans than for individual health plans. As a result, the deductible for Maria's group plan probably will be less than if she purchased an individual plan.*

5. *True*.

Tax Treatment of Group Health Plans

As an incentive for employers to provide health insurance benefits to their employees, the federal government grants favorable tax treatment to group plans. Let's briefly review this treatment.

Taxation of Group Health Premiums

Employers are entitled to take a tax deduction for premium contributions they make to a group health plan, as long as the contributions represent an ordinary and necessary business expense. By the same token, individual participants do not include employer contributions made on their behalf as part of their taxable income.

As a general rule, individual premium contributions to a group health plan are not tax deductible. Only when unreimbursed medical expenses—expenses that can include any individual contributions to a group medical plan—exceed 7.5 percent of an individual's adjusted gross income can a tax deduction be taken. The deduction is limited to the amount exceeding 7.5 percent of adjusted gross income.

✓ **Take Note:** Any premiums the individual contributes for group disability or group AD&D coverage are not considered qualifying medical expenses when determining this excess.

Taxation of Group Health Benefits

Any benefits an individual receives under a medical expense plan are not considered taxable income, because they are provided to cover losses the individual incurred. It is a somewhat different story with disability income plans, however. Disability benefit payments that are attributed to employee contributions are not taxable, but benefit payments that are attributed to employer contributions are taxable.

✓ **For Example:** Anne is a participant in a contributory group disability income plan in which her employer pays two-thirds of the premium and Anne pays one-third. Her employer qualifies for a tax deduction for its share of the premium and, as is true with employer contributions to all group health plans, Anne is not taxed on those contributions. The premium portion that Anne pays does not qualify for a tax deduction for her.

Now assume Anne becomes disabled and receives disability income benefits of $900 a month. One-third of the monthly benefit—$300—would be tax free, because it is attributed to the premium she paid; the remaining two-thirds of the payment—$600—would be taxable income, because it is attributed to the premium her employer paid.

Summary

Group health insurance—like group life insurance—is evidenced by one master contract that covers multiple lives. Virtually any health insurance product available as an individual contract also is available under the group umbrella. Thus, medical expense insurance, disability income insurance and accidental death and dismemberment insurance all are common group plans. In addition, there are a number of coverages, like vision and dental care, that are available only to groups.

Of utmost concern to insurance regulators is that employees be protected from loss of their insurance coverage if their job is terminated. Accordingly, nearly all states have provisions in their insurance laws that require group life and medical expense policies to provide a conversion option to terminating participants. The federal government also has exercised its regulatory prerogative by passing laws, like COBRA, that protect terminated employees and that guarantee maternity cases will be treated the same as any other medical condition.

Key Concepts

In preparing for their licensing examination, students should be familiar with the following concepts:

master policy

contributory vs. noncontributory
  plans

group major medical expense

group AD&D

conversion privilege

COBRA

MSA

certificate of insurance

group basic medical expense

group disability income

group health underwriting

preexisting conditions

taxation of group health insurance

Lesson Exam Twenty-three

1. Which of the following statements about group health insurance is CORRECT?

   A. The insurer, not the employer, stipulates the minimum number of persons that must be covered under a group plan.
   B. Group health plans provide more extensive benefits than individual health plans.
   C. If a group plan provides medical expense benefits, it must be with a comprehensive policy.
   D. COBRA requirements are directed at employers with 20 or fewer employees.

2. Which type of group health coverage typically does NOT contain a conversion privilege?

   A. Basic medical expense
   B. Comprehensive medical expense
   C. Disability income
   D. Accidental death and dismemberment

3. Which of the following can an individual include as *qualifying expenses* for purposes of determining a medical tax deduction?

   A. Premium contributions paid by the employer to a group medical expense plan
   B. Premium contributions paid by the employer to a group disability plan
   C. Premium contributions paid by the individual to a group medical expense plan
   D. Premium contributions paid by the individual to a group disability plan

4. An individual purchased group credit accident and health insurance to cover a car loan. Following an accident two months later, the individual was disabled for eight months. Which of the following benefits were paid under the policy?

   A. Monthly income benefits to the insured
   B. An amount equal to eight months of the loan payment to the insured's creditor
   C. An amount equal to 10 months of the loan payment to the insured's creditor
   D. Monthly income benefits to the insured and an amount equal to eight months of the loan payment to the insured's creditor

5. Dan is a participant in his company's group health plan. One of the plan's provisions specifies that, in the event he is eligible for benefits under another policy, his group plan will serve as the primary plan. What is this provision called?

   A. Excess coverage
   B. Coordination of benefits
   C. Other insurance with this insurer
   D. Double indemnity

6. A vacation cruise line that wants group health coverage for its passengers would purchase what kind of insurance?

   A. Franchise health
   B. Wholesale health
   C. Blanket health
   D. Credit health

7. The purpose of COBRA requirements concerns

   A. coordination of health benefits
   B. continuation of health insurance
   C. Medicare supplement coverage
   D. nondiscrimination in group health plans

8. Sally is covered by her employer's noncontributory group disability income plan, the premium for which is $50 a month. If she were to become disabled and receive $1,000 a month, how much of each benefit payment would be taxable income to her?

    A. $0
    B. $50
    C. $950
    D. $1,000

9. Which of the following statements regarding group disability income plans is NOT correct?

    A. Benefits are specified in terms of a percentage of the participant's earnings.
    B. Benefits paid under the group plan are supplemental to workers' compensation benefits.
    C. Employees covered under both a short-term and long-term plan collect benefits from each simultaneously.
    D. A minimum length of service may be required before an employee is eligible to participate in the plan.

10. Which of the following statements about COBRA is CORRECT?

    A. The premium for continued group medical coverage may be up to 102 percent of the premium that otherwise would be charged.
    B. The employer must pay the cost of the continued group coverage.
    C. The schedule of benefits during the continuation period may be different than those provided under the group plan.
    D. COBRA permits an employee to convert a group certificate to an individual policy.

Answers & Rationale

1. **B.** Group health plans generally provide more extensive benefits than individual plans. For example, some group plans offer individual benefit maximums of $1 million; others do not set any maximum benefit limits.

2. **D.** Group basic medical expense, comprehensive medical expense and disability income insurance all typically contain a conversion privilege that allows the insureds to convert their group certificate to an individual policy when they leave their employment. Group AD&D policies do not contain conversion privileges.

3. **C.** Individual premium contributions to a group medical expense plan are deductible only when they and other unreimbursed medical expenses exceed 7.5 percent of an individual's adjusted gross income. Premium contributions made by the employer and those made by an employee for group disability coverage cannot be considered for purposes of determining a medical tax deduction.

4. **B.** A group credit accident and health plan is designed to help an insured pay off a loan if he or she becomes disabled. In this case, if the insured is disabled for eight months, the policy will pay an amount equal to eight months of the loan payment to the insured's creditor.

5. **B.** A coordination of benefits provision establishes which plan is the primary plan when an insured is covered by another health plan.

6. **C.** A vacation cruise line would purchase blanket health insurance to provide group health insurance coverage for its passengers. This type of insurance is issued to cover a group that may be exposed to the same risks, but whose members are changing constantly.

7. **B.** COBRA requires employers to continue group medical expense coverage for terminated workers (and their families) for up to 36 months after termination.

8. **D.** Because Sally does not contribute toward the cost of the premium for the group disability income plan, all of the benefits she receives will be attributed to the premium her employer paid. As a result, she will have to report all of her monthly benefits ($1,000) as taxable income.

9. **C.** If an employer provides both a short-term and long-term disability plan, the long-term plan typically begins paying benefits only after the short-term benefits cease. Employees would not collect benefits from each plan simultaneously.

10. **A.** COBRA does not require the employer to pay for the cost of continued group coverage. The terminated employee can be required to pay the premium, which may be up to 102 percent of the premium that otherwise would be charged.

24

Uses of Health Insurance

INTRODUCTION

At first glance, it might seem that the uses of health insurance are self-explanatory: a person buys health insurance to protect against the cost of health care—or, more accurately, health insurance provides protection against the costs associated with losing one's health. However, health insurance plans can be used in a variety of ways to meet an individual's or business' unique needs. Individuals, for example, need to have a comprehensive health insurance plan in place to insure against the financial consequences of illness or disability. Similarly, health insurance also is necessary to protect a business against the risks it faces, including losses due to a key employee's death or disability. Businesses also commonly offer health insurance as part of an employee benefits program. In this lesson, we will take a closer look at some of the ways in which individuals and businesses use health insurance.

LESSON OBJECTIVES

When you complete this lesson you should be able to:

- describe the importance of medical expense insurance and disability income insurance in an individual's total health insurance plan;
- explain how group health and disability insurance differ from individual coverage;
- list the advantages of offering health insurance as part of an employee benefits plan; and
- explain how business overhead expense insurance, health insurance and disability buy-out plans are used to help businesses continue if an owner becomes disabled or injured.

A Proper Health Insurance Program

In order to design the proper health insurance program, several questions must be addressed. First, who is to be covered? The insurance needs of individuals, families and businesses vary widely, as do the insurance products available to each. Second, is the needed coverage currently provided by a group plan or social insurance program? Third, how much responsibility for medical care expenses is the policyowner able (and willing) to assume through policy deductibles and coinsurance in exchange for reduced premiums? Only through a careful consideration of these and other questions can an insurance producer develop an insurance program that satisfies the distinctive needs of business, family, and individual clients.

Individual Needs for Health Insurance

At one time it was acceptable to expect one's family to provide support when illness or disability struck. Those days are now long past; today, we all must prepare for and assume the responsibility of covering the cost of medical care for ourselves. However, unless one is independently wealthy, the prospect of covering costs out-of-pocket is not an attractive one; indeed, it can be downright terrifying.

The loss of one's health can have wide-ranging consequences. Not only does the cost of medical care come with a high price tag, but the loss of income that often accompanies a disabling illness or injury can compound the devastating effects of the health loss. Current demographics, which show that both parents in most families are working, emphasize the importance of considering both parents' income needs when designing a complete health insurance program.

Medical Expense Insurance Needs

While it is difficult to measure the importance of one type of insurance over another, it is fair to presume that a health insurance program must begin with an adequate amount of medical expense insurance. Without proper protection devoted to these potential costs, even the most basic medical care can exhaust an individual's savings quickly; a catastrophic claim can spell financial disaster.

At one time, most medical policies were the basic medical expense type. However, today it is more common to find most Americans covered under some form of a major medical policy or a service plan such as Blue Cross/Blue Shield or an HMO. If the policyowner can afford the cost, an ideal policy is a combination plan in which a basic plan is enhanced by a supplementary major medical plan. Under this approach, the insured obtains the first dollar benefits of the basic plan and also has the expansive protection offered by the major medical plan.

Most policyowners, of course, are concerned with the cost of their health insurance and find that some financial sacrifice may be required. For example, an individual major medical plan with a $100 individual deductible is going to cost more than a comparable plan with a $500 deductible. A plan with an 80/20 coinsurance provision will cost more than a comparable plan with a 75/25 coinsurance provision. The question the policyowner must answer is, Am I willing to assume more of the cost risk of possible future claims in exchange for the definite cost savings offered by a plan with a higher deductible or coinsurance limit?

Group vs. Individual Coverage

More Americans are protected under group medical expense policies than individual policies. The benefit to the group member, even assuming the plan is contributory, is the significantly reduced out-of-pocket cost compared to an individual plan. The group plan participant can take comfort in knowing that even if he or she should terminate employment, continued coverage is guaranteed through the conversion privilege built into every group health policy.

Disability Income Insurance Needs

The importance of protecting one's earnings sometimes is overlooked in the insurance needs analysis process—a regrettable fact for the many people who become disabled every year. Americans too often assume that Social Security will provide the income necessary to survive if disability strikes. This is an unfortunate assumption; not only is the definition of disabled to qualify for Social Security benefits extremely narrow, but no assurance exists that the benefits will meet the disabled person's needs.

✓ *Take Note:* Social Security disability income should be viewed as a possible source of income to augment a personal plan. Whether the personal plan is based on a group policy or an individual policy, it should be regarded as the primary source of income if earnings are lost due to disability.

Policyowners can control the premium cost of a disability income plan by electing a longer elimination period than might otherwise be desired. The length of the benefit period also has a direct impact on the premium.

Because of the favorable tax treatment given to individually funded disability income policies, a plan that provides about 60 percent of predisability gross earnings can be considered sufficient. This is because disability income benefits are income tax free if the individual insured paid the premiums.

✓ **For Example:** An individual who earns $3,000 each month may only take home $2,000 after taxes. Consequently, a disability plan that provides a monthly tax-free benefit of $1,800 likely would be sufficient.

In the case of group disability income plans, the group member has little choice as to the level of benefits provided; the plan document must have a schedule of benefits that identifies what the participant will receive if he or she is disabled. On the other hand, the group member benefits to the extent the employer contributes to the disability income premiums.

If both parents in a family are employed, then disability income must be considered for each. If each parent's income is indispensable for the financial support of the family, then it is safe to assume that the loss of either income would present a financial problem.

Business Needs for Health Insurance

Many health insurance producers have found a niche servicing the business market. There is a good, practical reason for this—the health insurance needs of the business market are as great as the needs of individuals.

Business uses of health insurance can be divided broadly into two categories: *employee benefit plans* and *business continuation plans*.

Employee Benefit Plans

Although any given employee benefit plan can offer a wide variety of benefits—life insurance, a pension or profit-sharing plan, vacation pay, deferred compensation arrangements, funeral leave, sick time—such plans almost always include some kind of provision for health insurance or health benefits. The large and rapid increases in the cost of health care likely are the primary reasons for the popularity of employer-sponsored health plans, and many people rely on these plans as their sole source of health insurance.

Group Health Insurance   As we have learned, a group health plan can consist of medical insurance, disability income insurance, and accidental death and dismemberment insurance alone or in any combination. In fact, it is not uncommon to find all of these coverages included in a single group insurance plan.

✓ **Take Note:** By providing its employees with a plan for health insurance, an employer derives a number of benefits:

- The plan contributes to employee morale and productivity.
- The plan enables the employer to provide a needed benefit that employees otherwise would have to pay for with personal after-tax dollars (this helps hold down demands for wage increases).
- The plan places the employer in a competitive position for hiring and retaining employees.
- The employer can obtain a tax deduction for the cost of contributing to the plan.
- The plan enhances the employer's image in both public and employee relations.

Cafeteria Plans

Many times, employer-provided health insurance benefits are part of a cafeteria plan. As the name implies, cafeteria plans (also known as Section 125 plans) are benefit arrangements in which employees can pick and choose from a menu of benefits, thus tailoring their benefits package to their specific needs. Employees can select the benefits they value or need and forgo those of lesser importance to them. The employer allocates a certain amount of money to each employee to purchase the benefits he or she desires. If the cost of the benefits exceeds the allocation, the employee may contribute the balance.

The types of flexible benefits usually available under a cafeteria plan include medical coverage, accidental death and dismemberment insurance, short-term and long-term disability, life insurance and dependent care. Some plans provide for choices within the choices: an employee may have the option of selecting from levels of medical plans or choosing from a variety of HMOs, for instance.

Business Continuation Plans

Just as life insurance provides a way to help a business continue in the event an owner or key employee dies, health insurance also serves continuation purposes in the event of a disabling sickness or injury. It does so through the following plans.

Business Overhead Expense Insurance

Business overhead expense insurance is designed to reimburse a business for overhead expenses in the event a business owner becomes disabled. It is sold on an individual basis to professionals in private practice, self-employed business owners, partners and occasionally close corporations.

Overhead expenses include rent or mortgage payments, utilities, telephones, leased equipment, employees' salaries and the like—all the expenses that must be paid regardless of the owner's disability.

✓ **Take Note:** Business overhead expense policies do not include any compensation for the disabled owner. They are designed to help the day-to-day operation of his or her business continue during the period of disability.

The benefits payable under these kinds of policies are limited to the covered expenses incurred or the maximum that is stated in the policy.

✓ **For Example:** Dr. Miller is the insured under a business overhead expense policy that pays maximum monthly benefits of $4,500. If Dr. Miller became disabled and actual monthly expenses were $3,950, the monthly benefits paid would be $3,950. If Dr. Miller's actual expenses were $4,700, the benefits payable would be $4,500.

The premium for business overhead insurance is a legitimate, tax-deductible business expense. The benefits when paid, however, are treated as taxable income.

Business Health Insurance

Business health insurance is available to indemnify a business for the loss of the services of a key employee, a partner or an owner should disability strike. In the event of a disability, this insurance provides the business with funds to bridge the period necessary to secure and train a worthy successor.

Determining the precise economic loss a business will face if a key individual becomes disabled is somewhat difficult; the cost of securing an experienced, competent replacement or the income the employee or owner currently earns are two common approaches to making this determination.

Disability Buy-Outs

A disability buy-sell agreement operates in much the same way as a life insurance buy-sell agreement. However, in this case, the plan sets forth the terms for selling and buying a partner's or stock owner's share of a business in the event he or she becomes disabled and is unable to participate in the business. It is a legal, binding arrangement, funded with a disability income policy.

Unlike typical disability income insurance plans that pay benefits in the form of periodic payments, the buy-out plan usually contains a provision allowing for a lump-sum payment of the benefit, thereby facilitating the buy-out of the disabled's interest. However, if the owners desire, the plan often permits the buy-out to occur through the use of periodic income payments.

Disability buy-out plans are characterized by lengthy elimination periods, often as long as two years. The reason for this is simple: because the plan involves the sale of a disabled partner's or owner's interest in the business, it is important to be quite sure that the disabled person will not be able to return to the business.

Considering the fact that a disabled partner can represent a double liability—the remaining partners must not only take up the slack left by the disabled partner's absence but usually must pay him or her an income as well—it is understandable that the disability buy-out plan is popular with business owners.

Summary

The uses of health insurance—notably medical expense and disability income—are as varied as the need for it is vital. Both the personal market and the business market have many uses for these important insurance products. Often the insured's concern is not whether he or she needs it, but whether he or she can afford it. Fortunately, every type of health insurance plan offers some way for the owner to reduce premium costs, including increasing the deductible or lengthening the elimination period.

Key Concepts

In preparing for their licensing examination, students should be familiar with the following concepts:

individual vs. group health
   insurance
business overhead expense
   insurance

disability buy-out insurance
employee benefit plans
business health insurance

Lesson Exam Twenty-four

1. All of the following are methods of keeping premium costs to a minimum in a health policy EXCEPT

   A. modifying benefit amounts
   B. increasing the deductible
   C. waiving the right to receive benefit payments when due
   D. extending the elimination period

2. Fred owns a small hardware store and is covered under a business overhead expense policy. If he becomes disabled, he can expect all the following expenses to be covered EXCEPT

   A. his employees' salaries
   B. his salary
   C. utility bills
   D. property and liability insurance premiums

3. Which of the following characteristics is associated with disability buy-out plans?

   A. A short elimination period
   B. The option to elect a lump-sum payment
   C. Provisions to cover the business' overhead expenses
   D. Irrevocable agreements

4. What is the income tax consequence if Marie's employer pays for her group disability income coverage?

   A. The premium payments are taxable income to her.
   B. The premium payments are tax deductible by her.
   C. The employer receives the disability income benefits tax free.
   D. The employer can take a tax deduction for the cost of premiums it pays.

5. With regard to health insurance policies, which of the following statements is CORRECT?

   A. A major medical plan with a $100 deductible is less expensive than one with a $500 deductible.
   B. More Americans are covered by an individual medical expense policy than a group policy.
   C. The appropriate benefit payable under a disability income policy should equal the insured's monthly gross income.
   D. A disability policy with a six-month elimination period is less expensive than one with a 60-day elimination period, all other factors being equal.

Answers & Rationale

1. **C**. A person can minimize premium costs by modifying benefit amounts, increasing the deductible and extending the elimination period. Waiving the right to receive benefit payments when due will not minimize premium expenses.

2. **B**. Business overhead expense insurance is designed to help a business' day-to-day operations continue during the owner's disability. As a result, Fred's policy would cover his employees' salaries, the utility bills and the store's property and liability insurance premiums. His policy would not, however, cover his own compensation.

3. **B**. A disability buy-sell plan usually contains a provision allowing for benefits to be paid in a lump sum. However, if the owners desire, a plan may permit the buy-out to occur through using periodic income payments.

4. **D**. If Mary's employer pays for her group disability income coverage, it can take a tax deduction equal to the cost of its premiums. The premium payments will not constitute taxable income to Mary, nor will she be able to take a tax deduction for them.

5. **D**. Policyowners can control the premium cost of a disability income plan by electing a longer elimination period. As a result, a disability policy with a six-month elimination period will be less expensive than one with only a 60-day period, all other factors being equal.

Final Exam

Remember to read the entire question before selecting an answer. Some of the responses may seem correct, but a careful reading may prove otherwise. Words like "all," "may," "shall," "not," and "except" can change the answer. All questions have a single correct response and are based on information found in this text.

General Principles

1. In the insurance business, risk can best be defined as

   A. sharing the possibility of a loss
   B. uncertainty regarding the future
   C. uncertainty regarding financial loss
   D. uncertainty regarding when death will occur

2. Which of the following risks is insurable?

   A. Pure
   B. Gambling
   C. Speculative
   D. Investing

3. Buying insurance is one of the most effective ways of

   A. avoiding
   B. transferring
   C. reducing
   D. retaining

4. Which of the following best describes the function of insurance?

   A. It is a form of legalized gambling.
   B. It spreads financial risk over a large group to minimize the loss to any one individual.
   C. It protects against living too long.
   D. It creates and protects risks.

5. Which of the following statements about insurable risk is NOT correct?

   A. The loss must be due to chance.
   B. The loss must be predictable.
   C. The loss must be catastrophic.
   D. The loss must have a determinable value.

6. The amount of money an insurer sets aside to pay future claims is called the

   A. premium
   B. reserve
   C. dividend
   D. accumulated interest

7. Which of the following constitutes an insurable interest?

   A. The policyowner must expect to benefit from the insured's death.
   B. The policyowner must expect to suffer a loss when the insured dies or becomes disabled.
   C. The beneficiary, by definition, has an insurable interest in the insured.
   D. The insured must have a personal or business relationship with the beneficiary.

8. Which of the following statements describes the parol evidence rule?

   A. A written contract cannot be changed once it is signed.
   B. An oral contract cannot be modified by written evidence.
   C. A written contract cannot be changed by oral evidence.
   D. An oral contract takes precedence over any earlier written contracts.

9. Which of the following factors determines whether policy dividends will be paid on a participating policy?

   A. Reserves and experience
   B. Expenses and claims costs
   C. Interest and benefits
   D. Premiums and renewability

10. Whom does licensed agent legally represent?

    A. The insurer
    B. The applicant/insured
    C. The state insurance department
    D. Himself or herself

11. Which of the following statements regarding policy replacement is NOT correct?

    A. Replacement involves convincing a policyholder to lapse or terminate an existing policy and purchase another.
    B. Interrupting one cash value insurance plan to begin another could cause serious financial problems for the policyowner.
    C. Even if the customer wants to replace his or her existing policy, an agent can effect a policy replacement only by following the replacement regulations in his or her state.
    D. Premiums for replacement policies are lower generally than premiums for the existing policies they replace.

12. With regard to insurable risks, which of the following statements is NOT correct?

    A. Only pure risks are insurable.
    B. An insurable risk must involve loss that is within the insured's control.
    C. Insurers will not insure risks that are catastrophic in nature.
    D. An insurable risk must be measurable.

13. On August 9, Albert made an application for life insurance that his agent submitted a day later without a premium payment. On August 21, the insurer issued the policy as applied for, and on August 24, the agent delivered the policy and collected the initial premium. On what day was the contract offer made?

    A. August 9
    B. August 10
    C. August 21
    D. August 24

14. All statements made by an applicant in an application for life insurance are considered to be

    A. warranties
    B. affirmations
    C. representations
    D. declarations

15. Which of the following legal terms indicates that a life insurance contract contains the enforceable promises of only one party?

    A. Adhesion
    B. Unilateral
    C. Conditional
    D. Aleatory

16. Which of the following types of agent authority is specifically set forth in writing in the agent's contract?

    A. Express
    B. Implied
    C. Apparent
    D. Personal

17. If a home catches fire after it is struck by lightning and the fire destroys its structure and contents, by insurance definition, the fire is the

    A. risk
    B. hazard
    C. peril
    D. proximate cause

18. What constitutes *consideration* for a life insurance policy?

    A. Application and initial premium
    B. Agent's commission
    C. Adhesion feature of the contract
    D. Policy's benefits

19. Statements made by an applicant for life insurance that are guaranteed to be true are

    A. warranties
    B. material statements
    C. representations
    D. declarations

20. Which of the following types of insurance company is owned by its policyholders?

    A. Service insurer
    B. Stock insurer
    C. Reinsurer
    D. Mutual insurer

Principles of Life Insurance

21. With regard to life insurance, which of the following statements is NOT correct?

    A. All individuals are considered to have insurable interests in themselves.
    B. Spouses are automatically considered to have insurable interests in each other.
    C. A creditor has an insurable interest in a debtor.
    D. Insurable interest must be maintained throughout the life of the contract.

22. A life insurance company is organized in Chicago where it maintains its home office. In Illinois, the company is classified as what kind of company?

    A. Domestic
    B. Local
    C. Foreign
    D. Preferred

23. A life insurance company organized in Illinois, with its home office in Philadelphia, is licensed to conduct business in Wisconsin. In Wisconsin, this company is classified as what kind of company?

    A. Domestic
    B. Alien
    C. Foreign
    D. Regional

24. To whom does the cash value of a life insurance policy belong?

    A. Policyowner
    B. Insured
    C. Insurer
    D. Beneficiary

25. Frank is the insured in a $40,000, five-year level term policy issued in 1995. He died in 2001. His beneficiary received

    A. $0
    B. $20,000
    C. $40,000
    D. the cash value of the policy

26. Which of the following statements regarding assignment of a life insurance policy is NOT correct?

    A. To secure a loan, the policy can be transferred temporarily to the lender as security for the loan.
    B. The policyowner must obtain approval from the insurance company before a policy can be assigned.
    C. The life insurance company assumes no responsibility for the validity of an assignment.
    D. The life insurance company must be notified in writing by the policyowner of any assignment.

27. After a family's breadwinner dies, the *blackout period* generally can be defined as the period

    A. during which children are living at home
    B. that begins when the youngest child turns 16 and ends when the surviving parent retires
    C. during which children are in school
    D. from the surviving parent's retirement to death

28. A company with three partners is considering a buy-sell plan. Which of the following statements pertaining to buy-sell plans and this partnership is NOT correct?

    A. An insured entity buy-sell agreement would be funded with five life insurance policies.
    B. If they choose a cross-purchase plan, each partner would have to purchase two policies for a total of six plans.
    C. No benefits will accrue to the partnership from the buy-sell agreement until one of the partners dies.
    D. If they choose an entity buy-sell agreement, the business would be party to the agreement.

29. Bill names his church as the beneficiary of his $300,000 life insurance policy. When Bill dies, who is responsible for the income taxes payable on the lump-sum proceeds received by the church?

    A. His estate
    B. His church
    C. No income tax is payable on the death proceeds
    D. His estate and church split the tax

30. Which provision of a life insurance policy states that the application is part of the contract?

    A. Consideration clause
    B. Insuring clause
    C. Entire contract clause
    D. Incontestable clause

31. Ron, the insured, dies during the grace period for his $100,000 life insurance policy. Considering that the premium on the policy has not been paid, what happens?

    A. The premium is canceled because the insured died during the grace period.
    B. The amount of the premium is deducted from the policy proceeds paid to the beneficiary.
    C. The premium due, plus a 10 percent penalty, is charged against the policy.
    D. The beneficiary must pay the premium after the death claim is paid.

32. Which of the following is stated in the consideration clause of a life insurance policy?

    A. Insured's risk classification
    B. Insured's general health condition
    C. Amount and frequency of premium payments
    D. Benefits payable upon the insured's death

33. John stopped paying premiums on his permanent life insurance policy eight years ago though he never surrendered it. He is still insurable and has no outstanding loan against the policy. The company probably will decline to reinstate the policy because the time limit for reinstatement has expired. The limit usually is

    A. six months
    B. one year
    C. two years
    D. three to seven years

34. Which of the following statements pertaining to reinstatement of a life insurance policy is NOT correct?

    A. A suicide exclusion period is renewed with a reinstated policy.
    B. When reinstating a policy, the insurer may charge the policyowner for past-due premiums.
    C. When reinstating a policy, the insurer may charge the policyowner for interest on past-due premiums.
    D. A new contestable period usually becomes effective in a reinstated policy.

35. Leland elects to surrender his whole life policy for a reduced paid-up policy. The cash value of his new policy will

    A. continue to increase
    B. decrease gradually
    C. remain the same as in the old policy
    D. decrease by 50 percent immediately

36. Kevin, the insured in a $200,000 life insurance policy, and his sole beneficiary, Lynda, are killed instantly in a car accident. Under the Uniform Simultaneous Death Act, to whose estate will the policy proceeds be paid?

    A. Lynda's
    B. Kevin's
    C. Both Kevin's and Lynda's equally
    D. The state

37. When a policyowner cannot exercise his or her rights of ownership without the policy beneficiary's consent, the beneficiary is designated

    A. vested
    B. contractual
    C. irrevocable
    D. primary

38. Which of the following statements about term insurance is NOT correct?

    A. It pays a benefit only if the insured dies during a specified period.
    B. Level, decreasing, and increasing are basic forms of term insurance.
    C. Cash values build during the specified period.
    D. It provides protection for a temporary period of time.

39. Bob purchases a $50,000 five-year level term policy. Which of the following statements about Bob's coverage is NOT correct?

    A. The policy provides a straight, level $50,000 of coverage for five years.
    B. If the insured dies at any time during the five years, his beneficiary will receive the policy's face value.
    C. If the insured dies after the specified five years, only the policy's cash value will be paid.
    D. If the insured lives beyond the five years, the policy expires and no benefits are payable.

40. Mrs. Williamson purchases a five-year $50,000 decreasing term policy with an option to renew. Which of the following statements about the policy's renewability is CORRECT?

    A. The premium for the renewal period will be the same as the initial period.
    B. The premium for the renewal period will be higher than the initial period.
    C. The premium for the renewal period will be the same as the initial period, but a one-time service charge will be assessed upon renewal.
    D. The premium for the renewal period will be lower than the initial period.

41. Joanna and her husband, Tom, have a $40,000 annuity that pays them $200 a month. Tom dies and Joanna continues receiving the $200 monthly check as long as she lives. When Joanna dies, the company ceases payment. This is an example of what kind of annuity?

    A. Installment refund
    B. Joint and full survivor
    C. Life
    D. Cash refund

42. Which of the following statements about the incontestable clause in a life insurance policy is NOT correct?

    A. The clause gives people assurance that when their policies become claims, they will be paid without delays or protests.
    B. The incontestable clause means that after a certain period, an insurer cannot refuse to pay the proceeds of a policy or void the contract.
    C. Incontestable clauses usually become effective two years from the issue date of the policy.
    D. Insurers can void a contract even after the specified period provided they can prove the policy was purchased fraudulently.

43. Which of the following statements does NOT describe the purpose of Social Security?

    A. To provide basic protection against financial problems accompanying death, disability and retirement.
    B. To augment a sound personal insurance plan.
    C. To provide a source of income for a meaningful standard of living.
    D. To protect workers, their spouses and dependent children.

44. Ralph owns a $50,000 nonpar whole life policy. Its cash value has accumulated to $15,000, and he has paid a total of $9,500 in premiums. If he surrenders the policy for its cash value, how will it be taxed?

    A. He will receive the $15,000 tax free.
    B. He will receive $5,500 tax free; the $9,500 balance is taxable as income.
    C. He will receive $9,500 tax free; the $5,500 balance is taxable as income.
    D. He will receive the $15,000 as taxable income.

45. Which of the following would NOT apply when a life insurance policy is reinstated after a lapse?

    A. All back premiums must be paid.
    B. All outstanding loans must be paid.
    C. A new contestable period goes into effect.
    D. A new suicide exclusion period goes into effect.

46. Jane, age 35, has just purchased a 20-pay whole life policy. When she turns 55, she will

    A. receive the policy's face amount benefit
    B. have a fully matured policy
    C. cease paying premiums
    D. no longer be covered by the policy

47. If a life insurance applicant is given a binding receipt, when does his or her coverage become effective?

    A. Date the policy is issued
    B. Date the applicant proves to be insurable
    C. Date the receipt is given
    D. Date the policy is delivered

48. Who performs the function of risk selection in determining an individual's insurability for policy issue?

    A. Actuary
    B. Agent
    C. Fiduciary
    D. Underwriter

49. Regular notices sent to policy-owners for payment of their life insurance policy premiums reflect

    A. gross premium
    B. net level premium
    C. net single premium
    D. none of the above

50. In which of the following situations would the premium payor of a life insurance policy be able to deduct the premium payments for tax purposes?

    A. Joe, the sole proprietor of a grocery store, purchases and pays premiums on a $75,000 term life policy on his life and names his wife as beneficiary.
    B. Leland, a local board member of the United Way, assigns his $25,000 whole life policy to that organization, but continues to make the premium payments.
    C. Michelle, the legal guardian of five-year-old Angela, makes the premium payments on Angela's $5,000 juvenile life insurance policy.
    D. Bob takes over the premium payments on his son's $30,000 whole life policy after his son declares bankruptcy.

51. At what point does a whole life policy mature or endow?

    A. When the policy's cash value equals the face amount
    B. When premiums paid equal the policy's face amount
    C. When premiums paid equal the policy's cash value
    D. When the policy's cash value equals the loan amount

52. If four individuals, all age 30, purchase the following life insurance policies, and all policies are still in force ten years later, who will have the largest cash value in his policy?

    Bob $100,000 straight whole life
    Dennis $100,000 life paid-up at 65
    Ralph $100,000 20-pay life
    Jack $100,000 life paid-up at 55

    A. Bob
    B. Dennis
    C. Ralph
    D. Jack

53. Who designates the beneficiary of a life insurance policy?

    A. Insured
    B. Policyowner
    C. Underwriter
    D. Fiduciary

54. A retirement plan that is not employer-sponsored allows single workers who earn up to $25,000 a year to contribute up to $2,000 and deduct the contribution from their taxes in 2001. The plan described is a(n)

    A. 401(k)
    B. SEP
    C. HR-10
    D. IRA

55. When an insured dies, who stands first to receive the policy's proceeds?

    A. Policyowner
    B. Primary beneficiary
    C. Insured's creditors
    D. Insured's estate

56. What is the basic source of information for life insurance underwriting and policy issue?

    A. Consumer reports
    B. Medical Information Bureau
    C. Application
    D. Physician reports

57. Jerry has just purchased a life insurance policy and is taking time to review the policy's provisions. He will find that his policy excludes death by all of the following means EXCEPT

    A. suicide
    B. accident
    C. aviation
    D. war

58. A life insurance policy provides for monthly income payments if the insured dies at any time during the first ten years. The income period begins when the policy is issued and ends ten years later. What kind of policy is this?

    A. Modified endowment
    B. Modified whole life
    C. Family income
    D. Family maintenance

59. Randy's premium payment was due on June 1, but the company did not receive it until June 28. Which policy provision kept Randy's policy from lapsing?

    A. Reinstatement
    B. Facility of payment
    C. Grace period
    D. Automatic premium loan

60. Which of the following statements regarding policy assignments is CORRECT?

    A. The policyowner must notify the insurer of the assignment and receive the insurer's permission.
    B. The procedure required for policy assignment is explained in the policy's insuring clause.
    C. A policy that has named an irrevocable beneficiary cannot be assigned without that beneficiary's agreement.
    D. Insurable interest must exist between the insured and the assignee at the time of assignment.

Principles of Health Insurance

61. On August 1, Roger completed an application for a major medical policy, gave his agent a check for the initial premium and received an insurability receipt from the agent. No medical examination was required. On August 3, the agent submitted Roger's application and premium to the insurance company. On August 6, Roger was involved in an accident and admitted to a hospital. On August 12, the agent received Roger's policy from the insurance company. Which of the following statements concerning this situation is CORRECT?

    A. Roger's coverage will begin when he receives the policy from the agent.
    B. Roger's coverage began when he received the insurability receipt.
    C. Roger's coverage began the day the insurance company received the application and premium from the agent.
    D. Roger's coverage began the day the agent sent the application and premium to the insurance company.

62. Beth's health insurance policy contains a provision that allows her to renew coverage up to age 65. However, the policy also states that should Beth lose her job, the insurance company will cancel the policy, regardless of Beth's age. In terms of renewability, what type of policy does Beth have?

    A. Cancelable
    B. Optionally renewable
    C. Guaranteed renewable
    D. Conditionally renewable

63. HMOs are known for stressing which of the following?

    A. Preventive care
    B. Health care and services on a fee-for-services-rendered basis
    C. Health care and services in hospital settings
    D. Health care and services to government employees

64. Which of the following statements is NOT true of PPOs?

    A. A PPO is a group of health care providers, such as doctors, hospitals and ambulatory health care organizations, that contracts with a group to provide their services.
    B. PPOs operate on a prepaid basis.
    C. PPO members select from among the preferred providers for needed services.
    D. Groups that contract with PPOs are employers, insurance companies or other health insurance benefits providers.

65. All of the following benefits are available under Social Security EXCEPT

    A. welfare
    B. death
    C. old age or retirement
    D. disability

66. Which of the following kinds of assistance is provided by Medicaid?

    A. Funds to states for the provision of medical care to the aged
    B. Funds to states to assist their medical public assistance programs
    C. Funds to charitable organizations for providing medical benefits to poor people
    D. Medical benefits to those who contributed to its funding through payroll taxes

67. Mr. Ritchie, a taxidermist, is insured under a business overhead expense policy that pays maximum monthly benefits of $2,000. His actual monthly expenses are $2,700. If Mr. Ritchie becomes disabled, the monthly benefit payable under his policy will be

    A. $1,300
    B. $2,000
    C. $2,350
    D. $2,700

68. Which of the following statements about Medicare supplement (Medigap) policies is NOT correct?

    A. Medigap policies supplement Medicare benefits.
    B. Medigap policies cover the cost of extended nursing home care.
    C. Medigap policies pay most, if not all, Medicare deductibles and copayments.
    D. Medigap policies pay for some health care services not covered by Medicare.

69. Which of the following is NOT a typical type of long-term care coverage?

    E. Skilled nursing
    F. Home health
    G. Hospice
    H. Residential

70. All of the following are mandatory provisions in health insurance policies EXCEPT

    A. proof of loss
    B. entire contract
    C. change of beneficiary
    D. misstatement of age

71. Under the notice of claims provision of a health insurance policy, a policyowner must provide notification of loss within a reasonable period of time, usually how long?

    A. 10 days after an occurrence or a commencement of a loss
    B. 20 days after an occurrence or a commencement of a loss
    C. One month after an occurrence or a commencement of a loss
    D. No later than three months after an occurrence or a commencement of a loss

72. Paul is hospitalized with a back injury and, upon checking his disability income policy, learns that he will not be eligible for benefits for at least 60 days. This would indicate that his policy probably has a 60-day

    E. elimination period
    F. probationary period
    G. disability period
    H. blackout period

73. Major risk factors in health insurance underwriting include all of the following EXCEPT

    A. physical condition
    B. habits or lifestyle
    C. marital status
    D. occupation

74. Which of the following is known for stressing preventive health care?

    A. Administrative-services-only providers
    B. Blue Cross/Blue Shield
    C. HMOs
    D. Commercial insurers

75. Leonard owns a major medical health policy which requires him to pay the first $200 of covered expenses each year before the policy pays its benefits. The $200 is the policy's

    A. coinsurance amount
    B. deductible
    C. stop-loss amount
    D. annual premium

76. Basic hospital expense insurance provides coverage for all of the following EXCEPT

    A. hospital room and board
    B. anesthesia and use of the operating room and supplies
    C. physician services
    D. drugs and x-rays

77. All of the following approaches are used by insurers to determine benefits payable under basic surgical expense insurance EXCEPT

    A. relative value scale approach
    B. traditional net cost method
    C. reasonable and customary approach
    D. surgical schedule method

78. Basic surgical expense policies generally provide coverage for all of the following EXCEPT

    A. anesthesiologist services
    B. surgeon services
    C. postoperative care
    D. miscellaneous expenses, such as lab fees and x-rays

79. A waiver of premium provision may be included with which kind of health insurance policy?

    A. Hospital indemnity
    B. Major medical
    C. Disability income
    D. Basic medical

80. The minimum number of persons to be insured under a group health insurance plan is established by

    A. the NAIC
    B. state law
    C. federal law
    D. the employer

81. Alice has a major medical policy with a $500 deductible and an 80/20 coinsurance provision. If she receives a hospital bill for $7,500 of covered expenses, how much of that bill will she have to pay?

    A. $1,400
    B. $1,900
    C. $2,000
    D. $2,400

82. Which of the following reimburses its insureds for covered medical expenses?

    A. HMOs
    B. PPOs
    C. Commercial insurers
    D. Blue Cross/Blue Shield

83. Individual health insurance policies are typically written on which basis?

    A. Participating
    B. Nonparticipating
    C. Experience-rated
    D. Claims-rated

84. Workers' compensation covers income loss resulting from

    A. work-related disabilities
    B. plant and office closings
    C. job layoffs
    D. job terminations

85. As it pertains to group health insurance, COBRA stipulates that

    A. retiring employees must be allowed to convert their group coverage to individual policies
    B. terminated employees must be allowed to convert their group coverage to individual policies
    C. group coverage must be extended for terminated employees up to a certain period of time at the employee's expense
    D. group coverage must be extended for terminated employees up to a certain period of time at the employer's expense

86. Which of the following statements regarding morbidity tables is CORRECT?

    A. They indicate the average number of individuals from a given group who will die in a given year.
    B. They indicate the average number of individuals from a given group who will become disabled.
    C. They indicate the gender and number of individuals from a given group who will die in a given year.
    D. They indicate the gender and number of individuals from a given group who will become disabled in a given year.

87. All of the following are primary health insurance premium factors EXCEPT

    A. interest
    B. expense
    C. policy benefits
    D. morbidity

88. When a group disability insurance plan is paid entirely by the employer, benefits paid to disabled employees are

    A. taxable income to the employee
    B. deductible income to the employee
    C. deductible business expenses to the employer
    D. taxable income to the employer

89. Harry, the owner of a convenience store, is the insured under a business overhead policy. Were Harry to become disabled, the policy would cover all of the following EXCEPT

    A. his salary
    B. the store manager's salary
    C. the rent
    D. utility bills

90. All of the following are mandatory health insurance policy provisions EXCEPT

    A. change of occupation
    B. entire contract
    C. grace period
    D. reinstatement

91. Which renewability provision allows an insurer to terminate a health insurance policy on any date specified in the policy and to increase the premium for any class of insureds?

    A. Conditionally renewable
    B. Optionally renewable
    C. Guaranteed renewable
    D. Cancelable

92. What does the time of payment of claims provision require?

    A. Claims must be paid after the insurer is notified of a loss.
    B. Claims must be paid after the insurer is notified and receives proof of loss.
    C. The insured must submit proof of loss within a specified time, or the claim may be denied.
    D. The insured must periodically submit proof of loss in order to receive the claim.

93. By most insurers' definitions, *partial disability* is the

    A. loss of one or more limbs
    B. ability of a disabled insured to work at any job for which he or she is reasonably suited
    C. inability of the insured to work at his or her own job
    D. inability of the insured to perform certain important duties of his or her job

94. What is the period of time immediately following a disability during which benefits are not payable?

    A. Elimination period
    B. Probationary period
    C. Residual period
    D. Short-term disability period

95. All of the following are characteristics of group health insurance plans EXCEPT

    A. their benefits are more extensive than those under individual plans
    B. the parties to a group health contract are the employer and the employees
    C. employers may require employees to contribute to the premium payments
    D. the cost of insuring an individual is less than what would be charged for comparable benefits under an individual plan

96. Bill's medical expense policy states that it will pay him a flat $50 a day for each day he is hospitalized. The policy pays benefits on which basis?

    A. Reimbursement
    B. Indemnity
    C. Service
    D. Partial

97. After a week in the hospital, Lola receives a bill for $9,000 of covered expenses. Her major medical policy has a $250 deductible and a 75/25 coinsurance feature. How much of the total expense will Lola's policy cover?

    A. $2,063
    B. $6,063
    C. $6,563
    D. $8,753

98. A basic surgical expense policy that covers surgeons' fees on a schedule approach

    A. bases its benefits on what is customary for a particular area
    B. assigns a set of points to each surgical procedure
    C. assigns a dollar amount to each surgical procedure
    D. bases its benefits on a percentage of hospital room and board expenses

99. A stop-loss feature in a major medical policy specifies the maximum

    A. benefit amount the policy provides each year

    B. benefit amount the policy provides in a lifetime

    C. amount the insured must pay in premiums

    D. amount the insured must pay toward covered expenses

100. Which of the following is a standard optional provision for health policies?

    A. Grace period

    B. Physical exam and autopsy

    C. Change of beneficiary

    D. Misstatement of age

General Principles Answers & Rationale

1. **C.** The concept of insurance developed from the need to minimize the adverse effects of risk associated with the probability of financial loss.

2. **A.** Only pure risks are insurable because they involve merely the chance of loss. They are pure in the sense that they do not mix both profits and losses. Insurance is concerned with the economic problems created by pure risks.

3. **B.** Buying insurance is one of the most effective ways of transferring risk. Through the insurance contract, the burden of carrying the risk and indemnifying the financial loss is transferred from the individual to the insurance company.

4. **B.** The function of insurance is to safeguard against financial loss by having the losses of the few paid by the contributions of the many who are exposed to the same risk.

5. **C.** One of the criteria for an insurable risk is that it not be catastrophic. A principle of insurance holds that only a small portion of a given group will experience loss at any one time. Risks that would adversely affect large numbers of people or large amounts of property—wars or floods, for example—typically are not insurable.

6. **B.** Reserves can be defined as the amounts set aside to fulfill the insurance company's obligation to pay future claims. The reserve is compiled from past premium payments and interest.

7. **B.** Insurable interest requires the policyowner to benefit from the insured's continued life or good health or to suffer a loss from the insured's death or disability.

8. **C.** The parol evidence rule states that when parties put their agreement in writing, all previous verbal statements come together in that writing, and a written contract cannot be changed or modified by parol (oral) evidence.

9. **B.** If expenses and claims costs are less than expected, dividends are likely to be paid.

10. **A.** An agent is an individual who has been authorized by an insurer to be its representative to the public and to offer for sale its goods and services.

11. **D.** The new policy will probably be at a higher premium rate because it will be based on the insured's then-attained age.

12. **B.** To be insurable, a risk must involve a chance of loss that is fortuitous and outside the insured's control.

13. **C.** If an applicant does not submit an initial premium with the application, he or she is inviting the insurance company to make a contract offer. The insurer can respond by issuing a policy (the offer) that the applicant can accept by paying the premium when the policy is delivered.

14. **C.** Most states require that life insurance policies contain a provision which stipulates that all statements made in the application be deemed representations, not warranties. A representation is a statement made by the applicant that he or she believes to be true. A warranty is a statement made by the applicant that is guaranteed to be true. If an insurance company rejects a claim on the basis of a representation, the company bears the burden of proving materiality.

15. **B.** Insurance contracts are unilateral in that only one party—the insurer—makes any kind of enforceable promise.

16. **A.** Express authority is the authority a principal gives to its agent. It is granted by means

of the agent's contract, which is the principal's appointment of the agent to act on its behalf.

17. **C.** A peril is the immediate specific event causing loss and giving rise to risk. When a building burns, fire is the peril.

18. **A.** Consideration is the value given in exchange for the promises sought. In an insurance contract, consideration is given by the applicant in exchange for the insurer's promise to pay benefits and it consists of the application and the initial premium.

19. **A.** A warranty in insurance is a statement made by the applicant that is guaranteed to be true. It becomes part of the contract and, if found to be untrue, can be grounds for revoking the contract. Warranties are presumed to be material because they affect the insurer's decision to accept or reject an applicant.

20. **D.** Mutual insurers are owned by the policyholders. Anyone purchasing insurance from a mutual insurer is both a customer and an owner.

Principles of Life Insurance Answers & Rationale

21. **D.** Insurable interest is required only when a contract is issued; it does not have to be maintained throughout the life of the contract, nor is it necessary at the time of claim.

22. **A.** An insurer is termed *domestic* in a state when it is incorporated in that state.

23. **C.** A foreign company operates in a state in which it is not chartered and in which its home office is not located.

24. **A.** The accumulation that builds over the life of a policy is called the cash value, and it belongs to the policyowner, who may or may not be the insured.

25. **A.** In this case, the insured died after his term policy had expired. As a result, his beneficiary received nothing.

26. **B.** Policyowners actually own their policies and may do with them as they please. They can even give them away, just as they can give away any other kind of property they own. Nevertheless, they must notify the insurance company in writing of any transfers of ownership (assignments). The company must then accept the validity of the assignments without question.

27. **B.** The *blackout period* is the time during which no Social Security benefits are payable to a surviving spouse. This period begins when the youngest child reaches age 16 and continues until the spouse retires.

28. **C.** A buy-sell plan offers several advantages to the partners while they are all living. The partners know they will have a legal right to buy a deceased partner's share of the business, and the family and heirs of the partners know that the partnership interest will be disposed of at a fair price. Further, the money needed to purchase the deceased partner's interest will be available when

needed. All this adds up to security and peace of mind for all involved, including employees of the business.

29. **C.** Lump-sum proceeds payable upon the death of the insured are not subject to income tax, no matter who the beneficiary is.

30. **C.** The entire contract clause states that the policy document, the application, which is attached to the policy, and any attached riders constitute the entire contract. The policy cannot refer to any outside documents as part of the contract.

31. **B.** If the premium of a policy has not been paid and the insured dies during the grace period, the policy benefit is payable. However, the premium amount due is deducted from the benefits paid to the beneficiary.

32. **C.** The consideration clause specifies the amount and frequency of premium payments that the policyowner must make to keep the insurance in force.

33. **D.** There is a limited period of time in which policies may be reinstated after lapse. This period is usually three years, but in some cases may be as long as seven years.

34. **A.** When reinstating a life policy, no new suicide exclusion period goes into effect.

35. **A.** When Leland surrenders his whole life policy for a reduced paid-up policy, the face value is reduced but the cash value continues to increase.

36. **B.** Under the Uniform Simultaneous Death Act, if the insured and primary beneficiary are killed in the same accident and there is not sufficient evidence to show who died first, the policy proceeds are to be distributed as if the insured

died last. Kevin's estate would receive the proceeds because Lynda, the beneficiary, was deemed to have predeceased Kevin and no other beneficiary was named.

37. **C.** If a beneficiary is named irrevocable, the policyowner gives up his or her right to change that beneficiary and, unless otherwise specified in the policy, the owner cannot take any action that would affect the right of that beneficiary to receive the full amount of the insurance at the insured's death. This includes taking out a policy loan or surrendering the policy.

38. **C.** There are no cash values in term policies.

39. **C.** If the insured lives beyond the five-year period, the policy expires and no benefits are payable. There are no cash values in term policies.

40. **B.** Premiums for the renewal period will be higher because of the insured's advanced age and, thus, increased risk.

41. **B.** The joint and full survivor option provides for payment of the annuity to two people. If either person dies, the same income payments continue to the survivor for life. When the surviving annuitant dies, no further payments are made to anyone.

42. **D.** After the policy has been in force for the specified period, the company cannot contest a death claim or refuse payment of the proceeds even on the basis of a material misstatement, concealment or fraud.

43. **C.** The purpose of the Social Security system is to provide a basic floor of protection, to augment—not replace—a sound personal insurance plan. Many expect Social Security to fulfill all their financial needs and provide a meaningful standard of living. The consequences of this misunderstanding has been disillusionment by many Americans who found they were inadequately covered when they needed life insurance, disability income or retirement income.

44. **C.** A policyowner is allowed to receive tax free an amount equal to what he or she paid into the policy over the years in the form of premiums.

45. **D.** There is no new suicide exclusion period when a policy is reinstated.

46. **C.** Limited pay whole life policies have level premiums that are limited to a certain period (less than life), after which no more premiums are owed.

47. **C.** Under a binding receipt (or temporary insurance agreement), coverage is guaranteed at the time of application for the amount of insurance applied for. The temporary coverage continues until the policy is issued as requested, until the company offers a different policy or until the company rejects the application, but in no event for more than 60 days from the date the agreement was signed.

48. **D.** Risk selection is performed by insurance company underwriters.

49. **A.** Gross premium equals net single premium plus expense. The gross premium is what the policyowners are required to pay.

50. **B.** Premiums paid for life insurance owned by a qualified charitable organization are deductible.

51. **A.** Whole life insurance is designed to mature at age 100. At age 100, the cash value of the policy has accumulated to the point that it equals the face amount of the policy, as it was actuarially designed to do. At that point the policy has completely matured or endowed. No more premiums are owed; the policy is completely paid up.

52. **C.** The larger the face amount of the policy, the larger the cash values; the shorter the premium-payment period, the quicker the cash values grow; and the longer the policy has been in force, the greater the build-up in cash values.

53. **B.** One of the rights of owning a life insurance policy is the right to designate and change the beneficiary of the policy proceeds.

54. **D.** Anyone under the age of 70½ who has earned income may open an IRA and contribute an amount up to $2,000 or 100 percent of compensation, whichever is less, in 2001. Contributions grow tax free until they are withdrawn.

55. **B.** A primary beneficiary is the party designated to receive the proceeds of a life insurance policy when they become payable.

56. **C.** The application for insurance is the basic source of insurability information. It is the first source of information to be reviewed, and it is reviewed thoroughly.

57. **B.** Most life insurance policies exclude the following risks: war, aviation, hazardous occupation or hobbies, commission of a felony and suicide.

58. **C.** A family income policy is a combination of whole life and decreasing term covering a select period of years. If the insured dies within the specified period, the policy provides a certain monthly income from the date of death until the end of the specified period. This period is known as the *income period* and the monthly payments are accomplished by the term insurance. At the end of the specified period, the face amount of the whole life policy is payable to the beneficiary. If the insured lives beyond the specified income period, only the face amount of the whole life policy is payable.

59. **C.** If policyowners forget or neglect to pay their premiums by the date they are due, the grace period allows an extra 30 days or one month during which premiums may be paid to keep policies in force.

60. **C.** When beneficiaries are designated *irrevocable*, the policyowner gives up the right to change them. Irrevocable beneficiaries have a vested right in the policy and the policyowner cannot exercise his or her rights of ownership without the beneficiary's consent.

Principles of Health Insurance Answers & Rationale

61. **B.** The insurability type of conditional receipt provides that when an applicant pays the initial premium, coverage is effective—on the condition that the applicant proves to be insurable—either on the date the application was signed or the date of the medical examination, if one is required.

62. **D.** A conditionally renewable policy allows an insurer to terminate the coverage, but only in the event of one or more conditions stated in the contract. These conditions cannot apply to the insured's health. Most frequently, they are related to the insured reaching a certain age or losing gainful employment.

63. **A.** HMOs stress preventive care to reduce the number of unnecessary hospital admissions and duplication of services.

64. **B.** Unlike HMOs, PPOs usually operate on a fee-for-service-rendered basis, not a prepaid basis.

65. **A.** Social Security provides death benefits, old age or retirement benefits and disability benefits to eligible workers. Social Security is an entitlement program, not a welfare program.

66. **B.** Medicaid provides matching federal funds to states for their medical public assistance programs to help needy persons, regardless of age.

67. **B.** Business overhead expense insurance reimburses business for the covered expenses incurred or the maximum that is stated in the policy. If Mr. Ritchie's monthly expenses were $1,700, his plan would have paid a monthly benefit of $1,700. However, because Mr. Ritchie's expenses exceeded his maximum coverage, the policy pays the maximum benefit stated in the policy, $2,000.

68. **B.** Medigap policies do not cover the cost of extended nursing home care.

69. **C.** Long-term care services are designed for senior citizens, and hospice services are for terminally ill persons and their families.

70. **D.** Misstatement of age is an optional provision of health insurance policies.

71. **B.** Under the notice of claims provision, an insured must provide notification of loss 20 days after an occurrence or a commencement of a loss.

72. **A.** Similar in concept to a deductible, the elimination period is the time immediately following the start of a disability when benefits are not payable.

73. **C.** Physical condition, habits or lifestyle (moral hazards) and occupation are major risk factors in health insurance. Marital status is not a risk factor.

74. **C.** Health maintenance organizations stress preventive care to promote patient health and to control the use of health care resources, particularly expensive resources like hospitals.

75. **B.** A deductible is a stated initial dollar amount that the individual insured is required to pay before insurance benefits are paid.

76. **C.** Physicians' services are not covered under a basic hospital expense policy, even in the case of surgery. The cost for a physician is covered under a basic surgical expense or basic physician's (nonsurgical) expense policy.

77. **B.** The traditional net cost method is a way of comparing costs of similar policies.

78. **D.** Miscellaneous expenses are covered under basic hospital expense policies. These

extras include drugs, x-rays, anesthesia, lab fees, dressings, use of the operating room and supplies.

79. **C.** A waiver of premium rider generally is included with guaranteed renewable and noncancelable individual disability income policies. It is a valuable provision because it exempts the policyowner from paying the policy's premiums during periods of total disability.

80. **B.** State laws specify the minimum number of persons to be covered under a group policy. One state may stipulate 15 persons as a minimum number, while another state may require a minimum of 10. (10 is the most typical minimum requirement.)

81. **B.** Alice's responsibility for payment is calculated in the following manner:

Total expenses	$ 7,500
Deductible Alice pays	− 500
Basis for insurer's payment	$ 7,000
	× .80
Amount insurer pays	$ 5,600
Coinsurance amount Alice pays	$ 1,400
Deductible	+ 500
Total Alice pays	$ 1,900

82. **C.** Commercial insurance companies function on the reimbursement approach. Policyowners obtain medical treatment from whatever source they feel is most appropriate and, per the terms of their policy, submit their charges to their insurer for reimbursement.

83. **B.** Most individual health insurance is issued on a nonparticipating basis.

84. **A.** All states have workers' compensation laws, which were enacted to provide mandatory benefits to employees for work-related injuries, illness or death.

85. **C.** COBRA requires employers with 20 or more employees to continue group medical expense coverage for terminated workers (as well as their spouses, divorced spouses and dependent children) for up to 18 months (or 36 months, in some situations) following termination. However, the terminated employee can be required to pay the premium, which may be up to 102 percent of the premium that would otherwise be charged.

86. **B.** Whereas mortality rates show the average number of persons within a larger group of people who can be expected to die within a given year at a given age, morbidity tables indicate the average number of individuals at various ages who can be expected to become disabled each year due to accident or sickness. They also reveal the average duration of disability.

87. **C.** There are three primary factors that affect health insurance premiums: morbidity, interest and expenses.

88. **A.** Disability benefit payments that are attributed to employee contributions are not taxable, but benefit payments that are attributed to employer contributions are taxable.

89. **A.** Business overhead expense policies do not include any compensation for the disabled owner.

90. **A.** Change of occupation is an optional provision.

91. **B.** The renewability provision in an optionally renewable policy gives the insurer the option to terminate the policy on the date specified in the contract. Furthermore, this provision allows the insurer to increase the premium for any class of optionally renewable insureds.

92. **B.** The time of payment of claims provision provides for immediate payment of the claim after the insurer receives notification and proof of loss.

93. **D.** By most definitions, partial disability is the inability of the insured to perform one or more important duties of his or her job.

94. **A.** The elimination period is the time immediately following the start of a disability when benefits are not payable. Elimination

periods eliminate claims for short-term disabilities for which the insured can usually manage without financial hardship and save the insurance company from the expense of processing and settling small claims.

95. **B.** The contract for coverage is between the insurance company and the employer, and a master policy is issued to the employer.

96. **B.** Indemnity medical expense policies do not pay expenses or bills; they merely provide the insured with a stated benefit amount for each day he or she is confined to a hospital as an in-patient. The money may be used by the insured for any purpose.

97. **C.** Lola's responsibility for payment is calculated in the following manner:

Total expenses	$ 9,000
Deductible Lola pays	– 250
Basis for insurer's payment	$ 8,750
	× .75
Amount insurer pays	$ 6,563
Coinsurance Lola pays	$ 2,187

98. **C.** Under the surgical schedule method, every surgical procedure is assigned a dollar amount by the insurer. When a claim is submitted to the insurer, the claims examiner reviews the policy to determine what amount is payable; if the surgeon's bill is more than the allowed charge set by the insurer, it is up to the insured to pay the surgeon the difference. If the surgeon's bill is less than the allowed charge, the insurer will pay only the full amount billed; the claim payment will never exceed the amount charged.

99. **D.** To provide a safeguard for insureds, many major medical policies contain a stop-loss feature that limits the insured's out-of-pocket expenses. This means that once the insured has paid a specified amount toward his or her covered expenses—usually $1,000 to $2,000—the company pays 100 percent of covered expenses after that point.

100. **D.** Misstatement of age is one of eleven optional policy provisions. Companies may ignore them or use them in their policy forms.

Glossary

A

absolute assignment A policy assignment under which the assignee (person to whom the policy is assigned) receives full control over the policy and also full rights to its benefits. Generally, when a policy is assigned to secure a debt, the owner retains all rights in the policy in excess of the debt, even though the assignment is absolute in form. *See also* assignee; assignment; assignor.

accelerated benefits rider A life insurance rider that allows for the early payment of some portion of the policy's face amount should the insured suffer from a terminal illness or injury.

acceptance One party's agreement to the purchase offer of another party, such that a legal contract is formed and both parties are contractually bound. With an insurance contract, acceptance generally takes place when the agent binds coverage or the policy is issued. *See also* offer and acceptance.

accidental bodily injury provision A disability income or accident policy provision that requires that the injury be accidental in order for benefits to be payable.

accidental death and dismemberment (AD&D) This is insurance that provides payment if the insured's death results from an accident, if the insured accidentally severs a limb above the wrist or ankle joints or totally and irreversibly loses his or her eyesight.

accidental death benefit rider A life insurance policy rider that provides for payment of an additional benefit related to the face amount of the base policy when death occurs by accidental means.

accidental dismemberment Often defined as *the severance of limbs at or above the wrists or ankle joints, or the entire irrevocable loss of sight.* Loss of use in itself may or may not be considered dismemberment.

accidental means provision The unforeseen, unexpected or unintended cause of an accident; requirement of an accident-based policy that the cause of the mishap be accidental for any claim to be payable.

accident and health insurance An insurance policy under which benefits are payable in case of disease, accidental injury or accidental death. Also called health insurance, personal health insurance and sickness and accident insurance.

accumulation unit The premiums an annuitant pays into a variable annuity are credited as accumulation units. At the end of the accumulation period, accumulation units are converted to annuity units.

acquired immune deficiency syndrome (AIDS) A life-threatening condition brought on by the human immunodeficiency virus; insurers must adhere to strict underwriting and claims guidelines in regard to AIDS risks and AIDS-related conditions.

acute illness A serious condition, such as pneumonia, from which the body can fully recover with proper medical attention.

adhesion A life insurance policy is a contract of adhesion because buyers must adhere to the terms of the contract already in existence. They have no opportunity to negotiate terms, rates, values, etc.

adjustable life insurance This products combines features of both term and whole life coverage and has adjustable lengths of coverage and amounts of accumulated cash value. Premiums may be increased or decreased to fit specific needs. Such adjustments are not retroactive and apply only to the future.

administrative-services-only (ASO) plan An arrangement under which an insurance company or an independent organization, for a fee, handles the administration of claims, benefits and other administrative functions for a self-insured group.

admitted insurer An insurance company that has met the legal and financial requirements for operation within a given state.

adult day care A type of care offered in care centers (usually custodial) designed for individuals who require assistance with various activities of daily living while their primary caregivers are absent.

adverse selection The tendency of insureds who present a higher probability of loss to purchase or renew insurance more often than those who present a lower probability; selection against the best interests of the insurance company (e.g., people near rivers purchasing flood insurance); tendency of policyowners to take advantage of favorable options in insurance contracts.

advertising code The rules established by the National Association of Insurance Commissioners (NAIC) to regulate insurance advertising.

agency The legal principle that allows an individual or organization to represent another individual or organization.

agent A person licensed by the state insurance authority to sell insurance products. The agent represents the insurance company in all transactions. *See also* broker; producer.

agent's report The section of an insurance application where the agent reports his or her personal observations about the applicant.

aleatory A kind of contract in which one party may obtain greater value under the agreement than the other party and in which payment depends upon a fortuitous event. An insurance contract is an aleatory contract.

alien insurer An insurance company incorporated and organized under the laws of a foreign nation, state, province or territory, rather than under the laws of the United States.

ambulatory surgery Surgery performed on an outpatient basis.

Amicable Society for a Perpetual Assistance Office England's first successful life insurance company; founded in 1705.

amount at risk The difference between the face amount of the policy and the reserve or policy value at a given time. In other words, the dollar amount over what the policyowner has contributed of cash value toward payment of his or her own claim. Because the cash value increases every year, the net amount at risk decreases until it finally reaches zero, at which time the cash value or reserve becomes the face amount.

annually renewable term (ART) A form of renewable term insurance that provides coverage for one year and allows the policyowner to renew his or her coverage each year without evidence of insurability. Also called yearly renewable term (YRT).

annuitant A person to whom an annuity is payable, or upon the continuance of whose life further payment depends.

annuity A contract that provides a stipulated sum payable at certain regular intervals (1) during the lifetime of one or more persons or (2) for a specified period only.

annuity unit The number of annuity units denotes the share of funds an annuitant will receive from a variable annuity account after the accumulation period ends and benefits begin. A formula is used to convert accumulation units to annuity units.

any occupation A definition of total disability that requires the insured to be unable to perform any job for which he or she is, "reasonably suited by reason of education, training or experience," in order to receive disability income benefits.

apparent authority The authority the general public assumes an agent has due to his or her actions, regardless of whether the authority has been given to the agent by law or contract.

application Form supplied by the insurance company, usually filled in the by the agent and medical examiner (if applicable) on the basis of information received from the applicant. It is signed by the applicant and is part of the insurance policy if it is issued. It gives information to the home office underwriting department so it may consider whether an insurance policy will be issued and, if so, in what classification and at what premium rate.

appointment The authorization or certification of an agent to act for or represent an insurance company.

approval receipt Rarely used today, this is a type of conditional receipt that provides that coverage is effective as of the date the application is approved (before the policy is delivered).

Armstrong Investigation An investigation of a large number of insurance companies in the United States in 1905 that led to the enactment of stricter state supervision and insurance requirements.

assessment insurance A plan by which either the amount of insurance or the number and amount of the assessments are variable. It is offered by either pure or advance assessment associations.

assessment mutual insurer An insurance company characterized by member-insureds who are assessed an individual portion of each loss that occurs. No premium payment is payable in advance.

assignee A person (including a corporation, partnership or other organization) to whom a right or rights under a policy are transferred by means of an assignment

assignment The legal transfer of a policyowner's rights or interests in an insurance policy to another party. The insured requests the assignment, and, barring state law, the company can either accept or reject the request.

assignment provision (health contracts) A commercial health policy provision that allows the policyowner to assign benefit payments from the insurer to directly to the health care provider.

assignor A person (including a corporation, partnership or other organization or entity) who transfers a right or rights under an insurance policy to another by means of an assignment.

attained age With reference to an insured, the current insurance age.

authority The actions and deeds an agent is authorized to conduct on behalf of an insurance company, as specified in the agent's contract.

authorized company An insurer that meets the licensing criteria of the state it wishes to do business in and has received a certificate of authority. Also known as an admitted company.

automatic premium loan provision This authorizes insurer to pay any premium in default automatically at the end of the grace period and charge the amount so-paid against the life insurance policy as a policy loan.

average indexed monthly earnings (AIME) The basis used for calculating the primary insurance amount (PIA) for Social Security benefits.

average monthly wage (AMW) The average wage base for computing virtually all Social Security benefits prior to 1979.

aviation exclusion This excludes from coverage certain deaths or disabilities due to aviation for those, "other than fare-paying passengers." May be attached by rider or included in standard policy language.

B

back dating The practice of making a policy effective at a date earlier than the present.

basic medical expense policy This is a health insurance policy that provides first dollar benefits for specified (and limited) health care, such as hospitalization, surgery or physician services and that is characterized by limited benefit periods and relatively low coverage limits.

beneficiary A person to whom the proceeds of a life or accident policy are payable when the insured dies. The various types of beneficiaries are: primary (those first entitled to proceeds), secondary (those entitled to proceeds if no primary beneficiary is living when the insured dies) and tertiary (those entitled to proceeds if no primary or secondary beneficiaries are alive when the insured dies).

benefit May be either the money or the right(s) given to the policyowner if the conditions set out in the policy come to pass.

benefit period The maximum length of time that insurance benefits will be paid for any one accident, illness or hospital stay.

Best's Insurance Report A guide, published by A.M. Best, Inc., that rates insurers' financial integrity and managerial and operational strengths.

binder A written note that temporarily obligates an insurer to provide insurance in the amount of $1 million or more; it effectively puts insurance into force before a contract has been written or the premium paid. A binder is usually good for 90 days.

binding receipt This is given by a company upon an applicant's first premium payment. The policy, if approved, becomes effective from the date of the receipt.

blackout period The period following the death of a family breadwinner during which no Social Security benefits are available to the surviving spouse.

blanket policy This covers a number of individuals who are exposed to the same hazards, such as members of an athletic team, company officials who are passengers in the same company plane, etc.

Blue Cross Independent, nonprofit membership organization providing protection against the costs of hospital care in a limited geographical area. Benefit payments are made directly to the hospital; benefits vary among Blue Cross organizations.

Blue Shield Independent, nonprofit membership organization providing protection against the costs of surgery and other items of medical care in a limited geographical area. Benefit payments are made directly to the company.

broker A licensed insurance representative who does not represent a specific company, but places business among various companies. Legally, the broker is usually regarded as a representative of the insured rather than the company.

business continuation plan Arrangements between the businessowners that provide that the shares owned by any one of them shall be sold to and purchased by the other co-owners or the business in the event of death or disablement.

business health insurance This is insurance issued primarily to indemnify a business for the loss of services of a key employee, partner or active close corporation stockholder.

business overhead expense insurance A form of disability income coverage designed to pay necessary business overhead expenses, such as rent, should the insured businessowner become disabled.

buyer's guides Informational consumer guide books that explain insurance policies and insurance concepts; in many states, they must be given to applicants when certain types of coverages are being considered.

buy-sell agreement An agreement that a decreased businessowner's interest will be sold and purchased at a predetermined price or according to a predetermined formula.

C

cafeteria plan An employee benefit arrangement in which employees can select from a range of benefits.

cancelable contact A health insurance contract that may be terminated by the company or renewed at its option.

capital sum The amount provided for accidental dismemberment or loss of eyesight. Indemnities for loss of one member or sight of one eye are percentages of the capital sum.

career agency system A method of marketing, selling and distributing insurance, represented by agencies or branch offices committed to the ongoing recruitment and development of career agents.

carrier Another term for an insurer or an entity responsible for the payment of benefits under an insurance policy; i.e., an insurer *carries* the risk for the policyowner(s).

case management The professional arrangement and coordination of health services through assessment, service plan development and monitoring.

cash or deferred arrangements A qualified employer retirement plan under which employees can defer amounts of their salaries into a retirement plan. These amounts are not included in the employee's gross income and so are tax-deferred. Also called 401(k) plans.

cash refund annuity This provides that, upon the death of an annuitant before payments totaling the purchase price have been made, the excess of the amount paid by the purchaser over the total annuity payments received will be paid in one sum to designated beneficiaries.

cash surrender option A nonforfeiture option that allows whole life insurance policyowners to receive a payout of their policy's cash values.

cash surrender value Amount available to the owner when a life insurance policy is surrendered to the company. During the early policy years, the cash value is the reserve less a surrender charge; in later policy years, it usually equals or closely approximates the reserve value at time of surrender.

cash value The equity amount or savings accumulation in a whole life policy.

chronic condition A treatable but incurable illness, such as arthritis or hypertension.

class designation A beneficiary designation. Rather than specifying one or more beneficiaries by name, the policyowner designates a class or group of beneficiaries. For example, "my children."

classification Occupational category of a risk.

cleanup fund A basic use for life insurance; this is a reserve to cover costs of last illness, burial, legal and administrative expenses, miscellaneous outstanding bills, etc. Also called a final expense fund.

close corporation A corporation owned by a small group of stockholders, each of whom usually has a voice in operation the business.

closed-panel HMO A group of physicians who are salaried employees of an HMO and who work in facilities provided by the HMO.

Consolidated Omnibus Budget Reconciliation Act (COBRA) of 1985 This law extended group health coverage to terminated employees and their families for up to 18 or 36 months.

coinsurance (percentage participation) The principle under which the company insures only part of the potential loss, and the policyowners paying the other part. For instance, in a major medical policy, the company may agree to pay 75 percent of the insured expenses, and the insured must pay the other 25.

collateral assignment The assignment of a policy to a creditor as security for a debt. The creditor is entitled to be reimbursed out of policy proceeds for the amount owed. The beneficiary is entitled to any excess of policy proceeds over the amount due the creditor in the event of the insured's death.

combination company A company whose agents sell both weekly premium life and health insurance as well as ordinary life insurance.

commercial health insurers Insurance companies that function on the reimbursement approach, which allows policyowners first to seek medical treatment and then to submit the charges to the insurer for reimbursement.

commissioner The head of a state insurance department; public officer charged with supervising the insurance business in a state and administrating insurance laws. Called "superintendent" in some states, and "director" in others.

commissioner's standard ordinary (CSO) table The table of mortality based on intercompany experience over a period of time, which is legally recognized as the mortality basis for computing maximum reserves on policies issued within past years. The 1980 CSO Table replaced the 1958 CSO Table.

common disaster provision This is sometimes added to a policy and designed to provide an alternative beneficiary in the event that both the insured and the original beneficiary die as the result of a common accident.

competent parties A person capable of understanding the contract being agreed to; to be enforceable, a contract must be entered into by competent parties.

comprehensive major medical insurance This is designed to give the protection offered by both a basic medical expense and major medical policy. It is characterized by a low deductible amount, coinsurance clause and high maximum benefits.

concealment The deliberate withholding of material facts that would affect the validity of an insurance policy or a claim under the policy.

conditional contract A contract that is in force only if certain obligations are met or events come to pass. In regard to an insurance contract, the payment of benefits is dependent on or a condition of the occurrence of the risk insured against.

conditionally renewable contract A health insurance policy that provides that the insured may renew the contract from period to period or continue it to a stated date or an advanced age, subject to the right of the insurer to decline renewal under the conditions defined in the contract.

conditioned receipt This is given to the policyowners when they pay a premium at the time of application. Such receipts bind the insurance company if the risk is approved as applied for, subject to any other conditions stated on the receipt.

conservation The activities involved in taking over and managing the affairs of a financially troubled insurer; the efforts involved in keeping insurance policies in force and/or reinstating lapsed policies.

consideration The inducement to complete a contract, for example, the premium paid by the insured and the promise to pay made by the insurer.

consideration clause The part of an insurance contract that sets forth the amount of initial and renewal premiums and frequency of future payments.

contestable period The period during which the company may contest a claim on a policy because of misleading or incomplete information furnished in the application.

contingent beneficiary The person or persons named to receive proceeds in case the original beneficiary is no longer living. Also referred to as secondary or tertiary beneficiary.

contract An agreement (offer and acceptance) between two parties who have legal capacity to contract that involves valuable consideration and that does not violate any statute or other legal rule.

contract of agency A legal document that contains the terms of the contract between the agent and company, signed by both parties. Also called an agency agreement.

contributory plan A group insurance plan issued to an employer under which both the employer and employees contribute to the cost of the plan. Generally, 75 percent of the eligible employees must be insured. *See also* noncontributory plan.

conversion privilege This allows the policyowner, before an original insurance policy expires, to elect to have a new policy issued that will continue the insurance coverage. Conversion may be effected at attained age (premiums based on the age attained at time of conversion) or at original age (premiums based on age at time of original issue).

convertible term An insurance contract that may be converted to a permanent form of insurance without medical examination.

coordination of benefits (COB) provision This is designed to prevent duplication of group insurance benefits. It limits benefits from multiple group health insurance policies in a particular case to 100 percent of the expenses covered and designates the order in which the multiple carriers are to pay benefits.

corridor deductible In superimposed major medical plans, this is the deductible amount between the benefits paid by the basic plan and the beginning of the major medical benefits.

cost of living (COL) rider A rider available with some policies that provides for an automatic increase in benefits (typically tied to the Consumer Price Index) to offset the effects of inflation.

coverage requirements The standards of coverage that prevent retirement plans from discrimination in favor of highly compensated employees. A plan must pass an IRS coverage test to be considered qualified.

covering note A written note prepared by an agent or broker, usually good for 90 days, that informs the insured that coverage is in effect before a contract has been written or the premium paid. *See also* binder.

credit accident and health insurance This pays policy premiums during the disability period or pays off an outstanding loan if the insured debtor becomes totally disabled due to an accident or sickness. May be individual or group policy.

credit life insurance This is usually written as decreasing term on a relatively small decreasing balance installment loan that may reflect direct borrowing or a balance due for merchandise purchased. If the borrower dies, benefits pay the balance due. May be individual or group policy.

credit report A summary of an insurance applicant's credit history, made by an independent organization that has investigated the applicant's credit standing.

cross-purchase plan An agreement that provides that upon a businessowner's death, surviving owners will purchase the deceased interest, often with funds from life insurance policies owned by each principal on the lives of all other principals.

currently insured A status of limited eligibility under Social Security that provides only death benefits.

custodial care The level of health or medical care given to meet daily personal needs, such as dressing, bathing, getting out of bed, etc. Though it does not require medical training, it must be administered under a physician's order.

D

death rate The proportion of persons in each age group who die within a year; usually expressed as so many deaths per thousand persons. *See also* expected mortality.

debit insurer *See* home service insurer.

decreasing term insurance This is term life insurance on which the face value slowly decreases in scheduled steps from the date the policy comes into force to the date the policy expires, while the premium remains level. The intervals between decreases are usually monthly or annual.

deductible The amount of expense or loss to be paid by the insured before a health insurance policy starts paying benefits.

deferred annuity This provides for the postponement of the commencement of an annuity until after a specified period or until the annuitant attains a specified age. May be purchased either on single-premium or flexible premium basis.

deferred compensation plan The deferral of an employee's compensation to some future age or date. These plans are frequently used to provide fringe benefits, such as retirement income, to selected personnel.

defined benefit plan A pension plan under which benefits are determined by a specific benefit formula.

defined contribution plan A tax-qualified retirement plan in which annual contributions are determined by a formula set for those in the plan. Benefits paid to a participant vary with the amount of contributions made on his or her behalf and the length of service under the plan.

delayed disability provision A disability income policy provision that allows a certain amount of time after an accident for a disability to result during which the insured remains eligible for benefits.

dental insurance A relatively new form of health insurance coverage typically offered on a group basis. It covers the costs of normal dental maintenance as well as oral surgery and root canal therapy.

dependency period The period following the death of the breadwinner up until the youngest child reaches maturity.

deposit term An insurance product with a modest endowment feature. It is normally sold for ten-year terms with a higher first-year premium than for subsequent years. If policy lapses, insured forfeits his or her deposit and receives no refund.

disability A physical or mental impairment that makes a person incapable of performing one or more duties of his or her occupation.

disability buy-sell agreement An agreement between business co-owners that provides that shares owned by any one of them who becomes disabled shall be sold to and purchased by the other co-owners or by the business using funds from disability income insurance.

disability income insurance A type of health insurance coverage that provides for the payment of regular, periodic income should the insured become disabled illness or injury.

disability income rider This is typically a rider to a life insurance policy that provides benefits in the form of income in the event the insured becomes totally disabled.

discrimination In insurance, this is the act of treating certain groups of people unfairly in the sale or pricing of policies; or of treating any of a given class of risk differently from other like risks. Discrimination is expressly prohibited in most state insurance codes.

dividend The policyowner's share in the divisible surplus of a company issuing insurance on the participating plan.

dividend options The different ways in which the insured under a participating life insurance policy may elect to receive surplus earnings: in cash, as a reduction of premium, as additional paid-up insurance, left on deposit at interest, or as additional term insurance.

domestic insurer An insurance company that writes business in the state or province of its incorporation or charter.

dread disease policy *See* limited risk policy.

E

elimination period The duration of time between the beginning of an insured's disability and the commencement of the period for which benefits are payable.

employee benefit plans Plans through which employers offer employees benefits such as coverage for medical expenses, disability, retirement and death.

employee stock ownership plan (ESOP) A form of defined contribution profit-sharing plan that ESOP invests primarily in the securities or stock of the employer.

endowment A contract that provides for payment of the face amount at the end of a fixed period, at a specified age of the insured or at the insured's death before the end of the stated period.

endowment period The period specified in an endowment policy during which, if the insured dies, the beneficiary receives a death benefit. If the insured is still living at the end of the endowment period, he or she receives the endowment as a living benefit.

enhanced whole life A whole life insurance policy issued by a mutual insurer, in which policy dividends are used to provide extra death benefits or to reduce future premiums.

enrollment period The period during which new employees can sign up for coverage under a group insurance plan.

entire contract provision An insurance policy provision that states that the application and policy contain all provisions and constitute the entire contract.

entity plan An agreement in which a business assumes the obligation of purchasing a deceased owner's interest in the business, thereby proportionately increasing the interests of surviving owners.

equity-indexed annuity A fixed deferred annuity that offers the traditional guaranteed minimum interest rate and an excess interest feature that is based on the performance of an external equities market index.

errors and omissions (E&O) insurance This is professional liability insurance that protects an insurance producer against claims arising from service he or she rendered or failed to render.

estate This is, most commonly, the quantity of wealth or property remaining at an individual's death.

estate tax The federal tax imposed on the value of property transferred by an individual at his or her death.

estoppel The legal impediment to denying the consequences of one's actions or deeds if they lead to detrimental actions by another.

evidence of insurability Any statement or proof of a person's physical condition, occupation, etc., that affects acceptance of the applicant for insurance.

examiner A physician authorized by the medical director of an insurance company to make medical examination person assigned by a state insurance company.

excess interest The difference between the rate of interest the company guarantees to pay on proceeds left under settlement options and the interest actually paid on such funds by the company.

exclusion ratio A fraction used to determine the amount of annual annuity income exempt from federal income tax. The exclusion ratio is the total contributions or investment in the annuity divided by the expected ratio.

exclusion rider A health insurance policy rider that waives the insurer's liability for all future claims on a preexisting condition.

exclusions These are specified hazards listed in a policy for which benefits will not be paid.

exclusive provider organization (EPO) A variation of the PPO concept, an EPO contracts with an extremely limited number of physicians and typically only one hospital to provide services to members; members who elect to get health care from outside the EPO receive no benefits. *See also* preferred provider organization.

expected mortality The number of deaths that theoretically should occur among a group of insured persons during a given period, according to the mortality table in use. Normally, a lower mortality rate is anticipated and generally experienced.

experience rating The review of the previous year's claims experience for a group insurance contract in order to establish premiums for the next period.

express authority The authority given to an agent or agency directly by means of the agency agreement or contract.

extended term insurance A nonforfeiture option that provides for the cash surrender value of a policy to be used as a net single premium (at the insured's attained age) to purchase term insurance for the face amount of the policy, less indebtedness, for as long a period as possible (but no longer than the term of the original policy.)

extra percentage tables Mortality or morbidity tables that indicate the percentage amount increase of premium for certain impaired health conditions.

F

face amount This commonly refers to the principal sum involved in the insurance contract. The actual amount payable may be decreased by loans or increased by additional benefits payable under conditions specified or stated in the rider.

facility of payment provision A clause permitted under a uniform health insurance policy provision that allows the company to pay up to $1,000 in benefits or proceeds to any relative who appears entitled to it if there is no named beneficiary or if the insured or beneficiary is a minor or legally incompetent.

facultative reinsurance The reinsurance of individual risks at the reinsurer's option. *See also* reinsurance; treaty reinsurance.

fair credit reporting act A Federal law requiring an individual to be informed if he or she is being investigated by an inspection company.

family income policy A combination of ordinary life and decreasing term insurance covering a period of 5,10,15, or 20 years. The term insurance is sufficient to provide (often when supplemented by interest on the ordinary life insurance) a specified monthly income from the date of death until the end of the specified income period. The principal sum of the ordinary insurance is payable when monthly income from the term insurance ceases or upon subsequent death.

family maintenance (family protection) policy Similar to the family income policy, this combines ordinary and term insurance, but without the decreasing insurance feature. Beginning at the insured's death, it provides for payment of an income for a fixed period of 10, 15 or 20 years from the date of death (not from the date of issue, as in the family income policy), with payment of the principal sum of the ordinary insurance at the end of the fixed period.

family plan policy An all-family plan of protection, usually with permanent insurance on the primary wage earner's life and with spouse and children automatically covered for lesser amounts of protection, usually term, all included for one premium.

Federal Insurance Act (FICA) The contributions made by employees and employers to fund Social Security benefits.

fiduciary A person who occupies a position of special trust and confidence regarding the handling or supervision of the affairs or funds of another. Examples are trustees, executors, administrators, corporate directors and insurance agents.

final expense fund *See* cleanup fund.

fixed-amount settlement option A life insurance settlement option whereby the beneficiary instructs that proceeds be paid in regular installments of a fixed dollar amount. The number of payment periods is determined by the policy's face amount, the amount of each payment and the interest earned.

fixed annuity A type of annuity that provides a guaranteed fixed benefit amount payable for the life of the annuitant.

fixed-period settlement option A life insurance settlement option in which the number of payments is fixed by the payee, with the amount of each payment determined by the amount of proceeds.

flat deductible The amount of covered expenses that must be paid by the insured before medical benefits are payable.

foreign insurer An insurance company that operates in a state other than the one in which it is incorporated or chartered.

franchise insurance A life or health insurance plan for covering groups of persons with individual policies uniform in provisions, although perhaps different in benefits. Solicitation usually takes place in an employer's business with the employer's consent. It is generally written for groups too small or qualify for regular group coverage. May be called wholesale insurance when the policy is life insurance.

fraternal benefit insurer A nonprofit benevolent organization that provides insurance to its members.

fraud An intentional concealment or false representation of a material fact that intends to take something of value or to force the surrender of a right. Fraud can only be determined by a court of appropriate jurisdiction.

free look A provision required in most states whereby policyholders have either 10 or 20 days to examine their new policies at no obligation.

fully funded In a retirement plan, a status in which the funds necessary to meet the financial obligations of the plan are accumulated in a reserve while the plan is in operation.

fully insured A status of complete eligibility for the full range of Social Security benefits: death benefits, retirement benefits, disability benefits and Medicare benefits.

funding In a retirement plan, the setting aside of funds for the payment of benefits.

G

general agent An independent agent with the authority, under contract with the company, to appoint soliciting agents within a designated territory and fix their compensation.

gift tax A Federal tax imposed on the (lifetime) transfer of property for less than full consideration.

government insurer An organization that, as an extension of the federal or state government, provides a program of social insurance.

grace period The period of time after the due date of a premium during which the policy remains in force without penalty.

graded premium whole life This is a variation of a traditional whole life contract that provides for lower than normal premium rates during the first few policy years, with premiums increasing gradually each year. After the preliminary period, premiums level off and remain constant.

gross premium The total premium paid by the policyowner, it generally consists of the net premium plus the expense of operation minus interest.

group credit insurance A form of group insurance issued by insurance companies to creditors to cover the lives of debtors for the amounts of their loans.

group insurance This is insurance that provides coverage for a group of persons, usually employees of a company, under one master contract.

group model HMO *See* closed-panel HMO.

guaranteed insurability (guaranteed issue) A arrangement, usually provided by rider, whereby additional insurance may be purchased at various times without evidence of insurability.

guaranteed renewable contract A health insurance contract that the insured has the right to continue in force by payment of premiums for a substantial period of time during which the insurer has a unilateral right to make any change in any provision, other than a change in premium rate for classes of insureds.

guaranty association An association established by each state to support insurers and protect consumers in the case of insurer insolvency. They are funded by insurers through assessments.

H

hazard A specific situation or condition that increases the probability or severity of a loss.

health insurance This is insurance against loss through sickness or accidental bodily injury. Also called accident and health, accident and sickness, sickness and accident or disability insurance.

health maintenance organization (HMO) Health care management that stresses preventive health care, early diagnosis and treatment on an outpatient basis. Persons generally enroll voluntarily by paying a periodic fixed fee.

home health care Skilled or unskilled care provided in an individual's home, usually on a part-time basis.

home service insurer An insurer that offers relatively small policies with premiums payable on a weekly basis, collected by agents at the policyowner's home.

hospital benefits The benefits payable for charges incurred while the insured is confined to or treated in a hospital, as defined in a health insurance policy.

hospital expense insurance Health insurance benefits subject to a specified daily maximum for a specified period of time while the inured is confined to a hospital, plus a limited allowance up to a specified amount for miscellaneous hospital expenses, such as operating room, anesthesia, laboratory fees, etc. Also called hospitalization insurance. *See also* medical expense insurance.

hospital indemnity A form of health insurance that provides a stipulated daily, weekly or monthly indemnity during hospital confinement; payable on an unallocated basis without regard to actual hospital expense.

human life value An individual's economic worth, measured by the sum of his or her future earnings that are devoted to his or her family.

I

immediate annuity This provides of the payment of an annuity benefit at one payment interval from date of purchase. Can only be purchased with a single payment.

implied authority Authority that, although it is not expressed in a contract (express authority) is necessary to perform the duties expressly authorized.

incidents of ownership Any power or interest over a life insurance policy that would subject the policy to inclusion in a decedent's gross estate.

incontestable clause This places a time limit (one to two years after issue) the insurer's right to void a policy or refuse benefits because of material misstatements made in the application.

increasing term insurance This is term life insurance in which the death benefit increases periodically over the policy's term. Usually purchased as a cost of living rider to a whole life policy. *See also* cost of living rider.

indemnity approach A method of paying health policy benefits to insureds based on a predetermined, fixed rate set for the medical services provided, regardless of the actual expenses incurred.

independent agency system A system for marketing, selling and distributing insurance in which independent brokers are not affiliated with any one insurer but represent any number of insurers.

indexed whole life A whole life insurance policy whose death benefit increases according to the rate of inflation. Such policies are usually tied to the Consumer Price Index (CPI).

individual insurance These are policies that provide protection to the policyowner, as distinct from group and blanket insurance. Also called personal insurance.

individual retirement account (IRA) A personal qualified retirement account through which eligible individuals accumulate tax-deferred income up to a certain amount each year, depending on their tax bracket.

industrial insurance A life insurance policy that provides modest benefits and a relatively short benefit period. Premiums are collected on a weekly or monthly basis by an agent calling at insured's homes. *See also* home service insurer.

inspection receipt A receipt obtained from an insurance applicant when a policy (upon which the first premium has not been paid) is left with him or her for further inspection. It states that the insurance is not in effect and that the policy has been delivered for inspection only.

inspection report An investigator report that provides facts required for a proper underwriting decision on applications for new insurance and reinstatements.

installment refund annuity An annuity income option that provides for the funds remaining at the annuitant's death to be paid to the beneficiary in the form of continued annuity payments.

insurability All conditions pertaining to individuals that affect their health, susceptibility to injury, or life expectancy; an individual's risk profile.

insurability receipt A type of conditional receipt that makes coverage effective on the date the application was signed or the date of the medical exam (whichever is later), provided the applicant proves to be insurable.

insurable interest The interest from which monetary loss will result if the peril insured against occurs; possibility of financial loss that can be protected against by insurance.

insurance A contractual means of transferring the risk of loss to an entity (insurer) that pools similar exposures.

insurance code The laws that govern the business of insurance in a given state.

insurer An entity that provides insurance coverage, typically through a contract of insurance. *See also* carrier.

insuring clause This defines and describes the scope of the coverage provided and limits of indemnification.

integrated deductible In superimposed major medical plans, this is a deductible amount between the benefits paid by the basic plan and those benefits paid by the major medical. All or part of the integrated deductible may be absorbed by the basic plan.

interest adjusted net cost method A method of comparing the costs of similar policies by using an index that takes into account the time value of money.

interest-only option (interest option) A mode of settlement under which all or part of the policy proceeds are left with the company for a definite period at a guaranteed minimum interest rate. Interest may either be added to the proceeds or paid annually, semiannually, quarterly or monthly.

interest-sensitive whole life A whole life policy whose premiums vary depending upon the insurer's underlying death, investment and expense assumptions.

interim term insurance Term insurance for a period of 12 months or less by special agreement of the company; it permits a permanent policy to become effective at a selected future date.

intermediate nursing care A level of health or medical care that is occasional or rehabilitative, ordered by a physician, and performed by skilled medical personnel.

irrevocable beneficiary A beneficiary whose interest cannot be revoked without his or her written consent, usually because the policyowner has made the beneficiary designation without retaining the right to revoke or change it.

J

joint and last survivor policy A variation of the joint life policy that covers two lives but pays the benefit upon the death of the second insured.

joint and survivor annuity This covers two or more lives and continues in force as long as any one of them survives.

joint life policy This covers two or more lives and provides for the payment of the proceeds at the death of the first among those insured, at which time the policy automatically terminates.

juvenile insurance This is written on the lives of children who are within specified age limits and generally under parental control.

K

Keogh plans These are designed to fund retirement of self-employed individuals; the name is derived form the author of the Keogh Act (HR-10), under which contributions to such plans are given favorable tax treatment.

key-person insurance This provides protection of a business against financial loss caused by the death or disablement of a vital number of the company, usually individuals possessing special managerial or technical skill or expertise.

L

lapse Termination of a policy because of the nonpayment of premiums.

law of large numbers A statistical principle which states that the larger the number of observations, the more accurate and reliable a prediction will be.

legal purpose The concept that the purpose of a contract must be legal, moral and in the public good. *See also* contract.

legal reserve The standard levels for policy reserves established thorough the insurance laws of the various states.

level premium funding method The insurance plan (used by all regular life insurance companies) under which, instead of an annually increasing premium that reflects the increasing chance of death, an equivalent level premium is paid. Reserves that accumulate from more than adequate premiums paid in the early years supplement inadequate premiums in later years.

level term insurance this is term coverage on which the face value remains unchanged from the date the policy comes into force to the date the policy expires.

license The certification issued by a state insurance department that an qualifies individual to solicit insurance applications for the period covered; usually issued for one year, renewable on application without need for repeat on the original qualifying requirements.

licensed insurer *See* admitted insurer.

lien system A plan for issuing coverage for substandard risks. A standard premium is paid but there is a lien against the policy to reduce the amount of insurance if the insured dies from a cause that resulted in the substandard rating.

life annuity This is payable during the continued life of the annuitant. No provision is made for the guaranteed return of the unused portion of the premium.

life expectancy The average duration of the life remaining to a number of persons of a given age, according to a given mortality table. Not to be confused with *probable lifetime,* which refers to the difference between a person's present age and the age at which death is most probable, i.e., the age at which most deaths occur.

life income settlement option A settlement option that provides for life insurance or annuity proceeds to be used to buy an annuity payable to the beneficiary for life, often with a specified number of payments certain or a refund if payments don't equal or exceed premiums paid.

life insurance This is insurance against loss due to the death of a particular person (the insured) upon whose death the insurance company agrees to pay a stated sum or income to the beneficiary.

limited pay life insurance A form of whole life insurance characterized by premium payments only being made for a specified or limited number of years.

limited policies These restrict benefits to specified accidents or diseases, such as travel policies, dread disease policies, ticket policies and so forth.

limited risk policy This provides coverage for specific kinds of accidents or illnesses, such as injuries received as a result of travel accidents or medical expenses stemming from a specified disease. *See also* special risk policy.

Lloyd's of London An association of individuals and companies that underwrite insurance on their own accounts and provide specialized coverages.

loading The amount added to net premiums to cover the company's operating expenses and contingencies; includes the cost of securing new business, collection expenses and general management expenses.

loan value The amount that can be borrowed from the issuing company by the policyowner using the value of the life insurance policy as collateral.

long-term care The broad range of medical and personal services for individuals (often the elderly) who need assistance with daily activities for an extended period of time.

long-term care policy A health insurance policy that provides daily indemnity benefits for extended care confinement.

loss sharing A basic principle of insurance whereby a large number of insureds contribute to cover the losses of a few.

lump sum The payment of the entire proceeds of an insurance policy in one sum. This is the method of settlement provided by most policies unless an alternate settlement is elected by the policyowner or beneficiary.

M

major medical expense policy A health insurance policy that provides broad coverage and high benefits for hospitalization, surgery and physician services. Characterized by deductibles and coinsurance cost-sharing.

managed care A system of delivering health care and health care services characterized by arrangements with selected providers, programs of ongoing quality control and of utilization review and financial incentives for members to use providers and procedures covered by the plan.

mandatory second opinion Requires insureds to get a second opinion before receiving nonlife-threatening surgery in order to be eligible for benefits.

master policy A policy issued to the employer under a group plan; contains all the insuring clauses defining employee benefits. Individual employees participating in the group plan receive individual certificates that outline highlights of the coverage. Also called master contract.

material Having influence or effect; a representation relating to a matter that is so substantial as to influence an outcome or actions.

maturity value The proceeds payable on an endowment contract at the end of the specified endowment period, or payable on an ordinary life contract at the last age of the mortality table if the insured is still living at that age. Maturity value of a policy is the same as the face amount of the policy and is equal to the reserve value of the contract on this maturity date. Actual amount payable by the company may be increased by dividend additions or accumulated dividend deposits, or decreased by outstanding loans.

McCarran-Ferguson Act Also know as Public Law 15, this 1945 act exempted insurance from federal antitrust laws in all matters regulated by the states.

medicaid This provides medical care for the needy under joint federal-state participation (Kerr-Mills Act).

medical cost management The process of controlling how policyholders utilize their policies. *See also* mandatory second opinion, precertification, ambulatory surgery and case management.

medical examination This is usually conducted by a licensed physician; the medical report is part of the application, becomes part of the policy contract, and is attached to the policy. A "nonmedical" is a short-form medical report filled out by the agent. Various company rules, such as amount of insurance applied for or already in force, or applicant's age, sex, past physical history and data revealed by inspection report, etc., determine whether the examination will be "medical" or "nonmedical."

medical expense insurance This pays benefits for non-surgical doctors' fees commonly rendered in a hospital; sometimes pays for home and office calls.

Medical Information Bureau (MIB) A service organization that collects medical data on life and health insurance applicants for member insurance companies.

medical report A document completed by a physician or other approved examiner and submitted to an insure to supply medical evidence of insurability (or lack of insurability) or in relation to a claim.

medicare A federally sponsored health insurance and medical care program for persons age 65 or older; administered under provisions of the Social Security Act.

Medicare Part A This is compulsory hospitalization insurance that provides specified in hospital and related benefits. All workers covered by Social Security finance its operation through a portion of their FICA tax.

Medicare Part B A voluntary program designed to provide supplementary medical insurance to cover physician services, medical services and supplies not covered under Medicare Part A.

Medicare+Choice A program that offers a variety of Medicare managed care choices, a private fee-for-service plan (PFFS), a Medicare medical savings account plan (MSA) and religious fraternal benefit society plans. Also known as Medicare Part C.

medicare supplement policy This is health insurance that provides coverage to fill the gaps in Medicare coverage.

minimum deposit insurance A cash value life insurance policy having a first-year loan value that is available for borrowing immediately upon payment of the first-year premium.

minimum premium plan (MPP) Designed to support a self-insured plan, a minimum premium plan helps insure against large, unpredictable losses that exceed the self-insured level.

miscellaneous expenses Hospital charges, other than for room and board, e.g., x-rays, drugs, laboratory fees, etc., in connection with health insurance.

misrepresentation The act of making, issuing, circulating or causing to be issued or circulated, an estimate, illustration, circular or statement of any kind that does not represent the correct policy terms, dividends or share of the surplus or the name or title for any policy or class of policies that does not in fact reflect its true nature.

misstatement of age or sex provision This provides that, if the insured's age or sex is misstated in an application for insurance, the benefit payable usually is adjusted to what the premiums paid should have purchased.

misuse of premium The improper use of premiums collected by an insurance producer.

modified endowment contract (MEC) A life insurance policy under which the amount a policyowner pays in during the fist years exceeds the some of net level premium that would have been payable to provide paid-up future benefits in seven years.

modified whole life A whole life insurance with premium payable during the first few years (usually five) only slightly larger than the rate of term insurance. Afterwards, the premium is higher for the remainder of life than the premium for ordinary life at the original age of issue, but lower than the rate at the attained age at the time of charge.

money-purchase plan A type of qualified plan under which contributions are fixed amounts or fixed percentages of the employees' salary. An employee's benefits are provided in whatever amount the accumulated or current contributions will produce for him or her.

moral hazard Effect of person reputation, character, associates, personal living habits, financial responsibility and environment (as distinguished from physical health) upon an individual's general insurability.

morale hazard The effect(s) indifference concerning loss has on the risk to be insured.

morbidity The relative incidence of disability due to sickness or accident within a given group.

morbidity rate This shows the incidence and extent of disability that may be expected from a given large group of persons; used in computing health insurance rates.

mortality The relative incidence of death within a group.

mortality table A listing of the mortality experience of individuals by age; permits an actuary to calculate, on average, how long a male or female of a given age group may be expected to live.

mortgage insurance A basic use of life insurance, so-called because many breadwinners leave insurance to pay off any mortgage balance outstanding at their death. The insurance generally is made payable to a family beneficiary instead of to the mortgage holder.

multiple employer trust (MET) This is made up of several small groups of individuals that need life and health insurance but do not qualify for true group insurance who band together under state trust laws to purchase insurance at a more favorable rate.

multiple employer welfare arrangement (MEWA) This is similar to a multiple employer trust (MET) with the exception that in a MEWA, a number of employers pool their risks and self-insure.

multiple protection policy A combination of term and whole life coverage that pays some multiple of the face amount of the basic whole life portion (such as $10 per month per $1,000) throughout the multiple protection period (such as to age 65).

mutual insurer An insurance company that is owned by its policyholders and managed by a board of directors.

N

National Association of Health Underwriters (NAHU) An organization of health insurance agents that is dedicated to supporting the health insurance industry and to advancing the quality of service provided by insurance professionals.

National Association of Insurance Commissioners (NAIC) An association of state insurance commissioners active in the analysis of insurance regulations and in the formation and recommendation of uniform and model regulations and legislation.

National Association of Insurance and Financial Advisors (NAIFA) An organization of life insurance agents that is dedicated to supporting the life insurance industry and to advancing the quality of service provided by insurance professionals.

National Service Life Insurance (NSLI) Created by Congress in 1940 to provide policies for individuals on active duty in military service. Persons entering military service after December 31, 1956 cannot purchase this insurance. However, persons discharged with a service-connected disability may purchase it within a certain time limit.

natural group A group formed for a reason other than to obtain insurance.

needs approach A method for determining how much insurance protection a person should have by analyzing a family's or business' needs and objectives should the insured die, become disabled or retire.

net premium This is calculated on the basis of a given mortality table and a given interest rate, without any allowance for loading.

nonadmitted insurer An insurance company that has not been licensed to operate within a given state.

noncancelable and guaranteed renewable contract A health insurance contract that the insured has the right to continue in force by payment of premiums set forth in the contract for a substantial period of time, during which the insurer has no right to make unilaterally any change in any contract provision.

noncontributory plan An employee benefit plan under which the employer bears the full cost of the employees' benefits; must insure 100 percent of eligible employees.

nondisabling injury An injury that requires medical care, but does not result in loss of time from work.

nonduplication provision This stipulates that insureds shall be ineligible to collect for charges under a group health plan if the charges are reimbursed under their own or spouse's group plan.

nonforfeiture options The privileges allowed under terms of a life insurance contract after cash values have been created.

nonforfeiture values Those benefits in a life insurance policy that by law the policyowner does not forfeit even if he or she discontinues premium payments; usually cash value, loan value, paid-up insurance value and extended term insurance value.

nonmedical insurance This is issued on a regular basis without requiring a regular medical examination. In passing on the risk, the company relies on the applicant's answers to questions regarding his or her physical condition and on personal references or inspection reports.

nonparticipating This is insurance under which the insured is not entitled to share in the divisible surplus of the company.

nonqualified plan A retirement plan that does not meet federal government requirements and is not eligible for favorable tax treatment.

notice of claims provision A policy provision that describes the policyowner's obligation to provide notification of loss to the insurer within a reasonable period of time.

O

offer and acceptance The offer may be made by the applicant by signing the application, paying the first premium and, if necessary, submitting to a physical examination. Policy issuance, as applied for, constitutes acceptance by the company. Or, the offer may be made by the company when no premium payment is submitted with application. Premium payment on the offered policy then constitutes acceptance by the applicant.

Old Age, Survivors, Disability and Hospital Insurance (OASDI) Retirement, death, survivor's disability income, health and hospital insurance benefits provided under the Social Security system. It is better known as Social Security.

open certificate This stipulates that rates and policy provisions may be changed. Fraternal benefit societies are required by law to issue this type of certificate. Also called open policy.

open-panel HMO A network of physicians who work out of their own offices and participate in the HMO on a part-time basis.

optionally renewable contract A health insurance policy in which the insurer reserves the right to terminate the coverage at any anniversary or, in some cases, at any premium due date, but does not have the right to terminate coverage between such dates.

ordinary insurance Life insurance of commercial companies not issued on the weekly basis; amount of protection usually is $1,000 or more.

Occupational Safety and Health Administration (OSHA) This establishes federal work safety guidelines.

other insureds rider A term rider that covers a family member other than the insured and that is attached to the base policy covering the insured.

outline of coverage The informational material about a specific plan or policy of insurance that describes the policy's features and benefits; in many states, an outline of coverage is required to be given to consumers when certain types of coverages are being considered.

overhead insurance A type of short-term disability insurance that reimburses the insured for specified, fixed, monthly expenses, normal and customary in operating the insured's business.

overinsurance An excessive amount of insurance; an amount of insurance that would result in payment of more than the actual loss or more than incurred expenses.

own occupation A definition of total disability that requires that the insured must be unable to work at his or her own occupation in order to receive disability income benefits.

P

paid-up additions The additional life insurance purchased by policy dividends on a net single premium basis at the insured's attained insurance age at the time additions ar purchased.

paid-up policy A contract on which no further premiums are to be paid and for the benefits of which the company is held liable.

parol evidence rule A rule of contract law that brings all verbal statements into the written contract and disallows any changes or modifications to the contract by oral evidence.

partial disability An illness or injury that prevents an insured from performing at least one or more, but not all, of their occupational duties.

participating An insurance plan under which the policyowner receives shares (commonly called dividends) of the divisible surplus of the company.

participating physician A doctor or physician who accepts Medicare's allowable or recognized charges and will not charge more than this amount.

participation standards The rules that must be followed for determining employee eligibility for a qualified retirement plan.

partnership A business entity that allows tow or more people to strengthen their effectiveness by working together as co-owners.

payor rider This is available under certain juvenile life insurance policies, upon payment of an extra premium; provides for the waiver of future premiums if the person responsible for paying them dies or is disabled before the policy becomes fully paid or matures as a death claim, or as an endowment, or the child reaches a specific age.

per capita rule This stipulates that death proceeds from an insurance policy are to be divided equally among the living primary beneficiaries.

peril The immediate, specific event that causes loss and gives rise to risk.

period certain annuity An annuity income option that guarantees a definite minimum period of payments.

periodical publication group A group representative of those eligible for blanket life insurance; in this case, the policy is issued to a newspaper, farm paper, magazine or other periodical. The policy insures independent contractors and others engaged in the marketing and delivery of periodical publications.

permanent flat extra premium A fixed charge added per $1,000 of insurance for substandard risks.

personal producing general agency system (PPGA) A method of marketing, selling and distributing insurance in which personal producing general agents (PPGAs) are compensated for business they personally sell and business sold by agents with whom they subcontract. Subcontracted agents are considered employees of the PPGA, not the insurer.

per stirpes rule This stipulates that death proceeds from an insurance policy are to be divided equally among the named beneficiaries. If a named beneficiary is deceased, his or her share then goes to the living descendants of that individual.

policy The insurance contract and all attached endorsements.

policy loan A loan made by the insurance company to the policyowner with the policy's cash value assigned as security. One of the standard nonforfeiture options.

policy provisions The term or conditions of an insurance policy as contained in the policy clauses.

precertification The insurer's approval of an insured's entering a hospital. Many health policies require precertification as part of an effort to control costs.

preexisting condition An illness or medical condition that existed before a policy's effective date; usually excluded from coverage through the policy's standard provisions or by waiver.

preferred provider organization (PPO) An association of health care providers, such as doctors and hospitals, that agree to provide health care services to members of a particular group at fees negotiated in advance.

preferred risk A risk whose physical condition, occupation, mode of living and other characteristics indicate a prospect for longevity or an unimpaired life.

preliminary term insurance This is term insurance attached to a newly issued permanent life insurance policy that extends term coverage of a preliminary period of 1 to 11 months, until the permanent insurance becomes effective. The purpose is to provide full life insurance premium and the anniversary to a later date.

premium The periodic payment required to keep an insurance policy in force.

premium factors The three primary factors considered when computing the basic premium for insurance: mortality, expense and interest.

Presbyterian Minister's Fund The oldest life insurance company in existence; founded in 1759 as "A Corporation for the Relief of Poor and Distressed Presbyterian Ministers and of Poor and Distressed Widows and Children of Presbyterian Ministers."

prescription drug coverage This is usually offered as an optional benefit to group medical expense plans and covers some or all of the cost of prescription drugs.

presumptive disability benefit A disability income policy benefit that provides that if an insured experiences a specified disability, such as blindness, he or she is presumed to be totally disabled and entitled to the full amount payable under the policy, whether or not he or she is able to work.

primary beneficiary In life insurance, this is the beneficiary designated by the insured as the first to receive policy benefits.

primary insurance amount (PIA) Amount equal to a covered worker's full Social Security retirement benefit at age 65 or disability benefit.

principal A person whose obligations are guaranteed under a bond (also called the obligor); the applicant for or subject of insurance; the one (usually the insurer) from whom an insurance agent derives authority.

principal sum The amount under an AD&D policy that its payable as a death benefit if death is due to an accident.

private insurer An insurer that is not associated with federal or state government.

probationary period The specified number of days after an insurance policy's issue date during which coverage is not afforded for sickness. Standard practice for group coverages.

proceeds The net amount of money payable by the company at the insured's death or at policy maturity.

producer A general term applied to an agent, broker, personal producing general agent, solicitor or other person who sells insurance.

professional liability insurance *See* errors and omissions insurance.

profit-sharing plan Any plan whereby a portion of a company's profits is set aside for distribution to employees who qualify under the plan.

proof of loss A mandatory health insurance provision stating that the insured must provide a completed claim form to the insurer within 90 days of the date of loss.

proper solicitation A high professional standard that requires an agent to identify himself or herself properly as an agent soliciting insurance on behalf of an insurance company.

pure endowment A contract providing for payment only upon survival of a certain person to a certain date and not in event of that person's prior death. This type of contract is just the opposite of a term contract, which provides for payment only in event that a certain person dies within the term period specified.

pure risk The uncertainty as to whether loss will occur; offers no chance for gain. Insurance may be provided against many types of pure risk.

Q

qualified plan A retirement or employee compensation plan established and maintained by an employer that meets specific guidelines spelled out by the IRS and consequently receives favorable tax treatment.

R

Railway Passengers Assurance Company Founded in 1848, this company made the first real attempt to protect the general public against accidents by writing ticket insurance to railway passengers for injury or death while riding the railways.

rate-up in age A system of rating substandard risks that involves assuming the insured to be older than he or she really is and charging a correspondingly higher premium.

rating The premium classification given an applicant for life or health insurance.

reasonable and customary charge The charge for a heath care service consistent with the going rate of charge in a given geographical area for an identical or similar service.

rebating The act of returning part of the commission or giving anything else of value to the insured as an inducement to buy the policy. It is illegal and cause for license revocation in most states. In some states, both the agent and the person receiving the rebate may be punished.

reciprocal insurer An association of individuals known as subscribers, managed by an attorney-in-fact, who agree to exchange insurance risks.

recurrent disability provision A disability income policy provision that specifies the period of time during which the reoccurrence of a disability is considered a continuation of a prior disability.

reduced paid-up insurance A nonforfeiture option contained in most life insurance polices that allows the insured to elect to have the cash surrender vale of the policy used to purchase a paid-up policy for a reduced amount of insurance.

re-entry option An option in a renewable term life policy under which the policyowner is guaranteed, at the end of the term, to be able to renew his or her coverage without evidence of insurability at a premium rate specified in the policy.

refund annuity This provides for the continuance of the annuity during the annuitant's lifetime at least until total payment equal to the purchase price have been made by the company.

rehabilitation benefit This is offered as an optional benefit to a disability income policy is designed to cover the cost of retraining in order to reenter the work force following a period of disability.

reimbursement approach The payment of health policy benefits to insured based on actual medical expenses incurred.

reinstatement The act of putting a lapsed policy back in force by producing satisfactory evidence of insurability and paying any past-due premiums required.

reinsurance The act of sharing or spreading a risk that is too large for one insurer by transferring part of the risk to a reinsurer. The insurance company obtaining the reinsurance is called the ceding company; the insurance company issuing the reinsurance is called the reinsurer.

relative value scale A method for determining the benefits payable under a basic surgical expense policy. Points are assigned to each surgical procedure and a dollar per point amount, or conversion factor, is used to determine the benefit.

renewable term A term policy prove that may be renewed on the same plan for one or more years without medical examination, but with rates based on the insured's advanced age.

renewable option An option that allows the policyowner to renew a term policy before its termination date without having to provide evidence of insurability.

replacement The act of replacing one life insurance policy with another; may be done legally under certain conditions. *See also* twisting.

representation A statement of material fact that is reasonably accepted as substantially true.

reserve Funds held by the company to help fulfill future claims.

reserve basis In life insurance, this is the mortality table and assumed interest rate used in computing rates.

residential care A type of health or medical care designed to provide a benefit for elderly individuals who live in a retirement community; addresses full-time needs, both social and medical.

residual disability benefit A disability income payment based on the proportion of income the insured has actually lost, taking into account the fact that he or she is able to earn some income.

respite care A type of health or medical care designed to provide a short rest period for a caregiver. Characterized by its temporary status.

results provision *See* accidental bodily injury provision.

retention The act of keeping a policy in force and "on the books."

revocable beneficiary A beneficiary whose right in a policy are subject to the policyowner's reserved right to revoke or change the beneficiary designation and the right to surrender or make a loan on the policy without the beneficiary's consent.

rider Strictly speaking, a rider adds something to a policy. However, the term is used loosely to refer to any supplemental agreement attached to and made a part of the policy, whether the policy's conditions are expanded and additional coverages added, or a coverage or conditions is waived.

risk The uncertainty regarding loss; a term indicating the person or property insured. *See also* pure risk; speculative risk.

risk pooling *See* loss sharing.

risk selection The method a home office underwriter uses to choose applicants that the insurance company will accept. The underwriter must determine whether risks are standard, substandard or preferred and adjust the premium rates accordingly.

rollover IRA An individual retirement account established with funds transferred from another IRA or qualified retirement plan that the owner had terminated.

S

salary continuation plan An arrangement whereby an income, usually related to an employee's salary, is continued upon employee's retirement, death or disability.

salary reduction SEP (SARSEP) A qualified retirement plan limited to companies with 25 or fewer employees. It allows employees to defer part of their pretax income to the plan, lowering their taxable income. *See also* Simplified Employee Pension Plan.

savings incentive match plan for employees (SIMPLE) A qualified employer retirement plan that allows small employers to set up tax-favored retirement savings plans for their employees.

schedule A list of specified amounts payable, usually for surgical operations, dismemberment, fractures, etc.

secondary beneficiary An alternative beneficiary designated to receive payment, usually in the event the original beneficiary predeceases the insured.

Section 457 plans Deferred compensation plans for employees of state and local governments in which amounts deferred will not be included in gross income until they are actually received or made available.

Self-Employed Individuals Retirement Act Passed by Congress in 1962, this act enables self-employed persons to establish qualified retirement plans similar to those available to corporations.

self-insurance Provided by a non-insurance company that has the financial ability to retain the risk of loss without the use of an insurance policy.

self-insured plan A health insurance plan under which an employer (usually a large one), labor union, fraternal organization or other group retains the risk of covering its employees' medical expenses.

service insurers Companies that offer prepayment plans for medical or hospital services; well-known examples are Blue Cross/Blue Shield plans and health maintenance organizations.

servicemembers' group life insurance (SGLI) All servicemembers on active duty are automatically covered for a specified amount of this group term life insurance, unless they elect no coverage or lesser amounts. The insurance is written by commercial companies and premiums are shared by insured and federal government.

service provider An organization that provides health coverage by contracting with service providers, to provide medical services to subscribers, who pay in advance through premiums. Examples of such coverages are HMOs and Blue Cross/Blue Shield plans.

settlement options Optional modes of settlement provided by most life insurance policies in lieu of lump-sum payment. Usual options are lump-sum cash, interest-only, fixed-period, fixed-amount and life income.

simplified employee pension plan (SEP) A type of qualified retirement plan under which the employer contributes to an individual retirement account set up and maintained by the employee.

single dismemberment The loss of one hand, one foot or the sight of one eye.

single-premium whole life insurance This is whole life insurance for which the entire premium is paid in one sum at the beginning of the contract period.

skilled nursing care The daily nursing care ordered by a doctor; often medically necessary. It can only be performed by or under the supervision of skilled medical professionals and is available 24 hours a day.

Social Security The programs first created by Congress in 1935 and now composed of Old Age, Survivors and Disability Insurance (OASDI), Medicare, Medicaid and various grants-in-aid, which provide economic security to nearly all employed people.

sole proprietorship The simplest form of business organization whereby one individual owns and controls the entire company.

special agent An agent who represents an insurance company in a given territory.

special class These are applicants who cannot qualify for standard insurance, but may secure policies with riders waiving payment for losses involving certain existing health impairments.

special questionnaires The forms used when, for underwriting purposes, the insurer needs more detailed information from an applicant regarding aviation or avocation, foreign residence, finances, military service or occupation.

special risk policy This provides coverage for unusual hazards normally not covered under accident and health insurance, such as a concert pianist insuring his or her hands for a million dollars. *See also* limited risk policy.

specified disease insurance *See* limited risk policy.

speculative risk A type of risk that involves the chance of both loss and gain; not insurable.

spendthrift provision This stipulates that, to the extent permitted by law, policy proceeds shall not be subject to the claims of creditors of the beneficiary or policyowner.

split-dollar life insurance An arrangement between two parties where life insurance is written on the life of one, who names the beneficiary of the net death benefits (death benefits less cash value), and the other is assigned the cash value, with both sharing premium payments.

spousal IRA An individual retirement account that persons eligible to set up IRAs for themselves may set up jointly with a nonworking spouse.

standard provisions The forerunners of the Uniform Policy Provisions in health insurance policies today.

standard risk A person who, according to a company's underwriting standards, is entitled to insurance protection without extra rating or special restrictions.

stock bonus plan A plan under which bonuses are paid to employees in shares of stock.

stock insurer An insurance company owned and controlled by a group of stockholders whose investment in the company provides the safety margin necessary in issuance of guaranteed, fixed premium, nonparticipating policies.

stock redemption plan An agreement under which a close corporation purchases a deceased stockholder's interest.

stop-loss provision This is designed to stop the company's loss at a given point, as an aggregate payable under a policy, a maximum payable for any one disability or the like; also applies to individuals, placing a limit on the maximum out-of-pocket expenses an insured must pay for health care, after which the health policy covers all expenses.

straight life income annuity (straight life annuity, life annuity) An annuity income option that pays a guaranteed income for the annuitant's lifetime, after which time payments stop.

straight whole life insurance *See* whole life insurance.

subscriber The policyowner of a health care plan underwritten by a service insurer, such as Blue Cross/Blue Shield.

substandard risk A person who is considered an under-average or impaired insurance risk because of physical condition, family or personal history of disease, occupation, residence in unhealthy climate or dangerous habits. *See also* special class.

successor beneficiary *See* secondary beneficiary.

suicide provision This provides that if the insured commits suicide within a specified period, usually two years after the issue date, the company's liability will be limited to a return of premiums paid.

supplemental accident coverage This is often included as part of a group basic or major medical plan and is designed to cover expenses associated with accidents to the extent they are not provided under other coverages.

supplementary major medical policy A medical expense health plan that covers expenses not included under a basic policy and expenses that exceed the limits of a basic policy.

surgical expense insurance This provides benefits to pay for the cost of surgical operations.

surgical schedule A list of cash allowances payable for various types of surgery, with the respective maximum amounts payable based upon severity of the operations; stipulated maximum usually covers all professional fees involved, e.g., surgeon, anesthesiologist.

surplus The amount by which assets exceed liabilities.

surplus lines broker An individual licensed to place coverage not available in his or her state (or not available in sufficient amount) through insurers not licensed or not admitted to do business in the state where the broker operates.

surrender value *See* cash surrender value.

T

taxable wage base The maximum amount of earnings upon which FICA taxes must be paid.

tax-sheltered annuity An annuity plan reserved for nonprofit organizations and their employees. Funds contributed to the annuity are excluded from current taxable income and are only taxed later, when benefits begin to be paid. Also called tax-deferred annuity and 403(b) plan.

temporary flat extra premium A fixed charge per $1,000 of insurance added to substandard risks for a specified period of years.

temporary insurance agreement *See* binding receipt.

term insurance This provides protection during a limited number of years and expires without value if the insured survives the stated period, which may be one or more years.

term of policy The period for which the policy runs. In life insurance, this is to the end of the term period for term insurance, to the maturity date for endowments and to the insured's death (or age 100) for permanent insurance. In most other kinds of insurance, it is usually the period for which a premium has been paid in advance; however, it may be for a year or more, even though the premium is paid on a semiannual or other basis.

tertiary beneficiary A beneficiary designated as third in line to receive the proceeds or benefits if the primary and secondary beneficiaries do not survive the insured.

third-party administrator (TPA) An organization outside the members of a self-insurance group which, for a fee, processes claims, completes benefits paperwork and often analyzes claims information.

third-party applicant A policy applicant who is not the prospective insured.

three-year rule Under estate tax law, this rule brings into the gross estate the value of any life insurance policy in which the decedent had incidents of ownership if the policy had been transferred within three years of his or her death.

time limit on certain defenses A provision stating that an insurance policy is incontestable after it has been in force a certain period of time. It also limits the period during which an insurer can deny a claim on the basis of a preexisting condition.

total disability A disability that prevents insureds from performing any duty of their usual occupations or any occupation for remuneration; actual definition depends on policy wording.

traditional net cost method A method of comparing costs of similar policies that does not take into account the time value of money.

travel-accident policies These provided coverage limited to indemnities for accidents while traveling, usually by common carrier.

treaty reinsurance An arrangement under which two or more insurers agree to share large insurance risks; the reinsurer automatically reinsures risks of a certain type written by the other, subject to the agreement.

trust Arrangement in which property is held by a person or corporation (trustee) for the benefit of others (beneficiaries). The grantor (person transferring the property to the trustee) gives legal title to the trustee, subject to terms set forth in a trust agreement. Beneficiaries have equitable title to the trust property.

trustee A person who holds legal title to property for the benefit of another; may be either an individual or a company, such as a bank and trust company.

twisting The practice of inducing a policyowner with one company to lapse, forfeit or surrender a life insurance policy for the purpose of taking out a policy in another company. Generally classified as a misdemeanor, subject to fine, revocation of license and sometimes imprisonment. *See also* misrepresentation.

U

unallocated benefit A reimbursement provision, usually for miscellaneous hospital and medical expenses, that does not specify how much will be paid for each type of treatment, examination, dressing, etc., but only sets a maximum that will be paid for all such treatments.

underwriter A company that receives premiums and accepting responsibility for fulfilling the policy contract or a company employee who decides whether or not the company should assume a particular risk; the agent who sells the policy.

underwriting The process through which an insurer determines whether, and on what basis, an insurance application will be accepted.

Unfair Trade Practices Act A model act written by the National Association of Insurance Commissioners (NAIC) and adopted by most states empowering state insurance commissioners to investigate and issue cease and desist orders and penalties to insurers for engaging in unfair or deceptive practices, such as misrepresentation or coercion.

Uniform Individual Accident and Sickness Policy Provisions Law An NAIC model law that established uniform terms, provisions and standards for health insurance policies covering loss resulting from sickness or from bodily injury or death by accident or both.

Uniform Simultaneous Death Act A model law that states that when an insured and beneficiary die at the same time, it is presumed that the insured survived the beneficiary.

unilateral A characteristic of an insurance contract in that only one party, the insurance company, makes an enforceable promise.

uninsurable risk A person who is not acceptable for insurance due to excessive risk factors.

universal life A flexible premium, two-part contract containing renewable term insurance and a cash value account that generally earns interest at a higher rate than a traditional policy. The interest rate varies. Premiums are deposited in the cash value account after the company deducts its fee and a monthly cost for the term coverage.

urgent care center A health care establishment that allows patients to see a physician without an appointment at any time; serves as an alternative to a hospital emergency room.

utilization review A technique used by health care providers to determine after the fact if health care was appropriate and effective.

V

valued contract A contract of insurance that pays a stated amount in the event of a loss.

variable annuity Similar to a traditional, fixed annuity in that retirement payments will be made periodically to the annuitants, usually over the remaining years of their lives. Under the variable annuity, there is no guarantee of the dollar amount of the payments; they fluctuate according to the value of an account invested primarily in common stocks.

variable life insurance this provides a guaranteed minimum death benefit. Actual benefits paid may be more, however, depending on the fluctuating market value of investments behind the contract at the insured's death. The cash surrender value also generally fluctuates with the market value of the investment portfolio.

variable universal life (VUL) insurance A life insurance policy combining characteristics of universal and variable life policies. A VUL policy contains unscheduled premium payments and death benefits and a cash value that vary according to the underlying funds whose investment portfolio is managed by the policyowner.

vesting The right of employees under a retirement plan to retain part or all of the annuities purchased by the employer's contributions on their behalf or, in some plans, to receive cash payments or equivalent value, on termination of their employment, after certain qualifying conditions have been met.

veterans' group life insurance (VGLI) This is low-cost nonrenewable, but convertible, five-year term insurance to which Servicemembers' Group Life Insurance (SGLI) is converted automatically at the time an insured servicemember is discharged, separated or released from active duty. At the end of the five-year period, the veteran may convert his or her VGLI to an individual policy with any company participating in the program.

vision insurance An optional coverage available with group health insurance plans, vision insurance typically pays for charges incurred during eye exams; eyeglasses and contact lenses are usually excluded.

void contract An agreement without legal effect; an invalid contract.

voidable contract A contract that can be made void at the option of one or more parties to the agreement.

voluntary group AD&D A group accidental death and dismemberment policy paid for entirely by employees, rather than an employer.

W

waiting period *See* elimination period.

waiver An agreement waiving the company's liability for a certain type or types of risk ordinarily covered in the policy; a voluntary giving up of a legal, given right.

waiver of premium A rider or provision included in most life insurance policies and some health insurance policies that exempts the insured from paying premiums after he or she has been disabled for a specified period of time, usually six months in life policies and 90 days or six months in health policies.

war clause This relieves or reduces the insurer's liability for specified loss caused by war.

warranties Statements made on an application for insurance that are warranted to be true; that is, they are exact in every detail as opposed to representations. Statements on applications for insurance are rarely warranties, unless fraud is involved. *See* representation.

whole life insurance This is permanent level insurance protection for the "whole of life," from policy issue to the death of the insured. Characterized by level premiums, level benefits and cash values.

wholesale insurance *See* franchise insurance

workers' compensation The benefits paid to workers for injury, disability or disease contracted in the course of their employment. Benefits and conditions are set by law, although in most states the insurance to provide the benefits may be purchased from regular insurance companies. A few states have monopolistic state compensation funds.

Y

yearly renewable term insurance (YRT) *See* annually renewable term.

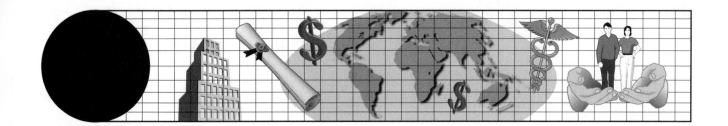

Appendix

This appendix contains both a sample whole life participating life insurance policy and sample application, as well as a sample health insurance policy and sample application. They are both representative of typical policies and applications issued by insurance companies in the United States and contain the standard language and provisions found in actual forms.

SUPERIOR MUTUAL LIFE INSURANCE COMPANY OF AMERICA

Superior Mutual agrees, in accordance with the provisions of this policy, to pay to the beneficiary the death proceeds upon receipt at the Home Office of due proof of the insured's death.

Ten-Day Right To Examine Policy You may return this policy by delivering it to the Home Office or to an agent of the Company within 10 days after receiving it. Immediately on such delivery, the policy will be void as of the date of issue and any premium paid will be refunded.

Anthony Caruso
President

Genevieve Berman
Secretary

Insured:	Daniel K. Williams
Policy Number:	0000-0000-00
Policy Date:	November 5, 2001

CONTENTS

INDEX

Insured: Daniel K. Williams   Age: 39 Male
Policy Number: 0000-0000-00   Risk: Standard
Date of Issue: November 5, 2001
Sum Insured: $50,000

SCHEDULE OF BENEFITS AND PREMIUMS

Benefit	Amount of Benefit	Annual Premium Amount Payable
Whole Life	$50,000	$809.00 for life

Total initial annual premium—nonsmoker basis $809.00

Whole life insurance policy. Death proceeds payable at death of insured.
Premiums payable during insured's lifetime. Annual dividends.

Male Insured: Daniel K. Williams   Age at Issue: 39
Policy Number: 0000-0000-00

TABLE OF GUARANTEED VALUES

End of Policy Year	Cash Value	Amount of Paid-Up Insurance	Extended Term Insurance Years	Extended Term Insurance Days
1	$ 0.00	*	0	0
2	0.00	*	0	0
3	365.50	*	1	120
4	981.00	*	3	67
5	1,616.50	*	4	260
6	2,537.50	*	6	252
7	3,486.50	11,450	8	128
8	4,464.00	13,950	9	265
9	5,471.50	16,350	10	320
10	6,511.50	18,550	11	304
11	7,584.50	20,650	12	217
12	8,690.50	22,550	13	68
13	9,832.00	24,400	13	230
14	11,008.00	26,100	13	345
15	12,219.50	27,650	14	59
16	13,258.50	28,700	14	32
17	14,316.00	29,600	13	349
18	15,393.00	30,450	13	283
19	16,489.00	31,150	13	198
20	17,607.00	31,800	13	94
Age 55	14,316.00	29,600	13	349
Age 60	19,537.50	33,650	12	340
Age 65	24,341.50	37,650	11	285

* Not available; benefit less than $10,000

Basis of Values: All cash values and net single premiums, except as otherwise provided under dividends, are based on:

The Commissioner's 1980 Standard Ordinary Mortality Table, smoker and nonsmoker, male and female, except that values for extended term insurance are based on the Commissioner's 1980 Extended Term Insurance Table, smoker and nonsmoker, male and female.

GENERAL PROVISIONS

Entire Contract—This policy is a contract between the owner and Superior Mutual. This policy, with a copy of the application attached to it, is the entire contract. Agents are not permitted to change this contract or extend the time for paying premiums.

All statements in the application are considered representations and not warranties. Superior Mutual will not use any statement to contest this policy or defend a claim unless the statement is in the application.

Incontestability—Except for failure to pay premiums, this policy cannot be contested after it has been in force during the insured's lifetime for two years from its date of issue. This time limit does not apply to any waiver of premium rider that may be a part of this policy.

Suicide Exclusion—The risk of suicide of the insured, while sane or insane, within two years of the date of issue of this policy, is not assumed. The beneficiary will receive the sum of the premiums paid, less debt.

Misstatement of Age or Sex—If the insured's age or sex is misstated, the amount payable under this policy will be that which the premiums paid would have purchased at the correct age and sex. This provision as it relates to a misstatement of sex does not apply if this policy is issued in a unisex premium class as shown on page 3.

Protection of Proceeds—To the extent allowed by law, the proceeds of this policy and any payments made under it will be exempt from attachment by the claims of creditors of the payee. No beneficiary can assign, transfer, anticipate or encumber the proceeds or payments unless you give them this right.

OWNER AND BENEFICIARY

Owner—The insured is the owner of this policy unless another is named as owner in the application. The owner may exercise the following rights without the consent of any beneficiary:

- obtain a loan to pay the premiums on this policy;
- elect a different dividend option;
- withdraw dividend accumulations;
- surrender dividend additions;
- change the method of premium payment with the consent of the Company; and
- change the ownership of this policy.

You may exercise all other rights and options granted by this policy, subject to the consent of any irrevocable beneficiary. The consent of any revocable beneficiary is not required.

Assignment—This may be assigned by written request. An absolute assignment will transfer ownership of the policy from you to the assignee. The policy may also be collaterally assigned as security. The limitations on your ownership rights while a collateral assignment is in force are set forth in the assignment. An assignment will take place only when recorded at the Home Office. When recorded, the assignment will take effect as of the date the written request was signed. Any rights created by the assignment will be subject to any payments made or actions taken by Superior Mutual before the change is recorded.

Superior Mutual will not be responsible for the validity of any assignment. If you assign this policy as collateral, any excess of the amount due the assignee will accrue to those otherwise entitled to it.

Beneficiary—The beneficiary is named by you in the application to receive the death proceeds. The interest of any beneficiary will be subject to any assignment. You may declare your choice of any beneficiary to be revocable or irrevocable. A revocable beneficiary may be changed by you at a later time. An irrevocable beneficiary must consent in writing to any change. Unless otherwise indicated, the beneficiary will be revocable.

A change of beneficiary may be made by written request while the insured is living. The change will take place as of the date the request is signed even if the insured is not living on the day the request is received. Any rights created by the change will be subject to any payments made or actions taken by Superior Mutual before the written request is received.

The interest of a beneficiary who dies before the insured will pass to the surviving beneficiaries in proportion to their share in the proceeds unless otherwise provided. If all beneficiaries die before the insured, the death proceeds will pass to the owner.

PREMIUMS

Premiums—The payments to Superior Mutual to keep this policy in force are the premiums. This policy will not be in force until the first premium is paid.

Premium due dates are computed from the date of issue. Premiums are payable in advance either at the Home Office or to the agent. The annual premium amounts are shown on page 3. A receipt signed by a Company officer will be given on request after payment.

Premiums may be paid annually, semi-annually, quarterly or by any other method allowed by Superior Mutual. You may change the method of premium payments only with the prior consent of the Company.

Grace Period—A premium may be paid during a period of 31 days beginning on the premium due date. The policy will remain in force during this grace period.

Nonpayment of Premium—Any premium that is not paid by its due date, either directly or by an automatic premium loan, is in default. A lapse occurs if the premium remains unpaid at the end of the 31-day grace period. After lapse, the policy will be continued in force under one of the following guaranteed insurance benefit options if there is a net cash value available.

Paid-Up Insurance Option—This is insurance for the insured's lifetime with no further premiums due. The amount of paid-up insurance is that amount that can be purchased for a net single premium at the insured's age on the date of default by the total of the cash value of the policy plus any dividend accumulations less any debt.

Paid-up insurance shares in dividends. Any dividend additions not subject to debt will continue in force.

If the paid-up insurance benefit is less than $10,000, this option will not be available. In such event, the net cash value will be used to purchase extended term insurance.

Extended Term Insurance Option—This is insurance for a limited period of time with no further premiums due. The amount of extended term insurance will equal the sum insured, plus any dividend additions or dividend accumulations, less any debt. The length of time the insured will be covered will be that which the net cash value will buy as a net single premium at the insured's age on the date of default. Extended term insurance does not share in dividends.

Applicable Benefit—Paid-up insurance will apply in the following situations if the amount of paid-up insurance is $10,000 or more:

- the amount of paid-up insurance equals or exceeds the amount of extended term insurance; or
- the policy is not in a standard premium class; or
- by written request, you elect paid-up insurance. This request may be made at any time, but not later than 62 days after the due date of the unpaid premium.

Extended term insurance will be the automatic benefit if the paid-up insurance benefit does not apply.

Automatic Premium Loan Option—This option will be in effect if elected in the application or by written request before the premium due date. You may withdraw this election at any time by written request.

While this option is in effect and the policy has a loan value, a loan will automatically be made on the premium due date to pay the unpaid premium. Interest will be waived if the automatic premium loan is repaid within 31 days of the date it is made.

The automatic premium loan option is subject to the following conditions:

- Any dividend accumulations will first be used to pay the unpaid premium unless you request otherwise. The balance of the unpaid premium will be paid by a policy loan.
- If the loan value of this policy is insufficient to pay the premium due, a loan will be made to pay the premium due for a shorter period of time.
- Regardless of the method of premium payment, if the loan value of this policy is not sufficient to pay the premium for a three-month period, no loan will be made. In that case, no premium will be paid and there will be a lapse.

SURRENDER OF THE POLICY

Surrender—Upon written request while the insured is living, you may surrender this policy for its net cash value. The policy will terminate on the date of the request. You may receive the net cash value in a lump sum or you may apply it under a payment option.

Superior Mutual may postpone payment of the net cash value for up to 6 months from the date you apply for it. If payment is postponed for 30 days or more, the proceeds will earn interest during the period of postponement at a rate not less than 3½% per year.

REINSTATEMENT

Reinstatement Following Lapse—You may reinstate this policy during the lifetime of the insured if the policy has lapsed and has not been surrendered. If you reinstate the policy within 62 days following the date of default, you must pay the premium that was due. You may reinstate more than 62 days after the date of default, but not more than five years after that date, by providing Superior Mutual with the following:

- evidence of insurability;
- payment of all past due premiums plus interest compounded annually at the rate of 6% from the date of default; and
- payment or reinstatement of any debt outstanding on the date of default. Interest is payable on

this debt from the date of default to the date of reinstatement at the loan interest rates that would have been applicable during said period in the absence of default.

The Company will waive evidence of insurability for reinstatement of the policy (but not any riders attached to it) if:

- the insured is in a standard premium class;
- the policy is in force as extended term insurance; and
- the period of time remaining for such extended term insurance coverage on the date of reinstatement is at least five years.

CHANGE OF PLAN

Exchange of Policy—If no premium is in default, you may exchange this policy for a new policy on another plan of insurance. Superior Mutual will not require evidence of insurability. The cash value of the new policy must exceed the cash value of this policy.

The new policy will be issued by Superior Mutual:

- on any whole life policy being issued on the date of issue;
- on the life of the insured only;
- with the same age, date of issue, sum insured and risk class as this policy; and
- at premium rates in use on the date of issue.

Riders will be available subject to evidence of insurability and consent of the Company.

The new policy will be subject to any debt and assignments outstanding on this policy.

Exchange Cost—If you exchange this policy within one year of the date of issue, you must pay any increase in the total premiums. Superior Mutual will not give credit for any premium paid for riders issued with this policy unless such riders are issued with the new policy.

If you exchange this policy one year or more after the date of issue, you must pay an amount equal to the increase in cash values on the date of exchange.

Any dividend additions that exist on the date of the exchange will be surrendered and their cash value applied to the payment. However, if the exchange is to a limited payment whole life plan, you may transfer dividend additions to the new policy.

CASH VALUES

Cash Value—The policy's guaranteed cash values are shown in the Table of Values. These values assume that all premiums have been paid. They do not include dividends or debt.

The values during a policy year will make allowance for full policy months elapsed and any premiums paid for that year. Values for policy years not shown are calculated on the same basis as those in the Table of Values. These values will be furnished on request.

Within 62 days from the due date of any unpaid premium, the policy's net cash value will be its net cash value on that premium due date.

The cash value for any paid-up insurance (including dividend additions) or extended term insurance will be the net single premium for that insurance at the insured's attained age. For 31 days after each policy anniversary, the cash value will not be less than the cash value on that anniversary.

Benefits provided by any rider attached to this policy will be excluded in determining policy values, unless stated otherwise in the rider.

Net Cash Values—The net cash value of this policy is the cash value, plus the value of any dividend additions and dividend accumulations, less any debt.

POLICY LOANS

Policy Loan—Loans may be obtained by request to the Home Office on the sole security of this policy.

When Available—Loans are available while this policy is in force other than as extended term insurance. For up to six months from the date of the request, Superior Mutual may delay granting a loan, other than to pay premiums on policies it has issued.

Amount Available—A loan may be for any amount up to the loan value less existing debt. The loan value is the amount that, with interest at the applicable loan rates then in effect, equals the cash value of the policy and the cash value of any dividend additions as of the next policy anniversary or premium due date, whichever is earlier. Any unpaid premium will be deducted from the amount loaned.

Loan Interest Rate—The loan interest rate is adjustable each year. On each January 1, Superior Mutual will establish an interest rate applicable to new and existing policy loans for that calendar year commencing on said date. You will be notified of the policy loan interest rate:

- when a policy loan is requested;
- not later than 60 days after an automatic premium loan has been made; and
- not less than 30 days in advance if a loan exists on the policy and the interest rate is changed.

The annual loan interest rate will not exceed the maximum rate allowable, which is the higher of:

- the Published Monthly Average for October of the prior year; or
- the rate used by the Company to compute the cash surrender values under the policy during the applicable period plus 1% per year.

Published Monthly Average means:

- Moody's Corporate Bond Yield Average— Monthly Average Corporates as published by Moody's Investors Services, Inc., or any successor to it; or
- a substantially similar average set by regulation issued by the Department of Insurance if Moody's Corporate Bond Yield Average—Monthly Average Corporates is no longer published.

The Company may raise the annual loan interest rate on January 1 if that rate is ½% or more below the maximum rate allowable. The Company shall lower the annual loan interest rate on January 1 if it is ½% or more above the maximum rate allowable.

In no event will the loan interest rate exceed the maximum rate allowed by law of the state in which this policy is delivered.

Loan Interest Payments—Interest on a loan is payable at the end of each policy year at the rates in effect for such policy year or on a pro rata basis

POLICY LOANS (continued)

for such shorter period as the loan may exist. Interest not paid when due will be added to the loan principal and bear interest at the loan rates established by Superior Mutual.

Repayment—Loans made prior to lapse may only be repaid prior to lapse of this policy. Loans made after lapse on paid-up insurance may be repaid while this policy is in force as paid-up insurance.

Foreclosure—If the debt exceeds the cash value of this policy and the cash value of any dividend additions, the policy will terminate. If debt exceeds cash value during a policy year solely because of a change in interest rate made during the policy year, the policy will not terminate during that policy year prior to the date it would have terminated if the interest rate had not changed. A notice of pending termination will be mailed to you at your last known address and to the last known address of any asisgnee. If the excess debt is not paid within 31 days after the notice is mailed, the policy will terminate with no value.

DIVIDENDS

Annual Dividends—This policy is entitled to share in the divisible surplus as determined each year by Superior Mutual. The Company will distribute this share as a dividend beginning at the end of the first policy year. Dividends are payable only while the policy is in force other than as extended term insurance. Each dividend may be applied in one of the following ways:

- paid in cash;
- used to reduce premium;
- used to buy participating paid-up insurance (called dividend additions); or
- left with Superior Mutual as a fund (called dividend accumulations) to earn interest at a rate set by the Company. The annual interest rate will not be less than 3½%.

If you make no election, the dividend will be used to buy dividend additions.

Purchase Price of Dividend Additions—The purchase price of dividend additions will be set by Superior Mutual. The purchase price will be the net single premium for the benefit provided at the insured's attained age. Superior Mutual may change the purchase price for dividend additions, but any change will apply only to dividend additions purchased after the date of change.

Cash Value of Dividend Additions—The cash value of dividend additions equals the net single premium for the paid-up insurance at the insured's attained age. This net single premium was determined on the same basis as was used for the purchase price of those dividend additions.

Basis of Net Single Premiums for Dividend Additions—All net single premiums are based on

tality Table, Smoker or Nonsmoker, male, female or Table B for unisex (or appropriate increases in such tables for non-standard risks). Interest will not be less than the rate used to calculate cash values.

Dividend at Death—A pro rata share of any dividend apportioned by the Company for the year of death will be added to the death proceeds if:

- the insured dies after the first policy year; and
- the policy is in force on the date of death.

Withdrawal of Dividend Accumulations—You may withdraw all or a part of the dividend accumulations at any time. If the automatic premium loan option has been elected, dividend accumulations will be used to pay unpaid premiums before a loan is made. You may request that dividend accumulations not be used to pay premiums.

Surrender of Dividend Additions—You may surrender dividend additions for their net cash value at any time if their value has not been otherwise used under the terms of this policy.

Paid-Up Privilege—You may exercise this privilege when the sum of the cash value of the policy, the cash value of any dividend additions and any dividend accumulations equals or exceeds the net single premium at the insured's age for the sum insured. At such time, on written request, this policy may be endorsed as fully paid-up. The dividend additions and dividend accumulations will be surrendered and their value applied to the cost of the paid-up policy. Any debt will continue in force. The net single premium and the basis of values for the paid-up insurance policy will be the same as that in use for dividend additions at the time the policy becomes fully paid-up.

PAYMENT OF PROCEEDS

Death Proceeds—The amount payable upon the death of the insured will be the sum insured plus any dividend, dividend accumulations, dividend additions and any one year term insurance in force on the date of death. Any premium paid for the period beyond the end of the policy month of the insured's death will be added to the death proceeds. Premiums that were waived will not be added to the death proceeds. Any debt and any premium due for the policy month in which the insured dies will be deducted from the death proceeds.

If a payment option is selected, the beneficiary, when filing proof of claim, may pay to the Company any amount that would otherwise be deducted from the proceeds.

Interest will be paid on lump-sum death proceeds at a rate not less than 3½% per year or the minimum rate set by law, if greater. Interest will be paid from the date of death to the payment date.

Payment Options—Upon written request, all or part of the death proceeds may be placed under one or more of the payment options below or any other option offered by the Company. Also, on surrender of this policy, the net cash value may be placed under one o more of the options instead of being paid in one sum.

The amounts payable under a payment options for each $1,000 of value applied will be the greater of:

(a) the rate per $1,000 of value applied based on the Company's non-guaranteed current payment option rates for this class of policies; or

(b) the rate in this policy for the applicable payment option.

Option A: Payments for a Specified Number of Years. (Table A) The Company will make equal payments for any selected number of years (not greater than 30). Payments may be made annually, semi-annually, quarterly or monthly.

Option B: Lifetime Monthly Payments. (Table B) Payments are based on the payee's age on the date the first payment will be made. One of three variations may be chosen. Depending upon this choice, payments will end:

(1) upon the death of the payee, with no further payments due (Life Annuity); or

(2) upon the death of the payee, but not before the sum of the payments equals or exceeds the amount applied under this options (Life Annuity with Installment Refund); or

(3) upon the death of the payee, but not before a selected period (5, 10 or 20 years) has elapsed (Life Annuity with Period Certain).

Option C: Interest Payments. The rate of interest will be determined by the Company each year but will not be less than 3½%. Payments may be made annually, semi-annually, quarterly or monthly. Payments will end when the amount left with the Company has been withdrawn. However, payments will not continue after the death of the payee. Any unpaid balance plus accrued interest will be paid in a lump sum.

Option D: Payments for a Specified Amount. Payments will be made until the unpaid balance is exhausted. Interest will be credited to the unpaid balance. The rate of interest will be determined by the Company each year but will not be less than 3½%. Payments may be made annually, semi-annually, quarterly or monthly. The payment level selected must provide for the payment each year of at least 8% of the amount applied.

Option E: Lifetime Monthly Payments for Two Payees. (Table E) One of three variations may be chosen. After the death of one payee, payments will continue to the survivor:

(1) in the same amount as the original amount;

(2) in an amount equal to ⅔ of the original amount; or

(3) in an amount equal to ½ of the original amount.

Payments are based on the payee's ages on the date the first payment is due. Payments will end upon the death of the surviving payee.

Selection of Payment Options—The amount applied under any one option for any one payee must be at least $5,000. The periodic payment for any one payee must be at least $50.

Subject to the owner and beneficiary provisions, you may change any option selection before the proceeds become payable. If you make no selection, the beneficiary may select an option when the proceeds become payable.

PAYMENT OF PROCEEDS (continued)

You may give the beneficiary the right to change from Option C or D to any other option at any time. If the payee selects Option C or D when this policy becomes a claim, the right may be reserved to change to any other option. The payee who elects to change options must be a payee under the option selected.

Additional Deposits—An additional deposit may be added to any proceeds when they are applied under Option B or E. A charge not to exceed 3% will be made. The Company may limit the amount of this deposit.

Rights and Limitations—A payee does not have the right to assign any amount payable under any option. A payee does not have the right to commute any amount payable under Option B or E. A payee will have the right to commute any amount payable under Option A only if the right is reserved in the written request selecting the option. If the right to commute is exercised, the commuted values will be computed at the interest rates used to calculate the benefits. The amount left under Option C, and any unpaid balance under Option D, may be withdrawn by the payee only as set forth in the written request selecting the option.

A corporate or fiduciary payee may select only Option A, C or D. Such selection will be subject to the consent of the Company.

Payment Dates—The first payment under any option, except Option C, will be due on the date this policy matures by death or otherwise, unless another date is designated. Payments under Option C begin at the end of the payment period selected, measured from policy maturity.

The last payment under any option will be made as stated in the description of that option. However, should a payee under Option B or E die prior to the due date of the second monthly payment, the amount applied less the first monthly payment will be paid in a lump sum or under any option other than Option E. Such payment will be made to the surviving payee under Option E or the succeeding payee under Option B.

Payment Rates—The Payment Option Tables show payment rates for Options A, B and E. For policy proceeds placed under these options within five years of the date of surrender or the date the proceeds are otherwise payable, the more favorable of the rates contained in this policy or the rates in use by the Company as of the date the proceeds are applied will be the basis for the periodic payments. Payments that commence more than five years after such date or as a result of additional deposits will be based on the rates in use by the Company as of the date the first payment is due.

PAYMENT OPTIONS

TABLE A

Payments for Specified Number of Years
Payments Per $1,000 Applied
Based on Interest at 3½% Per Year

YEARS	ANNUAL	SEMI-ANNUAL	QUARTERLY	MONTHLY
1	1,000.00	504.30	253.23	84.65
2	508.60	256.49	128.79	· 43.05
3	344.86	173.91	87.33	29.19
4	263.04	132.65	66.61	22.27
5	213.99	107.92	54.19	18.12
6	181.32	91.44	45.92	15.35
7	158.01	79.69	40.01	13.38
8	140.56	70.88	35.59	11.90
9	127.00	64.05	32.16	10.75
10	116.18	58.59	29.42	9.83
11	107.34	54.13	27.18	9.09
12	99.98	50.42	25.32	8.46
13	93.78	47.29	23.75	7.94
14	88.47	44.62	22.40	7.49
15	83.89	42.31	21.24	7.10
16	79.89	40.29	20.23	6.76
17	76.37	38.51	19.34	6.47
18	73.25	36.94	18.55	6.20
19	70.47	35.54	17.85	5.97
20	67.98	34.28	17.22	5.75
21	65.74	33.15	16.65	5.56
22	63.70	32.13	16.13	5.39
23	61.85	31.19	15.66	5.24
24	60.17	30.34	15.24	5.09
25	58.62	29.56	14.85	4.96
26	57.20	28.85	14.49	4.84
27	55.90	28.19	14.15	4.73
28	54.69	27.58	13.85	4.63
29	53.57	27.02	13.57	4.53
30	52.53	26.49	13.30	4.45

PAYMENT OPTIONS (continued)

TABLE B

**Monthly Payments Per $1,000 Applied
Based on Interest at 3½% Per Year**

Age	OPTION B (1) Life Annuity	OPTION B (2) Instal. Refund Annuity	OPTION B (3) Life Annuity With 5 Years Certain	OPTION B (3) 10 Years Certain	OPTION B (3) 20 Years Certain	Age	OPTION B (1) Life Annuity	OPTION B (2) Instal. Refund Annuity	OPTION B (3) Life Annuity With 5 Years Certain	OPTION B (3) 10 Years Certain	OPTION B (3) 20 Years Certain
0-5	3.09	3.09	3.09	3.09	3.09						
6	3.10	3.10	3.10	3.10	3.10	46	3.98	3.91	3.98	3.97	3.92
7	3.11	3.11	3.11	3.11	3.11	47	4.03	3.95	4.03	4.01	3.96
8	3.12	3.11	3.12	3.12	3.12	48	4.08	4.00	4.08	4.06	4.00
9	3.13	3.12	3.13	3.13	3.13	49	4.14	4.05	4.13	4.11	4.05
10	3.14	3.13	3.14	3.14	3.14	50	4.19	4.10	4.19	4.17	4.10
11	3.15	3.14	3.15	3.15	3.15	51	4.25	4.15	4.25	4.23	4.14
12	3.16	3.15	3.16	3.16	3.16	52	4.32	4.20	4.31	4.29	4.20
13	3.17	3.16	3.17	3.17	3.17	53	4.38	4.26	4.38	4.35	4.25
14	3.18	3.17	3.18	3.18	3.18	54	4.46	4.32	4.45	4.42	4.30
15	3.19	3.19	3.19	3.19	3.19	55	4.53	4.38	4.52	4.49	4.36
16	3.21	3.20	3.21	3.20	3.20	56	4.61	4.45	4.60	4.56	4.42
17	3.22	3.21	3.22	3.22	3.21	57	4.69	4.52	4.68	4.64	4.48
18	3.23	3.22	3.23	3.23	3.23	58	4.78	4.59	4.77	4.72	4.54
19	3.25	3.24	3.25	3.24	3.24	59	4.88	4.67	4.86	4.81	4.60
20	3.26	3.25	3.26	3.26	3.25	60	4.98	4.75	4.96	4.90	4.66
21	3.27	3.26	3.27	3.27	3.27	61	5.09	4.83	5.07	5.00	4.73
22	3.29	3.28	3.29	3.29	3.28	62	5.20	4.92	5.18	5.10	4.79
23	3.31	3.29	3.31	3.30	3.30	63	5.32	5.02	5.30	5.21	4.86
24	3.32	3.31	3.32	3.32	3.32	64	5.46	5.12	5.42	5.33	4.93
25	3.34	3.33	3.34	3.34	3.33	65	5.60	5.22	5.56	5.44	4.99
26	3.36	3.35	3.36	3.36	3.35	66	5.74	5.33	5.70	5.57	5.06
27	3.38	3.36	3.38	3.38	3.37	67	5.90	5.45	5.85	5.70	5.12
28	3.40	3.38	3.40	3.40	3.39	68	6.07	5.57	6.02	5.84	5.18
29	3.42	3.40	3.42	3.42	3.41	69	6.26	5.70	6.19	5.98	5.24
30	3.44	3.42	3.44	3.44	3.43	70	6.45	5.84	6.37	6.13	5.30
31	3.46	3.44	3.46	3.46	3.45	71	6.66	5.98	6.57	6.29	5.35
32	3.49	3.47	3.49	3.48	3.47	72	6.89	6.14	6.78	6.45	5.41
33	3.51	3.49	3.51	3.51	3.50	73	7.13	6.30	7.00	6.62	5.45
34	3.54	3.52	3.54	3.54	3.52	74	7.39	6.47	7.23	6.79	5.49
35	3.57	3.54	3.57	3.56	3.55	75	7.68	6.65	7.48	6.97	5.53
36	3.60	3.57	3.59	3.59	3.58	76	7.98	6.84	7.75	7.14	5.57
37	3.63	3.60	3.63	3.62	3.60	77	8.30	7.04	8.03	7.33	5.60
38	3.66	3.62	3.66	3.65	3.63	78	8.65	7.25	8.32	7.51	5.62
39	3.69	3.65	3.69	3.69	3.66	79	9.02	7.47	8.64	7.69	5.65
40	3.73	3.69	3.73	3.72	3.70	80	9.43	7.71	8.96	7.87	5.67
41	3.76	3.72	3.76	3.76	3.73						
42	3.80	3.75	3.80	3.79	3.76						
43	3.84	3.79	3.84	3.83	3.80						
44	3.89	3.83	3.88	3.88	3.84						
45	3.93	3.87	3.93	3.92	3.88						

Rates for ages 81 and over
are the same as those for age 80.

PAGE 13

PAYMENT OPTIONS (continued)

TABLE E(1)

Monthly Payments Per $1,000 Applied
Joint & Survivor
Based on Interest at 3½% Per Year

OLDER AGE

YOUNGER AGE	50	55	60	65	70	75	80
50	3.70	3.77	3.82	3.86	3.89	3.91	3.93
55		3.92	4.01	4.08	4.14	4.17	4.20
60			4.22	4.34	4.43	4.50	4.54
65				4.61	4.77	4.90	4.98
70					5.16	5.38	5.54
75						5.92	6.23
80							7.00

TABLE E(2)

Initial Monthly Payments Per $1,000 Applied
Joint & ⅔ Survivor
Based on Interest at 3½% Per Year

OLDER AGE

YOUNGER AGE	50	55	60	65	70	75	80
50	4.30	4.16	4.31	4.47	4.65	4.83	5.02
55		4.33	4.50	4.69	4.89	5.10	5.32
60			4.72	4.95	5.19	5.44	5.69
65				5.25	5.55	5.87	6.18
70					5.99	6.39	6.79
75						7.03	7.57
80							8.50

TABLE E(3)

Monthly Payments Per $1,000 Applied
Joint & ½ Survivor
Based on Interest at 3½% Per Year

OLDER AGE

YOUNGER AGE	50	55	60	65	70	75	80
50	4.22	4.39	4.60	4.85	5.14	5.47	5.83
55		4.56	4.79	5.06	5.38	5.74	6.13
60			5.02	5.32	5.68	6.08	6.52
65				5.65	6.05	6.51	7.02
70					6.52	7.05	7.65
75						7.75	8.48
80							9.52

Payment rates for combinations of ages not shown may be
obtained from the Company upon request.

NOTICE

The insured, by virtue of this policy, is a member of the SUPERIOR MUTUAL LIFE INSURANCE COMPANY OF AMERICA, and is entitled to vote, either in person or by proxy, at any and all meetings of the Company. The Annual Meetings are held at the Company's Home Office on the third Wednesday of June in each year, at ten o'clock A.M.

Whole Life Insurance Policy. Death proceeds payable at death of insured. Premiums payable for the period shown on page 3. Annual dividends.

PAGE 15

LIFE INSURANCE APPLICATION

Superior Mutual Life Insurance Company

PART 1   The following questions relate to the person proposed for insurance

1. Proposed insured - First name, middle initial, last name ☐ Male ☐ Female	16. Beneficiary

16. Beneficiary

Class	Name(s) (please print clearly)	Relationship to insured

2. Date of birth   month   day   year

3. Age nearest birthday

4. Place of birth

5. Telephone numbers   Day: Night:

6. Address for premium notices (bills will be sent to owner at this address)

If two or more beneficiaries are named state the class: 1, 2, 3, etc. Surviving beneficiaries in the lowest class share equally. All decisions made by SMLI in good faith as to the identity of beneficiaries not designated by name shall be conclusive as to SMLI's liability and any payment made in accordance therewith shall, to the extent thereof, discharge SMLI of it's obligation for such payment.

7. Residence of insured (if different)

17. Will coverage applied for replace or change any existing life insurance or annuity (other than SBLI)? If "Yes" submit form A-52.   ☐ Yes   ☐ No

8. Social Security number of the insured

9. Amount of existing SMLI Insurance $

18. If group insurance conversion:
Group name _____
Date group insurance terminated _____
☐ Policy terminated
☐ Employment terminated
Note: Part 2 on the reverse side should be completed only if Waiver of Premium is requested in question 12 or #5 in question 13.

10. Any other name now or previously known by (incl. maiden name, if applicable)

11. Within the last 12 months has the insured smoked: Cigarettes? ☐ Yes ☐ No   (a urine test may be required)   Cigars or a pipe? ☐ Yes ☐ No

19. Conversion or exchange of existing SMLI insurance (other than group):
Total Face Amount _____ Plan _____
Policy numbers:

12. Insurance Amount & Plan

Basic Policy $ _____ Plan _____

Insured Rider $ _____ Plan _____

Children Rider $ _____   Term to age 22 Insurance (complete Child Rider questionnaire)

Waiver of Premium ☐ Yes ☐ No   (issue ages 15-55 only)

The above policies are hereby tendered (1) for endorsement, if a rider insurance conversion, or (2) for surrender, if basic policy conversion or exchange; in consideration for and effective as of the date of issue of the insurance herein applied for. If a surrender, pay any cash or dividend values to me. (The above policies must accompany this application.)

For Term Conversions, Part 2 on the reverse side should be completed only if #5 is selected in question 13 or if Waiver of Premium is requested in question 12.

For Exchanges, Part 2 on the reverse side must be completed in all cases unless notified otherwise.

13. Dividends (if selection is missing or not available, #4 will be effective)

1 ☐ Pay in Cash
2 ☐ Reduce amount due - any excess dividend as ☐ #4 ☐ #3 ☐ #1
3 ☐ Purchase paid-up life additions (not available on term insurance)
4 ☐ Accumulate at interest
5 ☐ Purchase one-year term additions (not available on term insurance)

14. Premium payment frequency   ☐ Annual ☐ Semi-annual ☐ Quarterly

Automatic Premium Loan Provision to be effective on permanent insurance unless requested otherwise.

20. Special Requests

15. Owner (if no owner is shown, the applicant will be the owner.)

Class	Name (please print clearly)	Age	Relationship to insured
1			
2			
3			

21. How did you hear about SMLI
☐ Family member has SMLI ☐ Newspaper ☐ Radio ☐ TV ☐ Mail insert
☐ Bank lobby sign ☐ Friend or relative ☐ Other:

22. Changes made by SMLI

23. Issuing bank: No. _____ Name: _____

1. Under penalty of perjury, I certify that the Social Security Number(s) is/are correct and that I am not subject to backup withholding.
2. I hereby certify that the statements above are correct and agree that SMLI, believing them to be correct, shall rely and act on them.
3. If SBLI makes a change in space 22, it will be approved by my acceptance of the policy.
4. I agree that the insurance applied for shall not take effect until the first full premium is paid and the policy delivered while each person to be insured is in good health. Once submitted, this application will remain the property of SMLI

Date _____   X _____ Signature of Insured (if age 15 or over)

X _____ Signature of First Owner in question 15, if any

X _____ Signature of Applicant (if other than Insured) If Insured is under 15 check if: ☐ Mother ☐ Father ☐ Guardian

Social Security No. of Owner, if any, otherwise Applicant _____

Action	Date	By		Agent No.	Agent Signature
R/R				Agency	Source, if diff.	Initial Premium Rec'd. $	Date Received

Name of Proposed Insured (print)

PART 2 — To be completed by the SMLI agent if non-medical. (If this is to be a medical application, the examiner will complete this section.)

1. (a) Employer's name and address

(b) Job title and exact duties

| (c) Years so employed | (d) Change in occupation contemplated? | ☐ Yes | ☐ No |
| | Other occupations last 2 years? | ☐ Yes | ☐ No |

Details of "YES" answers. Identify the question number. Include diagnosis, dates, duration, names and addresses of all attending physicians and medical facilities. Give reason for checkup, treatment, and medication.

2.   **Yes** **No**

(a) Do you intend to reside or travel outside the United States and Canada except for vacations? ☐ ☐

(b) Have you ever made claim for or received any pension or disability benefits? ☐ ☐

(c) Have you ever had an application for life or health insurance declined, postponed, modified or offered at other than regular premiums for your age? ☐ ☐

3. (a) Do you participate in parachuting, motor racing or any other hazardous avocations? ☐ ☐

(b) Do you own, operate or are you licensed to operate an airplane? ☐ ☐

(c) How many flights have you made in the past twelve months in other than commercial airlines/airplanes?   #If any _____ ☐ None

4. Have you ever consulted any doctor or practitioner for, or suffered from any illness or disease of: **Yes** **No**

(a) The brain or nervous system? ☐ ☐

(b) The heart, blood vessels, or lungs? ☐ ☐

(c) The stomach or intestines? ☐ ☐

(d) The skin, glands, middle ear, hearing, eyes, or vision? ☐ ☐

5. Have you ever had or been advised to have an electrocardiogram, X-ray, or other diagnostic test? ☐ ☐

6. Have you ever had or been treated for rheumatism, bone disease, cancer, syphilis or other venereal disease, or any disorder of the muscles or bones, including the spine, back, or joints? ☐ ☐

7. Have you ever had or been treated for: chest pain, dizziness, fainting, convulsions, allergies, asthma, shortness of breath, persistent cough, repeated headache, paralysis, stroke, or diabetes? ☐ ☐

8. Have you ever been treated for or had any known indication of:

(a) Alcoholism? ☐ ☐

(b) Mental or nervous disorder? ☐ ☐

(c) Any deformity or congenital disorder? ☐ ☐

9. Have you ever used or dealt in barbiturates, excitants or hallucinogens, narcotics or other habit forming drugs? ☐ ☐

10. Are you now being treated or taking medicine for any condition or disease? ☐ ☐

11. Have you ever consulted a doctor or practitioner for, or had any known indication of, any illness, disease, or physical defect or disorder not included in the above questions? ☐ ☐

12. Other than above, within the past 3 years, have you had a checkup, consultation, illness, injury, surgery, or been a patient in a hospital, clinic, sanitarium or other medical facility? ☐ ☐

13. Females age 15 and over only:

(a) Ever had any disorder of menstruation, pregnancy, or of the female organs or breasts? ☐ ☐

(b) Are you now pregnant? ☐ ☐

(c) Ever had a caesarean section? ☐ ☐

(d) Are uterine functions now irregular? ☐ ☐

(e) Number of children _____

15. Family History - Indicate below any diabetes, cancer, high blood pressure, heart or kidney disease, mental illness or suicide.

Family Member	Age if Living	State of Health (If not good, give details or cause of death.)	Age at Death
Father			
Mother			
Brothers & Sisters			
No. Living _____			
No. Dead _____			

14. Height (in shoes) _____ ft. _____ in. Weight (clothed) _____ lbs.

Has weight changed in the past two years? ☐ Yes ☐ No

If "Yes": Gain _____ lbs., Loss _____ lbs. How long at present weight? _____

_____   X _____
Date   Signature of Examiner (Agent if non-medical)

I hereby certify that the above answers and statements are correct and I agree that SMLI believing them to be correct shall rely and act on them. I agree that they shall be a part of my application for insurance or policy change request. I acknowledge receipt of the attached **Disclosure Notice and MIB Notification.**

I HEREBY AUTHORIZE any licensed physician, medical practitioner, hospital, clinic or other medical or medically related facility, insurance company, the Medical Information Bureau or other organization, institution or person, that has any records or knowledge of the Proposed Insured or his/her health to give to the Medical Director, Superior Mutual Life, any such information.

A photographic copy of this authorization shall be as valid as the original.

_____ _____ X _____
Name of Proposed Insured (please print)   Date   Signature of Proposed Insured (Parent or Guardian if insured under age 15)

PART 3 — To be completed by an Examiner authorized by SMLI. Omit if Non-Medical.

16. Males only	17. Blood Pressure	18. Pulse	19. Urinalysis
Chest (inspiration) _____ in.	Systolic	Rate _____	Albumin _____
Chest (expiration) _____ in.	Diastolic (All sound ceases)	Quality _____	
Waist _____ in.		Irregularities per minute _____	Sugar _____
	If over 138/88, repeat twice 3 minutes apart		

20. For question 14 answers	21. Did you observe any indication of physical or mental impairment or abnormality not indicated in Part 2? ☐ Yes ☐ No
Did you measure? ☐ Yes ☐ No	If "Yes" explain:
Did you weigh? ☐ Yes ☐ No	

I have personally seen the person whose name appears in part 2. I am satisfied as to the identity of that person. I certify that the answers in Part 2 were correctly recorded by me.

Paramed Stamp:

_____   X _____   _____
Date   Examiner

A consumer inspection report, if we request one, may include information obtained through personal interviews with your neighbors, friends or others with whom you are acquainted. This inquiry includes information as to your character, general reputation, personal characteristics and mode of living. You have the right to make a written request within a reasonable period of time to receive additional, detailed information about the nature and scope of this investigation. Please direct any such request to Medical Director, Superior Mutual Life.

Information regarding your insurability will be treated as confidential. We may, however, make a brief report thereon to the Medical Information Bureau (MIB), a nonprofit membership organization of insurance companies, which operates an information exchange on behalf of its members. If you apply to another MIB member company for life or health insurance coveage, or a claim for benefits is submitted to such a company, MIB, upon request, will supply such company with the information in its files.

We will not reject your application because of data furnished by MIB; it may simply alert us to the possible need for further information. MIB files do not contain medical reports from doctors or hospitals, nor do they indicate whether any insurance applications have been accepted or rejected.

Upon receipt of a request from you, MIB will arrange disclosure of any information it may have in your file. (Medical information will be disclosed only to your attending physician.) If you question the accuracy of the information in the MIB file, you may contact MIB and seek a correction in accordance with the procedures set forth in the Federal Fair Credit Reporting Act. The address of the MIB office is P.O. Box 105, Essex Station, Boston MA 02112, telephone (617) 426-3660. We may also release information in our file to other life insurance companies to whom you apply for life or health insurance, or to whom a claim for benefits may be submitted.

**ERIE HEALTH INSURANCE
COMPANY OF AMERICA**

Erie Health agrees, in accordance with the provisions of this policy, to pay the benefits provided in this policy due to injury or sickness.

Twenty-Day Right to Examine Policy   You may return this policy by delivering it to the Home Office or to an agent of the Company within 20 days after receiving it. Immediately on such delivery, the policy will be void as of the date of issue and any premium paid will be refunded.

Robert Johnson
President

John Birdy
Secretary

Insured:	Bill Dempsy
Policy Number:	0000-0000-00
Policy Date:	November 5, 2001

Individual Health Policy

Contents

Index

DEFINITIONS

"You," "Your" and "Yours" means the insured named on the Policy Schedule. "Time," "Us" and "Ours" means the Company.

COVERED PERSON: Covered person means the insured and all eligible dependents shown on the policy schedule, or added by endorsement.

CUSTODIAL CARE means care given to a covered person if the person:

1. is mentally or physically disabled and such disability is expected to last for an indefinite time;
2. needs a protected, monitored and/or controlled environment;
3. needs help to support the essentials of daily living; and
4. is not under active and specific medical, surgical and/or psychiatric treatment, which will reduce the disability to the extent necessary for the person to function outside a protected, monitored and/or controlled environment.

DENTAL SERVICE means any medical or surgical procedure that involves the hard or soft tissue of the mouth that requires treatment as a result of a disease or condition of the teeth and gums. Treatment for neoplasms is not considered a dental service.

DISABLED DEPENDENTS: This section amends the Eligible Dependents section. An unmarried child who cannot support himself due to mental incapacity or physical handicap may continue to be insured. This child must be fully dependent upon you for support. The Company may inquire of you two months prior to attainment by a dependent of the limiting age set forth in this policy, or at any reasonable time thereafter, whether such dependent is in fact a disabled and dependent person. In the absence of proof submitted within 60 days of such inquiry that such dependent is a disabled and dependent person, the Company may terminate coverage of such person at or after attainment of the limiting age. In the absence of such inquiry, coverage of any disabled and dependent person shall continue through the term of such policy or any extension or renewal thereof.

EFFECTIVE DATE OF COVERAGE; A covered person's effective date of coverage is: (1) the policy date, if the covered person is listed on the application and the policy schedule; or (2) the date of policy endorsement, if the covered person is added

ELIGIBLE DEPENDENTS: Eligible dependents are those dependents shown on the policy schedule or added by endorsement. This may include: (1) Your lawful spouse; and (2) Unmarried dependent children, including step-children and adopted children (or children who are in your custody pursuant to an interim court order of adoption), if they are legally dependent on you for their support and under 21 years of age.

Your newborn children, born while the policy is in force, will be covered for 60 days after birth. For coverage beyond 60 days after birth, written application must be made to the Company within that 60-day period. An additional premium will be required retroactive to date of birth. Other eligible dependents may be added by you upon evidence of insurability satisfactory to the Company. Additional premium will be required.

ELIGIBLE FOR MEDICARE means that the covered person is either:

1. covered by both Part A and Part B of Medicare; or
2. not covered for both Part A and Part B of Medicare because of:
   a. a failure to enroll when required;
   b. a failure to pay any premium that may be required for full coverage of the person under Medicare; or
   c. a failure to file any written request, claim or document required for payment of Medicare benefits.

HOSPICE PROGRAM means a coordinated interdisciplinary program for meeting the special physical, psychological, spiritual and social needs of dying covered persons and their immediate families. The covered person must be enrolled in the program by a physician.

HOSPITAL means a place other than a convalescent, nursing or rest home, that:

- provides facilities for medical, diagnostic and acute care on an inpatient basis. If these services are not on its own premises, they must be available through a prearranged contract;
- provides 24-hour nursing care supervised by registered nurses;
- has X ray and lab facilities either on its premises or available through a prearranged contract;
- charges for these services.

A special ward, floor or other accommodation for convalescent, nursing or rehabilitation purposes is not considered a hospital.

IMMEDIATE FAMILY means you, your spouse, and the children, brothers, sisters and parents of either you or your spouse.

INJURY: Injury means accidental bodily injury sustained by a covered person while covered under this policy.

MEDICALLY NECESSARY CARE means confinement, treatment or service that is rendered to diagnose or treat a sickness or injury. Such care must be (1) prescribed by a physician; (2) considered to be necessary and appropriate for the diagnosis and treatment of the sickness or injury; and (3) commonly accepted as proper care or treatment of the condition by the U.S. medical community. Medically necessary care does not include care considered to be: (1) experimental or investigative in nature by any appropriate technological assessment body established by any state or federal government; (2) provided only as a convenience to the covered person or provider; and (3) in excess (in scope, duration or intensity) of that level of care which is needed to provide safe, adequate and appropriate diagnosis and treatment. The fact that a physician may prescribe, order, recommend or approve a service or supply does not, of itself, make the service or supply medically necessary.

MEDICARE: Medicare means the Health Insurance for the Aged Act, Title XVIII of the Social Security Act as amended.

MENTAL ILLNESS: Mental illness means a mental or nervous disorder, including neuroses, psychoneurosis, psychopathy, psychosis and other emotional disorders. Affective disorders (including bipolar disorders and major depression), alcoholism, drug addiction and chemical dependency are also included in this definition.

OTHER HEALTH INSURANCE PLAN: This means any plan that provides insurance, reimbursement or service benefits for hospital, surgical or other medical expenses. This includes: (1) individual or group health insurance policies; (2) nonprofit health service plans, including Blue Cross and Blue Shield; (3) health maintenance organization subscriber contracts; (4) self-insured group plans; (5) welfare plans; (6) medical coverage under homeowners or automobile insurance; and (7) service provided or payment received under laws of any national, state or local government. This does not include Medicaid.

If coverage is provided on a service basis, the amount of benefits under such coverage will be taken as the cost of the service in the absence of such coverage.

PART A means the Hospital Insurance Benefits for the Aged portion of Medicare.

PART B means the Supplementary Medical Insurance for the Aged portion of Medicare.

PHYSICAL MEDICINE means the diagnosis and treatment of physical conditions relating to bone, muscle or neuromuscular pathology.

PHYSICIAN: A person licensed by the state to treat the kind of injury or sickness for which a claim is made. The physician must be practicing within the limits of his or her license.

POLICY OWNER: The insured shown on the policy schedule unless someone else is designated the owner on the application.

PREEXISTING CONDITIONS: A preexisting condition is a condition not fully disclosed on the application for insurance:

1. for which the covered person received medical treatment or advice from a physician within the six-month period immediately preceding that covered person's effective date of coverage; or
2. which produced signs or symptoms within the six-month period immediately preceding that covered person's effective date of coverage.

    The signs or symptoms must have been significant enough to establish manifestation or onset by one of the following tests:
    a. The signs or symptoms would have allowed one learned in medicine to make a diagnosis of the disorder; or
    b. The signs or symptoms should have caused an ordinarily prudent person to seek diagnosis or treatment.

Preexisting conditions will be covered after the covered person has been insured for two years, if the condition is not specifically excluded from coverage.

REASONABLE AND CUSTOMARY CHARGE means the lesser of:

1. The actual charge;
2. What the provider would accept for the same service or supply in the absence of insurance; or

3. The reasonable charge as determined by the Company, based on factors such as:
   a. the most common charge for the same or comparable service or supply in a community similar to where the service or supply is furnished;
   b. the amount of resources expended to deliver the treatment and the complexity of the treatment rendered; and
   c. charging protocols and billing practices generally accepted by the medical community or specialty groups; or
   d. inflation trends by geographic region.

SICKNESS: Sickness means an illness, disease or condition of a covered person that manifests itself after the covered person's effective date of coverage. For sickness that manifests itself during the first 15 days following the effective date, coverage is provided only for covered expense incurred after that 15-day period.

SKILLED NURSING FACILITY means a nursing home, licensed as a skilled nursing facility, operating in accordance with the laws of the state in which it is located and meeting the following requirements:

1. Is primarily engaged in providing room, board and skilled nursing care for persons recovering from sickness or injury;
2. Provides 24-hour-a-day skilled nursing service under the full-time supervision of a physician or graduate registered nurse;
3. Maintains daily clinical records;
4. Has transfer arrangements with a hospital;
5. Has a utilization review plan in effect;
6. Is not a place for rest, the aged, drug addicts, alcoholics or the mentally ill; and
7. May be a part of a hospital.

COVERAGE DESCRIPTION

DEDUCTIBLE AMOUNT: The deductible amount for each covered person during each calendar year is the larger of:

- the basic deductible amount shown in the policy schedule; or
- the amount of benefits paid for covered expenses by any other health insurance plan as defined in the policy.

The deductible amount must be:

- incurred each calendar year; and
- deducted from covered expenses.

A calendar year begins on January 1 and ends December 31.

MAXIMUM FAMILY DEDUCTIBLE AMOUNT: A maximum family deductible amount equal to three times the basic deductible amount will satisfy the deductible requirements for all covered persons in a family during a calendar year.

FAMILY CAP MAXIMUM: The maximum expense amount incurred per family for covered expense will not exceed the family cap maximum shown in the policy schedule for any calendar year.

CARRY-OVER DEDUCTIBLE: Any covered expense incurred and applied to a covered person's basic deductible amount during the last three months of a calendar year may also be used to

reduce that person's basic deductible amount for the next calendar year.

The maximum family deductible and the carry-over deductible provisions will not apply if the benefits paid by other health insurance are used as the deductible.

RIGHT TO CHANGE DEDUCTIBLE AMOUNT: You may apply for an increase or decrease in the basic deductible amount within a 60-day period after a premium rate change, or during the first 30 days of a calendar year, provided that: (1) the new basic deductible amount is one that is available on this form, (2) a request for the change is made in writing to the Company, and (3) no claims have been incurred during that calendar year.

If you request a decrease in the deductible amount, the Company will require proof of continued insurability of all covered persons.

PAYMENT OF BENEFITS: Benefits for covered expense incurred will be paid in accordance with Sections A and B of the covered expense provision.

If benefits paid by other health insurance are used as the deductible amount, all covered expense will be paid at 100 percent, but payment will not exceed the amount that would have been paid in the absence of other health insurance.

Where applicable, the rate of payment starts again for each covered person each new calendar year after the deductible amount has been met. The Company will pay up to the lifetime maximum benefit shown in the policy schedule for each covered person.

If the payment by other health insurance is used as the deductible amount, the lifetime maximum benefit will be increased. The maximum benefit will be increased by $3 for each $1 paid by other coverage over the basic deductible.

PAYMENT OF BENEFITS WHEN ELIGIBLE FOR MEDICARE: When any covered person is eligible for Medicare, he or she will be deemed to have Part A and Part B Medicare coverage that is primary to the coverage under this policy. Services covered by Medicare will not be covered by this policy to the extent that benefits are payable by Medicare. If there is remaining covered expense after Medicare pays for assigned services, benefits will be paid at 100 percent up to the amount approved by Medicare; for unassigned services, benefits will be paid at 100 percent up to our reasonable and customary charge limit. Payment of benefits for services not covered by Medicare will be determined by the terms and limits of this policy.

COVERED EXPENSE: Covered expense means expense that is (a) incurred for services, treatment or supplies prescribed by a physician and described in Section A or B below; (b) incurred by a covered person as the result of sickness or injury as defined; (c) incurred for medically necessary care; and (d) incurred while the covered person's coverage is in force. Covered expense does not include any charge in excess of the reasonable and customary charge.

A. The following items of covered expense are subject to the deductible and rate of payment as described in this policy and shown in the policy schedule.

1. Room, board and general nursing care while confined in a semi-private room, ward, coronary care or other intensive care unit in a hospital. For confinement in a private room, the covered expense is limited to the hospital's most common daily charge for a semi-private room.

2. Other hospital services including services performed in a hospital outpatient department or in a free-standing surgical facility.

3. Physician services and surgical services, including second surgical opinions by board-certified specialists. This does not include services rendered by members of your immediate family.

4. Reconstructive surgery to restore function for conditions resulting from accidental injury provided the injury occurred while the covered person is insured under this plan. Reconstructive surgery that is incidental to or follows covered surgery performed as the result of trauma, infection or other diseases of the involved part.

Reconstructive surgery for congenital defects provided the covered person has been insured continuously under this plan since the time of birth.

5. Hospice programs when (a) the physician projects a life expectancy of six months or less; and (b) the physician enrolls a covered person in the program. Notification is to be made in writing to the Company within seven days of admission to a licensed hospice facility. Covered expense includes up to 30 days of inpatient treatment at a hospice facility. Hospice home care is covered in addition to benefits provided under item 6. Benefits for services that include inpatient hospice services, hospice home care and counselling under the authorized hospice program are limited to $15,000 during the covered person's lifetime.

6. Up to 40 home health care visits in any 12-month period. One visit consists of up to four hours of home health aide service within a 24-hour period by anyone providing services or evaluating the need for home health care.

For home health care to be a covered expense, the physician must certify that:

a. hospitalization or confinement in a skilled nursing facility would otherwise be required;

b. medically necessary care is not available from members of the covered person's immediate family or persons living with the covered person without causing undue hardship; and

c. the home health care will be provided by a state-licensed or Medicare-certified home health agency.

Home health care does not include:

a. services not included in the home health care plan established for the covered person by the physician;

b. services provided by the covered person's immediate family or anyone residing with the covered person;

c. homemaker services; or

d. custodial care.

7. Professional ambulance service to the nearest hospital that is able to handle the sickness or injury. One trip to a hospital for a covered person for each sickness or injury is covered.

8. X ray, radioactive treatment, laboratory tests and anesthesia services.

9. Outpatient physical medicine benefits to a maximum of $500 for each covered person per calendar year. Physical medicine benefits include but are not limited to: rehabilitative speech, physical, occupational and cognitive therapies; biofeedback; sports medicine; cardiac exercise programs; adjustments and manipulations. The limitation does not apply to the treatment of burns, fractures, complete dislocations; joint replacements or related conditions for which a covered person is hospitalized for surgery and physical medicine that immediately follows hospitalization.

10. Rental, up to the purchase price, or purchase, when approved in advance by the Company, of (a) a basic wheelchair, basic hospital bed or basic crutches; (b) the initial permanent basic artificial limb, eye or external breast prosthesis; and (c) oxygen and the equipment needed to administer oxygen.

Casts, orthopedic braces, splints, dressings and sutures.

Dental braces, dental appliances, corrective shoes, orthotics or repairs to or replacement of prosthetic devices are not covered expenses.

11. Drugs that require the written prescription of a licensed physician. However, if a prescription drug benefit rider is attached to this policy, covered drugs will be paid under that rider (to age 65 or prior Medicare eligibility) instead of under this policy.

12. Whole blood, blood plasma and blood products, if not replaced.

13. Dental service for an injury to a sound natural tooth when the expense is incurred within six months following the injury.

"Sound" is defined as:

a. organic and formed by nature;

b. not extensively restored or endodontically treated; and

c. not extensively decayed or involved in periodontal disease.

14. Treatment of mental illness. Expense incurred by a covered person while confined as an inpatient to a hospital or psychiatric hospital for mental illness as defined in the policy. Coverage is limited to a maximum benefit of $2,500 for a covered person during a calendar year. Outpatient treatment, drugs or medications are not covered.

15. Sterilization, if the covered person has been insured on this policy for at least two years.

16. Treatment of temporomandibular joint dysfunction except for: crowns that correct vertical dimension; splints, orthopedic repositioning appliances, biteplates and equilibration treatments (including splint equilibration and adjustments); bite functional or occlusal registration, with or without splints, and kinesiographic analysis; any orthodontic treatment, including extraction of teeth; study models, except for the complete model made necessary when surgical intervention is completed. Surgical charges for correction of orthognathic conditions are covered.

B. The following items 1, 2 and 3 of covered expense will not be subject to the basic deductible amount of the 80 percent rate of payment. Covered expense will be considered for payment under this section before it is considered under any other section of the policy. Covered expense for which a benefit is payable under this section will not be considered for payment under any other section of the policy.

1. Skilled nursing care: Medically necessary care in a skilled nursing facility for up to 30 days provided (a) the covered person enters the skilled nursing facility within 14 days after discharge from an authorized hospital confinement; (b) the skilled nursing facility confinement is for the same condition that required the hospital confinement; and (c) such care is authorized by the Company within seven days following admission to the skilled nursing facility. The daily benefit for confinement in a skilled nursing facility will not exceed one-half of the semi-private hospital room rate for the area.

2. Second and third opinions required by the Company's authorization service. Only an exam, X ray and lab work, and a written report by the physician rendering the opinion are

included. You will be supplied with a list of three recommended physicians from whom the second or third opinion may be sought. The service may allow another physician to be consulted if the physician is (a) a board-certified specialist in the field of the proposed treatment; (b) is not financially associated with the first physician; and (c) does not perform the treatment.

3. Pre-admission testing. X rays and lab work performed on an outpatient basis before an authorized hospital admission provided (a) the tests are related to a scheduled admission; (b) the charges for the tests would have been covered expense if the individual was confined as an inpatient in a hospital; and (c) the tests were not repeated in or by the hospital, or elsewhere.

HUMAN ORGAN/TISSUE TRANSPLANT OR REPLACEMENT: Covered expense incurred by a covered person for the following human organ or tissue transplants or replacements if the procedure is authorized as indicated below, to a maximum lifetime benefit of $250,000 for each covered person.

Human organ transplant. The following procedures are covered if the procedure is authorized in writing by the Company prior to the beginning of the donor search and selection:

a. Bone marrow transplant
b. Heart transplant
c. Liver transplant

No benefits will be paid if the procedure has not been authorized by the Company prior to the beginning of the donor search and selection. To begin the authorization process, the physician or the physician's assistant must contact the Company's authorization service.

Tissue transplant or replacement. The following procedures are covered if authorized according to the procedures outlined in the authorization provision:

a. Cornea transplant
b. Prosthetic tissue replacement, including joint replacement
c. Vein or artery graft
d. Heart valve replacement
e. Implantable prosthetic lens in connection with cataracts

Donor Expenses. Expense incurred for surgery, storage and/or transportation service related to

donor organ acquisition is also covered, up to a maximum benefit of $10,000 per covered procedure.

If the transplanted organ is from a live donor, expense incurred by the donor that is not paid by any other plan of insurance will be covered as though the donor's expense were the expense of the covered person.

No benefits will be paid for any transplant not authorized in writing by the Company prior to the beginning of donor search and selection or any transplant or replacement procedure not specifically listed above.

Kidney Disease or End Stage Renal Disease. Expense incurred for dialysis, transplantation and donor-related services to a maximum of $30,000 for each covered person during a calendar year. The transplant must be authorized in writing by the Company prior to the beginning of the donor search and selection. No benefits will be paid if the procedure has not been authorized by the Company prior to the beginning of such search.

Together with expense for dialysis and/or transplantation, expense incurred for surgery, storage and/or transportation service related to donor organ acquisition is limited to the $30,000 annual maximum. If the transplanted organ is from a live donor, expense incurred by the donor that is not paid by any other plan of insurance will be covered as though the donor's expense were the expense of the covered person, and included in the $30,000 annual maximum.

The limits in this provision for kidney disease or end stage renal disease provide for coordination with the governmental coverage for end stage renal disease.

COVERED COMPLICATIONS OF PREGNANCY: You, your spouse or a dependent child are covered for complications of pregnancy as defined below. Benefits are provided on the same basis as any covered sickness. Covered complications of pregnancy are limited to:

1. Conditions (when pregnancy is not ended) whose diagnoses are distinct from pregnancy, but are caused or adversely affected by pregnancy. Some examples: acute nephritis, nephrosis and cardiac decompensation.
2. Non-elective caesarean section
3. Ectopic pregnancy that is terminated
4. Spontaneous termination of pregnancy (mis-

carriage) that occurs before the 26th week of gestation; or missed abortion

Covered complications of pregnancy do not include: high-risk pregnancy or delivery, false labor, premature labor, occasional spotting, physician prescribed rest, morning sickness, pre-eclampsia or placenta previa.

CONGENITAL ILLNES OR DEFECT OF A NEWBORN CHILD: Congenital illness or defect of a child of the insured born while this policy is in force will not be considered a preexisting condition. Benefits will be provided on the same basis as any other sickness.

AUTHORIZATION PROVISION

This plan requires pre-authorization of all hospital admissions, inpatient surgeries, outpatient surgeries and transplants. The payment of benefits for covered expense described under the "Coverage Description" section of this policy may be reduced if the authorization procedure described below is not followed.

AN AUTHORIZATION DOES NOT GUARANTEE THAT BENEFITS WILL BE PAID. PAYMENT OF BENEFITS WILL BE DETERMINED BY THE TERMS AND LIMITS OF THE POLICY.

ELECTIVE ADMISSION OR SURGERY: For non-emergency hospital confinement, inpatient surgery, outpatient surgery or day surgery performed in a hospital, you must have the physician ordering the confinement or surgery obtain authorization before the patient is admitted to the hospital or has surgery performed. The authorization is obtained by the physician or physician's assistant from the Company's authorization service. The service can be reached by telephone during normal business hours, each Monday through Friday. A toll-free number and the name of the Company's authorization service is provided on the ID card given to you by the Company. You must instruct the physician to obtain the authorization by using the authorization form provided by the Company.

The service may require a second opinion prior to granting authorization. In such cases, you will be supplied with a list of three recommended physicians from whom the second opinion may be sought. However, the service may allow another physician to be consulted who (a) is a board-certified specialist in the field of the proposed treatment or surgery; (b) is not financially affiliated with the first physician; and (c) does not perform the surgery or provide the treatment. If the second opinion confirms the need for admission, then the admission will be considered AUTHORIZED. If the second opinion does not confirm the need for surgery or treatment, the service may allow a third

opinion to be sought from a physician meeting the qualifications described for second opinions.

The physician may proceed with treatment on the basis of verbal authorization from the service. This will be followed by a written authorization sent to you, the hospital and the physician. The authorization remains valid for 60 days from the date of the written authorization. For treatment beginning after the 60-day period, a new authorization must be obtained.

EMERGENCY ADMISSIONS: Emergency admissions are admissions for life-threatening conditions or for a condition for which the absence of immediate treatment would cause permanent disability. An emergency admission must also be authorized in the same manner as an elective admission or surgery, as soon as it is reasonably possible to give notice of such confinement. Otherwise that portion of an emergency confinement occurring beyond 48 hours after admission (excluding Saturdays, Sundays and legal holidays) is considered UNAUTHORIZED.

UNAUTHORIZED ADMISSION, CONFINEMENT, OR SURGERY: If authorization is obtained in accordance with the above procedures, the hospital admission or surgery will be considered authorized; otherwise, it will be considered UNAUTHORIZED. An admission, confinement or surgery for which authorization was obtained shall be considered UNAUTHORIZED if (a) the authorization is no longer valid when confinement begins or surgery is performed; or (b) the type of treatment, admitting physician or hospital differs from the authorized treatment, physician or hospital.

Also, that portion of a hospital confinement, whether non-emergency or emergency, that exceeds the number of authorized days will be considered UNAUTHORIZED, unless an extension is granted. To receive an extension, the physician must call the Company's authorization service at least 24 hours prior to the originally scheduled discharge date and request an extension. The authorization service may or may not authorize an extension. Unauthorized extensions will be considered on the same basis as an unauthorized admission.

REDUCTION OF PAYMENT: The first $500 of covered expense incurred for unauthorized hospital admissions, confinements (or the unauthorized portion thereof) or any surgery shall not be paid by the Company; nor will that $500, or any portion thereof, be applied to the basic deductible amount requirement or rate of payment determination. As described under the Coverage Description section, to be a covered expense, the services, treatment and supplies must be medically necessary and the resulting charges reasonable and customary.

EXCLUSIONS AND LIMITATIONS

EXPENSES NOT COVERED BY THIS POLICY: This policy does not provide benefits for the following:

1. preexisting conditions during the first two years coverage is in force; except as provided by the policy;
2. expense incurred for a sickness during the first 15 days after a covered person's effective date of coverage;
3. intentionally self-inflicted injury, suicide or suicide attempt, whether sane or insane;
4. care, treatment or services while in a government hospital, unless the covered person is legally required to pay for such services in the absence of insurance;
5. injury or sickness to the extent that benefits are paid by Medicare or any other government law or program (except Medicaid); or any Motor Vehicle No-Fault Law;
6. injury or sickness covered by any Worker's Compensation Act or Occupational Disease Law;
7. war or any act of war; injury or sickness while in the military service of any country (any premium paid for a time not covered will be returned pro-rata);
8. treatment of Temporomandibular Joint Dysfunction except as provided in item 16 of the covered expense provision;
9. dental service including X rays, care or treatment except as provided under item 13 of the covered expense provision;
10. treatment for infertility; confinement, treatment or services related to artificial insemination; restoration of fertility, reversal of sterilization or promotion of conception; or expense incurred for genetic counselling, testing or treatment.
11. eyeglasses, contact lenses, hearing aids, eye exams, eye refraction or eye surgery for correction of refraction error;
12. normal pregnancy or childbirth (except as may be provided by rider), routine well-baby care including hospital nursery charges at birth; abortion or caesarean section except as provided in the Covered Complications of Pregnancy provision;
13. expense incurred for weight reduction or weight-control programs, including surgery; treatment, medication or hormones to stimulate growth;
14. reconstructive or plastic surgery that is primarily a cosmetic procedure, including medical or surgical complications therefrom; except as provided in item 4 of the covered expense provision;
15. the first $500 of otherwise covered expense incurred during any unauthorized hospital confinement or the unauthorized portion of a confinement or unauthorized surgery (see Reduction of Payment Provision);
16. treatment, removal or repair of tonsils or adenoids during the first six months of coverage, except on an emergency basis;
17. expense incurred due to injury or sickness due to committing a felony or while under the influence of illegal narcotics;
18. sales tax or gross receipt tax;
19. custodial care.

CLAIMS

NOTICE OF CLAIM: If a covered person incurs covered expense, you must give the Company written notice of claim. The notice must be given within 60 days after the claim begins, or as soon as is reasonably possible. The notice must be given to the Company or its agent, and must include your name and policy number.

CLAIM FORMS: When notice of claim is received, the Company will send you claim forms. If you do not receive the forms within 15 days after the giving of such notice, you shall be deemed to have complied with the proof of loss requirements if: (1) you give the Company a written statement of the nature and the extent of the loss for which claim is made; and (2) such statement is given within the time limit stated in the Proofs of Loss provision.

PROOFS OF LOSS: You must give the Company written proof of loss within 90 days after the covered expense is incurred. If written proof is not given in the time required, this will not make the claim invalid as long as the proof is given as soon as reasonably possible. In no event, except in the absence of legal capacity, may proof be given later than one year from the time otherwise required.

PAYMENT OF CLAIMS: Benefits will be paid to you unless you have assigned them to a doctor, hospital or other provider. Any benefits unpaid and unassigned at your death will be paid to the designated beneficiary or your estate.

TIME OF PAYMENT OF CLAIMS: Benefits for covered expense will be paid promptly upon receipt of written proof of loss. If not paid within 30 days of receipt of proof of loss, interest at the rate of 8 percent per annum will be paid, in addition, after the 30th day.

PHYSICAL EXAMINATION: While a claim is pending, the Company has the right to have a covered person examined as often as reasonably necessary. This will be at the Company's expense.

CONTRACT

CONSIDERATION: This policy is issued on the basis of the statements and agreements in the application and payment of the required premium. Premium payment in advance on or before the policy date will keep this policy in force from the policy date until the first renewal date. The premium is set out in the policy schedule. Each renewal premium is due on its due date subject to the grace period. All periods of insurance will begin and end at 12:01 A.M., standard time, at your residence.

ENTIRE CONTRACT; CHANGES: This policy, your attached application and any endorsements constitute the entire contract. No change in this policy is valid unless approved by an executive office of the Company. The approval must be endorsed by the officer and attached to the policy. No agent can change this policy or waive any of its provisions.

TIME LIMIT ON CERTAIN DEFENSES: After two years from the effective date of coverage, no misstatement made in the application (unless fraudulent) will be used to void the policy or deny any claim beginning after the two year period.

No claim for expense incurred by a covered person that begins more than two years from that person's effective date of coverage will be reduced or denied on the grounds that a disease or physical condition (not excluded from coverage by name or specific description) had existed prior to the covered person's effective date.

GRACE PERIOD: There is a grace period of 31 days for the payment of each premium due after the first premium. The policy will stay in force during this grace period. If the premium is not paid by the end of the grace period, this policy will lapse. No coverage will be provided during the grace period if the covered person has similar coverage available through another carrier and does not pay premium to the Company.

NON-RENEWAL: The grace period does not apply if the Company has given you written notice that it will not renew the policy. This notice must be sent to you at least 30 days before the premium is due. Notice will be mailed to your last known address in the Company's records. Coverage will continue for any period for which premium has been accepted.

The Company can only decline to renew the policy on the renewal date occurring on, or after and nearest, each anniversary. The anniversary will be based on the policy date or last reinstatement date. This does not apply if premiums are not paid. Non-renewal will not prejudice any expense incurred while the policy was in force.

LEGAL ACTION: You cannot bring legal action to recover on this policy before at least 60 days have passed from the time written proof has been given to the Company. No action can be brought after three years from the time written proof has been given to the Company. The time limit is five years in Kansas; six years in South Carolina.

TERMINATION OF INSURED'S COVERAGE: Your coverage will end on the date the policy lapses or is non-renewed.

TERMINATION OF DEPENDENT COVERAGE: Coverage will end for your dependent children on the date the policy lapses or is non-renewed, or on the premium due date following the earliest to occur of (a) the date of their marriage, (b) the date they reach age 21 (or age 25 if the dependent is enrolled in and actively pursuing a full-time course of study at an accredited institution of higher learning), or (c) the date they are no longer dependent on you. Coverage will end on your spouse: (a) on the date the policy lapses or is non-renewed; or (b) on the premium due date following the date of a divorce. Benefits will still be paid to the end of the time for which premiums were accepted.

CONVERSION: A spouse or a dependent child who is no longer eligible for coverage on this policy can obtain a similar policy. No proof of good health will be required, but written application must be made within 60 days after that person's coverage terminates.

MISSTATEMENT OF AGE OR SEX: If any age or sex has been misstated, an adjustment in the benefits payable will be made to recover any past premiums due.

REINSTATEMENT: If you do not pay a renewal premium within the time granted, your policy will lapse. It will be reinstated if the Company or its agent accepts the premium without requiring an application.

If the Company or its agent requires an application for reinstatement, and the application and one modal premium are received within six months of the lapse date, the policy will be reinstated when approved by the Company. The Company has 45 days to act on your application. Your policy will be reinstated unless the Company notifies you in writing of its disapproval.

You will be covered for an injury sustained on or after the reinstatement date. You will be covered for a sickness that begins more than ten days after the reinstatement date.

After the policy is reinstated, you and the Company will have the same rights as existed just before the due date. These rights are subject to any provisions endorsed or attached to the policy. Premium cannot be required for more than 60 days before the date.

CONFORMITY WITH STATE STATUTES: If this policy, on its effective date, is in conflict with any laws in your state of residence, it is changed to meet the minimum requirements of such laws.

MAJOR MEDICAL INSURANCE APPLICATION

Name _____ Occupation _____ Sex _____
　　　Last　　　　　　　　　　First　　　　　　　　Middle　　　　　　　　　　　　　　　　　　　　　　　　　　M/F

Billing Address _____ Height _____ Weight _____
　　　　　　　Street　　　　　　　　　　　　City　　　　　State　　Zip Code　　　　　Ft. In.　　　　Lbs.

Date of Birth _____ Place of Birth _____ Phone (_____) _____
　　　　　Mo./Day/Yr.　　　　　　　　　　　City/State　　　　　　　　　　Area Code　　Number

Social Security # _____ Business Phone (_____) _____
　　　　　　　　　　　　　　　　　　　　　　　　　　　　　Area Code　　Number

1) I am a member actively at work at least 30 hours a week　❑ Yes　❑ No

YOUR CHOICE OF DEDUCTIBLE:　❑ PLAN A–$250　❑ PLAN B–$500　❑ PLAN C–$1,000

HOW WOULD YOU LIKE YOUR PREMIUM BILLED:　❑ Monthly　❑ Quarterly

WHICH PLAN ARE YOU APPLYING FOR:　❑ Comprehensive　❑ Basic

If you wish to include your spouse and/or eligible dependent children, complete this section:

NAME (First, Middle, Last)	SEX	DATE OF BIRTH	HEIGHT	WEIGHT
Your Spouse				
Your Children				

THE FOLLOWING QUESTIONS ARE TO BE ANSWERED FOR EACH PERSON APPLYING FOR COVERAGE. ANY MISSTATEMENTS MAY AFFECT YOUR COVERAGE—GIVE FULL DETAILS TO ALL "YES" ANSWERS IN THE SPACE PROVIDED.

In the last 10 years, has any person proposed for insurance been diagnosed, treated by or consulted a licensed physician or practitioner for any of the following:

	Yes	No			Yes	No
a. Abnormal blood pressure, chest pain, stroke, heart attach or murmur or any other heart, blood or circulatory disorder	❑	❑	f. Ulcers, colitis, rectal disorder or any disorder of the digestive system, liver or gallbladder		❑	❑
b. Cancer, tumor, growth, enlarged lymph nodes, skin disorder or discolored areas or lesions of the skin or mouth	❑	❑	g. Diabetes, thyroid disorder, speech impairment or disorder of the eyes, ears, nose or throat		❑	❑
c. Emphysema, lung or respiratory disorder	❑	❑	h. Seizures or neurological disorder, mental, nervous or emotional disorder, psychiatric or psychological counseling or treatment		❑	❑
d. Arthritis, or any disorder of the back or neck, muscles, bones or joints	❑	❑	i. Alcoholism, drug or chemical dependency or substance abuse		❑	❑
e. Kidney or urinary system disorder, disorder of the prostate or reproductive system, or breast disorder	❑	❑	j. Acquired Immune Deficiency Syndrome or AIDS Related Complex (ARC)		❑	❑

Continued

For Office Use Only	Eff. _____	Ren. Date _____	Paid _____
	CC _____	Cert. No. _____	

NOTICE OF INSURANCE INFORMATION PRACTICES

TO PROPERLY UNDERWRITE AND ADMINISTER YOUR INSURANCE COVERAGE A CERTAIN AMOUNT OF INFORMATION MUST BE COLLECTED. THE APPLICATION FOR INSURANCE CONTAINS INFORMATION OBTAINED FROM YOU NECESSARY FOR THIS PURPOSE. IN ADDITION, AS PART OF OUR REGULAR UNDERWRITING PROCEDURE, OTHER INFORMATION MAY BE COLLECTED FROM OTHER SOURCES ABOUT YOU OR YOUR ELIGIBLE DEPENDENTS WHO MAY BE PROPOSED FOR INSURANCE.

GENERALLY, DISCLOSURE OF PERSONAL INFORMATION WILL NOT BE MADE TO THIRD PARTIES. HOWEVER, IN SOME CIRCUMSTANCES, THE INSURANCE COMPANY OR YOUR AGENT WILL MAKE DISCLOSURE OF PERSONAL INFORMATION WITHOUT YOUR AUTHORIZATION TO THIRD PARTIES. THIS MIGHT INCLUDE THE DISCLOSURE OF PERSONAL INFORMATION TO PERSONS OR ORGANIZATIONS WHO MAY WISH TO MARKET PRODUCTS OR SERVICES, INCLUDING AFFILIATES OF THE INSURANCE COMPANY, BUT ONLY IF YOU HAVE NOT INDICATED TO US IN WRITING THAT YOU OBJECT TO OUR DOING SO.

YOU HAVE THE RIGHT TO OBTAIN ACCESS TO PERSONAL INFORMATION ABOUT YOU OR YOUR ELIGIBLE DEPENDENTS, IF PROPOSED FOR INSURANCE, COLLECTED BY THE COMPANY OR YOUR AGENT, EXCEPT INFORMATION RELATING TO A CLAIM, CIVIL OR CRIMINAL PROCEEDING. MEDICAL INFORMATION WILL ONLY BE RELEASED THROUGH A DOCTOR, PRACTITIONER, OR OTHER MEDICAL PROFESSIONAL SELECTED BY YOU WHO IS LICENSED TO PROVIDE PROFESSIONAL CARE RELEVANT TO THE NATURE OF THE INFORMATION. YOU ALSO HAVE THE RIGHT TO SEEK CORRECTION OF INFORMATION YOU BELIEVE TO BE INACCURATE.

	Yes	No
2) Are you or any of your dependents currently pregnant? **If yes, list name and due date.**	❑	❑
3) In the last 2 years, has any person proposed for insurance taken prescription medication for more than 30 days? **If yes, state condition, name of medication, dosage and frequency in space provided below.**	❑	❑
4) In the last 5 years, have you or any of your dependents to be insured had any physical disorder, illness, injury, surgery, or check-up, or consultation other than admitted above?	❑	❑

Complete the following for each "YES" answer to questions 1 through 4:

Ques. No.	Name of Person	Date of Treatment From	Date of Treatment To	Reason for Checkup, Diagnosis, Illness or Condition Frequency of Attacks	Treatment or Findings, Medication, Recommendations, Hospitalization and/or Surgery Degree of Recovery	Name and Address of Each Physician, Practitioner and Medical Facility

If additional space is needed use a separate sheet. Sign, date and return it with this form.

	Yes	No
5) Has any person proposed for insurance had health insurance declined, postponed, ridered, rated, cancelled or had reinstatement or renewal refused? **If yes, state the name of the company, action, reason and date in the space below.**	❑	❑
6) Does any person proposed for insurance now carry health insurance or have an application pending with another company? **If yes, state name of applicant, company, type and amount of coverage in the space provided below.**	❑	❑
7) Will the coverage you are applying for replace any coverage listed above? **If yes, give details below.**	❑	❑

I understand and agree that the statements and answers in this application are complete and true to the best of my knowledge and belief and shall form a part of the contract of insurance. I also understand and agree that the insurance applied for, if issued, shall be subject to such statements and answers and will take effect on the effective date stated on the schedule provided the applicable first premium has been paid.

I AUTHORIZE any physician, medical practitioner, hospital, clinic, other medical or medically related facility, insurance or reinsuring company, Medical Information Bureau, consumer reporting agency, employer, or the Veterans Administration, having information available as to advice, diagnosis, treatment, or care of any physical or mental condition concerning me, my spouse, or my minor children, including information about drugs, alcoholism, or mental illness, and any other non-medical information concerning me, my spouse, or my minor children to give to the Company, its affiliates, its legal representative, or its reinsurers any and all such information.

I UNDERSTAND the information obtained by use of the Authorization will be used by the Company or its affiliates to determine eligibility for insurance.

I KNOW that I may request to receive a copy of this Authorization.

I ACKNOWLEDGE having received and read the Notice Regarding Medical Information Bureau and the Notice of Insurance Information Practices (where applicable).

I AGREE that a copy of this Authorization shall be as valid as the original.

I AGREE that this Authorization shall remain valid for two years from the date shown below.

_____	X _____	X _____
DATE	SIGNATURE OF PROPOSED INSURED	SIGNATURE OF SPOUSE (IF APPLYING)

The National Association of Insurance and Financial Advisors

Code of Ethics

PREAMBLE: Those engaged in offering insurance and other related financial services occupy the unique position of liaison between the purchasers and the suppliers of insurance and closely related financial products. Inherent in this role is the combination of professional duty to the client and to the company as well. Ethical balance is required to avoid any conflict between these two obligations. Therefore,

I Believe It To Be My Responsibility

To hold my profession in high esteem and strive to enhance its prestige.

To fulfill the needs of my clients to the best of my ability.

To maintain my clients' confidences.

To render exemplary service to my clients and their beneficiaries.

To adhere to professional standards of conduct in helping my clients to protect insurable obligations and attain their financial security objectives.

To present accurately and honestly all facts essential to my clients' decisions.

To perfect my skills and increase my knowledge through continuing education.

To conduct my business in such a way that my example might help raise the professional standards of those in my profession.

To keep informed with respect to applicable laws and regulations and to observe them in the practice of my profession.

To cooperate with others whose services are constructively related to meeting the needs of my clients.

Adopted September 1999
NAIFA Board of Trustees

NAHU—America's Benefit Specialists

Code of Ethics

To hold the selling, servicing, and distribution of Disability Income and Health Insurance Plans as a professional and a public trust and do all in my power to maintain its prestige.

To keep the needs of those whom I serve paramount.

To respect my client's trust in me, and never do anything which would betray that trust or confidence.

To give all service possible when service is needed.

To present policies factually and accurately—providing all information necessary for the issuance of sound insurance coverage to the public I serve.

To use no advertising which may be false or misleading.

To consider the sale of Disability Income and Health Insurance Plans as a career, know and abide by the insurance laws of my state, and seek constantly through study to increase my knowledge and improve my ability to meet the needs of my client.

To be fair and just to my competitors, and engage in no practice which might reflect unfavorably on myself or my industry.

To treat prospects, clients, and companies fairly by submitting applications which reveal all available information pertinent to the underwriting of a policy.

To be loyal to my clients, associates, fellow agents and brokers, and the company or companies whose products I represent.

Index

This index is designed to make this Passtrak® product more useful to you. Together with the glossary, the table of contents and your own reading notes, it will allow you to find needed information quickly and easily. Here are a few hints to help you use the index fully:

1. Multiple word entries and sub-entries are listed alphabetically according to key words and key concepts. For example, the entry for "cancelable renewability provisions of health insurance" would be "health insurance, renewability provisions, cancelable." If you are having trouble finding a term, try looking under other possible variations (i.e., "renewability provisions" and "provisions, renewability").
2. If an entry has more than one common designation, the alternative designation(s) will point you to "*see*" the proper term; if an entry is related to other terms, it will point you to "*see also*" these other terms.
3. Boldface entries and sub-entries appear in the glossary; boldface page numbers indicate figures.

Dear Student,

What did you think of your Dearborn PASSTRAK study materials? We'd like to know!

We invite you to complete the PASSTRAK survey below. Your responses will help us to develop even better exam preparation materials. Please tear this page out of your book, fold it into thirds, seal it and mail it to us. We'll pay the postage. Your comments are greatly appreciated.

Dearborn™
Financial Services

A **Kaplan Professional** Company
155 North Wacker Dr
Chicago, IL 60606-1719

Book title and edition number: _____

Please rate the PASSTRAK materials using the following scale:

1 = Poor   2 = Satisfactory   3 = Very Good

License Exam Manual				Questions & Answers			
Easy to read	1	2	3	Challenging	1	2	3
Easy to understand	1	2	3	Number of questions	1	2	3
Organized	1	2	3	Accurate	1	2	3
Up-to-date	1	2	3	Up-to-date	1	2	3
Complete	1	2	3	Matches the test	1	2	3
Accurate	1	2	3				

How well do you believe the PASSTRAK materials prepared you for the exam?   1   2   3

What did you like about the PASSTRAK materials?

What would you like us to do to improve the PASSTRAK materials?

Which topic or subject did you find most difficult to study?

What other Dearborn products do you use? Please check them here:

Classroom _____   AnswerPhone _____   Online Drill & Practice _____ Continuing Education Materials _____

Practice Finals _____ Diagnostic Exams _____ Course software _____   Audiotapes _____

How likely would you be to use an online product? Very likely _____ Somewhat likely _____ Not likely _____

Did you take the licensing exam?   No _____ Yes _____   Date _____   Score _____

Name (optional): _____

State of Residence _____   Firm _____

May we contact you?
If so, please provide us with your phone number or email address: _____

You can reach us with your comments and questions at Dearborn's AnswerPhone, a toll-free service.
Securities AnswerPhone: (800) 621-9621, ext. 3598
Insurance AnswerPhone: (800) 621-9621, ext. 2444

You can also contact us at our website, www.dearborn.com.

▼ Important—please fold over and tape before mailing ▼

BUSINESS REPLY MAIL

FIRST-CLASS MAIL   PERMIT NO. 88175   CHICAGO, IL

POSTAGE WILL BE PAID BY ADDRESSEE

ATTN FINANCIAL SERVICES MARKETING
DEARBORN FINANCIAL SERVICES
155 N WACKER DRIVE
CHICAGO IL 60606-1719

▲ Important—please fold over and tape before mailing ▲

Please cut along dotted line